CLINICIAN'S GUIDE TO COCAINE ADDICTION

THE GUILFORD SUBSTANCE ABUSE SERIES

EDITORS

HOWARD T. BLANE, PhD
Research Institute on Alcoholism, Buffalo

THOMAS R. KOSTEN, MD
Yale University School of Medicine, New Haven

Clinician's Guide to Cocaine Addiction

Theory, Research, and Treatment

Thomas R. Kosten
Herbert D. Kleber
Editors

THE GUILFORD PRESS
New York / London

© 1992 The Guilford Press
A Division of Guilford Publications, Inc.
72 Spring Street, New York, NY 10012

Printed in the United States of America

This book is printed on acid-free paper.

Last digit is print number: 9 8 7 6 5 4 3 2 1

Library of Congress Cataloging-in-Publication Data

Clinician's guide to cocaine addiction: theory, research, and treatment
    / edited by Thomas R. Kosten, Herbert D. Kleber.
        p.   cm. — (The Guilford substance abuse series)
    Includes bibliographical references and index.
    ISBN 0-89862-192-5
    1. Cocaine habit.   2. Cocaine—Physiological effect.   3. Cocaine
habit—Treatment.   I. Kosten, Thomas R.   II. Kleber, Herbert
D.   III. Series.
    [DNLM: 1. Cocaine—pharmacology.   2. Substance
Dependence—therapy.   WM 280 C641]
RC568.C6C55   1992
616.8647—dc20
DNLM/DLC
for Library of Congress   92-1521
                                                            CIP

Contributors

S. KELLY AVANTS, PhD, Assistant Professor of Psychology, Yale University School of Medicine; Staff Psychologist, West Haven VA Hospital, West Haven, Conn.

DANA BEITNER-JOHNSON, PhD, Pre-Doctoral Fellow in Psychiatry, Yale University School of Medicine, New Haven, Conn.

JED BLACK, MD, Post-Doctoral Fellow in Psychiatry, Yale University School of Medicine; Chief Resident, Connecticut Mental Health Center, New Haven, Conn.

ROBERT BYCK, MD, Professor of Psychiatry and Pharmacology, Yale University School of Medicine; Director, Consultation Liaison Service, Yale New Haven Hospital, New Haven, Conn.

KATHLEEN M. CARROLL, PhD, Assistant Professor of Psychiatry, Yale University School of Medicine; Director, Treatment Enhancement Project, Substance Abuse Treatment Unit, New Haven, Conn.

GRACE CHANG, MD, MPH, Assistant Professor of Psychiatry, Harvard University, Cambridge, Mass.; Attending Psychiatrist, Brigham and Women's Hospital, Boston, Mass.

MARY H. CLOSSER, DO, Assistant Professor of Psychiatry, University of Michigan; Director Substance Abuse Inpatient Program, Ann Arbor, Mich.

FRANK H. GAWIN, MD, Clinical Associate Professor of Psychiatry, University of California at Los Angeles; Associate Chief of Research, Brentwood VA Medical Center, Los Angeles, Calif.

JUDY GROSSMAN, DRPH, Associate Research Scientist in Psychiatry, Yale University School of Medicine; Director, Mother' Project, Substance Abuse Treatment Unit, New Haven, Conn.

ADAM JAFFE, PHD, Associate Research Scientist in Psychiatry, Yale University School of Medicine; Substance Abuse Research Center, New Haven, Conn.

PETER JATLOW, MD, Professor and Chairman of Laboratory Medicine and Professor of Psychiatry, Yale University School of Medicine; Chief of Laboratory Medicine, Yale New Haven Hospital, New Haven, Conn.

HERBERT D. KLEBER, MD, Professor of Psychiatry and Director, Division on Substance Abuse, Columbia University, College of Physicians and Surgeons, New York, N.Y.

THERESE A. KOSTEN, PHD, Research Scientist in Psychiatry, Yale University School of Medicine; Substance Abuse Research Center, New Haven, Conn.

THOMAS R. KOSTEN, MD, Associate Professor of Psychiatry, Yale University School of Medicine; Director, Substance Abuse Research Center, New Haven, Conn.

SUNIYA LUTHAR, PHD, Assistant Professor of Psychology in Psychiatry, Yale University School of Medicine; Substance Abuse Research Center, New Haven, Conn.

ARTHUR MARGOLIN, PHD, Associate Research Scientist in Psychiatry, Yale University School of Medicine; Substance Abuse Research Center, New Haven, Conn.

CHRISTOPHER J. MCDOUGLE, MD, Assistant Professor of Psychiatry, Yale University School of Medicine; Associate Director, Clinical Neuroscience Research Unit, Connecticut Mental Health Center, New Haven

DAVID F. MUSTO, MD, Professor of Child Psychiatry, Yale University School of Medicine; Senior Consultant, Substance Abuse Treatment Unit, New Haven, Conn.

ERIC J. NESTLER, MD, PHD, Mears Associate Professor of Psychiatry and Pharmacology, Yale University School of Medicine; Acting Director, Ribicoff Research Center, Connecticut Mental Health Center, New Haven

PATRICK G. O'CONNOR, MD, MPH, Assistant Professor of Medicine, Yale University School of Medicine; Director, Outpatient General Medical Services, Yale New Haven Hospital, New Haven, Conn.

H. ROWLAND PEARSALL, MD, Assistant Professor of Psychiatry, Yale University School of Medicine; Associate Director, Inpatient Services, Connecticut Mental Health Center, New Haven

LAWRENCE H. PRICE, MD, Associate Professor of Psychiatry, Yale University School of Medicine; Director, Clinical Neuroscience Research Unit, Connecticut Mental Health Center, New Haven

MARC I. ROSEN, MD, Assistant Professor of Psychiatry, Yale University School of Medicine; Director, Inpatient Research, Treatment Research Unit, Connecticut Mental Health Center, New Haven

BRUCE J. ROUNSAVILLE, MD, Associate Professor of Psychiatry, Yale University School of Medicine; Director, Psychosocial Research, Substance Abuse Treatment Unit, Connecticut Mental Health Center, New Haven

SALLY SATEL, MD, Assistant Professor of Psychiatry, Yale University School of Medicine; Director, Inpatient Substance Abuse Treatment, West Haven VA Hospital, West Haven, Conn.

RICHARD SCHOTTENFELD, MD, Associate Professor of Psychiatry, Yale University School of Medicine; Director, Substance Abuse Treatment Unit, Connecticut Mental Health Center, New Haven

JULIA SHI, MD, Post-Doctoral Fellow in Medicine, Yale University School of Medicine; Substance Abuse Treatment Unit, Connecticut Mental Health Center, New Haven, Conn.

SUSAN M. STINE, MD, PHD, Assistant Professor of Psychiatry, Yale University School of Medicine; Director, Outpatient Substance Abuse Treatment, West Haven VA Hospital; West Haven, Conn.

DOUGLAS M. ZIEDONIS, MD, Assistant Professor of Psychiatry, Yale University School of Medicine; Medical Director, Substance Abuse Treatment Unit Outpatient Services, Connecticut Mental Health Center, New Haven, Conn.

Preface

THIS BOOK AROSE out of a longtime interest by the faculty at Yale University School of Medicine in the clinical aspects and theoretical basis of cocaine abuse. Many Yale investigators have been excited by the challenge of work with cocaine and its abusers, and the aim of this book is to convey the excitement of active research in the laboratory and clinic and show how it has informed and improved clinical practice. The book is unique because it draws from the faculty of a single institution—the Yale Substance Abuse Research Center. It therefore has a coherence based on years of regular interaction among one group of investigators, some of whom have now moved on to other institutions.

We are indebted to the National Institute on Drug Abuse for funding, which has allowed the Yale Center to have a sustained focus on the national public health problem of cocaine abuse. The Center was formed near the beginning of the cocaine epidemic, and its staff have contributed many seminal works on the theory and treatment of cocaine abuse. It has indeed been a privilege for both of us to work with these investigators, who, though from many disciplines, have all been concerned with the same problem in the last decade: the cocaine epidemic.

This book discusses the scientific basis of clinical practice as well as specific treatment approaches, to help the reader understand the links between these areas. Other books have covered one or the other area, but the integration of these preclinical and clinical areas is rarely found in a single text, particularly one whose authors have spent so many years in collaboration. In twenty chapters this book covers the history of cocaine research, the pharmacology and phenomenology of cocaine, and the treatment of cocaine abuse. Chapters on the neurobiology of cocaine and on cognitive, conditioning, and family/genetic factors in cocaine abuse provide the scientific basis for later chapters on pharmacotherapy, psychotherapy, emergency management, comorbid psychopathology, and the pregnant cocaine abuser. A final chapter overviews the treatment approaches and provides a framework for matching patients to various treatments.

The format of each chapter has been individually developed to suit the optimal presentation of material in each field of study. Thus the preclinical chapters frequently have figures and diagrams that illustrate important principles of medication and neurotransmitter or psychological action relevant to cocaine abuse and its treatment, while the clinical chapters use case examples and interview extracts to clarify key points in the management of patients. In many examples the preclinical basis of a clinical intervention is illustrated to help the reader develop his or her own ideas for innovative treatment approaches.

This book will be of interest to a wide range of clinicians who treat cocaine-abusing patients. The chapter on medical complications and emergency management is intended to help physicians who treat patients in crisis, but at the same time provides important understanding of these life-threatening problems for all clinicians who treat cocaine abusers. The chapters on neurobiology and pharmacotherapy are targeted toward physicians, but will also interest nurses and psychologists who believe medications enhance treatment response. The chapters on conditioning and cognitive factors and psychotherapy will be useful to all clinicians, and the chapter on dual diagnosis treatment will be of broad interest to mental health professionals because of the co-occurrence of substance abuse in nearly 50% of patients with other psychiatric disorders. Special treatment populations such as pregnant women and methadone-maintained patients are also given attention. Finally, the role of the clinical laboratory provides critical information on the use of urine drug screens, which are the basis of most clinical monitoring—an important subject for all clinicians treating substance abusers. As a textbook or resource book for courses on substance abuse, this is a comprehensive single source on cocaine—one of the most prevalent drugs of abuse. This book also provides an excellent introduction to and overview of the field for counselors or other health care providers newly entering the field.

Thomas R. Kosten, MD
Yale University

Herbert D. Kleber, MD
Columbia University

Contents

PART ONE

HISTORY OF
COCAINE RESEARCH

CHAPTER ONE

America's First Cocaine Epidemic: What Did We Learn?

David F. Musto, MD

"I HAVE TESTED [the] effect of coca," wrote a youthful Sigmund Freud in his famed essay "On Coca" (1885/1974), "which wards off hunger, sleep, and fatigue and steels one to intellectual effort, some dozen times on myself." Like other doctors who had tested the drug, he found that the euphoria it induced was not followed by depression or any other unpleasant aftereffects. Furthermore, wrote Freud, "a first dose or even repeated doses of coca produce no compulsive desire to use the stimulant further."

With obvious wonder, Freud described the remarkable experiments of 78-year-old Sir Robert Christison, a world-famous toxicologist at the University of Edinburgh: "During the third experiment he chewed two drams of coca leaves and was able to complete [a 15-mile] walk without the exhaustion experienced on the earlier occasions; when he arrived home, despite the fact that he had been nine hours without food or drink, he experienced no hunger or thirst, and woke the next morning without feeling at all tired."

Freud's "song of praise to this magical substance," as he described it, was only one of many that were sung by various medical authorities before the turn of the century. Indeed, Freud had become interested in coca because American physicians, the drug's earliest and heartiest enthusiasts, had "discovered" that it reduced the cravings of opiate addicts and alcoholics. Freud's interest was not academic. He was seeking a cure for

The author gratefully acknowledges *Connecticut Medicine* and *The Wilson Quarterly* for permission to reprint two earlier articles, with alterations, in the form of one chapter here.

of his colleague, Ernst von Fleischl-Marxow. "At present,"
d in 1885, "there seems to be some promise of widespread
ad use of coca preparations in North America, while in
s scarcely know them by name."

COCAINE IN AMERICA

In America, where the cocaine fad would reach greater heights than in
Europe, the ability to cure opiate addiction was regarded as only one of
cocaine's marvelous powers. While morphine and other torpor-inducing
opiates were beginning to seem positively un-American, cocaine seemed
to increase alertness and efficiency, much-prized qualities in the
industrializing nation. In 1880, Dr. W. H. Bentley, writing in Detroit's
Therapeutic Gazette, hailed coca as "the desideratum . . . in health and
disease." The *Gazette*'s editors, quoting another medical journal, cheerily
endorsed this view: "'One feels like trying coca, with or without the
opium-habit. A harmless remedy for the blues is imperial.' And so say
we."

Encouraged by the nation's leading medical authorities, and with
no laws restricting the sale, consumption, or advertising of cocaine (or
any other drugs), entrepreneurs quickly made cocaine an elixir for the
masses. Lasting from 1885 to the 1920s, America's first great cocaine
epidemic went through three phases: the introduction during the 1880s,
as cocaine rapidly gained acceptance; a middle period, when its use
spread and its ill effects came to light; and a final, repressive stage after
the turn of the century, when cocaine became the most feared of all illicit
drugs.

North Americans, to be sure, were not the first inhabitants of this
hemisphere to discover or extol the powers of the "magical leaf." For
centuries before (and after) the arrival of the Europeans, the natives of the
Andes had chewed coca leaves to gain relief from hunger and fatigue.
The drug spread beyond South America only after 1860, when an
Austrian chemist named Albert Niemann learned how to isolate the
active ingredient, cocaine. When Freud published this first praise of the
elixir, pure cocaine, along with the milder coca, was already available to
Americans in drug and grocery stores, saloons, and from mail-order
patent-medicine vendors. By 1885, the major U.S. manufacturer, Parke,
Davis & Co., of Detroit and New York, was selling cocaine and coca in
15 forms, including coca-leaf cigarettes and cheroots, cocaine inhalant,
a coca cordial, cocaine crystals, and cocaine in solution for hypodermic
injection.

COCAINE EASILY AVAILABLE

Parke, Davis reported that it had repeatedly stepped up production during 1885 in order to satisfy the public's growing appetite. A Parke, Davis advertisement informed doctors of the drug's uses:

> An enumeration of the diseases in which coca and cocaine have been found of service would include a category of almost all the maladies that flesh is heir to . . . Allowing for the exaggeration of enthusiasm, it remains the fact that already cocaine claims a place in medicine and surgery equal to that of opium and quinine, and coca has been held to be better adapted for use as a popular restorative and stimulant than either tea or coffee.

The American craving for cocaine was not satisfied by domestic producers alone. From Paris came a variety of popular cocaine concoctions manufactured by Angelo Mariani. "Vin Mariani," a mixture of wine and coca, arrived on the drug store shelf with a raft of celebrity endorsements, including those of Pope Leo XIII, Thomas Edison, Sarah Bernhardt, Emile Zola, Henrik Ibsen, and the Prince of Wales. "Since a single bottle of Mariani's extraordinary coca wine guarantees a lifetime of a hundred years," exclaimed novelist Jules Verne, "I shall be obliged to live until the year 2700" (Mariani, 1901). Mariani boasted that Ulysses S. Grant took another of his products, "Thé Mariani," once a day during this last illness in 1885, allowing the ex-president to complete his famous *Memoirs*.

For consumers on a budget, the new wonder drug was available in less exalted forms. Coca-Cola, for example, contained a minute amount of cocaine—enough to provide a noticeable lift, if not a "high." (Coca-Cola's cocaine content was 0.0025 percent in 1900 and may have been greater during the 1880s.) The "real thing" began life as a coca wine in 1885. In deference, ironically, to the widespread temperance sentiment of the day, the company eliminated the alcohol content of the drink and later added soda water, which allowed it to market Coke as a healthful "soft drink"—a "brain tonic" to relieve headaches and cure "all nervous affections." With the successful marketing of Coca-Cola and similar refreshers, the neighborhood drugstore soda fountain of late-19th-century America came to serve as the poor man's Saratoga Springs. There, the weary citizen could choose from among dozens of soda pop pick-me-ups, including Cola Coke, Rocco Cola, Loca Nola, Nerv Ola, Wise Ola, and one with the simple and direct name, Dope.

Cocaine also was offered as an asthma remedy and an antidote for toothache pain. (Other patent medicines contained opiates, such as morphine and heroin.) Dr. Nathan Tucker's Asthma Specific, a popular catarrh powder, or snuff, considered to be an excellent cure for hay fever and asthma, contained as much as half a gram of pure cocaine per package. Thanks to its remarkable ability to shrink the nasal mucous membranes and drain the sinuses, cocaine became the official remedy of the American Hay Fever Association.

In the six states and innumerable counties that were "dry" during the mid 1890s, working men found snuffs, soft drinks, and other cocaine products a cheap substitute for hard liquor. In states where teetotalers had not prevailed, bartenders often put a pinch of cocaine in a shot of whiskey to add punch to the drink. Peddlers sold it door to door. And some employers in the construction and mining industries found practical uses for the drug, reportedly distributing it to their workers to keep them going at a high pitch.

How much cocaine did Americans consume? Judging from its wide legal availability, and given its seductive appeal, it is safe to assume that they were using substantial amounts by the turn of the century. The limited import statistics for the leaf and manufactured cocaine suggest that use peaked shortly after 1900, just as cocaine was being transformed in the public mind from a tonic into a terror. It is also difficult to determine how many Americans were addicted to cocaine. Because they can live with their addictions for 20 or 30 years, opium addicts (of whom there were perhaps 250,000 around the turn of the century) are a relatively stable population and thus easier to count. Legal imports of coca leaves during that period averaged about 1.5 million pounds annually and the amount of cocaine averaged 200,000 ounces. (Today the United States has roughly three times the population it did in 1900 but consumes, the government estimates, more than 10 times as much cocaine—perhaps 2.5 million ounces annually.)

At first there were few reports of chronic cocaine abuse. Confronted with one example in 1887, Dr. William A. Hammond, former Surgeon General of the Army and one of the most prominent cocaine advocates of the era, dismissed it as a "case of preference, and not a case of irresistible habit." By 1892, however, the *Medical Record* cited more than 200 cases of habit in the medical literature,some among people being treated, as Freud and others had recommended, for addiction to morphine and other opiates (Mattison, 1892).

In fact, Freud himself watched his friend Ernst von Fleischl-Marxow disintegrate into a state of "cocainist" delirium before he died in 1891. Freud claimed that he had not intended for von Fleischl-Marxow to inject the drug, and he withdrew his support for its use as a treatment for morphine addiction. But he never publicly renounced other uses of the drug.

By the turn of the century, cocaine was becoming more and more suspect. A thorough investigation by a committee of the Connecticut State Medical Society in 1896 concluded that cocaine cures for hay fever and other ailments had been a major cause of drug dependency, and "the danger of addiction outweighs the little efficacy attributed to the remedy." It recommended that cocaine be made available only to physicians, for use as a local anesthetic. Scattered newspaper reports ("Another Physician a Victim to the Baneful Drug"), books such as Annie Meyer's *Eight Years in Cocaine Hell* (1902), word of mouth, and articles in *Ladies' Home Journal*, *Collier's*, and other popular magazines brought more bad news. The debilitating effects of Sherlock Holmes's cocaine habit were familiar enough to earn a place in an 1899 Broadway play bearing the name of the brilliant British detective.

HISTORY OF THE LEGAL STATUS OF COCAINE

What was the legal status of cocaine in the United States during this first epidemic and its aftermath, and what impact did changes in legal status have on the price of illicit cocaine? This price impact can be quite informative in comparison with current illicit cocaine prices. Cocaine's legal status has passed through three stages: it could be legally obtained by anyone from the time of its introduction in 1884 until about 1900; then, a movement at both state and local levels restricted its availability subject to a physician's judgment; and finally, after 1914, severe constraints on access to cocaine were enacted by the federal government. During the middle stage, responsibility for cocaine availability was assigned to the health professions. From an examination of illicit and licit prices in New York City during that middle stage, some interesting conclusions can be drawn about the potential impact of legislation to regulate cocaine medically.

When cocaine became commercially available in the United States in 1884, its purveyors were allowed an open market. Until the early 20th century, regulation of medical and pharmaceutical practice was reserved to the police powers of the states and was not an appropriate arena for federal legislation. As a result, the first legal controls on the distribution of cocaine occurred at the local and state level.

One reason there was no initial restriction on the availability of cocaine is that it was considered by prominent authorities to be a harmless tonic without any untoward side effects or aftereffects, as reviewed earlier in this chapter. As demand soared, pharmaceutical manufacturers rapidly increased production (see Musto,1987; 1989). The initial wholesale price for cocaine hydrochloride was $15 per gram, but dropped within 2 years to a much lower figure, about $0.25, and thereafter generally followed the rate of inflation.

The early approval of cocaine gradually changed to concern and eventually to fear of its effects on the mind and behavior of users ("Want Cocaine . . . ," December 1896). New York State legislators turned to the wisdom of health professionals as a defense against the cocaine problem. In 1907, Alfred E. Smith, then a member of the Assembly, led a legislative attack on cocaine . The subsequent Smith anticocaine law restricted cocaine availability to a physician's prescription and required record-keeping, but the law placed no restriction on the amount or purpose of the prescriptions (Act to Amend the Penal Code . . . , 1907).

These steps, however, did not bring cocaine under control to a degree satisfactory to the public or legislature. Some physicians and pharmacists provided cocaine without the professional restraint antici- pated by lawmakers. In spite of this liberality, cocaine was still being sold on the streets of New York. One loophole regarding possession without a prescription was addressed by an amendment in 1910 (Act to Amend the Penal Law . . . , 1910). Then, in 1913, after continued frustration over the easy access to cocaine, an even stricter anticocaine law was passed with support from Smith, now Speaker of the New York Assembly. This Act imposed severe restrictions on the health professions as well as penalties for any "patient" having cocaine without a certificate of authorization provided by a pharmacist or physician (Act to Amend the Penal Law . . . , 1913).

The final stage of control, limiting the freedom of the health profession in dispensing cocaine and ending any latitude in its possession, had been reached to the extent feasible in New York State. The following year, the federal Harrison Act would bring an unprece- dented restriction of cocaine's availability to the entire nation. More than alcohol, even during a national campaign which would lead to Prohibition in 1920, cocaine stood out as a fearful substance almost universally condemned.

In 1906, the Pure Food and Drug Act had required that the existence of an amount of cocaine in over-the-counter remedies be revealed on the label, although the amount was unregulated (Young, 1967). Then, on March 1, 1915, the Harrison Narcotics Act of 1914 came into force. It required that records be kept of all opiates and cocaine from the importer or manufacturer down to the patient's prescription. Unlike the Pure Food and Drug Act, it also limited the amount of opiates— while prohibiting any cocaine—in nonprescription remedies. The Act required that physicians prescribe these drugs only "in the course of professional practice" and "in good faith" (Musto, 1987). With the passage of the Harrison Act and that of various state anticocaine laws, the high-water mark of restrictions on cocaine in the first wave of cocaine use had been reached.

Eventually cocaine use faded in the United States. The gap between the beginning of the current wave of cocaine use, about 1970, and the waning years of previous use, the 1930s, was so long that the earlier experience has been practically forgotten.

The current resurgence of cocaine led to calls for legalization in the 1970s on the basis of its apparent harmlessness, whereas in recent years legalization proposals have stressed the economic argument to reduce the profits from illegal cocaine sales. Legal cocaine, according to this reasoning, would undercut costs, eliminate turf wars between rival drug sellers, and reduce the economic motivation for enlisting new cocaine users. Some have suggested turning cocaine distribution over to health professionals, an idea which has echoes of the Al Smith Law of 1907, and which was still associated with a significant illicit cocaine market. To examine this market, I have estimated illicit cocaine prices during the first cocaine epidemic and compared them to current prices.

ESTIMATING ILLICIT COCAINE PRICES

To estimate the illicit price of cocaine during what might be called the "medical" phase of cocaine control, in New York City from 1908 through 1914, and to compare that price with illicit cocaine prices in the 1980s, the average industrial hourly wage was chosen as a comparison for purchasing power.

1908–1914

The wholesale price of cocaine in the earliest period, after a rapid fall from 1884 to 1886, settled down at a fairly steady level. Interestingly, the cost per gram at the wholesale level ($0.25) stayed close to the average hourly wage for industrial workers. Also, the price ($0.25) of the illicit street unit, or "deck," from 1908 until 1914 approximated the hourly wage.

New York City street market prices for cocaine during the period before 1908 have not been located. Following passage of the Smith anticocaine law, prices began to be reported in the newspapers as arrests were made. The street or illicit price of a "deck" appears to have remained steady over the 7 years between the Smith law and the coming into force of the Harrison Act, March 1, 1915.

That the typical street unit was a deck for 25 cents is concluded from newspaper accounts. In one of the early arrests under the Smith Act, it was reported in the *New York Times* that a seller provided cocaine at the rate of 26 [sic] cents a package to "any one—man, woman or boy" ("Held as Cocaine Vendor," 1908). The State Department report of 1910 (*Opium Problem*) also gave 25 cents as the typical package. The *New York Tribune* ("Refuge for Drug Victims," 1912) reported in detail the process of making "decks" to sell for 25 cents. The following year, the *Tribune* reported more street sales at the rate of 25 cents each ("Cocaine Law Potent," 1913). In 1914, the *Tribune* ("Follow Girl") reported the arrest of a cocaine dealer while weighing out 25-cent "decks" of cocaine.

The amount of cocaine in a deck is estimated as about 80 mg. In the Federal government's report, *Opium Problem*, submitted to Congress in February 1910, the amount of cocaine in an envelope is estimated to be "one to two grains" (65–130 mg). The *New York Tribune* account of December 2, 1912 ("Refuge") estimated the amount of cocaine in a "deck" to be 1.3 grains (85 mg). This amount has been taken as a reasonable estimate of cocaine in the illicit street unit.

The rate for a gram of cocaine on the street market would be about $2.75, 11 times the unit price and, for the period under analysis, about 10 times the average hourly industrial wage.

According to newspaper reports, a well-established illicit pricing scheme as well as profiteering organizations existed during the "medical" phase of control ("Police Blind," 1912; "Gangs of Gunmen," 1912).

1982–1989

In 1982, the DEA began compiling statistics based on the sale of cocaine at the street level and also providing estimates of cocaine costs at higher levels of the drug trade.

The prices of bulk and street unit cocaine have been drifting down since the early 1980s. By now the street unit cost of cocaine—often stated to be $5–15—approximates the average industrial hourly wage. The cost per gram on the street has declined from about 10 times to (if we take the lowest price reported by the DEA for 1989) about 4 times the wage level. The wholesale price of a gram of cocaine has leveled off the last 3 years near the average hourly industrial wage of $10 per hour.

The street cost of a gram of cocaine can be compared between the two time periods by dividing the hourly wage into the price. There is a striking similarity between the two eras, except that the cost of cocaine at the street level is now lower, in terms of actual buying power, than it was on the streets of New York City prior to the Harrison Act and while the legal control of cocaine was vested in the judgment of health professionals. From 1907 to 1914, this ratio ranged from 10:1 to 12:1, and from 1982 to 1985 this ratio was virtually identical at 10:1 to 12:1. Since 1985 the ratio has dropped, however, and gone from 10:1 down to about 4:1 in 1989, a substantial drop in relative price.

STABLE ILLICIT MARKET BEFORE 1914

Whether there was an illicit market for cocaine prior to the earliest state laws has not been determined. The prices in New York City found for the period 1907–1914 were reported as a result of police arrests of illegal distributors, but prior to 1907 there were accounts of voluntary restrictions by local pharmacists and physicians (Musto, 1987; "Want Cocaine," 1896). Further research may clarify the question as to when an illicit market could be sustained owing to the creation of voluntary restrictions and the beginning of popular condemnation.

The question of a previous "street market" for cocaine is significant because, if the assumptions about the cost and content of a "deck" are valid, there does not seem to have been a period of adjustment to market demand after enactment of the 1907 Smith law. The postlaw market apparently maintained a fairly steady price for a "deck" of cocaine for nearly 8 years.

The existence of this illicit market while the regulation of cocaine was turned over to the judgment of physicians and pharmacists suggests that this measure did not affect the supply or the availability of cocaine outside professional distribution. A gram of cocaine continued to cost on the street about 10 times the average industrial hourly wage, a multiple as high as, or higher than, cocaine has cost on the street since 1982. In this regard, it is reasonable to conclude that syndicates that provided illicit cocaine before the Harrison Act had profit margins comparable to those of our own day.

One of the most interesting comparisons between the pre–World War I unit price on the street, 25 cents, and the more recent street unit prices, $5–15, is their coincidental similarity to the hourly wage. Perhaps the wages for an hour's work is a natural market rate for the street unit. Until the Harrison Act, the United States had no national uniform law for the legal distribution of cocaine. That the street price in New York City could be maintained at such a high level before the Harrison Act is further evidence that reliance on health professions failed to eliminate an illicit market.

The reasons for this failure appear to be several. Visits to a physician were assumed to keep access to cocaine under the watchful eye of a professional. This requirement, however, would add the cost of a prescription to the cost of cocaine from a pharmacist. Also, drug users may have had a disinclination to become involved with formal and official suppliers then as now. Whatever reasons one might want to assign, the hurdle presented by professional contact and record keeping was apparently sufficient to maintain a stable illicit market in cocaine. Significantly, this illicit market was sustained in the face of some health professionals who dispensed and prescribed liberally.

There is evidence that the price of cocaine after World War I was much higher, even taking inflation into account, than in the era before the Harrison Act—$1.50/deck ("Addicts Picket," 1921) and $2.00/deck ("Arrested at Movie," 1923). An important component of this rise in price and gradual decline in demand is the prolonged length of time required for the shift in consumption pattern. If we assume the time required now for a change in popular demand for cocaine may be roughly similar to the time taken for the previous episode, the curve in the cocaine price has been the opposite in each era. The shape of the price curve over the earlier wave of cocaine use resembled the shape of a J (extending the price curve into the apparent rise after World War I) and, while the current price curve is incomplete, we know that the recent curve has been the very reverse of that before 1915, starting high in the early 1970s and going lower. It will be interesting to see whether we are in a trough that will begin to rise and form a U shape, or whether the decline of cocaine prices will continue. If the condemnation and reaction against cocaine continues, it is possible the price will rise as a reflection of domestic restrictions, both social and legal, as it did after the anticocaine consensus established 70–80 years ago.

THE TIMING OF ANTICOCAINE LAWS

Unlike the current cocaine episode, which began about 1970, laws were not in place during the earlier "epidemic" until the public and legislators demanded controls. Escalating legal severity after 1907 in New York State and the rest of the nation paralleled popular opinion. A report President Taft transmitted to Congress in 1910 described cocaine as "more appalling in its effects than any other habit-forming drug used in the United States" ("Opium Problems," 1910). A further reflection of the fear of cocaine is that the section of the Harrison Act of 1914 that permitted some opiates, even heroin, in over-the-counter remedies, allowed no cocaine.

The contrast between the attempts to control cocaine in the two waves of use is striking. Even after the substantial decline of cocaine use by World War II, increasingly harsh penalties for cocaine use were placed on the statute books (Musto, 1987). These laws created a dramatic disparity between the fairly relaxed attitude toward cocaine in the mid-1970s and the severe penalties. The conflict between severe laws and widespread toleration of cocaine use meant that we experienced about 15 years of additional controversy over cocaine and controls until a consensus was once again established against the use of cocaine in the mid-1980s.

In this second cocaine era, we have had anticocaine laws from the beginning of its renewed popularity and availability, whereas cocaine use in the last century began in the absence of laws restricting it. After 1884, only as cocaine use continued and its damage was seen did laws against the drug begin to be enacted and gradually strengthened. Since 1970, in contrast, the extended controversy over controls on cocaine—the prolonged disharmony between anticocaine laws on the books and more tolerant public attitudes—may be reflected in the frustration that has led to calls for drastic measures on opposite sides: Those who propose legalizing cocaine believe it is time we all admitted to 20 years of failure in controlling it, whereas others call for draconian penalties that aim to sharply and quickly curtail drug use through punishment. The quest for a simple answer to the drug problem does not take into account the gradual fall in demand for cocaine that, at least in the past, followed the establishment of a popular anticocaine attitude. The decline phase may last 15–20 years. Reasonable policies might not appear effective as quickly as the public wishes, but impatiently rejecting these measures for extreme criminal justice measures will flood courts and jails, legitimize extravagant interdiction methods, and lead to a psychology of scapegoating foreign nations and domestic groups, such as the inhabitants of the inner cities—all without substantially affecting the rate of decline in cocaine use.

On the other hand, the foregoing price analysis suggests that anything less than open access to cocaine, even the apparently liberal public health position of turning over responsibility to the flexible judgment of physicians and pharmacists, still supports an illicit market with prices comparable with our own day.

THE COCAINE QUANDARY

The public faces the quandary of fearing cocaine too much to allow open access, but being outraged by the corruption and profits that are products of the illicit trade in drugs. In the previous wave of drug use, this cocaine impasse was resolved by an almost total elimination of the demand for cocaine through public experience with the drug and its users. In spite of profiteering in the illicit market, cocaine eventually faded away in the United States. This awareness of cocaine's dangers was not effectively passed on to later generations—although severe penalties did persist—and by 1970 cocaine reappeared in the United States as fresh and exciting, an apparently useful tonic, stimulant, or ideal recreational substance.

The period of cocaine's availability after the mid-1880s and before action began to be taken against it, about 20 years, and the stage of increasing control, about 10 more years, followed finally by about two more decades during which the problem subsided, suggests that cocaine use is not quickly corrected by simple, dramatic actions. Neither reverting to free access, the very condition that brought on demands for control, nor a simple reliance on punishment offers hope for a speedy solution.

REFERENCES

Act to amend the penal code, in relation to the sale of certain drugs, Laws of New York oo 424 (1907).

Act to amend the penal law, in relation to the sale of cocaine and eucaine, Laws of New York oo 131 (1910).

Act to amend the penal law, in relation to the sale or possession of coaine or eucaine, Laws of New York oo 470 (1913).

Addicts picket drug purveyor. (1921, July 28). New York Tribune, p. 20.

Arrested at movie as vendor of drugs. (1923, January 4). New York Times, p. 8.

Bentley, W. H. (1880, December 15). Erythoxylon coca. Therapeutic Gazette, IV, 350–351.

Cocaine law potent; seek "men higher up." (1913, November 10). New York Tribune, p. 1, 5.

Connecticut Medical Society. (1896). Report of the Committee on Matters of Professional Interest in the State: 1. Cocaine. Proceedings, 253–264.

Erythoxylon coca as an antidote to the opium habit [Editorial]. (1880, June 15). Detroit Therapeutic Gazette. In R. Byck (Ed.) (1974), Cocaine papers by Sigmund Freud (pp. 19–21). New York: Stonehill.

Follow girl to drug den; seize 5. (1914, July 1). New York Tribune, p. 2.

Freud, S. (1974). On coca. In R. Byck (Ed.), Cocaine papers by Sigmund Freud (pp. 49–73). New York: Stonehill. (Original work published 1885)

Gangs of gunmen protect sellers from competition. (1912, December 2). New York Tribune, p. 2.

Hammond, W. A. (1887, November). Coca: Its preparations and their therapeutical qualities, with some remarks on the so-called "cocaine habit." Transactions of the Medical Society of Virginia.

Harrison Narcotics Act, 38 Stat. 785. (1914).

Held as cocaine venders. (1908, August 3). New York Times, p. 5.

Mariani, A. (Ed.). (1901). *Contemporary celebrities from an album of Mariani.* New York: Mariani & Co.

Mattison, J. B. (1892, October 22). Cocainism. *Medical Record, 42,* 474–477.

Meyers, A. (1902). *Eight years in cocaine hell.* Chicago: Press of the St. Luke Society.

Musto, D. F. (1987). *The American disease* (exp. ed.). New York: Oxford University Press.

Musto, D. F. (1989). America's first cocaine epidemic. *Wilson Quarterly, 13,* 59–64.

Opium problem. (1910). *Message from the President of the United States.* 61st Cong., 2d sess., S. Doc. 377, p. 49.

Police blind to cocaine selling. (1912, December 2). *New York Tribune,* p. 1.

Pure Food and Drug Act, 34 Stat. 768. (1906)

Refuge for drug victims under noses of police. (1912, December 2). *New York Tribune,* p. 2.

Want cocaine at any cost. (1896, December 29). *Ansonia Sentinel,* p. 2.

Young, J. H. (1967). *The medical messiahs.* Princeton, NJ: Princeton University Press.

CHAPTER TWO

Cocaine Research at Yale

Robert Byck, MD

THE MOST RENOWNED comment on cocaine from Yale was voiced in 1934 by Cole Porter. "I get no kick from cocaine," penned the songwriter, but his later colleagues disagreed. A search of the literature for the 21 years from 1966 to 1987 indicates that a full 1% of the world literature on cocaine came from Yale. A modern review of the actions of cocaine (not written by a Yale investigator) uses about 10% Yale references.[*] Why this preoccupation with the most seductive of drugs by the most stolid of institutions?

The discovery of Machu Pichu by Yale's Hiram Bingham in 1911 first brought representatives of the institution in contact with coca. Bingham was not particularly interested in coca or cocaine but his expedition did observe and photograph the Peruvian Indians' use of the substance. Coca tea is a sustenant for all who visit the Andes, and so we could expect that Bingham indulged when it was offered. This beverage was provided to David Musto, Murdoch Ritchie, Peter Jatlow, David Paly and me when we visited Cuzco for the Conference on Coca and Cocaine in 1979. Dr. Jatlow later examined a specimen and found no significant amount of cocaine in this hot water extract of coca leaves.

David Musto had written about the history of cocaine and its regulation in "The American Disease." He had also made Yale's most heralded contribution to the cocaine literature, in an article for the

---

[*]Fischman, M. W. (1987). Cocaine and the amphetamines. In H. Y. Meltzer (Ed.), *Psychopharmacology: The third generation of progress* (pp. 1543–1554). New York: Raven Press.

Journal of the American Medical Association, by creating the concept of a cocaine-addicted Sherlock Holmes going to Sigmund Freud for treatment. Moriarty in this conception was Holmes's cocaine-driven paranoid delusion. Freud's treatment of Holmes led Freud, according to the Musto creation, to discover the technique of psychoanalysis. These ideas were converted by another author to the well-known novel and movie, *The Seven Per Cent Solution.* Unfortunately, Musto had only the joy of creation and no mundane profit from this literary venture.

Although the recent establishment of a Center for the Study of Opiate and Cocaine Abuse under the direction of Herbert Kleber has crystallized cocaine research at Yale, involvement in cocaine research goes much further back. Two present Yale chairpersons, Peter Jatlow and Paul Barash, were part of the original Cocaine Project supported by the National Institute of Drug Abuse (NIDA) in 1974. The story of that project also parallels my personal involvement in cocaine research.

I had been interested in central stimulants since I was a medical student. My first research project overlapped with interests of Gordon Alles, the discoverer of amphetamine and some of its hallucinogenic derivatives. Alles, who had his own laboratories of pharmacology, was a drug taster. This was an important virtue for someone who was interested in orally active antiallergy drugs, but it led him to some terrific bellyaches. The tradition of testing for drug effect by ingestion has had a long and fruitful history but is now out of fashion. It is not the drug laws or the Institutional Review Board that dampened the drug tasters but rather the discovery of the neurotoxic compounds such as 6-hydroxy-dopamine. Alles had originally felt that abuse of amphetamine was unlikely. Strangely enough, amphetamine abuse was a rare phenomenon until after World War II. The wide availability of central stimulants during wartime gave them an implied cachet of safety. The road from suggested safety to widespread abuse is a very short one, as we have seen with cocaine.

Implied safety was the issue in 1974. There had been a resurgence of cocaine abuse after 40 years of relative indifference to the drug. I had become involved with cocaine through The New York Times. A Times reporter had suggested me as a possible editor of Sigmund Freud's Cocaine Papers and, after much travail, I had completed the book. This restimulated my interest in the central stimulants. Herb Kleber brought to my attention a NIDA research request for proposal. Because Murdoch Ritchie, the author of the chapter on cocaine in Goodman and Gilman's *The Pharmacological Basis of Therapeutics* was a close colleague and Paul Barash was interested in a new project, we assembled a group to respond to the request for proposal. Craig Van Dyke, at that time a new assistant professor working with me on the Psychiatric Consultation Service, was interested in participating, as was Peter Jatlow of the Department of Laboratory Medicine.

The first problem to be attacked was that of devising a sensitive and accurate assay for cocaine in body fluids. Peter Jatlow and David Bailey did this successfully with gas-liquid chromatography and a nitrogen detector. This, and the concomitant discovery that the primary metabolism of cocaine was by esterases in the blood, opened up an entirely new era in cocaine research. Specimens could be preserved from esteritic breakdown by the addition of fluoride to the collecting tubes. Pseudocholinesterase deficiency might be the cause of some cocaine toxicities and, although no cases had been found, we warned of that possibility at the time. This issue is now being pursued by Peter Jatlow in collaboration with Florida investigators. The group then examined the time course of metabolite excretion with the use of surgical patients receiving cocaine in the course of their anesthetic management.

The physiological laboratory began work on establishing dose–effect relationships for cocaine in humans and on as examining the time course of the physiological effects of cocaine. Various psychological measures were devised, and old scales used in psychological research were adapted to fit the needs of the project. A sophisticated computerized laboratory allowed us to evaluate data. David Stagg, now director of the Biomedical Computing Unit, was instrumental in creating the computer systems for the lab. That laboratory, still operating, was the prototype for the many "drug challenge" labs now proliferating around the country and at Yale.

It is hard to realize today the extreme anxiety investigators then felt in administering cocaine to normal subjects. We were ready with anesthesiologists and resuscitation equipment,only to find that the effects of the drug were quite unremarkable in the laboratory. The human subject issues were of great moment at the time, and we had to be extremely cautious in our subject recruiting. We secretly shared with the two other groups working on cocaine the reality of the unspectacular nature of the drug response. Whenever this was reported publicly, a great storm of protest would arise. Sometimes it was better to be quiet about results. We did a series of experiments on the effects of cocaine on exercise performance that have never been published. There is a political dimension to cocaine research that does not exist in most other scientific endeavors.

The group was the first to correlate plasma level and drug effect for cocaine. An interest in the old literature led us to examine the established belief, canonized by textbooks, that cocaine, being hydrolyzed in the stomach, was ineffective by mouth. Because Peruvian

Indians had been chewing coca leaves for centuries, this seemed improbable. Of course it turned out that old tradition was more reliable than modern textbooks, and we could demonstrate that cocaine was, in fact, more effective when taken orally than intranasally. The group led by Peter Jatlow examined the metabolites of cocaine as found in the urine and later defined the pharmacokinetics of oral and intranasal cocaine. Later pharmacokinetic work with Raphael Zahler, now a cardiologist in the Department of Internal Medicine, permitted us to collaborate with an econometrician and a mathematician in creating a way to predict the effects of drugs based on the past history of the plasma level curves.

A new dimension was added to our work when a medical student, David Paly, now an anesthesiologist, approached me with the idea of going to Peru to measure plasma levels of cocaine in Peruvian Indians. I pointed out that we could gather the same information by having subjects chew coca leaves in the laboratory, but Paly preferred Cuzco to New Haven and raised the money to travel. We had established contact with a Peruvian neurosurgeon, Fernando Cabieses, who paved the way for experiments with coca chewers and helped us in recruiting subjects and providing facilities for our work in South America. A neuropsychiatrist, Dr. Raul Jeri, became involved and so Paly's path was facilitated with official contacts since Jeri was, incidentally, a general in the Guardia Civil (the Peruvian analogue to our Public Health Service). Paly eventually traveled to Peru several times, but his first trip brought him into contact with the new habit of cocaine smoking. He not only did remarkable field work on coca chewing but brought back the specimens that allowed us to publish the first papers in the English language on cocaine smoking. The results of the Paly trips led to papers on both cocaine smoking and coca chewing. Indians in Peru have always added an aliquot of burned shells (llipta, or alkali lime) to the quid of chewed coca leaves. The Paly data on coca chewing demonstrated for the first time that the alkali lime used by the Indians raised the effective plasma levels of cocaine by a 10-fold factor. Once again, primitive indigenous pharmacology proved its wisdom. In the course of these travels David Paly established the unique distinction of smuggling cocaine *into* Peru. Doped plasma samples had to be made up to check for deterioration in transit. It was thus necessary to bring very small amounts of cocaine "the wrong way."

In 1979, we were invited to the First Interamerican Conference on Coca and Cocaine held in Lima, Peru. Musto, Ritchie, Jatlow, Paly, and I attended the conference. Little did we know this was a critical international event and was intended to have greater political than scientific content. Arriving early, my wife and I were invited to attend a horse race held in honor of the conference. We sat in the presidential box to view this bizarre event amongst the bejewelled and befurred representatives of Lima society.

Later, when the conference was about to begin, Dr. Jeri asked me to "greet the delegates." After I agreed, he explained that the speech had to be in Spanish, a language of which I was entirely innocent. A badly typewritten Spanish text on flimsy paper was my fluttering guide as I spoke in dim light to the mayor of Lima, the ministers of culture and public health and a substantial cohort of *generales*. The diplomatic corps was present as were a few vastly amused scientists. Fortunately my pronunciation was so pitiful that no one even suspected that I had any knowledge of the language. As I finished and sank gratefully to my chair, I was rewarded with applause, and the National Chorus burst into song.

The conference highlighted to us the political importance of cocaine in South America. A volume of papers from the conference with 4 of 16 scientific papers from our group was eventually published with State Department and Pan American Health organization support. The niceties of publishing the country by country political statements were adeptly handled by Dr. Jeri, who edited the volume. Our paper on coca chewing was a subject of intense dispute by those who were not willing to accept that coca chewing leads to significant plasma cocaine levels.

Straightforward findings can become controversial in cocaine research. We generated a dispute with the publication of the finding that small single doses of intranasal lidocaine could not be distinguished from similarly administered doses of cocaine. This finding, although technically correct, would come back to haunt us, as would the publication of data showing that low doses of cocaine and placebo could not be distinguished.

Craig Van Dyke had always wanted to publish an article in *Scientific American*, and the editors responded positively to his inquiry. Since we had reviewed various aspects of cocaine pharmacology several times, he and I jointly prepared an article for publication in the journal. What we, like other authors, found out was that writing for popular magazines was different from writing for medical journals. The editors decided, without our approval, what would stay and what would go. The result was a highly political piece which, although it contained many of our words, gave an impression that was contrary to our intent. Sometimes they used descriptions we had never written, and so a comparison between cocaine and potato chips was ascribed to Van Dyke and Byck. We had never included such a comparison in our text and asked the editors of *Scientific American* to remove it. They refused. The article caused a storm in the press, and we were big news for a week or so. The newspapers concentrated on the cocaine–placebo similarity without mentioning that this was true for all drugs at low doses. The newspapers misread the comments about addiction and headlined the idea that we had found cocaine to be nonaddicting. This, of course, was nonsense. It was contrary to the text of the article, and we had never done any work on the addiction potential of cocaine. In a small community such as Yale, explaining things to your colleagues can be more work than doing the research. Publicity seems to be an intrinsic part of doing research in cocaine, and the newspapers never quite get it right.

When he was a resident at Yale, Mark Gold came to me with a story of a patient who had ceased cocaine use when he was put on lithium treatment. We published this together, but this was just a beginning for Mark, who has since published voluminously on cocaine. He later "founded" the 1-800 COCAINE hotline and wrote a book with that name.

Fueled by publicity and aided by a significant South American cocaine industry, the resurgence of cocaine in the early 1980s created a great need for treatment programs and strategies for cocaine abuse. Frank Gawin and Herb Kleber began to investigate treatment strategies for the many patients who were arriving at substance abuse clinics. They first characterized the phases of the development of cocaine dependence and then, after some investigation of the neuroendocrine correlates of cocaine use, started controlled investigations of the effects of desipramine in cocaine abuse treatment. Kleber, Tom Kosten, and Bruce Rounsaville reviewed their experience with cocaine abuse treatments, and Kosten published on the differential diagnosis of depression in cocaine addicts based on the Dexamethasone Suppression Test. In an article in *Psychopharmacology*, Gawin noted that chlorpromazine did block paranoia but not euphoria.

Van Dyke, now in California, extended cocaine research to the immune system and published work indicating that cocaine enhanced the immune response. Although my own work has been mainly concerned with the pharmacology of cocaine in humans, the Yale output includes work by Michael Davis, Norman Gillis and others on the animal pharmacology of cocaine.

David Musto has continued his interest in cocaine and has published widely on the policy issues and history of the drug as well as the regulations governing its use. A recent article by Musto in the Scientific American brings our relationship with that journal full circle.

In the mid-1980s, James Jekel began a fruitful collaboration with a group in the Bahamas examining the epidemic of cocaine abuse that had suddenly developed in these islands. In 1986, a critical article in *Lancet* documented these efforts. David Allen, who had been on the Yale faculty in psychiatry and divinity, and who is now in the Bahamas with the National Drug Council, published *The Cocaine Crisis*, about the growing problem of cocaine in the Caribbean area. Gawin and Jekel contributed to this volume as well.

Frank Gawin and I found that changes in the brains of heavy cocaine abusers could be documented with magnetic resonance imaging. A number of new research proposals on cocaine were funded in 1987 and even more in later years. Gawin left Yale, and Kleber became a national leader in the nation's effort against drug abuse. Tom Kosten took over most of the research direction of projects that had grown in the late 1980s. It seems that Yale's interest in cocaine has not diminished. The present chapter, originally written in 1987, tells our local history only to that date. The bibliography extends to the middle of 1991, and it is obvious that there is no diminution in the continued fascination of this Freudian "cure for the blues" for the Blues.

Although this chapter is not referenced specifically, what follows is as complete a Yale bibliography as I could gather. All forms of publication were included up to 1987, but only archival materials appear after that date. Presumably, the list is more inclusive of articles from our group than others and contains only work done at Yale. Searches were done in various data bases for mention of "Haven" in the address listings and "cocaine" in the text. These searches were supplemented by our own cocaine data base searches on authors known to me. Since 1987, the Medline data base contained addresses, and so "Yale" could be searched as well. If, despite these efforts, I have left out certain publications, I would welcome additions or corrections, and I apologize in advance for any articles that were overlooked.

APPENDIX 2.1.
A CHRONOLOGICAL LIST OF YALE CONTRIBUTIONS TO SCHOLARSHIP ON COCAINE

1. Musto, D. F. (1968). Sherlock Holmes and Sigmund Freud. A study in cocaine. *Journal of the American Medical Association, 204,* 125–130.

2. Musto, D. F. (1973). *The American disease: Origins of narcotic control.* New Haven: Yale University Press. (Expanded edition, Oxford University Press, 1987.)

3. Byck, R. (Ed.). (1974). *Cocaine papers: Sigmund Freud.* New York: Stonehill. (Paperback: New York, New American Library, 1975; French edition: Brussels, Editions Complexe, 1976; Portuguese Edition: Rio de Janeiro, Espaco e Tempo 1989.)

4. Jatlow, P. I., & Bailey, D. N. (1975). Gas chromatographic analysis for cocaine in human plasma, with use of a nitrogen detector. *Clinical Chemistry, 21,* 1918–1921.

5. Jatlow, P. I., & Bailey D. N. (1975). Gas chromatographic measurement of cocaine in plasma using a nitrogen detector. *Clinical Chemistry, 21,* 946.

6. Byck, R. (1975, June 27). The drug muddle. *The New York Times,* p. 35.

7. Van Dyke, C., Barash, P. G., Jatlow, P. I., & Byck, R. (1975). Cocaine: Plasma levels after topical anesthesia in man. *The Pharmacologist, 17,* 82.

8. Byck, R., Jatlow, P. I., Barash, P., & Van Dyke, C. (1976). Cocaine: Blood levels, excretion and physiological effect after intranasal application in man. *Psychopharmacology Bulletin, 12,* 47–48.

9. Jatlow, P. I., Barash, P. G., Van Dyke, C., & Byck, R. (1976). Impaired hydrolysis of cocaine in plasma from succinylcholine sensitive individuals. *Clinical Research, 24,* 255A.

10. Van Dyke, C., Barash, P. G., Jatlow P. I., & Byck R. (1976). Cocaine: Plasma concentrations after intranasal application in man. *Science, 191,* 859–861.

11. Jatlow, P. I. (1976). Analysis of cocaine and its metabolites in biological fluids. In S. J. Mule (Ed.), *Cocaine, chemical, biological, clinical, social and treatment aspects* (pp. 59–70). Cleveland: CRC Press.

12. Barash, P. G., Kopriva, C. J., Stahl, A., Langou, R., Van Dyke, C., Jatlow, P. I., & Byck, R. (1977). Is cocaine a sympathetic stimulant under general anesthesia? *Proceedings of the American Society of Anesthesiologists, 71–72.*

13. Byck, R., Jatlow, P. I., Barash, P., & Van Dyke, C. (1977). Cocaine: blood concentration and physiological effect after intranasal application in man. In E. H. Ellinwood & M. M. Kilbey (Eds.), *Cocaine and other Stimulants* (pp. 629–645). New York: Plenum Press.

14. Byck, R., & Van Dyke, C. (1977). What are the effects of cocaine in man? In R. C. Petersen & M. Stillman (Eds.), *Cocaine 1977* (National Institute on Drug Abuse Research Monograph No. 13, pp. 97–117). Washington, DC: U. S. Government Printing Office.

15. Van Dyke, C., & Byck, R. (1977). Cocaine: 1884–1974. In E. H. Ellinwood & M. M. Kilbey (Eds.), *Cocaine and other stimulants.* New York: Plenum Press.

16. Van Dyke, C., Byck, R., Barash, P. G., & Jatlow, P. I. (1977). Urinary excretion of immunologically reactive metabolite(s) after intranasal administration of cocaine, as followed by enzyme immunoassay. *Clinical Chemistry, 23,* 241–244.

17. Wilkinson, P. K., Van Dyke, C., Barash, P. G., Jatlow, P. I., & Byck, R. (1977). Cocaine pharmacokinetics following intranasal application of five different doses in man. *Abstracts of the 23rd National Meeting of the Academy of Pharmaceutical Sciences, 7,* 116.

18. Barash, P., Cronau, L., Mandel, S., Jatlow, P. I., Van Dyke, C., Byck, R., & Gillis, C. N. (1978). Does cocaine block norepinephrine uptake in man? *Proceedings of the American Society of Anesthesiologists,* pp. 357–358.

19. Gold, M. S., & Byck, R. (1978). Lithium, naloxone, endorphins and opiate receptors: possible relevance to pathological and drug-induced manic-

euphoric states in man. In R. C. Petersen (Ed.), *The International Challenge of Drug Abuse* (National Institute on Drug Abuse Research Monograph No. 19, pp. 192–209). Washington, DC: U. S. Government Printing Office.

20. Jatlow, P. I., Van Dyke, C., Barash, P., & Byck, R. (1978). Measurement of benzoylecgonine and cocaine in urine, and separation of various cocaine metabolites using reversed- phase high-performance liquid chromatography. *Journal of Chromatography, 152,* 115–121.

21. Van Dyke, C., Jatlow. P. I., Ungerer, J., Barash, P. G., & Byck, R. (1978). Oral cocaine: Plasma concentrations and central effects. *Science, 200,* 211–213.

22. Van Dyke, C., Jatlow, P. I., Ungerer, J., Barash, P., & Byck, R. (1978). Comparative psychological effects after intranasal application of local anesthetics: Lidocaine and cocaine. *Proceedings of the 40th Annual Meeting on Problems of Drug Dependence,* pp. 322–332.

23. Byck, R., Paly, D., Van Dyke, C., Jeri, F. R., & Jatlow, P. I. (1979). Cocaine: Plasma levels after coca paste smoking. *Abstracts of the Annual Meeting, New Research Section, American Psychiatric Association.*

24. Jatlow, P. I., Barash, P., Van Dyke, C., Radding, J., & Byck, R. (1979). Cocaine and succinylcholine sensitivity: A new caution. *Anesthesia Analgesia, 58,* 235–239.

25. Paly, D., Van Dyke, C., Jatlow, P. I., Cabieses, F., & Byck, R. Cocaine: Plasma concentrations in coca chewers. *Clinical Pharmacology and Therapeutics, 25,* 240.

26. Van Dyke, C., Jatlow, P. I., Ungerer, J., Barash, P., & Byck, R. (1979). Cocaine and lidocaine have similar psychological effects after intranasal application. *Life Sciences, 24,* 271–274.

27. Catravas, J. D., & Gillis, C. N. (1980). Pulmonary clearance of [^{a}14C]-5-hydroxytryptamine and [^{a}3H]norepinephrine in vivo: Effects of pretreatment with imipramine or cocaine. *Journal of Pharmacology and Experimental Therapeutics, 213,* 120–127.

28. Barash, P. G., Kopriva, C. J., Langou, R., Van Dyke, C., Jatlow, P. I., Stahl, A., & Byck, R. (1980). Is cocaine a sympathetic stimulant during general anesthesia? *Journal of the American Medical Association, 243,* 1437–1439.

29. Byck, R., Van Dyke, C., Jatlow, P. I., & Barash P (1980). Clinical pharmacology of cocaine. In F. R. Jeri (Ed.), *Cocaine 1980: Proceedings of International Seminar on Coca and Cocaine* (pp. 250–256). Lima, Peru: Pacific Press.

30. Byck, R. (1980). Cocaine: A major drug issue of the seventies. *Hearings, 96th Congress, Committee on Narcotic Abuse and Control* (pp. 58–69, 88–83). Washington, DC: U. S. Government Printing Office.

31. Jatlow, P. I., Van Dyke, C., Barash, P., Wilkinson, P., & Byck, R. (1980). Analysis of cocaine and its metabolites in biological fluids: Technical, metabolic, and pharmacokinetic considerations. In F. R. Jeri (Ed.), *Cocaine 1980: Proceedings of International Seminar on Coca and Cocaine* (pp. 111–119). Lima, Peru: Pacific Press.

32. Paly, D., Van Dyke, C., Jatlow, P. I., Jeri, F. R., & Byck, R. (1980). Cocaine: Plasma levels after cocaine paste smoking. In F. R. Jeri (Ed.), *Cocaine*

1980: Proceedings of International Seminar on Coca and Cocaine (pp. 106–110). Lima, Peru: Pacific Press.

33. Paly, D., Jatlow, P. I., Van Dyke, C., Cabieses, F., & Byck, R. (1980). Plasma levels of cocaine in native Peruvian coca chewers. In F. R. Jeri (Ed.), *Cocaine 1980: Proceedings of International Seminar on Coca and Cocaine* (pp. 86–89). Lima, Peru: Pacific Press.

34. Wilkinson, P., Van Dyke, C., Jatlow, P. I., Barash, P., & Byck, R. (1980). Intranasal and oral cocaine kinetics. *Clinical Pharmacology and Therapeutics, 27,* 386–394.

35. Byck, R. (1980, Aug–Sept). Subject recruiting in 1913: Yale investigates Peru. *IRB: A Review of Human Subjects Research, 2*(7), 2–3.

36. Byck, R., Ruskis, A., Ungerer, J., & Jatlow, P. I. (1982). Naloxone potentiates cocaine effect in man. *Psychopharmacology Bulletin, 18,* 214–215.

37. Paly, D., Jatlow, P. I., Van Dyke, C., Jeri, F. R., & Byck, R. (1982). Cocaine paste smoking: Plasma levels and effects. *Life Sciences, 30,* 731–738.

38. Van Dyke, C., & Byck, R. (1982). Cocaine. *Scientific American, 246,* 128–141.

39. Van Dyke, C., Ungerer, J., Jatlow, P. I., Barash, P., & Byck, R. (1982). Intranasal cocaine: Dose relationships of psychological effects and plasma levels. *International Journal of Psychiatry in Medicine, 12,* 1–13.

40. Zahler, R., Wachtel, P., Jatlow, P. I., & Byck, R. (1982). Kinetics of drug effect by distributed lag analysis: An application to cocaine. *Clinical Pharmacology and Therapeutics, 31,* 775–782.

41. Gawin, F. H., & Kleber, H. D. (1983). Cocaine abuse treatment. *Yale Psychiatric Quarterly, 6,* 4–13.

42. Van Dyke, C., & Byck, R. (1983). Cocaine in man. In N. K. Mello (Ed.), *Advances in substance abuse* (pp. 1–24). Greenwich, CT: Jai Press.

43. Gawin, F. H., Gore, J. C., Newton, T. F., Sostman, H. D., Holcombe, W., & Byck, R. (1984). Magnetic resonance imaging studies of cocaine abusers. *Abstracts of the Annual Meeting of the American College of Neuropsychopharmacology,* p. 98.

44. Gawin, F. H., & Kleber, H. D. (1984). Cocaine abuse treatment. Open pilot trial with desipramine and lithium carbonate. *Archives of General Psychiatry, 41,* 903–909.

45. Khantzian, E. J., Gawin, F., Kleber, H. D., & Riordan, C. E. (1984). Methylphenidate (Ritalin) treatment of cocaine dependence—a preliminary report. *Journal of Substance Abuse Treatment, 1,* 107–112.

46. Gawin, F. H., & Kleber, H. D. (1984). Cocaine abuse treatment: An open trial with lithium and desipramine. *Archives of General Psychiatry, 41,* 903–910.

47. Kleber, H. D., & Gawin, F. H. (1984). *Cocaine abuse: A review of current and experimental treatments* (National Institute on Drug Abuse Research Monograph No. 50, pp. 111–129). Washington, DC: U. S. Government Printing Office.

48. Kleber, H. D., & Gawin, F. H. (1985). The spectrum of cocaine abuse and its treatment. *Journal of Clinical Psychiatry, 45,* 18–23.

49. Gawin, F., Riordan, C., & Kleber, H. D. (1985). Methylphenidate

treatment of cocaine abusers without attention deficit disorder: A negative report. *American Journal of Drug and Alcohol Abuse, 11,* 193–197.

50. Rounsaville, B. J., Gawin, F. H., & Kleber, H. D. (1985). Interpersonal psychotherapy adapted for ambulatory cocaine abusers. *American Journal of Drug and Alcohol Abuse, 11,* 171–191.

51. Harty, T. P., & Davis, M. (1985). Cocaine: Effects on acoustic startle and startle elicited electrically from the cochlear nucleus. *Psychopharmacology, 87,* 396–399.

52. Ritchie, J. M., & Greene, N. M. (1985). Local anesthetics. In L. Goodman & A. Gilman (Eds.), *The pharmacological basis of therapeutics* (7th ed., pp. 300–320). New York: Macmillan.

53. Davis, M. (1985). Cocaine: excitatory effects on sensorimotor reactivity measured with acoustic startle. *Psychopharmacology* [Berlin], *86,* 31–36.

54. Gawin, F. H., Byck, R., & Kleber, H. D. (1985, December). Double blind comparison of desipramine and placebo in cocaine abuse treatment: Preliminary results. *Abstracts of Panels and Posters Presented at Annual Meeting of the American College of Neuropsychopharmacology,* p. 169.

55. Gawin, F. H., & Kleber, H. D. (1985). Neuroendocrine findings in chronic cocaine abusers: A preliminary report. *British Journal of Psychiatry, 147,* 569–573.

56. Gawin, F., & Kleber, H. D. (1985). *Cocaine use in a treatment population: Patterns and diagnostic distinctions* (National Institute on Drug Abuse Research Monograph No. 61, pp. 182–192). Washington, DC: U. S. Government Printing Office.

57. Gawin, F. H., & Kleber, H. D. (1986). Pharmacological treatments of cocaine abuse. *Psychiatric Clinics of North America, 9,* 573–583.

58. Kosten, T. R., Gawin, F. H., Rounsaville, B. J., & Kleber, H. D. (1986). Cocaine abuse among opioid addicts: Demographic and diagnostic factors in treatment. *American Journal of Drug and Alcohol Abuse, 12,* 1–16.

59. Gawin, F. H., & Kleber, H. D. (1986). Abstinence symptomatology and psychiatric diagnosis in cocaine abusers. Clinical observations. *Archives of General Psychiatry, 43,* 107–113.

60. Gawin, F. H. (1986). Neuroleptic reduction of cocaine- induced paranoia but not euphoria. *Psychopharmacology* [Berlin], *90*(11), 142–143.

61. Byck, R. (1986). "Crack" cocaine. *Hearings, Permanent Subcommittee on Investigations of the Committee on Governmental Affairs, United States Senate, 99th Congress.* Washington, DC: U. S. Government Printing Office, 86–92.

62. Jekel, J. F., Allen, D. F., Podlewski, H., Clarke, N., Dean-Patterson, S., & Cartwright, P. (1986). Epidemic freebase cocaine abuse. *The Lancet, 1,* 459–462.

63. Musto, D. F. (1986, June 11). Lessons of the first cocaine epidemic. *The Wall Street Journal,* p. 30.

64. Byck, R. (1986). The effects of cocaine on complex performance in humans. *Alcohol, Drugs and Driving, 2,* 1–4.

65. Gawin, F. H., Byck, R., & Kleber, H. D. (1986). Desipramine

augmentation of cocaine abstinence: Initial results. *Clinical Neuropharmacology,* 9, 202–204.

66. Gawin, F. H. (1986). New uses of antidepressants in cocaine abuse. *Psychosomatics, 27,* 24–29.

67. Van Dyke, C., & Byck, R. (1986). Cocaine. In R. E. Long (Ed.), *Drugs and American society* (pp. 60–75). New York: H. W. Wilson (a corrected version of an article originally published in *Scientific American*).

68. Kosten, T. R., Gawin, F. H., Rounsaville, B. J., & Kleber, H. D. (1986). *Abuse of cocaine with opioids: Psychosocial aspects of treatment* (National Institute on Drug Abuse Research Monograph No. 67, pp. 278–282). Washington, DC: U. S. Government Printing Office.

69. Kleber, H. D., & Gawin, F. H. (1986). Cocaine. In R. Millman (Ed.), *Psychiatric Update* (Vol. 5, pp. 160–185). Washington, DC: American Psychiatric Association Press.

70. Kosten, T. R., Rounsaville, B. J., & Kleber, H. D. (1987). A 2.5 year follow-up of cocaine use among treated opioid addicts—have our treatments helped? *Archives of General Psychiatry, 44,* 281–284.

71. Byck, R. (1987). Cocaine, marijuana and the meanings of addiction. In R. L. Hamowy (Ed.), *On dealing with drugs: Problems of government control* (pp. 221–245). San Francisco: Pacific Press.

72. Byck, R. (1987). Cocaine use and research: Three histories. In S. Fisher, A. Raskin, & E. H. Uhlenhuth (Eds.), *Cocaine: Clinical and behavioral aspects* (pp. 3–20). New York: Oxford University Press.

73. Carroll, K., Keller, D. S., Fenton, L., & Gawin, F. H. (1987). Psychotherapy for cocaine abusers. In D. A. Allen (Ed.), *The cocaine crisis* (pp. 75–106). New York: Plenum Press.

74. Jekel, J. F. (1987). Public Health approaches to the cocaine problem: Lessons from the Bahamas. In D. A. Allen (Ed.), *The cocaine crisis* (pp.–119). New York: Plenum Press.

75. Gawin, F. H., & Kleber, H. D. (1987). Issues in cocaine abuse treatment research. In S. Fisher, A. Raskin, & E. H. Uhlenhuth (Eds.), *Cocaine: Clinical and behavioral aspects* (pp. 174–192). New York: Oxford University Press.

76. Jekel, J. F., & Allen, D. F. (1987). Trends in drug abuse in the mid-1980's. *Yale Journal of Biology and Medicine, 60,* 45–52.

77. Gawin, F. H. (1987). Laboratory assessment in substance abuse treatment: Distinctions in utilization and effects on treatment design. *Clinical Chemistry, 33,* 95B–101B.

78. Kosten, T. H., Schumann, B., Wright, D. R., & Gawin, F. H. (1987). Desipramine reductions of cocaine abuse in a methadone maintenance population. *Journal of Clinical Psychiatry, 48*(11), 442–444.

79. Gawin, F. H. (1987). Laboratory assessments in treatments of substance abuse: utilization and effects on treatment design. *Clinical Chemistry, 33,* 95B–100B.

80. Jatlow, P. I. (1987). Drug of abuse profile: Cocaine. *Clinical Chemistry, 33,* 66B–71B.

81. Kosten, T. R., Schumann, B., Wright, D., Carney, M. K., & Gawin, F. H. (1987). A preliminary study of desipramine in the treatment of cocaine abuse in methadone maintenance patients. *Journal of Clinical Psychiatry, 48,* 442–444.

82. Kosten, T. R., Rounsaville, B. J., Babor, T. F., Spitzer, R. L., & Williams, J. B. (1987). Substance-use disorders in DSM-III-R. Evidence for the dependence syndrome across different psychoactive substances. *British Journal of Psychiatry, 151,* 834–843.

83. Kleber, H. D., & Gawin, F. H. (1987). Cocaine withdrawal. *Archives of General Psychiatry, 44,* 297–298.

84. Kleber, H. D., & Gawin, F. H. (1987). The physiology of cocaine craving and "crashing." *Archives of General Psychiatry, 44,* 299–300.

85. Kleber, H. D., & Gawin, F. H. (1987). Pharmacological treatment of cocaine abuse. In A. M. Washton & M. S. Gold (Eds.), *Cocaine.* New York: Guilford Press.

86. Gawin, F. H. (1988). Chronic neuropharmacology of cocaine: Progress in pharmacotherapy. *Journal of Clinical Psychiatry, 49,* 11–16.

87. Gawin, F. H., & Ellinwood, E. H., Jr. (1988). Cocaine and other stimulants. Actions, abuse, and treatment. *New England Journal of Medicine, 318,* 1173–1182.

88. Gawin, F. H., & Kleber, H. D. (1988). Evolving conceptualizations of cocaine dependence. *Yale Journal of Biology and Medicine, 61,* 123–136.

89. Gradman, A. H. (1988). Cardiac effects of cocaine: A review. *Yale Journal of Biology and Medicine, 61,* 137–147.

90. Jatlow, P. (1988). Cocaine: Analysis, pharmacokinetics, and metabolic disposition. *Yale Journal of Biology and Medicine, 61,* 105–135.

91. Morgan, C., Kosten, T., Gawin, F., & Kleber, H. A. (1988). *Pilot trial of amantadine for ambulatory withdrawal for cocaine dependence* (National Institute on Drug Abuse Research Monograph No. 81, pp. 81–85). Washington, DC: U. S. Government Printing Office.

92. Kleber, H. D. (1988). Cocaine abuse: Historical, epidemiological, and psychological perspectives. *Journal of Clinical Psychiatry, 49,* 3–610.

93. Kosten, T. R., & Kleber, H. D. (1988). Differential diagnosis of psychiatric comorbidity in substance abusers. *Journal of Substance Abuse Treatment, 5,* 201–206.

94. Kosten, T. R., & Kleber, H. D. (1988). Rapid death during cocaine abuse: A variant of the neuroleptic malignant syndrome? *American Journal of Drug and Alcohol Abuse, 14,* 335–346.

95. Kosten, T., Rounsaville, B., & Kleber, H. (1988). *A 2.5 year follow-up of abstinence and relapse to cocaine abuse in opioid addicts* (National Institute on Drug Abuse Research Monograph No. 81, pp. 231–236). Washington, DC: U. S. Government Printing Office.

96. Kosten, T. R., Rounsaville, B. J., Kleber, H. D. (1988). Antecedents and consequences of cocaine abuse among opioid addicts. A 2.5 year follow-up. *Journal of Nervous and Mental Disease, 176,* 176–181.

97. Weiss, R., & Gawin, F. H. (1988). Protracted detection of cocaine metabolites. *Americal Journal of Medicine, 85,* 879–888.

98. Ellinwood, E. H., & Gawin, F. H. (1988). What we don't know about cocaine. *American Association for the Advancement of Science Observer, 1,* 5–6.

99. Thatcher, S. S., Corfman, R., Grosso, J., Silverman, D. G., & DeCherney, A. H. (1989). Cocaine use and acute rupture of ectopic pregnancies. *Obstetrics and Gynecology, 74,* 478–931.

100. Musto, D. F. (1989). America's first cocaine epidemic. *Wilson Quarterly, 13,* 59–64.

101. Satel, S. L., & Gawin, F. H. (1989). Migraine like headache and cocaine use. *Journal of the American Medical Association, 261,* 2995–2996.

102. Satel, S. L., & Gawin, F. H. (1989). Seasonal cocaine abuse. *American Journal of Psychiatry, 146,* 534–535.

103. Musto, D. F. (1989). Evolution of American attitudes toward substance abuse. *Annuals of the New York Academy of Sciences, 562,* 3–7.

104. Moghaddam, B., & Bunney, B. S. (1989). Differential effect of cocaine on extracellular dopamine levels in rat medial prefrontal cortex and nucleus accumbens: Comparison to amphetamine. *Synapse, 4,* 156–161.

105. Kosten, T. R., Kleber, H. D., & Morgan, C. (1989). Role of opioid antagonists in treating intravenous cocaine abuse. *Life Sciences, 44,* 887–892.

106. Kosten, T. R., Rounsaville, B. J., & Foley S. H. (1989). *Inpatient vs. outpatient cocaine abuse treatments* (National Institute on Drug Abuse Research Monograph No. 95, pp. 312–313). Washington, DC: U. S. Government Printing Office.

107. Kosten, T. R., Kleber, H. D., & Morgan, C. (1989). Treatment of cocaine abuse with buprenorphine. *Biological Psychiatry, 26,* 637–639.

108. Kosten, T. R. (1989). Pharmacotherapeutic interventions for cocaine abuse. Matching patients to treatments. *Journal of Nervous and Mental Disease, 177,* 379–389.

109. Kosten, T. R., Morgan, C. J., & Kleber, H. D. (1989). *Buprenorphine treatment of cocaine abuse* (National Institute on Drug Abuse Research Monograph No. 95, p. 461). Washington, DC: U. S. Government Printing Office.

110. Kosten, T. A. (1989). *Cocaine attenuates opiate withdrawal in human and rat* (National Institute on Drug Abuse Research Monograph No. 95, pp. 361–362). Washington, DC: U. S. Government Printing Office.

111. Jaffe, A. J., & Kilbey, M. M. (1989). *The Cocaine Expectancy Questionnaire (CEQ): Its construction and predictive utility* (National Institute on Drug Abuse Research Monograph No. 95, p. 456). Washington, DC: U. S. Government Printing Office.

112. Gawin, F. H., Kleber, H. D., Byck, R., Rounsaville, B. J., Jatlow, P. I., & Morgan, C. (1989). Desipramine facilitation of initial cocaine abstinence. *Archives of General Psychiatry, 46,* 117–121.

113. Gawin, F. H., & Ellinwood, E. H., Jr. (1989). Cocaine dependence. *Annual Review of Medicine, 40,* 149–161.

114. Gawin, F. H. (1989). Cocaine abuse and addiction. *Journal of Family Practice, 29,* 193–197.

115. Gawin, F. H., Allen, D., & Humblestone, B. (1989). Outpatient treatment of "crack" cocaine smoking with flupenthixol decanoate. A preliminary report. *Archives of General Psychiatry, 46,* 322–325.

116. Gawin, F. H., Morgan, C., Kosten, T. R., & Kleber, H. D. (1989). Double-blind evaluation of the effect of acute amantadine on cocaine craving. *Psychopharmacology* (Berlin), *97*, 402–403.

117. Bradberry, C. W., & Roth, R. H. (1989). Cocaine increases extracellular dopamine in rat nucleus accumbens and ventral tegmental area as shown by in vivo microdialysis. *Neuroscience Letters, 103*, 97–102.

118. Berger, P. A., Gawin, F. H., Kosten, T. R. (1989). Mazindol treatment for cocaine craving. *Lancet, 1*, 283–284.

119. Gawin, F. H., & Ellinwood, E. H. (1989). Stimulant abuse treatment. In H. D. Kleber & T. B. Karasu (Eds.), *Treatments of psychiatric disorders: A Task Force Report of the American Psychiatric Association* (pp. 1218–1241). Washington, DC: American Psychiatric Association Press.

120. Berger, P., Elsworth, J. D., Reith, M. E., Tanen, D., & Roth, R. H. (1990). Complex interaction of cocaine with the dopamine uptake carrier. *European Journal of Pharmacology, 176*, 251–252.

121. Berger, P., Elsworth, J. D., Arroyo, J., & Roth, R. H. (1990). Interaction of [3H]GBR 12935 and GBR 12909 with the dopamine uptake complex in nucleus accumbens. *European Journal of Pharmacology, 177*, 91–94.

122. Bracken, M. B., Eskenazi, B., Sachse, K., McSharry, J. E., Hellenbrand, K., & Leo-Summers, L. (1990). Association of cocaine use with sperm concentration, motility, and morphology. *Fertility and Sterility, 53*, 315–322.

123. Gawin, F. H., & Ellinwood, E. H. (1990). Clinical correlates and consequences of chronic cocaine abuse. In N. Volkow & A. Swan (Eds.), *Cocaine and the brain*. New Brunswick, NJ: Rutgers University Press.

124. Carroll, K., & Rounsaville, B. (1990). *Can a technology model of psychotherapy research be applied to cocaine abuse treatment?* (National Institute on Drug Abuse Research Monograph No. 104, pp. 91–104). Washington, DC: U. S. Government Printing Office.

125. Musto, D. F. (1990). Illicit price of cocaine in two eras: 1908–1914 and 1982–1989. *Connecticut Medicine, 54*(6), 321–326.

126. Fleming, J. A., Byck, R., & Barash, P. G. (1990). Pharmacology and therapeutic applications of cocaine. *Anesthesiology, 73*, 518–531.

127. Jatlow, P., & Nadim, H. (1990). Determination of cocaine concentrations in plasma by high-performance liquid chromatography *Clinical Chemistry, 36*, 1436–1439. [Published erratum appears in *Clinical Chemistry* (1991, June), *37*(6), 886.]

128. Kashkin, K. B., & Kleber, H. D. (1989). Hooked on hormones? An anabolic steroid addiction hypothesis. *Journal of the American Medical Association, 262*, 3166–3170.

129. Kosten, T. R., Morgan, C., & Kosten, T. A. (1990). Depressive symptoms during buprenorphine treatment of opioid abusers. *Journal of Substance Abuse Treatment, 7*, 51–54.

130. Kosten, T. R., Gawin, F. H., Morgan, C., Nelson, J. C., & Jatlow, P. (1990). Evidence for altered desipramine disposition in methadone-maintained patients treated for cocaine abuse. *American Journal of Drug and Alcohol Abuse, 16*, 329–336.

131. Kosten, T. A. (1990). Cocaine attenuates the severity of naloxone-precipitated opioid withdrawal. *Life Sciences, 47,* 1617–1623.

132. Kosten, T. A., & Kosten, T. R. (1990). The dependence syndrome concept as applied to alcohol and other substances of abuse. *Recent Developments in Alcoholism, 8,* 47–68.

133. Nestler, E. J., McMahon, A., Sabban, E. L., Tallman, J. F., & Duman, R. S. (1990). Chronic antidepressant administration decreases the expression of tyrosine hydroxylase in the rat locus coeruleus. *Proceedings of the National Academy of Sciences, USA, 87,* 7522–7526.

134. Nestler, E. J., Terwilliger, R. Z., Walker, J. R., Sevarino, K. A., & Duman, R. S. (1990). Chronic cocaine treatment decreases levels of the G protein subunits Gi alpha and Go alpha in discrete regions of rat brain. *Journal of Neurochemistry, 55,* 1079–1082.

135. O'Malley, S. S., & Gawin, F. H. (1990). *Abstinence symptomatology and neuropsychological impairment in chronic cocaine abusers* (National Institute on Drug Abuse Research Monograph No. 101, pp. 179–190). Washington, DC: U. S. Government Printing Office.

136. Diakogiannis, I. A., Steinberg, M., & Kosten, T. R. (1991). *Mazindol treatment of cocaine abuse. A double- blind investigation* (National Institute on Drug Abuse Research Monograph No. 105, p. 514). Washington, DC: U. S. Government Printing Office.

137. Jatlow, P., Elsworth, J. D., Bradberry, C. W., Winger, G., Taylor, J. R., Russell, R., & Roth, R. H. (1991). Cocaethylene: A neuropharmacologically active metabolite associated with concurrent cocaine-ethanol ingestion. *Life Sciences, 48,* 1787–1794.

138. Jatlow, P., Hearn, W. L., Elsworth, J. D., & Roth, R. H. (1991). *Cocaethylene inhibits uptake of dopamine and can reach high plasma concentrations following combined cocaine and ethanol use* (National Institute on Drug Abuse Research Monograph No. 105, pp. 572–573). Washington, DC: U. S. Government Printing Office.

139. Kosten, T. R., Morgan, C. H., & Schottenfeld, R. S. (1991). *Amantadine and desipramine in the treatment of cocaine abusing methadone maintained patients* (National Institute on Drug Abuse Research Monograph No. 105, pp. 510–511). Washington, DC: U. S. Government Printing Office.

140. Kosten, T. A., Kosten, T. R., & Rounsaville, B. J. (1991). *Cocaine symptoms are predicted by familial psychopathology* (National Institute on Drug Abuse Research Monograph No. 105, pp. 603–604). Washington, DC: U. S. Government Printing Office.

141. Margolin, A., Kosten, T., Petrakis, I., Avants, S. K., & Kosten, T. (1991). *An open pilot study of bupropion and psychotherapy for the treatment of cocaine abuse in methadone- maintained patients* (National Institute on Drug Abuse Research Monograph No. 105, pp. 367–368). Washington, DC: U. S. Government Printing Office.

142. Pacholczyk, T., Blakely, R. D., & Amara S. G. (1991). Expression cloning of a cocaine- and antidepressant-sensitive human noradrenaline transporter. *Nature, 350,* 350–354.

143. Pickett, G., Kosten, T. R., Gawin, F. H., Byck, R., Fleming, J.,

Silverman, D., Kosten, T. A., & Jatlow, P. (1991). *Concurrent effects of acute intravenous cocaine in context of chronic desipramine in humans* (National Institute of Drug Abuse Research Monograph No. 105, pp. 508–509). Washington, DC: U. S. Government Printing Office.

144. Rounsaville, B. J., Anton, S. F., Carroll, K., Budde, D., Prusoff, B. A., & Gawin, F. (1991). Psychiatric diagnoses of treatment-seeking cocaine abusers. *Archives of General Psychiatry, 48,* 43–51.

145. Satel, S. L., & Kosten, T. R. (1991). Designing drug efficacy trials in the treatment of cocaine abuse. *Journal of Nervous and Mental Diseases, 179,* 89–96.

146. Satel, S. L., Southwick, S. M., & Gawin, F. H. (1991). *Clinical features of cocaine induced paranoia* (National Institute on Drug Abuse Research Monograph No. 105, p. 371). Washington, DC: U. S. Government Printing Office.

147. Terwilliger, R. Z., Beitner-Johnson, D., Sevarino, K. A., Crain, S. M., Nestler, E. J. (1991). A general role for adaptations in G-proteins and the cyclic AMP system inmediating the chronic actions of morphine and cocaine on neuronal function. *Brain Research, 548,* 100–110.

148. Gawin, F. H. (1991). Cocaine addiction: Psychology and neurophysiology. *Science, 251,* 1580–1586.

149. Musto, D. F. (1991). Opium, cocaine and marijuana in American history. *Scientific American, 265*(1), 40–48.

Evolving Conceptualizations of Cocaine Dependence

Frank H. Gawin, MD
Herbert D. Kleber, MD

IN 1980, cocaine was considered a benign euphoriant (Grinspoon & Bakalar, 1989; National Commission on Marihuana and Drug Abuse, 1973). Cocaine's popularity was increasing, but broad distribution of cocaine began only in the late 1970s, and little time had elapsed to allow the development of extreme cocaine abuse, so cocaine abusers rarely appeared seeking treatment. By 1982, cocaine abusers had begun to appear at the Substance Abuse Treatment Unit of Yale University and the Addiction Prevention and Treatment Foundation, and we founded the Yale cocaine abuse treatment and research program when the number of primary cocaine abusers in the treatment unit reached four (the average census is now over 60 cocaine abusers). The establishment of a unit devoted to cocaine dependence led to a continuing, systematic research effort that has advanced new conceptualizations of cocaine dependence and of the appropriateness of pharmacological treatment strategies. This chapter reviews the recent evolution of our understanding of cocaine dependence.

EVOLUTION OF CLINICAL UNDERSTANDING

In 1980, the *Comprehensive Textbook of Psychiatry* stated that "taken no more than two or three times per week, cocaine creates no serious

---

This chapter was previously published in a slightly different form in the *Yale Journal of Biology and Medicine*. The author retains the copyright.

problems" (Grinspoon & Bakalar, 1980). The *Diagnostic and Statistical Manual-III* (DSM-III) of the American Psychiatric Association (APA) reflected the prevailing perception that withdrawal or tolerance to cocaine did not occur and the DSM-III did not list cocaine dependence as a substance abuse problem (APA, 1980). Case reports of cocaine dependence from the turn of the century were considered aberrant exaggerations. Experts claimed that cocaine produced, at worst, "minor psychological disturbances" and "psychological" addiction only in some addiction-prone abusers (reviewed in Gawin & Kleber, 1986b). Moreover, this psychological addiction was considered a relatively minor clinical condition amenable to treatment with psychotherapy, in contrast to the "physiological" addiction associated with narcotics, alcohol, and sedative-hypnotics.

This clinical consensus existed despite the lack of systematic clinical studies of cocaine abusers. Our initial clinical studies were intended, therefore, to reconcile the disparity between the clinical wisdom of the time, that cocaine was not supposed to produce true addiction, and the fact that it was being cited increasingly by patients as the direct cause of compulsive drug taking and seeking treatment.

We employed direct clinical observation of subjects in treatment, using semistructured interviews as well as structured assessments of cocaine craving and use. These studies showed that cocaine produced a dependence similar, in magnitude and resistance to treatment, to that of other drugs of abuse such as alcohol and opiates, but that cocaine dependence differed substantially in the pattern of abuse development and in clinical presentation.

Four areas of clinical importance were targeted by these initial investigations: (1) details of the progression of dyscontrol over cocaine use (Kleber & Gawin, 1984b), (2) patterns of cocaine use (Gawin & Kleber, 1985a), (3) abstinence symptomatology (Gawin & Kleber, 1986a), and (4) the role played by comorbid psychiatric disorders (Gawin & Kleber, 1986a; Gawin, 1986). Most of these initial observations took place in a very carefully followed subsample of 30 cocaine abusers who were treated between 1982 and 1984. Details of sample characteristics appear elsewhere (Gawin & Kleber, 1985a; Gawin & Kleber, 1985b; Gawin & Kleber, 1986d).

The Progression to Cocaine Dependence
(Kleber & Gawin, 1984b; Gawin & Ellinwood, 1988)

Our cocaine abusers related that, as in earlier descriptions of the developing amphetamine dependence (Ellinwood, 1977), dyscontrol over cocaine use occurred gradually, within a social context. Initially, low cocaine doses enhance social enjoyment or vocational performance (Kleber & Gawin, 1984b; Gawin & Ellinwood, 1988). Few negative consequences of such use were initially apparent; however, lengthening episodes of use, sleep disruption, dosage escalation, and increased social isolation all gradually became accompaniments of cocaine use. Between initial exposure to cocaine and treatment seeking, 2 to 5 years usually elapsed, which accounts for the lag between cocaine's initial populariza-tion and the latter appearance of reports of addiction. Compulsive, uncontrolled binge use began when availability increased (e.g., because of increased funds, improved supply sources, engaging in cocaine commerce), or following a switch to an administration route of higher intensity, which delivered increased doses to the brain (smoking or intravenous route). The extreme euphoria produced by such binges produced vivid memories that formed the foundation for later stimulant craving.

The human cocaine addicts we studied described binges that paralleled the repeated rapid cocaine self-administration observed in animals provided unlimited access (reviewed in Johanson, 1984). Thoughts of loved ones, safety, responsibilities, and morality did not enter consciousness during binges. Only thoughts of stimulant effects and supplies persisted. Although a similar gradual progression to dyscontrol has been described for other abused drugs, such as opiates and alcohol, the time course for dependence has generally been longer (Kleber, 1974), and simple availability of large amounts of the abused drug played a less central role, especially in alcohol abuse, than in cocaine abusers.

A widespread belief in the early 1980s was that intranasal cocaine did not cause addiction; the fact that 50% of the abusers we studied were exclusive intranasal users, showed this perception to be erroneous. The clinical presentation of intranasal abusers did not differ from that of other abusers, with the same severity of dependence (Gawin & Kleber, 1985).

Patterns of Cocaine Use in Dependence
(Gawin & Kleber, 1985a)

Continual, daily use of alcohol or opiates is considered the normal pattern in opiate or alcohol dependence. Use is generally repeated within a day of the last use, to ameliorate rapidly appearing withdrawal symptoms. Because many cocaine abusers did not use cocaine daily, the absence of a daily use pattern was considered evidence that cocaine produced a less severe and intractable addiction. Whereas many of the cocaine users we studied described daily use within the year that preceded their seeking treatment, over 90% described a transition to binge abuse on developing dyscontrol. The binge pattern became more pronounced as attempts to curtail use were initiated, and several extra days of abstinence more often separated binges. By the time of treatment seeking, users averaged one to three binges per week, lasting from 8–24 hours. Counterintuitively, abusers described that their earlier daily use was associated with some control over cocaine intake: Use could be stopped although some cocaine supplies remained, in order to allow normal sleep to occur. When dyscontrol occurred, users were unable to refrain until supplies were exhausted, and use throughout the night took place, resulting in prolonged binges followed by intervals of abstinence. This observation established that the absence of daily use pattern in a cocaine abuser did not indicate decreased impairment and often indicated the opposite, providing a crucial clinical distinction between cocaine addiction and alcohol or opiate dependence.

A pattern of unceasing cocaine bingeing, as described previously by Seigel (1982) also occurred, but in less than 10% of the sample. In such abuse, brief periods (3–6 hours) of sleep interrupted continual, long-term, high-dose intake (Seigel, 1982), but this pattern required almost unlimited access to cocaine ($100,000/year cocaine expense).

Abstinence Symptoms
(Gawin & Kleber, 1986a)

We observed a triphasic cocaine abstinence pattern that helped dispel the perception that cocaine use produces no withdrawal. The three phases are summarized below.

Crash (Phase 1): Other investigators had emphasized an immediate postcocaine depression following a binge (Seigel, 1982; Anonymous, 1984). This "crash" of mood and energy was also described by our patients immediately after cessation of a cocaine binge. Cocaine craving, depression, agitation, and anxiety rapidly intensified. We were intrigued, however, by descriptions that, over approximately 1–4 hours, cocaine craving was supplanted by mounting fatigue and craving for sleep; further use was then often strongly rejected, unlike parallel points after several hours of opiate, sedative, or alcohol withdrawal. The cocaine abusers administered alcohol, anxiolytics, sedatives, opiates, or marijuana to induce sleep. Once sleep occurred, prolonged hypersomnolence followed. The crash's length was related to the duration and intensity of the preceding binge. The exhaustion, depression, and hypersomnolence of the crash probably reflect acute neurotransmitter depletion caused by the preceding cocaine binge (Gawin & Kleber, 1986a). Clinical recovery from the crash depends in part on sleep, diet, and, probably, time for neurotransmitter synthesis and repletion. Usual management included nutrition and rest. When the abuser awakens from the hypersomnolence, few crash residua persisted, and the offset of the crash is therefore self-limited.

The crash had sometimes been confused with withdrawal from cocaine by prior investigators (Seigel, 1982; Khantzian, 1983; Dackis, Gold, & Sweeney, 1987). This confusion had resulted in the erroneous perceptions that (1) withdrawal symptoms ended with resolution of the crash; (2) no withdrawal treatment was needed, because the crash was self-limited; and (3) withdrawal symptoms in cocaine abuse were intense but short. Other investigators questioned whether the crash was even a withdrawal equivalent. Instead they considered it an acute reaction to the massive stimulation of the cocaine binge, concluding that no neurophysiological adaptation to cocaine occurred and that therefore no withdrawal treatment was necessary (Anker & Crowley, 1982). We hypothesized instead that the crash was like the acute withdrawal of the alcohol "hangover" (Gawin & Kleber, 1986a; Kleber & Gawin, 1987a) and concurred that it does not contribute to long-term abuse. Because of the striking consistency of several-day intervals between cocaine binges, however, we then further evaluated whether other withdrawal symptoms with delayed emergence might be present.

Withdrawal (Phase 2): The usual manifestations of physiological withdrawal symptoms (e.g., hypertension, tachycardia, diaphoresis, pilo-erection, seizures, cramps) that are produced by abused drugs such as opiates or alcohol are absent in cocaine abusers, which led to the belief that cocaine's addiction was purely "psychological." We observed the gradual onset of a significant protracted dysphoric syndrome, including decreased activation, amotivation, and intense boredom with limited pleasure from the environment (anhedonia), after a variable, brief (1–5 days) euthymic interval following the crash. These subtle psychological symptoms were less dramatic than those of the crash and went unrecognized by most early observers. We observed no gross physiological alterations. The symptoms were generally not constant or severe enough to meet psychiatric diagnostic criteria for major mood disorders. Such symptoms nonetheless frequently led to resumption of cocaine use and repetition of a cyclical pattern: binge–crash–euthymic interval–anhedonia–relapse–binge.

Of additional importance was our observation that abusers were often able to withstand the anhedonia of this phase until confronted with classically conditioned cues that evoke memories of cocaine euphoria. Conditioned cocaine cravings were cued by varied, idiosyncratic objects or events that had been temporally paired with cocaine euphoria. Cues included specific persons, locations, or events (e.g., birthdays), or seeing abuse objects (e.g., money, glass pipes, mirrors, syringes, and single-edged razor blades, among many others). Internal cues also evoke craving (e.g., mild alcohol intoxication, or mood states such as anxiety caused by interpersonal strife, which the user had previously soothed by cocaine use). In contrast to the user's limited ability to experience pleasure during cocaine withdrawal, cues evoked vivid memories of extreme euphoria, inducing severe stimulant craving and, hence, resumption of use. Once abstinence was sustained, however, anhedonic symptoms lifted within 2–10 weeks.

Because the anhedonic state was directly related to craving and resumption of use, it paralleled "withdrawal" from other abused substances, except for the absence of gross physiological changes, and thus we termed it cocaine "withdrawal." As with other drugs of abuse, the withdrawal syndrome from cocaine was an inversion of acute drug effects. Cocaine acutely amplifies normal pleasure to produce exaggerated euphoria; cocaine chronically produces a withdrawal state of dampened euphoric response to produce anhedonia. The concordance of these symptoms with several types of data on neurophysiological and behavioral alterations after chronic stimulants in animals (reviewed below), and to pharmacotherapy effects (also reviewed below) led us to conceptualize this state as a plausible psychological manifestation of neuroadaptation to chronic perturbation of brain reward systems by cocaine, and hence to hypothesize that its origins were physiological despite its primarily psychological symptom expression.

Extinction (Phase 3): Despite resolution of the craving related to withdrawal anhedonia, intermittent recurrence of cocaine craving was reported by long-abstinent cocaine abusers, based on cued memories of cocaine euphoria. As we followed our sample over time, craving based on conditioned cues was reported months or even years after last cocaine use. The craving was episodic, lasting only hours. Lasting recovery from cocaine dependence appeared to depend on experiencing this intermittent conditioned craving without relapsing. The previous pairing of cues with euphoria would not occur, and, as expected in a classical conditioning phenomenon, extinction of craving gradually followed. Relapse caused by classically conditioned craving and withdrawal had previously been extensively described in opiate and nicotine withdrawal, so their appearance in cocaine abuse was unsurprising. The clinical impression we formed, however, was that evoked cocaine craving was more intense than that occurring with other commonly abused substances, a not unexpected finding given cocaine's extreme potency as a reinforcer in animal models, and the established linkage in animal experiments between strength of reinforcement and magnitude of classical conditioning. This finding led to a substantial appreciation of the importance of managing such cues, and to a focus on techniques to attenuate safely the potency of such cues in psychotherapy treatment and research efforts (reviewed below).

Psychiatric Comorbidity
(Gawin & Kleber, 1986a, Gawin, 1986)

Weiss and colleagues (Weiss, Mirin, Michael, & Sollogub, 1986; Weiss, Mirin, Michael, Guggin, & Sollogub, 1987) at MacLean Hospital conducted research on psychiatric disorder in inpatient cocaine abusers at the same time that we conducted similar studies in outpatients at Yale (Gawin & Kleber, 1986a; Kleber & Gawin, 1987a). Research from both groups indicated that DSM-III Axis I interview timing and application had to be modified when applied to cocaine abuse and that, whereas some cocaine abusers suffer primarily from an addictive disorder, a substantial proportion might be self-medicating psychiatric disorders such as depression.

Modification of interview timing was needed because crash symptoms mimic those of depressed states in affective disorders. In the diagnostic studies cited, DSM-III criteria were applied, but clinical assessments were delayed until crash symptoms should have abated, before diagnostic assessments took place. Significantly, applications of this delay resulted in acceptable diagnostic validity (Weiss et al., 1986).

In the two sets of two studies done by Weiss et al. (Weiss et al., 1986; Weiss et al., 1987) and ourselves (Gawin & Kleber, 1985a, 1986a), Axis I affective disorders were present in 30–50% of cocaine abuse treatment-seeking populations, and attention-deficit disorder-residual type (ADD-RT) was present in 3–5%. These findings suggested significant implications regarding predisposition to cocaine abuse. Anxiety or panic disorders and schizophrenia were almost absent, indicating that dysphoric effects of cocaine in these populations may select against the development of abuse. Conversely, the prevalence of cyclical mood disorder (cyclothymic disorder and bipolar disorder) may be 10 times higher in cocaine abuse treatment populations compared with opiate and alcohol abuse populations, suggesting preferential selection for cocaine in such individuals.

It should be noted that, because of the coexistence of chronic cocaine abuse, it is impossible to be certain whether these disorders represented preabuse psychopathology exacerbated by cocaine, or cocaine-induced disorders. Similarly, the permanence of such states during long-term abstinence has not yet been determined. But, regardless of uncertainties over etiology or stability, the observation of diagnostically discrete subpopulations in cocaine abuse treatment populations has led to important clinical assessments of appropriate pharmacotherapies. In turn, remarkable amelioration of cocaine abuse has been reported in cyclical and attention deficit disorder cocaine abusers treated appropriately with, respectively, lithium and stimulant medications, whereas no response to these agents is found in cocaine abusers without these diagnoses (reviewed in Gawin & Kleber, 1986c).

Continuing and Future Research on the Clinical Phenomenology of Cocaine Abuse

The studies reviewed created a foundation for investigation of cocaine abuse that helped clarify essential clinical research questions to be addressed in further, more rigorous studies and future research. Numerous investigators are currently examining the clinical characteristics of cocaine dependence. In studies now underway, we and colleagues are evaluating (1) distinctions between cocaine users who have not sought treatment and those in our treatment programs, in order to learn about potential factors creating the transitions to dependence and the motivation to seek treatment; (2) the range of abuse patterns and their development, in order to quantify severity and potentially to predict prognosis, as well as to facilitate development of accurate animal models of cocaine dependence (discussed below);(3) whether cocaine abstinence symptoms are amenable to structured, systematic assessment; the findings reviewed thus far have been substantiated by other clinical investigators but were not subjected to structured research evaluations. Both behavioral (e.g., ratings of withdrawal symptoms by blind raters) and neurochemical indices of cocaine withdrawal are being investigated. Furthermore, the application of new instruments developed for other psychiatric disorders (such as anhedonia scales developed for depression) to cocaine abusers is being assessed in clinical studies. (4) Factors that influence the time course and intensity of abstinence symptoms, such as total cocaine abuse history, recent use, co-use of other substances, and Axis I comorbidity, are also being assessed in clinical studies. (5) The interrelationship of anhedonic craving for cocaine and craving evoked by cues is being explored. In opiate abuse, cues have been demonstrated to evoke not only a desire for opiate euphoria, but also withdrawal symptoms that, in turn, superimpose additional desire for opiates to relieve these symptoms. Whether cocaine cues can evoke or worsen anhedonia, in addition to provoking desire for cocaine euphoria, remains to be assessed.

EVOLVING APPLICATIONS OF PRECLINICAL RESEARCH TO CLINICAL PROBLEMS

When our studies began, it was assumed that neuroadaptation did not occur in human cocaine abuse and that cocaine was only "psychologically" addicting. Nonetheless, the brain's prototypical response to persistent, drug-induced neurochemical perturbations is homeostatic compensatory neuroadaption. We consequently evaluated available preclinical data to determine if the abstinence symptomatology we observed might be based in neurophysiological adaptations to chronic cocaine administration.

Substantial preclinical research (reviewed in Wise & Bogarth, 1987; Spyraki, Fibiger, & Phillips, 1982; Gawin, 1986) had established that cocaine and amphetamine facilitate activity of a central nervous system reward system, presumably by increasing neurotransmission in mesolimbic and/or mesocortical dopaminergic tracts. In humans, activation of these pathways would produce sensations of euphoria. Lesions in these pathways block cocaine effects in animal experiments. Dopamine receptor blockers, which should disrupt transmission in these pathways, also attenuate cocaine effects in animals. Furthermore, electrical self-stimulation using electrodes placed in these pathways produces behavior identical to that observed in cocaine self-administration experiments.

Although less preclinical research on chronic cocaine administration had taken place than on acute cocaine effects, most reports described neurophysiological alteration from chronic administration of cocaine or the very similar abused stimulant, amphetamine. A crucial concordance existed between animal models of pleasure and our clinical observations of cocaine withdrawal. Intracranial electrical self-stimulation (ICSS) in animals, of the same dopaminergic reward pathways that are activated by acute cocaine administration, had previously been used as a model for human pleasure. Chronic stimulants decreased ICSS reward indices (reviewed in Gawin & Ellinwood, 1988). These ICSS decrements implied that chronic cocaine abuse could produce a neurophysiological down-regulation of the brain reward regions activated by acute cocaine use. Such down-regulation would be consistent with our clinical observations of protracted anhedonia in abstinent stimulant abusers. Complementary findings existed in neuroreceptor adaptation studies. Central dopaminergic, α-adrenergic, and β-adrenergic receptor supersensitivity were demonstrated after chronic cocaine administration (reviewed in Gawin & Kleber, 1984), but presynaptic and postsynaptic receptor changes were not differentiated in these studies. We hypothe-

size that relative autoreceptor supersensitivity would decrease dopaminergic neurotransmission and might provide a foundation both for the
ICSS changes demonstrated in animals and the anhedonia observed in
humans (Gawin & Kleber, 1986a).

The concordance of clinical and preclinical data provided a
foundation for the new hypothesis that clinical cocaine dependence was
associated with sustained neurophysiological changes, but in brain
systems that regulate only psychological processes—particularly, hedonic responsivity or pleasure—and therefore involved a true physiological addiction and withdrawal, but one whose clinical expression appears
primarily psychological.

Despite the compelling concordance and parsimony of generalizing
between preclinical finding and clinical findings on cocaine, the
existence of a neuroadaptive withdrawal state in cocaine abusers remains
a not yet proven working hypothesis. Before this hypothesis can be
considered proven or disproven, not only will broader investigations of
cocaine's consequences be needed, but also advances in research
methodology: In particular, two fundamental research areas, both the
foci of ongoing work, will require exploration.

The first area of investigation concerns whether the administration
conditions in animal studies generalize to human abuse. Prior chronic
animal paradigms have employed administration patterns that do not
reflect human abuse patterns (Gawin & Kleber, 1986b). The chronic
stimulant studies in animals involve daily intraperitoneal drug administration that may not accurately reflect the consequences of multidose
binges and the multiple-day, cocaine-free intervals that characterize
human abuse. Administration duration is also usually only 1–3 months
in such experiments and may not accurately reflect the consequences of
multiple years of cocaine abuse. Hence more accurate reproductions of
human drug self-administration are needed in future preclinical research.

Second, does evidence of neuroadaptation exist in human beings
who abuse cocaine? Although we (Gawin & Kleber, 1985b; Kleber &
Gawin, 1987b) and others (Dackis, Gold, & Sweeney, 1987; Giannini,
Malone, Giannini, Price, & Loiselle, 1987) have conducted studies of
neuroendocrine indices and neurotransmitter metabolite levels, as
indices of dopaminergic function, that appear to be consistent with
animal data, such indirect peripheral indices can be confounded by
multiple sources. For example, other drugs abused, altered sleep cycles,
concurrent medical or psychiatric disorder, and diet might all alter
peripheral indices of central neurotransmitter function, as might
duration of abstinence, intensity of abuse, and genetic heterogeneity,

among many others (Gawin & Kleber, 1985b). These confounds caused by differences in antecedent history can, at present, only be resolved by chronic cocaine studies in animals that control for all variables other than cocaine administration. Advances in imaging, particularly in vivo imaging of humans, may soon obviate the problems of examining animals or peripheral indices in humans, by directly evaluating metabolism and neurochemistry in the brains of cocaine abusers. The spatial resolution of current positron emission tomographic scanning and magnetic resonance spectroscopic imaging are currently insufficient to demarcate brain function in the dopaminergic reward regions of principal interest in cocaine abuse studies, but rapid advances in these imaging technologies may soon make such studies possible. Preliminary imaging studies of cocaine abusers in withdrawal have already been done (Baxter, 1987).

Finally, future research supporting the hypothesis of a neuroadaptive withdrawal state should also be able to quantify the extent of neuroadaptation. Our preliminary clinical observations indicate that both symptom severity and duration were related to the length and intensity of the preceding chronic abuse. Predisposing psychiatric disorders also amplified withdrawal (Gawin & Kleber, 1986a). Conversely, in infrequent "recreational" cocaine users without psychiatric disorders, withdrawal may not occur. High-intensity "binge" cocaine use and coinciding neuroadaptation might be required before withdrawal occurs. Basic research is thus needed to determine how to "stage" neurophysiological alterations produced by cocaine abuse, and to determine the extent to which interindividual differences exist in susceptibility to, and recovery from, cocaine neuroadaptation. Such information would aid in providing a precise scientific foundation for a cocaine abuse treatment design.

EVOLVING TREATMENT STRATEGIES

As cocaine abusers began to appear for treatment throughout the United States, available drug treatments, usually alcohol or opiate abuse psychotherapies, were applied without adaptation for specific problems, such as anhedonia or conditioned craving, in cocaine dependence (Kleber & Gawin, 1984a, 1984b).

Cocaine abuse treatment, like other substance abuse treatment, can be subdivided into two phases, abstinence initiation and relapse prevention. These correspond to the withdrawal and extinction phases of cocaine abstinence (Gawin & Kleber, 1986b).

Abstinence Initiation Strategies

Continued cycles of stimulant binges or of daily use are likely as long as anergic and anhedonic symptoms are present. Hospitalization, group and individual psychotherapy, and treatment contracts involving aversive contingencies for continued drug use have long been employed to facilitate abstinence in varied substance abuse populations and have been routinely employed in cocaine abuse treatment. Of these, only hospitalization has the advantage of ensuring abstinence. Hospitalization, however, also has the simultaneous disadvantage of isolation from the cue-rich environment, precluding extinction during an inpatient stay.

We and others considered these approaches either inadequate or too costly and sought new alternatives to treatment of cocaine anhedonia, exploring pharmacological treatment aimed at reversing the hypothesized deficits in dopaminergic reward systems.

Anhedonia is a common symptom in multiple psychiatric disorders, especially unipolar and bipolar depression. Tricyclic antidepressants (TCAs), while having broad effects on numerous depressive symptoms, also effectively reverse the anhedonia of severe depression. Although only 10% of cocaine abusers in treatment samples met criteria for severe depression, most cocaine abusers reported anhedonic symptoms, and we reasoned that such agents might have specific antianhedonic effects in this population. Preclinical data strengthened this possibility. Chronic TCA effects on neurophysiology are generally opposite to those of chronic cocaine: They induce receptor subsensitivity rather than supersensitivity. In particular, TCAs produce autoreceptor subsensitivity in dopaminergic systems and increase dopaminergic transmission, which would oppose the dopaminergic autoreceptor supersensitivity we hypothesized to underlie cocaine anhedonia. More important, in a little-noticed study done in 1974, Simpson, investigating whether stimulant-induced ICSS deficits might provide a useful model for severe depressive disorders, demonstrated that chronic desipramine treatment increased sensitivity to electrical stimulation in ICSS animals pretreated with stimulants, thereby reversing the stimulants' chronic effect (Simpson & Annau, 1977). The same findings were later extended to other closely related TCAs (Kokkinidis, Zacharko, & Predy, 1980). These results not only had implications as a model for affective disorder but also had direct implications for stimulant abuse treatment. Regardless of whether autoreceptor changes in dopaminergic tracts are responsible for ICSS changes and their reversal by TCAs, or whether some other mechanism is responsible, these data implied that cocaine anhedonia could be reversed by TCAs.

Despite the presence of significant suggestive animal data from electrophysiology and neurochemistry research, a decade passed before clinicians began to explore the possible utility of TCAs in human stimulant abusers. Shortly after establishing the cocaine clinic in 1982, we began a series of pharmacotherapy pilot trials in cocaine abusers. In addition to evaluating the efficacy of a TCA, desipramine, we studied two other agents. Methylphenidate was evaluated because of the possibility that it might rapidly restore dopaminergic reward functioning, analogous to methadone treatment for heroin abusers, and lithium was evaluated because of anecdotal accounts that is had benefited some stimulant abusers.

The first two trials were open-label comparisons. Subjects in other open trials were psychotherapy resistant, outpatient cocaine abusers. The first study (Gawin & Kleber, 1984) compared desipramine plus psychotherapy, lithium carbonate plus psychotherapy, and psychotherapy alone in chronic cocaine abusers who had failed to stop cocaine abuse with the help of psychotherapy alone. Six desipramine patients (200 mg/day) uniformly decreased and ultimately ceased their cocaine use during the 12-week trial. Craving did not change from pretreatment until the third week of pharmacotherapy, consistent with the delayed efficacy of TCAs in depression and the delay before receptor changes take place in TCA animal studies (Charney, Menkes, & Heninger, 1981). By the end of week three, craving scores were reduced to one third of their pretreatment value. Declines in cocaine use paralleled the craving scores. Decreases in use and craving occurred regardless of other coexisting psychiatric disorders. Subjects without depressive disorders appeared to benefit from a subtle but consistent increase in the ability to respond to pleasurable stimuli. Desipramine was uniformly well tolerated. In addition to these six patients who were being studied in the formal pilot trial, we reported on an additional six cocaine abusers treatment with desipramine, and the results were essentially the same. Taken collectively, the pilot study found that desipramine decreased cocaine craving and resulted in abstinence in 11 out of 12 chronic cocaine abusers (92%).

All of the subjects being treated with psychotherapy alone reported persistent subjective cravings for cocaine. Only one of them (17%) was able to abstain totally from cocaine, and only half the group showed any improvement. Six patients received a combination of lithium plus psychotherapy. Only subjects with cyclothymic disorder became abstinent in this group.

We continued evaluating TCAs in a second open pilot trial (Gawin, 1986a; Gawin, Byck, & Kleber, 1986) in which the subjects consisted only of individuals without diagnoses of affective disorders, so as to assess further whether TCA responses occurred in subjects who did not meet criteria for depression. Twenty-six patients without major affective disorders were selected. The methods employed were otherwise the same as in the first trial. Six patients declined pharmacotherapy and were used as a nonmedication comparison group. Open pharmacological treatment was added to the psychotherapy treatment regimen in the remaining 20 patients, who were randomly assigned either to desipramine or to a comparison active treatment (lithium or methylphenidate).

Desipramine hydrochloride produced abstinence in over 80% of the desipramine group, compared with less than 40% in comparison groups who were given other agents (lithium and methylphenidate) or who continued in psychotherapy without medication. As in our first study, craving and cocaine use decreased in the desipramine group after a typical tricyclic time lag. Methylphenidate produced rapid reductions in craving during the first week, which then reversed. As methylphenidate tolerance developed, subjects described conditioned craving as a result of mild methylphenidate stimulation. The methylphenidate trial was stopped after five subjects had been treated for 4 weeks because all five deteriorated clinically (Gawin, Riordan, & Kleber, 1985). Subsequent subjects were given lithium.

Similarly promising results occurred in an independent, simultaneous open trial conducted by Rosecan (1983) in an unselected population using another tricyclic drug, imipramine. By 1985, four groups had reported open-trial data that TCAs facilitated recovery from cocaine abuse.

These promising early results led to a substantial effort to evaluate these findings using double-blind methods. Giannini et al. (1986) completed the first double-blind trial in 24 cocaine abusers, contrasting desipramine to an active placebo, diphenhydramine. Ongoing, double-blind, placebo-controlled studies by ourselves and O'Brien have also reported midpoint data; these investigations have confirmed that desipramine produces statistically and clinically significant increases in abstinence rates (Gawin et al., 1986; O'Brien, 1987) and decreases in cocaine use, craving, and symptom scores (Gawin et al., 1986; Giannini et al., 1986; O'Brien, 1987).

Although these findings remain tentative, in that two of the studies require completion, they imply that a generally effective pharmacotherapy to facilitate abstinence initiation exists. Three additional groups have recently initiated double-blind TCA trials, and a complete assessment of the value of TCAs in the abstinence initiation phase of cocaine abuse treatment will shortly exist. If proven effective by this collective research, an extremely important, new, effective, inexpensive, and expedient modality for cocaine abuse treatment will be available for the first time.

Other experimental pharmacological research strategies, all based on a rationale of increasing reward transmission in dopaminergic reward systems, are also in preliminary stages of investigation. Most are attempts to increase dopaminergic neurotransmission directly, using dopamimetic agents like amantidine (Tennant & Sagherian, 1987), bromocriptine (Dackis & Gold, 1985), tyrosine (Gold, Pottash, & Annitto, 1983), and, as described above, methylphenidate (Gawin, Riordan, & Kleber, 1985). These agents have all been reported to produce acute decreases in cocaine craving in small, short-term open trials, lending further substantiation to the hypothesis that cocaine produces a neuroadaptation that can be affected pharmacologically. The clinical utility of these treatments, however, is less clear than for TCAs. Tennant and colleagues conducted a double-blind comparison of amantidine and bromocriptine in 14 cocaine abusers (Tennant & Sagherian, 1987), but 71% of the bromocriptine subjects dropped out because of side effects, rendering the amantidine findings difficult to interpret. Giannini has reported double-blind reductions in symptom scores in bromocriptine-treated subjects compared with those given placebo but did not report abstinence or craving data (Giannini et al, 1986).

Relapse Prevention Strategies

Although relapse prevention pharmacotherapies exist for opiate and alcohol abuse (naltrexone and disulfiram, respectively), no similar pharmacotherapy has yet emerged for cocaine dependence (possible stimulant blockade has also been tried using lithium [Gawin & Kleber, 1984], trazodone [Rowbotham, Jones, Benowitz, & Jacob, 1984], imipramine, and neuroleptics [Gawin, 1986], but these experiments have not yet demonstrated a clinically useful blockade of cocaine effects for any pharmacotherapy).

Beginning studies are now under way in our treatment programs to elucidate which psychotherapeutic techniques best preclude relapse in cocaine abusers. The approaches under study are generally comparable to those used after withdrawal in other substance abuse treatments (Marlatt & Gordon, 1980). The goal of relapse prevention is gradually to decrease the external controls placed on the abuser, by family and therapist, during initiation of abstinence, and gradually to facilitate development of the abuser's internal controls. Relapse prevention techniques include extinguishing conditioned cues, reducing external dysphoria and stress, developing drug-free socialization networks, predicting situations of high relapse risk, rehearsing avoidance strategies, and connecting memories of negative consequences of cocaine abuse to positive memories of cocaine in order to counteract evoked memories of cocaine euphoria. Idiosyncratic needs in the addict's life that the stimulant may have met, albeit dysfunctionally, are also explored, and constructive alternatives to meeting these needs are pursued (Rounsaville, Gawin, & Kleber, 1985).

Although conceptually attractive and clinically expedient, such techniques have not yet been systematically evaluated. Using precisely applied research psychotherapy methodologies, fundamental questions are now being assessed as to whether systematic application of these straightforward relapse prevention techniques improves outcome compared with less directive psychotherapy. Examples of questions being addressed by current studies include: (1) What is the relative value of each of the relapse techniques listed above? (2) Can internal cues (e.g., those evoked by mood states or interpersonal strife) be extinguished as readily as external cues (e.g., locations where cocaine was used) that are more easily reproduced and controlled? (3) When should return to the cue-rich environment be avoided, and when should it be advocated? (4) Do such treatments have additive or interactive effects when combined with pharmacotherapies? While this research is in its infancy, it promises guided, rational applications of psychotherapy to prevent relapse.

CONCLUSION

The advent of cocaine dependence as a drug-dependence disorder without gross physiological withdrawal symptoms forces reconceptualization of "classic" drug abuse constructs such as dependence, tolerance, and withdrawal. These constructs are based on gross physiological measures and have remained unchanged for decades. There exist for benzodiazepines, alcohol, and opiates excellent antiwithdrawal agents that reverse gross physiological withdrawal symptoms, but these agents have not solved the problem of addiction to these drugs. This implies that other symptoms contribute to unrelenting abuse. These symptoms may be of the same order as the psychological symptoms expressed in cocaine withdrawal and may also be neurophysiological in origin. The lack of broad clinical applicability of "classic" constructs of withdrawal, tolerance, and dependence based on gross physiological parameters has led the World Health Organiza- tion to discard old terms in favor of the more physiologically precise "neuroadaptation" (World Health Organization, 1981), and recently led the APA to define drug dependence in behavioral rather that gross physiological terms for the first time (Rounsaville, Spitzer, & Williams, 1986).

The concept of cocaine dependence has evolved, within one decade, from that of a nonexistent disorder to that of a complexly regulated disorder with interwoven behavioral, psychological, and neurophysiological components. It is unlikely that a shift of similar magnitude will result from our research efforts or those of others during the next decade; instead, future research, at Yale's cocaine abuse clinic and elsewhere, will provide increasingly precise depictions of the details of the development, expression, and management of cocaine abuse.

REFERENCES

American Psychiatric Association. (1980). *Diagnostic and Statistical Manual of Mental Disorders* (3rd ed.). Washington, DC: Author.

Anker, A. L., & Crowley, T. J. (1982). *Use of contingency in speciality clinics for cocaine abuse* (National Institute on Drug Abuse Research Monograph No. 41, pp. 452–459). Washington, DC: U. S. Government Printing Office.

Anonymous. (1984). Adverse effects of cocaine abuse. *Medical Letter on Drugs and Therapeutics, 26,* 51–52.

Baxter, L. R. (1987, September). *Localization of the neurochemical effects of cocaine and other stimulants in the human brain.* Paper presented at the North American Conference on Cocaine Abuse and Its Treatment, Washington, DC.

Charney, D. S., Menkes, D. B., & Heniger, G. R. (1981). Receptor sensitivity and the mechanism of action of antidepressant treatment. *Archives of General Psychiatry, 38,* 1160–1180.

Dackis, C. A., & Gold, M. S. (1985). Bromocriptine for cocaine withdrawal [letter]. *Lancet, i,* 1151–1152.

Dackis, C. A, Gold, M. S., & Sweeney, D. R. (1987). The physiology of cocaine craving and "crashing" [letter]. *Archives of General Psychiatry, 44,* 298–300.

Ellinwood, E. H., & Petrie, W. M. (1977). Dependence on amphetamine, cocaine and other stimulants. In S. N. Pradhan (Ed.), *Drug Abuse: Clinical and Basic Aspects* (pp. 248–262). St. Louis, MO: CV Mosby.

Gawin, F. H. (1986a). New uses of antidepressants in cocaine abuse. *Psychosomatics, 27,* s24–s29.

Gawin, F. H. (1986b). Neuroleptic reduction of cocaine-induced paranoia but not euphoria? *Psychopharmacology, 90,* 142–143.

Gawin, F. H, Byck, R., & Kleber, H. D. (1986). Desipramine augmentation of cocaine abstinence: Initial results. *Proceedings in Clinical Neuropharmacology, 9*(Suppl 4), 202–204.

Gawin, F. H., & Ellinwood, E. H. (1988). Cocaine and other stimulants: Actions, abuse, and treatment. *New England Journal of Medicine, 318*(18), 1173–1182.

Gawin, F. H., & Kleber, H. D. (1984). Cocaine abuse treatment: Open trial with desipramine and lithium carbonate. *Archives of General Psychiatry, 42,* 903–910.

Gawin, F. H., & Kleber, H. D. (1985a). *Cocaine use in a treatment population: Patterns and diagnostic distinctions* (National Institute on Drug Abuse Research Monograph No. 61, pp. 182–192). Washington DC: U. S. Government Printing Office.

Gawin, F. H., & Kleber, H. D. (1985b). Neuroendocrine findings in chronic cocaine abusers. *British Journal of Psychiatry, 147,* 569–573.

Gawin, F. H., & Kleber, H. D. (1986a). Abstinence symptomatology and psychiatric diagnosis in chronic cocaine abusers. *Archives of General Psychiatry, 43,* 107–113.

Gawin, F. H., & Kleber, H. D. (1986b). Issues in cocaine abuse treatment research. In S. Fisher, B. Raskin, & R. Uhlenhuth (Eds.), *Cocaine: Clinical and biobehavioral aspects* (pp. 169–187). New York: Oxford University Press.

Gawin, F. H., & Kleber, H. D. (1986c). Pharmacological treatment of cocaine abuse. *Psychiatric Clinics of North America 9,* 573–583.

Gawin, F. H., Riordan, C., & Kleber, H. D. (1985). Methyphenidate use in non-ADD cocaine abusers—A negative study. *American Journal of Drug Alcohol Abuse, 11,* 193–197.

Giannini, A. J, Malone, D. A., Giannini, M. C., Price, W. A., & Loiselle, R. H. (1986). Treatment of Depression in chronic cocaine and phencyclidine abuse with desipramine. *Journal of Clinical Pharmacology, 25,* 211–214.

Giannini, A. J, Malone, D. A., Loiselle, R. H., & Price, W. A. (1987). Blunting of TSH response to TRH in chronic cocaine and phencyclidine abusers. *Journal of Clinical Psychiatry, 48,* 25–26.

Gold, M. S., Pottash, A. L. C., & Annitto, W. D. (1983, November 7). *Cocaine withdrawal: Efficacy of tyrosine.* Paper presented at the Society for Neuroscience, 13th annual meeting, Boston MA.

Grinspoon, L., & Bakalar, J. B. (1980). Drug dependence: Non-narcotic agents. In H. I. Kaplan, A. M. Freedman, B. J. Sadock (Eds.), *Comprehensive Textbook of Psychiatry, 3rd edition.* Baltimore: Williams and Wilkins.

Johanson, C. E. (1984). *Assessment of the dependence potential of cocaine in animals* (National Institute on Drug Abuse Research Monograph No. 50, pp. 54–71). Washington, DC: U. S. Government Printing Office.

Khantzian, E. J. (1983). Cocaine dependence: An extreme case and marked improvement with methylphenidate treatment. *American Journal of Psychiatry, 140,* 784–785.

Kleber, H. D. (1974). Drug abuse. In L. Bellak (Ed.), *A Concise Handbook of Community Mental Health.* New York: Grune and Stratton.

Kleber, H. D., & Gawin, F. H. (1984a). *Cocaine abuse: A review of current and experimental treatments* (National Institute on Drug Abuse Research Monograph No. 50, pp. 111–129). Washington, DC: U. S. Government Printing Office.

Kleber, H. D., & Gawin, F. H. (1984b). The spectrum of cocaine abuse and its treatment. *Journal of Clinical Psychiatry, 45,* 18–23.

Kleber, H. D., & Gawin, F. H. (1987a). Cocaine withdrawal [reply]. *Archives of General Psychiatry, 44,* 298–299.

Kleber, H. D., & Gawin, F. H. (1987b). The physiology of cocaine craving and "crashing" [reply]. *Archives of General Psychiatry, 44,* 300–301.

Kokkinidis, L., Zacharko, R. M., & Predy, P. A. (1980). Post-amphetamine depression of self-stimulation responding from the substantianigra: Reversal by tryclic antidepressants. *Pharmacology, Biochemistry and Behavior, 13,* 379–383.

Marlatt, G. A., & Gordon, J. R. (1980). Determinants of relapse: Implications for the maintenance of behavior change. In P. O. Davidson & S. M. Davidson (Eds.), *Behavioral medicine: Changing health lifestyles* (pp. 410–452). New York: Brunner/Mazel.

National Commission on Marihuana and Drug Abuse. (1973, March). *Drug use in America: Problems in perspective* (Second Report of the National Commission of on Marihuana and Drug Abuse). Washington, DC: National Institute on Drug Abuse.

O'Brien, C. (1987, September 16). *Controlled studies of pharmacologic and behavioral treatments of cocaine dependence* Paper presented at North American Conference on Cocaine Abuse and Its Treatment, Washington, D. C.

Rosecan, J. (1983, July 14–19). *The treatment of cocaine abuse with imipramine, L-tyrosine, and L-tryptophan.* Paper presented at the VII World Congress of Psychiatry, Vienna, Austria.

Rounsaville, B. J., Gawin, F. H., & Kleber, H. D. (1985). Interpersonal psychotherapy (IPT) adapted for ambulatory cocaine abusers. *American Journal of Drug Alcohol Abuse, 11,* 171–191.

Rounsaville, B. J., Spitzer, R. L., & Williams, J. B. (1986). Proposed changes in DSM-III substance use disorders: Description and rationale. *American Journal of Psychiatry, 143,* 463–468.

Rowbotham, M., Jones, R. T., Benowitz, N., & Jacob, P. (1984). Tranzodone-oral cocaine interactions. *Archives of General Psychiatry, 41,* 895–899.

Seigel, R. K. (1982). Cocaine smoking. *Journal of Psychoactive Drugs, 14,* 321–337.

Simpson, D. M., & Annau, Z. (1977). Behavioral withdrawal following several psychoactive drugs. *Pharmacology, Biochemistry and Behavior, 7,* 59–64.

Spyraki, C., Fibiger, H. C., & Phillips, A. C. (1982). Cocaine-induced place preference conditioning: Lack of effects of neuroleptics and 6 hydroxydopamine lesions. *Brain Research, 253,* 195–203.

Tennant, F. S., Jr., & Sagherian, A. A. (1987). Double-blind comparison of amantadine and bromocriptine for ambulatory withdrawal from cocaine dependence. *Archives of Internal Medicine, 147,* 109–112.

Weiss, R. (1984). *Neural mechanisms of the reinforcing actions of cocaine* (National Institute on Drug Abuse Research Monograph No. 50, pp. 15–53). Washington, DC: U. S. Government Printing Office.

Weiss, R. D., Mirin, S. M., Michael, J., Griggin, M., & Sollogub, A. (1987, May 12). *Psychopathology in drug abusers and their families.* Paper presented at the 140th meeting of the American Psychiatric Association, Chicago.

Weiss, R. D., Mirin, S. M., Michael, J. L., & Sollogub, A. C. (1986).

Psychopathology in chronic cocaine abusers. *American Journal of Drug Alcohol Abuse, 12,* 17–29.

Wise, R. A., & Bogarth, M. A. (1987). A psychomotor stimulant theory of addiction. *Psychological Review, 94,* 469–492.

World Health Organization. (1981). WHO Expert Committee on Addiction-Producing Drugs: Nomenclature and classification of drug and alcohol–related problems. *Bulletin of the World Health Organization, 39,* 225–242.

PART TWO

PHARMACOLOGY AND PHENOMENOLOGY

Basic Neurobiology of Cocaine: Actions within the Mesolimbic Dopamine System

Dana Beitner-Johnson, PhD
Eric J. Nestler, MD, PhD

C OCAINE IS a potently reinforcing drug with an extremely high abuse liability. The acute pharmacological and behavioral actions of cocaine have been studied extensively, but the neurobiological basis of the drug's high addiction potential, especially after repeated use, remains uncertain. The aim of this chapter is to examine possible cellular and intracellular processes by which cocaine exerts its rewarding effects.

COCAINE ADDICTION AND THE MESOLIMBIC DOPAMINE SYSTEM

Much progress has been made in the past decade toward identifying specific regions in the brain that are involved in cocaine addiction. A considerable body of evidence, based largely on self-administration studies in laboratory animals, implicates the mesolimbic dopamine system as one of the primary sites of the reinforcing actions of cocaine. The mesolimbic dopamine system consists of dopaminergic neurons in the ventral tegmental area (VTA) and their projections to the nucleus accumbens (NAc) and other cortical and limbic structures, including the medial prefrontal cortex and olfactory tubercle (see Figure 4.1). In contrast, other major dopaminergic systems in brain, such as the nigrostriatal dopamine pathway (which consists of dopaminergic neurons in the substantia nigra and their projections to the caudate–

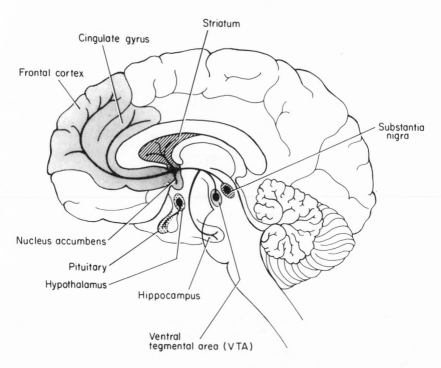

FIGURE 4.1. Major dopamine systems in the human brain. Dopaminergic cell bodies in the ventral tegmental area (VTA) (also termed A10 cells) are shown projecting to the nucleus accumbens (NAc) and other limbic and prefrontal cortical areas. These brain regions have been strongly implicated in the rewarding effects of drugs of abuse. Other major dopamine systems in brain include dopaminergic cell bodies in the substantia nigra (SN) (also termed A9 cells) that project to the caudate–putamen, and dopaminergic cell bodies in the hypothalamus that project to the pituitary. From *Molecular Foundations of Psychiatry: An Introductory Text* by S. E. Hyman and E. J. Nestler, in press. Copyright 1992 by the American Psychi·· ·ic Press. Reprinted by permission.

putamen) and the tuberoinfundibular dopamine pathway (which consists of dopaminergic neurons in the hypothalamus and their projections to the pituitary), are generally not thought to be involved in brain reward processes (Bozarth, 1986; Koob & Bloom, 1988; Liebman & Cooper, 1989).

The most persuasive evidence for a central role of the mesolimbic dopamine system in the rewarding actions of stimulants are the findings that dopamine-depleting lesions of the NAc (Lyness, Friedle, & Moore, 1979; Roberts, Corcoran, & Fibiger, 1977) or VTA (Roberts & Koob, 1982) attenuate cocaine or amphetamine self-administration. Moreover, dopaminergic receptor antagonists block the reinforcing effects of self-administered cocaine or amphetamine (for a review see Koob & Bloom, 1988; Liebman & Cooper, 1989), whereas selective dopamine agonists facilitate the reinforcing effects of self-administered cocaine (Woolverton, Goldberg, & Ginos, 1984; Wise, Murray, & Bozarth, 1990) and it also has been reported that rats will self-administer dopamine agonists, including dopamine itself, directly into the NAc (Dworkin, Goeders, & Smith, 1986). Rats will also work for electrical stimulation of the VTA, which is presumably rewarding because it results in increased dopamine release in the NAc and/or other projection areas (Bozarth, 1986). In addition to the VTA and NAc, other structures within the mesolimbic dopamine system are thought to be involved in drug reward processes. For example, lesions of the ventral pallidum, a major output of the NAc, attenuate cocaine self-administration (Hubner & Koob, 1990), and rats have been reported to self-administer cocaine directly into the medial prefrontal cortex (Goeders & Smith, 1983). Based on these types of studies, the mesolimbic dopamine system and several of its projection areas have been termed "dopaminergic brain reward regions."

The mesolimbic dopamine system appears to play a critical role in mediating the reinforcing properties not only of cocaine, but of many other drugs of abuse as well. Lesions of the VTA-NAc pathway attenuate opiate self-administration (Zito, Vickers, & Roberts, 1985; Bozarth, 1986), and opiates have been reported to be self-administered directly into these brain regions (Bozarth, 1986). Moreover, virtually all drugs abused by humans and laboratory animals, including stimulants like cocaine and amphetamine, opiates, alcohol, nicotine, and cannabinoids, all acutely increase extracellular levels of dopamine in the NAc (DiChiara & Imperato, 1989; Chen et al., 1990). These findings suggest that many classes of drugs of abuse may produce their reinforcing effects at least in part via common actions on the mesolimbic dopamine system. Because these various addictive drugs have diverse primary sites of action, as will be seen later, intracellular targets of the drugs may be a convergence point at which they exert similar effects on mesolimbic dopamine function.

Because the brain's mesolimbic dopamine system is thought to be a primary site of the rewarding, and presumably addicting, actions of cocaine, this chapter focuses on the effects of cocaine on this brain system. Understanding the neuropharmacological actions of cocaine mediated via dopaminergic brain reward regions, at the cellular and intracellular levels, will improve our understanding of the mechanisms underlying cocaine addiction and help design novel pharmacological treatments for this formidable clinical problem.

BASIC PHARMACOLOGICAL PROPERTIES OF COCAINE

Cocaine has a number of acute pharmacological actions. One is its ability to block nerve impulse conduction: It acts as a potent local anesthetic by disrupting the function of voltage-sensitive sodium channels in all excitable cells (Ritchie & Greene, 1990). However, this local anesthetic action does not appear to be related to cocaine's addictive properties, in that other local anesthetics, like procaine and lidocaine, are not reinforcing (Clouet, Asghar, & Brown, 1988).

Cocaine also acts to inhibit the reuptake of the monoamine neurotransmitters dopamine, serotonin, and norepinephrine into nerve terminals. Such reuptake is the major mechanism by which monoaminergic signals at the synapse are turned off (Cooper, Bloom, & Roth, 1991). As a result, drugs like cocaine, which inhibit the reuptake process, potentiate monoaminergic function. Cocaine inhibits monoamine reuptake by binding to, and thereby inhibiting the function of, specific proteins, termed transport proteins, located on the plasma membrane of monoaminergic nerve terminals. These proteins serve to transport the monoamine from the synaptic cleft back into the nerve terminal where it is processed for subsequent rerelease (Figure 4.2). Thus cocaine binds with high affinity to the specific transport proteins for dopamine, serotonin, and norepinephrine. Because the transport proteins are of very low abundance in brain, they have been difficult to characterize biochemically. However, several complementary DNA sequences that correspond to the norepinephrine, dopamine, and serotonin transporters have recently been isolated and expressed (Bannon, Xue, Shibeta, Dragovic, & Kapatos, 1990; Pacholczyk, Blakely, & Amara, 1991). The studies should enable a better understanding of how cocaine inhibits the transport proteins and could aid in the development of novel drugs that interact with these transporters in such a way as to block cocaine action.

The majority of evidence suggests that the reinforcing properties of cocaine are more related to its ability to inhibit dopamine reuptake rather than norepinephrine or serotonin reuptake, although it is clear that cocaine has significant actions on the brain's serotonin and norepinephrine systems (Pitts & Marwah, 1987; Clouet et al., 1988; Pan & Williams, 1989). Using a large number of drugs with varying degrees of dopamine reuptake blocking activity, it has been shown that the behavioral potency of the drugs in self-administration studies is correlated most closely with their relative ability to bind to the dopamine transporter (Ritz, Lamb, Goldberg, & Kuhar, 1987). In contrast, no such relationship was found with respect to the ability of these drugs to inhibit serotonin or norepinephrine reuptake (Ritz et al., 1987). Furthermore, whereas selective dopamine antagonists block and selective dopamine agonists facilitate cocaine reward (see preceding section), antagonists and agonists that act selectively on the serotonin or norepinephrine transmitter systems do not have these properties (Woolverton, 1987; Porrino et al., 1989; Wise & Bozarth, 1987). Finally, whereas specific dopaminergic lesions block cocaine self-administration (see preceding section), lesions of the brain's serotonergic or noradrenergic systems do not (Roberts et al., 1977; Leccese & Lyness, 1984). Based on this evidence, it is now generally accepted that facilitation of dopaminergic transmission, via inhibition of dopamine reuptake into nerve terminals, is the primary mechanism by which cocaine is reinforcing (Kuhar, Ritz, & Boja, 1991).

Cocaine is considered an indirect dopamine agonist: It potentiates the synaptic actions of endogenously released dopamine by inhibiting dopamine reuptake. This is in contrast to direct agonists which interact directly with one or another type of dopamine receptor. As a result, cocaine would be expected to activate all dopamine receptors (see Figure 4.2), as opposed to many direct agonists, which exert selective

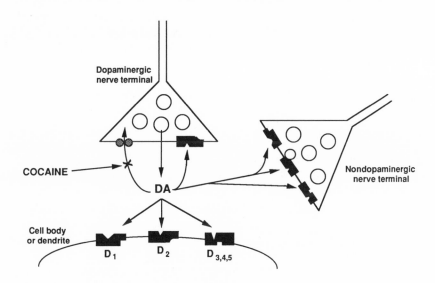

FIGURE 4.2. Schematic illustration of the acute actions of cocaine at dopaminergic synapses. Cocaine binds to the dopamine transporter and blocks the reuptake of dopamine into nerve terminals. This results in prolonged presynaptic and postsynaptic actions of dopamine at multiple receptor types. The presynaptic actions include those on both dopaminergic and nondopaminergic nerve terminals.

actions at various dopamine receptor subtypes. Dopamine receptors were initially categorized as D1 or D2 subtypes based on their relative ability to bind a large number of ligands and to regulate the enzyme adenylate cyclase (which catalyzes the synthesis of cAMP) (Stoof & Kebabian, 1981). Dopamine D1 receptors are positively coupled to adenylate cyclase (that is, they stimulate the enzyme and increase cAMP levels) and are localized on cell bodies, dendrites, and axon terminals of dopaminoceptive cells. Dopamine D2 receptors, at least in most brain regions, are negatively coupled to adenylate cyclase and are found on dendrites, cell bodies, and nerve terminals of the dopamine neurons themselves (hence these are termed autoreceptors); they are also present on dopaminoceptive neurons (Bunney, Sessak, & Silva, 1987; Roth, Wolf, & Deutch, 1987). With the recent molecular cloning of the D3, D4, and D5 dopamine receptors, and of subtypes of the D1 and D2 receptors (Sokoloff, Giros, Martres, Bouthenet, & Schwartz, 1990; Van Tol et al., 1991; Sunahara et al., 1991), each of which has unique regional distributions in brain and potentially unique regulatory features, it appears that the dopamine system is considerably more complex than initially thought. The D3 dopamine receptor has a particularly interesting regional distribution, in that it is enriched in limbic areas of the brain, including the NAc (Sokoloff et al., 1990). This raises the possibility that some of the reinforcing effects of cocaine (and dopamine itself) that occur within in the NAc may be due to activation of D3 receptors in addition to D1 and D2 receptors also prevalent in this brain region. It is not yet known what intracellular second messenger systems these novel dopamine receptor subtypes act upon. Nevertheless, the heterogeneity of dopamine receptors indicates that the precise pharmacological actions of indirect (and therefore nonselective) dopamine agonists like cocaine vary greatly depending on the particular brain region, cell type, and receptor subtype under consideration.

ACUTE EFFECTS OF COCAINE IN VIVO

Pharmacological Effects of Acute Cocaine

Acute cocaine inhibition of monoamine reuptake leads to numerous physiological effects in the central and peripheral nervous systems. For example, inhibition of norepinephrine reuptake, and the resulting potentiation of sympathetic function, presumably accounts for much of the hypertensive and cardiotoxic effects of the drug.

Cocaine augmentation of dopaminergic transmission in the brain can be observed readily in vivo with microdialysis techniques (Church & Justice, 1987; Pettit, Pan, Parsons, & Justice, 1990). This method involves inserting a small dialysis probe into discrete regions of the brain, collecting extracellular fluid from these regions, and measuring levels of dopamine and other neurotransmitters and their metabolites in the dialysates. An advantage of this technique is that it can be used in awake, behaving animals. The administration of a single dose of cocaine elicits a transient elevation in extracellular dopamine levels in dopaminergic terminal field areas of the brain, like the NAc and caudate–putamen. Cocaine is a relatively short-acting drug, such that, in response to a single intraperitoneal injection, for example, dopamine levels are increased markedly within minutes, peak within a half hour, and return to normal within 1–2 hours (Pettit et al., 1990). These very rapid "on and off" rates of cocaine probably contribute significantly to its great abuse potential. The ability of cocaine to increase extracellular levels of serotonin and norepinephrine is more difficult to measure directly, due to the much lower levels of these neurotransmitters, compared with dopamine, in limbic and prefrontal cortical regions.

Behavioral Effects of Acute Cocaine

Acute administration of cocaine to animals and humans produces a well-characterized motor-activating effect very similar to that seen with other psychostimulants like amphetamine (Johanson & Fischman, 1989). In rodents, cocaine produces an alerting response consisting of increases in exploration, locomotion, grooming, gnawing, and stereotypy (Johanson & Fischman, 1989). Much of the behavioral locomotor activation is thought to be mediated by the mesolimbic dopamine system, as psychostimulant-induced locomotor activation is blocked by pretreatment with dopamine receptor antagonists and by specific neurotoxic lesions of dopaminergic nerve terminals in the NAc (Kelley, Seviour, & Iverson, 1975; Roberts et al., 1977). Moreover, microinjection of cocaine locally into the NAc elicits the locomotor activating response (Delfs, Schreibner, & Kelley, 1990). In contrast, cocaine-induced stereotypy appears to be mediated largely via the nigrostriatal dopamine system.

Electrophysiological Effects of Acute Cocaine

The acute electrophysiological effects of dopamine (and cocaine) in the brain have been studied extensively. In electrophysiological studies, dopamine has been found to act primarily, but not exclusively, as an inhibitory neurotransmitter. The electrophysiological actions of cocaine within the two major midbrain dopaminergic systems are quite similar. Cocaine inhibits dopaminergic cell bodies in the substantia nigra and ventral tegmental area via indirect activation of D2 autoreceptors (Wachtel, Hu, Galloway, & White, 1989). In the dopaminergic terminal field areas (e.g., NAc and caudate–putamen), the effects of cocaine can be considerably more complex, due to multiple dopamine receptor subtypes on both presynaptic and postsynaptic neurons and to the heterogeneity of the cell types in these brain regions (Bunney et al., 1987; Roth et al., 1987). White and colleagues have studied the effects of dopamine in the NAc in vivo and have attempted to distinguish actions at specific dopamine receptor subtypes using selective antagonists (White & Wang, 1986). They found that the effect of dopamine on both D1 and D2 receptors was primarily inhibitory in anesthetized rats. However, North and colleagues specifically studied cocaine actions on rat NAc neurons in an in vitro brain slice preparation and reported that cocaine inhibits these cells via indirect activation of D1 receptors, but excites them via indirect activation of D2 receptors (Uchimura & North, 1990). These results are quite similar to earlier reports of the effects of dopamine on NAc neurons in guinea pig brain slices (Uchimura, Higashi, & Nishi, 1986). These discrepancies in the reported functional effects of D2 receptors on NAc neurons may be due in part to the different preparations used (in vivo versus in vitro). An alternative explanation is the fact that the NAc is a highly heterogeneous structure that contains multiple neuronal cells types, including microtopographical differences in cell type (Pickel, Towle, Joh, & Chan, 1988), neuropeptides (Zahm & Heimer, 1988; Voorn, Gerfen, & Groenewegen, 1989), and dopamine receptor subtypes (Allin, Russell, Lamm, & Taljaard, 1989; Sokoloff et al., 1990); it is conceivable that these various subpopulations of NAc neurons might respond very differently to cocaine.

Biochemical and Molecular Actions of Acute Cocaine

Because cocaine exerts its effects on brain function via indirect activation of dopaminergic (and serotonergic and noradrenergic) receptors, a complete understanding of cocaine action requires analysis of the consequences of such receptor activation on neuronal function. It is now known that dopamine and most other neurotransmitters produce many of their physiological effects in target neurons through a complex cascade of intracellular messengers involving G proteins (Gilman, 1987), which couple extracellular receptors to intracellular effector systems, and the effector systems themselves, which include second messengers, protein kinases, and phosphoproteins (Figure 4.3). From this perspective, acute cocaine acts initially on the dopamine transporter to inhibit dopamine reuptake. This leads to increases in synaptic dopamine levels and to activation of dopamine receptors, which, in turn, leads to effects on G proteins, the cAMP second messenger system, and to multiple physiological effects in the target neuron. Activation of D1 receptors stimulates adenylate cyclase via coupling to the stimulatory G protein, Gs, whereas activation of D2 receptors inhibits adenylate cyclase via coupling to the inhibitory G protein, Gi (see Stoof & Kebabian, 1981; Gilman, 1987; Innis & Aghajanian, 1987). Altered levels of cAMP, in turn, lead to alterations in cAMP-dependent protein kinase activity and to alterations in the phosphorylation state of a multitude of phosphoprotein substrates including receptors, ion channels and pumps, neurotransmitter synthetic enzymes, cytoskeletal proteins, and many other proteins that control neuronal function in cell bodies, dendrites, and nerve terminals (Nestler & Greengard, 1989). Activation of D2 receptors also leads to direct stimulation of K^+ channels via a Gi-like protein (Innis & Aghajanian, 1987). As mentioned above, intracellular second messenger systems to which the D3, D4, and D5 dopamine receptors are linked remain to be established.

Increasing evidence indicates that one role of these intracellular messenger pathways is to mediate neurotransmitter regulation of gene expression in target neurons (see Hyman & Nestler, in press). Neurotransmitter regulation of gene expression is thought to occur, in large part, via second messenger–dependent phosphorylation and/or induction of a class of proteins termed transcription factors—proteins that bind to specific DNA sequences (response elements) in the promoter regions of genes and thereby increase or decrease the rate at which those genes are transcribed. Interestingly, acute cocaine has been shown to have actions at this level of transcriptional regulation. By acting at dopamine D1 receptors, cocaine induces the transcription factor fos and several other fos-related proteins in rat striatal tissues (Graybiel, Moratella, & Robertson, 1990; Young, Porrino, & Iadarola, 1991), presumably by activation of the intracellular cAMP system. A major current interest is to identify the numerous target genes that are turned on or off via cocaine regulation of these transcription factors.

This discussion of the intracellular actions of cocaine illustrates that, although cocaine acts directly upon only a small number of proteins (i.e., monoaminergic transporters), a single acute dose actually alters diverse cellular processes and thereby exerts numerous effects on neuronal function.

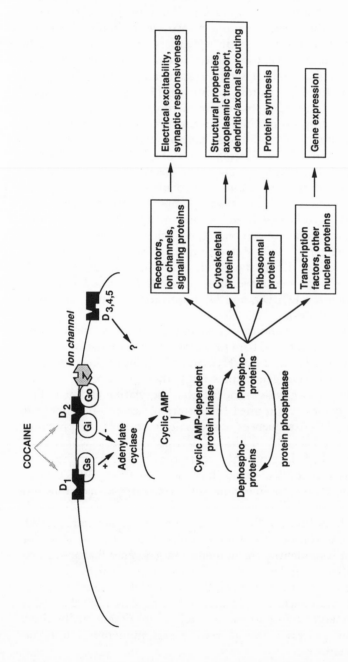

FIGURE 4.3. Schematic illustration of the acute actions of cocaine on intracellular messenger systems. By acting at dopamine D1 or D2 receptors, cocaine interacts with the adenylate cyclase system and alters intracellular levels of the second messenger cyclic AMP (cAMP). Alterations in cAMP levels, in turn, affect the phosphorylation state of a multitude of phosphoprotein substrates that regulate virtually all aspects of neuronal function. It is not yet known what second messenger systems the D3, D4, and D5 dopamine receptors are coupled to, or whether more than one type of dopamine receptor coexists at specific synapses within the same cells, as depicted here.

CHRONIC EFFECTS OF COCAINE IN VIVO

Behavioral Sensitization

In addition to its acute effects on brain function, cocaine has prominent actions after chronic use. In animal studies, one of the most striking features of chronic cocaine exposure is the phenomenon termed behavioral sensitization. This refers to the observation that chronic administration of cocaine increases the degree of locomotor activity and stereotypic behaviors in response to a subsequent acute dose of the drug (Post & Rose, 1976; Kilbey & Ellinwood, 1977). There is neurochemical evidence that sensitization to the locomotor-activating effects of cocaine may be mediated at least in part via the mesolimbic dopamine system (Kalivas, Duffy, DeMars, & Skinner, 1988; Pettit et al., 1990; Steketee, Striplin, Murray, & Kalivas, 1991). Microdialysis studies have shown that after chronic cocaine treatment, increased amounts of dopamine are released in the NAc in response to an acute cocaine injection (Pettit et al., 1990), and this could account for the increased locomotor activation observed in animals treated chronically with cocaine (Post & Rose, 1976; Kalivas et al., 1988; Clouet et al., 1988). However, this potentiation of dopamine release may be due to an altered pharmacokinetic disposition of the drug after chronic administration, possibly peculiar to the intraperitoneal route used in these animal studies (Pettit et al., 1990; Chen, Marmur, Paredes, Pulles, & Gardener, 1991).

There is also some evidence in animals that chronic exposure to stimulants can produce sensitization to the reinforcing effects of these drugs (Piazza, Deminiere, Le Moal, & Simon, 1989; Lett, 1989). These data certainly corroborate a strong clinical impression, namely, that craving for cocaine (and possibly other effects, e.g., paranoia) increases with chronic exposure to the drug. However, it remains entirely unknown whether cocaine sensitization with respect to locomotor activity, stereotypy, and dopamine levels in the NAc in rodents is in any way related to sensitization to drug reinforcement and craving.

Electrophysiological Studies of Chronic Cocaine

Electrophysiological studies of the mesolimbic dopamine system have shown that chronic cocaine has dramatic effects on these neurons, with a type of "cocaine sensitization" also observed in these studies in vivo. Chronic cocaine increases the responsiveness of D1, but not of D2, receptors to dopamine agonists in the rat NAc; that is, D1 receptors become supersensitive (Henry & White, 1991). However, no consistent changes in levels or affinity of D1 dopamine receptors have been observed in the NAc in response to chronic cocaine (see Clouet et al., 1988; Peris et al., 1990), suggesting that this supersensitivity may be occurring via a postreceptor mechanism. Henry, Greene, & White (1989) have also shown that D2 receptors within the VTA become subsensitive to dopamine following chronic cocaine administration. In addition, there are a greater number of spontaneously active VTA neurons, and their firing rates are significantly higher in cocaine-treated rats than in controls. This increased activity could be due to a decrease in the inhibitory influence of dopamine, acting at D2 receptors, on these neurons. These studies demonstrate that chronic cocaine seems to have very different actions on dopaminergic cell bodies and their terminal fields: while dopamine cell bodies in the VTA are activated after chronic cocaine and are subsensitive to dopamine, the NAc is supersensitive to the inhibitory actions of dopamine.

Biochemical and Molecular Studies of Chronic Cocaine

Several studies have examined dopamine receptor binding after chronic cocaine treatment; however, no consistent changes in levels or affinity of dopamine receptors or transporters have been reported within the mesolimbic dopamine system or elsewhere (Clouet et al., 1988; Peris et al., 1990). The inconsistent findings may be due, in part, to the different treatment durations and drug doses used by different laboratories. Also, it is now known that previous studies of dopamine receptors have been limited by the lack of specific ligands, antibodies, or clones for the multiple dopamine receptor subtypes. The possibility of chronic cocaine regulation of dopamine receptors needs to be reassessed using more specific probes for the large number of dopamine receptors now known to exist in brain.

Catecholamines and catecholamine metabolite levels have also been studied after chronic cocaine or amphetamine treatment. Although there are some discrepancies in this literature as well, several groups report that levels of catecholamines and their metabolites are reduced in terminal fields of the mesolimbic dopamine system after chronic stimulant treatment (Ellison, 1983; Robertson, Leslie, & Bennett, 1991). Interestingly, similar results have been found in rats that received cocaine chronically via intravenous self-administration. Bozarth (1989) reported that after 3 weeks of cocaine self-administration there was a marked reduction in dopamine content in the VTA and NAc but not in the substantia nigra or caudate–putamen. Hurd, Weiss, Koob, & Ungerstedt (1989) found that after a 9-day period of cocaine self-administration, extracellular dopamine overflow in the NAc was diminished compared with dopamine levels in rats that had acutely self-administered cocaine. These data are consistent with the view that chronic cocaine induces a state of relative dopamine deficiency in terminal field areas of the mesolimbic dopamine system. Such a dopamine deficiency might be expected to elicit a compensatory supersensitivity to the physiological actions of dopamine, as indeed has been observed in electrophysiological studies for D1 receptor function in the NAc (see preceding section).

Studies at the biochemical level in our laboratory have provided a possible molecular basis for the neurochemical and electrophysiological findings discussed above. We have demonstrated that chronic cocaine treatment up-regulates the cAMP system, at several levels, in the NAc. Chronic cocaine increases levels of adenylate cyclase and cAMP-dependent protein kinase activity (Terwilliger, Beitner-Johnson, Sevarino, Crain, & Nestler, 1991a), and decreases levels of the inhibitory G proteins Gi–Go (Nestler, Terwilliger, Walker, Sevarino, & Duman, 1990), specifically in this brain region. As D1 receptors act through stimulation of the cAMP pathway, the observed up-regulation of adenylate cyclase and cAMP-dependent protein kinase, together with a decrease in Gi–Go (without a change in Gs), could in part underlie the D1 receptor supersensitivity observed electrophysiologically.

We have also shown that chronic cocaine decreases levels of Gi–Go in the VTA (Nestler et al., 1990). As D2 receptors are thought to exert their actions on target neurons via Gi–Go coupling to specific ion channels and/or inhibition of adenylate cyclase, the cocaine-induced decreases in levels of these G protein subunits in VTA neurons could account for the subsensitivity of D2 receptors, as observed in electrophysiological studies. Further evidence for a role of decreased levels of Gi–Go in cocaine action on VTA neurons is the finding that in vivo inhibition of Gi–Go function in the VTA via local application of pertussis toxin mimics the ability of chronic cocaine to facilitate the locomotor activating effects of an acute cocaine challenge (Steketee et al., 1991).

In addition to studying G proteins and the cAMP system, we have also studied the actions of cocaine on the next step in this signal transduction pathway, namely, cAMP-dependent protein phosphorylation, in the VTA and NAc. One of the phosphoproteins studied has been tyrosine hydroxylase, the rate-limiting enzyme in dopamine biosynthesis, which can provide information about the state of dopaminergic transmission in specific brain regions (Cooper, Bloom, & Roth, 1991). We found that chronic, but not acute, cocaine increases levels of tyrosine hydroxylase in the VTA (Beitner-Johnson & Nestler, 1991). As tyrosine hydroxylase levels are correlated with cellular activity in catecholaminergic cells (for references, see Guitart et al., 1990), increased tyrosine hydroxylase expression in the VTA in response to chronic cocaine may reflect the elevated level of VTA neuronal activity reported electrophysiologically. Chronic cocaine did not alter tyrosine hydroxylase levels in dopaminergic neurons of the substantia nigra (Beitner-Johnson & Nestler, 1991).

Chronic cocaine also produces an apparent dephosphorylation of tyrosine hydroxylase, without a change in its total amount, in the NAc. Inasmuch as cAMP-dependent protein kinase and other protein kinases are known to phosphorylate and activate tyrosine hydroxylase, dephosphorylation of the enzyme would suggest reduced catalytic activity and, as a result, decreased dopamine synthesis, in response to chronic cocaine. This molecular event could therefore account for the relative deficiency in synaptic dopamine levels seen in the terminal fields of the mesolimbic dopamine system in the chronic cocaine state. Since tyrosine hydroxylase present in the NAc is located in dopaminergic nerve terminals derived from the VTA, these results further support the idea, stated above, that chronic cocaine exerts differential effects on VTA cell bodies and their nerve terminals. In contrast to the NAc, no changes in tyrosine hydroxylase phosphorylation state or total amount were observed in the caudate–putamen in response to chronic cocaine (Beitner-Johnson & Nestler, 1991).

We have also identified a number of other cocaine-regulated phosphoproteins in the mesolimbic dopamine system. Prominent among these are neurofilament (NF) proteins with molecular weights of 200, 160, and 68 kd, designated NF-200, NF-160, and NF-68. We found that chronic, but not acute, cocaine treatment decreases the total amounts of these three neurofilament proteins specifically in the VTA, with no effects observed elsewhere in brain (Beitner-Johnson, Guitart, & Nestler, 1992). Neurofilaments are components of the neuronal cytoskeleton and are thought to play a role in axonal transport (Hoffman & Lasek, 1980), dendritic sprouting (Hall, Lee, & Kosik, 1991), and determination of neuronal morphology (Hoffman, Griffith, & Price, 1984). Cocaine-induced alterations in neurofilaments could therefore impede dopaminergic neurotransmission in the VTA–NAc pathway, influence local dopaminergic function within the VTA itself, and even alter the structural integrity of VTA neurons. As one example, decreased levels of neurofilaments would be expected to be associated with decreases in axonal caliber and axonal transport rates. This could result in decreased transport of tyrosine hydroxylase from cell bodies to nerve terminals, which could, in turn, account for the fact that higher levels of tyrosine hydroxylase in the VTA are not seen in the NAc in the chronic cocaine state. It is therefore possible that cocaine-induced decreases in neurofilaments may be a critical event in the process by which the various biochemical and electrophysiological adaptations described above occur in the VTA–NAc pathway. Studies are currently underway to determine whether cocaine regulation of neurofilament proteins are long lasting or if they can be reversed after cocaine discontinuation.

The ability of chronic cocaine to alter the total amounts of G proteins, tyrosine hydroxylase, neurofilaments, and possibly other proteins in the mesolimbic dopamine system suggests that these actions of cocaine may be mediated, at least in part, at the level of gene expression. In this regard, it is interesting to note that we have recently demonstrated that chronic cocaine dramatically decreases the ability of a subsequent acute injection of cocaine to regulate c-fos and fos-like transcription factors (Hope, Kosofsky, Hyman, & Nestler, in press). Although the functional significance of these findings are not yet known, the results underscore a critical point, namely, that a complete understanding of the chronic actions of cocaine on brain function will ultimately require knowledge of cocaine action at the genetic transcriptional level.

Common Biochemical Actions of Chronic Cocaine and Chronic Morphine

Many of the biochemical alterations described above, which occur in response to chronic cocaine treatment, also occur in response to chronic morphine treatment. This is somewhat surprising, in that the two drugs elicit a number of very different acute actions in vivo. The drugs act upon different receptor systems (cocaine inhibits monoamine reuptake proteins, whereas morphine acts as an opiate receptor agonist), and cocaine is a stimulant, whereas morphine is a sedating analgesic (although at low doses morphine does have some stimulatory effects). Moreover, whereas acute cocaine inhibits VTA neurons, acute morphine excites the neurons (Matthews & German, 1984). These different acute behavioral and electrophysiological actions are in contrast to the observation that the two drugs are reinforcing acutely and chronically and can induce a similar type of behavioral sensitization after chronic exposure, and that the VTA–NAc pathway may be involved in these acute and chronic actions of both drugs (see Bozarth, 1986; Shippenberg & Herz, 1987; Kalivas & Duffy, 1988). It is, therefore, of considerable interest that we have identified a number of common chronic actions of cocaine and morphine in the mesolimbic dopamine system. In the NAc, chronic morphine, like chronic cocaine, up-regulates the cAMP system, with increases in adenylate cyclase and cAMP-dependent protein kinase, and decreases in Gi, as shown in Figure 4.4 (Terwilliger et al., 1991a), and decreases in the phosphorylation state of tyrosine hydroxylase (Beitner-

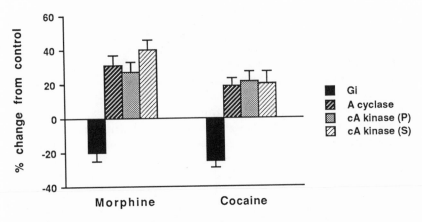

FIGURE 4.4. Chronic morphine and cocaine produce similar adaptations in G-proteins and the cAMP system in the NAc. Rats were treated chronically with either morphine (1 subcutaneous pellet of morphine daily for 5 days [75 mg, NIDA]), or cocaine (15 mg/kg intraperitoneal injections twice daily for 14 days). Rats were then sacrificed on day 6 for morphine, or day 15 for cocaine. The NAc was dissected from control and treated rats, and duplicate aliquots of tissue extracts were analyzed for levels of Giα, adenylate cyclase activity, or cAMP-dependent protein kinase activity in particulate (P) and soluble (S) fractions. The data are expressed as percent change from control ± SEM (n = 8–14). All changes shown are statistically significant (p < .05 by χ^2 test). Data are from Nestler, Terwilliger, Walker, Sevarino, and Duman (1990) and Terwilliger, Beitner-Johnson, Sevarino, Crain, and Nestler (1991a).

Johnson & Nestler, 1991). In the VTA, chronic morphine, like chronic cocaine, increases tyrosine hydroxylase levels (Beitner-Johnson & Nestler, 1991) and decreases neurofilament levels (Beitner-Johnson et al., 1992).

GENETIC DETERMINANTS OF COCAINE ADDICTION

Genetic factors clearly play a role in a number of mental disorders, including alcoholism. The involvement of genetic factors in other drug addictions is less clear, but generally presumed to contribute to individual differences in susceptibility to drug addiction in both animals and people (Pickens & Svikis, 1988). Recent studies have demonstrated that individual differences in acquired levels of amphetamine self-administration in an outbred Sprague-Dawley strain of rats can be predicted accurately by individual differences in locomotor responses to a novel environment (Piazza et al., 1989). Based on the role of the mesolimbic dopamine system in such locomotor responses (see above), these studies suggest that the VTA-NAc may be involved in a predisposition to drug addiction. More recent studies by the same group have also implicated the activity of the hypothalamic–pituitary–adrenal axis in controlling an individual's locomotor responsiveness and amphetamine self-administration (Piazza et al., 1991). Locomotor responses to cocaine and amphetamine also differ among individuals in an outbred strain of Wistar rats (Hooks, Jones, Smith, Neill, & Justice, 1991), which may reflect a genetic predisposition to drug self-administration in these animals as well.

Fischer and Lewis Rats: A Model System of Genetic Factors in Cocaine Addiction

Another model system to study possible genetic factors involved in drug addiction are Fischer 344 and Lewis rats, two inbred rat strains that show, respectively, lower and higher levels of self-administration of cocaine, opiates, and alcohol (Li & Lumeng, 1984; Suzuki, George, & Meisch, 1988; George & Goldberg, 1989). Lewis rats also develop greater degrees of conditioned place preference to systemic cocaine and opiates (Guitart, Beitner-Johnson, & Nestler, in press). In an effort to understand the biological basis of these strain differences in drug preference, we studied G proteins, the cyclic AMP system, tyrosine hydroxylase, and neurofilaments in brain dopamine systems of the two rat strains.

Interestingly, in every case examined, levels of these proteins in drug-naive Lewis rats, compared to drug-naive Fischer rats, parallel the effects of chronic cocaine or chronic morphine on outbred Sprague-Dawley rats. Thus the NAc of drug-naive Lewis rats displayed higher levels of adenylate cyclase and cAMP-dependent protein kinase, and lower levels of Gi, compared with drug-naive Fischer rats (Terwilliger et al., 1991b). The VTA of drug-naive Lewis rats exhibited ≈45% higher levels of tyrosine hydroxylase immunoreactivity than drug-naive Fischer rats, whereas the NAc contained ≈45% lower levels of the enzyme (Beitner-Johnson, Guitart, & Nestler, 1991). (Note that the lower enzyme levels in the NAc of Lewis versus Fischer rats is functionally similar to the cocaine- and morphine-induced decrease in enzyme phosphorylation and catalytic activity.) Finally, Lewis rats contained lower levels of neurofilament proteins in the VTA compared with Fischer rats. The striking similarities between the levels of tyrosine hydroxylase and neurofilaments in the VTA in response to chronic morphine or chronic cocaine, and in Lewis versus Fischer rats, are summarized in Figure 4.5. The strain differences observed in levels of G proteins, adenylate cyclase, cAMP-dependent protein kinase, tyrosine hydroxylase, and neurofilaments showed regional specificity to the mesolimbic

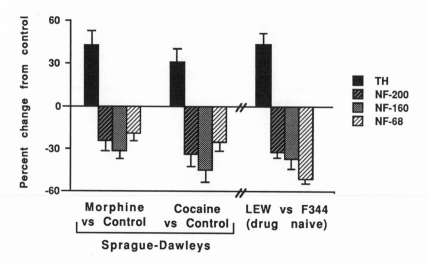

FIGURE 4.5. Similar regulation of phosphoproteins in the VTA in response to chronic morphine or chronic cocaine or in drug-naive Lewis versus Fischer 344 rats. Sprague-Dawley (outbred) rats were treated chronically with either morphine or cocaine as described in the legend to Figure 4.4. Drug-naive Lewis rats were compared to drug-naive Fischer 344 rats. Tyrosine hydroxylase (TH) and neurofilaments (NFs) were measured by immunoblotting techniques. Data are expressed as percent change from control (for morphine- and cocaine-treated rats), or percent change from Fischer 344 levels (for Lewis rats). Shown are levels of tyrosine hydroxylase (TH) and neurofilaments 200, 160, and 68 kD (NF-200, NF-160, and NF-68) (see text). Data are expressed as mean ± SEM and represent the results from 8-16 rats in each group, and are taken from Beitner-Johnson, Guitart, and Nestler (1991, 1992b).

dopamine system in that no strain differences in levels of these proteins were seen in the nigrostriatal dopamine system or elsewhere in the brain. Taken together, these findings raise the possibility that aspects of cocaine and morphine addiction, and a genetic predisposition to drug addiction, may manifest themselves via similar biochemical mechanisms.

CONCLUSIONS AND PERSPECTIVES FOR FUTURE RESEARCH

Role in Mediating the Rewarding Properties of Cocaine

Although these studies are at the relatively early stages of development, the biochemical changes that occur in response to chronic cocaine treatment are likely to be related to the reinforcing and addicting properties of cocaine for several reasons. First, it appears that these changes in second messenger systems, tyrosine hydroxylase, and neurofilament proteins are long-term adaptations that occur in the VTA and NAc in response to repeated exposure to cocaine, in that these changes are not seen in response to acute cocaine treatment. Second, chronic cocaine alters tyrosine hydroxylase, the rate-limiting enzyme in dopamine biosynthesis, in the VTA and NAc, where dopamine is thought to play a central role in drug reward mechanisms. Third, the biochemical changes could account for the known chronic electrophysiological effects of cocaine on VTA and NAc neurons. Fourth, the various biochemical alterations show regional specificity, in that they are not seen in the nigrostriatal dopamine system which is structurally similar to the mesolimbic dopamine system, but generally not correlated with drug reward. Fifth, these changes are not produced by chronic treatment of rats with haloperidol or imipramine, two psychotropic drugs that are not reinforcing. In contrast, the effects of chronic cocaine are highly similar to the effects of chronic morphine on G proteins, the cAMP system, tyrosine hydroxylase, and neurofilaments in the mesolimbic dopamine system. Finally, the effects of chronic cocaine and chronic morphine are similar to differences seen in dopaminergic brain reward regions of drug-naive Fischer and Lewis rats, two genetically inbred rat strains which show, respectively, lower and higher levels of drug preference for cocaine, morphine, and alcohol.

Based on the remarkably similar biochemical profiles of the mesolimbic dopamine system in morphine-treated rats, cocaine-treated rats, and drug-naive Lewis rats (compared with Fischer rats), we would propose that a drug-addicted (or drug-preferring) state is associated with higher levels of tyrosine hydroxylase and lower levels of neurofilaments in dopaminergic cell bodies of the VTA, and with decreased levels of tyrosine hydroxylase activity and an up-regulated cAMP pathway in the NAc. These results and interpretations are summarized in Figure 4.6. Although aspects of this scheme clearly remain hypothetical, the model defines a number of future experiments that promise to better define the precise mechanisms by which cocaine and other drugs of abuse produce drug addiction and craving, as well as the molecular basis for individual differences in susceptibility to drug addiction.

Possible Clinical Applications

These findings have implications for the treatment of human drug addiction. Our indication that tyrosine hydroxylase activity is decreased in the NAc after chronic cocaine exposure, along with the corroborating neuropharmacological evidence, suggests that long-term cocaine use

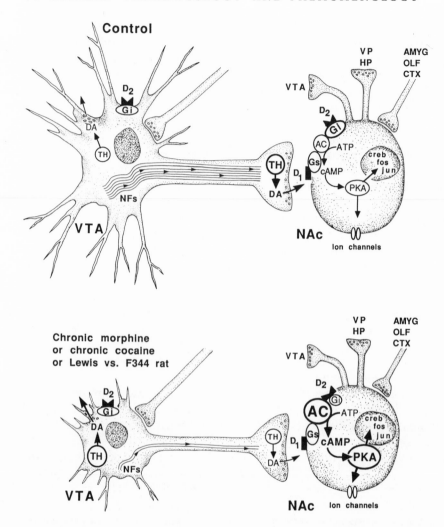

FIGURE 4.6. Schematic summary of similar biochemical manifestations of the "drug-addicted" and "drug-preferring" state. The top Figure depicts a control VTA neuron projecting to the NAc. Shown in the VTA cell are tyrosine hydroxylase (TH), dopamine (DA), presynaptic dopamine receptors (D2) coupled to G proteins (Gi), and neurofilaments (NFs). Shown in the NAc are, in addition to TH and DA, dopamine receptors (D1 and D2), G proteins (Gi and Gs), components of the intracellular cyclic AMP system (AC, adenylate cyclase activity; PKA, cAMP-dependent protein kinase activity; and possible substrates for the kinase—ion channels and nuclear transcription factors creb, fos, and jun), as well as major inputs and outputs of this region (VP, ventral pallidum; HP, hippocampus; AMYG, amygdala; OLF, olfactory cortex; CTX, other cortical regions).

The bottom Figure depicts a VTA neuron projecting to the NAc after chronic morphine or cocaine treatment, or from a Lewis (drug-preferring) rat as compared with may produce a relative dopamine deficiency state in this brain region. Similar ideas have been proposed previously (e.g., see Dackis & Gold, 1985). In humans, dopamine receptor blockers are generally unpleasant and dysphoric, suggesting that dopamine depletion would exert similar effects. It is possible that a cocaine-induced dopamine deficit in the mesolimbic dopamine system represents part of the mechanism underlying the dysphoria and anhedonia that often accompany cocaine withdrawal. This deficiency state may also contribute to cocaine craving (Wise, 1982; Wise & Bozarth, 1987), although it remains unknown as to whether craving solely reflects attempts to "treat" the dysphoria or whether it is a distinct process. Drugs that act as direct (e.g., bromocriptine) or indirect (e.g., mazindol or bupropion) dopamine agonists have been considered as potential therapies for cocaine addiction, although convincing clinical evidence for their efficacy is lacking. However, this treatment strategy must be viewed with caution, as any drug that can substitute for cocaine by acting on the brain's dopamine system is also a potentially reinforcing, and perhaps addicting, drug itself.

Another strategy in developing new treatments for cocaine addiction would be to target drugs at postreceptor steps known to be involved in drug reward mechanisms. For example, we would predict, based on our biochemical findings in the NAc, that drugs that influence specific types of G proteins or activity of the cAMP pathway could potentially alter

---

a Fischer (F344) rat. In the drug-addicted or drug-preferring animal, TH levels are increased in the VTA, and decreased in the NAc (owing to either decreased phosphorylation, for morphine and cocaine, or decreased enzyme levels, in Lewis versus F344 rats). NF levels are decreased in the VTA in the drug-addicted or drug-preferring state. This decrease in NFs may be associated with alterations in neuronal structure, decreases in axonal caliber, and/or decreases in axonal transport rate in these cells, as indicated in the Figure. This hypothetical decrease in axonal transport may account for the lack of correspondingly increased levels of TH in dopaminergic terminals in the NAc. Decreased TH in the NAc implies decreased dopamine synthesis and may result in lower dopaminergic transmission in this brain region. In the NAc of the the drug-addicted or drug-preferring state, Gi is decreased, and adenylate cyclase and cAMP-dependent protein kinase activities are increased—changes that could account for D1 receptor supersensitivity observed electrophysiologically (Henry & White, 1991).

It should be noted that alterations in dopaminergic transmission probably influence many cell types within the NAc, as well as other nerve terminals in the NAc. Similarly, altered local dopaminergic transmission in the VTA could also influence other nerve terminals in this brain region. Thus biochemical alterations in the mesolimbic dopamine system could potentially lead to altered neuronal function in many other brain regions as well. From Beitner-Johnson, Guitart, and Nestler, in press, "The Neurobiology of Drug and Alcohol Addiction," *Annals of the New York Academy of Sciences, 654.* Copyright 1992 by the Annals of the New York Academy of Sciences. Reprinted by permission.

drug reinforcement. So far, however, very few drugs have been available that directly act on these intracellular messenger proteins, although such compounds represent a major current focus of developmental therapeutic programs. Conceivably, drugs that are found to influence postreceptor steps—that is, G proteins, the cAMP system, protein kinases, or even neurofilaments—may represent novel approaches to the treatment of drug addiction.

A striking aspect of our findings is that chronic cocaine and morphine treatments alter neurofilament levels in the VTA. Although tentative, our findings suggest the possibility that chronic drug use leads to profound alterations in the structural features of mesolimbic dopamine neurons, which could reduce the ability of these cells to transmit dopaminergic signals to postsynaptic cells in the NAc and elsewhere. Long-term cocaine and opiate use may thereby impair the brain's endogenous reward system. This could have a profound impact on motivation, affect, and stress responses, as discussed above. A major focus of future investigations will be to determine the mechanisms by which these chronic drug treatments alter neurofilament levels in the VTA and the precise changes that occur as a result in VTA neuronal structure and function.

Clearly, a better understanding of the mechanisms underlying the actions of cocaine on mesolimbic dopamine neurons and other brain regions involved in drug reward will lead to the development of increasingly efficacious pharmacological agents that prevent or reverse aspects of drug addiction. Studies of drug-regulated intracellular second messenger systems and specific phosphoproteins in brain reward regions promise to lead to an improved understanding of such mechanisms, as well as to the identification of some of the factors that contribute to individual vulnerability to drug addiction.

REFERENCES

Acquas, E., Carboni, E., & DiChiara, G. (1991). Profound depression of mesolimbic dopamine release after morphine withdrawal in dependent rats. *European Journal of Pharmacology, 193,* 133–134.

Allin, R., Russel, V., Lamm, M., & Taljaard, J. (1989). Regional distribution of dopamine D1 and D2 receptors in the nucleus accumbens of the rat. *Brain Research, 501,* 389–391.

Bannon, M. J., Xue, C.-H., Shibata, K. L., Dragovic, J., & Kapatos, G. (1990). Expression of a human cocaine-sensitive dopamine transporter in Xenopus laevis oocytes. *Journal of Neurochemistry, 54,* 706–708.

Beitner-Johnson, D., & Nestler, E. J. (1991). Morphine and cocaine exert common chronic actions on tyrosine hydroxylase in dopaminergic brain reward regions. *Journal of Neurochemistry, 57,* 344–347.

Beitner-Johnson, D., Guitart, X., & Nestler, E. J. (1991). Dopaminergic brain reward regions of Lewis and Fischer rats display different levels of tyrosine hydroxylase and other morphine- and cocaine-regulated phosphoproteins. *Brain Research, 561,* 147–150.

Beitner-Johnson, D., Guitart, X., & Nestler, E. J. (1992). Neurofilament proteins and the mesolimbic dopamine system: Common regulation by chronic morphine and chronic cocaine in the rat ventral tegmental area. *Journal of Neuroscience, 12,* 2165–2176.

Beitner-Johnson, D., Guitart, X., & Nestler, E. J. (in press). Common intracellular actions of morphine and cocaine in dopaminergic brain reward regions. *Annals of New York Academy of Sciences, 654.*

Bozarth, M. A. (1986). Neural basis of psychomotor stimulant and opiate reward: Evidence suggesting the involvement of a common dopaminergic system. *Behavioral Brain Research, 22,* 107–116.

Bozarth, M. A. (1989). New perspectives on cocaine addiction: Recent findings from animal research. *Canadian Journal of Physiology and Pharmacology, 67,* 1158–1167.

Brock, J. W., Ng, J. P., & Justice, J. B., Jr. (1990). Effect of chronic cocaine on dopamine synthesis in the nucleus accumbens as determined by microdialysis with NSD-1015. *Neuroscience Letters, 117,* 234–239.

Bunney, B. S., Sesack, S. R., & Silva, N. L. (1987). Midbrain dopaminergic systems: neurophysiology and elecrophysiological pharmacology. In H. Y. Meltzer (Ed.), *Psychopharmacology: The third generation of progress* (pp. 81–94). New York: Raven Press.

Chen, J., Marmur, R., Paredes, W., Pulles, A., & Gardener, E. L. (1991). Systemic cocaine challenge after chronic cocaine treatment yields cocaine sensitization of extracellular dopamine content in nucleus accumbens but direct cocaine perfusion into nucleus accumbens does not—in vivo microdialysis studies. *Society for Neuroscience Abstracts, 17,* p. 823.

Chen, J., Paredes, W., Li, J., Smithe, D., Lowinson, J., & Gardener, E. L. (1990). Δ 9-tetrahydrocannabinol produces naloxone-blockable enhancement of presynaptic basal dopamine efflux in nucleus accumbens of conscious, freely-moving rats as mesured by intracerebral microdialysis. *Psychopharmacology, 102,* 156–162.

Church, W. H., & Justice, J. B., Jr. (1987). Rapid sampling and determination of extracellular dopamine in vivo. *Analytical Chemistry, 59,* 712–716.

Clouet, D., Asghar, K., & Brown, R. (Eds.). (1988). *Mechanisms of cocaine abuse and toxicity* (Research Monograph No. 88). National Institute on Drug Abuse. Rockville, MD.

Cooper, J. R., Bloom, F. E., & Roth, R. H. (1986). *The biochemical basis of neuropharmacology* (6th ed.). New York: Oxford University Press.

Dackis, C., & Gold, M. (1985). New concepts in cocaine addiction: The dopamine depletion hypothesis. *Neuroscience Biobehavioral Review, 9,* 469–477.

Delfs, J. M., Schreibner, L., & Kelley, A. E. (1990). Microinjection of cocaine into the nucleus accumbens elicits locomotor activation in the rat. *Journal of Neuroscience, 10,* 303–310.

DiChiara, G., & Imperato, A. (1988). Drugs abused by humans preferentially increase synaptic dopamine concentrations in the mesolimbic system of freely moving rats. *Proceedings of the National Academy of Sciences, USA, 85,* 5274–5278.

Dworkin, S. I., Goeders, N. E., & Smith, J. E. (1986). The reinforcing and rate effects of intracranial dopamine administration. In L. S. Harris (Ed.), *Problems of drug dependence, 1985* (Vol. 67, pp. 242–248). Washington, DC: U. S. Government Printing Office.

Einhorn, L. C., Johansen, P. A., & White, F. J. (1988). Electrophysiological effects of cocaine in the mesoaccumbens dopamine system: studies in the ventral tegmental area. *Journal of Neuroscience, 8,* 100–112.

Ellison, G. (1983). Phasic alterations in dopamine metabolites following continuous administration of amphetamine. *Brain Research, 268,* 387–389.

Fibiger, H. C. (1978). Drugs and reinforcement mechanisms: A critical review of the catecholamine theory. *Annual Review of Pharmacology and Toxicology, 18,* 37–56.

George, F. R., & Goldberg, S. R. (1989). Genetic approaches to the analysis of addiction processes. *Trends in Pharmacological Sciences, 10,* 78–83.

Gilman, A. G. (1987). G proteins: Transducers of receptor-generated signals. *Annual Review of Biochemistry, 56,* 615–649.

Goeders, N. E., & Smith, J. E. (1983). Cortical dopaminergic involvement in cocaine reinforcement. *Science, 221,* 773–775.

Graybiel, A. M., Moratella, R., & Robertson, H. A. (1990). Amphetamine and cocaine induce drug-specific activation of the c-fos gene in striosome-matrix compartments and limbic subdivisions of the striatum. *Proceedings of the National Academy of Sciences, USA, 87,* 6912–6916.

Guitart, X., Beitner-Johnson, D., & Nestler, E. J. (in press). Fischer and Lewis rat strains differ in basal levels of neurofilament proteins and their regulation by chronic morphine in the mesolimbic dopamine system. *Synapse.*

Guitart, X., Hayward, M., Nisenbaum, L. K., Beitner-Johnson, D. B., Haycock, J. W., & Nestler, E. J. (1990). Identification of MARPP-58, a morphine- and cyclic AMP-regulated phosphoprotein of 58 kDa, as tyrosine hydroxylase: Evidence for regulation of its expression by chronic morphine in the rat locus coeruleus. *Journal of Neuroscience, 10,* 2649–2659.

Hall, G. F., Lee, V. M.-Y., & Kosik, K. S. (1991). Microtublule destabilization and neurofilament phosphorylation precede dendritic sprouting after close axotomy of lamprey central neurons. *Proceedings of the National Academy of Sciences, USA, 88,* 5016–5020.

Henry, D. J., & White, F. J. (1991). Repeated cocaine administration causes persistent enhancement of D1 dopamine receptor sensitivity within the rat nucleus accumbens. *Journal of Pharmacological and Experimental Therapeutics, 258,* 882–890.

Henry, D. J., Greene, M. A., & White, F. J. (1989). Electrophysiological effects of cocaine in the mesoaccumbens dopamine system: Repeated administration. *Journal of Pharmacological and Experimental Therapeutics, 251,* 833–839.

Hoffman, P. N., & Lasek, R. J. (1980). Axonal transport of the cytoskeleton in regenerating motor neurons: constancy and change. *Brain Research, 202,* 317–333.

Hoffman, P. N., Griffin, J. W., & Price, D. L. (1984). Control of axonal caliber by neurofilament transport. *Journal of Cell Biology, 99,* 705–714.

Hooks, M. S., Jones, G. H., Smith, A. D., Neill, D. B., & Justice, J. B., Jr. (1991). Individual differences in locomotor activation and sensitization. *Pharmacology, Biochemistry and Behavior, 38,* 467–470.

Hope, B., Kosofsky, B., Hyman, S. E., & Nestler, E. J. (in press). Regulation of IEG expression and AP-1 binding by chronic cocaine in the rat nucleus accumbens. *Proceedings of the National Academy of Sciences.*

Hubner, C. B., & Koob, G. F. (1990). The ventral pallidum plays a role in mediating cocaine and heroin self-administration in the rat. *Brain Research, 508,* 20–29.

Hurd, Y. L., Weiss, F., Koob, G. F., And, N.-E., & Ungerstedt, U. (1989). Cocaine reinforcement and extracellular dopamine overflow in rat nucleus accumbens: An in vivo microdialysis study. *Brain Research, 498,* 199–203.

Hyman, S. E. & Nestler, E. J. (in press). *Molecular foundations of psychiatry: An introductory text.* Washington, DC: American Psychiatric Press.

Innis, R. B., & Aghajanian, G. K. (1987). Pertussis toxin blocks autoreceptor-mediated inhibition of dopaminergic neurons in rat substantia nigra. *Brain Research, 411,* 139–143.

Johanson C.-E., & Fischman, M. W. (1989). The pharmacology of cocaine related to its abuse. *Pharmacological Reviews, 41,* 3–52.

Kalivas, P. W., & Duffy, P. (1988). Effects of daily cocaine and morphine treatment on somatodendritic and terminal field dopamine release. *Journal of Neurochemistry, 50,* 1498-1504.

Kalivas, P. W., Duffy, P., DuMars, L. A., & Skinner, C. (1988). Behavioral and neurochemical effects of acute and daily cocaine administration in rats. *Journal of Pharmacology and Experimental Therapeutics, 245,* 485–492.

Kelly, P. H., Seviour, P. W., & Iverson, S. D. (1975). Amphetamine and apomorphine responses in the rat following 6-OHDA lesions of the nucleus accumbens septi and corpus striatum. *Brain Research, 94,* 507–522.

Kilbey, M. M., & Ellinwood, E. H. (1977). Administration of stimulant drugs: Response modification. In E. H. Ellinwood & M. M. Kilbey (Eds.), *Cocaine and other stimulants* (pp. 404–429). New York: Plenum Press.

Koob, G. F., & Bloom, F. E. (1988). Cellular and molecular mechanisms of drug dependence. *Science, 242,* 715–723.

Kuhar, M. J., Ritz, M. C., & Boja, J. W. (1991). The dopamine hypothesis of the reinforcing properties of cocaine. *Trends in Neurosciences, 14,* 299–302.

Leccese, A. P., & Lyness, W. H. (1984). The effects of putative-5-hydroxytryptamine receptor active agents on d-amphetamine self-administration in controls and rats with 5,7-dihydroxytryptamine median forebrain bundle lesions. *Brain Research, 303,* 153–162.

Lett, B. T. (1989). Repeated exposures intensify rather than diminish the rewarding effects of amphetamine, morphine, and cocaine. *Psychopharmacology* [Berlin], *98,* 357–362.

Li, T.-K., & L. Lumeng, (1984). Alcohol preference and voluntary alcohol intakes of inbred rat strains and the NIH heterogeneous stock of rats. *Alcoholism, Clinical and Experimental Research, 8,* 485–486.

Liebman, J. M., & Cooper, S. J. (Eds.). (1989). *The neuropharmacological basis of reward.* New York: Oxford University Press.

Lyness, W. H., Friedle, N. M., & Moore, K. E. (1979). Destruction of dopaminergic nerve terminals in nucleus accumbens: Effect of d-amphetamine self-administration. *Pharmacology, Biochemistry and Behavior, 11,* 553–556.

Matthews, R. T., & German, D. C. (1984). Electrophysiological evidence for excitation of rat ventral tegmental area dopamine neurons by morphine. *Neuroscience, 11,* 617–625.

Nestler, E. J., & Greengard, P. (1989). Protein phosphorylation and the regulation of neuronal function. In G. Siegel, B. Agranoff, R. W. Albers, and P. Molinoff (Eds.), *Basic Neurochemistry* (4th ed., pp. 373–398). New York: Raven Press.

Nestler, E. J., Terwilliger, R. Z., Walker, J. R., Sevarino, K. A., & Duman, R. S. (1990). Chronic cocaine treatment decreases levels of the G protein subunits Giα and Goα in discrete regions of the rat brain. *Journal of Neurochemistry, 55,* 1079–1082.

Ng, J. P., Hubert, G. W., & Justice, J. B., Jr. (1991). Increased stimulated release and uptake of dopamine in nucleus accumbens after repeated cocaine administration as measured by in vivo voltammetry. *Journal of Neurochemistry, 56,* 1485–1492.

Pacholcyzk, T., Blakely, R. D., & Amara, S. G. (1991). Expression cloning of a cocaine-sensitive and antidepressant-sensitive human noradrenaline transporter. *Nature, 350,* 350–354.

Pan, H.-T., Menacherry, S., & Justice, J. B., Jr. (1991). Differences in the pharmacokinetics of cocaine in naive and cocaine-experienced rats. *Journal of Neurochemistry, 56,* 1299–1306.

Pan, Z. Z., & Williams, J. T. (1989). Differential actions of cocaine and amphetamine on dorsal raphe neurons in vitro. *Journal of Pharmacology and Experimental Therapeutics, 251,* 56–62.

Peris, J., Boyson, S. J., Cass, W. A., Curella, P., Dwoskin, L. P., Larson, G., Lin, L.-H., Yasuda, R. P., & Zahniser, N. R. (1990). Persistence of neurochemical changes in dopamine systems after repeated cocaine administration. *Journal of Pharmacology and Experimental Therapeutics, 253,* 38–44.

Pettit, H. O., Pan, H., Parsons, L. H., & Justice, J. B., Jr. (1990). Extracellular concentrations of cocaine and dopamine are enhanced during chronic cocaine administration. *Journal of Neurochemistry, 55,* 798–804.

Piazza, P. V., Deminiere, J.-M., Le Moal, M., & Simon, H. (1989). Factors that predict individual vulnerability to amphetamine self-administration. *Science, 245,* 1511–1513.

Piazza, P. V., Maccari, S., Deminiere, J.-M., Le Moal, M., Mormede, P., & Simon, H. (1991). Corticosterone levels determine individual vulnerability to amphetamine self-administration. *Proceedings of the National Academy of Sciences, USA, 88,* 2088–2092.

Pickel, V. M., Towle, A. C., Joh, T. H., & Chan, J. (1988). Gamma-aminobutyric acid in the medial rat nucleus accumbens: ultrastructural localization in neurons receiving monosynaptic input from catecholaminergic afferents. *Journal of Comparative Neurology, 272,* 1–14.

Pickens, R. W., & Svikis, D. S. (1988). *Biological vulnerability to drug abuse* (NIDA Research Monograph No. 89). Rockville, MD: National Institute on Drug Abuse.

Pitts, D. K., & Marwah, J. (1987). Electrophysiological actions of cocaine on noradrenergic neurons in rat locus ceruleus. *Journal of Pharmacological and Experimental Therapeutics, 240,* 345–351.

Porrino, L. J., Ritz, M. C., Goodman, N. L., Sharpe, L. G., Kuhar, M. J., & Goldberg, S. R. (1989). Differential effects of the pharmacological manipulation of serotonin systems on cocaine and amphetamine self-administration in rats. *Life Sciences, 45,* 1529–1535.

Post, R. M., & Rose, H. (1976). Increasing effects of repetitive cocaine administration in the rat. *Nature, 260,* 731–732.

Ritchie, J.M., & Greene, N. M. (1990). Local Anesthetics. In A. G. Gilman, T. W. Rall, A. S. Nies, & P. Taylor (Eds.), *The pharmacological basis of therapeutics* (pp. 311–331). New York: Permagon Press.

Ritz, M. C., Lamb, R. J., Goldberg, S. R., & Kuhar, M. J. (1987). Cocaine receptors on dopamine transporters are related to self-administration of cocaine. *Science, 237,* 1219–1223.

Roberts, D. C. S., Corcoran, M. E., & Fibiger, H. C. (1977). On the role of ascending catecholaminergic systems in intravenous self-administration of cocaine. *Pharmacology, Biochemistry and Behavior, 6,* 615–620.

Robertson, M. W., Leslie, C. A, & Bennet, J. P., Jr. (1991). Apparent synaptic dopamine deficiency induced by withdrawal from chronic cocaine treatment. *Brain Research, 538,* 337–339.

Roth, R. H., Wolf, M. E., & Deutch, A. Y. (1987). Neurochemistry of midbrain dopamine systems. In H. Y. Meltzer (Ed.), *Psychopharmacology: The third generation of progress* (pp. 113–126). New York: Raven Press.

Shippenberg, T. S., & Herz, A. (1987). Place preference conditioning reveals the involvement of D1-dopamine receptors in the motivational properties of m and k-opioid agonists. *Brain Research, 436,* 169–172.

Sokoloff, P., Giros, B., Martres, M.-P., Bouthenet, M.-L., & Schwartz, J.-C. (1990). Molecular cloning and characterization of a novel dopamine receptor (D3) as a target for neuroleptics. *Nature, 347,* 146–151.

Steketee, J. D., Striplin, C. D., Murray, T. F., & Kalivas, P. W. (1991). Possible role for G-proteins in behavioral sensitization to cocaine. *Brain Research, 545,* 287–291.

Stoof, J. C., & Kebabian, J. W. (1981). Opposing roles for D1 and D2 dopamine receptors in efflux of cyclic AMP from rat neostriatum. *Nature, 294,* 366–368.

Sunahara, R. K., Guan, H.-C., O'Dowd, B. F., Seeman, P., Laurier, L. G., Ng, G., George, S. R., Torchia, J., Van Tol, H. H. M., & Niznik, H. B. (1991). Cloning of the gene for a human dopamine D5 receptor with a higher affinity for dopamine than D1. *Nature, 350,* 614–619.

Suzuki, T., George, F. R., & Meisch, R. A. (1988). Differential establishment and maintenance of oral ethanol reinforced behavior in Lewis and Fischer 344 inbred rat strains. *Journal of Pharmacology and Experimental Therapeutics, 245,* 164–170.

Terwilliger, R., Beitner-Johnson, D., Sevarino, K. A., Crain, S. M., & Nestler, E. J. (1991a). A general role for adaptations in G-proteins and the cyclic AMP system in mediating the chronic actions of morphine and cocaine on neuronal function. *Brain Research, 548,* 100–110.

Terwilliger, R., Bradberry, C., Guitart, X., Beitner-Johnson, D., Marby, D., Kosten, T. A., & Nestler, E. J. (1991b). Lewis and Fischer 344 rats and drug addiction: Behavioral and biochemical correlates, *Society of Neurosciences Abstracts, 17,* 823.

Uchimura, N., & North, R. A. (1990). Actions of cocaine on rat nucleus accumbens neurones in vitro. *British Journal of Pharmacology, 99,* 736–740.

Uchimura, N., Higashi, H., & Nishi, S. (1986). Hyperpolarizing and depolarizing actions of dopamine via D1 and D2 receptors on nucleus accumbens neurons. *Brain Research, 375,* 368–372.

Van Tol, H. H. M., Bunzow, J. R., Guan, H.-C., Sunahara, R. K., Seeman, P., Niznik, H. B., & Civelli, O. (1991). Cloning of the gene for a human D4 receptor with high affinity for the antipsychotic clozapine. *Nature, 350,* 610–614.

Voorn, P., Gerfen, C. R., & Groenewegen, H. J. (1989). Compartmental organization of the ventral striatum of the rat: immunohistochemical distribution of enkephalin, substance P, dopamine, and calcium binding protein. *Journal of Comparative Neurology, 289,* 189–201.

Wachtel, S. R., Hu, X.-T., Galloway, M. P., & White, F. J. (1989). D1 dopamine receptor stimulation enables the postsynaptic, but not autoreceptor, effects of D2 dopamine agonists in nigrostriatal and mesoaccumbens dopamine systems. *Synapse, 4,* 327–346.

White, F. J., & Wang, R. Y (1986). Electrophysiological evidence for the existence of both D1 and D2 dopamine receptors in the rat nucleus accumbens. *Journal of Neuroscience, 8,* 274–280.

Wise, R. A. (1982). Neuroleptics and operant behavior: The anhedonia hypothesis. *Behavioral and Brain Sciences, 5,* 39–87.

Wise, R. A., & Bozarth, M. A. (1987). A psychomotor stimulant theory of addiction. *Psychological Review, 94,* 469–492.

Wise, R. A., Murray, A., & Bozarth, M. A. (1990). Bromocriptine self-administration and bromocriptine-reinstatement of cocaine-trained and heroin-trained lever pressing in rats. *Psychopharmacology, 100,* 355–360.

Woolverton, W. L. (1987). Evaluation of the role of norepinephrine in the reinforcing effects of psychomotor stimulants in rhesus monkeys. *Pharmacology, Biochemistry and Behavior, 26,* 834–839.

Woolverton, W. L., Goldberg, L. I., & Ginos, J. Z. (1984). Intravenous self-administration of dopamine receptor agonists by rhesus monkeys. *Journal of Pharmacology and Experimental Therapeutics, 230,* 687–683.

Young, S. T., Porrino, L. J., & Iadarola, M. J. (1991). Cocaine induces striatal c-Fos-immunoreactive proteins via dopaminergic D1 receptors. *Proceedings of the National Academy of Sciences, USA, 88,* 1291–1295.

Zahm, D. S., & Heimer, L. (1988). Ventral striatopallidal parts of the basal ganglia in the rat: 1. Neurochemical compartmentation as reflected by the distributions of neurotensin and substance P immunoreactivity. *Journal of Comparative Neurology, 272,* 516–535.

Zito, K., Vickers, G., & Roberts, D. C. S. (1985). Disruption of cocaine and heroin self-administration following kainic acid lesions of the nucleus accumbens. *Pharmacology, Biochemistry and Behavior, 23,* 1029–1036.

Animal Models
for Cocaine Abuse

Therese A. Kosten, PhD

I N THE PAST two decades, cocaine abuse has become a matter of great concern. To develop useful methods for preventing and treating cocaine abuse, we need to better understand its etiology and phenomenology. One approach is to use animal models to manipulate and control the parameters of the drug's effects. When promising results are obtained with animal models, they can be tested on human, addict populations. In addition, information obtained from the addicts through clinical observations or controlled studies should be tested in the animal models. This provides a validity check of the models as well as a basis for more detailed exploration of the various phenomena involved in cocaine abuse.

This chapter examines how animal models can be used to further our understanding of cocaine abuse. First, we will discuss the rationale and role of animal models for clinical applications. Second, we will outline the variety of cocaine's behavioral properties that must be considered in order to develop and interpret animal model studies. Third, we will discuss the psychological constructs, such as conditioning, upon which animal models are based. Fourth, we will present several techniques that are used as animal models of cocaine's effects. Finally, we will discuss how to link the data obtained from animal work to humans. This last purpose is both the most important and the most difficult because it involves making links across different species and across different disciplines.

RATIONALE AND ROLE OF ANIMAL MODELS

Rationale

There are several reasons why animals are used in behavioral research; and the benefits and rationale for this approach have been eloquently detailed elsewhere (Miller, 1985; Gallup & Suarez, 1985). Briefly, one advantage of animal research is that it permits control over various factors such as genetic background, prior experience, and environmental conditions. Animal research is more efficient, particularly for developmental or genetic studies. And there are of course many biological manipulations that can be tested on animals but not on humans.

Animal models have led to many successful treatments for medical syndromes. The role of animal models to test these syndromes is more directly applicable to the human situation than it is for psychiatric syndromes because the etiology and mechanisms of behavioral disorders are much less clear.

Animal Models in Psychiatry

In psychiatry, clinical syndromes are defined by their behavioral or symptom aspects, not by underlying mechanisms or etiology (e.g., DSM-III-R). There are multiple possible causes, differing courses, and spectra of illnesses, as well as a variety of treatment approaches for psychiatric syndromes. Moreover, because of the complexity of human behavior, there are great individual differences in the behavioral aspects of any given syndrome. Thus it is impossible to have one single animal model for a psychiatric syndrome that would be parallel in all aspects. No existing or possible animal model should be expected to be an ideal match to the human behavioral disorder. Rather,the human disorder should be assessed using a variety of animal models that necessarily vary in the ways in which they resemble the human disorder.

Developing animal models of substance abuse is somewhat less complicated than developing animal models of other psychiatric disorders, in one aspect. In substance abuse, we know one of the etiological factors or commonalities among cases: exposure to drugs and their effects. This, of course, only explains a small piece of the etiological puzzle. Drug abuse reflects the interaction of social, behavioral, and other biological factors besides the drug effects such as genetic or physiological factors. Nonetheless, animal models of substance abuse will all involve exposing the animals to the drug. Yet, even this aspect is not uniform in nature because parameters such as length, timing, dose, and other conditions of drug exposure will vary across models and studies.

Types of Animal Models

Henn and McKinney (1987) categorized animal models into four kinds, based on their specific purpose in helping to understand the human disorder: (1) those based on behavioral similarity; (2) those designed to test an etiology; (3) those designed to test mechanisms (e.g., neurobiological mechanisms); and (4) those used to test potential pharmacological treatments. Each type of animal model has specific features in which one aspect of the disorder can be evaluated in a controlled, systematic manner.

Categorizing animal models of substance abuse with this classification system will aid our understanding of their purpose. First, testing behavioral similarity has led to animal models designed to assess drug-taking behavior and are used to test abuse liability of new compounds. The degree of similarity to which the new compound affects behavior as do established drugs of abuse provides an estimate of whether this drug may be abused by humans. Second, an animal model can test possible etiological factors, such as genetic factors. Third, animal models can test mechanisms, such as delineating neural mechanisms of drug using behavior. Finally, when animal models are used to test potential pharmacological treatments they must use established behavioral paradigms and test pharmacological agents suggested by the etiologic or mechanistic studies.

THE EFFECTS OF COCAINE ON BEHAVIOR

Positive Reinforcement

Generally, animal models are based on the assumption that cocaine alters behavior because it is positively reinforcing. The assumption is similar for humans in that cocaine's ability to induce euphoria or to be rewarding is believed to be the basis of cocaine addiction (Edwards, Arif, & Hodgson, 1981). Cocaine, the putative reinforcer, leads to increases in behaviors associated with it or with those behaviors needed to obtain cocaine again.

We assess the degree of positive reinforcement by quantifying an increase in behavior associated with the drug. However, as in all behavioral research, we measure performance, not the underlying processes. Many things can affect an animal's capacity to perform a behavior; thus, rigorous methods must be used to assess whether performance was altered owing to factors other than positive reinforcement.

Other Acute Properties of Cocaine

Although reward or positive reinforcement is an important property of cocaine's ability to establish and sustain use, this drug has other properties that will affect behavior. It is a psychomotor stimulant and, in rats, low doses will produce grooming, locomotion, and rearing (Scheel-Kruger, Braestrup, Nielson, Golembiowska, & Mogilnicka, 1977; Snoddy & Tessel, 1985). Low doses will probably affect the behavior under study by increasing its output. At large doses, cocaine can cause stereotypy (Lewander, 1974; Tyler & Tessel, 1979) that may limit expression of the behavior under study. Cocaine has anesthetic properties that, although fairly localized, may alter pain or other sensory thresholds (O'Connor, Kuwada, DePalma, Stanford, & Tasman, 1990). Finally, cocaine has aversive properties, which are described for humans in the Chapter 9 of this book, and can be studied in animals as well.

Chronic Effects of Cocaine

In addition to these acute effects of cocaine, chronic cocaine exposure can alter behavior. Some effects of cocaine, such as motor effects, may be enhanced with chronic use (sensitization), whereas others may be attenuated (tolerance). Moreover, abrupt cessation from chronic cocaine exposure may be associated with withdrawal discomfort in humans (Gawin & Kleber, 1986) and in animals. Withdrawal distress occurs with cessation from chronic opiate use and is believed to sustain, in part, further opiate use (Jaffe, 1985). The relief from discomfort that the drug provides is an example of negative reinforcement which is described in the following section.

Thus the multiple aspects of cocaine's effects must be considered in order to interpret and understand the data obtained from animal model studies as well as from human studies. Although the working assumption is that cocaine leads to, and sustains, addiction owing to its positive reinforcing property, other properties may contribute to cocaine addiction as well.

PSYCHOLOGICAL CONSTRUCTS USED IN ANIMAL MODEL RESEARCH

Operant Conditioning

Many animal models are based on operant conditioning. Skinner (1938) defined this construct as behavior that is controlled by its consequences, which, if they result in an increase in behavior, are known as "reinforcers." Positive reinforcers are those for which the presentation of the stimulus (i.e. the drug) is reinforcing and negative reinforcers are those where the removal of the stimulus (i.e. drug withdrawal) is reinforcing.

In operant conditioning, the reinforcement is contingent upon emitting a behavior to obtain the reinforcement. For example, an animal could learn to press a bar to get a drug injection. First, the experimenter will present the drug (reinforcer) when the animal nears the bar (shaping) until the animal presses the bar on its own to receive the drug. Because animals have no inherent interest in bar pressing, it assumed that the consequence of receiving the drug controls the bar-pressing behavior. Then, through many conditioning trials, the behavior is established and the removal of this reinforcement contingency will result in decreased responding or "extinction." If, after extinction, the reinforcement contingency is presented again, the response will develop more quickly ("reinstatement").

There are many methods by which the strength of the operant response is assessed to provide a measure of the degree of reinforcement. Some possible measures include rate of responding, probability of emitting a discrete response in a choice paradigm (Skinner, 1938), latency or speed of emitting a response (Hull, 1943), and proportion of time emitting a response (Baum & Rachlin, 1969). The use and limitations of these measures are described in the following section.

The strength and pattern of operant behavior is influenced by the schedule of reinforcement. A range of schedules can be used that generate different patterns of responding (see Ferster & Skinner, 1957). Two types of schedules are used in animal models of substance abuse: the "ratio" schedule, in which the number of responses needed to obtain the reinforcer is specified, and the "interval" schedule, in which the interval between the availability of two successive reinforcers is specified. These schedules can be "fixed," so that the reinforcer is available on a constant basis, or "variable" where the reinforcer is available on an average basis . For example, a fixed interval 5 schedule is one in which the drug will be available every 5 seconds, provided the animal bar-presses during that time. A variable ratio 30 schedule is one in which, on the average, 30 responses are required to obtain the reinforcer. These "partial reinforcement" schedules produce greater response strength and are associated with slower extinction than are schedules of continuous reinforcement (Mackintosh, 1974). These methods of operant conditioning were developed with food and shock reinforcers. The differences in patterns of operant behavior between these reinforcers and drugs will be discussed later.

Classical Conditioning

Classical conditioning, the basis of other animal models of substance abuse, occurs when stimuli present in the environment at the time of the reinforcement acquire the capacity to maintain a given response. In classical conditioning, in contrast to operant conditioning, the animal is not required to make a response to get the reinforcement in classical conditioning. Stimuli that acquire conditioning are originally neutral but with successive pairings with the reinforcer become "conditioned stimuli" (CSs). CSs are capable of eliciting a "conditioned response" (CR) that is usually similar in type, but not magnitude, to the "unconditioned response" (UCR).

Classical conditioning was first described by Pavlov (1927), whose salivating dog experiment is often cited. In this example, the conditioned stimulus (CS) is a bell that rings before the presentation of food. The food, or unconditioned stimulus (UCS), elicits salivation. After several pairings of the bell, or CS, with the food, or UCS, the bell presentation alone elicits the conditioned salivatory response.

Animal models of drug reinforcement, based on classical conditioning, include conditioned place preference (CPP) and conditioned taste aversion (CTA). These models assess the positive reinforcing and aversive aspects of drug abuse, respectively. Both models use indirect measures of the conditioned response. For the former, the degree of approaching the CS is used to assess reinforcement, and in the latter, the degree of avoiding the CS is measured.

Other aspects of drug use besides reinforcement have been proposed to be due to classical conditioning. Classically conditioned stimuli may elicit drug withdrawal (Wikler, 1973) or drug tolerance (Siegel, 1979). This work is important for interpreting results from studies in which drugs are given. First, either tolerance to some properties of cocaine or withdrawal of the drug may distort the measures of positive reinforcement obtained. Second, Siegel's work shows that the conditioned responses may not be in the same direction as the unconditioned responses. For example, a stimulus that was paired with morphine presentation will come to elicit physical responses that are opposite to the physical responses caused by the morphine itself. Whereas morphine causes a decrease in heart rate, stimuli associated with it elicit an *increase* in heart rate.

This phenomenon may be explained by delineating what response was conditioned. Eikelboom and Stewart (1982) propose that the drug injection itself should not be considered the unconditioned response, as is often the assumption. Rather, the central nervous system events that occur owing to the drug effects should be deemed the unconditioned responses. These events include the autonomic nervous system's responses to restore homeostasis, such as returning body temperature or heart rate to normal levels.

Thus to interpret animal studies of cocaine use we should consider the drug effects as the reinforcer, not the drug injection itself. Moreover, tolerance, sensitization, and, possibly, withdrawal may become conditioned along with the behaviors used to assess reinforcement, thus confounding the interpretation of the results.

Motivation and Other Related Constructs

Another construct that can be used to explain drug-taking behavior is motivation. This explains why an animal behaves in a specific way given circumstances such as the incentive available, the difficulties of obtaining the goal, and its internal state. Motivation can be innate, as in the feeding drive that occurs owing to food deficiency, or acquired, as in drug-taking behavior.

The role of motivation in drug-taking behavior was addressed by Solomon and Corbit (1974) in a theoretical model. However, little empirical work in animal models of substance abuse has used motivational concepts. Some of the techniques developed in feeding behavior (e.g., Miller, 1967) could be modified for substance abuse. One possible paradigm would be to measure how much an animal will overcome shock grids to obtain the drug goal.

Other related constructs that could be used to guide the development of animal models of substance abuse include arousal, which was used by Hebb (1955) as a term for general motivation, and affective arousal, which was introduced by Young (1959) as a concept to supplement motivation theories. Because drugs of abuse influence arousal, either by increasing it or decreasing it, and alter affect, these constructs may be useful for future animal model studies of substance abuse. At present, most research using animal models of drug addiction have been based on either operant or classical conditioning constructs, as discussed below.

TECHNIQUES USED TO STUDY COCAINE REINFORCEMENT

Self-Administration

One of the most widely used techniques to assess cocaine reinforcement in animals is the drug self-administration (SA) technique. In this technique, animals are implanted with intravenous catheters and trained to bar-press to receive a drug injection through this catheter. Pickens and Thompson (1968) found that animals would press a lever if doing so was followed by an injection of cocaine. Their experiments also exemplify the rigorous methods needed to assess whether this behavior was indeed due to the reinforcing property of cocaine. First, they showed that when the cocaine was replaced with saline, the bar-pressing behavior declined. Second, if the cocaine was delivered automatically, that is, the contingency of receiving cocaine was not dependent on bar pressing, responding declined. Finally, when two levers were available where pressing only one resulted in cocaine delivery, little responding on the other lever was seen; reversing this contingency led to the appropriate modification in behavior.

Many studies have replicated this original study of cocaine SA, and these findings have been demonstrated in a number of different species, including rats (Pickens & Thompson, 1968), rhesus monkeys (Woods & Schuster, 1968), baboons (Griffiths, Findley, Brady, Dolan-Gutcher, & Robinson, 1975), cats (Balster, Kilbey, & Ellinwood, 1976), dogs (Risner & Jones, 1975), and humans (Fischman, 1984). This remarkable concordance across species suggests several things. First, cocaine is an efficacious reinforcer. Second, the neural mechanisms by which cocaine's reinforcing actions occur are probably similar across species. Finally, it demonstrates the validity and usefulness of the animal model of self-administration.

In addition to this procedural validity of the SA method, it has face validity because the SA technique often uses similar administration routes as those used by humans (i.e., intravenous route). However, cocaine SA has been shown to occur through a number of routes of administration including intragastrically (Woolverton & Schuster, 1983), smoking (Siegel, Johnson, Brewster, & Jarvik, 1976), intranasally (Foltin, Fischman, Pedroso, & Pearlson, 1988), and intramuscularly (Goldberg, Morse, & Goldberg, 1976). Although this demonstrates that cocaine is reinforcing when it is administered through a variety of routes, the degree and length of reinforcement does vary across methods (Van Dyke, 1978).

As discussed previously, a number of different procedures, such as schedules of reinforcement, can be used to study cocaine SA. In addition, there are several ways to measure the animal's response to the cocaine including tabulating the number of bar presses. Because of the vast array of behavioral tests and measures used in these studies, there have been difficulties in interpreting the results. Another consideration is that behavioral responses will differ during "acquisition" versus during "maintenance" of SA. All of these issues are particularly important for animal model studies that were designed to assess mechanisms or pharmacological interventions.

Different behavioral responses are seen because of the nature of the schedule of reinforcement. A fixed interval schedule leads to a "scallop" response curve over time with low responding toward the beginning of the interval and progressively higher responding as the end of the interval approaches. Variable interval schedules, on the other hand, result in more stable responding. These response profiles are characteristic of operant schedules of reinforcement in general and are not specific to drug SA. However, distinctions between "traditional" reinforcers, such as food and water, and drug reinforcers have been found. For example, cocaine maintains responding under ratio schedules (Balster & Schuster, 1973; Goldberg, Woods, & Schuster, 1971), but the rate of responding has been low compared with that of the traditional reinforcers. Moreover, the dose–response relationship is inverse such that higher doses of cocaine result in lower response rates.

There are explanations for these peculiar results from cocaine SA studies and a number of recommendations for improved response measures have been made (see Johanson & Fischman, 1989). The main reason for discrepant or irreconcilable results from various studies is that using the rate of responding as a response measure is problematic. In a SA paradigm, after the animal responds for a cocaine injection, all subsequent responses are then affected by the previous drug injections. Because cocaine is also a psychomotor stimulant, these behavioral measurements that presumably reflect reinforcement are distorted. Moreover, the reinforcing and motor effects of the cocaine may change differentially with chronic use as tolerance and/or sensitization develop.

Several alternative procedures have been developed to avoid the problems of using rate of responding as a measure of drug reinforcement. One method is to have a time-out period after each injection to allow the drug effects to wear off (Downs & Woods, 1974; Winger & Woods, 1985). This addresses the interpretation problem caused by the acute effects of cocaine, but not the issues of tolerance and sensitization.

Another common method of assessing the reinforcing aspect of cocaine as distinct from its general activating aspect, is to measure cocaine responding and food responding in the same session (Herling, Downs, & Woods, 1979). If the two behaviors are affected similarly, then we are seeing an effect on general activation, not an effect on cocaine reinforcement. Herling et al. (1979) demonstrated that the rate of responding for both cocaine and food decreased with subsequent cocaine administration. This provides evidence that changes in rate of responding for cocaine may be due, for the most part, to cocaine's effects on activity. The premise behind this study is that measuring food reinforcement, as distinct from cocaine reinforcement, will show the selectivity of the drug effect. Indeed, many SA studies use this comparison as a control procedure. However, this premise may be flawed if one views reinforcement as an integrated, general phenomenon (e.g., Olds, 1969). Although the evidence suggests that several pathways are involved in various aspects of reinforcement (Stein, 1983; Everitt, Robbins, Evenden, & Marston, 1987), it is very likely that enough overlap of systems exists between feeding and cocaine reinforcement so as to make it improbable to distinguish these effects behaviorally.

A number of other alternative procedures to assess cocaine's reinforcement appear to be less sensitive to the motoric effects of cocaine. One procedure is use second-order conditioning, where one conditioned stimulus is presented with the cocaine injections and another, second-order, stimulus is paired with this first conditioned stimulus. The second-order stimulus takes on some of the characteristics of the first CS, and because the second-order stimulus is not presented with the drug injections, measures of how it affects behavior are not confounded by the drug's actions on performance. Goldberg and colleagues (Goldberg, 1973; Kelleher & Goldberg, 1977) found high response rates for cocaine with this method that resembled the type of responding seen for other natural reinforcers.

Another alteration of the conditioning paradigm that may be less sensitive to motor effects is the progressive ratio schedule (Mello, Lucas, Bree, & Mendelson, 1988). In this procedure, the average number of responses required to receive the drug injection increases once the behavior has become established. The point at which responding decreases to some criterion is called the "breaking point." This measure of reinforcement reflects how much work the animal is willing to do to receive the drug. The breaking points for cocaine have been shown to be a direct function of dose (Yanagita, 1973; Griffiths, Brady, & Snell, 1978).

Another approach to evaluating cocaine's reinforcing property without the confounding motor effects is to use measures of choice or relative frequency of response in a choice paradigm. Johanson and Schuster (1975) showed that when animals were given a choice between two levers that delivered two different doses of cocaine and the response measure was the number of trials one lever was chosen relative to the other, a direct dose–response curve was generated. Other choice procedures that have demonstrated the efficacy of cocaine reinforcement are providing the animal with the choice of receiving cocaine injections versus a number of other options. For example, monkeys given a choice between food and cocaine will prefer cocaine (Aigner & Balster, 1978). However, Carroll, Lac, and Nygard (1989) found that if the alternative to cocaine is sugar solutions or even saccharin, the acquisition and maintenance of cocaine SA was disrupted.

One other approach to assessing cocaine's reinforcing efficacy is to measure its resistance to punishment (e.g., shock). This procedure has been studied extensively on many behaviors controlled by reinforcement (Azrin & Holz, 1966). Generally, the intensity of punishment is related to the degree of behavioral suppression for the reinforcer. Other factors such as the schedule of reinforcement and the time between response and punishment also affect the outcome. However, it is assumed that the greater the resistance to decreases in self-administration that is followed by punishment, the greater the strength of the reinforcement. Using a punishment procedure, Grove and Schuster (1974) found that responding to cocaine decreased as a function of shock intensity.

The various approaches to assessing cocaine's reinforcing effects described above, were useful for demonstrating that these models can be used to understand behavioral similarity, the first category of animal models presented earlier. However, it becomes even more important to understand the limitations and possible confounds from these procedures when we use them to assess mechanisms and test pharmacological interventions. This is because the additional manipulations required in these types of studies can also distort the response measures and lead to erroneous conclusions.

Self-Stimulation

The discovery of intracranial self-stimulation (ICSS) by Olds and Milner (1954) had a profound effect on behavioral neuroscience in general and on the development of animal models of drug addiction. In this paradigm, animals work to receive electrical stimulation in certain areas of the brain, chiefly along the medial forebrain bundle (MFB). The type of work rats perform to receive the opportunity to get this stimulation includes running uphill, jumping over hurdles at the end of an alley, and bar pressing (Edmonds & Gallistel, 1974). These behaviors were characterized by rapid learning and rapid extinction as well as an intense execution that often overrode other motivated behaviors such as feeding. Because this stimulation controlled these behaviors by increasing their output, the neural areas that support the ICSS were considered "reward" areas. As suggested by the similarity in language used to describe self-administration techniques, ICSS is also an operant paradigm. As such, many of the issues of techniques and interpretation of results that were addressed in the last section are also applicable to ICSS behavior.

Olds (1969) initially interpreted the behavioral and neuroanatomical data as suggesting that there was a common neural substrate for all motivated behaviors, but latter studies refuted this (Valenstein, 1964). In spite of the evidence against a common basis for "reward" in general, the common notion among animal models of drug addiction is that there is a common mechanism among all drugs of abuse. Advances in both pharmacological and psychological fields of study have drawn the focus to the dopamine system as the basis of reward (Wise, 1989).

Most ICSS studies are conducted because of the interest in understanding the behavior and its neural substrates in their own right. However, ICSS has been used as an animal model to understand the processes underlying drug addiction. Kornetsky and colleagues (Kornetsky, Esposito, McLean, & Jacobson, 1979; Kornetsky & Esposito, 1979) argue that alterations in ICSS by putative drugs of abuse will have implications for the abuse liability of these drugs. Specifically, if a drug lowers the threshold for ICSS, then it has a high potential for abuse because the drug works through the same mechanism as the ICSS. Indeed, cocaine was shown to produce decreases in the current threshold for ICSS (Esposito, Motola, & Kornetsky, 1978; Kornetsky & Esposito, 1981; Wauquier & Niemegeers, 1974). Similar results have been demonstrated for opiates (Marcus & Kornetsky, 1974; Kornetsky et al., 1979; Kornetsky & Esposito, 1979), drugs that are also abused by humans and self-administered by animals. However, the specificity of this effect for abused drugs is called into question by the finding that tricyclic antidepressants, which are not associated with abuse or positive reinforcement, also lower ICSS thresholds (McCarter & Kokkinidis, 1988). Yet another interpretation of this effect of antidepressants on ICSS is that if ICSS works through similar neural mechanisms as cocaine-use behavior, then this finding is consistent with the clinical results that show some efficacy for desipramine in the treatment of cocaine abuse (Gawin et al., 1989).

Conditioned Place Preference

Another behavioral paradigm that has been used to assess the reinforcing aspects of drugs is the conditioned place preference (CPP) procedure. This procedure is an example of a classically conditioned behavior because the animal does not execute a response in order to receive the reinforcing agent (e.g., the drug). Rather, originally neutral cues are paired with the drug effects that are administered by the experimenter. Specifically, the animal is exposed to a chamber that has at least two distinctive sides. Training is done by placing the animal in one side (conditioned stimulus) and then injecting the drug. The animal is exposed to the other side on the same or alternate days and given a vehicle injection. As few as two to four sessions are required to produce CPP

(Reid, Marglin, Mattie, & Hubbell, 1989). To test CPP and the presumed reinforcing effects of the drug, the animal is placed in the chamber with access to both sides. The amount of time spent on the reinforced side, or the increase in this time over baseline, is the measure of CPP. Thus CPP has the advantage of testing the reinforcing aspects of drugs when the animal is drug-free. Moreover, because many fewer drug exposures are necessary than in self-administration procedures, tolerance, sensitization, and toxicity play a lesser role in the CPP behavior.

The CPP procedure was first investigated by Beach (1957) who showed that rats will prefer the compartment that has been associated with morphine treatment. This investigation was prompted by the observation of Olds & Milner (1954) that rats that bar-pressed for ICSS would tend to remain in the area of the lever associated with the ICSS treatment.

An extensive literature exists for the CPP procedure that shows its usefulness as an animal model of substance abuse. Most of the early studies of CPP focused on morphine and other opioids that were found to produce CPP (Mucha, van der Kooy, O'Shaugnessy, & Bucenieks, 1982). More recently, cocaine has been studied using this technique, and it too produces CPP (Mackey & van der Kooy, 1985; Spyraki, Fibiger, & Phillips, 1982; Morency & Beninger, 1986). There is evidence that the CPP effect is related to classical conditioning because extinction occurs when the animal is exposed to the conditioning environment in the absence of the drug administration (Bardo, Niesewander, & Miller, 1986). The importance of other procedural variables has been demonstrated for cocaine CPP by Nomikos and Spyraki (1988). In particular, these investigators showed that the conditioning of the behavior to cocaine injections that are given intraperitoneally may be due to local anesthetic effects, not to reinforcing effects.

The CPP procedure has been questioned as to its validity as an animal model of drug addiction. One question is that CPP lacks the excellent face validity of the SA model, which better represents the addict's behavior of taking the abused drug to receive its reinforcing effects. However, both classical conditioning in general (Siegel, 1979; Wikler, 1973) and environmental cues in particular (Marlatt & Gordon, 1985) are strongly related to drug abuse and relapse. Another question about the CPP procedure is that its measure, time spent in the reinforced chamber, may be distorted and not reflect reinforcement. Other factors may influence this measure, including (1) fear or preference for novel stimuli (if a habituation session is not used) (2) habituation (if this session is used) or (3) a possible conditioned motor effect. Alternative measures are the number of entries into the conditioned chamber or the mean duration of the stays in this environment. The CPP procedure has also been criticized because it often uses intraperitoneal injections instead of the route used by human drug addicts (e.g., inhalation, intravenous). The results of the Nomikos & Spyraki (1988) study described above underscore this problem. CPP could therefore be improved by injecting the drugs through in-dwelling intravenous catheters to better reflect the pharmacokinetics of human drug abuse. Despite these issues, the best advantage of the CPP procedure is that it tests the behavior when the animal is drug-free, thus eliminating many of the interpretation difficulties and methodological complexities associated with the SA procedure.

Other Paradigms

A number of other paradigms can be used to assess the behavioral effects of cocaine, although the three paradigms discussed above are the most common and were all designed to assess the reinforcing effects of cocaine. However, other paradigms can be used to assess aspects of cocaine use that are not associated with positive reinforcement, as discussed below.

The conditioned taste aversion (CTA) paradigm, which was described under classical conditioning, has been used with cocaine. This behavior, first described by Garcia, Kimeldorf, and Koelling (1955), shows that after a novel and preferred taste solution is paired with aversive consequences, originally believed to be gastrointestinal malaise, the taste solution will subsequently be avoided. Many psychoactive substances that are abused by humans can induce CTA (Cappell & LeBlanc, 1978), including cocaine (Foltin & Schuster, 1982; Foltin, Preston, Wagner, & Schuster, 1981; Goudie, Dickins, & Thornton, 1978). Thus the assumption that gastrointestinal malaise is the common factor underlying the CTA has been questioned. In fact, it has been difficult to reconcile the findings that drugs normally associated with positive reinforcement can also be associated with negative consequences. However, Wise, Yokel, and DeWit (1976) showed that amphetamine can be associated with both positive reinforcement, as assessed by SA, and aversion, as assessed by CTA, in the same animal. These findings suggest that other psychoactive drugs of abuse can have both reinforcing and aversive properties at the same time.

Because many drugs and other manipulations can induce a conditioned taste aversion, this suggests that there is more than one mechanism underlying the effect. However, it is difficult to differentiate these aversive effects in the CTA paradigm because the actual responses (conditioned and unconditioned) are rarely assessed. Those studies that did measure these responses found that the CTA behavior was associated with conditioned hypothermia (Zahorik, 1973) and with a conditioned decrease in heart rate (Kosten & Contreras, 1989). The work of Parker and Cawell (1984) has suggested that when the measure of solution rejection is based on the facial expression methods of Grill and Norgren (1978), that drugs of abuse show a different pattern of facial expression compared with the more standard drugs used in CTA experiments, such as lithium chloride. Thus using physiological measures in addition to behavioral ones is an important step toward helping our understanding of the aversive aspects of cocaine use.

Another procedure that can be used to assess the positive reinforcement aspects of cocaine use, and which is based on operant conditioning, is the operant place conditioning paradigm (Crowder & Hutto, in press). In this procedure, an animal is placed in a T maze and trained to run to one side in order to receive the drug reinforcement. Numerous studies have employed a T maze to measure conditioning when food or water were used as reinforcers (Miller & Kessen, 1952; Miller, Dicara, & Wolf, 1968). To test conditioning, and by definition, the power of the reinforcer, latency to get to the conditioned side or the number of trials to learn the task can be used. This technique has the following advantages. First, the behavior probably reflects both the operant conditioning of an approach response to get the reinforcement and the classical conditioning of associating a specific environment with the reinforcement. Second, it has the ability to space the drug injections over time so as to lessen the possibility of distorted measures owing to motor effects. Third, the experimenter has more control over studying chronic or acute drug effects, depending on the training schedule chosen. Fourth, it is unlikely that there are conditioned motor effects on the performance. Finally, the behavior is tested when the animal is drug-free, which is similar to the CPP procedure, but unlike the SA procedure.

Linking Animal Work to Understanding Human Cocaine Addiction

The animal model procedures discussed in this chapter, although disparate in their origins, have shown a good deal of convergence in their findings. As described earlier, the SA, ICSS, and CPP procedures have all shown that cocaine is a potent reinforcer. The behavioral similarities between these models also extend to the human population, wherein cocaine has been found to be extremely addicting. Although more research is necessary to further test the validity of these models and to refine the type of measures used to assess reinforcement, it is clear that they provide a useful tool for studying the etiology, mechanisms, and pharmacological manipulations of cocaine reinforcement.

The results obtained from animal studies have in many ways influenced clinical applications for treating substance abuse. The role of conditioning factors in maintaining cocaine use behavior has been incorporated into the relapse prevention psychotherapies pioneered by Marlatt (Marlatt & Gordon, 1985). Another aspect of conditioning that has been used therapeutically is to give repeated exposures to the conditioned cues of drug use without subsequent drug effects, in order to extinguish drug use behavior. Although this showed some efficacy for opiate use (O'Brien, Greenstein, Ternes, McLellan, & Grabowski, 1980; Meyer & Mirin, 1982), its usefulness for treating cocaine has been less effective (Childress, McLellan, Ehrman, & O'Brien, 1988; Rohsenow, Niaura, Childress, Abrams, & Monti, 1990). However, this cue reactivity technique combined with psychophysiological measures may provide useful information on the role of drug craving in treatment efficacy. For more detail on these techniques, see Chapter 6, this volume.

Another application of animal models of cocaine abuse to the human situation is to examine etiological factors in drug abuse. Although the etiology of cocaine abuse is multifactorial and includes social, personality, environmental, and biological factors, few of these factors can be assessed in animals. Indeed, animal models tend to be limited to assessing the biological factors involved in the etiology of this disorder. However, the results from this application of animal models has shown that genetic factors are important in determining susceptibility to cocaine or other drug addiction.

For example, the Lewis strain of rats shows a greater tendency to self-administer cocaine compared with the typical strain of rats used in these experiments, the Sprague-Dawley rats. Another strain of rats, the Fisher rats, shows a lesser tendency for cocaine SA (Clouet, Asghar, & Brown, 1988). We have also shown that the Lewis and Fisher rats differ in the ability to condition a place preference to cocaine (Terwilliger et al., 1991) with the Lewis rats showing a much greater CPP. Even within the Sprague-Dawley strain, typically used these experiments, we and others (L. D. Reid, personal communication, February 1991) have noticed striking individual differences in rats' ability to develop cocaine CPP. Further investigation of the biochemical bases of this presumed genetic susceptibility is being pursued (see Chapter 4, this volume).

The information gained from these genetic or physiological vulnerability studies in animals will be useful adjuncts to the genetic studies of human drug abuse. A number of human studies have provided evidence that alcohol abuse shows familial transmission (see Goodwin, 1989, for review). The few family studies of substance abuse that have been done also suggest that the tendency to abuse drugs has familial patterns (Rounsaville et al., 1991; Kosten, Rounsaville, Kosten, &

Merikangas, 1991; Mirin, Weiss, Sollogub, & Michael, 1984). Because these twin, adoption, and other family studies are costly and difficult to perform, animal models provide a more efficient way to gather preliminary information on the neurochemical correlates of the tendency to abuse drugs.

The third role of animal models in psychiatric research is to test mechanisms underlying cocaine abuse. This is one of the dominant areas of research in this field. Numerous studies have investigated the neural mechanisms involved in "reward" in general and in cocaine use behavior in particular. These studies have demonstrated that specific areas of the brain, notably the ventral tegmental area (VTA) and the nucleus accumbens (NAc) are important for cocaine use behavior. Lesions of the VTA and NAc block systemic self-administration of cocaine, and local administration of cocaine into the NAc has been reported to lead to place preference (Aulisi & Hoebel, 1983; Petit, Ettenberg, Bloom, & Koob, 1984; Zito, Vickers, & Roberts, 1985).

Cocaine is thought to act indirectly on these neural systems by increasing synaptic neurotransmitter levels. This increase is due to inhibition of the reuptake carriers for dopamine, serotonin, and norepinephrine, an important mechanism for the functional inactivation of these neurotransmitter signals (Cooper, Bloom, & Roth, 1986). A dominant theory of the pharmacological basis of cocaine's positive reinforcing effects is that it occurs through dopaminergic pathways (Wise & Rompre, 1989). Presumably, cocaine exerts reinforcing actions by inhibiting dopamine reuptake in the VTA which would lead to enhanced stimulation of D1 and D2 dopamine receptors located on the cell bodies or nerve terminals in the NAc or other areas to which the VTA projects. In addition to these dopaminergic mechanisms, the serotonin and opioid systems have been implicated in cocaine's reinforcing actions. For more detail on these neural mechanisms, see the Chapter 4, this volume.

The information gained from these mechanistic studies using animal models of cocaine use behavior has suggested many potential pharmacological treatment agents for human cocaine addicts. One approach to developing pharmacological agents for cocaine abuse is that an agent that "blocks" the positive reinforcing effect of cocaine has potential treatment efficacy (Kosten & Kosten, 1991). These animal studies suggested that dopaminergic antagonists should block cocaine's reinforcing properties. However, a number of dopamine receptor antagonists have been found to *not* block cocaine CPP, including pimozide, haloperidol, and α-flupenthixol (Mackey & van der Kooy, 1985; Spyraki et al., 1982). The studies using SA have similarly not, in general, given support for the attenuation of the reinforcing effects of cocaine by dopaminergic antagonists (Katz, 1989). Whether these results with cocaine reflect limitations in the behavioral techniques, in the neurobiological hypotheses, or in the specific dopamine antagonists tested thus far is not clear.

A number of pharmacological agents have been assessed for treating cocaine addicts, including dopamine antagonists (see Chapter 20, this volume). Interestingly, buprenorphine, which is not a dopamine antagonist, showed some efficacy in reducing cocaine use in a nonrandomized study (Kosten, Morgan, & Kleber, 1989). Buprenorphine, a mixed opiate agonist–antagonist, has subsequently been shown to reduce cocaine SA in rhesus monkeys (Mello, Mendelson, Bree, & Lucas, 1989) and to attenuate cocaine CPP in rats (Kosten, Marby & Nestler, 1991). Thus there is some convergence of evidence for at least one pharmacological treatment agent across human clinical studies and two different animal models of cocaine behavior.

To test potential pharmacological treatment agents in human studies requires randomized, placebo-controlled, and double-blind procedures with many subjects. In addition, the high dropout rates of these studies increase the number of subjects needed to make reasonable conclusions. Thus the most efficient way to investigate the potential efficacy of the myriad of possible pharmacological agents is to test them in animal models. Animal models permit the rapid screening of many potential medications and provide an experimental framework within which to investigate the neurobiological basis of cocaine addiction.

Acknowledgment

Support was provided by the National Institute on Drug Abuse Center Grant.

REFERENCES

Aigner, T. G., & Balster, R. L. (1978). Choice behavior in rhesus monkeys: Cocaine versus food. *Science, 210,* 534–535.

American Psychiatric Association (1987). *Diagnostic and statistical manual of mental disorders* (3rd ed., rev.). Washington DC: Author.

Aulisi, E. F., & Hoebel, B. G. (1983). Rewarding effects of amphetamine and cocaine in the nucleus accumbens and block by alpha-flupenthixol. *Society for Neurosciences Abstracts, 9,* 121.

Azrin, N. H., & Holz, W. C. (1966). Punishment. In W. K Honig (Ed.), *Operant behavior: Areas of research and application* (pp. 380–447). New York: Appleton-Century-Crofts.

Balster, R. L., Kilbey, M. M., & Ellinwood, E. H., Jr. (1976). Methamphetamine self-administration in the cat. *Psychopharmacologia, 46,* 229–233.

Balster R. L., & Schuster, C. R. (1973). Fixed-interval schedule of cocaine reinforcement: Effect of dose and infusion duration. *Journal of Experimental Analysis of Behavior, 20*, 119–129.

Bardo, M. T., Neisewander, J. L., & Miller, J. S. (1986). Repeated testing attenuates conditioned place preference with cocaine. *Psychopharmacology, 89*, 239–243.

Baum, W. M., & Rachlin, H. C. (1969). Choice as time allocation. *Journal of the Experimental Analysis of Behavior, 12*, 861–874.

Beach, H. D. (1957). Morphine addiction in rats. *Canadian Journal of Psychology, 11*, 104–112.

Cappell, H. D., & LeBlanc, A. E. (1978). Gustatory avoidance conditioning by drugs of abuse: Relationships to general issues in research on drug dependence. In N. W. Milgram, K. Krane, & T. M. Alloway (Eds.), *Food aversion learning* (pp. 133–167). New York: Plenum Press.

Carroll, M. E., Lac, S. T., & Nygarrd, S. T. (1989). A concurrently available nondrug reinforcer prevents the acquisition or decreases the maintenance of cocaine-reinforced behavior. *Psychopharmacology, 97*, 23–29.

Childress, A. R., McLellan, A. T., Ehrman, R., & O'Brien, C. P. (1988). Classical conditioned responses in opioid and cocaine dependence: A role in relapse? In B. A. Ray (Ed.), *Learning factors in substance abuse* (National Institute on Drug Abuse Research Monograph No. 84, pp. 25–43). Washington, DC: U. S. Government Printing Office.

Clouet, D., Asghar, K., & Brown, R. (Eds.). (1988). *Mechanisms of cocaine abuse and toxicity* (National Institute on Drug Abuse Research Monograph No. 88). Washington, DC: U. S. Government Printing Office.

Cooper, J. R., Bloom, F. E., & Roth, R. H. (1986). *Biochemical basis of neuropharmacology* (5th ed.). New York: Oxford University Press.

Crowder, W. F., & Hutto, C. W. (in press). Operant place conditioning measures examined using morphine reinforcement. *Pharmacology, Biochemistry and Behavior*.

Downs, D. A., & Woods, J. H. (1974). Codeine-and cocaine-reinforced responding in rhesus monkeys: Effects of dose on response rates under a fixed-ratio schedule. *Journal of Pharmacology and Experimental Therapeutics, 191*, 179–188.

Edmonds, D. E., & Gallistel, C. R. (1974). Parametric analysis of brain stimulation reward in the rat: 3. Effect of performance variables on the reward summation function. *Journal of Comparative and Physiological Psychology, 87*, 876–884.

Edwards, G., Arif, A., & Hodgson, R. (1981). Nomenclature and classification of drug-and alcohol-related problems: A WHO memorandum. *Bulletin of the World Health Organization, 59*, 225–242.

Eikelboom, R., & Stewart, J. (1982). Conditioning of drug-induced physiological responses. *Psychological Review, 89*, 507–528.

Esposito, R. U., Motola, A. H. D, & Kornetsky, C. (1978). Cocaine: Acute effects on reinforcement thresholds for self-stimulation behavior to the medial forebrain bundle. *Pharmacology, Biochemistry and Behavior, 8*, 437–439.

Everitt, B. J., Robbins, T. W., Evenden, J. L., & Marston, H. M. (1987). The effects of excitotoxic lesions of the substantia innominata, ventral and dorsal globus pallidus on the acquisition and retention of a conditional visual discrimination: Implications for cholinergic hypotheses of learning and memory. *Neurosciene, 22*, 441–469.

Ferster, C. B., & Skinner, B. F. (1957). *Schedules of reinforcement.* New York: Appleton-Century-Crofts.

Fischman, M. W. (1984). The behavioral pharmacology of cocaine in humans. In J. Grabowski (Ed.), *Cocaine: Pharmacology, effects, and treatment of abuse* (National Institute on Drug Abuse Research Monograph No. 50, pp. 72–91). Washington, DC: U. S. Government Printing Office.

Foltin, R. W., Fischman, M. W., Pedroso, J. J., & Pearlson, G. D. (1988). Repeated intranasal cocaine administration: Lack of tolerance to pressor effects. *Drug and Alcohol Dependence, 15*, 71–74.

Foltin, R. W., Preston, K. L., Wagner, G. C., & Schuster, C. R. (1981). The aversive stimulus properties of repeated infusions of cocaine. *Pharmacology, Biochemistry and Behavior, 15*, 71–74.

Foltin, R. W., & Schuster, C. R. (1982). The effects of cocaine in a gustatory avoidance paradigm: A procedural analysis. *Pharmacology, Biochemistry and Behavior, 16*, 347–352.

Gallup, G. G., & Suarez, S. D. (1985). Alternatives to the use of animals in psychological research. *American Psychologist, 40*, 1104–1111.

Garcia, J., Kimeldorf, D. J., & Koelling, R. A. (1955). A conditioned aversion towards saccharin resulting from exposure to gamma radiation. *Science, 122*, 157–159.

Gawin, F. H., & Kleber, H. D. (1986). Abstinence symptomatology and psychiatric diagnosis in cocaine abusers. *Archives of General Psychiatry, 43*, 107–113.

Gawin, F. H., Kleber, H. D., Byck, R., Rounsaville, B. J., Kosten, T. R., Jatlow, P. I., & Morgan, C. (1989). Desipramine facilitation of initial cocaine abstinence. *Archives of General Psychiatry, 46*, 117–121.

Goldberg, S. R. (1973). Comparable behavior maintained under fixed-ratio and second-order schedules of food presentation, cocaine injection, or d-amphetamine injection in the squirrel monkey. *Journal of Pharmacology and Experimental Therapeutics, 186*, 18–30.

Goldberg, S. R., Woods, J. H., & Schuster, C. R. (1971). Nalorphine-induced changes in morphine self-administration in rhesus monkeys. *Journal of Pharmacology and Experimental Therapeutics, 176*, 464–471.

Goldberg, S. R., Morse, W. H., & Goldberg, D. M. (1976). Behavior maintained under a second-order schedule by intramuscular injection of morphine or cocaine in rhesus monkeys. *Journal of Pharmacology and Experimental Therapeutics, 199*, 278–286.

Goodwin, D. W. (1988). *Is alcoholism hereditary?.* New York: Ballantine Books.

Goudie, A. J., Dickins, D. W., & Thornton, E. W. (1978). Cocaine-induced conditioned taste aversions in rats. *Pharmacology, Biochemistry and Behavior,* 8, 757–761.

Griffiths, R. R., Brady, J. V., & Snell, J. D. (1978). Progressive ratio performance maintained by drug infusions: Comparison of cocaine, diethylproprion, chlorphentermine and fenfluramine. *Psychopharmacology,* 56, 5.

Griffiths, R. R., Findley, J. D., Brady, J. V., Dolan-Gutcher, K., & Robinson, W. W. (1975). Comparison of progressive-ratio performance maintained by cocaine, methylphenidate, and secobarbital. *Psychopharmacologia, 43,* 81–83.

Grill, H. J., & Norgren, R. (1978). The taste reactivity test: 1. Mimetic responses to gustatory stimuli in neurologically normal rats. *Brain Research, 143,* 263–279.

Grove, R. N., & Schuster, C. R. (1974). Suppression of cocaine self-administration by extinction and punishment. *Pharmacology, Biochemistry and Behavior, 2,* 199–208.

Hebb, D. O. (1955). Drives and the CNS (conceptual nervous system). *Psychological Review, 62,* 243–254.

Henn, F. A., & McKinney, W. T. (1987) Animal models in psychiatry. In H. Y. Meltzer (Ed.), *Psychopharmacology: The third generation of progress* (pp. 687–696). New York: Raven Press.

Herling, S., Downs, D. A., & Woods, J. H. (1979). Cocaine, d-amphetamine, and pentobarbital effects on responding maintained by food or cocaine in rhesus monkeys. *Psychopharmacology, 64,* 261–269.

Hull, C. L. (1943). *Principles of behavior.* New York: Appleton-Century-Crofts.

Jaffe, J. H. (1985). Drug addiction and drug abuse. In L. S. Goodman & A. Gilman (Eds.), *The pharmacological basis of therapeutics* (5th ed., pp. 532–584). New York: Macmillan.

Johanson C. E., & Fischman, M. W. (1989). The pharmacology of cocaine related to its abuse. *Pharmacological Reviews, 41,* 3–52.

Johanson, C. E., & Schuster, C. R. (1975). A choice procedure for drug reinforcers: Cocaine and methylphenidate in the rhesus monkey. *Journal of Pharmacology and Experimental Therapeutics, 193,* 676–688.

Katz, J. L. (1989). Drugs as reinforcers: Pharmacological and behavioural factors. In J. L. Liebman & S. J. Cooper (Eds.), *The neuropharmacological basis of reward* (pp. 164–213). Oxford: Clarendon Press.

Kelleher, R. T., & Goldberg, S. R. (1977). Fixed-interval responding under second-order schedules of food presentation or cocaine injection. *Journal of the Experimental Analysis of Behavior, 28,* 221–231.

Kornetsky, C., & Esposito, R. U. (1979). Euphorigenic drugs: Effects on the reward pathways of the brain. *Federation Proceedings, 38,* 2473–2476.

Kornetsky, C., & Esposito, R. U. (1981). Reward and detection thresholds for brain stimulation: Dissociative effects of cocaine. *Brain Research, 209,* 496–500.

Kornetsky, C., Esposito, R. U., McLean, S., & Jacobson, O. (1979). Intracranial self-stimulation thresholds: A model for the hedonic effects of drugs of abuse. *Archives of General Psychiatry, 36,* 289–292.

Kosten T. A., & Contreras, R. J. (1989). Deficits in conditioned heart rate and taste aversion in area postrema-lesioned rats. *Behavioral Brain Research, 35,* 9–21.

Kosten T. A., & Kosten, T. R. (1991). Pharmacological blocking agents for treating substance abuse. *Journal of Nervous and Mental Disease, 179,* 583–592.

Kosten, T. A., Marby, D. W., & Nestler, E. J. (1991). Cocaine conditioned place preference is attenuated by chronic buprenorphine treatment. *Life Sciences, 49,* P201–P206.

Kosten, T. R., Morgan, C., & Kleber, H. D. (1989). Role of opioid antagonists in treating intravenous cocaine abuse. *Life Sciences, 44,* 887–891.

Kosten, T. R., Rounsaville, B. J., Kosten, T. A., & Merikangas, K. (1991). Gender differences in the specificity of alcoholism transmission among the relatives of opioid addicts. *Journal of Nervous and Mental Disease, 179,* 392–400.

Lewander, T. (1974). Effect of chronic treatment with central stimulants on brain monoamines and some behavioral and physiological functions in rats, guinea pigs, and rabbits. *Advances in Biochemistry and Psychopharmacology, 12,* 221–239.

Mackey, W. B., & van der Kooy, D. (1985). Neuroleptics block the positive reinforcing effects of amphetamine but not of morphine as measured by place conditioning. *Pharmacology, Biochemistry and Behavior, 22,* 101–105.

Mackintosh, N. J. (1974). *The psychology of animal learning.* New York: Academic Press.

Marcus, R., & Kornetsky, C. (1974). Negative and positive intracranial reinforcement thresholds: Effects of morphine. *Psychopharmacologia, 38,* 1.

Marlatt, G. A., & Gordon, J. R. (1985). *Relapse prevention.* New York: Guilford.

McCarter, B. D., & Kokkinidis, L. (1988). The effects of long-term administration of antidepressant drugs on intracranial self-stimulation responding in rats. *Pharmacology, Biochemistry and Behavior, 31,* 243–247.

Mello, N. K., Lucas, S. E, Bree, M. P., & Mendelson, J. H. (1988). Progressive ratio performance maintained by buprenorphine, heroin and morphine in macque monkeys. *Drug and Alcohol Dependence, 21,* 81–97.

Mello, N. K., Mendelson, J. H., Bree, M. P., & Lucas, S. E. (1989). Buprenorphine suppresses cocaine self-administration by rhesus monkeys. *Science, 245,* 859–862.

Meyer, R. E., & Mirin, S. M. (1982). *The heroin stimulus: Implications for a theory of addiciton.* New York: Plenum Press.

Miller, N. E. (1967). Behavioral and physiological techniques: Rational and experimental designs for combining their use. In Werner, H. (Ed.), *The handbook of physiology, Volume 6. The alimentary canal.* Washington, DC: American Physiological Society.

Miller, N. E. (1985). The value of behavioral research on animals. *American Psychologist, 40,* 423–440.

Miller, N. E., DiCara, L. V., & Wolf, G. (1968). Homeostasis and reward: T-maze learning induced by manipulating antidiuretic hormone, *American Journal of Physiology, 215*, 684–686.

Miller, N. E., & Kessen, M. L. (1952). Reward effects of food via stomach fistual compared with those of food via mouth. *Journal of Comparative and Physiological Psychology, 45*, 555–564.

Mirin, S. M., Weiss, R. D., Sollogub, A., & Michael, J. (1984). Psychopathology in families of drug abusers. In S. M. Mirin (Ed)., *Substance abuse and psychopathology* (pp. 79–106). Washington DC: American Psychiatric Press.

Morency, M. A., & Beninger, R. J. (1986). Dopaminergic substrates of cocaine-induced place conditioning. *Brain Research, 399*, 33–41.

Mucha, R. F., van der Kooy, D., O'Shaughnessy, M., & Bucenieks, P. (1982). Drug reinforcement studied by the use of place conditioning in rat. *Brain Research, 243*, 91–105.

Nomikos, G., & Spyraki, C. (1988). Cocaine-induced place conditioning: Importance of route of administration and other procedural variables. *Psychopharmacology, 94*, 119–125.

O'Brien, C. P., Greenstein, R., Ternes, J., McLellan, A. T., & Grabowski, J. (1980). Unreinforced self-injections: Effects on rituals and outcome in heroin addicts. In L. S. Harris (Ed.), *Problems of drug dependence 1979* (National Institute on Drug Abuse Research Monograph No. 27). Rockville, MD: U. S. Department of Health and Human Services.

O'Connor, S., Kuwada, S., DePalma, N., Stanford, T., & Tasman, A. (1990). Amplitude modulated frequency response during acute cocaine intoxication in rabbits. In *Problems of Drug Dependence Proceedings of the 51st Annual Scientific Meeting* (National Institute on Drug Abuse Reserch Monograph No. 95, pp. 331–332). Rockville MD: U. S. Dept. Health & Human Services.

Olds, J. (1969). The central nervous system and reinforcement of behavior. *American Psychologist, 24*, 114–132.

Olds, J., & Milner, P. (1954). Positive reinforcement produced by electrical stimulation of septal area and other regions of the brain. *Journal of Comparative and Physiological Psychology, 47*, 419–425.

Parker, L. A., & Carvell, T. (1984). Orofacial and somatic responses elicited by lithium-, nicotine-, and amphetamine-paired sucrose solutions. *Pharmacology, Biochemistry and Behavior, 24*, 883–887.

Pavlov, I. P. (1927). *Conditioned reflexes* (G. V. Anrep, trans.). London: Oxford University Press.

Petit, H. O., Ettenberg, A., Bloom, F. E., & Koob, G. F. (1984). Destruction of dopamine in the nucleus accumbens selectively attenuates cocaine but not heroin self-administration in rats. *Psychopharmacology, 84*, 167–173.

Pickens, R., & Thompson, T. (1968). Cocaine-reinforced behavior in rats: Effects of reinforcement magnitude and fixed-ratio size. *Journal of Pharmacology and Experimental Therapeutics, 161*, 122–129.

Reid, L. D., Marglin, S. H., Mattie, M. E., & Hubbell, C. L. (1989). Measuring morphine's capacity to establish a place preference. *Pharmacology, Biochemistry and Behavior, 33,* 765–775.

Risner, M. E., & Jones, B. E., (1975). Self-administration of CNS stimulants by dog. *Psychopharmacologia, 43,* 207–213.

Rohsenow, D. J., Niaura, R. S., Childress, A. R., Abrams, D. B., & Monti, P. M. (1990). Cue reactivity in addictive behaviors: Theoretical and treatment implications. *International Journal of the Addictions, 25,* 957–993.

Rounsaville, B. J., Kosten, T. R., Weissman, M. M., Prusoff, B. A., Pauls, D., Anton, S. F., & Merikangas, K. (1991). Psychiatric disorders in the relatives of probands with opioid addiction. *Archives of General Psychiatry, 48,* 33–42.

Scheel-Kruger, J., Braestrup, C., Nielson, M., Golembiowska, K., & Mogilnicka, E. (1977). Cocaine: Discussion on the role of dopamine in the biochemical mechanisms of action. In E. H. Ellinwood & M. M. Kilbey (Eds.), *Cocaine and other stimulants* (pp. 373–408). New York: Plenum.

Siegel, R. K., Johnson, C. A., Brewster, J. M., & Jarvik, M. E. (1976). Cocaine self-administration in monkeys by chewing and smoking. *Pharmacology, Biochemistry and Behavior, 4,* 461–467.

Siegel, S. (1979). The role of conditioning in drug tolerance and addiction. In J. D. Keehn (Ed.), *Psychopathology in animals: Research and clinical applications* (pp. 143–168). New York: Academic Press.

Skinner, B. F. (1938). *The behavior of organisms.* New York: Appleton-Century-Crofts.

Snoddy, A. M., & Tessel, R. E. (1985). Prazosin: Effect on psychomotor-stimulant cues and locomotor activity in mice. *European Journal of Pharmacology, 116,* 221–228.

Solomon, R. L., & Corbit, J. D. (1974). An opponent-process theory of motivation: 1. Temporal dynamics of affect. *Psychological Review, 81,* 119–145.

Spyraki, C., Fibiger, H. C., & Phillips, A. G. (1982). Cocaine-induced place preference conditioning: Lack of effects of neuroleptics and 6-hydroxydopamine lesions. *Brain Research, 253,* 195–203.

Stein, L. (1983). The chemistry of positive reinforcement. In M. Zuckerman (Ed.), *Biological bases of sensation seeking, impulsivity and anxiety* (pp. 151–180). New York: Plenum.

Terwilliger, R. Z., Bradberry, C., Guitart, X, Beitner-Johnson, D., Marby, D., Kosten, T. A., Roth, R. H., & Nestler, E. J. (1991). Lewis and Fischer 344 rats and drug addiction: Behavioral and biochemical correlates. *Society for Neurosciences Abstract, 17,* 823.

Tyler, T. D., & Tessel, R. E. (1979). Amphetamine's locomotor-stimulant and norepinephrine-releasing effects: Evidence for selective antagonism by nisoxetine. *Psychopharmacology, 64,* 291.

Valenstein, E. S. (1964). Problems of measurement and interpretation with reinforcing brain stimulation. *Psychological Review, 71,* 415–437.

Van Dyke, C., Jatlow, P., Ungerer, J., Barash, P. G., & Byck, R. (1978). Oral cocaine: Plasma concentrations and central effects. *Science, 200,* 211–213.

Wauquier, A., & Niemegeers, C. J. E. (1974). Intracranial self-stimulation in rats as a function of various stimuli parameters: 5. Influence of cocaine on medial forebrain bundle stimulation with monopolar electrodes. *Psychopharmacologia, 38,* 201–210.

Wikler, A. (1973). Dynamics of drug dependence. *Archives of General Psychiatry, 28,* 611–616.

Winger, G. D., & Woods, J. H. (1985). Comparison of fixed-ratio and progressive ratio schedules of maintenance of stimulant drug-reinforced responding. *Drug and Alcohol Dependence, 15,* 123–130.

Wise, R. A., & Rompre, P. P. (1989). Brain dopamine and reward. In M. R. Rosenzweig & L. W. Porter (Eds.), *Annual review of psychology* (pp. 191–226). Palo Alto, CA: Annual Reviews.

Wise, R. A., Yokel, R. A., & DeWit, H. (1976). Both positive reinforcement and conditioned aversion from amphetamine and from apomorphine in rats. *Science, 191,* 1273–1275.

Woods, J. H., & Schuster, C. R. (1968). Reinforcement properties of morphine, cocaine, and SPA as a function of unit dose. *International Journal of the Addictions, 3,* 231–237.

Woolverton, W. L., & Schuster, C. R. (1983). Intragastric self-administration in rhesus monkeys under limited access conditions: Methodological studies. *Journal of Pharmacological Methods, 10,* 93–106.

Yanagita, T. (1973). An experimental framework for evaluation of dependence liability in various types of drugs in monkeys. *Bulletin on Narcotics, 25,* 57–64.

Young, P. T. (1959). The role of affective processes in learning and motivation. *Psychological Review, 66,* 104–125.

Zahorik, D. M. (1973). Conditioned physiological changes associated with learned aversions to tastes paired with thiamine deficiency in the rat. *Journal of Comparative and Physiological Psychology, 79,* 189–200.

Zito, K. A., Vickers, G., & Roberts, D. C. (1985). Disruption of cocaine and heroin self-administration following kainic acid lesions of the nucleus accumbens. *Pharmacology, Biochemistry and Behavior, 23,* 1029–1036.

Cue-Reactivity and Cocaine Addiction

Arthur Margolin, PhD

S. Kelly Avants, PhD

A HANDFUL of inpatients, chronic opiate addicts, sit in a circle, participating in a group therapy session. They are reminiscing about making a score—buying dope, going to their customary shooting-up place, mixing and injecting the drug. Some members of the group say they feel uncomfortable; they begin to exhibit symptoms of mild opiate withdrawal—tearing, nausea, yawning. Seeing what's happening, other members of the group quickly change the subject.

Although the patients in this vignette are opiate addicts, this is nevertheless a relevant place to begin a discussion of cue reactivity in cocaine addiction. Models of relapse to opiate use have had a significant influence upon the conceptualization of cocaine addiction in general and on cocaine cue-reactivity in particular. This influence stems, in part, from an intersection of the principles of conditioning with clinical research into opiate addiction. At the locus of this intersection, with respect to drug addiction research, resides Abraham Wikler, a physician and researcher at the Addiction Research Center at Lexington, Kentucky. Wikler, over a number of years, gave a detailed, influential explanation concerning the physiological responses experienced by the group therapy members described in the example above (Wikler, 1948, 1973, 1980).

Wikler's account begins with the proposition that the group's discussion of previous opiate use served to evoke memories not only of the direct effects of opiates, but also of experiences of opiate withdrawal. Such talk, then, constituted a complex conditioned stimulus, eliciting conditioned withdrawal responses in some of these chronic opiate users.

Based on this proposition, Wikler (1973) propounded a comprehensive model of relapse to drug use. The detoxified opiate addict, returning to his former drug-using environment after treatment, is bombarded with stimuli that elicit conditioned withdrawal responses. The chronic drug user knows well the anodyne to this aversive state: drug use. Thus he relapses.

Given its simplicity and comprehensiveness, the influence of this model upon drug addiction research is not surprising, extending beyond opiates to other substances including cocaine and alcohol. Consider the following example.

Mark has been in treatment for cocaine addiction for 6 weeks and, although a long-term cocaine user, has been abstinent for 3 weeks. This is the longest period of time he has not used cocaine in several years. Twice a week he has been attending "relapse prevention" group therapy sessions, and, judging from his active participation in the group, seems committed to maintaining abstinence. In the first session of the fourth week he reports to the group that on his way home from work on a Friday, his payday, he "blanked out" walking home from the bus stop, and woke up Sunday afternoon, exhausted, having spent the weekend getting high. He claims that, walking home, he was not thinking of using and cannot comprehend what happened. The group does not doubt the veracity of his story.

One question we will be discussing later in this chapter is whether cocaine addicts such as Mark, like the opiate inpatients as explained by Wikler, use their drug of choice because they experience conditioned withdrawal, and if not, what psychophysiological responses they might have to environmental stimuli that lead to relapse.

ASSUMPTIONS IN CUE-REACTIVITY STUDIES

The thumbnail sketches above—Mark and the opiate group members— are illustrative of the striking yet hardly uncommon clinical material that theories of addiction must grapple with and ultimately account for. These examples raise the question: What sustains addictive behavior? Studies of cue-reactivity seek to illuminate one aspect of this question— the effect of drug-related cues on sustaining addiction, that is, on relapse. The brevity of these sketches, however, belies the complexity of conducting research in this area. To begin with, researchers must make assumptions that necessarily simplify the naturalistic object domain— the addict's life as it unfolds in real time in real environments. Thus cue-reactivity protocols hypothesize that the continuous flux of the addict's real-world environment contains discrete moments that are crucial to sustaining addictive behavior. What characterizes these discrete moments is that in them objects and events that have been associated with drug use have a critical impact upon the addict such that the near-term course of that individual's behavior is deflected toward drug use.

Stemming in part from Wikler's influence, and in part from the procedural clarity offered by stimulus–response paradigms in laboratory research, cue-reactivity research has been guided primarily by models of learning based upon respondent and operant conditioning (Grabowski & O'Brien, 1981; Drummond, Cooper, & Glautier, 1990). The laboratory procedures that follow from these models include the elicitation of temporally bounded subject reactions to the presentation of temporally bounded cues. Typically, objects associated with a subject's drug and route of administration are presented to the subject as stimuli, and the drug-related behavior—or some laboratory stand-in for it, such as craving, or a discriminative physiological profile—constitutes the response. Thus Wikler's influence has had two important consequences: the application of conditioning models to the investigation of relapse in clinical populations, and, until relatively recently, an emphasis upon withdrawal-based conditioned responses in the relapse process.

That the phenomenon of relapse will be illuminated when studied according to these strictures has more than a *prima facie* plausibility. The cases cited above are apparently clear instances of an addict's exposure to environmental cues precipitating drug use. Just as the group discussion functioned as a conditioned stimulus eliciting drug-related withdrawal states, so we may surmise that Mark's environment, as he walked home from work on Friday afternoon, contained conditioned stimuli that elicited conditioned responses in Mark that led to his actual drug use.

CUE-REACTIVITY IN COCAINE ADDICTION

Laboratory studies have shown that cocaine addicts respond differentially to cocaine-related cues compared with neutral cues. Researchers at the University of Pennsylvania have found that cocaine addicts exhibit a decrease in skin temperature and an increase in skin conductance level when presented with cocaine-associated objects (Childress, McLellan, Ehrman, & O'Brien, 1988). In addition, cocaine addicts have been found to report significant craving for cocaine in the presence of cocaine-related cues (Childress et al., 1988; O'Brien, Childress, McLellan, & Ehrman,

1990; Negrete, Emil, & Abrahamovicz, 1991; Rohsenow, Niaura, Childress, Abrams, & Monti, 1991). These findings have been corroborated by Kranzler and Bauer (1989, 1990) who found that cocaine-related cues (a video of cocaine objects and people smoking cocaine) precipitated an increase in self-reported craving and a decrease in respiratory sinus arrhythmia, a measure of parasympathetic influence upon heart rate. Another team of researchers (Pretorius, Newlin, Wong, & Better, 1991) found a significant negative correlation between baseline heart rate and self-reported craving to cocaine cues in cocaine addicts, suggesting the possibility of a trait-like, rather than a situational, response to cocaine-related stimuli.

The studies cited above collected data from two domains: physiological responses and self-reported craving. The ultimate utility of the craving construct in addiction research is a topic of some debate among researchers in this field (Kozlowski & Wilkinson, 1987). One view is that a subject's self-report on such a complex, subjective state such as craving is likely to be so confounded by demand characteristics, as well as individual differences in self-awareness of internal states, as to be of no utility whatsoever. Another view is that cue-elicited craving taps into what is perhaps the primary internal state related to actual drug use—the addict's desire to use the drug. Given the complexity of the material, and the fact that the utility of craving ratings in predicting actual drug use behavior is still an open question (Bauer, 1991), we find the view espoused by Baker, Morse, and Sherman (1987) to be highly judicious. They suggest that feelings of craving, like feelings of fear—although bearing an intricate and variable relationship to actual behavior—are manifestations of, and hence potentially illuminate, important internal affective and motivational processes contributing to drug use.

CUE-REACTIVITY RESEARCH AT YALE

In 1989 we established a psychophysiology laboratory at Yale's Substance Abuse Treatment Unit. One of our goals was to create a protocol that would reliably elicit craving in cocaine addicts in order to use subjects' reactivity scores as part of pre–post assessments in pharmacotherapy trials. The protocol we developed was based on previous research by the University of Pennsylvania group (Childress et al., 1988). In our protocol the subject is presented sequentially with films and objects related to neutral and cocaine cues. During the presentation of the cues, skin conductance level and skin temperature are concurrently measured. Self-reported craving at multiple time points is also assessed.

The Cues

The subject watches a video of people handling the cues and then is presented with the objects themselves to handle. The cocaine and neutral videos we use in our protocol are each 2 minutes long. The cocaine video contains scenes of people handling cocaine and cocaine-related paraphernalia, and using cocaine. The cocaine-related objects consist of several well-used freebase pipes, a vial containing a cocaine-like powder, a container of baking soda, and a butane torch (in our area, freebasing is the predominant route by which addicts smoke cocaine). The neutral video contains scenes of people handling neutral, non-drug-related, objects. The neutral objects include fossils, rocks, and seashells, objects we thought would be unlikely to have many drug-related associations.

CUE-REACTIVITY PARADIGMS IN PHARMACOTHERAPY TRIALS

We included pre-treatment and post-treatment cue-reactivity measures in a study of the "second-generation" antidepressant bupropion, for the treatment of cocaine addiction (Margolin, Kosten, Petrakis, Avants, & Kosten, 1990; Margolin, Avants, Ziedonis, Petrakis, & Kosten, in press). In this 8-week study, patients were maintained on bupropion 100 mg *t.i.d.* and participated in weekly group or individual psychotherapy. Bupropion is a suitable agent to be used in research designs that assess psychophysiological changes with treatment because it does not seem to have a direct pharmacological affect upon autonomic or cardiovascular systems (Peck & Hamilton, 1983).

The inclusion of the cue-reactivity paradigm in the bupropion pharmacotherapy study permitted us to test the effectiveness of our protocol in eliciting reactivity and to examine the influence of treatment upon reactivity. We found that our cue-reactivity protocol successfully elicited craving and differential physiological response to cocaine-related cues in these cocaine abusing subjects (Margolin et al., 1990). The neutral cues did not elicit significant levels of self-reported craving or physiological reactivity relative to baseline levels.

Given the hypothesized association between relapse and cue-reactivity (both physiological responses and self-reported craving), we hypothesized that subjects who stopped using cocaine in the study and who reported low levels of self-reported craving to drug cues would also exhibit reduced autonomic reactivity to drug cues posttreatment. Conversely, subjects who continued using would exhibit continued reactivity in both objective and subjective domains. To the best of our knowledge, this important hypothesis had not been tested in a pre–post treatment design. We found that although subjects who successfully achieved abstinence in our study reported reduced levels of craving posttreatment in the presence of drug cues, they did not exhibit significantly lower levels of autonomic reactivity. In fact, in some cases reactivity increased. Thus successful abstainers experienced reduced craving while simultaneously exhibiting physiological reactivity to the cues. Is this evidence for conditioning of physiological responses in our subjects, and, if so, what is the nature of the response interpreted in terms of conditioning theory?

CONDITIONING FACTORS IN DRUG ABUSE

Drugs of abuse, because they affect a multiplicity of systems, behavioral, psychological, and physiological, are extremely complex stimuli (Eikelboom & Stewart, 1982). What to count as the stimulus and what to count as the response in this dynamic landscape is partly an empirical question and partly a matter of definition. For example, if the recognition of the drug by a receptor is considered to be the stimulus, then each drug will generate a multitude of stimuli as it is received by different receptors in different organ tissues at different times after administration. The response, too, is usually multivariate, including alterations in physiological functioning—which, in turn, may elicit homeostatic adjustments— and, of course, for drugs of abuse, a time course of subjective effects usually including a feeling of euphoria or relief.

The responses cited in the example of the opiate addicts —yawning, nausea, diarrhea—are usually considered to be "opposite" to the direct effects of opiates. Different theories have suggested different explanations of what may be happening here. Wikler (1948) proposed that these responses are evidence of conditioned withdrawal. Other researchers, however, have proposed a model that would regard them as an instance of a conditioned "compensatory" response (Macrae, Scoles, & Siegel, 1987; Siegel, 1983). Compensatory responses, by counteracting the drug's effects, may decrease the time for the organism to reestablish homeostasis (Siegel, 1983). The response is adaptive insofar as it precipitates this counteraction at or before the time that the drug is actually administered.

Whereas some responses seem to "oppose" a drug's effects, other responses seem to "mirror" the drug's effects, an isodirectional response. Clinicians and researchers will be familiar with examples of cocaine abusers responding to cocaine-related paraphernalia with cocaine-like symptoms—racing heart, sweaty palms, and so forth, and, subjectively, a feeling of being light-headed or even high. Why certain drugs elicit predominantly conditioned opposite and others predominantly conditioned isodirectional responses is therefore an interesting and perplexing question, of theoretical and practical import in drug addiction research. Eikelboom and Stewart (1982) have suggested that the direction of the conditioned response is a function of whether a drug acts upon the efferent or afferent arm of the central nervous system. They suggest that drugs such as cocaine may bypass normal receptor mechanisms that engender adaptive counterresponses.

Cocaine and opiates may differ in operant conditioning factors as well as classical conditioning factors. Because withdrawal distress is a prominent unconditioned effect of opiate administration, the act of self-administering an opiate may become strongly associated with avoidance or relief of withdrawal distress. In this case, the drug functions as a *negative reinforcer*; by relieving the distress, it reinforces the drug-using behavior. Drugs of abuse obviously also have important properties as *positive reinforcers*, promoting drug use not by terminating discomfort but by producing pleasurable states that the addict will desire to recreate. Eikelboom and Stewart (1982) have proposed an appetitive motivational model of drug use, which suggests that drug-addictive behavior can be accounted for in terms of the incentive value of drug use influencing motivational systems governing approach behavior. Other investigators point out that in drug addiction these positive and negative reinforcement systems will interact in complex ways to shape behavior (cf. the model proposed by Niaura et al., 1988). (For a more detailed discussion of conditioning models, the reader is referred to Chapter 5 by Therese Kosten, in the present volume.)

In light of the various conditioning models that have been put forth to account for addictive behavior—conditioned withdrawal model, conditioned compensatory model, appetitive motivational model—the interpretation of the physiological responses of subjects in cue-reactivity paradigms is by no means straightforward. A cocaine addict presented with cocaine-related cues may respond with increased skin conductance and heart rate, and decreased skin temperature—a typical "stress" response, which may mimic the predictions of a variety of conditioning models. Given that drug cues are stressors for most drug-addicted subjects, this stress response is a major confound in assessing the predictions of conditioning models concerning autonomic reactivity to drug cues (Niaura et al., 1988). To our knowledge, no cue-reactivity studies controlling for stress responses have yet been conducted on cocaine addicts (cf. Sherman, Zinser, & Sideroff, 1985).

NEUROBIOLOGICAL PATHWAYS OF
APPROACH AND AVOIDANCE

Recent work in the neurobiology of punishment and reward systems has shed some light on the brain mechanisms that may underlie appetitive and avoidance motivational states. There is increasing evidence that drug addiction is mediated by a positive reinforcement system centered in the medial forebrain bundle, which links the medial basal forebrain to the ventral tegmental area of the midbrain. This positive reinforcement system is thought to be anatomically and functionally distinct from the site of the negative reinforcing system in the brainstem (Wise, 1988). The positive reinforcement system generates approach behaviors based on incentive motivation independent of the reduction of dysphoric states, such as unconditioned or conditioned opiate withdrawal. Research into positive and negative reinforcement systems points to drug-seeking behavior as governed by fundamental motivational systems that have been protected by evolution because of their intrinsic survival functions. Animal studies suggest that the "artificial" drug activation of the reward system, a system which has evolved for adaptive functioning when activated by natural reinforcers such as food, sex, and social attachment, may constitute a profoundly and unnaturally powerful stimulation that evolution has not equipped mammals to deal with (Wise, 1988).

It is especially important for drug addiction clinicians to recognize that approach behaviors to maladaptive goals are not necessarily the result of neurophysiological disregulation, or of a lack of motivation on the patient's part to achieve abstinence. Rather, they may be the direct result of normal brain mechanisms having been activated by intensely pleasurable stimuli. Hence cocaine addiction, unlike opiate addiction, may have significant commonalities with "behavioral" addictions such as gambling or sexual addiction (Marks, 1990). In these addictions, a "withdrawal" phase is not a prominent feature of the syndrome, although the individual may be exhausted, guilty, and generally dysphoric after protracted participation in them. However, the memories of the intense reward associated with these activities may then come to dominate behavior. Indeed, Wise (1987) has suggested that cocaine addiction might be better regarded as a "disorder of memory" than as a disorder of neurobiology. This suggests that a useful treatment approach to cocaine addiction may be one based on helping patients develop approach systems focused on rewarding non-drug-related objects and memories, which would then compete with the drug-related approach systems. We will return to this point later in the chapter.

As the above discussion suggests, researchers have recently been focusing on the ways in which addictive behavior is a manifestation of appetitive behavior, rather than, as in Wikler's model, avoidance behavior with respect to conditioned withdrawal distress. The ascendancy of appetitive models stems in part from a lack of evidence for the role of conditioned withdrawal in relapse (Baker et al., 1987), even as it may apply to relapse opiates. Opiate addicts, for example, rarely give withdrawal-related symptoms as a reason for their relapse (Chaney, Roszell, & Cummings, 1982). Furthermore, research has shown that craving seems to peak just after opiate administration, which is not consistent with the withdrawal model (Meyer & Mirin, 1979). The potential usefulness of applying a Wiklerian withdrawal model to cocaine addiction is further diminished by the fact that the very existence of a pharmacologically based cocaine withdrawal syndrome is still an unsettled question. Unlike substances such as opiates and alcohol, cocaine may possess a far more subtle withdrawal syndrome, if any. Gawin and Kleber's (1986) three-phase model of cocaine withdrawal—crash, dysphoria, craving—has been difficult to confirm when the subjects are inpatients isolated from drug cues (Weddington et al., 1990). Research has not supported the existence of conditioned withdrawal responses in cocaine addicts: In response to cocaine-related cues, cocaine addicts most frequently report appetitive craving responses (Childress et al., 1988) or cocaine-like "high" symptoms (Kranzler & Bauer, 1990). In general, of the various conditioning models put forth to account for relapse to drug use, the appetitive motivational model (Stewart, deWitt, & Eikelboom, 1984) seems to be the best supported, across many addictive substances (Niaura et al., 1988; Rohsenow et al., 1991). However, it should be pointed out that the relation of this or any conditioning model to relapse is still an open question (Drummond et al., 1990).

As well as a shift away from withdrawal-based models of drug use, there has also been a shift away from strict "conditioned response" models, as evidenced by the fact that some researchers now speak instead of "cue-reactivity," a term that makes no commitment concerning the precise provenance of the response. This terminological shift is due in part to the difficulty of documenting an elicited response as "conditioned" in the absence of a comprehensive knowledge of a given subject's drug-using history, and in the absence, as discussed above, of adequate control conditions. It may also be due in part to the increased recognition that multiple factors, internal and external, physiological, emotive, and cognitive, interact in complex ways to promote addictive behavior (Niaura et al., 1988; Shiffman, 1989).

THE ROLE OF INTERNAL STATES AND CONTEXTUAL CUES

We draw the reader's attention once again to the case of Mark. During his walk home he was presumably exposed to many conditioned stimuli for cocaine use. Yet, he had walked home this way many days after work that week and did not use cocaine. What may have been different this time was context. It was Friday, the end of the workweek, a time, perhaps, to celebrate, and he had his paycheck in his pocket. That he claimed to be unaware, either at the time or afterwards, of what led to his use is not necessarily evidence of his mendacity—it is consistent with the activation of an unconscious drug use script, as Tiffany (1990) has suggested.

In Mark's case, the context included internal and external cues. Two brief examples from our own clinical experience illustrate that internal mood states alone may have a powerful influence on craving and drug use.

Gail is a methadone patient who has been in treatment for cocaine abuse for several months. She lives with her ex-husband, who is not addicted to opiates but who abuses cocaine in their house and in her presence. She maintains that her desire to use cocaine is greatest not when she sees her ex-husband using it, but when they argue, especially if he threatens her, when she feels the need to use to be almost unbearable.

Joan is also a patient in treatment for cocaine addiction. She has spent most of her life living by her wits on the street. Last year she met a non-drug-using man whom she loves and respects and who seems to reciprocate these feelings. They plan to get married. She reports that her desire to use cocaine is wholly dependent on her mood: When particularly elated, she develops an intense craving to use and often sneaks out of the house and goes to a nearby town where she can buy cocaine.

In these cases, the patient's internal environment appears to be the origin of drug use, not the sight of drug paraphernalia. For Gail, drug use, by ameliorating her emotional distress, may function as a negative reinforcer (Khantzian, 1985). For Joan, positive emotional states, states associated with the effects of cocaine use, also function as conditioned stimuli leading to drug use. That internal mood states alone can elicit craving has been shown in a number of studies, including surveys (Chaney et al., 1982; Wallace, 1989) and laboratory experiments (Childress, McLellan, Natale, & O'Brien, 1987). The model of relapse proposed by Baker et al. (1986), cited above, suggests that both positive and negative mood states can become conditioned stimuli eliciting appetitive motivation toward drug use. Positive mood states, particularly in the case of stimulants, may mimic the drug's effects (Stewart et al., 1984), and act as internal conditioned stimuli for drug use, whereas negative mood states increase the incentive value of the drug, increasing the addict's expectation that it will terminate the negative condition. According to this theory, both routes enhance drug-directed appetitive motivational states.

Because conditioning models more readily lend themselves to investigations of the external constraints on behavior, there seems to be a need for models which, when applied to cue-reactivity paradigms, would allow researchers to interpret the subjects' behavior in terms of their internal processing of the cues. Such models would facilitate an investigation of the internal processes of the patient in interpreting what the patient in cue-reactivity experiments is doing.

CONTROL THEORY AND CUE-REACTIVITY

Cue-reactivity paradigms, because they are based upon stimulus–response methodology, tend to be "open-loop" models— that is, the subject's response to the cues is not regarded as feeding back to, and influencing, the subsequent presentation of the stimulus. This is a significant departure from real-world dynamics in which individuals more often stand in a "closed-loop" relation to their environments: Stimuli are usually followed by behavior that alters the way in which the stimuli are in turn presented. Germane to this perspective was an observation we made in our posttreatment reactivity session. Some of the subjects who achieved abstinence, when presented with the drug cues, averted their gaze, sometimes turning their head completely away from the cues, as well as manifesting expressions of disgust. A stimulus–response, open-loop interpretation of these phenomena would hold that the cues "caused" these "effects," and would not posit any further interaction between them. A closed-loop interpretation of the behavior of these subjects suggests that they were actively attempting to "control" the cues by minimizing their exposure to them. Turning the head, averting the eyes, removes the cues from the subject's perceptual field. The perspective that in cue-reactivity sessions the subject is actually attempting to control his exposure to, and perception of, the cues, rather than the cues in some sense "controlling" the subject, is a point of view that control theorists have been urging for years (Carver & Scheier, 1982; Markin, 1988; Powers, 1973).

In control theory, an individual may be regarded as a negative feedback loop whose behavior is governed by the goal of minimizing deviations from a set-point, or internal reference state. In these terms, the behavior of subjects in cue-reactivity experiments may be understood as attempts to counteract the disturbance to their internal reference states precipitated by the drug cues. (For an introduction to the application of the principles of control theory to psychology, see Powers, 1973). We see control theory as a fruitful heuristic for the investigation of cue-reactivity. It suggests the need for methods of assessing subject's internal reference states and for measuring subjects' attempts to keep these reference states from going out of range in cue-reactivity paradigms (cf. Niaura et al., 1988). Such assessment may provide a clinically meaningful explanation of the finding of continued physiological reactivity co-occurring with reduced craving and cocaine abstinence.

ASSESSMENT OF INTERNAL STATES: DIRECTIONS FOR FUTURE RESEARCH

Several methods for assessing subjects' internal reference states suggest themselves. The following are those we are currently using in our cue-reactivity studies. To give us more insight into changes that may occur in the subject's internal motivational state with successful treatment, we videotape the subject's facial expressions in the presence of the drug cues (Ekman & Friesen, 1975). In addition, we have modified our craving scale to include a cocaine "revulsion" rating. In these ways, we hope to gain access to aspects of the subject's motivation, both avoidance and approach. Because cue-reactivity may also be influenced by the subject's current level of motivation to cease using cocaine, we have also incorporated Prochaska and DiClemente's (1986) four-stage model of change (precontemplation, contemplation, action, and maintenance) in our assessments.

By videotaping the subject's pretreatment and posttreatment behavior, obtaining cocaine revulsion ratings, and assessing the subject's current stage of change, we hope that the nature of the subject's physiological reactivity to drug cues may be clarified. However, in order to examine what internal reference states may govern the approach or avoidance responses pretreatment and posttreatment, we felt that another instrument was needed. For this purpose, we selected and modified the Selves Questionnaire (Higgins, Bond, Klein, & Strauman, 1986). As modified, this instrument asks subjects to generate up to 10 attributes to describe their actual self, their ideal self, and their addict self, and to indicate how much they have experienced themselves as each sense of self during the previous week. The questionnaire is based on self-discrepancy theory (Higgins, 1987, 1989a) which proposes a view of the self as a dynamic multi-faceted structure comprised of numerous self-representations (see Higgins, 1987, 1989a, 1989b). Chronic discrepancies among self-states are hypothesized to form cognitive schematic structures that, when activated, lead to the activation of other related constructs (e.g., specific negative emotional states such as depression or anxiety), which are linked to the self-discrepancy constructs in an associative memory network (Higgins, 1989b). Higgins's theory hypothesizes that a failure to live up to one's ideals (an actual-self:ideal-self discrepancy) constitutes an absence of positive outcomes and leads to dejection-related emotions (such as disappointment, sadness, dissatisfaction, shame, depression). In our research, we have found that cocaine addicts have higher actual-self:ideal-self discrepancies than nonusers or opiate users (Avants, Singer, & Margolin, 1992). However, cocaine addicts in treatment who achieve abstinence demonstrate a shift in their self-concept reference state. They became discrepant with their addict self, more congruent with their ideal self, and less depressed (Avants, 1992; Avants, Margolin, Kosten, & Singer, 1991). Thus, with successful treatment, cognitive–affective, as well as behavioral, changes occur. We propose that these cognitive–affective changes may contribute to the nature of the posttreatment physiological reactivity that the subjects exhibit when exposed to drug cues; they will also influence whether or not such reactivity places the subject at risk for relapse. To illustrate these points, we present the following case:

MH is a 28-year-old college educated single white male who owns a small business. At the time of entering outpatient treatment he had been using cocaine regularly for the past 2 years. During the past year he used an average of 2 grams of cocaine weekly. Pretreatment assessments revealed that MH had a Beck depression score of 17, placing him in the range of borderline clinical depression. His current self-concept was highly congruent with his "addict" self-concept and was highly discrepant with his "ideal" self. At this time he used the following words to describe himself: ashamed, guilty, selfish, depressed, liar, unreliable, irresponsible, lazy, uncaring. These adjectives closely matched the way he described his "addict" self. Totally discrepant with both his current self- concept and his addict self was his description of his ideal self as healthy, caring, giving, reliable, responsible, hardworking, considerate, prompt, fun, and aggressive. During the pretreatment cue-reactivity assessment, MH exhibited heightened physiological reactivity—increased skin conductance levels, and decreased skin temperature—and he reported moderate to high levels of craving in the presence of drug cues.

MH was placed on bupropion 100 mg *t.i.d.* and received weekly psychotherapy which focused on establishing a life-style incompatible with drug use. By the end of the 8th week of the study, MH had been abstinent from cocaine use for 6 consecutive weeks. His abstinence was verified by twice-weekly urine screens for cocaine metabolites. Posttreatment assessments revealed that MH was still highly reactive physiologically to cocaine cues. In fact, his mean posttreatment skin conductance level in the presence of the drug cues (6.02 μmhos) was higher than his mean pretreatment level (3.85 μmhos). Posttreatment, however, he reported little craving in the presence of these cues, and in fact showed expressions of extreme discomfort in their presence. His Beck depression score decreased to zero following treatment, and his self-concept was more congruent with his ideal self and was vastly discrepant with his addict self. Posttreatment, MH described himself as happy, healthy, responsible, caring, hardworking, energetic, patient, and thoughtful.

This case is illustrative of what we have observed frequently in our laboratory. Before treatment, when the patient is depressed and his internal reference state is that of "drug addict," exposure to cocaine-related cues may precipitate an approach response—a turning toward the drug cues, a fascination with handling the paraphernalia—that manifests itself in increased autonomic arousal. After successful treatment, when the patient is no longer depressed and no longer perceives himself as the type of person who uses drugs, exposure to cocaine-related cues may precipitate an avoidance response—turning away from the drug cues, expressions of disgust—which also manifests itself in the same pattern of increased physiological arousal.

Use of a control theory framework to examine cue-reactivity before and after treatment for cocaine addiction suggests that concomitants of successful treatment (achieved abstinence) will include posttreatment identification with nonaddict senses of self and avoidance behaviors in the presence of the drug cues. The first half of this proposition has already been supported (Avants et al., 1991); we are in the process of testing the latter half.

IMPLICATIONS FOR TREATMENT

In this chapter we have examined stimulus–response conditioning models as they may apply to an understanding of cue-reactivity in cocaine addiction. We have pointed out what appear to be some limitations of these models, and have suggested that the supplementation of conditioning models with other paradigms such as control theory will be fruitful when applied to the understanding of the effect of drug-related cues upon addicts. These considerations suggest that treatment for cocaine addiction may usefully contain some of the following components. Treatment can be initiated by stabilizing the patient's affective state through the use of antidepressant pharmacotherapy. In our clinical experience, bupropion stabilizes mood state within 24–72 hours of the first dosage. Antidepressants also have an important role as "anticraving" agents; the stabilization of mood state eliminates the patient's need for cocaine in order to regulate negative emotional states. Cognitive–behavioral psychotherapy can be instituted that focuses on shifting the patient's sense of self away from drug-using and non-drug-using internal scripts and reference states (Avants, 1992; cf. Tiffany, 1990). Hence, one object of psychotherapy is the creation of a non-drug-related system of rewards that is strong enough to compete with, and dominate, the pretreatment drug-focused system (McAuliffe, Albert, Cordill-London, & McGarraghy, 1991). This treatment goal is also implied by the literature on behavioral theories of choice, in which drug-taking behavior is analyzed in the context of, and relative to, the availability of alternative reinforcers (Vuchinich & Tucker, 1988). Systematic exposure to drug cues may have an important role in treatment both for desensitization training (O'Brien et al., 1990), and for bolstering self-efficacy in the face of drug-related stimuli and thoughts (Marlatt, 1990). Finally, the patient can be taught to reinterpret continued autonomic reactivity to drug cues as compatible with the existence of avoidance rather than approach motivational states, and not as evidence of a lack of resolve to remain abstinent.

Many drug addicts, particularly inner-city addicts, find it difficult to create benefits in their lives worth stopping drug use for. They have few pleasures in their lives, other than a drug-induced state. This is the result of, or produces, a vicious circle in that the production of this state involves addicts in activities that further degrade physiological and psychosocial systems. Pretreatment and posttreatment assessment of addicts' internal reference states through the use of the Selves Questionnaire (Avants et al., 1991) and the development of a psychotherapy focused on facilitating change in addict reference states (Avants, 1992) was a first attempt to assess the addict's self-representation in their own words, and to make the process of change in self-representation to a non-drug-using self state a deliberate, conscious process. The measurement of various subject characteristics involving self-definition, cognitive scripts, and emotive states represents attempts by many researchers to assess and specify those internal states that determine behavior in the face of fluctuating environmental cues. We believe that this approach can be fruitfully applied to the examination of a drug addict's physiological behavior in the presence of drug-related cues. Many years of research have failed to show that a more narrow construal of cue-reactivity will suffice to illuminate addictive behavior in *homo sapiens.*

REFERENCES

Avants, S. K. (1992). *Self-discrepancies in cocaine and opiate addicted individuals*. Unpublished doctoral dissertation, Yale University, New Haven, CT.

Avants, S. K., Margolin, A., Kosten, T. R., & Singer, J. E. (1991). *A multidimensional approach to treatment outcome research with cocaine dependent patients*. Manuscript submitted for publication.

Avants, S. K., Singer, J. E., & Margolin, A. (1992). *Self-belief discrepancies in cocaine and opiates abusers*. Manuscript submitted for publication.

Baker, T. B., Morse, E., & Sherman, J. E. (1987). The motivation to use drugs: A psychobiological analysis of urges. In C. Rivers (Ed.), *The Nebraska symposium on motivation: Alcohol use and abuse* (pp. 257–323). Lincoln, NE: University of Nebraska Press.

Bauer, L. (1991). Psychology of craving. In J. Lowinson, P. Ruiz, & R. Millman (Eds.), *Comprehensive textbook of substance abuse*. New York: Williams & Wilkins.

Carver, C. S., & Scheier, M. F. (1982). Control theory: A useful conceptual framework for personality—social, clinical, and health psychology. *Psychological Review, 92*, 111–135.

Chaney, E. F., Roszell, D. K., & Cummings, C. (1982). Relapse in opiate addicts: A behavioral analysis. *Addictive Behaviors, 7*, 291–297.

Childress, A. R., McLellan, A. T., Ehrman, R., & O'Brien, C. P. (1988). Classical conditioned responses in opioid and cocaine dependence: A role in relapse? In B. A. Ray (Ed.), *Learning factors in substance abuse* (National Institute on Drug Abuse Research Monograph No. 84, pp. 25–43). Washington, DC: U. S. Government Printing Office.

Childress, A. R., McLellan, A. T., Natale, M., & O'Brien, C. P. (1987). Mood states can elicit conditioned withdrawal and craving in opiate abuse patients. In L. S. Harris (Ed.), *Problems of drug dependence, 1987* (National Institute on Drug Abuse Research Monograph No 76, pp. 137–144). Washington, DC: U. S. Government Printing Office.

Drummond, D. C., Cooper, T., & Glautier, S. P. (1990). Conditioned learning in alcohol dependence: Implications for cue exposure treatment. *British Journal of Addiction, 85*, 725–743.

Eikelboom, R., & Stewart, J. (1982). Conditioning of drug-induced physiological responses. *Psychological Review, 89*, 507–528.

Ekman, P., & Friesen, W. V. (1975). *Unmasking the face*. Palo Alto, CA: Consulting Psychologists Press.

Gawin, F. H., & Kleber, H. D. (1986). Abstinence symptomatology and psychiatric diagnosis in cocaine abusers. *Archives of General Psychiatry, 43*, 107–113.

Grabowski, J., & O'Brien, C. P. (1981). Conditioning factors in opiate abuse. In N. K. Mello (Ed.), *Advances in substance abuse* (pp.69–121). Greenwich, CT: Jai Press.

Higgins, E. T. (1987). Self-discrepancy: A theory relating self and affect. *Psychological Review, 94*, 319–340.

Higgins, E. T. (1989a). Self-discrepancy theory: What patterns of self-beliefs cause people to suffer. *Advances in Experimental Social Psychology, 22,* 93–136.

Higgins, E. T. (1989b). Knowledge accessibility and activation: Subjectivity and suffering from unconscious sources. In J. S. Uleman & J. A. Bargh (Eds.), *Unintended thought.* New York: Guilford Press.

Higgins, E. T., Bond, R. N., Klein, R., & Strauman, T. (1986). Self-discrepancies and emotional vulnerability: How magnitude, accessibility, and type of discrepancy influence affect. *Journal of Personality and Social Psychology, 51,* 5–15.

Khantzian, E. J. (1985). The self-medication hypothesis of addictive disorders: Focus on heroin and cocaine dependence. *The American Journal of Psychiatry, 142,* 1259–1264.

Kozlowski, L. T., & Wilkinson, D. A.(1987). Use and misuse of the concept of craving by alcohol, tobacco, and drug researchers. *British Journal of Addiction, 82,* 31–36.

Kranzler H., & Bauer, L. (1989). A laboratory procedure for evaluation of pharmacotherapy for cocaine dependence. In L. S. Harris (Ed.), *Problems of drug dependence 1989* (National Institute on Drug Abuse Research Monograph No 95, pp. 324–325). Washington, DC: U. S. Government Printing Office.

Kranzler, H., & Bauer, L. (1990). Effects of bromocriptine on subjective and autonomic responses to cocaine-associated stimuli. *Problems of drug dependence 1990* (National Institute on Drug Abuse Research Monograph No. 105, pp. 505–506). Washington, DC: U. S. Government Printing Office.

Macrae, J. R., Scoles, M. T., & Siegel, S. (1987). The contribution of Pavlovian conditioning to drug tolerance and dependence. *British Journal of Addiction, 82,* 371–380.

Margolin, A., Avants, S. K., Ziedonis, D., Petrakis, I., & Kosten, T. R. (in press). *Pre- and post-treatment cue-reactivity in cocaine addicts treated with bupropion* (National Institute on Drug Abuse Research Monograph). Washington, DC: U. S. Government Printing Office.

Margolin, A., Kosten, T. R., Petrakis, I., Avants, S. K., & Kosten, T. S. (1990). An open pilot study of bupropion and psychotherapy for the treatment of cocaine abuse in methadone-maintained patients. In L. Harris (Ed.), *Problems of drug dependence, 1990* (National Institute on Drug Abuse Research Monograph No. 95, pp. 367–368). Washington, DC: U. S. Government Printing Office.

Margolin, A., Kosten, T. R., Petrakis, I., Avants, S. K., & Kosten, T. S. (1991). Bupropion reduces cocaine abuse in methadone-maintained patients. *Archives of General Psychiatry, 48,* 87.

Markin, R. S. (1988). The nature of behavior: Control as fact and theory. *Behavioral Science, 33,* 196–206.

Marks, I. (1990). Behavioral (non-chemical) addictions. *British Journal of Addiction, 85,* 1389–1394.

Marlatt, A. G. (1990). Cue exposure and relapse prevention in the treatment of addictive behaviors. *Addictive Behavior, 15,* 395–399.

McAuliffe, W. E., Albert, J., Cordill-London, G., & McGarraghy, T. K. (1991). Contributions to a social conditioning model of cocaine recovery. *The International Journal of the Addictions, 25*(9A & 10A), 1141–1177.

Meyer, R. E., & Mirin, S. M. (1979). *The heroin stimulus.* New York: Plenum Press.

Monti, P. M., Rohsenow, D. J., Abrams, D. B., & Binkoff, J. A. (1988). Social learning approaches to alcohol relapse: Selected illustrations and implications. In B. A. Ray (Ed.), *Problems of drug dependence 1988* (National Institute on Drug Abuse Research Monograph No. 84, pp. 141–159). Washington, DC: U. S. Government Printing Office.

Negrete, J. C., Emil, S. G. S., & Abrahamovicz, M. (1991). *Arousal responses to cocaine cues: Factors of variance and clinical significance.* Paper presented at the annual meeting of the Committee on Problems of Drug Dependence, Palm Beach, FL.

Niaura, R. S., Rohsenow, D. J., Binkoff, J. A., Monti, P. M., Pedraza, M., & Abrams, D. B. (1988). Relevance of cue reactivity to understanding alcohol and smoking relapse. *Journal of Abnormal Psychology, 97(2),* 133–152.

O'Brien, C. P., Childress, A. R., McLellan, T., & Ehrman, R. (1990). Integrating systematic cue exposure with standard treatment in recovering drug dependent patients. *Addictive Behaviors, 15,* 355–365.

O'Brien, C. P., Childress, A. R., Mclellan. T., Ehrman, R., & Ehrman, R. (1988). Types of conditioning found in drug-dependent humans. In B. A. Ray (Ed.), *Problems of drug dependence 1988* (National Institute on Drug Abuse Research Monograph No. 84, pp. 44–61). Washington, DC: U. S. Government Printing Office.

Peck, A. W., & Hamilton, M. (1983). Psychopharmacology of bupropion in normal volunteers. *The Journal of Clinical Psychiatry, 44,* 202–205.

Powers, W. T. (1973). *Behavior: The control of perception.* New York: Aldine De Gruyter.

Pretorius, M. B., Newlin, D. B., Wong, C. J., & Better, W. E. (1991). *Individual differences in cocaine-craving: Physiological and affective correlates.* Paper presented at the annual meeting of the Committee on Problems of Drug Dependence, Palm Beach, FL.

Prochaska, J. O., & DiClemente, C. C. (1986). Toward a comprehensive model of change. In W. R. Miller and N. Heather (Eds.), *Treating addictive behaviors. Processes of change.* New York: Plenum Press.

Rohsenow, D. J., Niaura, R. S., Childress, A. R., Abrams, D. B., & Monti, P. M. (1991). Cue reactivity in addictive behaviors: Theoretical and treatment implications. *International Journal of the Addictions, 25*(7A & 8A), 957–994).

Sherman, J. E., Zinser, M. C., & Sideroff, S. (1985). *Subjective reports of craving, withdrawal sickness and mood induced by boring, anxiety-provoking, or heroin-associated stimuli among drug-free addicts in treatment.* Paper presented at the meeting of the American Psychological Association, Los Angeles. [Discussed in Baker, Morse, & Sherman, 1986]

Shiffman, S. (1989). Conceptual issues in the study of relapse. In M. Gossop (Ed.), *Relapse and addictive behaviour* (pp. 149–179). London: Tavistock/ Routledge.

Siegel, S. (1983). Classical conditioning, drug tolerance, and drug dependence. In Y. Israel, F. B. Glaser, H. Kalant, R. E. Popham, W. Schmidt, & R. G. Smart (Eds.), *Research advances in alcohol and drug problems* (Vol.7, pp. 207–246). New York: Plenum Press.

Stewart, J., deWit, H., & Eikelboom, R. (1984). The role of unconditioned and conditioned drug effects in the self- administration of opiates and stimulants. *Psychological Review, 91,* 251–268.

Tiffany, S. T. (1990). A cognitive model of drug urges and drug-use behavior: Role of automatic and nonautomatic processes. *Psychological Review, 97,* 147–168.

Vuchinich, R. E., & Tucker, J. A. (1988). Contributions from behavioral theories of choice to an analysis of alcohol abuse. *Journal of Abnormal Psychology, 97*(2), 181–195.

Wallace, B. C. (1989). Psychological and environmental determinants of relapse in crack cocaine smokers. *Journal of Substance Abuse Treatment, 6,* 95–106.

Weddington, W. W., Brown, B. S., Haertzen, C. A., Cone, E. J., Dax, E. M., Herning, R. I., Michaelson, B. S. (1990). Changes in mood, craving, and sleep during short-term abstinence reported by male cocaine addicts: A controlled, residential study. *Archives of General Psychiatry, 47,* 861–868.

Wikler, A. (1948). Recent progress in research on the neurophysiological basis of morphine addiction. *American Journal of Psychiatry, 105,* 329–338.

Wikler, A. (1973). Dynamics of drug dependence. *Archives of General Psychiatry, 28,* 611–616.

Wikler, A. (1980). *Opioid dependence: Mechanisms and treatment.* New York: Plenum Press.

Wise, R. A. (1987). The role of reward pathways in the development of drug dependence. *Pharmacotherapy and Therapeutics, 35,* 227–263.

Wise, R. A. (1988). The neurobiology of craving. *Journal of Abnormal Psychology, 97*(2), 118–132.

CHAPTER SEVEN

Cognitive Factors Associated with Cocaine Abuse and Its Treatment: An Analysis of Expectancies of Use

Adam Jaffe, PhD

ADDICTION TO COCAINE, like addiction to any substance, can be conceptualized as a multidirectional process between the individual, the environment, and the substance itself (Rosecan, Spitz, & Gross, 1987). Within this multidirectional process, the role of the individual can be studied from several perspectives: this chapter will focus on the cognitive factors that promote and sustain cocaine abuse.

THE IMPORTANCE OF CONSIDERING COGNITIVE FACTORS

The study of cognitive variables associated with substance abuse has developed into an approach of primary importance, as it has contributed greatly to our understanding of substance use behavior. Goldman and colleagues (1987) state that the importance of examining cognitive variables in drug research has been understood for decades, as evidenced by the use of placebo-controlled studies specifically designed to control for cognitive variables. However, although cognitive factors were identified as important determinants of substance abuse early on, these early studies only treated cognitions as potential confounding factors. It was not until the 1970s and 1980s that cognitive variables associated with alcohol and drug abuse were viewed as important to explore in their own right, rather than merely controlled for as potential confounds. Indeed, cognitive variables seem to be a major factor in initiating and sustaining drug use, and determining some drug effects (Goldman et al., 1987).

A study of the entire realm of cognitive variables involved in cocaine use is potentially limitless. In order to provide organizational structure and some parameters to look at cognitive factors, it will be helpful to apply a theoretical model with which to examine such research. Potential theories from which to choose run the gamut from psychodynamic theories (see review by Khantzian & Khantzian, 1984) to learning-based theories. Social learning theory will be used in this chapter to illustrate in a coherent manner the cognitive factors involved in cocaine use. Social learning theory was selected over other theories of several reasons: (1) This theory focuses on cognitive factors without ignoring the environmental and substance context for these factors. (2) Research on substance abuse using this model over the past 20 years is plentiful. (3) Comprehensive treatment models for cocaine abuse using this theoretical framework have been developed recently and are available. Thus, rather than attempting to be all-encompassing, cognitive variables involved in cocaine abuse will be organized within the social learning model, as well as defined and limited by parameters set by recent research findings.

In general, social learning theory postulates that cognitive–mediational factors play a central role in learning and behavior (Bandura, 1977). In specific, this theory makes similar claims about the role that cognitive factors play in the learning and behavior associated with drug use. Environment, behavior, and personal factors (i.e., cognitive–mediational factors) are viewed as interdependent determinants of each other. Consequently, within the social learning model, causality is seen as a multidirectional process between the individual, the environment, and the substance itself (Abrams & Niaura, 1987; Rosecan et al., 1987). In this causal process, behavior and the environment interact with basic cognitive capabilities (i.e., symbolizing capability, forethought capability, vicarious capability, self-regulatory capability, and self-reflective capability (Abrams & Niaura, 1987; Bandura, 1977b, 1985).

Before we turn to the specific social learning model of drug use, we need to look at how social learning theory explains the central questions of (1) how thought affects action and (2) how individuals select particular patterns of behavior, such as drug use.

A cognitive concept central to social learning theory is self-efficacy (Bandura, 1982), or one's self-perceived ability to carry out a particular task. Beliefs about the probability that a given behavior will lead to a given outcome are referred to as efficacy expectations. According to Bandura (1977a), efficacy expectations can be learned from vicarious experience (modeling effects), social persuasion, physiological states, as well as from performance accomplishments (learning from experience). A person's self-efficacy for a particular task or behavior is a strong predictor of whether or not that task or behavior will be initiated and sustained, even in the presence of obstacles.

Social learning theory suggests that using a substance such as cocaine is initiated and continued through social reinforcement, modeling effects, anticipated drug effects (expectancies), direct experience with the drug's effects, as well as through the perception of these effects as reinforcing or punishing (Abrams & Niaura, 1987). Drug use can be seen as behavior that can be maintained by the consequences of its use. Because consequences that strengthen a particular pattern of behaviors are reinforcers, drug-taking behavior may be reinforced by the drug's ability to induce pleasurable effects (positive reinforcement) or by its ability to end an aversive situation (negative reinforcement) (Jaffe, 1987). Using cocaine and achieving euphoria or using cocaine and alleviating an aversive emotional state (such as depression or anxiety) are examples of consequences that may strengthen cocaine use. Consequently, drug use within social learning theory is conceptualized as involving

> persons with particular social learning histories, placed in specific situations, in a certain state, and with personal needs and expectations (cognitive–emotional and biological/physiological) so that the substance chosen is seen as the 'optimal' method of coping. In this context, it is clear that cognitive factors play a central role in determining if and when drug use will occur, how much of the substance will be used, and, in some instances, what behaviors will result (Abrams & Niaura, 1987, p. 157).

Clearly, within this theoretical framework, cognitive variables are of primary importance. And, more specifically, of the set of cognitive variables, the variable receiving the most research attention over the past 15 years is substance-related expectations (Abrams & Niaura, 1987).

RESEARCH ON DRUG RELATED EXPECTATIONS

The term expectancy has been used in many different contexts, but the common definitional theme has been that of a cognitive intervening variable referring to "the anticipation of a systematic relationship between events or objects. . . . This relationship is usually of an 'if-then' nature. If a certain event or object is registered, then a certain event is expected to follow" (Goldman et al., 1987). Moreover, expectancies can be inferred to have causal status, since an individual may actually produce a certain consequence upon noting that an "if" condition is fulfilled (Goldman et al., 1987). In relation to drug abuse, expectancies refer to an individual's specific beliefs about the effects of cocaine, alcohol, or other drugs. Such expectations are the result of the individual's particular learning history.

The earliest studies with direct implications for expectancy theory in substance abuse involved the administration of alcohol in both placebo and balanced placebo designs, in order to infer the role of expectancies in alcohol-related behavior.

One important early study with direct implications for expectancy theory was conducted by Merry (1966), who administered alcohol to inpatient alcoholics without their knowledge by placing vodka in their morning orange juice. He found ratings of craving were not affected by this manipulation. Engle and Williams (1972) told subjects that they either were or were not receiving alcohol and administered alcohol independently of this. They measured cravings before, during, and after the placebo/alcohol administration and found that the most salient factor in ratings of craving was the instructional set, regardless of whether alcohol was actually received. Subjects who were told that they had received alcohol reported greater subsequent craving, regardless of actual alcohol or placebo consumption.

Marlatt, Demming, and Reid (1973), also using a balanced placebo design, looked at actual alcohol consumption in a taste-rating task. They found that alcoholics craved and drank more subsequent to drinking a placebo that they believed to be alcohol than when they in fact received alcohol but believed their drink to be nonalcoholic.

In combination, the results of these and other similar studies lent initial support to the importance of nonpharmacological factors in alcohol craving and consumption.

More recent studies have suggested that expectancies mediate the behavioral effects of alcohol in many areas, including aggressive behavior (Lang, Goeckner, Adesso, & Marlatt, 1975; Pihl, Smith, & Farrell, 1984), food consumption (Polivy, Schueneman, & Carlson, 1976), social anxiety (Abrams & Wilson, 1979), and ability to delay gratification (Abrams & Wilson, 1983). In the area of sexual functioning, expectancies have been shown to mediate subjective sexual arousal (Briddell & Wilson, 1976; Wilson & Lawson, 1976; Wilson, Lawson, & Abrams, 1978) as well as to counteract the decreased penile and vaginal responsiveness to erotic stimuli normally seen with alcohol consumption

(Briddell & Wilson, 1976; Lansky & Wilson, 1981; Wilson & Lawson, 1976).

In sum, these studies suggest that expectancies are frequently as instrumental in determining behavioral consequences of alcohol use as are the actual pharmacological effects of alcohol. In these studies, however, it was necessary to infer the expectations from behavioral outcomes observed (Goldman et al., 1987). For example, if a subject behaved more aggressively after he believed he consumed alcohol, then the expectancy that alcohol increases aggressiveness was inferred by the experimenters. Since then, investigation of alcohol-related expectancies has been refined by specifying the components of individual expectancies through multifactorial questionnaires that inquire about an individual's beliefs about alcohol (Christiansen et al., 1989).

Investigators using different samples and similar test construction techniques have identified similar areas of alcohol expectancies. Using interviews and factor analytic techniques, Brown, Goldman, Inn, and Anderson (1980) found six alcohol expectancy factors: alcohol as (1) a global positive transforming agent, (2) enhancing social and physical pleasure, (3) enhancing sexual experience, (4) increasing power and aggression, (5) increasing social assertiveness, and (6) promoting relaxation. Using similar methodology to Brown et al. (1980), Southwick, Steele, Marlatt, and Lindell (1981) obtained three expectancy dimensions: perceived dominance, pleasure/disinhibition, and behavior impairment. Leigh (1987) obtained five areas of expectancies: nastiness, disinhibition, cognitive/physical impairment, gregariousness, and depressant effects. Numerous studies using these and similar instruments have since been conducted with implications for the assessment, treatment, and etiology of alcohol abuse (see reviews by Goldman et al., 1987; Leigh, 1989; Wilson, 1987).

EXPECTANCIES AND COCAINE RESEARCH: MOTIVATIONALLY RELEVANT BELIEFS ABOUT COCAINE

Although there is a vast literature suggesting that people hold many expectations regarding the effects of cocaine, only recently have these beliefs been explored within an expectancy paradigm (Jaffe & Kilbey, 1990, 1991; Jaffe, Kilbey, & Rosenbaum, 1989, 1990; Jaffe & Lohse, 1991). These expected effects include improved sexual performance (Gay, 1981; McConnel, 1985), increased excitement, grandiosity, and youthfulness (McConnel, 1985), enhanced physical performance (Fischman & Schuster, 1980; Resnick, Kestenbaum, & Schwartz, 1980), increased aggressiveness (Grinspoon & Bakalar, 1977), and increased feelings of stimulation and euphoria (Fischman, 1984; Post, 1975; Siegel, 1980; Seecof & Tennant, 1986; Spotts & Shontz, 1984). Exploration of beliefs about cocaine and identification of cocaine expectancies provide a paradigm for clarifying the relationship between particular beliefs held about cocaine and the etiology, assessment, and treatment of cocaine abuse and dependence. A review of studies that explore potentially motivating beliefs about cocaine follows.

Although beliefs or expectations regarding cocaine use are clearly not independent of cocaine's actual effects, the goal here is to focus on expected effects from cocaine rather than actual effects of administration. For a comprehensive review of the phenomenology of cocaine administration, the reader is referred to Chapter 6 (this volume).

A large part of cocaine's mystique comes from its association with sex. Users frequently report a belief that cocaine is a powerful aphrodisiac (Resnick & Resnick, 1984). Its street names connote sensuality and sex: "lady," "girl," "her," "la dona blanca," "candy," "blow," "the pimp's drug." In the Haight-Ashbury Center in San Francisco, cocaine is called the "champagne of sexual drugs." It is identified as the premier enhancer of sexuality and sexual pleasure in the young drug- and sex-sophisticated population (Gay, 1981). Fifty percent of callers to the COCAINE hotline in New York report that sexual stimulation is a major reason they become compulsive users (McConnel, 1985). Cocaine is often used orally and topically during sex. Although the central nervous system stimulation and increased energy can, at times, enable prolonged sex, topical application acts as a local anesthetic, thus inhibiting physical stimulation, and prolonged use can cause impotence or loss of sexual desire (Gold, Dackis, Pottash, Extein, & Washton, 1986). Despite the prevalence of users' expectancy of sexual enhancement, experimental findings have never demonstrated any sexually enhancing effects of cocaine (Gay, 1981).

Washton, after compiling information on thousands of callers to the COCAINE hotline, identified subsets of individuals who appear to use cocaine for different reasons that seem to be related to different beliefs about what cocaine does for them. For example, Washton identified subsets of users who expect cocaine to increase their excitement, their feelings of invincibility, or their feelings of youthfulness (McConnell, 1985). Washton states that these beliefs persist despite the fact that, with continued use, cocaine actually seems to be impairing their functioning in most areas.

Gold et al. (1986) report that patterns of escalating cocaine use frequently arise from attempts to recapture the expected "ephemeral euphoric state" that in actuality occurs less frequently with chronic use.

Finally, the belief that cocaine is a drug that has been associated with privilege and the privileged class has frequently been cited as a motivating factor for use.

Self-reports of cocaine users often involve the insistence that they can do anything better under the influence of cocaine (Fischman, 1984). O'Malley, Johnston, & Bachman (1985) surveyed high school seniors who had used cocaine in the last 12 months. They identified the following reasons (in order) as the top six self-reported reasons given for their cocaine use: to experiment, to feel good, to have a good time with my friends, to get more energy, to relax, and to stay awake. Self-reports from cocaine users typically refer to the motivationally relevant feelings of enhanced physical, mental, and sexual capabilities (Gold et al., 1986).

Resnick and Resnick (1984) used a semistructured clinical interview to discern what users regard as the most desirable and motivating effects of cocaine. They found that the most highly motivating effects are those related to cocaine stimulant properties and its facilitation of emotional expressiveness. Users reported beliefs that cocaine makes them feel more alert, energetic, sociable, and talkative. In addition, this sample believed that cocaine creates an aura of being more loving, conciliatory, caring, and socially related.

Spotts and Shontz (1984) interviewed cocaine users about their reasons for using the drug and their recollection of cocaine's effects. Users reported beliefs that cocaine made their "mind feel clear, quicker, alert, and more effective in managing transactions in the environment" (p. 130) In addition, beliefs about cocaine's physical effects included quicker, more accurate, and more precise reflexes, greater agility, and decreased feelings of fatigue and pain.

To assess the actual effects of cocaine on new learning, Fischman (1978) measured acquisition of behavior after cocaine administration. She reported that, at sufficient doses, cocaine interferes with tasks involving the acquisition of new behavior patterns, despite the widespread belief to the contrary among users.

Cocaine users frequently report that the drug enhances physical performance. This has been investigated experimentally on only a few occasions (Fischman, 1984). Resnick et al. (1980) reported that neither 10 mg nor 25 mg of cocaine administered intranasally or intravenously affected hand grip strength. Fischman and Schuster (1980) reported that inhalation of 96 mg of cocaine did not affect the performance of rested subjects on a reaction-time task. However, they report some indication that inhalation of cocaine can reverse or partially reverse fatigue-induced decrements in performance.

Much of the literature relevant to expectancies has focused on positive valenced expectations. Beliefs about the negative effects of cocaine use have been explored but to a lesser degree. However, certain negative expectations have been found to be important predictors of drinking behavior, are positively correlated with some drinking variables (for a review, see Leigh, 1989), and have been shown to concurrently predict cocaine behavior (Jaffe & Kilbey, 1992; Jaffe et al., 1990). Thus the exploration of negative expectations should not be ignored.

Cocaine has often been linked to physical aggression. It is reasoned that because cocaine increases energy and confidence, and can produce irritability and paranoia, the cocaine–aggression link is a logical one. We know of no human laboratory work in this area. However, numerous examples of self-report and correlational relationships between cocaine and aggression/violence exist (e.g., Inciardi, 1990; Brody, 1990; Dembo et al., 1990). Given the illegal and violent nature of the subculture surrounding cocaine, the direction of causality is hard to establish through these reports. Animal studies, however, have demonstrated that cocaine can increase aggression in some cases with some doses, but there is not a consistent relationship (e.g., Emley & Hutchinson, 1983; Hadfield, 1982; Hadfield, Nugent, and Mott, 1982; O'Donnel & Miczek, 1980). It seems that cocaine, like caffeine and nicotine, often increases nonattack behavior produced by a noxious stimulus as often as it increases attack behavior (Grinspoon & Bakalar, 1977). Thus the cocaine–aggression link is suggested but inconclusive.

Resnick and Resnick (1984) reported that in a sample of 430 cocaine users the most frequently expected negative effects were feeling nervous, fearful, irritable, depressed, paranoid, nauseated, and having a rapid heartbeat. In addition, compulsive users frequently report trying in vain to reexperience the expected euphoria that they remember but instead experience anxiety, depression, and paranoid ideation. Satel, Southwick, and Gawin (1991) found that 34 of 50 (68%) cocaine-dependent men reported experiencing highly distressing transient paranoid states in the context of cocaine use. These reported paranoid experiences became more severe with continued cocaine use. In the laboratory, Sherer, Kumor, Cone, & Jaffe (1988) administered an IV dose of 40–80 mg of cocaine followed by 4-hour continuous IV infusions of cocaine or placebo (saline) to experienced cocaine users. They reported that observers rated the subjects' behavior as moderately suspicious following the 4-hour cocaine infusion and saw no suspiciousness following saline infusion. However, the subjects themselves did not report feeling an increase in suspiciousness during any of the conditions. Thus clinical self-report suggests clear expectations and experience of paranoia, and laboratory findings offer supportive evidence of paranoid behavior.

Chitwood (1985) asked cocaine users retrospectively to indicate whether they believed that cocaine caused the particular physical conditions they were experiencing. Decreased appetite, headache, decreased interest in sex, insomnia, and dizziness are the negative effects that this group believed to be caused by cocaine.

Seecof and Tennant (1986) used a questionnaire consisting of a list of 20 emotions that past literature and anecdotal reports suggest are "associated with the cocaine rush." The study was designed to investigate the expected effects of cocaine among heroin abusers. Thus this questionnaire was given to heroin abusers with a history of at least a single episode of IV cocaine use. Subjects were asked to remember previous cocaine use experiences and to indicate whether each emotion described was remembered as strong, weak, or missing. They found both males and females rated excitement, pleasure, thirst, strength, and anxiety as the top six emotions experienced with cocaine use. Of the respondents, 43–81% experienced each of these effects. Some differences between males' and females' responses were noted. Males rated power quite high, ranking this second, whereas females rated power significantly lower at rank order 10. Females ranked satisfaction 5th, warmth 6th, and relaxation 12th. Rank order for these three variables were much higher than for males who ranked them 15th, 16th, and 17th, respectively.

SIGNIFICANCE OF NEGATIVE EXPECTATIONS

We have seen throughout this chapter that negative expectations regarding cocaine are prominent among users and nonusers alike. Negative expectations have been found to be important predictors of substance use (Jaffe et al., 1989; Jaffe & Kilbey, 1991; Leigh, 1987, 1988). Thus, much of the alcohol and cocaine literature looking at motivationally relevant beliefs suggests that expectations of negative consequences also seem to be important variables.

Although it is clear that individuals hold both positive and negative expectations regarding cocaine, it is less clear where such negative expectations fit into a social-learning or motivational perspective of cocaine use.

In specific, if we are to attribute direct motivational significance to expectancies, it is somewhat surprising to find such strong negative expectations in cocaine abusers (Jaffe et al., 1989). In addition, expectancy theory must be able to explain why particular negative expectancies, such as anxiety and decrements in sexual performance, are held more strongly by abusers than experimental users or nonusers as well as why other negative expectancies (e.g., depression) are held more strongly by abusers and experimental users than by nonusers (Jaffe & Kilbey, 1992).

Conversely, why particular positive expectations, such as grandiosity and euphoria, are held more strongly by experimental and nonusers than by abusers also needs to be explained by expectancy theory.

Leigh (1989) suggests that such effects may be part of an opponent process model of acquired motivation proposed to explain addiction to various drugs and experiences (Shipley, 1987). Positive versus negative expectations may also be related to individuals' distinction between proximal and distal consequences across substances (e.g., alcohol and cocaine), in that many positive effects are relatively immediate, and negative effects such as depression are more delayed (Leigh, 1989).

Expectancy theory suggests that expectancies reflect cultural stereotypes about a drug's effects as well as information derived from personal experience. Hence negative expectations may reflect, in part, greater experience with cocaine, increased doses, or chronicity of use and thus more experience with the negative consequences of use. It is important to note that, because we have gained most of our knowledge about abusers' expectations from treatment populations, one cannot discount the effects of treatment on such expectations.

ASSESSMENT OF COCAINE EXPECTATIONS: THE COCAINE EXPECTANCY QUESTIONNAIRE (CEQ)

Jaffe et al. (1989, 1991) systematically and empirically assessed the domains of cognitive expectations that adults hold about cocaine use. To construct a questionnaire assessing these expectations, cocaine abusers, experimental users, and nonusers were interviewed, and the literature was reviewed to determine the general themes of cocaine expectations. This questionnaire was administered to a sample of 852 people (87 cocaine abusers, 78 experimental users, and 596 college students). The answers were then factor-analyzed in order to determine the overall categories of expectations that users and nonusers hold regarding cocaine.

The cocaine related expectations held by the cocaine-abusing and college populations, as measured by the CEQ, include (1) grandiosity/euphoria; (2) enhancement of cognitive, social, and physical abilities; (3) anxiety and anxiety-related physiological sensations; (4) depression, (5) improved mood; (6) sexual enhancement; (7) antisocial and aggressive behavior; (8) paranoia; (9) tension reduction; (10) increased energy/arousal; (11) desire for other drugs; and (12) decrements in sexual performance. With the use of multivariate prediction techniques, expectancies measured by the CEQ have demonstrated highly significant discriminative power between groups of abusers, experimental users, and nonusers. Eight of the 12 expectancy factors accounted for significant unique between group variance.

Finally, subjects' scores on the expectancy factors or categories as measured by the CEQ demonstrated highly significant differences between groups of abusers, experimental users, and nonusers. Finding significant differences between these groups on the relative strength with which they hold the identified expectancies lays the groundwork for preliminary theorizing for the motivational or etiological relevance of specific expectancies.

In essence, when compared with previous studies that explored cocaine-related beliefs or expectations in a more rudimentary fashion, the CEQ appeared to capture the major features of these beliefs as a whole. Both positive and negative expectations are represented. The measurement of expectations with the CEQ allows this construct to be more easily used in empirical studies. In addition, the CEQ makes it possible to assess and use individual's beliefs about cocaine in the prevention and treatment of cocaine abuse.

EXPECTANCIES AND A RELAPSE PREVENTION MODEL

One model of substance abuse based on social learning theory principles is that of Marlatt and Gordon (1985). These authors focus on the relapse process across substances of abuse. According to them, the relapse process primarily involves encounters with high risk-situations in which the person is exposed to environmental factors, such as a bar or drug party, that increase the likelihood of a relapse. In their model, Marlatt and Gordon (1985) argue that in such situations, individuals with no coping response for the situation at hand will experience a decreased sense of self-efficacy. When this is experienced together with a positive outcome expectancy for drug use, the likelihood of drug use increases. After substance use, individuals experience various cognitive reactions that are subsumed under the term abstinence violation effect (Marlatt & Gordon, 1985). Basically, the abstinence violation effect involves the experience of cognitive dissonance and negative self-attribution. In this case, cognitive dissonance refers to the perceived contrast between one's desired self-image as a non–substance user and one's immediate behavior of drug use. Thus the person makes self-attributions of helplessness, loss of control, or failure that lead to further use.

Conversely, consider persons who experience high-risk situations but have coping skills at hand with which to respond and have less positive expectations for the use of the substance. These persons will tend to have a greater sense of self-efficacy and less motivation to use the substance, making them less likely to relapse. As the basis for a therapeutic approach to substance abuse, Marlatt and Gordon (1985) suggest cognitive behavioral techniques such as self-monitoring of high-risk situations, coping skills training, efficacy-enhancing imagery, and cognitive restructuring that addresses expectancies and the abstinence violation effect.

CRAVING, EXPECTANCIES, AND RELAPSE

The concept of craving is a psychobiological concept that can be understood on different levels and within different theoretical frameworks. Theories range from noncognitive classical conditioning (Luding & Wikler, 1974; Stockwell, Hodgson, Rankin, & Taylor, 1982; Poulos, Hinson, & Siegel, 1981) to cognitive–social learning analyses (see Chapter 6 in the volume for a thorough discussion of this topic). The most developed cognitive analysis of craving is the expectancy approach of Marlatt (Wilson, 1987). Marlatt and Gordon (1985) defined craving as a "subjective state that is mediated by the incentive properties of positive outcome expectancies" (p. 138). More specifically, Gawin and Kleber (1986) hypothesize that drug craving is fueled by dysphoric states and by selective recall of the expected euphoria (and by the likely presence of environmental cues). Hence, positive outcome expectations that a substance will "transform subjective experience and dysphoric emotional states" are experienced by the individual as a craving (Wilson, 1987). Whereas cognitive–social learning theory suggests that outcome expectations in particular situations depend on judgments (efficacy expectations) of one's ability to cope, craving becomes especially strong in high-risk (cocaine) situations. In such situations, the person has deficient alternative coping skills and little self-efficacy (Marlatt, 1985; Wilson, 1987), combined with positive expectations that cocaine will improve his or her situation. According to Marlatt's expectancy approach, the probability of the initial use of cocaine (followed by the abstinence violation effect) and a full-blown relapse is highest under these conditions.

To further specify cognitive craving and relapse precipitants (triggers), Wallace (1989) questioned 35 cocaine abusers returning for a second inpatient treatment and performed a content analysis of their responses. Wallace found that 40% of their relapses were associated with identified negative emotional states, including feelings of emptiness, boredom, loneliness, depression, frustration, or anger, and 24% of relapses involved interpersonal stress as a determinant. This is consistent with "triggers" found across substances of abuse (Marlatt & Gordon, 1985). In sum, negative emotional states and interpersonal stressors have been consistently identified as relapse precipitants across various substances of abuse.

From this discussion of craving and relapse, it is clear that cocaine-related expectancies play a central role in the cognitive aspect of craving. Beyond this determination, what can such an analysis of the craving and relapse process add to our knowledge of the likely content of these expectancies? If negative emotional states (i.e., anger, depression, and loneliness) and interpersonal stress are related to increases in craving and relapse, it may be inferred that people hold expectations that cocaine can reduce the discomfort of these negative emotional states and interpersonal stressors. Specifically, such expectations may include a belief in cocaine's ability to improve ones's mood, relieve interpersonal stress, or promote general tension reduction. Confirmation of the role of specific expectations in craving and relapse await further validation. However, such a cognitive conceptualization of the craving and relapse process gives us added insight into the likely content of relevant expectations, and suggests that expectancies are of central importance to this process.

EXPECTANCIES AND SELF-EFFICACY

We have previously noted that feelings of low self-efficacy (limited self-perceived ability to cope with given situations), coupled with positive outcome expectancies for drug use, are likely to lead to substance use or relapse (Marlatt & Gordon, 1985). However, beyond this assertion, it is clear that many of the positive expectations regarding cocaine are directly relevant to one's actual feeling of self-efficacy. Indeed, the primary or most prevalent expectation from both the literature review and the CEQ seems to be grandiosity/euphoria. Items endorsed on this scale of the CEQ include: People feel powerful when they use cocaine; people feel more important when they use cocaine; cocaine makes a person feel almost God-like; and cocaine makes a person feel they can do no wrong. Other expectations that appear throughout the literature are enhancement of cognitive, social, and physical abilities; sexual enhancement; tension reduction; and increased energy. This suggests that a significant cognitive variable or expectation for cocaine use is a somewhat generalized feeling of enhanced self efficacy across a variety of situations. Without referring to this concept directly, Spotts and Shontz (1984) succinctly summarized the self-efficacy expectation.

They state that heavy cocaine abusers report believing that cocaine "mobilizes [them], sharpens [their] vision, reaction time, and thinking, and makes [them] feel stronger, more powerful, and better able to cope with the world" (p. 134). Thus, the relationship between expectancies and self-efficacy is multilayered.

Expectations that cocaine will help one accomplish a task, coupled with a weak self-perceived ability to accomplish the task without cocaine, lead to a greater likelihood of using/relapsing (Marlatt & Gordon, 1985). Different individuals are likely to have different self-efficacy profiles combined with different expectations regarding cocaine's ability to improve these deficits. This has implications for where, when, and why an individual may use cocaine. In sum, self efficacy must be considered in conjunction with expectations for the prevention and treatment of cocaine abuse.

IMPLICATIONS FOR PREVENTION AND TREATMENT

Major prevention and treatment implications of expectancies involves their predictive power. The alcohol literature has shown that expectancies predict drinking behavior concurrently (Brown, 1985a; Christiansen & Goldman, 1983) and over time (Smith, Roehling, Christiansen, & Goldman, 1986). To date, the cocaine literature has shown the concurrent predictive power of expectancies (Jaffe et al., 1989, 1991). Thus, expectations can be useful for early intervention strategies by identifying individuals at risk for problematic substance use.

Given that expectancies are related to treatment outcome and that expectancies are potentially modifiable, they have profound implications for treatment. In terms of treatment, higher expectations of reinforcement from alcohol were associated with poor treatment outcome and 1-year drinking measures (Brown, 1985b). Goldman et al. (1987) state that direct attempts to change expectations should have an impact on substance use behavior. In essence, the treatment implications from the expectancy literature point to the need to assess and understand the person's cocaine-related expectations in the context of other relevant cognitive variables, such as perceived high-risk situations, efficacy expectations, and craving in designing clinical interventions.

Empirical assessment of individuals' beliefs and expectations of cocaine use with adolescents and young adults may allow the development of an effective primary intervention strategy. Longitudinal studies with these populations would allow the development of expectancy profiles that are predictive of future cocaine use. Instruments such as the

Cocaine Expectancy Questionnaire (Jaffe et al., 1989; Jaffe & Kilbey, 1992) could then be used to identify high-risk individuals. Primary intervention strategies involving attempts to alter the expectancies of high-risk groups could then be attempted.

Because beliefs about cocaine are strong concurrent predictors of use, altering cocaine expectancies may have an impact on substance use behavior. By targeting high risk beliefs about cocaine's effects and attempting to modify these beliefs in therapy, it may be possible to reduce a person's likelihood of using. Goldman et al. (1987) suggest that such expectancy changes could be facilitated by first teaching individuals about the role of expectancies in shaping actual and perceived substance use consequences, and then training them to obtain their desired substance use consequences through alternative methods. The intervention model based upon cognitive expectancies can be illustrated by the following case example.

Case Example

Barry is a married professional in his 40s who used up to half a gram of cocaine, intranasally, two or three times per week. Upon entering treatment, Barry gave the superficial impression of adequate social and occupational functioning, and his cocaine use was unknown to his colleagues.

Barry is a somewhat rigid, tense man who admits to feeling awkward in social situations. His memory for recently learned material is occasionally faulty, a problem his professional colleagues and friends have begun to notice. Barry's physical health is unremarkable, though he is "pot-bellied," shuffles with a slight stoop, and has a slight stutter. This latter condition contributes to his feeling ill at ease in social situations.

A highly educated man who has spent many years in professional association with the health care community, Barry is aware of the dangers of cocaine use and sought treatment on his own initiative.

Preliminary assessment using the CEQ (Jaffe et al., 1989, 1991) revealed Barry's expectations that cocaine promotes relaxation, enhances social behavior, and improves cognitive functioning. Follow-up interviews revealed the closely corresponding clinical history described above.

Treatment was carried out in a framework of relapse prevention and coping skills (Marlatt & Gordon, 1985). Here we will focus on those aspects of therapy most directly relevant to cocaine-related expectancies in the context of social learning theory.

Therapy focused on addressing the patient's cocaine expectations on multiple levels. With direction provided by the assessment of the patient's cocaine expectations, therapy attempted to improve Barry's sense of self-efficacy and efficacy expectations in given situations without using cocaine. In addition, therapy attempted to alter the patient's motivationally relevant cocaine-related expectancies.

Self-monitoring and a functional analysis of time, place, situation, internal dialogue, and craving was carried out early in therapy (Marlatt & Gordon, 1985). From this analysis, it became clear that various situations, such as social gatherings, were "high risk" for Barry, in large part because of his self-perceived inability to cope effectively with this situation, coupled with his belief that cocaine would help him to cope effectively. Thus he experienced increased cocaine craving. This specific situational craving could be decreased by improving his ability to cope with the situation effectively and/or decreasing his expectation that cocaine will improve his ability to do so. To accomplish this, the patient was provided with effective strategies for achieving the effects he was looking for from cocaine, namely improved relaxation, social skills, and cognitive functioning. Concurrent with this approach, a psychoeducational component and cognitive restructuring techniques designed to "debunk" erroneous cocaine expectations in the targeted areas were used. The resulting increased sense of self-efficacy, efficacy expectations and positive outcome expectations, coupled with diminished positive cocaine expectations, helped to decrease Barry's relapses.

Specifically, relaxation was promoted through skills training; Barry proved particularly adept at using breathing exercises and soothing imagery for relaxation. Also helpful was cognitive restructuring to explore the irrational social anxiety that Barry felt, and to change his cocaine-related expectations. The patient often worried that others made value judgments about his memory problems and knew about his previous cocaine problems. This caused enormous anxiety in his social interactions, which led to further cocaine use. Barry was taught to identify such thoughts, challenge these irrational beliefs, relabel his anxiety as a signal that his thinking pattern needed to be changed, and to come up with more adaptive thoughts such as, "These are my friends," "We support one another," "Others focus on my strengths rather than on my weaknesses." Roleplaying and modeling were also used to provide training in initiating social interaction, conversational skills, and nonverbal communication.

The same approach was used to attack the patient's mistaken cocaine expectations. First, as noted previously. Barry and the therapist identified the patient's expectations with the CEQ, which included beliefs that cocaine would decrease his anxiety, improve his cognitive abilities, and facilitate his social interactions. Next, Barry was taught to challenge these thoughts with factual information to the contrary, such as that cocaine is a stimulant and unlikely to increase relaxation, cocaine only makes one *feel like* one is performing better mentally and socially, and so on. The patient's original expectations were then relabeled as "traps" that had led him to further use. More adaptive thoughts were developed, such as "I can improve my social interactions through practice," "Using my relaxation skills will decrease my anxiety," "Cocaine will only increase my anxiety and hurt my social performance," and so forth.

In addition, Barry was given assistance in developing pragmatic strategies for dealing with remaining cognitive losses. For example, at work he gave presentations based on material that had been well practiced, to avoid difficulty in recalling new material. In addition, concrete problem-solving skills were taught, modeled, and rehearsed. For instance, Barry was taught a simple five-step problem-solving strategy. This strategy included (1) identifying the problem, (2) brainstorming alternative solutions, (3) considering pros and cons of each solution, (4) choosing an alternative, and (5) evaluating the results. Once the patient learned this method, the therapist demonstrated its use through a hypothetical example. Next, the patient and therapist chose several persisting problems that the patient was currently experiencing with others, such as arguments with colleagues, limited social support network, and poor communication with his wife. The patient rehearsed the use of the above model, aloud and in writing, while the therapist provided structured feedback about his performance. Barry was able to effectively "solve" several problems in this manner. This approach helped the patient to generalize the application of such efficacy-enhancing solutions across situations.

Self-monitoring identified a clear abstinence violation effect (cognitive dissonance and guilt/shame) after cocaine slips. It also became clear that the client's expectations played an integral role in his experience of the abstinence violation effect. Contrary to his expectations of relaxation, the client experienced a significant increase in situational and generalized anxiety after a slip. He became concerned that others would find out about his slip; he interpreted his increased heart rate and pulse as signs of anxiety; he began to ruminate about his failure (slip); and he became increasingly anxious generally. Paradoxically, this increased anxiety became a trigger to use more cocaine. Indeed, because he expected cocaine to decrease his anxiety (despite his experience to the contrary), upon experiencing the anxiety that accompanied his slip he craved and used cocaine to achieve his expected tension reduction.

In sum, intervention included providing Barry with factual information and cognitive restructuring techniques designed to debunk his positive expectations. Intervention also consisted of psychotherapeutic techniques designed to help Barry achieve in a healthy way what he previously expected from cocaine: relaxation, improved social skills, and improved cognitive functioning.

Self-report and clinical observation suggest that focusing on cognitive expectations in this manner improved the patient's sense of self-efficacy and cocaine free outcome expectations. In addition, the intensity and frequency of the patient's situationally specific craving decreased over the course of treatment. Specifically, the patient's internal dialogue in various social and anxiety-provoking situations no longer included such craving-increasing thoughts as "If I use cocaine I will feel more relaxed and function better socially." In terms of cocaine use, a 6-month follow-up interview revealed only a few circumscribed slips. A recent reassessment using the CEQ revealed that his expectations regarding cocaine use are now more in line with what is known about cocaine's pharmacology, particularly with regard to relaxation and social comfort. As a consequence, desires for relaxation or social comfort are less likely to lead to future cocaine craving or use.

However, it should be noted that some of the patient's inaccurate expectancies remained unchanged. In particular, 6 months after treatment the CEQ revealed that the patient continued to expect cocaine to improve his cognitive abilities. This suggests that expectancies are "sticky"; they are not necessarily changed quickly or easily. A comprehensive treatment approach beyond mere education is needed in order to effect a lasting change in expectancies.

Although Barry's is a relatively mild case of cocaine addiction treated in its early stages, it illustrates the use of cocaine-related expectancies in the rigorous assessment, formulation, and implementation of a social learning–based relapse prevention model of therapeutic intervention.

CONCLUSION

Social learning theory was presented as a model for understanding cognitive factors in cocaine abuse, in general, and expectancies, in particular. Cognitive expectations involved in cocaine abuse were explored in relation to recent research findings and were considered in the context of other cognitive variables within the social learning framework. It was argued that expectations of cocaine use are central to cognitive models of substance abuse. Additionally, a systematic and empirical way of assessing cocaine-related expectancies, namely, the CEQ (Jaffe et al., 1989; Jaffe & Kilbey, 1992) was examined. Instruments such as this one make it possible to assess and use beliefs about cocaine in the prevention and treatment of cocaine abuse. Finally, expectancies were considered in the context of a relapse prevention model of treatment (Marlatt & Gordon, 1985), and a case example was presented. Consideration of social learning theory and a relapse prevention model of treatment suggest that cognitive variables such as expectancies are variables of central importance for both the prevention and treatment of cocaine abuse. It is important for comprehensive intervention efforts to assess and address cocaine-related expectations directly. It is hoped that both theorists and practitioners will be able to use the expectancy construct with greater understanding and ease.

REFERENCES

Abrams, D. B., & Niaura, R. S. (1987). Social learning theory. In H. T. Blane & K. E. Leonard (Eds.), *Psychological theories of drinking and alcoholism* (pp. 181–220). New York: Guilford Press.

Abrams, D. B., & Wilson, G. T. (1979). Effects of alcohol on social anxiety in women: Cognitive versus physiological processes. *Journal of Abnormal Psychology, 88,* 161–173.

Abrams, D. B., & Wilson, G. T. (1983). Alcohol, sexual arousal, and self-control. *Journal of Personality and Social Psychology, 45,* 188–198.

alcoholics: An experimental analogue. *Journal of Abnormal Psychology, 81,* 233–241.

Bandura, A. (1977a). Self-efficacy: Toward a unifying theory of behavioral change. *Psychological Review, 84,* 191–215.

Bandura, A. (1977b). *Social learning theory.* Englewood Cliffs, NJ: Prentice Hall.

Bandura, A. (1982). Self-efficacy mechanism in human agency. *American Psychologist, 37,* 122–147.

Bandura, A. (1985). *Social foundations of thought and action.* Englewood Cliffs, NJ: Prentice Hall.

Briddell, D. W., & Wilson, G. T. (1976). Effects and expectancy set on male sexual arousal. *Journal of Abnormal Psychology, 85,* 225–234.

Brody, S. L. (1990). Violence associated with acute cocaine use in patients admitted to a medical emergency department. *National Institute on Drug Abuse Research Monographs, 103,* 44–59.

Brown, S. A. (1985a). Expectancies versus background in the prediction of college drinking patterns. *Journal of Consulting and Clinical Psychology, 53,* 123–130.

Brown, S. A. (1985b). Reinforcement expectancies and alcoholism treatment outcome after a one year follow up. *Journal of Studies on Alcohol, 46,* 304–308.

Brown, S. A., Goldman, M. S., Inn, A., & Anderson, L. (1980). Expectations of reinforcement from alcohol: Their domain and relation to drinking patterns. *Journal of Consulting and Clinical Psychology, 48,* 419–426.

Chitwood, D. D. (1985). Patterns and consequences of cocaine use. *National Institute on Drug Abuse Research Monographs, 61,* 111–129.

Christiansen, B. A., & Goldman, M. S. (1983). Alcohol related expectancies versus demographic/background variables in the prediction of adolescent drinking. *Journal of Consulting and Clinical Psychology, 51,* 249–257.

Christiansen, B. A., Smith, G. T., Roehling, P. V., & Goldman, M. S. (1989). Using alcohol expectancies to predict adolescent drinking behavior after one year. *Journal of Consulting and Clinical Psychology, 57,* 93–99.

Dembo, R., Williams, L., Wothke, W., Schmeidler, J., Getreu, A., Berry, E., Wish, E. D., & Christensen, C. (1990). The relationship between cocaine use, drug sales, and other delinquency among a cohort of high-risk youths over time. *National Institute on Drug Abuse Research Monographs, 103,* 112–135.

Emley, G. S., & Hutchinson, R. R. (1983). Unique influences of ten drugs upon post-shock biting attack and pre-shock manual responding. *Pharmacology, Biochemistry and Behavior, 19*(1), 5–12.

Engle, K. B., & Williams, T. K. (1972). Effect of an ounce of vodka on alcoholics' desire for alcohol. *Quarterly Journal of Studies on Alcohol, 33,* 1099–1115.

Fischman, M. W. (1978). Cocaine and amphetamine effects on repeated acquisition in humans. *Federal Proceedings, 37,* 618.

Fischman, M. W. (1984). The behavioral pharmacology of cocaine in humans. *National Institute on Drug Abuse Research Monographs, 50,* vii–viii.

Fischman, M. W., & Schuster, C. R. (1980). Cocaine effects in sleep-deprived humans. *Psychopharmacology, 72,* 1–8.

Gawin, F. H., & Kleber, H. D. (1986). Abstinence symptomatology and psychiatric diagnosis in cocaine abusers. *Archives of General Psychiatry, 43,* 107–113.

Gay, G. R. (1981). You've come a long way baby! Coke time for the new American lady of the eighties. *Journal of Psychoactive Drugs, 13,* 287–318.

Gold, M. S., Dackis, C. A., Pottash, A. L. C., Extein, I., & Washton, A. (1986). Cocaine update: From bench to bedside. *Advances in Alcohol and Substance Abuse, 5,* 35–60.

Goldman, M. S., Brown, S. A., & Christiansen, B. A. (1987). Expectancy theory: Thinking about drinking. In H. T. Blane & K. E. Leonard, *Psychological theories of drinking and alcoholism* (pp. 181–220). New York: Guilford Press.

Grinspoon, L., & Bakalar, J. D. (1977). Cocaine. In R. Dupont, A. Goldstein, & J. O'Donnel (Eds.), *Handbook on drug abuse* (National Institute on Drug Abuse Research Monograph). Washington, DC: U. S. Government Printing Office.

Hadfield, M. G. (1982). Cocaine: Peak time of action on isolation-induced fighting. *Neuropharmacology, 21*(7), 711–713.

Hadfield, M. G., Nugent, E. A., & Mott, D. E. (1982). Cocaine increases isolation-induced fighting in mice. *Pharmacology, Biochemistry and Behavior, 16*(2), 359–360.

Inciardi, J. A. (1990). The crack–violence connection within a population of hard-core adolescent offenders. *National Institute on Drug Abuse Research Monographs, 103,* 92–111.

Jaffe, A. J., & Kilbey, M. M. (1990). The Cocaine Expectancy Questionnaire (CEQ). *National Institute on Drug Abuse Research Monographs, 95,* 456–457.

Jaffe, A. J., & Kilbey, M. M. (1992). The Cocaine Expectancy Questionnaire (CEQ): Its construction and predictive utility. Manuscript submitted for publication.

Jaffe, A. J., & Kilbey, M. M., & Rosenbaum, G. R. (1989). Cocaine related expectancies: Their domain and implications for treatment. *Pharmacology, Biochemistry, and Behavior, 32*(4), 1094.

Jaffe, A. J., & Lohse, C. M. (1991). Expectations regarding cocaine use: Implications for prevention and treatment. *Addiction and Recovery, 11,* 9–12.

Jaffe, A. J., Kilbey, M. M., & Rosenbaum, G. R. (1990). Predictive power of the Cocaine Expectancy Questionnaire (CEQ). *Pharmacology, Biochemistry and Behavior, 36,* 435.

Lang, A. R., Goeckner, D. J., Adesso, V. T., & Marlatt, G. A. (1975). The effects of alcohol on aggression in male social drinkers. *Journal of Abnormal Psychology, 84,* 508–518.

Lansky, D., & Wilson, G. T. (1981). Alcohol, expectations, and sexual arousal in males: An information processing analysis. *Journal of Abnormal Psychology, 90,* 35–45.

Leigh, B. (1987). Beliefs about the effects of alcohol on self and others. *Journal of Studies on Alcohol, 48,* 467–475.

Leigh, B. C. (1989). In search of the seven dwarves: Issues of measurement and meaning in alcohol expectancy research. *Psychological Bulletin, 105,* 361–373.

Levy, S. J., & Pierce, J. P. (1989). Predicting intention to use cocaine in teenagers in Sydney, Australia. *Addictive Behaviors, 14,* 105–111.

Ludwig, A. M., & Wikler, A. (1974). "Craving" and relapse to drink. *Quarterly Journal of Studies on Alcohol, 35,* 108–130.

Marlatt, G. A., & Gordon, J. R. (Eds.). (1985). *Relapse prevention: Maintenance strategies in the treatment of addictive behaviors.* New York: Guilford Press.

Marlatt, G. A., Demming, B., & Reid, J. B. (1973). Loss of control in

McConnel, H. (Ed.). (1985, February). Cocaine new epidemic, says U. S. researchers. *The Journal,* 16–17.

Merry, J. (1966). The "loss of control" myth. *Lancet, i,* 1257–1258.

O'Donnel, J. M., & Miczek, K. A. (1980). No tolerance to antiaggressive effect of d-amphetamine in mice. *Psychopharmacology* [Berlin], *68*(2), 191–6.

O'Malley, P. M., Johnston, L. D., & Bachman, J. G. (1985). Cocaine use among

American adolescents and young adults. *National Institute on Drug Abuse Research Monographs, 61,* 50–75.

Pihl, R. O., Smith, M., & Farrell, B. (1984). Alcohol and aggression in men: A comparison of brewed and distilled beverages. *Journal of Studies on Alcohol, 45,* 278–282.

Polivy, J., Schueneman, A. L., & Carlson, K. (1976). Alcohol and tension reduction: Cognitive and physiological effects. *Journal of Abnormal Psychology, 85,* 595–606.

Post, R. M. (1975). Cocaine psychosis: A continuum model. *American Journal of Psychiatry, 133,* 3.

Poulos, C. X., Hinson, R. E., & Siegel, S. (1981). The role of Pavlovian processes in drug tolerance and dependence: Implications for treatment. *Addictive Behaviors, 6,* 205–211.

Resnick, R. B., & Resnick, E. B. (1984). Cocaine abuse and its treatment. *Psychiatric Clinics of North America, 7*(4), 713–728.

Resnick, R. B., Kestenbaum, R. S., & Schwartz, L. K. (1980). Acute systemic effects for cocaine in man: A controlled study by intranasal and intravenous routes. In F. R. Jeri (Ed.), *Cocaine 1980* (pp. 17–20). Lima, Peru: Pacific Press.

Rosecan, J. J., Spitz, H. I., & Gross, B. (1987). Contemporary issues in the treatment of cocaine abuse. In H. I. Spitz & J. J. Rosecan (Eds.), *Cocaine abuse: New directions in treatment and research* (pp. 299–323). New York: Brunner/Mazel.

Satel, S. L., Southwick, S. M., & Gawin, F. H. (1991). Clinical features of cocaine-induced paranoia. *American Journal of Psychiatry, 148*(4), 495–498.

Seecof, R., & Tennant, F. S., Jr. (1986). Subjective perceptions to the intravenous "rush" of heroin and cocaine in opioid addicts. *American Journal of Drug and Alcohol Abuse, 12*(1&2), 79–87.

Sherer, M. A., Kumor, K. M., Cone, E. J., & Jaffe, J. H. (1988). Suspiciousness induced by four-hour intravenous infusions of cocaine. *Archives of General Psychiatry, 45*(7), 673–677.

Shipley, T. E. (1987). Opponent process theory. In H. T. Blane & K. E. Leonard (Eds.), *Psychological theories of drinking and alcoholism* (pp. 346–387). New York: Guilford Press.

Siegel, R. K. (1980). Long term effects of recreational cocaine use: A four year study. In F. R. Jeri (Ed.), *Cocaine 1980* (pp. 11–16). Lima, Peru: Pacific Press.

Smith, G. T., Roehling, P. V., Christiansen, B. A., & Goldman, M. S. (1988). *Alcohol expectancies versus demographics to predict adolescent drinking longitudinally.* Paper presented at the American Psychological Association Convention, Washington, DC.

Southwick, L. L., Steele, C. M., Marlatt, G. A., & Lindell, M. (1981). Alcohol-related expectancies: Defined by phase of intoxication and drinking experience. *Journal of Consulting and Clinical Psychology, 49,* 713–721.

Spotts, G. V., & Shontz, F. Z. (1984). Drug induces ego issues: 1. Cocaine:

Phenomenology and implications. *International Journal of the Addictions, 19(2),* 119–151.

Stockwell, T. R., Hodgson, R. J., Rankin, H. J., & Taylor, C. (1982). Alcohol dependence, beliefs and the priming effect. *Behavior Research and Therapy, 20,* 513–522.

Wallace, B. C. (1989). Psychological and environmental determinants of relapse in crack cocaine smokers. *Journal of Substance Abuse Treatment, 6,* 95–106.

Wilson, G. T. (1987). Cognitive studies in alcoholism. *Journal of Consulting and Clinical Psychology, 55(3),* 325–331.

Wilson, G. T., & Lawson, D. M. (1976). Expectancies, alcohol, and sexual arousal in male social drinkers. *Journal of Abnormal Psychology, 85,* 587–594.

Wilson, G. T., Lawson, D. M., & Abrams, D. E. (1978). Effects of alcohol on sexual arousal in male alcoholics. *Journal of Abnormal Psychology, 87,* 609–616.Khantzian, E. J., & Khantzian, N. J. (1984). Is there a psychological predisposition? *Psychiatric Annals, 14,* 753–759.

CHAPTER EIGHT

Clinical Neurobiology of Cocaine Administration and Abstinence

Jed Black, MD
Christopher J. McDougle, MD
Lawrence H. Price, MD

EMOTIONAL AND BEHAVIORAL manifestations of cocaine's neurobiological effects in humans have long been apparent. Centuries before cocaine was isolated from the coca plant (*Erythroxylon coca*) in the mid-1800s, natives in certain regions of South America chewed the dried coca leaves to achieve desired subjective effects on mood and energy. Even in this oral form, which is less addictive than present-day routes of administration (i.e., intranasal, intravenous, smoke inhalation), cocaine's powerful reinforcing effects on human behavior were evident. The Spaniards discovered that they could induce South American Incan slaves to work more diligently by allowing them to chew coca leaves, which sometimes served as payment for their labor.

Modern-day experience in both animals and humans clarifies the degree to which cocaine is able to effect sustained self-administration. Animals allowed unlimited access to intravenous cocaine will self-administer large amounts of the drug, often resulting in death within days to a few weeks. Humans have been known to rapidly deplete all personal property, including large fortunes, for the rewarding effects of cocaine. Many individuals will continue this repeated use despite knowledge of the risk of death that may accompany the purchase or use of cocaine.

Despite the lack of a prominent physical withdrawal syndrome, cocaine administration and abstinence clearly cause profound changes in brain function. It is this ability to alter central nervous system (CNS) activity, rather than some "character flaw" in the user, that underlies cocaine's tremendous abuse potential. A better understanding of cocaine's mechanism of action in the brain is needed to develop effective treatments for cocaine addiction.

Over the past 30 years, there has been a tremendous amount of preclinical work in animals investigating cocaine's CNS effects. Clinical studies in humans are much less abundant, in part because such studies are so readily confounded by a multitude of factors that are not easily controlled. Innate individual differences, variability in route and intensity of cocaine administration, and duration of abstinence from cocaine must be considered. In addition, other comorbid substance abuse, psychiatric disorders, or medical illnesses are potentially complicating variables. Despite these obstacles, substantial preliminary work has been accomplished in the areas of neurochemistry, neuroendocrinology, and brain metabolism.

The integration of animal studies with research in humans is essential in clarifying the relationship between clinical effects and underlying neurobiological mechanisms. However, tremendous differences exist between drug administration paradigms used in animal studies and human abuse patterns. Long-term (chronic) cocaine administration in animals is generally defined as 3–30 days, and occasionally up to 3 months, of daily (single or multiple) cocaine injections. Human abuse occasionally consists of daily cocaine use but is more commonly characterized by frequent bingeing interspersed with brief periods of abstinence. Most clinical studies select subjects who have abused cocaine consistently for at least 3–6 months.

Studies in which cocaine is administered either alone or in conjunction with other agents provide information on cocaine's acute effects. Studies performed during abstinence from cocaine help to determine cocaine's long-term effects and the brain's compensatory responses. Clinical studies of cocaine administration and abstinence have frequently assessed neurochemical and neuroendocrine function simultaneously. Also, brain imaging investigations have studied regional metabolism, blood flow, and neuroreceptor ligand distribution. Specific findings from such studies will be considered in respective sections of this chapter that review the neurochemistry, neuroendocrinology, and brain imaging of cocaine administration and abstinence.

NEUROCHEMISTRY

Cocaine potently inhibits presynaptic reuptake of a variety of neurotransmitters in the CNS. Neuronal reuptake of secreted neurotransmitter is a primary means of neurotransmitter removal from the synaptic cleft, serving as a mechanism of neuronal energy and substrate conservation. Reuptake blockade of neurotransmitter substances, including the monoamines dopamine (DA), norepinephrine (NE), and serotonin (5-HT), is thought to account for the major portion of cocaine's effects in the CNS.

Dopamine

Extensive research has been conducted on cocaine-induced alterations of CNS DA systems. The ability to block DA reuptake in certain CNS regions has been found to be important in animal studies of self-administration, and this mechanism may underlie the abuse potential of several substances in humans.

DA-containing neurons are concentrated in localized brain regions. The three DA systems most thoroughly studied with respect to cocaine are the nigrostriatal, tuberoinfundibular, and ventral tegmental–cortical/limbic (frequently termed mesocortical and mesolimbic) systems. In general, DA is synthesized in these neurons from the amino acid tyrosine by the rate-limiting enzyme tyrosine hydroxylase (TH) to form DOPA (3,4,-dihydroxyphenylalanine), which is then decarboxylated to DA and concentrated in neuronal granules. These granules are directed toward specific sites where DA is released, during tonic and stimulated neuronal firing, to bind with presynaptic or postsynaptic receptors. Released DA subsequently undergoes catabolism in the synaptic cleft and/or reuptake into the nerve terminal to be stored in vesicles or metabolized. DA system regulation occurs at a variety of points in this process, from precursor uptake and synthesis to catabolism.

Preclinical studies provide evidence that cocaine's ability to inhibit nerve terminal DA transporters, which results in reduced reuptake, can alter DA function in a variety of ways. These alterations include changes in DA synthesis and turnover, modifications in DA storage and release, and changes in presynaptic and postsynaptic receptor sensitivity. Cocaine is also known to exert other direct and indirect neurochemical effects on the DA system, which are beyond the scope of this brief review.

Findings from studies in animals provide evidence for increased TH activity following cocaine administration, suggesting increased DA synthesis, thought to occur as a compensatory response to increased DA release and catabolism. More recent studies have found a dramatic reduction of TH in distinct regions of rat brain following cessation of chronic cocaine administration. Increases, decreases, or no changes in the levels of DA and the DA metabolites dihydroxyphenylacetic acid (DOPAC) and homovanillic acid (HVA) have been found in numerous preclinical studies. Most evidence, however, demonstrates increased levels of extracellular DA during acute cocaine administration in both naive and chronically exposed animals, and decreased extracellular DA and DA metabolite levels following chronic exposure in a variety of DA-related brain regions. These preclinical findings have prompted a variety of hypotheses regarding cocaine's net effect on CNS DA activity. Dackis and Gold (1985) have postulated a functional "dopamine depletion" following chronic exposure to cocaine, which is consistent with the observed decrease in extracellular DA as well as with some of the other clinical and preclinical findings reviewed in this chapter. Other clinical and preclinical findings, however, are not explained by functional DA depletion occurring as a result of chronic cocaine administration.

In clinical studies, measurement of plasma concentrations of the DA metabolite HVA (pHVA) has revealed no change during acute cocaine administration, decreases or no change during cocaine abstinence, and an increased or normal response to DA agonist challenges during abstinence. Many differences exist in the designs of these clinical studies. Some studies have examined pHVA changes within cocaine subjects over time, others have compared pHVA in cocaine users versus controls, and a few studies have done both.

Plasma HVA response to cocaine administration has been assessed in a study of 13 males with a history of intravenous cocaine use within the preceding 3 months (Sherer, 1988). Intravenous cocaine (or placebo) was infused with a high (60—80 mg) or low (40 mg) loading dose followed by a 4-hour cocaine (or placebo) infusion. No significant pHVA responses were seen during a 2-hour period following either high- or low-dose cocaine infusion compared to placebo infusion. The authors note, however, that baseline pHVA prior to cocaine infusion was positively correlated with observer ratings of the subjects' suspiciousness. Of note, Martin, Yeragani, Lodhi, and Galloway (1989) found a correlation between changes in pHVA and craving for cocaine during a 3-week period of abstinence, despite pHVA values that remained within the normal range. Satel et al. (1991), however, found no correlation between pHVA and craving.

Extein et al. (1987) found a significant decrease from baseline pHVA levels following 30 days of abstinence in five chronic cocaine users compared with five age- and sex-matched controls, but no significant difference after two days of abstinence. In contrast, over a 3-week period of abstinence, no significant change was seen in pHVA concentrations in a study of six hospitalized chronic cocaine users (Martin et al., 1989). In a similar study, Gill, Gillespie, Hollister, Davis, and Peabody (1991) found pHVA concentrations to be within the normal range in 21 hospitalized chronic cocaine users tested at admission (within 3 days of cocaine use) and following 10–20 days of abstinence. No significant differences were found in pHVA between early and late abstinence. Satel et al. (1991) also found no significant change in pHVA during 3 weeks of abstinence in 22 inpatient cocaine users.

Hollander et al. (1990) performed DA agonist challenges using single subcutaneous injections of apomorphine (a direct-acting DA agonist) in a group of seven chronic cocaine users who had been abstinent less than 4 days, and a separate group of three subjects who had been abstinent for 1 week or more. The pHVA response to apomorphine did not significantly differ between the two groups. A significant negative correlation, however, was found between estimated total cocaine use and individual baseline pHVA levels, such that greater total cocaine use was associated with lower baseline pHVA.

In another challenge study, McDougle et al. (1991) compared pHVA response to a single dose of Sinemet (L-dopa/carbidopa 250 mg/25 mg) versus placebo during early (1–2 days) and late (15–16 days) abstinence from cocaine in six hospitalized chronic cocaine users. This study is unique in that all cocaine users were withdrawing from fixed repeated doses of cocaine that had been administered under controlled inpatient conditions for three days prior to the start of the challenge testing. No significant differences were found in baseline pHVA levels between early and late abstinence within the group of cocaine abusers. An increased pHVA response to Sinemet, however, was found during early abstinence when compared to late abstinence within the cocaine subjects.

An autopsy study of a chronic cocaine abuser identified significantly decreased levels of DA in subdivisions of the caudate, putamen, and nucleus accumbens, but normal levels in the substantia nigra (Wilson et al., 1990). Dopamine D2 receptor binding density and affinity, however, were within the normal range in the caudate and putamen. This variability in regional DA concentration parallels preclinical findings of regionally decreased extracellular DA in animal brain following chronic cocaine administration. Preclinical studies have found increases, decreases, or no change in striatal DA D2 receptor density following chronic cocaine.

Taken together, these clinical studies suggest no consistent pattern of alteration in pHVA during cocaine administration or abstinence. Certainly, differences in subject population and study design contribute to this variability. In addition, the degree to which plasma metabolite levels reflect brain neurotransmitter system activity is debatable. Both peripheral and central sources contribute to plasma metabolite pools, which may fluctuate on a diurnal basis and in response to multiple physiological factors. A full knowledge of the origin and significance of the metabolites does not exist, and information regarding the processes they reflect is incomplete. Some studies in animals have found little correlation between pHVA and HVA concentrations in discrete brain regions.

Despite these limitations, there are data showing differences in plasma and cerebrospinal fluid (CSF) levels of HVA between healthy controls and patients with various neuropsychiatric disorders in which a disturbance in DA function has been hypothesized. The findings of McDougle et al. (1991), which are theoretically relevant and consistent with several preclinical findings, demonstrate that highly controlled clinical studies are essential to the adequate assessment of available hypotheses. Carefully controlled clinical studies assessing DA metabolite concentrations during cocaine administration and abstinence may significantly enhance our understanding of cocaine's effects on human DA function.

Norepinephrine

Although cocaine is known to block NE reuptake and affect NE neurotransmission, preclinical research investigating acute and chronic effects of cocaine on central NE function is less abundant than that for DA. Few consistent findings have emerged in this area, but the NE metabolite 3-methoxy-4-hydroxyphenethyleneglycol (MHPG) has been reported to be increased following acute cocaine administration and decreased following chronic administration.

Clinical studies of NE function suggest decreases or no change in MHPG following acute cocaine administration or during abstinence. Reuptake blockade of NE by cocaine might be expected to result in temporarily increased MHPG levels. Sherer (1988), however, found reduced plasma MHPG (pMHPG) 30–60 minutes following intravenous cocaine infusion in chronic cocaine users. These values normalized within 4 hours even when the cocaine infusion remained continuous throughout the 4-hour period.

Tennant (1985) reported that 24-hour urinary excretion of MHPG was decreased in eight outpatient cocaine users compared with that of eight race-, sex-, and age-matched controls during acute abstinence (1–2 days). Urinary MHPG levels returned to normal following 20 days of abstinence in the two subjects retested. In contrast, Extein et al. (1987) found significant decreases in pMHPG after 30 days of abstinence, but not following 2 days of abstinence. Significant and persistent decreases in pMHPG were apparent during 4 weeks of abstinence in a study in which cocaine users were compared with normal controls (Krajewski, 1987). Also, Demer et al. (1989) reported decreased pMHPG in five cocaine users assessed between 6 and 27 days of abstinence; levels remained low in the three subjects retested following an additional 1–4 weeks of abstinence. Historical control data from another laboratory were used in this study for comparison, however, and as many as three of these subjects may have been taking desipramine, an NE reuptake inhibitor, which is likely to have confounded results.

In contrast to these studies, Martin et al. (1989) found pMHPG levels to be consistently within the normal range during 3 weeks of abstinence (see Dopamine). Similarly, Gill et al. (1991) found pMHPG concentrations to remain within the normal range over 10–20 days of abstinence (see Dopamine). In a study that controlled for cocaine dose prior to the initiation of abstinence, McDougle et al. (1990) found pMHPG to be significantly higher in cocaine users during early abstinence compared with late abstinence (see Dopamine). However, Sinemet-provoked pMHPG responses did not differ significantly in cocaine users between early and late abstinence.

These clinical studies evidence no consistent findings of MHPG level alteration during cocaine administration or abstinence. As previously noted, one must be cautious in inferring central changes from peripheral measures. However, it is thought that as much as 30–60% of circulating pMHPG may be derived from central sources. Net changes in central MHPG, therefore, may be reflected by more subtle changes in peripheral levels.

Serotonin

Clinical studies of central 5-HT function following acute and chronic cocaine administration have not been reported. Reduced 5-HT uptake in platelets of abstinent cocaine users has been described (Dackis & Gold, 1989).

Preclinical data indicate that cocaine administration results in an acute reduction in the firing rate of dorsal raphe neurons, consistent with cocaine's ability to inhibit 5-HT reuptake. Acute decreases in 5-HT synthesis and reduced concentrations of the 5-HT metabolite 5-hydroxyindoleacetic acid (5-HIAA) following chronic cocaine administration have also been reported. Whereas cocaine self-administration has been found to be associated with DA reuptake blockade, cocaine's reward and mood-altering properties may also be modulated by 5-HT mechanisms. These preclinical studies indicate that intact 5-HT neuronal function may be critical to cocaine's potent abuse potential.

Additional research is needed to clarify the importance of cocaine's acute and chronic effects on 5-HT function.

NEUROENDOCRINOLOGY

As reviewed above, there is substantial evidence of cocaine's effects on central DA, NE, and 5-HT systems. These neurotransmitter systems are known to have regulatory effects on endocrine function. The function of the pituitary gland, in particular, has been shown to be quite sensitive to changes in specific neurotransmitter systems. Pituitary gland activity, therefore, has been characterized as a "window to the brain," as changes in pituitary and other endocrine gland function may be reflective of more central neuronal activity.

Investigators have explored various aspects of endocrine function in chronic cocaine users during acute and/or prolonged abstinence. Preliminary clinical work on prolactin (PRL), growth hormone (GH), thyroid-stimulating hormone (TSH), and hypothalamic–pituitary–adrenal (HPA) axis function in abstinent cocaine users has been performed. We are unaware of studies of human endocrine function during cocaine administration.

These neuroendocrine studies have been performed with the goal of indirectly assessing alterations in specific central neurotransmitter systems in cocaine abusers. However, research in animals has shown clearly that cocaine-induced alterations in neurotransmitter function may vary between discrete brain regions. For example, cocaine-induced changes in striatal DA function appear to be quite different from those occurring in the tuberoinfundibular DA (TIDA) system, with some suggestion that cocaine-induced toxic effects may occur to a lesser degree in TIDA than in striatal neurons. Whereas changes in TIDA system function would seem likely to be reflected by changes in PRL regulation, striatal DA system changes might have no such effect.

Clinical neuroendocrine research initially focused on differences in basal hormone secretion in abstinent chronic cocaine users versus normal controls. Recently, however, challenge paradigm studies have been performed in which DA agonists have been administered to both groups to determine possible differences in hormonal secretion following provocation of the DA system.

Prolactin

Some neuronal systems exert their effects on endocrine function indirectly by regulating hypothalamic function. DA from TIDA neurons, however, acts directly on pituitary lactotrophs to tonically inhibit PRL secretion. Preclinical and clinical studies show that DA antagonists produce increases in PRL secretion, whereas DA agonists or agents that enhance DA release inhibit PRL secretion.

The acute administration of cocaine to rats and rhesus monkeys generally decreases plasma PRL concentrations. This decrease has been found in cocaine-naive animals as well as in animals chronically exposed to cocaine. Baseline PRL levels have been shown to increase over time in animals receiving extended daily cocaine administration. Although no controlled studies of PRL response to acute cocaine administration have been performed in humans, these preclinical findings are generally consistent with the findings during abstinence in humans.

Cocaine-induced alteration of pituitary PRL secretion during abstinence has been evaluated in a number of clinical studies. Most of these studies demonstrate elevated serum PRL levels in abstinent cocaine users, particularly during early abstinence. However, decreased, as well as normal, PRL levels have also been reported.

Dackis and Gold (1985) found mean PRL levels to be significantly greater in 20 cocaine users, 1–3 days abstinent, compared with 20 age-matched controls. These increased PRL levels subsequently decreased, although they did not completely normalize, after 2 weeks of abstinence. Mendelson et al. (1988) reported PRL levels in the "hyperprolactinemic range" in 9 of 14 cocaine-addicted, hospitalized males, 1–3 days abstinent. After 4 weeks of abstinence, no significant change in the elevated mean PRL levels was noted.

To further characterize possible cocaine-induced changes in PRL secretion, these investigators subsequently analyzed serum PRL levels at 10-minute intervals over 6 hours in eight normal controls and in eight chronic cocaine users during acute abstinence (12–24 hours) (Mendelson, Mello, Teoh, Ellingboe, & Cochin, 1989). Four of eight cocaine users had PRL levels in the hyperprolactinemic range, and the cocaine group showed significantly higher mean PRL levels than the control group. Increased PRL levels were also found by these investigators in four of five cocaine addicts within the first week of abstinence during a controlled study of desipramine treatment for cocaine abuse (Teoh et al., 1990). Hyperprolactinemia persisted in two patients for more than 3 months of abstinence, normalized after three weeks in one patient, and decreased toward normal after 4 weeks in the fourth patient. The duration or degree of hyperprolactinemia was independent of desipramine or placebo treatment. Others have reported increased basal PRL (Dax & Pilotte, 1990) or a trend toward increased PRL (Lee, Bowers, Nash, & Meltzer, 1990; Hollander et al., 1990) in chronic cocaine users during acute abstinence.

These studies provide evidence for elevated PRL secretion in chronic cocaine users during acute abstinence, which may normalize or remain elevated during sustained abstinence. Other investigators, however, report decreased or normal PRL levels in abstinent cocaine users. Gawin and Kleber (1985) reported decreased mean PRL levels in a group of 15 male, outpatient chronic cocaine users, abstinent 4–10 days, compared with normal controls. These levels normalized after 4 weeks of abstinence in subjects retested. PRL levels in a group of six female users in this study were highly variable. A trend for decreased basal PRL secretion in abstinent cocaine users has been observed by McDougle et al. (1990) (see Dopamine). Normal PRL levels were found by Swartz, Breen, and Leone (1990) in 23 of 23 hospitalized cocaine users abstinent 2–43 weeks. Satel et al. (1991) reported no significant differences in baseline PRL values between cocaine users and controls (see Dopamine). A trend toward significant PRL elevation, however, was seen in this inpatient group following 19–21 days of abstinence. Gill et al (1991) found no significant differences in mean PRL levels between early and late abstinence in hospitalized cocaine users (see Dopamine). Mean PRL levels were within the normal range, but were consistently higher (during both early and late abstinence) than the mean normative PRL values for the laboratory used in this study.

Neurobiological challenge studies assessing PRL responses to DA agonist administration have been performed in abstinent cocaine users. Hollander et al. (1990) found significant decreases in PRL compared with baseline, following administration of apomorphine in two groups of chronic cocaine users (separated according to abstinence duration), but no significant differences were found between groups (see Dopamine). However, a trend for less robust peak PRL decreases following apomorphine was found in cocaine users compared with historical controls.

In a placebo-controlled study, Lee et al. (1990) randomly administered subcutaneous apomorphine or saline to 16 inpatient cocaine users, abstinent 4–39 days, and 8 normal controls. PRL responses to apomorphine were not significantly different in cocaine users compared with controls. Although no correlation between abstinence duration and baseline neuroendocrine measures was found in the cocaine group, the wide range of abstinence duration may have obscured possible existing differences in neuroendocrine responsivity between the cocaine users and controls.

Clinical and preclinical findings together provide evidence for cocaine-induced alterations in TIDA neuronal function. If cocaine acts to block DA reuptake at TIDA nerve terminals, this could result in an increase in pituitary concentrations of circulating DA and a consequent acute inhibition of lactotroph secretion, manifested as reduced plasma PRL levels. If increased DA concentrations persisted, lactotroph DA receptor sensitivity might be expected to decrease. If, however, chronic cocaine use resulted in a net functional decrease in circulating DA, PRL levels might increase and lactotroph DA receptor sensitivity could also increase in a compensatory fashion. Such DA receptor supersensitivity in lactotrophs could account for preclinical findings of enhanced PRL inhibition during challenges with cocaine or DA agonists following chronic cocaine exposure.

In addition to DA, 5-HT has been shown to exert regulatory effects on PRL secretion. Some preclinical data indicate that 5-HT systems play an indirect stimulatory role, either by direct inhibition of TIDA neurons or via other systems, but there is also evidence of direct effects of 5-HT on PRL. NE is also thought to be capable of indirectly stimulating PRL secretion, although this has not been well characterized. Cocaine's effects on these systems are likely to affect alterations in PRL secretion as well.

Growth Hormone

The effects of chronic cocaine use on growth hormone (GH) secretion has also been a focus of clinical and preclinical research. Growth hormone secretion appears to be under the regulatory control of multiple neurotransmitter systems. The precise role of each system in GH regulation remains somewhat controversial. Species-specific differences in neuronal GH regulation, as well as conflicting findings within species, have been reported. In general, most stimuli that act to cause GH release appear to act via central α-adrenergic receptors. Both epinephrine and NE appear to exert stimulatory effects on GH secretion. Serotonin is thought to exert mild GH-releasing effects. Data exist that suggest that DA agonists stimulate GH secretion, possibly in part through α-adrenergic receptor stimulation, and that DA antagonists block GH release. This monoamine-induced stimulation of GH is thought to occur indirectly, through regulation of hypothalamic tuberoinfundibular neurons. However, some data suggest that certain DA agonists may act to decrease GH release, possibly by direct action at the pituitary somatotrope level.

Clinical studies in abstinent cocaine users have found significant increases, no change, or trend decreases in GH levels. Gawin and Kleber (1985) found increased GH levels in the group of cocaine users previously discussed (see Prolactin). Dax and Pilotte (1990) reported an increased mean 24-hour GH concentrations in abstinent male cocaine users compared with cocaine-naive males. The group of hospitalized cocaine users studied by Satel et al. (1991) showed no significant differences in GH levels from controls during 19–21 days of abstinence, and no changes were seen in mean levels within the cocaine subjects over this period (see Prolactin). Similarly, no significant differences in GH were found by Lee et al. (1990) between abstinent cocaine users and controls. A trend for lower GH levels in cocaine subjects during both early and late abstinence was reported by Hollander et al. (1990) (see Dopamine). McDougle et al. (1990) also observed a similar trend for decreased GH levels in cocaine users during early abstinence, but not during late abstinence (see Dopamine).

Neurobiological challenge studies of GH responsivity to DA agonist administration have also produced varied results. Hollander et al. (1990) found no significant differences in GH responsivity to apomorphine between a group of cocaine users during early abstinence and a separate group during late abstinence. Comparison of both groups to historical controls revealed a trend for less robust peak GH increases in the cocaine users (see Dopamine). Lee et al. (1990) reported no significant differences between abstinent cocaine users and controls (see Prolactin). In contrast, McDougle et al. (1990) assessed baseline GH levels and responsivity to Sinemet and found a significantly increased GH response to Sinemet during early, compared with late, cocaine abstinence (see Dopamine). If GH responsivity to Sinemet represents an indirect measure of DA function, increased GH response during early abstinence would suggest enhanced DA responsivity, perhaps reflecting increased presynaptic DA release or postsynaptic DA receptor supersensitivity, which might normalize over prolonged abstinence.

Thyroid Axis

Clinical and preclinical studies of neuronal thyroid axis regulation provide evidence for regulatory control by DA, NE, and 5-HT. DA agonists have been shown to inhibit TSH secretion, whereas DA antagonists stimulate TSH secretion in humans. However, direct hypothalamic administration of DA in animals has been shown to produce thyrotropin-releasing hormone (TRH) release, which stimulates TSH secretion. NE input has been found to generally exert a stimulatory effect on TSH, although α-agonist and α-antagonist effects in humans are inconclusive. Studies of 5-HT agonist and antagonist effects on TSH release in both humans and animals are also inconclusive.

These differences in TSH neuroregulatory findings notwithstanding, two controlled clinical studies have been reported that found consistent significant differences in TSH responsivity to TRH administration between abstinent cocaine users and controls. Dackis and Gold

(1985) reported significant blunting of the TSH response to TRH infusion in 17 cocaine users tested within 5 days of abstinence compared with controls. Similar findings were reported by Giannini, Malone, Loiselle, and Price (1987), who found blunted TSH responses to TRH infusion in 9 of 10 cocaine users following at least 48 hours of abstinence. None of 10 controls in this study evidenced TSH blunting.

Baseline triiodothyronine (T3), thyroxin (T4), and TSH did not differ between the cocaine subjects and controls in either study. The authors of both studies cite evidence that supports a stimulatory effect of catecholamines on TRH, and suggest that repeated cocaine-induced catecholamine release might cause repeated episodes of TRH elevation, resulting in thyrotroph TRH receptor down-regulation.

Hypothalamic–Pituitary–Adrenal Axis

Preclinical work provides evidence for alterations in the HPA axis induced by cocaine. Neurotransmitter regulation of corticotropin-releasing factor (CRF), adrenocorticotropic hormone (ACTH), and cortisol is complex. Findings from both clinical and preclinical studies indicate that the effect of NE on HPA axis function can be either inhibitory or stimulatory, depending on the HPA axis level or receptor subtype studied. DA regulation of the HPA axis is less well understood. The 5-HT precursor 5-hydroxytryptophan and 5-HT agonists produce elevations in animal and human plasma cortisol levels and have been shown to promote ACTH release; serotonin antagonism has been shown to decrease cortisol release in some animals. Acute and chronic cocaine administration in animals has resulted in increased ACTH and corticosterone secretion. Following repeated cocaine injections over many days in rats, ACTH and corticosterone levels have been elevated or unchanged, depending on the study. Also, chronic cocaine administration in rats has resulted in adrenocortical hypertrophy.

Studies evaluating HPA axis function during abstinence in chronic cocaine users are limited and have not produced consistent findings. Forty-two percent of the cocaine users studied by Gawin and Kleber (1985) exhibited "abnormal dexamethasone suppression" (see Prolactin). Cortisol levels were found to be normal in chronic cocaine users during early abstinence (Mendelson et al., 1989). Mendelson et al. (1988) also found normal cortisol levels in chronic cocaine users during a 4-week period of abstinence (see Prolactin). In addition, ACTH levels have been reported to be normal in male cocaine users during abstinence (Dax & Pilotte, 1990). Normal cortisol and ACTH levels have prompted some authors to suggest that chronic cocaine use does not alter HPA axis function; however, animal studies would suggest otherwise. More definitive studies are needed to clarify cocaine's effects on HPA axis function.

NEUROIMAGING

Clinical investigations using indirect measures of cocaine-induced changes in CNS function have been reviewed in the first two sections of this chapter. Great strides have been made during the past decade in the development and refinement of brain imaging strategies that facilitate direct assessment of central biochemical processes. Brain imaging techniques currently used to explore human brain biochemical function include positron emission tomography (PET), single photon emission computed tomography (SPECT), and magnetic resonance spectroscopy (MRS). To date, no studies using MRS to assess brain function in cocaine users have been reported. PET and SPECT investigations conducted in cocaine users are reviewed in this section.

PET is an analytical neuroimaging technique that requires the integration of the positron tomograph, radioactively labeled compounds (tracers), and tracer kinetic mathematic models to provide in vivo measurements of the rates and anatomical distribution of focused biochemical reactions. In brief, labeled compounds include drugs and other biomolecules that contain a radioisotope substitution of a natural isotope (e.g., carbon, nitrogen, oxygen, hydrogen). Radioisotopes used in PET have short half-lives, ranging from 2 minutes to 2 hours, and decay by the emission of positrons that combine with electrons to produce two gamma rays 180 degrees apart. Labeled compounds reach the brain via injections into the vascular system. Gamma rays easily penetrate the head, allowing for detection by the positron tomograph. This is accomplished by a process known as coincidence detection, which utilizes geometric information produced by the two gamma rays travelling simultaneously in opposite directions.

SPECT differs from PET in that tracer compounds used in SPECT imaging emit single photons or gamma rays; hence, no two gamma rays bear any geometric relationship to each other. This difference in gamma ray production results in a generally poorer resolution and decreased sensitivity with SPECT compared to PET. Another technical difference is that radioisotopes or radionuclides of SPECT radiotracers have much longer half-lives, ranging from a few hours to many days.

PET has generally been employed in humans to assess regional glucose or oxygen metabolism, regional blood flow, and regional distribution of neuroreceptor ligands; SPECT's use has generally been in the assessment of the latter two. Evaluation of neuronal protein synthesis, neuronal second messenger function, and neurotransmitter storage, release, uptake, and degradation are among the many other potential applications for PET or SPECT in humans. Ultimately, neuroimaging techniques that characterize global and regional aspects of brain physiological or biochemical function could aid in the clinical assessment of normal and altered brain functioning, as well as in the detection of experimental, treatment-related, or time -related changes.

Cocaine Administration

To date, only one study has been reported using PET to examine the acute effects of euphorigenic doses of cocaine in humans (London et al., 1990). In that study, eight male chronic cocaine users, abstinent for 7–10 days, received intravenous cocaine (40 mg) and placebo (saline) in a crossover design. Using the tracer [^{18}F]fluorodeoxyglucose (FDG), PET was performed following both cocaine and saline administration in each subject. Comparison of cocaine versus placebo scan results revealed a reduction in global and regional cerebral glucose utilization following cocaine administration in most areas sampled. No brain regions showed increased glucose metabolism. Of all cortical and subcortical areas examined, only the cerebellum and pons revealed no reduction in glucose metabolism. The observed decrease in regional glucose metabolic rates was not thought to be a result of cocaine-induced sympathomimetic effects, in that rates were calculated using a model designed to be insensitive to ischemia.

These results might seem counterintuitive if one expected a stimulant drug, such as cocaine, to increase cerebral metabolic activity, in contrast to such CNS depressants as benzodiazepines, barbiturates, and opiates, all of which have been reported to lower cortical glucose metabolism in PET studies. Moreover, preclinical studies have generally shown acute cocaine administration to stimulate global and regional glucose metabolism, although discrepancies in findings between human and animal studies may be related to differences in species, stimulant doses, or assessment techniques. However, lending support to the findings of London et al. (1990) are PET studies performed in chronic cocaine users during acute abstinence, which have demonstrated increased metabolic activity (see Cocaine Abstinence, below).

A decrease in cerebral metabolic rates during cocaine administration is not inconsistent with a dopaminergic action. Administration of haloperidol, a DA D2 receptor antagonist, has been shown to increase cortical glucose metabolic rates in schizophrenics. DA itself has been shown to exert both excitatory and inhibitory effects on different populations of postsynaptic neurons. In theory, both excitatory and inhibitory effects of a given neurotransmitter could result in decreases in regional metabolic rates, depending on the function of the affected postsynaptic neuronal system.

Clearly, cocaine's effects on CNS NE and 5-HT systems must also be considered when discussing cerebral metabolic rates and blood flow. NE neurons originating in the locus coeruleus have diffuse projections to the cerebral cortex. 5-HT neurons from the dorsal raphe nuclei also project extensively to cortical regions. The interactions of cocaine with these two neuronal systems, however, has not yet been evaluated by PET or SPECT.

Cocaine Abstinence

Preclinical studies have found both generalized increases and decreases in brain metabolic activity following cessation of chronic cocaine administration. Global and regional decrements in basal cerebral glucose metabolism that normalized with DA agonist administration have also been reported.

PET studies have been performed to assess aspects of human CNS function in chronic cocaine users during abstinence from cocaine use. In general, these studies have been performed within 1–30 days of cocaine use cessation.

PET studies in cocaine abstinence have measured distribution of blood flow, rates of cerebral oxygen or glucose metabolism, and regional distribution of neuroreceptor ligands. Volkow, Millani, Gould, Adler, and Krajewski (1988) reported multiple areas of reduced [^{15}O]water uptake in a number of regions of the anterior cerebral cortex, particularly in the prefrontal and left anterior temporal regions. More than one region of reduced [^{15}O]water uptake, indicative of reduced cerebral blood flow, was seen in 9 of 20 cocaine users scanned within 72 hours of admission and in 6 of 12 cocaine users from the same group who were scanned 10 days later. These findings were not observed in 24 control subjects. Although absolute cerebral blood flow was not quantitated, increased uptake ratios of cerebellum to whole brain in these cocaine users may indicate that the entire cortex was hypoperfused. These authors noted a similar pattern of decreased glucose metabolism in the prefrontal cortex in four of six cocaine users (number of days abstinent not reported) with PET scanning using FDG.

In contrast, no significant decrease relative to normal controls was observed in left lateral prefrontal cortical glucose metabolism in "a small number" of nondepressed cocaine users who underwent FDG PET scanning following 2–5 days of abstinence (Baxter et al., 1988). Based on previous PET studies in depressed patients, which had revealed decreased glucose metabolism in the lateral prefrontal cortex, these investigators suggested that cocaine users showing decreased frontal cortical blood flow, indicative of reduced glucose metabolic rates, might be suffering from concurrent major depression.

The discrepant PET findings in cerebral blood flow and glucose metabolic rates in abstinent cocaine users are paralleled in three SPECT studies. One report, using [^{123}I]isopropyl iodoamphetamine, revealed focal defects in cerebral blood flow in 11 of 12 cocaine users studied from 12 hours to 1.5 years following last cocaine use (Tumeh, Nagel, English, Moore, & Holman, 1990). None of five controls evidenced deficits. Holman et al. (1991) reported similar SPECT findings using technetium-99m hexamethylpropylenamine oxime (HMPAO). Abnormal perfusion patterns were seen in 16 of 18 chronic cocaine users abstinent 1–16 days. No abnormalities were found in 15 normal controls. Focal or general defects were not found by computed tomography (Tumeh et al., 1990) or magnetic resonance imaging (Homan et al., 1991) in the majority of cocaine users with SPECT perfusion abnormalities. The perfusion abnormalities identified in these studies were thought to represent subtle cerebrovascular lesions secondary to cocaine use.

Another reported study of SPECT in cocaine users found no focal defects or regions of decreased cerebral blood flow in 10 cocaine users compared with normal controls. Subjects were scanned using HMPAO within 24 hours and after 3–4 weeks of abstinence (Pearsall, Seibyl, Hoffer, & Woods, 1990). Formal analysis of this data is ongoing.

It is important to note that, under resting conditions, regional cerebral blood flow has been shown to correlate closely with regional glucose or oxygen metabolism, both of which are measures of regional neuronal activity. Chronic cocaine use, however, might cause cerebrovascular lesions resulting in reduced regional cerebral blood flow. Such cerebrovascular lesions could reduce glucose metabolic rates in nearby or distant areas independent of direct cocaine effects on neuronal activity. Within-subject comparisons of regional defects in cerebral blood flow and of cerebral glucose metabolism before and during cocaine administration might clarify these discrepancies.

A more recent study (Volkow et al., 1991), using FDG PET in 10 chronic cocaine users abstinent from 12 hours to 1 week, found elevated regional glucose metabolic rates compared with those of normal control subjects and those of five cocaine users studied following 2–4 weeks of abstinence. Specifically, glucose metabolic rates were significantly higher globally, in the orbitofrontal cortex, and in the basal ganglia of cocaine subjects less than 1 week abstinent compared with cocaine subjects 2–4 weeks abstinent, whose metabolic rates, in turn, showed no differences from those of normal controls. In fact, regression analysis revealed a significant relationship between the number of days abstinent from cocaine and normalization of glucose metabolic rates in the orbitofrontal cortex and basal ganglia over the 4-week period. It is notable that all but three cocaine users reported mild to severe depressive symptoms at the time of the study. These 15 cocaine users did not evidence defects in cerebral blood flow, nor did they show the decreased frontal cortical glucose metabolic rates that have been previously found in depressed patients.

In addition to research on cerebral blood flow and glucose metabolic rates in cocaine users, radioligand distribution abnormalities have also been evaluated with PET. Volkow et al. (1990), using PET, reported reduced uptake of [^{18}F] N-methylspiroperidol (a ligand with high affinity for postsynaptic DA receptors) in the striatum of cocaine users abstinent from cocaine 2–7 days compared to those abstinent 4–5 weeks. Those abstinent four to five weeks showed no differences in uptake when compared with normal controls. The authors suggested that this diminished uptake could represent a reduction in postsynaptic DA receptor concentration or affinity due to chronic cocaine use.

Another group observed significantly reduced striatal to cerebellar ratios of ^{18}F-Dopa with PET in two chronic cocaine users abstinent 4 and 5 days, respectively, compared with controls (Baxter et al., 1988). These preliminary results suggest that chronic cocaine use might impair striatal neuronal utilization of L-Dopa.

Finally, labeled cocaine has been used with PET to study cerebral regional distribution when tracer doses are administered to cocaine-naive healthy volunteers and baboons (Fowler et al., 1989). These doses, which were much too low to produce cocaine-related subjective effects, were used to determine distribution when administered alone and following monoamine reuptake inhibitor pretreatment. The six normal volunteers studied showed highest [^{11}C]cocaine uptake in the corpus striatum, which paralleled findings in baboons. Pretreatment with the NE reuptake inhibitor desipramine did not affect labeled cocaine distribution in the two volunteers studied. In baboons, however, pretreatment with the DA reuptake inhibitor nomifensine or with unlabeled cocaine produced decreases in striatal, but not cerebellar, [^{11}C]cocaine concentration. These results suggest that cocaine binds to striatal DA reuptake sites, consistent with the findings of other animal studies discussed above. NE reuptake blockade with desipramine appeared not to have affected labeled cocaine binding.

In summary, the single PET study of brain metabolism during cocaine administration has shown reduced global and regional glucose metabolism in both cortical and subcortical structures. PET studies of basal cerebral glucose metabolism in abstinent chronic cocaine users have shown decreases or no change in prefrontal cortical metabolic rates, and increases in global, orbitofrontal, and basal ganglia metabolic rates that normalize with sustained abstinence.

PET and SPECT studies of cerebral blood flow in abstinent cocaine users have shown either regional reductions, focal deficits, or no changes in cortical blood flow.

PET studies of cerebral neuroreceptor ligand distribution in early-abstinent cocaine users have demonstrated reduced striatal postsynaptic DA receptor binding, which normalizes with sustained abstinence, and decreased L-Dopa utilization in striatal neurons. Also, PET findings showed highest uptake of labeled cocaine to be in the striatum of normal volunteers, with probable binding activity at striatal DA reuptake sites.

The possible confounding factors of clinical cocaine studies previously noted must be considered when interpreting clinical neuroimaging findings. Direct cerebrovascular change or damage due to cocaine use and alterations in neuronal function secondary to vascular abnormalities could also confound imaging studies. These limitations notwithstanding, neuroimaging will undoubtedly prove to be an invaluable tool in facilitating the characterization of cocaine's neurobiological effects in humans.

CONCLUSION

Despite the frequent inconsistencies of the findings reviewed in this chapter, carefully controlled studies in humans have revealed significant neurobiological effects of cocaine administration, with differential effects between acute and prolonged abstinence from cocaine use. These preliminary observations extend the large body of preclinical research demonstrating selective and profound effects on neuronal activity. These initial studies suggest that more rigorous evaluations of neurobiological function in chronic cocaine users during cocaine administration and at different times during abstinence are essential to elucidating the multiple effects of cocaine on the human brain. Knowledge so obtained has great potential for furthering the development of effective treatments for those suffering the debilitating effects of cocaine addiction.

REFERENCES

Baxter, L. R., Jr., Schwartz, J. M., Phelps. M. E., Mazziotta. J. C., Barrio, J., Rawson, R. A., Engel, J., Guze, B. H., Selin, C., & Sumida, R. (1988). Localization of neurochemical effects of cocaine and other stimulants in the human brain. *Journal of Clinical Psychiatry, 49*(Suppl. 2), 23–26.

Dackis, C. A., & Gold, M. S. (1985). New concepts in cocaine addiction: The dopamine depletion hypothesis. *Neuroscience and Biobehavioral Review, 9,* 469–477.

Dax, E. M., Pilotte, N. S. (1990, June). Growth hormone (GH) release is altered in men who abruptly cease long-term cocaine. Abstract at the Second International Congress of Neuroendocrinology, Bordeaux, France.

Demer, J. L., Volkow, N. D., Ulrich, I., Krajewski, K., Davis, C. M., & Porter, F. I. (1989). Eye movements in cocaine abusers. *Psychiatry Research, 29,* 123–136.

Extein, I., Potter, W. Z., Gold, M. S., Andre, P., Rafuls, W. A., & Gross, D. A. (1987). "Persistent neurochemical deficit in cocaine abuse." *APA New Research Abstracts,* No.61, p. 52.

Fowler, J. S., Volkow, N. D., Wolf, A. P., Dewey, S. L., Schlyer, R. R., Hitzemann, R., Logan, J., Bendriem, B., Gatley, J., & Christman, D. (1989). Mapping cocaine binding sites in human and baboon brain in vivo. *Synapse, 4,* 371–377.

Gawin, F. H., & Kleber, H. D. (1985). Neuroendocrine findings in chronic cocaine abusers: A preliminary report. *British Journal of Psychiatry, 147,* 569–573.

Giannini, A. J., Malone, D. A., Loiselle, R. H., Price, W. A. (1987). Blunting of TSH response to TRH in chronic cocaine and phencyclidine abusers. *Journal of Clinical Psychiatry, 48,* 25–26.

Gill, K., Gillespie, H. K., Hollister, L. E., Davis, C. M., & Peabody, C. A. (1991). Dopamine depletion hypothesis of cocaine dependence: A test. *Human Psychopharmacology, 6,* 25–29.

Holman, B. L., Carvalho, P. A., Mendelson, J., Teah, S. K., Nardin, R., Hallgring, E., Hebben, N., & Johnson, K. A. (1991). Brain perfusion is abnormal in cocaine-dependent polydrug users: A study using technetium-99m-HMPAO and ASPECT. *Journal of Nuclear Medicine, 32,* 1206–1210.

Hollander, E., Nunes, E., DeCaria, C. M., Quitkin, F. M., Cooper, T., Wager, S., & Klein, D. F. (1990). Dopaminergic sensitivity and cocaine abuse: Response to apomorphine. *Psychiatry Research, 33,* 161–169

Krajewski, K. J. (1987). Cocaine abstinence symptomatology and MHPG. *Proceedings of the 14th Annual Meeting of the American Psychiatric Association,* 236

Lee, M. A., Bowers, M. M., Nash, J. F., & Meltzer, H. Y. (1990). Neuroendocrine measures of dopaminergic function in chronic cocaine users. *Psychiatry Research, 33,* 151–159.

London, E. D., Cascella, N. G., Wong, D. F., Phillips, R. L., Dannals, R. F., Links, J. M., Herning, R., Grayson, R., Jaffe, J. H., & Wagner, H. N. (1990) Cocaine-induced reduction of glucose utilization in human brain. *Archives of General Psychiatry, 47,* 567–574.

Martin, S. D., Yeragani, V. K., Lodhi, R., & Galloway, M. P. (1989). Clinical ratings and plasma HVA during cocaine abstinence. *Biological Psychiatry, 26,* 356–362

McDougle, C. J., Price, L. H., Palumbo, J. M., Kosten, T. R., Heninger, G. R., & Kleber, H. D. (1990). Clinical neurobiology of cocaine withdrawal. *APA New Research Abstracts, No. 551*, p. 258

Mendelson, J. H., Mello, N. K., Teoh, S. K., Ellingboe, J., & Cochin, J. (1989). Cocaine effects on pulsatile secretion of anterior pituitary, gonadal, and adrenal hormones. *Journal of Clinical Endocrinology and Metabolism, 69,* 1256–1260.

Mendelson, J. H., Teoh, S. K., Lange, U., Mello, N. K., Weiss, R., Skupny, A., & Ellingboe, J. (1988). Anterior pituitary, adrenal, and gonadal hormones during cocaine withdrawal. *American Journal of Psychiatry, 145,* 1094–1098.

Pearsall, H. R., Seibyl, J. P., Hoffer, P. B., & Woods, S. W. (1990). SPECT in psychiatry: 2. *Yale Psychiatric Quarterly, 13*(3&4), 2–12.

Satel, S. L., Price, L. H., Palumbo, J. M., McDougle, C. J., Krystal, J. H., Gawin, F., Charney, D. S., Heninger, G. R., & Kleber, H. D. (1991). The clinical phenomenology and neurobiology of cocaine abstinence: A prospective inpatient study. *American Journal of Psychiatry, 148,* 1712–1716.

Sherer, M. A. (1988). Intravenous cocaine: Psychiatric effects, biological mechanisms. *Biological Psychiatry, 24,* 865–885.

Swartz, C. M., Breen, K., & Leone, F. (1990). Prolactin levels during extended cocaine abstinence. *American Journal of Psychiatry, 147,* 777–779.

Tennant, F. S. (1985). Effect of cocaine dependence on plasma phenylalanine and tyrosine levels and on urinary MHPG excretion. *American Journal of Psychiatry, 142,* 1200–1201.

Teoh, S. K., Mendelson, J. H., Mello, N. K., Weiss, R., McElroy, S., McAfee, B. (1990). Hyperprolactinemia and risk for relapse of cocaine abuse. *Biological Psychiatry 28,* 824–828.

Tumeh, S. S., Nagel, J. S., English, R. J., Moore, M., & Holman, B. L. (1990). Cerebral abnormalities in cocaine abusers: Demonstration by SPECT perfusion brain scintigraphy. *Radiology, 176,* 821–824

Volkow, N. D., Fowler, J. S., Wolf, A. P., Hitzemann, R., Dewey, S., Bendriem, B., Alpert, R., & Hoff, A. (1991). Changes in brain glucose metabolism in cocaine dependence and withdrawal. *American Journal of Psychiatry, 148,* 621–626.

Volkow, N. D., Fowler, J. S., Wolf, A. P., Schlyer, D., Shine, C. Y., Alpert, R., Dewey, S. L., Logan, J., Bendriem, B., Christman, D., Hitzemann, R., & Henn, F. (1990). Effects of chronic cocaine abuse on postsynaptic dopamine receptors. *American Journal of Psychiatry, 147,* 719–724

Volkow, N. D., Mullani, N., Gould, L., Adler, S., & Krajewski, K. (1988). Cerebral blood flow in chronic cocaine users: A study with positron emission tomography. *British Journal of Psychiatry, 152,* 641–648.

Wilson, J. M., Deck, J., Shannok, K., Chang, L. J., DiStefano, L. M., & Kish, S. J. (1990). Markedly reduced striatal dopamine levels in brain of a chronic cocaine abuser. *Society for Neuroscience Abstracts 16,* No. 110.7, p. 252.

CHAPTER NINE

"Craving For and Fear of Cocaine": A Phenomenologic Update on Cocaine Craving and Paranoia

Sally Satel, MD

FREUD STATED that cocaine claimed "no victims of its own." He believed the drug was dangerous only when used to treat withdrawal from morphine and warned that morphine addicts, "already succumbed to the demon," would eventually come to "misuse (cocaine) in the same manner" (cited in Bernfeld, 1953). In his 1887 paper, "Craving For and Fear of Cocaine," Freud revised his position somewhat to warn against the abuse potential of cocaine if it were injected. Yet, later Freud insisted that addiction or abuse of cocaine was never found as a phenomenon in itself, but, rather only in individuals once addicted to morphine. He wrote that, in morphine addicts, cocaine could cause rapid physical and mental deterioration, paranoia and hallucinations when administered by any route.

Freud's first use of cocaine, one twentieth of a gram, promoted a cheerfulness that rescued him, temporarily, from one of his frequent episodes of despair. He continued to use it in "very small doses regularly against depression . . . with the most brilliant success" (quoted in Jones, 1953; cited in Byck, 1974, p. 7). Freud advocated cocaine's value as an antidepressant; he wrote of cocaine-induced "exhilaration and lasting euphoria, . . . in no way differs from the normal euphoria of a healthy person . . . you perceive an increase in self control and possess more vitality and capacity for work . . . you are simply normal and it is soon hard to believe that you are under the influence of any drug" (quoted in Jones, 1953; cited in Byck, 1974, p. 9). Indeed, even his scientific observations appeared colored by personal experience when he wrote that animals administered cocaine displayed "the most gorgeous excitement" (quoted in Jones, 1953; cited in Byck, 1974, p. 8)

The Viennese psychiatric and medical communities judged the situation differently, however. They observed that cocaine could produce uncontrolled craving for the drug, and even psychosis. In a campaign led by Erlenmeyer, cocaine was virtually eliminated from the pharmacopoeia, and Freud was darkly credited as having added to alcohol and morphine "the third scourge of humanity, cocaine" (Bernfeld, 1953).

Freud's generally benign perspective on cocaine stands in sharp contrast to the ways in which addicts describe the experience of cocaine and the devastating consequences of its abuse. It is ironic that he correctly described much of the phenomenology of cocaine intoxication but was profoundly wrong in his estimation of its abuse potential.

Playing somewhat on the title of Freud's 1887 paper, this chapter focuses on some of the phenomenologic issues surrounding craving for cocaine and cocaine-induced paranoia: a fear-like state experienced and dreaded by many high-intensity users (i.e.,> 5 g per week). These special topics have been chosen because they have been the focus of recent, interesting work. For example: What is the nature of cocaine craving and withdrawal? How does craving for cocaine compare with craving for other substances? What underlies the differential individual vulnerabilities to cocaine-induced suspiciousness/paranoia?

Craving for cocaine and its adverse effect of paranoia play major roles in the experience of severe cocaine addiction. An addict's "willingness" to sustain terrifying paranoia and dangerous medical complications arising from use is a compelling index of the drug's reinforcing power. I believe that an appreciation of the subjective effects associated with cocaine is essential to understanding cocaine dependence.

CRAVING

Disposition to use a drug is a complicated psychological state. Classically, it has been called *craving* and is conceptualized as having both "physiologic[al]" and "symbolic" dimensions (Kozlowki & Wilkinson, 1987). *Physiologic craving,* also called *narcotic hunger* (Ludwig, Wikler, & Stark, 1974) occurs in the context of withdrawal, and is a central aspect of models of cue-reactivity and relapse (Niaura et al., 1988). In Siegel's (1975) conditioned compensatory response model, contextual cues reliably associated with drug ingestion trigger a syndrome opposite to the direction of intoxication symptoms (withdrawal). This theoretical model is based on homeostatic concepts of internal regulation. The conditioned withdrawal model, put forth by Wikler (1973), proposes that the contiguity between stable environmental reminders of drug use and periodic episodes of withdrawal permits the latter to become a conditioned response dependent on the presence of salient reminders.

The term *negative reinforcement* has been used to describe a drug that terminates distress or dysphoria and returns the individual to a normal mood state; *positive reinforcement* refers to the action of a stimulus that produces pleasure or euphoria in an individual already experiencing a normal mood state (Wise, 1988). In physiological craving (withdrawal-linked desire for drug), readministration of the drug would have a negative reinforcing effect. In psychic craving, however, the drug that is craved may potentially serve either a negative or positive reinforcing function. The conditioned appetitive motivational model (Stewart, deWit, & Eikelboom, 1984) describes the seeking of drugs for pleasure, a disposition that can be initiated by external cues or by subjective states. This section outlines some of the clinically relevant differences between cocaine and other drugs with respect to these dimensions.

Many drugs that are compulsively self-administered by humans produce a physiological withdrawal syndrome when use is discontinued. This withdrawal syndrome is usually linked to desire for drug: alcoholics undergoing sweats and tremors seek alcohol, opiate users with cramps and diarrhea want heroin. Readministration of these drugs, or their pharmacologic equivalent, reduces the withdrawal symptoms. In this context, the drug is considered a negative reinforcer.

Abrupt discontinuation of cocaine, however, is not marked by physiological symptoms of autonomic arousal. Rather it has been viewed as a discrete neurobiological state expressed as disturbances of mood and psychic arousal (Ellinwood & Petrie, 1977; Dackis & Gold 1985; Gawin & Kleber, 1986; Brower & Paredes, 1987; Gawin & Ellinwood, 1990). First conceptualized as cocaine withdrawal by Gawin and Kleber (1986), a triphasic model of postbinge symptoms was named the "cocaine abstinence syndrome."

According to the model, the first phase ("crash," lasting 9 hours to 4 days) is marked by craving, irritability and agitation (early crash), yearning for sleep and exhaustion (middle), and hypersomnolence (late). As depression and desire for sleep increase, craving subsides. The crash is followed by a protracted period of milder withdrawal (lasting 1–10 weeks) during which time craving reemerges and anhedonia prevails. This is succeeded finally by an indefinite period of extinction characterized by no symptoms and episodic craving. These changes were believed to reflect disturbances in central dopamine function secondary to long-term cocaine use. However, the crash can occur in first-time stimulant users if the first-use episode is of sufficient duration and dosage (Kleber & Gawin, 1987).

Gawin, Khalsa, and Anglin (1991) collected data from a population of 250 cocaine-dependent males in a 21-day inpatient treatment program. The subjects were asked to report the presence or absence of 30 subjective symptoms presumably reflecting withdrawal, as they had stopped using cocaine within 1 week of data collection. Using factor analysis, four factors (i.e., sets of symptoms) were identified: dysphoria set, nervousness–activation set, craving set, and the physical problems set. Each set consisted of five or six symptoms. These symptom sets, according to the authors, represented a relatively early phase of cocaine withdrawal. However, in the absence of a comparison with other recently abstinent groups, it is possible that this myriad of symptoms actually reflected generalized distress following cessation of drug use rather than symptoms specifically produced by cocaine abstinence.

There are several interesting differences between the phenomenology of withdrawal from opiates and alcohol compared with that of cocaine withdrawal. For example, individuals undergoing opiate or alcohol withdrawal will obtain relief when given the respective substances. Indeed, agents with similar pharmacologic effects (e.g., methadone and Librium [chlordiazepoxide HCl], respectively) will mitigate or abolish withdrawal symptoms and are the mainstay of medical detoxification. By contrast, an individual who is crashing from cocaine following a binge is unlikely to experience much sustained relief even if cocaine were given. Indeed, many patients find the idea of consuming additional cocaine aversive. One man who freebased cocaine said: "By the time you're ending a run, you feel sickened and exhausted. You haven't eaten in a day, you're dehydrated except for the alcohol you might have drank [sic], your throat is raw, you've been paranoid for hours with your heart going like crazy. It's like you ran a marathon without moving a step. When it's ending, the last thing I want is more cocaine."

Recently, two groups of investigators have failed to observe the pattern of subjective features of the cocaine abstinence syndrome as described by Gawin and Kleber (1986) and other investigators. Weddington et al. (1990) documented the absence of cyclic or phasic changes in mood states, cocaine craving, and interrupted sleep in 12 cocaine-dependent inpatients examined during a 4-week period. At admission, subjects showed minimal evidence of clinically significant depression. All subjective symptoms of mood, craving, and arousal displayed a steady, gradual improvement over the course of the study. Similar subjective findings emerged from a study by Satel, Price, and coworkers (1991), in which 22 newly abstinent cocaine-dependent males were observed during a 21-day hospitalization. Over 21 days, objective ratings of mood and arousal showed gradual improvement from an unexceptional baseline. Although all subjects had consumed cocaine within 24 hours of admission, some claimed that they had slept prior to admission, and thus the crash phase may have been missed.

It may be important that the original conceptualization of the triphasic cocaine withdrawal was derived from observations of outpatients. The Weddington et al. (1990) and Satel, Price, et al. (1991) studies involved inpatients who were largely protected from environmental cues. Divergent findings may be accounted for, in part, by the phenomenon of *conditioned withdrawal*. Conditioned withdrawal, classically documented in opiate users but also reported in alcoholics (Rankin, Stockell, & Hodgson, 1982), represents actual physiological correlates of pharmacologic withdrawal (e.g., gooseflesh, diarrhea, cramps accompanied by intense craving for the drug) that is elicited in *drug-free* individuals upon exposure to reminders of drug use, such as visual and olfactory cues. Conceivably, the subjects studied by Gawin and Kleber (1986) experienced a more robust withdrawal because, as outpatients, they were constantly exposed to environmental reminders of drug use. Thus, symptoms of cocaine withdrawal may be largely limited to a crash phase, although it is quite possible that constant exposure to cues leads to a more clinically observable syndrome. The notion of environmental mediation of clinical withdrawal is compelling and may determine, in part, the severity of the observable manifestations of central changes in neuroreceptors and transmitters secondary to chronic cocaine use.

Conditioned withdrawal, however, does not seem to occur in cocaine dependent individuals in a manner analogous to opiate dependent individuals (see Chapter 6, this volume). Specifically, drug-free cocaine abusers do not report the precipitation of crash symptoms when they are exposed to old "copping" areas or drug paraphernalia. Rather, when exposed to these and other reminders of drug use, cocaine abusers frequently experience an intense craving for cocaine. These reminders, or cues, are considered major precipitants of relapse to cocaine, and reactivity to these cues can persist up to months or years after cocaine use has stopped (Dackis, Gold & Sweeney, 1987).

Indeed, even the meaning attributed to the word *craving* differs between cocaine abusers and opiate and alcohol abusers. Childress, McLellan, and O'Brien (1988) surveyed cocaine-dependent individuals and found that they tended to label as craving the positive (high-like) qualities of the cocaine intoxication experience. In contrast, opiate- and alcohol-dependent subjects were more likely to refer to the negative, withdrawal-associated features of these respective substances when asked to define the subjective experience of craving. Furthermore, in the laboratory drug-free cocaine abusers report desire for cocaine when presented with authentic drug paraphernalia; some even describe "tasting" cocaine at this time. Childress and coworkers (Childress, McLellan, Ehrman, & O'Brien, 1987; Childress, McLellan, Natale, & O'Brien, 1987) found that reactivity to cocaine cues results in changes in psychophysiological arousal—decreased galvanic skin response and decreased skin temperature, responses that are consistent with cocaine drug effects. However, opiate abusers also manifest this psychophysiological profile in response to relevant stimuli; thus their physiological response is more strongly reminiscent of opiate withdrawal than it is of opiate effect. Some opiate abusers initially report feeling "sick" when presented with paraphernalia. These data support the notion that subjective and physiological response to cocaine cues resembles cocaine drug effect (appetitive motivational model), whereas subjective and physiological responses to opiate-related cues may be more consistent with Wikler's conditioned withdrawal model.

Environmental cues that act as triggers for craving are varied and, at times, highly idiosyncratic. Shulman (1989) field-tested a "Cocaine Trigger Inventory" on 200 cocaine-dependent patients receiving treatment. A category of triggers called "people, places and things" was most likely to elicit craving; examples were "people one used (drugs) with," "presence of cocaine or cocaine-like material." Other common triggers included money, weekends, recollection of a cocaine high, loneliness, boredom, and depression. Perhaps the most powerful stimulus for appetitive craving is a small, priming dose of cocaine (Stewart et al., 1984; Jaffe, Cascella, Kumor, & Sherer, 1989). More idiosyncratic cues have included chalk dust, plaster dust, and "the smell of a pharmacy." In the laboratory, failure to respond to standard stimuli may be a function of the cues' lack of personal salience to that particular subject (O'Brien, Childress, & McLellan, 1988). Finally, positive emotional states may promote craving; presumably such an internal medium mimics cocaine's effect and is thus paired with a desire for cocaine. According to Wise (1988), pleasurable affect and the positive effect of a drug may be associated because they are centrally mediated by the same neural pathways that subserve reinforcement.

Indeed, internal (interoceptive) cues can be highly provocative triggers, as they are in opiate users (Sherman, Zinser, & Sideroff, 1985; Childress, McLellan, & O'Brien, 1986). Satel and Gawin (1989) described a series of patients with seasonal affective disorder who craved cocaine only in the depressive cycle of the year. However, triggering mood states need not attain the severity of major depression in order to serve as an internal cue. For example, one cocaine-using schizophrenic that we treated found that his craving for cocaine was greatest whenever he was given a neuroleptic for intercurrent psychotic symptoms. While his psychosis abated with the medication, he would develop neuroleptic-induced dysphoria. With removal of the neuroleptic, the iatrogenic mood state would resolve and he was better able to resist cocaine. Another patient, a 25-year-old woman, would crave cocaine most acutely whenever she perceived rejection from her boyfriend.

Whereas cocaine seeking frequently springs from a desire to experience pleasure (or to reduce emotional pain), the urge to use alcohol or opiates is not always paired with a longing for, or expectation of, the euphoriant effect of the drug. Indeed, many alcoholics have claimed that they "don't even like the taste of it, I do it so I won't get the shakes." A young woman opiate addict claimed that prior to entering treatment, she tried to stop, "wasn't even that interested in getting high anymore," but "I couldn't kick it because I was so afraid of getting dope sick." By contrast, heavy cocaine abusers may awake from a crash and "feeling okay, I reached for the pipe, since I wanted to feel even better." Further, if there is a negligible withdrawal from cocaine following the crash phase, then, for cocaine abusers, there are few adverse symptoms that might compel them to continue use for the primary purpose of mitigating those symptoms.

Thus appetitive motivation to use cocaine, rather than physiological craving based on alleviation of pharmacologic or conditioned withdrawal discomfort, may be most relevant to relapse and compulsive use of cocaine (Wise, 1988). The intense craving among heavy cocaine users is a product of their powerful recall of drug-induced pleasure. Such recall and the cues that trigger it are extremely compelling to the addict; it would seem that neither opiate nor alcohol initiation are as largely appetitively cue-driven as initiation of cocaine in an experienced user (Rohsenow, Childress, Monti, Niaura, & Abrams, 1990/1991). Indeed, it is our impression that cocaine abusers tend to have a greater awareness of their environment during intoxication; they are able to report with fair detail and accuracy the course and events of a recent binge. Unlike those intoxicated with opiates or alcohol intoxication, who tend to convey a vague and often jumbled account of the circumstances both during use and when questioned retrospectively, the cocaine user "is indeed master of everything, but everything matters intensely. With heroin . . . there is a loss of interest in the self that makes mastery of the environment irrelevant" (Grinspoon & Bakalar, 1976, p. 94)

How is it that cocaine cues are so deeply etched in memory and that euphoric recall is so palpable to many users? Several lines of evidence support the notion that the biology of memories of past positive drug effects as well as of withdrawal are central to the problem of drug craving (Collier, 1968; Jaffe & Sharpless, 1968; Wise, 1988) According to one view, variations in the strength of memories result, at least in part, from differences in the degree to which brain systems are activated during experience (McGaugh, 1990). Findings indicate that cognitive retention can be enhanced by electrical or pharmacologic stimulation of certain brain structures (Westbrook & McGaugh, 1964; Kesner, 1982). The noradrenergic system, which is also intimately involved in mediating cocaine's central effects, enhances learning in animals (Introini-Collison & McGaugh, 1986). By contrast, opiates impair retention of learned material. Thus it is tempting to speculate that memory storage (for cues and other experiences associated with cocaine use) is actually enhanced by the heightened noradrenergic transmission resulting directly from the acute pharmacologic effect of cocaine. Finally, this may also relate to the triggering by cues of withdrawal symptoms in opiate users. Rather than inducing primary desire to experience opiate-induced euphoria, cues are more likely to provide conditioned opiate withdrawal, because the original experience of pharmacologic withdrawal is "laid down" in the midst of autonomic arousal and adrenergic storm. Opiate euphoria, not accompanied by adrenergic discharge, is perhaps less strongly conditioned relative to the withdrawal because of the retention-impairing effects of opiate. It is likely that alcohol craving syndromes are more similar to opiate effects than to stimulant. Though highly speculative, this model of "drug-modified learning" is consistent with the predicted outcomes of the conditioned appetitive motivational model for cocaine and the conditioned withdrawal for opiate.

COCAINE-INDUCED PARANOIA

Descriptive Data

Psychosis, in general, and paranoia, in particular, are among the most dramatic psychiatric consequences of chronic stimulant use. Although high-dose amphetamine administration may be associated with the development of florid psychosis in users, chronic, high-dose cocaine consumption seems to produce a time-limited paranoid syndrome. The descriptive literature on cocaine-induced psychosis has been limited to extreme cases such as episodes of violence, suicide, murder and child abuse (Honer, Gewertz, & Turey, 1987; Budd, 1989; Lindenbaum, Carroll, Daskal, & Kapusnick, 1989; Goodwin & Gause, 1991). In some reports, it is unclear whether cocaine had precipitated psychoses in predisposed individuals or whether the effects were induced *de novo*. It is perhaps counterintuitive that intense craving for cocaine, as described above, persists in the face of such a highly distressing and predictable feature of "getting high."

In a recent study, Satel, Southwick, and Gawin (1991) examined 50 male cocaine abusers, with no other diagnosis of major psychopathology, electively admitted to a 21-day rehabilitation program. None of the subjects were currently psychotic, nor did they have a history of psychosis. The mean quantity of cocaine consumed in the month prior to admission was 17 g. Subjects were interviewed with the Cocaine Experiences Questionnaire, which was designed to elicit detailed self-reports on paranoid experiences in the context of cocaine use. Thirty-four subjects (68%) developed transient paranoid episodes ("binge" paranoia) during cocaine use; this is different from the prolonged psychotic and paranoid episodes previously described in amphetamine abusers (Angrist, 1990). All subjects used cocaine in binges (periods of sustained use lasting 8–72 hours) and in all but one, paranoia had resolved by the time of awakening from the crash (postcocaine hypersomnolence). In this one subject, the maximum paranoid experience extended 6–8 hours past the crash.

Typical paranoid ideation included the suspicion or belief that the police or drug dealers were about to apprehend the subject, or that others in the room were planning to attack and steal the cocaine. Frequently, actual stimuli (sounds and flashes of light) were misinterpreted as evidence that menacing individuals were immediately outside the door or window preparing to enter. All subjects found these experiences distressing and, not infrequently, terrifying. None described perceptual hallucinations or bizarre delusions. Frequently subjects described an overlapping of paranoia with the cocaine high, so that both were simultaneously experienced.

Slightly over half of the paranoid individuals (53%) acted on their paranoid ideation by checking activities (relocking doors, scanning out of windows) and hiding in closets or under the bed, or refusing to leave a contained place such as a car. Thirty-eight percent of subjects actually armed themselves with a gun or knife for protection. Over two thirds felt less paranoid when they used cocaine by themselves, and 87% reported that they felt much safer when they used it in familiar settings.

The paranoid group described the onset of binge-limited paranoia after a mean duration of 35 months of use. Although this period of time tended to be less than the lifetime duration of use by nonparanoid subjects (50 months), the difference was not significant. Similarly, although the quantity of cocaine to which the paranoid subjects were exposed *up until the onset of paranoia* tended to be less than the lifetime quantity to which nonparanoid subjects were exposed (0.82 kg vs. 1.34 kg), the difference was not significant.

These findings suggest that development of paranoia in heavy users is not a simple result of exceeding a threshold of usage and that affected individuals may possess a predisposition to this drug-induced state. Paranoia became more severe and developed more rapidly with continued use; this is consistent with a sensitization model of cocaine-induced paranoia. Other potential, yet unexplored, vulnerability factors for the development of cocaine-induced paranoia may include family history, personality traits, or neurophysiological features of individuals.

In a similar study, Brady, Lydiard, Malcolm, and Ballenger (1991) assessed 55 individuals consecutively admitted for treatment of cocaine dependence; none had primary psychotic or bipolar illness. Eighty-nine percent developed paranoia related to grounded fears associated with drug acquisition and apprehension, 7% developed paranoid delusions unrelated to drug use, and two subjects (3.6%) experienced auditory hallucinations but no paranoia. The majority reported auditory and visual illusions, misperceiving ordinary sounds or images as evidence of imminent danger. Cocaine-related psychosis was not associated with lifetime duration of use or amount of cocaine consumed in the month prior to admission. Almost half experienced psychosis reliably with each drug use, and 72% claimed greater likelihood of experiencing psychosis with use as addiction progressed and also with smaller amounts of cocaine over the course of addiction. Finally, males were more likely to report psychosis than were females.

In an effort to extend the investigation of predictive markers of vulnerability to cocaine-induced paranoia, Satel and Edell (1991) examined the presence of psychological markers in paranoia-prone users. A sample of 20 cocaine abusers (10 with a history of transient cocaine-induced paranoia and 10 without such a history) completed the Wisconsin Scales of Psychosis Proneness (Chapman & Chapman, 1987), to determine whether those with a history of transient cocaine-induced paranoia have a predisposition toward psychosis. No patient had a personal or family history of psychotic illness. The items on the Wisconsin Scales are intended to represent trait-like attributes; methods for their derivation were based on the work of Jackson (1970) and Meehl (1964). The subject is carefully instructed to answer according to his drug-free experience. Consequently, high scores of "proneness" are believed to represent *preexisting* disposition (trait) rather than "acquired" beliefs and attitudes secondary to cocaine use.

The absolute scores of the paranoid-prone group were high enough on the Wisconsin subscales of perceptual aberration and magical ideation to be considered in the psychosis-proneness range based on established norms for these scales. (Ratings on the other two subscales— physical anhedonia and sociopathy—were comparable for both groups). Eighty percent (8/10) of the group with a history of cocaine-induced paranoia scored in the psychosis-prone range, compared with only 1 in 10 individuals without such history. The between-group differences were highly significant statistically and suggest that heavy users who experience cocaine-induced paranoia may be predisposed to this symptom based on intrinsic vulnerability, and that, perhaps, with continued use of cocaine or other pharmacologic stress, they may be at higher risk for the eventual development of psychotic illness.

In so far as the study described above is cross-sectional and correlational, it is impossible to determine the direction of causality. That is, does the experience of cocaine-induced paranoia (or, perhaps, the drug-induced neurobiological changes underlying this symptom) increase the likelihood of having perceptual aberration and magical ideation, or are these latter experiences an expression of intrinsic vulnerability to paranoia that predated cocaine consumption in otherwise asymptomatic individuals? Only prospective data can provide definitive answers.

It is plausible to reason that individuals with characteristic paranoid tendencies, or those who would worry excessively about the illegal aspects of cocaine use, might tend to transform the perceptions of autonomic arousal and hyperalertness induced by cocaine into paranoia. A classic example of psychological disposition as a determinant of attribution involving internal stimuli is the notion that "the coward defines the rush of adrenalin as fear while the brave man defines it as the exhilaration of facing danger" (Grinspoon & Bakalar, 1976, p. 95). Schacter and Singer (1962) found that individuals' subjective responses to an injection of epinephrine were largely dependent upon the expectations of either anxiety or pleasure that were experimentally "suggested" by the investigators before receiving the drug.

Animal Studies

An approach to uncovering the nature of the vulnerability to drug-induced suspicious/paranoid behavior resides in experimental administration of cocaine to drug-naive individuals. Clearly this is not possible in humans, and there are few appropriate animal models for evaluating paranoia. However, an interesting model for studying the interaction between cocaine and an organism's innate "psychological" disposition comes from Crowley, Mikulich, Williams, Zerbe, and Ingersoll (1991) who worked with social nonhuman primates. These investigators assessed cocaine's effects on the social behavior of group-living ma-caques. Eight adult males housed in a large outdoor corral were treated with intramuscular (IM) doses of cocaine (1.5 mg per kg or less). Monkeys were observed for 4 hours following drug administration, which took place on 8 separate days (note that animals received IM saline "control" on 4 of the days).

Cocaine tended to suppress affiliative behaviors and induced bizarre stereotypies, hypervigilance, and panic-like flight. In addition to the individual differences expected among these non-inbred animals, dominance rank also contributed to behavioral differences among members of the social group. When all members of the group were given cocaine, higher ranking monkeys tended to climb to more elevated perches than usual and lower ranking ones assumed lower perches than usual when dosed with cocaine. The less dominant monkeys would exhibit panic-like escape behaviors with seemingly neutral stimuli during cocaine treatment; the time spent in a lying-down posture was significantly decreased in all monkeys who sat in a tense, rigid posture suggesting hypervigilance. When cocaine was given only to a particular individual, while others in the group remained cocaine-free, that monkey tended to stay remote from his fellows and climbed to high places in the corral, where he gazed intensely into the surrounding fields and appeared to be "checking." Cocaine did not increase aggressive or sexual behavior in any of the monkeys. Lastly, auto-grooming increased and self-care stereotypies developed in all monkeys.

Intriguing contrasts exist between these observations and the behaviors of cocaine abusers. First, cocaine-*naive* monkeys who received approximately 1.5 mg per kg (monkeys weighed 15 kg on average, so that a total daily dose of 22.5 mg was given) during a first exposure to cocaine behaved in a fashion similar to *experienced*, high-intensity cocaine users. That is, they appeared to become fearful and anxiously vigilant. Second, cocaine did not enhance social activity (as it often does in light-to-modest users) nor sexual behavior (as it commonly does in both modest and heavy cocaine users). Instead, the social withdrawal produced by cocaine is reminiscent of behaviors of chronic cocaine users who experience paranoia. Indeed, studies have found that one half to two thirds of experienced users preferred to use alone and in a familiar place because they experienced less paranoia and fear in these contexts (Satel, Southwick, & Gawin, 1991; Brady et al., 1991).

The meaning of the differences between humans and monkeys is not clear; indeed, it is not obvious how human and nonhuman primates can be matched in studies such as these. At minimum, the monkeys were passive and "unmotivated" recipients of the drug whereas addicts were purposeful users with specific expectations of drug effect. In this study, the human subjects were dependent upon cocaine and had used heavy amounts by the time they were studied; the monkeys were relatively drug naive. Species-specific differences in response to cocaine or in the pharmacokinetics of cocaine may play a role. Also, dosing patterns in the monkey study did not at all resemble human administration patterns; these and numerous other variables differ. Nevertheless, these data suggest that behavioral responses to cocaine may be influenced, in part, by psychosocial substrates such as social stature and that cocaine-induced suspiciousness. Other potential, yet unexplored, vulnerability factors for the development of cocaine-induced paranoia may reside in family history, individual personality traits, or individual neurophysiological features.

Human Experimental Data

The earliest placebo-controlled experimental administrations (challenges) of cocaine were performed in 1976 by Fischman, Schuster, and Resnekov (1976). This and subsequent studies have been concerned primarily with the subjective experiences of the high and crash, and the cardiovascular changes produced by intranasal, intravenous, or smoked cocaine. In the majority of these studies, a single administration of cocaine (or placebo) is given on a test day. To our knowledge, only one group (Sherer, Kumor, Cone, & Jaffe, 1988) has performed continuous cocaine infusions over several hours, although Isbell (1953) administered intravenous cocaine boluses intermittently over 12 hours (see below).

In general, the challenge studies have employed the Addiction Research Center Inventory (ARCI, short form; Martin, 1971) in evaluating subjective change. The short form consists of 49 items (out of an original 550; Haertzen, Hill, & Belleville, 1963) which has been shown to be sensitive to the effects of a number of different stimulant drugs. The short-form questions were taken from the Morphine–Benzedrine Group, Pentobarbital–Chlorpromazine–Alcohol Group, LSD Group, Benzedrine Group and Amphetamine Group scales of the 550-item ARCI. Of the 49 questions on the modified form, only 2 seem to be directly related to paranoid or psychotic symptomatology: item 46—"I feel anxious and upset," and item 35—"I have a weird feeling." Visual analogue scales have been used to assess subjective states (stimulated, high, anxious, sedated, down, hungry) and desire for substances (cocaine, alcohol, heroin, tobacco, marijuana). Each scale consists of a 10-cm line labeled *not at all* on the left side and *extremely* on the right side. Specific items related to suspiciousness or bizarre ideation are not included in these scales, nor are objective behavioral measures emphasized.

Although cocaine infusion studies have been conducted by numerous groups, there is surprisingly little data about cocaine-induced paranoia or altered ideation. The first cocaine challenge in which psychotic symptoms were prospectively induced was performed by Isbell in 1953 (cited in Angrist, 1990) and documented in a film made at the Addiction Research Center (Isbell, 1953) in Lexington, Kentucky, entitled *Clinical Manifestations of Cocaine Addiction*. The film depicted a subject who was given repeated 20-mg IV injections of cocaine at 30-minute intervals and increased the dose to 50 mg at 5–10 minute intervals. Over a 12 hour period, the subject received more than 2 g of cocaine and, at this point, began to manifest visual hallucinations (seeing bugs) and had the paranoid delusion of being watched by detectives.

Muntaner, Kumor, Nagashi, and Jaffe (1989) administered cocaine in single injections to eight experienced IV cocaine users; the main focus of this study was on the cardiovascular and euphoria/crash symptoms. Doses of 10, 20 and 40 mg were given on separate days. Cardiovascular effects were not consistently correlated with subjective responses. Suspiciousness, assessed by self-report only ("How suspicious do you feel?" "Can the staff tell what you are thinking?" "How uncomfortable do you feel?") was shown to increase following each administration irrespective of dose. Comparison of degree of suspiciousness induced after administration on separate test days was not performed.

Sherer and his colleagues (1988) have specifically focused on cocaine-induced changes in thought processes during controlled administration of the drug. This study was unique in its administration of cocaine over a sustained period of time as compared with other studies cited wherein a single injection was given. Eight experienced IV cocaine-using males were studied. Baseline diagnostic evaluations disclosed no primary Axis 1 pathology or dependence on other substances. Subjects participated in 5 test days and received, in randomized order, a loading dose of either low cocaine (40 mg) or high cocaine (60 or 80 mg) intravenously or a placebo, followed by an active or placebo infusion. The cocaine infusion was administered to maintain a plasma level approximately equal to the peak achieved with the loading dose; thus the 5 test days were as follows: low cocaine loading/infusion, low cocaine loading/placebo, high cocaine loading/infusion, high cocaine loading/placebo, placebo load/placebo infusion.

Thus a range of 25–43 mg per hour cocaine was infused in the subjects receiving the 40-mg loading dose and 37–65 mg per hour in the group given the 80-mg loading dose. Ratings (self-ratings and nurses' objective ratings) were performed at 30-minute intervals.

Half of the subjects manifested suspiciousness and, in one case, overtly bizarre behavior and ideation during infusions. Temporally, this tended to overlap with the initial induction of euphoria and well-being. Of note, none of the subjects reported feeling suspicious, but nurses' reports were often dramatic. For example, the subjects displayed various behaviors such as social withdrawal (four of four), expressed fears of doom and death (four of four), expressed fear of being robbed (one), sat with back to the wall (one), reported auditory hallucinations (one). One man smeared shaving cream on his face, claimed that he was disfigured, and threatened to sue the staff for injuring him. In these subjects, the onset of altered ideation was at 30 minutes (for the subject who claimed disfigurement), 60 minutes (one subject), 90 minutes (two subjects). There was no formal thought disorder noted, nor was there any clouding of consciousness. In three subjects, suspiciousness lasted for several hours after the infusion terminated, whereas for the subject who became frankly delusional, the symptoms lasted for 24 hours after infusion. Placebo infusions yielded no behavioral changes.

The authors found few clinical features predictive of the development of cocaine-induced suspiciousness. Variables such as history of cocaine and other drug use, clinical diagnosis of personality disorder, and plasma levels of cocaine were not associated with suspiciousness during the study. Cardiovascular changes produced by cocaine did not correlate with development of such symptoms. (Of interest, Satel, Southwick, & Charney [1990] did not find an association between reported experiences of "palpitations," "racing heart," or "jitteriness" and cocaine-induced paranoia. This suggests that cocaine-related paranoia may be a primary perception rather than a secondary attempt at making sense of a physiological response to a stimulant drug.)

Similarities and differences exist between the Sherer group's work and the retrospective descriptive studies by the Satel and Brady groups. For example, an overlapping of pleasurable and distressing reactions to cocaine occurred. Although the subjects in the Sherer study did not indicate suspiciousness or paranoid ideation in the self-ratings, they verbally reported or enacted their perceptions in the presence of the raters. Also, the time to onset of suspiciousness and paranoia took, on average, longer in the experimental than in the other samples, who were assessed in retrospective fashion. Whereas the accuracy and reliability of data retrospectively reported by drug abusers has been questioned (Chitwood, 1985), the consistency of responses in the studies by Satel et al. (1991) was striking. That is, virtually all subjects reported time to onset of paranoia as being 15 minutes or less once they had begun to experience it regularly.

To the extent that cocaine promotes hyperalertness, the threshold for developing paranoia may be lower when it is used in a street setting that provides multiple threatening stimuli. It is conceivable that the heavy addicts studied by Satel et al. became suspicious/paranoid quickly following administration because threatening stimuli in the environment were ever-present, thus allowing psychic contents to organize more rapidly around the predictable environmental variables (getting caught, being robbed or harmed). These same paranoia-prone individuals, taken into the safer, sanctioned laboratory, might perceive this new setting as unburdened with the realities and fantasies of street danger. In such a novel environment, suspicious responses—if they developed—might be less stereotyped because the nature of the threat was not as easily predictable. In the laboratory there may have been fewer alerting stimuli for the individual to focus upon and subsequently magnify into a paranoid state; thus suspiciousness and paranoia took longer to develop. As more drug was infused, however, the suspiciousness and paranoia, when they occurred, took more varied forms. (Of note, to our knowledge virtually none of the single-bolus cocaine challenge experiments produced overt suspiciousness, paranoia, or psychosis in their subjects. Isbell's study and that of Sherer et al., however, produced florid symptomatology, and these were the only two trials with continuous dosing. As such, they more accurately reproduced the patterns of cocaine administration used naturally.)

Comparison of the descriptive and experimental studies is compromised by lack of knowledge of subjects' usage history and prior responses to cocaine. In the Sherer study, for example, it is not clear whether the subjects undergoing laboratory infusion had a history of cocaine-induced paranoia "in the field." Given matched groups, it would be interesting to note whether the content of delusions is influenced by the setting in which the cocaine infusion is received; this has been shown to be the case for epinephrine administered to humans under differing experimental conditions (Schacter & Singer, 1962) The paranoid delusions reported by subjects in the Satel et al. (1991) and Brady et al. (1991) samples were fairly similar in nature. The content was invariably organized around drug-related fears such as apprehension by the police or others whom they had reason to fear (e.g., neighborhood dealer, local gang members). Behaviors such as checking, hiding, or arming oneself were consistent with the paranoid ideation. The subjects in the Sherer group's study, however, displayed more bizarre cocaine-induced thinking and behaviors that were not invariably rooted in fears of apprehension or harm.

As noted above, the study populations must be matched by history of exposure as well as clinical and demographic features. With respect to exposure to cocaine, it is especially difficult to compare groups because street use cannot be easily quantified. For example, Sherer et al. (1988) can report the average dosage (50 mg per hour) and plasma level. On the street, the typical heavy user may administer as much as 0.5–1.0 g per hour. Taking the local dilution factor into account, approximately 20–40% in 1989 (the year of our data collection in New Haven), higher amounts of active cocaine may have been administered per hour by our sample.

SUMMARY

We have presented, together, the phenomenologic features of craving for cocaine and of cocaine-induced paranoia. This juxtaposition serves to emphasize the compelling aspect of cocaine craving (believed, here, to stem largely from appetitive forces rooted in strong positive memories) in the face of an often terrifying complication of chronic-use paranoia. Although expected on theoretical grounds, there is little evidence that high-intensity cocaine use produces prolonged psychosis. In fact, subjects rarely report amphetamine-like bizarre psychoses but, rather, describe fairly consistent experiences of hypervigilance and fear during use. It is not clear why certain individuals are vulnerable to cocaine-induced thought disturbance whereas others, with matched usage histories and patterns, appear immune. Future experimental work, informed at the outset by careful descriptive studies, may elucidate the differential vulnerability to cocaine-induced paranoia.

REFERENCES

Angrist, B. (1990). Cocaine and prior stimulant epidemics. In N. D. Volkow & A. C. Swann (Eds.), *Cocaine in the brain.* New Brunswick, NJ: Rutgers University Press.

Bernfeld, S. (1953). Freud's studies on cocaine. *Journal of the American Psychoanalytic Association, 1,* 581–613.

Brady, K., Lydiard, L. B., Malcolm, R., & Ballenger, J. C. (1991). Cocaine-induced psychosis. *Journal of Clinical Psychiatry, 52,* 509–512.

Brower, K., & Paredes, A. (1987). Cocaine withdrawal [letter]. *Archives of General Psychiatry, 44,* 297–298.

Budd, R. D. (1989). Cocaine abuse and violent death. *American Journal of Drug and Alcohol Abuse, 15,* 375–382

Byck, R. (1974). *Cocaine papers by Sigmund Freud.* New York: Stonehill.

Chapman, L. J., & Chapman, J. P. (1987). The search for symptoms predictive of schizophrenia. *Schizophrenia Bulletin, 13,* 497–503.

Childress, A. R., McLellan, A. T., Ehrman, R., & O'Brien, C. P. (1987). Extinction of conditioned responses in abstinent cocaine or opioid users. In *Problems of drug dependence* (National Institute on Drug Abuse Research Monograph No. 76, pp. 189–195). Washington, DC: U. S. Government Printing Office.

Childress, A. R., McLellan, A. T., Natale, M. & O'Brien, C. (1987). Mood states can elicit conditioned withdrawal and craving in opiate abuse patients. In *Problems of drug dependence* (National Institute on Drug Abuse Research Monograph No. 76, pp. 137–144). Washington, DC: U. S. Government Printing Office.

Childress, A. R., McLellan, A. T., & O'Brien, C. P. (1986). Conditioned responses in a methadone population: A comparison of laboratory, clinic and natural setting. *Journal of Substance Abuse Treatment, 3,* 173–179.

Childress, A. R., McLellan, A. T., & O'Brien, C. P. (1988). Extinguishing conditioned responses in drug dependent persons. In B. Ray (Ed.), *Learning factors in drug dependence* (National Institute on Drug Abuse Research Monograph; DHHS Publication No. ADM-88-1576, pp. 137–144). Washington, DC: U. S. Government Printing Office.

Chitwood, D. O. (1985). Patterns and consequences of cocaine use. In N. J. Kozel & E. H. Adams (Eds.), *Cocaine use in America: Epidemiology and clinical perspectives* (National Institute on Drug Abuse Research Monograph Research Monograph No. 61). Washington, DC: U. S. Government Printing Office.

Collier, H. O. J. (1968). Supersensitivity and dependence. *Nature, 220,* 228–231.

Crowley, T. J., Mikulich, S. K., Williams, E. A., Zerbe, G. O., & Ingersoll, N. C. (1991). *Cocaine, social behavior and alcohol drinking in monkeys.* Unpublished manuscript.

Dackis, C. A., & Gold, M. S. (1985). New concepts in cocaine addiction: The dopamine depletion hypothesis. *Neuroscience and Biobehavioral Review, 9,* 469–477.

Dackis, C. A., Gold, M. S., & Sweeney, P. R. (1987). [Letter]. *Archives of General Psychiatry, 44,* 298–299.

Ellinwood, E. H., & Petrie, W. M. (1977). Dependence on amphetamine, cocaine and other stimulants. In S. N. Pradhan (Ed.), *Drug abuse: Clinical and basic aspects.* St. Louis, MO: C. V. Mosby.

Fischman, M. W., Schuster, C. R., & Resnekov, L. (1976). Cardiovascular and subjectives effects of intravenous cocaine administration in humans. *Archives of General Psychiatry, 33,* 983–989.

Gawin, F. M., & Kleber, H. D. (1986). Abstinence symptomology and psychiatric diagnosis in cocaine abusers: clinical observations. *Archives of General Psychiatry, 43,* 107–113

Gawin, F. H., & Ellinwood, E. H., Jr. (1990). Consequences and correlates of cocaine abuse: Clinical phenomenology. In N. D. Volkow & A. C. Swann (Eds), *Cocaine in the brain.* New Brunswick, NJ: Rutgers University Press.

Gawin, F. H., Khalsa, H., & Anglin, D. (1991, June). *Large scale investigation of subjective symptoms of cocaine withdrawal.* Abstract presented at the Committee on the Problems of Drug Dependence, Palm Beach, FL.

Grinspoon, L., & Bakalar, J. B. (1976). *Cocaine: A drug and its social evolution.* New York: Basic Books.

Goodwin, F. K., & Gause, E. M. (1991). From the Alcohol, Drug Abuse and Mental Health Administration. *Journal of the American Medical Association,* 265–1510.

Haertzen, C. A., Hill, H. E., & Belleville, R. E. (1963). Development of the Addiction Research Center Inventory, selection of items that are sensitive to the effects of various drugs. *Psychopharmacologia, 4,* 155–166.

Honer, W. H., Gewirtz, R., & Turey, H. (1987). Psychosis and violence in cocaine smokers [letter]. *Lancet, 2,* 451.

Introini-Collison, I., & McGaugh, J. L. (1986). Epinephrine modulates long term retention of an aversive motivated discrimination task. *Behavioral and Neural Biology, 45,* 358–365.

Isbell, H. (1953). Clinical manifestations of drug addiction [Film]. Lexington, KY: Addiction Research Center.

Jackson, D. N. (1970). A sequential system for personality scale development. In C. N. Spielberger (Ed.), *Current topics in clinical and community psychology* (Vol. 2). New York: Academic Press.

Jaffe, J. H., Cascella, N. G., Kumar, K. M., & Sherer, M. A. (1989). Cocaine-induced cocaine craving. *Psychopharmacology, 97,* 59–64

Jaffe, J. H., & Sharpless, S. K. (1968). Pharmacological denervation supersensitivity in the central nervous system: A theory of physical dependence. In A. H. Wikler (Ed.), *The addictive states.* Baltimore, MD: Williams & Wilkins.

Jones, E. (1974). The cocaine episode. In R. Byck (Ed.), *Cocaine papers by Sigmund Freud.* New York: Stonehill Press.

Kesner, R. P. (1982). Brain stimulation, effects on memory. *Behavioral and Neural Biology, 36,* 315–367.

Kleber, H. D., & Gawin, F. H. (1987). In reply to cocaine withdrawal [letter]. *Archives of General Psychiatry, 44,* 297–298.

Koslowski, L. T., & Wilkinson, D. A. (1987). Use and misuse of the concept of craving by alcohol, tobacco and drug researchers. *British Journal of Addictions, 82,* 31–36.

Lindenbaum, G. A., Carroll, S. F., Daskal, I., & Kapusnick, R. (1989). Patterns of alcohol and drug abuse in an urban trauma center: The increasing role of cocaine abuse. *Journal of Trauma, 29*(12), 1654–1658.

Ludwig, A. M., Wikler, A., & Stark, L. (1974). The first drink: psychobiological aspects of craving. *Archives of General Psychiatry, 30,* 539–547.

Maier, H. W. (1987). *Der Kokainismus {Cocaine addiction}* (O. J. Kalant, Trans.).

Toronto: Addiction Research Foundation. (Original work published 1928)

Martin, W. R., Sloan, J. W., Sapira, J., & Jasinski, D. R. (1971). Physiologic, subjective and behavioral effects of amphetamine, methamphetamine, ephedrine, phenmetrizine and methylphenidate in man. *Clinical Pharmacology and Therapeutics, 2,* 245–258.

McGaugh, J. L. (1990). Significance and remembrance: The role of neuromodulatory systems. *Psychological Science, 1,* 15–25.

Meehl, P. E. (1964). *Manual for use with Checklist of Schizotypic Signs.* Minneapolis: University of Minnesota, Psychiatric Research Unit.

Muntaner, C. Kumor, K., Nagoshi, C., & Jaffe, J. H. (1989). Intravenous cocaine infusions in humans: close responsivity and correlations of cardiovascular vs. subjective effects. *Pharmacology, Biochemistry and Behavior, 34,* 697–703.

Niaura, R. Rohsenow, D. J., Binkoff, J. A., Monti, P. M., Pedraza, M., & Abrams, D. B. (1988). Relevance of cue reactivity to understanding alcohol and smoking relapse. *Journal of Abnormal Psychology, 97,* 133–152.

O'Brien, C. P., Childress, A. R., & McLellan, A. T. (1988). Types of conditioning found in drug-dependent humans. In B. Ray (Ed.), *Learning factors in drug dependence* (National Institute on Drug Abuse Research Monograph; DHHS Publication No. ADM-88-1576, pp. 44–61). Washington, DC: U. S. Government Printing Office.

Rankin, H., Stockell, T., & Hodgson, R. (1982). Cues for drinking and degree of alcohol dependence. *British Journal of Addiction, 77,* 287–296.

Rohsenow, D. J., Childress, A. R., Monti, P. M., Niaura, R. S., & Abrams, D. B. (1990/1991). Cue-reactivity in addictive behaviors: theoretical and treatment implications. *International Journal of Addictions, 25,* 957–993.

Satel, S. L., & Edell, W. S. (1991). Cocaine-induced paranoia and psychosis proneness. *American Journal of Psychiatry, 148,* 1708–1711.

Satel, S. L., & Gawin, F. H. (1989). Seasonal cocaine abuse. *American Journal of Psychiatry, 146,* 534–536.

Satel, S. L., Price, L. H. Palumbo, J. C., McDougle, J. C., Krystal, J. H., Gawin, F. H., Charney, D. S., Heninger, G. R., & Kleber, H. D. (1991). Clinical phenomenology and neurobiology of cocaine abstinence: A prospective inpatient study. *American Journal of Psychiatry, 148,* 1712–1716.

Satel, S. L., Southwick, S. M., & Charney, D. S. (1990). *Cocaine-induced paranoia.* Presented at the Annual meeting of the American Psychiatric Association NY, NY.

Satel, S. L., Southwick, S. M., & Gawin, F. H. (1991). Clinical features of cocaine-induced paranoia. *American Journal of Psychiatry, 148,* 495–498.

Schacter, S., & Singer, J. (1962). Cognitive, social and physiologic determinants of emotional state. *Psychological Review, 63,* 379–399.

Sherer, M. A. Kumor, K. M., Cone, E. J., & Jaffe, J. H. (1988). Suspiciousness induced by four- hour intravenous infusions of cocaine. *Archives of General Psychiatry, 45,* 673–678.

Sherman, J. E., Zinser, M. C., & Sideroff, S. (1985). *Subjective reports of craving withdrawal sickness and mood induced by boring, anxiety-provoking, or heroin-associated stimuli among drug-free addicts in treatment.* Paper presented at the annual meeting of the American Psychoanalytic Association, Los Angeles.

Shulman, G. D. (1989). Experience with the Cocaine Trigger Inventory. *Advances in Alcohol and Substance Abuse, 8,* 71–85.

Siegel, S. (1975). Evidence from rats that morphine tolerance is a learned response. *Journal of Comparative Physiological Psychology, 89,* 498–506.

Stewart, J., de Wit, H., & Eikelboom, R. (1984). The role of unconditioned and conditioned drug effects with the self administration of opiates and stimulants. *Psychological Review, 91,* 257–268.

Weddington, W. W., Brown, B. S., Haertzen, C. A., Cone, E. J., Dax, E. M., Herning, R. I., & Michaelson, B. S. (1990). Changes in mood, craving and sleep during short-term abstinence reported by male cocaine addicts: a controlled residential study. *Archives of General Psychiatry, 47,* 861–868.

Westbrook, W. H., & McGaugh, J. L. (1964). Drug facilitation of latent learning. *Psychopharmacology, 5,* 440–446.

Wikler, A. (1973). Dynamics of drug dependence. *Archives of General Psychiatry, 28,* 611–616.

Wise, R. (1988). The neurobiology of craving: implications for the understanding of treatment and addiction. *Journal of Abnormal Psychology, 97,* 118–132.

CHAPTER TEN

The Role of Drug Analysis in Cocaine Abuse Treatment and Research

Peter Jatlow, MD

THE ANALYSIS of drugs and drug metabolites in body fluids, and perhaps in other biological materials, plays an essential role in drug abuse treatment and research. It is the only way to definitively establish that a given drug has been used. In clinical research, especially when a drug is administered by other than a systemic route, it is also the only way to reliably assess the amount of drug that has actually reached the systemic circulation, and to control for differences in bioavailability and pharmacokinetics between subjects.

The purposes of cocaine analysis in drug abuse treatment and research are varied, and include drug abuse screening, clinical evaluation of overdose, studies of drug pharmacokinetics, investigation of the relationship between dose (blood concentration) and response, and assessment of pharmacokinetic and pharmacodynamic interactions in the evaluation of pharmacological treatment modalities. These applications differ from one another in the use of the information obtained through drug analysis and, as a consequence, differ in choice of methodology, of biological fluid (urine or blood) for assay, target (parent drug or metabolite), and requirements for sensitivity and specificity. Regardless of the purpose, optimal interpretation of cocaine concentration data and design of research protocols are facilitated by some understanding of cocaine's metabolic disposition and pharmacokinetics.

Measurement of cocaine and/or its metabolites may be performed in a clinical or research context. Clinical applications—defining clinical in the broadest sense—include drug abuse screening as well as the diagnosis and acute management of the cocaine-intoxicated or overdosed patient. Measurement of plasma concentrations is fundamental to clinical research employing cocaine challenges for the purpose of defining pharmacokinetics or to establish pharmacokinetic–pharmacodynamic relationships. Various pharmacological agents are under evaluation for treatment of cocaine abuse. Identification or exclusion of pharmacokinetic interactions between such drugs and cocaine is important to help understand their mechanism of action. Finally, identification of dose–response relationships and useful plasma concentrations for potential therapeutic drugs may help to optimize therapy and facilitate interpretation of outcome data. Each of these applications of cocaine analysis is discussed in this chapter.

METABOLIC DISPOSITION AND PHARMACOKINETICS

Metabolism

The major routes for cocaine's metabolic disposition involve hydrolysis of each of its two ester groups, which results in the loss of pharmacological activity. Loss of the methyl group yields benzoylecgonine, which is the major urinary metabolite of cocaine. Benzoylecgonine accounts for about 40–60% of a cocaine dose and is the major target for drug abuse screening assays. Some benzoylecgonine is thought to arise through chemical hydrolysis of cocaine (Stewart, Inaba, Lucassen, & Kalow, 1979; Inaba, Stewart, & Kalow, 1978), although enzymatic pathways have not been excluded. Loss of the aromatic group yields the second major metabolite, ecgonine methyl ester. This compound is produced by the action of plasma cholinesterase as well as hepatic esterases on cocaine and accounts for about 30–40% of a cocaine dose. The hepatic esterases have a lower affinity but higher capacity for cocaine than does plasma cholinesterase (Stewart et al., 1979) but their relative in vivo importance is not established. In vitro, cocaine is rapidly hydrolyzed to ecgonine methyl ester when added to normal human plasma, but is stable in the plasma of individuals who are homozygous for the atypical plasma cholinesterase enzyme, (e.g., sensitive to succinylcholine) (Stewart et al., 1979; Jatlow, Barash, Van Dyke, Radding, & Byck, 1979). Whether or not individuals deficient in plasma cholinesterase activity are more sensitive to cocaine toxicity is unestablished. Fatal cocaine overdose most certainly does occur in individuals with a normal plasma cholinesterase phenotype and/or enzyme activity.

Microsomal pathways appear to be relatively unimportant in humans for the disposition of cocaine. A minute proportion of cocaine is N-demethylated to norcocaine which, with one exception, is the only known active metabolite of cocaine. Norcocaine is only slightly less active then cocaine as an inhibitor of monoamine reuptake (Hawks, Kopin, Colburn, & Thoa, 1974). This pathway appears to be of negligible significance in humans. Further oxidation of norcocaine to reactive or toxic intermediates is thought to mediate the cocaine-induced hepatotoxicity that has been observed in mice (Kloss, Rosen, & Rauckman, 1984; Thompson, Schuster, & Shaw, 1979). However, hepatotoxicity resulting from cocaine use has not been proven to occur in humans, and in any event is apparently uncommon.

Recent studies indicate that some cocaine is transesterified to cocaethylene when cocaine and ethanol are administered concurrently. Cocaethylene is equipotent to cocaine in blocking dopamine reuptake and in its binding to the dopamine transporter, increases locomotor activity in rodents, and is self-administered by primates (Hearn et al., 1991, Jatlow et al., 1991). In excess of 50% of cocaine abusers are reported to ingest alcohol during cocaine binges (Grant & Harford, 1990). Formation of an active metabolite with cocaine-like properties may be a factor in this particularly common form of polydrug abuse.

Pharmacokinetics

Cocaine is rapidly eliminated with a plasma half-life of approximately 1 hour (Cook, Jeffcoat, & Perez-Reyes, 1985; Wilkinson, Van Dyke, Jatlow, Barash, & Byck, 1980; Barnett, Hawks, & Resnick, 1981). Total body clearance and volume of distribution are reported to be in the range of 2 L per minute and 2 L per kg respectively. There appears to be somewhat less interindividual variation in cocaine's pharmacokinetics than is the case for many other psychotropic drugs, such as, for example, the tricyclic antidepressants, that are more dependent on microsomal pathways for their disposition. Because cocaine's in vitro disappearance from plasma is also rapid, it is imperative that a cholinesterase inhibitor such as a sodium fluoride be added to blood samples immediately following collection, if analysis of cocaine at a later time is intended. For the same reason, much data regarding plasma concentrations obtained in fatal overdoses may be an underestimation because of unavoidable delays in sample collection.

The major inactive metabolites, benzoylecgonine and ecgonine methyl ester, are eliminated more slowly (Ambre, 1985). With plasma half-lives of approximately 6 and 4 hours respectively, their identification allows for a much larger time window for detection of cocaine use.

Benzoylecgonine is the easier to measure, and is the accepted and preferred marker for cocaine use in most drug abuse screening programs (see below). Since these two metabolites are inactive, they cannot be used directly as indicators of behavioral effects or impairment.

Following intranasal administration of cocaine, plasma concentrations peak at about 1–2 hours (Wilkinson et al., 1980; Cook et al., 1985). Estimates of bioavailability by the intranasal route have ranged from 30–70% (Cook et al., 1985). Because cocaine is a potent vasoconstrictor, it can limit its own rate of absorption. Undoubtedly some drug is also swallowed and absorbed by the gastrointestinal route following intranasal administration. Peak blood levels after a single intranasal dose of 2 mg per kg are generally in the range of 300–400 ng per mL (Wilkinson et al., 1980). When cocaine is given by the oral route (not a usual route of administration), bioavailability and plasma concentrations are comparable to those following intranasal administration (Van Dyke, Barash, Jatlow, & Byck, 1976; Van Dyke, Jatlow, Ungerer, Barash, & Byck, 1978). Peak plasma concentrations of 500–700 ng per mL are seen following IV administration of 0.5 mg per kg. Smoking of cocaine free base (including crack) can be considered analogous to IV administration with respect to its rapid entry into the systemic circulation and the intensity of its effects (Perez-Reyes, Digiuseppe, Ondrusek, Jeffcoat, & Cook, 1982; Paly, Jatlow, Van Dyke, Jeri, & Byck, 1979). Bioavailability of that portion of smoked cocaine that reaches the lungs intact is high, and plasma concentrations in excess of 1000 ng per mL are easily and rapidly obtained.

DRUG ABUSE SCREENING

Urinary drug abuse screening was originally developed as an important adjunct to drug abuse treatment programs, particularly methadone programs for opiate abusers. Its role has since expanded, not only with respect to the variety of drugs of interest, but in types of applications as well. Aside from its use as an adjunct in drug abuse treatment, urinalysis for drugs of abuse is now used in such contexts as preemployment screening, monitoring of athletes, on-the-job screening in selected instances, and for management of prisoners and parolees. The intent of this section is not to debate the merit of drug abuse screening for nonmedical purposes, or such logistic details as custody, sample collection, and quality control, which have been amply reviewed elsewhere (Hawks & Chiang, 1986; DeCresce, Mazura, Lifshitz, & Tilson, 1990). Rather, the focus will be on the scientific aspects pertinent to cocaine.

All drug abuse screening procedures, with the exception of gas chromatography/mass spectrometry (GC/MS), have a small but important incidence of false positives. The lower the selected detection limits (greater the sensitivity), the higher the incidence of false positives (the less the specificity). Thus it is considered dogma that positives obtained with screening procedures must be confirmed by an independent assay based on a different principle, preferably GC/MS (Hawks & Chiang, 1986; DeCresce et al., 1989). Traditionally, although not universally, immunoassays are employed for first-step screening, with subsequent confirmation of positives by GC/MS. Immunoassays have the requisite sensitivity, and GC/MS adds the required specificity. Clinical programs, wherein the focus is not forensic, may use other approaches, including thin-layer, gas, and high-pressure liquid chromatography, especially when analyses cannot be limited to drugs of abuse.

Drug screening procedures focus on the identification of the urinary metabolite benzoylecgonine as a marker for cocaine use. Benzoylecgonine not only reaches much higher concentrations in urine, but with its longer half-life (see Pharmokinetics) persists in the urine for a much longer period of time than does the parent compound.

Widely used immunoassays for benzoylecgonine include enzyme immunoassay techniques (EMIT [SYVA Corporation, Palo Alto, CA] and others), fluorescent polarization (TDX [Abbott Corporation, Abbott Park, IL]), and radioimmunoassays (Hawks et al., 1986; DeCresce et al., 1989). Various other nonisotopic immunoassays have been applied to drugs of abuse including cocaine. Most commercially available procedures appear to be satisfactory, but all require confirmation of positives. Most cocaine assays use 300 ng per mL of benzoylecgonine as a lower cutoff or threshold for positivity. Greater sensitivity with higher yield is possible but, as indicated, entails a greater risk for false positives. Following a positive immunoassay, confirmation of the presence of benzoylecgonine by GC/MS is generally employed, although ecgonine methylester and sometimes the parent compound can also be detected following cocaine use, depending on the elapsed time prior to sampling.

Generally cocaine itself cannot be detected in urine for much longer than 12 hours after its use, but benzoylecgonine is usually detectable (using a 300 ng per mL cutoff) for about 72 hours (Van Dyke, Byck, Barash, & Jatlow, 1977; Hawks et al., 1986). However, the time during which benzoylecgonine is detectable following cocaine use will vary with the lower concentration cutoff used, quantity of cocaine consumed (Ambre, 1985), and individual differences in pharmacokinetics. Instances have been reported wherein low concentrations of benzoylecgonine have persisted in the urine for a week or longer (Weiss & Gawin, 1988). Whether such occurrences are a consequence of the quantity of cocaine consumed, reflect unusual pharmacokinetics, or indicate redistribution from a deep compartment is uncertain. However, considering the enormous amounts of cocaine that may be self-administered during a binge, it is not surprising that detectable concentrations of benzoylecgonine might sometimes persist in the urine for a considerable time. This is not a trivial issue, in that questions often arise as to whether the detection of benzoylecgonine in urine indicates recent and/or recurrent use (within the last several days) or residual metabolite from an earlier episode. In general, the presence of un-metabolized cocaine in urine tends to suggest relatively recent use, that is, within the last 12–24 hours.

Other biological materials have been used for drug abuse screening. Hair, in particular, has attracted considerable attention. It has been suggested that not only does cocaine and/or benzoylecgonine persist in hair for a much longer period than in urine, but that hair can also provide an chronological record of drug use over an extended period (Baumgartner, Black, Jones, & Blahd, 1982). In theory, drug found in the distal portion of the hair shaft may represent exposure at a relatively early time, and that near the root might reflect more recent use. It has been suggested that hair analysis might be particularly useful in screening of newborn infants for intrauterine exposure to cocaine (Graham, Koren, Klein, Schneiderman, & Greenwald, 1989). Meconium has also been recommended as superior to urine for the evaluation of newborns (Maynard, Amoruso, & Oh, 1991). The data on hair analysis is quite provocative, but further study to characterize this application, including such critical parameters as detection limits, recovery, and specificity in comparison with a "gold" standard such as GC/MS is needed (Bailey, 1990). It cannot be emphasized strongly enough that urine drug screening cannot be used to establish clinical condition or behavioral impairment at the time of sample collection, nor quantity of drug used, nor time of drug use. Urine drug abuse screening, with proven confirmation, can only establish that a drug or its metabolites are present (above a lower threshold concentration) or absent (below that concentration), and thus that the drug has either been used or not been used within a very approximate time window.

COCAINE BLOOD LEVELS

Most information available on the correlation between plasma blood concentrations and clinical or behavioral effects is based upon single-dose studies in a laboratory setting employing unequivocally safe doses. Subjects are attached to an intravenous line, along with various electronic monitors for measurement of physiological parameters. At frequent intervals, they may be asked to fill out various questionnaires designed to evaluate cocaine's subjective effects. At the same time, they are evaluated by trained observers. This paradigm is usually the only option for performing such studies and has yielded a great deal of valuable information. However, extrapolation of such data to a naturalistic setting more conducive to experiencing cocaine's effects, and wherein multiple, often much larger, doses are repeatedly self-administered during the course of a binge, is less than perfect. Some investigators (Foltin et al., 1990), have studied cocaine's effects in a more naturalistic experimental laboratory setting, with repeated administration.

It is probable that blood concentrations that occur during the course of a binge are well in excess of those observed in the laboratory. Acute tolerance, although a controversial issue, may also play a role in determining the behavioral and physiological correlates of cocaine blood concentrations (Fischman, Schuster, Javaid, Hatano, & Davis, 1985; Chou, Ambre, & Ruo, 1986). Most studies indicate that behavioral and physiological effects decay more rapidly than cocaine blood concentrations and that they are more intense during the rising portion of the blood level curve. Rapidly rising blood levels also appear to produce the most intense effects. Thus the same peak plasma levels occurring immediately after IV or pulmonary (smoking) administration are more intense than, and may even be qualitatively different from, those observed after intranasal (snorting) use. The effect of the route of administration on bioavailability and on rate of rise of plasma blood concentrations has been discussed above (see Pharmokinetics).

Evaluation of Cocaine Overdose

The laboratory is often asked to evaluate the possibility of cocaine intoxication in young patients presenting with acute psychosis, seizures, cardiac arrhythmias, myocardial ischemia, and a history suspicious for drug abuse in the absence of other likely causes. Clinical laboratories will usually address this problem through rapid analysis of urine for benzoylecgonine with an immunoassay. It is unlikely that anyone will manifest symptoms of acute cocaine intoxication in the absence of benzoylecgonine in the urine. However, the presence of this inactive metabolite in urine only indicates that cocaine has been used, probably within the last several days, and does not establish that the presenting clinical problem is a consequence of cocaine use. Finding of unchanged cocaine in the urine is somewhat more suggestive that cocaine has been used within the last 12–24 hours. However, because the effects of cocaine can dissipate quickly, even this information must be used with caution in attributing clinical findings to cocaine. For the same reason, the quantity of either cocaine or its metabolite in the urine may in itself be of limited use in explaining behavioral effects.

The measurement of cocaine in plasma is probably the best, although not perfect, option for drawing conclusions about the probability of acute cocaine intoxication. The data regarding cocaine, or, for that matter, most psychotropic drugs, is insufficient to permit definitive conclusions regarding correlation of blood concentrations with clinical effects. The time between ingestion and sampling; tolerance; presence of other, possibly unidentified central nervous system active drugs; and individual variations in pharmacokinetics and dynamics are all confounding factors. However, a plasma level greater than 100 ng per mL suggests that cocaine has been used within the last 6 hours, and this together with the clinical data, can enable reasonable clinical conclusions. Patients may present with evidence of myocardial ischemia or stroke at a time when cocaine is no longer measurable in the blood. In such instances, identification of cocaine metabolite in the urine may be helpful in placing a patient within a high-risk group.

Determination of plasma levels of cocaine is not available in most hospitals, and rarely, if ever, in such a manner as to be useful for clinical management. Thus, in the urgent clinical situation, understanding the uses and constraints of urine drug screening is probably more important than the ability to interpret plasma cocaine concentrations.

Plasma Cocaine Concentrations in Clinical Research

Several studies have measured plasma drug concentrations in the course of investigating cocaine's pharmacokinetics and pharmacodynamics following various routes of administration. Single-dose pharmacokinetics and dynamics of cocaine by all routes of administration (oral, intranasal, intravenous, and pulmonary) have been well established (Javaid, Fischman, Schuster, Dekirmenjian, & Davis, 1978; Fischman et al., 1985; Van Dyke et al., 1976; Van Dyke et al., 1978). Cocaine levels remain helpful in studies attempting to access the neurochemical effects of cocaine following acute and chronic use, and in studies of the effects of various pharmacological interventions on cocaine's pharmacodynamics. Cocaine concentrations are particularly important whenever nonsystemic (e.g., intranasal) routes of administration are employed wherein bioavailability is incomplete and variable. Ruling out of pharmacokinetic interactions of experimental drugs with cocaine is another indication for obtaining blood levels. For example, in a recent study of the effect of desipramine on the response to acute cocaine challenges, it was essential to verify that cocaine blood concentration in the active and placebo groups were approximately the same. Otherwise it would have been impossible to determine whether desipramine might have directly effected the response to cocaine or whether instead, it had altered the disposition of cocaine (Kosten et al., in press).

Drug analysis can also be important in the clinical evaluation of various pharmacological agents that are being considered for management of cocaine abuse. Because most of our data regarding blood concentrations of various psychotherapeutic drugs under investigation is based upon the treatment of non-drug-abuse disorders, their extrapolation to cocaine abuse may not be appropriate. Preliminary data suggests that there may be a therapeutic window for desipramine and that subjects with high desipramine levels (> 200 ng per mL), show a poor response (Gawin et al., in preparation). Possibly, high levels of desipramine elicit sufficient dopaminergic effects, to serve as a cue that enhances rather than reduces craving. In any event, establishment of a dose–response relationship is an accepted criteria for establishing cause and effect.

Even if definition of a therapeutic range is an unrealistic goal, monitoring of blood levels of therapeutic agents can serve several other useful purposes. The most obvious is assessment of drug compliance, potentially a problem in outpatient clinical trials in the drug-abusing population. Moreover, plasma drug concentrations can help to explain outcome. A subpopulation that shows poor response as a consequence of unusually high or low concentrations can confound the interpretation and cause a pessimistic evaluation of what may actually be a useful medication.

Measurement of blood levels can be useful in assessing interactions of cocaine and a therapeutic agent. For example, patients receiving concurrent methadone and desipramine treatment for poly-drug abuse with opiates and cocaine have much higher blood levels of desipramine than do either desipramine-treated cocaine abusers not receiving methadone, or a population of depressed non-drug-abusing patients. We found higher plasma-level-to-dose ratios in the methadone group, and lower relative concentrations of 2-hydroxy desipramine suggesting, although not proving, that methadone inhibits desipramine metabolism (Kosten et al., 1990). Excessively high desipramine levels might help explain a poor response in this group of patients. Investigation of carbamazepine for the management of cocaine abuse offers another example. Because carbamazepine is a strong microsomal enzyme inducer, it might lower methadone concentrations and increase the methadone dose required to successfully control opiate use and prevent withdrawal in patients concurrently treated for opiate abuse. On the other hand, the same individuals might require a reduction of methadone dose upon discontinuation of carbamazepine.

Analytical Methods

A variety of suitable methods have been reported for measurement of cocaine in plasma. These include GC/MS, gas chromatography using a nitrogen selected detector, and high-performance liquid chromatography (HPLC) (Jatlow & Bailey, 1975; Jatlow & Nadim, 1990; Jacobs, Elias-Baker, Jones, & Benowitz, 1984; Foltz, Fentiman, & Foltz, 1980). Probably the latter is the easiest to use and most suitable for "routine" analyses, either clinically or in research. Although immunoassays may be suitable for plasma cocaine analysis, they are more generally used for urine screening. Currently, plasma cocaine assays are available in some research centers and forensic laboratories. Most procedures are capable of quantifying cocaine concentrations as low as about 5 ng per mL. This is suitable for pharmacokinetics studies and is well below threshold concentrations associated with pharmacological effects. For both clinical and research purposes, it is often desirable to freeze samples for future assays. It should be remembered that cocaine disappears very rapidly in vitro in plasma if a cholinesterase inhibitor is not added. This is most easily accomplished by collecting samples in the usual gray-stoppered glucose collection tubes, which generally contain sufficient sodium fluoride to inhibit cholinesterase activity, providing samples are frozen within about 2 hours of collection.

CONCLUSIONS

Skepticism about the usefulness of plasma drug concentrations arises from the often inconsistent data regarding their clinical or pharmacological significance, and opinions that data obtained from populations may not be applicable to individuals. However, in any situation wherein dose is considered to be important, plasma concentrations can be viewed as a more precise expression of dosage, corrected for individual variations in pharmacokinetics. Considering the marked variation in human response to psychotropic drugs, measurement or detection of cocaine and/or its metabolites in the appropriate biological fluids is at present our best tool for establishing that cocaine has been used; how much has reached the systemic circulation and, implicitly, receptor sites in the brain and other target organs; and whether or not various observed effects might reasonably be attributed to cocaine.

REFERENCES

Ambre, J. (1985). The urinary excretion of cocaine and metabolites in humans: A kinetic analysis of published data. *Journal of Analytical Toxicology, 9,* 241–245.

Bailey, D. N. (1989). Drug screening in an unconventional matrix: Hair analysis. *Journal of the American medical Association, 262,* 3331.

Barnett, G., Hawks, R., & Resnick, R. (1981). Cocaine pharmacokinetics in humans. *Ethnopharmacology, 3,* 353–366.

Baumgartner, A. M., Black, C. T., Jones, P. F., & Blahd, W. H. (1982). Radioimmunoassay of cocaine in hair. *Journal of Nuclear Medicine, 23,* 790–792.

Chou, M. J., Ambre, J. J., & Ruo, T. I. Kinetics of cocaine distribution, elimination, and chronotropic effects. *Clinical Pharmacology and Therapeutics, 38,* 318–324.

Cook, C. E., Jeffcoat, R. J., & Perez-Reyes, M. Pharmacokinetic studies of cocaine and phencyclidine in man. In G. Barnett & C. N. Chiang (Eds.), *Pharmacokinetics and pharmacodynamics of psychoactive drugs* (pp. 48–74). Foster City, CA: Biomedical Publications.

DeCresce, R., Mazura, A., Lifshitz, M., & Tilson, J. (1990). Drug testing in the workplace. *American Society of Clinical Pathology.* Chicago: ASCP Press.

Fischman, M. W., Schuster, C. R., Javaid, J., Hatano, Y., & Davis, J. (1985). Acute tolerance development to the cardiovascular and subjective effects of cocaine. *Journal of Pharmacology and Experimental Therapeutics, 235,* 677–682.

Foltin, R. W., Fischman, M. W., Nestadt, G., Stromberger, H., Cornell, E. E., & Pearlson, G. D. (1990). Demonstration of naturalistic methods for cocaine smoking by human volunteers. *Drug and Alcohol Dependence, 26,* 145–154.

Foltz, R. L., Fentiman, A. F., & Foltz, R. B. (Eds.). (1980). *GC/MS assays for drugs in body fluid* (National Institute on Drug Abuse Research Monograph No. 32). Washington, DC: U. S. Government Printing Office.

Graham, K., Koren, G., Klein, J., Schneiderman, J., & Greenwald, M. (1989). Determination of gestational cocaine exposure by hair analysis. *Journal of the American Medical Association, 262*(23), 3328–3330.

Grant, B. F., & Harford, T. C. (1990). Concurrent and simultaneous use of alcohol with cocaine—results of a national survey. *Drug and Alcohol Dependence, 25,* 97–104.

Hawks, R. L., & Chiang, C. N. (Eds.). (1986). *Urine testing for drugs of abuse* (National Institute on Drug Abuse Research Monograph No. 73). Washington, DC: U. S. Government Printing Office.

Hawks, R. L., Kopin, I. J., Colburn, R. W., & Thoa, N. B. (1986). Norcocaine: A pharmacologically active metabolite of cocaine found in brain. *Life Sciences, 15,* 2189–2195.

Hearn, W. L., Flynn, D. D., Hime, G. W., Rose, S., Contino, J. C., Mantero-Atienza, E., Wetli, C. V., & Mash, D. C. (1991). Cocaethylene:

A unique cocaine metabolite displays high affinity for the dopamine transporter. *Journal of Neurochemistry, 56,* 698–701.

Jacobs, P., Elias-Baker, B. A., Jones, R. T., & Benowitz., N. L. (1984). Determination of cocaine in plasma by automated gas chromatography. *Journal of Chromatography, 306,* 173–181.

Inaba, T., Steward, D. J., & Kalow, W. (1978). Metabolism of cocaine in man. *Clinical Pharmacology and Therapeutics, 23,* 547–552.

Jatlow, P., & Bailey, D. (1975) Gas chromatographic analysis for cocaine in human plasma with use of a nitrogen detector. *Clinical Chemistry, 21,* 1918–1921.

Jatlow, P., Barash, P. G., Van Dyke, C., Radding, J., & Byck, R. (1979). Cocaine and succinylcholine sensitivity: A new caution. *Anesthesia and Analgesia 58,* 235–238.

Jatlow, P., Elsworth, J. D., Bradberry, C. W., Winger, J. H., Taylor, J. R., Russell, R., & Roth, R. H. (1991). Cocaethylene: A neuropharmacologically active metabolite associated with concurrent cocaine-ethanol ingestion. *Life Sciences, 48,* 1787–1794.

Jatlow, P., & Nadim, H. (1990). Determination of cocaine concentrations in plasma by high performance liquid chromatography. *Clinical Chemistry, 36,* 1436–1439.

Javaid, J. I., Fischman, M. W., Schuster, C. R., Dekirmenjiian, H., & Davis, J. M. (1978). Cocaine plasma concentrations: Relation to physiological and subjective effects in humans. *Science, 200,* 227–228.

Kloss, M. N., Rosen, G. M., & Rauckman, E. J. (1984). Cocaine mediated hepatotoxicity, a critical review. *Biochemical Pharmacology, 33,* 169–173.

Kosten, T. R., Gawin, F. H., Morgan, J. C., Nelson, J. C., & Jatlow, P. (1990). Evidence for altered desipramine disposition in methadone maintained patients treated for cocaine abuse. *American Journal of Drug and Alcohol, 16,* 329–336.

Kosten, T., Gawin, F. H., Silverman, D. G., Fleming, J., Compton, M., Jatlow, P., & Byck, R. (in press). Intravenous cocaine challenges during desipramine maintenance. *Neuropsychopharmacology.*

Maynard, E. C., Amoruso, L. P., & Oh, W. (1991). Meconium for drug testing. *American Journal of Diseases of Children, 145*(6), 650–652.

Paly, D., Jatlow, P., Van Dyke, C., Jeri, R., & Byck, R. (1982). Plasma cocaine concentrations during cocaine paste smoking. *Life Sciences, 30*(9), 731–738.

Perez-Reyes, M., Diguiseppi, S., Ondrusek, G., Jeffcoat, A. R., & Cook, C. E. (1982). Free base cocaine smoking. *Clinical Pharmacology and Therapeutics, 32,* 459–465.

Stewart, D. J., Inaba, T., Lucassen, M., & Kalow, W. (1979). Cocaine metabolism: Cocaine and norcocaine hydrolysis by liver and serum esterases. *Clinical Pharmacology and Therapeutics, 25,* 464–468.

Thompson, M. L., Shuster, L., & Shaw, K. (1979). Cocaine-induced hepatic necrosis in mice: The role of cocaine metabolism. *Biochemical Pharmacology, 28,* 2389–2395.

Van Dyke, C., Barash, P. G., Jatlow, P., & Byck, R. (1976). Cocaine: Plasma concentrations after intranasal application in man. *Science, 191*, 859–861.

Van Dyke, C., Byck, B., Barash, P., & Jatlow, P. (1977). Time course of urinary excretion of immunologically (EMIT) reactive metabolites following intranasal administration of cocaine. *Clinical Chemistry, 23*, 241–244.

Van Dyke, C., Jatlow, P., Ungerer, J., Barash, P. G., & Byck, R. (1978). Oral cocaine: Plasma concentrations and central effects. *Science, 200*, 211–213.

Weiss, R. D., & Gawin, F. H. (1988). Protracted elimination of cocaine metabolites in long-term high-dose cocaine abusers. *American Journal of Medicine, 85*(6), 879–880.

Wilkinson, P., Van Dyke, C., Jatlow, P., Barash, P., & Byck, R. (1980). Intranasal and oral cocaine kinetics. *Clinical Pharmacology and Therapeutics, 27*, 386–394.

HAPTER ELEVEN ▓▓▓▓▓▓▓▓▓▓▓▓▓▓▓▓▓▓▓▓▓▓▓▓

Family/Genetic Studies of Cocaine Abusers and Opioid Addicts

Bruce J. Rounsaville, MD
Suniya Luthar, PhD

WHAT IS TRANSMITTED IN FAMILIES OF DRUG ABUSERS?

Since 1983, we have pursued the hypothesis that drug abuse is transmitted in families. Numerous reports from families of drug abusers (Rounsaville, Kosten, et al. 1991; Stanton, 1979; Cadoret, Troughton, O'Gorman, & Heywood, 1978; Croughan, 1985; Mirin, Weiss, Sollogub, & Michael 1984) and alcoholics (Winokur & Clayton, 1968; Goodwin, 1979; Schuckit, 1986; Cloninger, 1978) suggest that substance abuse runs in families. However, a fundamental question is "What is being transmitted?" We have pursued two possible types of familially transmitted vulnerability: (1) individuals inherit a factor related to the mechanism of action or metabolism of psychoactive substances themselves, or (2) individuals inherit a factor that underlies a range of deviant behaviors of which substance abuse is one.

Within the first model, the familially transmitted factor may be broad or very specific. If it is broad, then what may be transmitted is something like an especially high level of positive reinforcement (or especially low level of negative reinforcement) (Rounsaville et al., 1991b) from a wide range of psychoactive substances. For even the most addictive drugs, only a fraction of those who use go on to develop a substance use disorder. This group may be those for whom the warning "It's so good, don't even try it once" may be said to apply. If the vulnerability is narrow, then what is being transmitted is a special sensitivity to specific classes of drugs such as sedatives, alcohol, opiates, stimulants, or hallucinogens, each of which is associated with different mechanisms of action.

Within the second model, substance abuse is indirectly transmitted in families by increased vulnerability to other disorders associated with drug abuse. Familially transmitted psychiatric disorders are a likely candidate for an intervening factor predisposing to drug abuse. For example, drug abuse has been hypothesized to be a form of self-treatment for dysphoric psychiatric symptoms such as anxiety or depression (Khantzian, 1985). Alternatively, drug abuse may fit well with the sensation-seeking traits of individuals with antisocial personality disorder or may be used to sustain the euphoric moods of mania.

HOW CAN WE EVALUATE WHAT IS BEING TRANSMITTED IN FAMILIES OF COCAINE ABUSERS?

In the remainder of this chapter, we will outline the types of evidence that might suggest whether familially transmitted vulnerability to cocaine abuse is (1) specific or general, and/or (2) mediated by psychopathology. In considering the different models for familial transmission of cocaine abuse, it should be noted that (1) the models are not mutually exclusive, so that there can be multiple familially transmitted pathways to cocaine abuse (e.g., depression plus or minus variants in dopaminergic systems), and (2) the population of cocaine abusers is likely to be heterogeneous so that, for example, some may have become cocaine abusers because of familial predisposition to antisocial personality, others in relationship to a familial predisposition to depression, and still others with no familial predisposing factors whatsoever (Meyer, 1986; Rounsaville, Weissman, Wilber, & Kleber, 1982).

To evaluate whether inherited vulnerability to substance abuse is drug-specific or general, we have studied families of separate groups of drug abusers who identify different substances including cocaine, opioids, and alcohol as their principal addiction. Alcoholics and their families remain the key comparison group because exposure to alcohol is nearly universal in Western societies, and a large literature already exists documenting genetic and familial factors that increase vulnerability to alcoholism (Winokur & Clayton, 1968; Goodwin, 1979; Schuckit, 1986; Cloninger, Christiansen, Reich, & Gottesman, 1978). Thus, if identical patterns of familial transmission occur with alcoholism and other drugs, this would suggest that findings from family and genetic studies of alcoholism can be extrapolated to apply to other types of drug abuse.

To provide evidence for a connection between inheritance of cocaine abuse and alcoholism, or between cocaine abuse and psychopathology, data can be evaluated from several lines of evidence: (1) studies showing an association of alcoholism and psychopathology with cocaine abuse (2) studies showing excess rates of alcoholism and psychiatric disorders in the families of cocaine abusers and also a more than expected co-occurrence of the two types of disorders within the families, and (3) studies showing excess rates of cocaine abuse in the families of those with alcoholism and other psychiatric disorders.

To what extent does this evidence exist at this time?

COMORBID ALCOHOLISM AND PSYCHIATRIC DISORDERS IN COCAINE ABUSERS

Evidence from both clinical and community surveys concurs in suggesting a strong association between cocaine abuse and other psychiatric disorders (Schottenfeld, Carroll, & Rounsaville, in press). In our survey of 298 treatment-seeking cocaine abusers (Rounsaville, Anton, et al. 1991) we found high lifetime rates of Major Depression 30.5%, Cyclothymia/Hyperthymia 19.9%, Mania/Hypomania 11.1%, Phobia 13.4%, Alcoholism 61.1% and Antisocial Personality 32.9%. These findings are consistent with numerous other reports from clinical samples (Chitwood & Morningstar, 1985; Gawin & Kleber, 1986; Griffin, Weiss, Mirin, & Lange, 1989; Nunes, Quitkin, & Klein, 1989; Weiss, Mirin, Griffin, & Michael, 1988; Weiss, Mirin, Michael, & Sollogub, 1986; Helfrich, Crowley, & Atkinson, 1982) in showing high rates of depression, bipolar disorders and anxiety disorders in treatment-seeking samples. Because these rates are derived from treatment-seeking groups, they may be artifactually high because having two disorders may predispose to treatment seeking. We evaluated this possibility by comparing treatment seekers with non-treatment-seeking cocaine abusers in the community and found that only rates of current Major Depression were higher (Carroll & Rounsaville, in press) suggesting that a current depressive episode may predispose to entering treatment. However, lifetime rates of major depression were elevated and nonsignificantly different in treated and untreated groups.

Because treatment-seeking groups are special in many ways, data from community samples are vital. Three studies from large-scale community surveys also document an association between psychopathology and cocaine abuse. Kandel, Murphy, and Karas (1985) reported on the results from a community survey of 1325 young adults in New York State who participated in earlier studies while still in high school. Based on a structured interview, their cross-sectional survey revealed that some cocaine users were less happy and had higher rates of psychiatric hospitalization, compared with women who did not use cocaine. No association was found between depression or psychiatric hospitalization, compared with women who did not use cocaine. No association was found between depression or psychiatric hospitalization and cocaine use among males. Newcomb, Bentler, and Fahey (1987) studied a community sample of 739 young adults in Los Angeles County, approximately one third of whom came from minority groups. The investigators used a 7-point scale to assess intensity of use among cocaine users, a category that included 37% of the men and 34% of the women out of the total sampled, 5% reported weekly cocaine use. Symptoms of anxiety and depression were associated with use of cocaine.

The best data regarding the co-occurrence of psychiatric and substance abuse disorders in community, as opposed to treatment-seeking, samples comes from the Epidemiological Catchment Area study (ECA), which used a structured psychiatric interview (the Diagnostic Interview Schedule) to assess psychopathology and substance use disorders in a carefully designed epidemiological sample of adults (Anthony & Trinkoff, 1988). In the ECA, the lifetime prevalence of drug abuse or dependence among males aged 18–44 years was 12.5%. Among men with a history of drug abuse/dependence compared with those without, lifetime rates of major depression were 14% versus 4%, rates for antisocial personality were 38% versus 10%, and rates for panic disorder were 3.2% versus 0.9%. Lifetime antisocial personality among those with drug abuse or dependence was 38% compared with 10% among those without these disorders. The lifetime prevalence of panic disorder was 3.2% among those with drug abuse or dependence compared with 0.9% among those without those disorders. In addition, data from the ECA on cocaine comorbidity document an increased lifetime prevalence of major depression among heavier users of cocaine. Among men aged 18–44, lifetime prevalence rates for major depression were 76% among those who never used cocaine or used it one to five times; 11% for those with a history of more than five times of cocaine use but no history of daily use; 14.6% for men with a history of daily use for 2 weeks or more but who did not meet DSM-III criteria for cocaine abuse; and 25.8% among men with a history of cocaine abuse. Similarly, a lifetime prevalence of panic disorder was considerably higher in men with a history of cocaine abuse (15.%) compared with men who had used zero to five times (1.7%), had used greater than five times but never daily

(2.4%), or had used daily for 2 weeks or more but did not meet criteria for cocaine abuse (2.3%). Alcohol dependence or abuse was diagnosed in 85% of those with cocaine abuse or dependence. Similar findings were found with regard to patterns of use for both marijuana and heroin.

In conclusion, the preponderance of evidence from both treatment-seeking and community samples of cocaine abusers suggests a strong association with alcoholism and other psychiatric disorders, particularly depressive disorders, anxiety disorders and antisocial personality. Because considerable evidence suggests that vulnerability to alcoholism (Winokur & Clayton, 1968; Goodwin, 1979; Schuckit, 1986), depression (Weissman et al. 1984; Winokur, Cadoret, Dorzab, & Baker, 1971; Winokur, Morrison, Clancy, & Crowe, 1973; Winokur, 1974), and criminality (Cloninger et al., 1978) is also transmitted in families, these are good candidates for disorders that may account for familial transmission of vulnerability to cocaine abuse.

DUAL DIAGNOSIS IN FAMILIES

There is little to review regarding findings that show excessive rates of cocaine abuse in the families of alcoholics, depressives, and individuals with antisocial personality. The reason for this lack of evidence may not be a lack of shared vulnerability between these disorders. Rather, it pertains to the important temporal and geographical trends in the epidemiology of cocaine abuse (see Chapter 12 in this volume). In contrast with alcohol use, which has been practiced by over 90% of the adult population in the United States for many generations, cocaine use has been comparatively rare until the 1980s, when over 25% of the 18–25-year-old group reported lifetime use of the drug in the NIDA-sponsored National Household Survey on Drug Abuse (Adams, Gfroerer, Rouse, & Kozel, 1986; NIDA, 1988). This contrasts with far lower rates for other age groups and with a rate of 9.1% lifetime use in the 18–25-year-old group in 1972, the first year the survey was conducted. Rates from prior years are likely to be at the 1972 level or lower. Moreover, these rates reflect use of cocaine and not cocaine abuse or dependence. The only survey to evaluate community rates of cocaine abuse or dependence was the ECA study, described above, in which overall lifetime rates of substance use disorders were over 5%. However, most of this was accounted for by marijuana abuse, and cocaine abuse was reported by less than 1% of the sample.

The large changes in rates of exposure to cocaine and the fact that cocaine is used only by a minority of the population place major constraints on the study of familial factors leading to cocaine abuse.

Older studies or those conducted in countries with low rates of cocaine use are uninformative, because exposure to cocaine is obviously necessary in order to develop cocaine abuse/dependence. This limitation applies to all of the landmark twin and adoption studies using Scandinavian samples and to most of the family studies evaluating biological relatives of those with depression, anxiety disorders, alcoholism or criminality. Hence lack of evidence from this literature does not mean that these familially transmitted disorders do not convey increased vulnerability to cocaine abuse. Rather, most subjects in these studies were protected by lack of exposure to cocaine.

Even in family studies of cocaine abusers, members of different generations or even siblings at different age levels within the same families may have widely varying risk for development of cocaine abuse owing to differential exposure to the drug. This contrasts with vulnerability to other psychiatric disorders or alcoholism for which exposure to environmental factors is not as essential or is nearly universal.

Because of these factors, there are no published studies at this time showing an excess of cocaine abuse in the biological relatives of those with alcoholism or other psychiatric disorders. Only two investigations have reported findings on rates of drug abuse, alcoholism, and other psychiatric disorders in the biological relatives of cocaine abusers. The first reports findings from the families of 160 drug abusers, of whom 36 were principally stimulant abusers (Mirin et al., 1984). In this study, rates exceeding those seen in community samples were found for alcohol abuse/dependence (males 15.2%, females 10.0%), drug abuse/dependence (males 12.2%, females 15.0%), and affective disorders (males 13.6%, females 26.7%). As well as far exceeding rates of these disorders found in community surveys such as the ECA study, these rates of disorders in families of stimulant abusers also exceeded those found in families of opioid addicts and of alcoholics. No data were presented regarding the degree to which comorbid alcoholism or depression in the stimulant-abusing probands was associated with elevated rates of these same disorders in their first-degree relatives.

RESULTS FROM THE YALE FAMILY/GENETIC STUDIES OF SUBSTANCE ABUSERS

In a study focusing on psychiatric disorders in treated cocaine abusers (Rounsaville, Anton, et al., 1991), we obtained psychiatric diagnoses using the Schedule for Affective Disorders and Schizophrenia (SADS) (Endicott & Spitzer, 1978) and Research Diagnostic Criteria (RDC) (Spitzer, Endicott, & Robins, 1978) on a sample of 298 patients in drug abuse treatment who identified cocaine as their principal drug of abuse. All met Research Diagnostic Criteria for cocaine abuse and over 99% also met DSM-III-R Criteria for Cocaine Dependence. We also obtained a family history of psychiatric disorders on all adult first-degree relatives using Family History Research Diagnostic Criteria (Andreason, Rice, Endicott, Reich, & Coryell, 1986). In all, we obtained diagnoses on 1,165 first-degree relatives including 673 siblings (355 males and 318 females) and 492 parents (236 males and 256 females). Missing data are accounted for by subjects who either did not know their family members or did not have sufficient information to respond to questions about relatives' psychiatric history.

To evaluate the issue of generalizability across families of those who abuse different types of drugs, we provide comparison data from a family/genetic study of opioid addicts in which 201 opioid-dependent probands and 877 first-degree relatives were diagnosed using similar methods. In the opioid study, we attempted to obtain direct interviews on first-degree relatives and were successful in interviewing a minority of them. In this study we found that being interviewed was associated with considerably higher rates of psychiatric disorders. Therefore, to provide a comparison group to cocaine abusers' relatives diagnosed from family history information, we will present findings from those opioid addicts' relatives who were not directly interviewed ($n = 743$).

We will evaluate findings from these samples as they relate to the two models for familial transmission described above. The specific trends expected, based on the two models, are as follows:

1. If vulnerability to substance abuse is transmitted, high rates of alcoholism and drug abuse would be expected in the relatives of drug-abusing samples in comparison to community rates derived from the New Haven sample of the Epidemiology Catchment Area Study (Robins et al., 1984). If a narrow vulnerability to abuse nonalcoholic drugs is being transmitted, we would expect high rates of drug abuse but not alcoholism in the relatives, except for the relatives of those cocaine- or opioid-addict probands who are also alcoholic themselves. Regarding the important issue of whether findings from alcoholics' families can be generalized to other samples of drug abusers, we will indirectly examine this issue by contrasting families of probands who abuse opioids and cocaine. If families of cocaine and opioid abusers are found to differ substantially in rates and patterns of substance abuse and psychopathology, this finding would suggest the need to conduct separate evaluations on familial vulnerability to different drugs of abuse.

2. If vulnerability to drug abuse is nearly always mediated by a vulnerability to another psychiatric disorder such as antisocial personality or depression, we would expect an excess of both types of conditions

TABLE 11.1. Demographic Characteristics of First-Degree Relatives of Cocaine and Opioid Abusers

Subjects	Cocaine		Opioid[a]	
	Male	Female	Male	Female
Probands				
n	206	92	95	106
Mean age	28.1	26.9	28.4	28.5
SD age	7.0	6.2	3.7	4.3
Relatives				
n	591	574	399	344
Mean age	40.9	40.9	44.2	44.2
SD age	15.12	14.2	16.4	14.8

[a]Only noninterviewed relatives included.

in the first-degree relatives of addicts, regardless of whether or not the proband has the psychiatric disorder as well. If drug abusers with comorbid psychopathology (e.g., depression) represent subgroups whose psychiatric disorders are independently transmitted, we would expect high rates of the comorbid disorders only in the families of dually diagnosed probands.

Demographic characteristics of the cocaine- and opioid-abusing probands and their relatives are presented in Table 11.1. As shown, the cocaine abusers differed from opioid addicts by having a larger proportion of males. Age, however, was similar. Regarding first-degree relatives, both samples of relatives were nearly evenly divided between males and females with an average age in their early 40s.

Rates of psychiatric disorders in relatives of cocaine abusers and opioid addicts are displayed in Table 11.2 along with rates in the New Haven Catchment Area from the ECA study. The ECA comparison group is presented as a general reference group in that diagnoses in this study were obtained using the Diagnostic Interview Schedule (Robins, Helzer, Croughan, & Ratcliffe, 1981) and scored according to DSM-III criteria. Most importantly, diagnoses were made from direct interview, a procedure which we have shown to result in rates of disorders more than twice those obtained through family history only. Hence, in comparison with the ECA sample, rates derived from first-degree relatives of cocaine and opioid abusers are likely to represent substantial underestimates of the true prevalence. Therefore, when rates of relatives' disorders exceed community rates, it is likely that the difference noted would be substantially greater, if relatives had been directly interviewed.

As shown in Table 11.2, comparisons with community rates of disorders in relatives of either cocaine abusers or opioid addicts indicate an excess of major depression, alcoholism, drug abuse, and antisocial

TABLE 11.2. Rates of Psychiatric Disorders Among First-Degree Relatives of Cocaine and Opioid Users Compared with Community Rates

	Cocaine relatives		Opioid relatives		ECA samples	
	Males	Females	Males	Females	Males	Females
n	591	574	399	344	8,211	10,971
Major depression	6.2	10.5[a]	8.8	16.3	2.6	7.0
Any anxiety (gener-alized, manic, phobic, obsessive compulsive)	1.4[a]	7.0	3.5	9.9	—	—
Alcoholism	35.0	15.9	29.1	14.5	13.5	2.8
Drug abuse	26.9[c]	14.4[c]	15.5	7.3	2.4	1.5
Antisocial personality	11.3[c]	2.31[b]	4.8	0.6	4.5	0.8

Note. ECA = Epidemiological Catchment Area.
[a]Rates among cocaine relatives < rates among same-sex opioid relatives at $p < .05$
[b]Rates among cocaine relatives > rates among same-sex opioid relatives at $p < .05$
[c]Rates among cocaine relatives > rates among same-sex opioid relatives at $p < .01$

personality. Hence relatives of these samples of drug abusers manifest an excess of the same disorders that are prevalent among the drug-abusing probands.

When relatives of cocaine abusers and opioid abusers are compared, we note a trend for opioid addicts' relatives to have higher rates of major depression and anxiety disorders and cocaine abusers' relatives to have higher rates of drug abuse and antisocial personality.

To evaluate the independence of transmission of psychiatric disorders in cocaine abusers' families, we contrasted the rates of disorders in relatives of cocaine abusers with and without specific psychiatric disorders. As shown in Table 11.3, proband alcoholism was not associated with an excess of any disorder in relatives; proband anxiety disorders were associated with a nearly two-fold (6.2% vs. 3.6%) risk for anxiety disorders, but not for other disorders; proband depression was associated with significantly higher rates of alcoholism (31.1% vs. 22.9%), drug abuse (25.4% vs. 18.4%), and depression (12.2% vs. 6.5%); and proband antisocial personality was not associated with considerably higher rates of any disorder.

CONCLUSIONS FROM THE YALE STUDIES

Regarding the models for familial transmission of substance abuse and comorbid psychopathology discussed, above the findings are consistent with the following conclusions:

TABLE 11.3. Specificity of Aggregation: Rates/100 Disorders in Relatives of Cocaine Probands by Comorbid Diagnosis in Proband

	Comorbid diagnosis in proband							
	Alcoholism		Any anxiety		Major depression		Antisocial personality	
	+	−	+	−	+	−	+	−
	n (%)	n (%)	n (%)	n (%)	n (%)	n (%)	n (%)	n (%)
Relatives	728	437	246	919	379	786	369	796
Alcoholism	192 (26.4)	105 (24.3)	67 (27.2)	231 (25.1)	118 (31.1)	180 (22.9)	106 (28.7)	192 (24.1)
Any anxiety (generalized panic, phobic, obsessive–compulsive)	28 (3.9)	20 (4.6)	15 (6.2)	33 (3.6)	20 (5.4)	28 (3.6)	17 (4.7)	31 (3.9)
Major depression	58 (8.1)	38 (8.8)	18 (7.4)	78 (8.6)	45 (12.2)	51 (6.5)	31 (8.5)	65 (8.2)
Antisocial personality	52 (7.2)	27 (6.2)	18 (7.4)	6.1 (6.7)	30 (8.1)	49 (6.3)	29 (8.0)	50 (6.3)
Drug abuse	147 (20.5)	91 (21.0)	47 (19.3)	191 (21.0)	94 (25.4)	144 (18.4)	87 (24.0)	151 (19.1)

1. Cocaine abusers' families manifest an excess vulnerability to a broad spectrum of substance abuse. Both alcohol and drug abuse were seen in high rates in relatives of cocaine abusers. Thus relatives were not only likely to abuse illicit drugs, but also to abuse alcohol. Moreover, the high rate of alcohol abuse in relatives was seen whether or not the proband abused alcohol. This finding suggests that alcohol and cocaine abuse are related to a shared familial vulnerability.

2. Cocaine abusers' families show an excess of a spectrum of psychiatric disorders, particularly antisocial personality and major depression, regardless of whether or not the proband manifests that disorder. This suggests cocaine abuse is related to familially transmitted vulnerability that is shared with antisocial personality and major depression.

3. Whereas families of cocaine abusers and opioid addicts are similar in displaying an excess of the same disorders as contrasted with community rates, they also differ significantly from each other. Notably, relatives of opioid addicts show higher rates of mood and anxiety disorders, whereas relatives of cocaine abusers have higher rates of drug abuse and antisocial personality. This suggests that choice of drug may be at least partially related to different patterns of familial aggregation.

The sedating effects of opioids may be sought to relieve painful anxiety and dysphoric symptoms, whereas the stimulating effects of cocaine may be more appealing to sensation-seeking, risk-taking individuals with antisocial tendencies. These differences in rates of disorders in families are similar to those seen for the probands themselves. Opioid addicts have generally been shown to have higher levels of psychopathology than cocaine abusers, particularly of depression (Rounsaville, Anton, et al., 1991; Malow, West, Williams, & Sutker, 1989).

The observed contrast between families of cocaine and opioid addicts suggests that separate investigations are needed to understand vulnerability to abuse of different types of drugs. Findings derived from the rich literature on family studies of alcoholics are not safely generalizable to families of individuals with other drugs of abuse.

4. Vulnerability to depression in cocaine abusers is somewhat independently transmitted in their families. Higher rates of depression, alcoholism, and drug abuse were seen in relatives of cocaine abusers who, themselves, met criteria for major depression. This suggests that cocaine abuse and depression are not simply alternative expressions of the same familially transmitted disorder. However, the disorders do not appear to be completely independent, in that families of depressed cocaine abusers exhibit an excess of substance abuse and depression. Thus depressed cocaine abusers come from families with generally greater rates of dysfunction. Notably, depressed cocaine abusers also show a poorer prognosis in treatment (Carroll & Rounsaville, 1992), suggesting that depression denotes a greater impairment that may be familially transmitted.

Because the rates of disorders in families are based on history from probands only, we cannot rule out the possibility that higher rates of disorders in families of depressives was related to biased reporting. Kendler et al. (1991) have recently shown that recognition of depression in family members is increased if the informant has had similar symptoms (i.e. "It takes one to know one."). However, findings from our family study of opioid addicts indicated that families of depressed opioid addicts showed higher rates of depression whether or not the family members had been directly interviewed (Rounsaville, Kosten, et al., 1991).

FUTURE DIRECTIONS FOR RESEARCH ON VULNERABILITY TO COCAINE ABUSE

As with any type of substance use disorder, the causes of cocaine abuse are likely to be determined by a broad range of factors including societal issues (e.g., drug availability, cultural values) along with individual differences in vulnerability. A role for family/genetic factors has been demonstrated for most types of psychiatric and substance use disorders on which data are available. Because widespread cocaine abuse is a relatively recent phenomenon in the United States, available findings regarding the unique features of cocaine abusers' families are sparse. Moreover, the very recency and volatility of the cocaine epidemic have placed severe restrictions on the ways that family factors can be studied for this particular type of drug abuse.

To disentangle familial effects that are environmental from those that are genetic, twin, adoption, and half-sibling studies provide powerful designs (Kidd & Matthysee, 1978; Weissman et al., 1986). Of these three types of studies, only half-sibling studies are practical, insofar as adoption and twin registries with substantial numbers of cocaine abusers are not available.

Another powerful design for evaluating genetically transmitted biological vulnerability to cocaine abuse could be provided by linkage studies, which have greatly increased in prominence with the availability of restriction fragment length polymorphism (RFLP) technology (Kidd, 1982). These methods have made it possible to pinpoint, in the case of single major locus genetic transmission, the actual location of the gene responsible for conferring risk for a given disorder. However, this research requires a subject pool of large, multigenerational families in which multiple family members manifest the disorder in each generation. Given the rarity of cocaine use and abuse until recent years, such families are unlikely to exist.

The most feasible type of study to evaluate familial contributions to vulnerability to cocaine abuse is the family/pedigree design (Weissman et al., 1986). In this type of study, families in which the disorder of interest is present are found through identified family members (probands) who have the disorder. All available relatives, including first-degree and second-degree relatives, are evaluated using either direct interview or the family history method. These studies do not allow for a strong separation of biological from environmental familial factors. However, the relative contribution of biological and environmental factors can be estimated statistically by models that include clearly environmental (e.g., ratings of family dynamics) and largely biological (e.g., distinction between full and half sibling) variables.

The highest yield from family/genetic studies of cocaine abusers is likely to result from longitudinal studies of children of cocaine-abusing probands compared with children of other types of drug abusers and of non-drug-abusers. These studies have two key strengths. First, children can be evaluated for abnormalities that are manifest before the development of cocaine abuse, allowing stronger inference about the direction of causality between a trait such as depression and cocaine abuse. For example, if a marker such as an electroencephalographic (EEG) abnormality (1) distinguishes cocaine-abusing adults from normals, (2) distinguishes cocaine abusers' children from children of normals, and (3) is associated with development of cocaine abuse by the children with the marker, then a relatively strong inference can be drawn that the marker is linked to a cause of cocaine abuse. Second, because children of different groups of drug abusers share a similar set of environmental risk factors (e.g., availability of cocaine), differences in rates of substance use or abuse in different groups of children are not likely to be accounted for by simple lack of exposure to drugs. We are currently conducting studies that compare the children of cocaine abusers, of opioid addicts, of alcoholics and of normals in an effort to detect biological and environmental factors transmitted in these families.

REFERENCES

Adams, E. H., Gfroerer, J. C., Rouse, B. A., & Kozel, N. J. (1986). Trends in prevalence and consequences of cocaine use. *Advances in Alcohol and Substance Abuse, 6,* 49–71.

Andreason, N. C., Rice, J., Endicott, J., Reich, T., & Coryell, W. (1986). The family history method approach to diagnosis: How useful is it? *Archives of General Psychiatry, 43,* 421–429.

Anthony, J. C., & Trinkoff, A. M. (1989). United States epidemiologic data on drug use and abuse: How are they relevant to testing abuse liability of drugs? In M. W. Fischman & N. K. Mello (Eds.), *Testing for abuse liability of drugs in humans.* (National Institute on Drug Abuse Research Monograph No. 92, pp. 241–266). Washington, DC: U. S. Government Printing Office.

Cadoret, R. J., Troughton, E., O'Gorman, T. W., & Heywood, E. (1978). An adoption study of genetic and environmental factors in drug abuse *Archives of General Psychiatry, 43,* 1131–1136.

Carroll, K. M., & Rounsaville, B. J. (in press). Contrast of treatment-seeking and untreated cocaine abusers. *Archives of General Psychiatry.*

Carroll, K. M., & Rounsaville, B. J. (1992). *Predictors of treatment retention and outcome in cocaine abusers.* Manuscript submitted for publication.

Chitwood, D. D., & Morningstar, P. C. (1985). Factors which differentiate cocaine users in treatment from nontreatment users. *The International Journal of the Addictions, 20,* 449–459.

Cloninger, C. R., Christiansen, K. O., Reich, T., & Gottesman, I. I. (1978). Implications of sex differences in the prevalence of antisocial personality, alcoholism, and criminality for models of familial transmission. *Archives of General Psychiatry, 35,* 841–851.

Croughan, J. L. (1985). The contributions of family studies to understanding drug abuse. In L. N. Robins (Ed.), *Studying drug abuse* (pp. 240–264). New Brunswick, NJ: Rutgers University Press.

Endicott, J., & Spitzer, F. L. (1978). A diagnostic interview: The Schedule for Affective Disorders and Schizophrenia. *Archives of General Psychiatry, 37,* 837–844.

Gawin, F. H., & Kleber, H. D. (1986). Abstinence Symptomatology and Psychiatry Diagnosis in Cocaine Abusers. *Archives of General Psychiatry, 43,* 107–113.

Goodwin, D. W. (1979). Alcoholism and heredity. *Archives of General Psychiatry, 36,* 57–61.

Griffin, M. L., Weiss, R. D., Mirin, S. M., & Lange, U. (1989). A comparison of male and female cocaine abusers. *Archives of General Psychiatry, 46,* 122–126,

Helfrich, A. A., Crowley, T. J., & Atkinson, C. A. (1983). A clinical profile of 136 cocaine abusers. In *Problems of drug dependence 1982* (National Institute on Drug Abuse Research Monograph, No. 43, pp. 343–350). Washington, DC: U. S. Government Printing Office.

Kandel, D. B., Murphy, D., & Karus, D. (1985). Cocaine use in young adulthood: Patterns of use and psychosocial correlates. In N. J. Kozel and E. H. Adams (Eds.), *Cocaine use in America: Epidemiologic and clinic perspectives* (National Institute on Drug Abuse Research Monograph No. 61, pp. 76–110). Washington, DC: U. S. Government Printing Office.

Kendler, K. S., Silberg, J. L., Neale, M. C., Kessler, R. C., Heath, A. C., & Eaves, L. J. (1991). The family history method: Whose psychiatric history is measured. *American Journal of Psychiatry, 148,* 1501–1504.

Khantzian, E. J. (1985). The self-medication hypothesis of addictive disorders: Focus on heroin and cocaine dependence. *American Journal of Psychiatry, 142,* 1250–1264.

Kidd, K. K. (1982). Genetic linkage markers in the study of psychiatric disorders. In E. Usdin and I. Harris (Eds.), *Biological markers in psychiatry and neurology* (pp. 459–466). Oxford: Pergamon Press.

Kidd, K. K., & Matthysee, S. (1978). Research designs for the study of gene-environment interactions in psychiatric disorders. *Archives of General Psychiatry, 35,* 925–932.

Malow, R. M., West, J. A., Williams, J. L., & Sutker, P. B. (1989). Personality disorders classification and symptoms in cocaine and opioid addicts. *Journal of Consulting and Clinical Psychology, 57,*(6), 765–767.

Meyer, R. E. (1986). How to understand the relationship between psychopathology and addictive disorders: Another example of the chicken and the egg. In R. E. Meyer (Ed.), *Psychopathology and addictive disorders* (pp. 3–16). Guilford Press: New York.

Mirin, S. M., Weiss, R. D., Sollogub, A., & Michael, J. (1984). Psychopathology in families of drug abusers. In S. M. Mirin (Ed.), *Substance abuse and psychopathology* (pp. 79–106). Washington, DC: American Psychiatric Press.

National Institute on Drug Abuse. (1988). *National Household Survey on Drug Abuse Main Findings, 1985* (DHHS Publication No. ADM 88-1586). Washington, DC: U. S. Government Printing Office.

Newcomb, M. D., Bentler, P. M., & Fahey, B. (1987). Cocaine use and psychopathology associations among young adults. *International Journal of the Addictions, 22,* 1167–1188.

Nunes, E. V., Quitkin, F. M., & Klein, D. F. (1989). Psychiatric diagnosis in cocaine abuse. *Psychiatry Research, 28,* 105–114.

Robins, L. N., Helzer, J. E., Croughan, J., & Ratcliffe, K. (1981). National Institute of Mental Health diagnostic Interview Schedule. *Archives of General Psychiatry, 38,* 381–389.

Robins, L. N., Helzer, J. E., Weissman, M. M., Orvaschel, H., Gruenberg, E., Burke, J. D., & Regier, D. A. (1984). Prevalence of specific psychiatric disorders in three sites. *Archives of General Psychiatry, 41,* 949–958.

Rounsaville, B. J., Anton, S. F., Carroll, K., Budde, D., Prusoff, B. A., & Gawin, F. (1991). Psychiatric diagnosis of treatment-seeking cocaine abusers. *Archives of General Psychiatry, 48,* 43–51.

Rounsaville, B. J., Kosten, T. R., Weissman, M. M., Prusoff, B., Pauls, D., Anton, S. F., & Merikangas, K. (1991). Psychiatric Disorders in Relatives of Probands with Opiate Addiction. *Archives of General Psychiatry, 48,* 33–42.

Rounsaville, B. J., Weissman, M. M., Wilber, C. H., & Kleber, H. D. (1982). Pathways to opiate addiction: An evaluation of differing antecedents. *British Journal of Psychiatry, 141,* 437–446.

Schottenfeld, R., Carroll, K. M., & Rounsaville, B. J. (in press). Comorbid psychiatric disorders and cocaine abuse. In F. Tims (Ed.), *Advances in cocaine treatment* (National Institute on Drug Abuse Research Monograph).

Schuckit, M. A. (1986). Genetic and clinical implications of alcoholism and affective disorder. *American Journal of Psychiatry, 143,* 140–147.

Spitzer, R. L., Endicott, J., & Robins, E. (1978). Research diagnostic criteria: Rationale and reliability. *Archives of General Psychiatry, 36,* 733–782.

Stanton, M. D. (1979). Drugs and the family. *Marriage and Family Review, 2,* 1–10,

Weiss, R. D., Mirin, S. M., Griffin, M. L., & Michael, J. (1988). Psychopathology in cocaine abusers: Changing trends. *Journal of Nervous and Mental Disease, 176,* 719–725.

Weiss, R. D., Mirin, S. M., Michael, J., & Sollogub, A. C. (1986). Psychopathology in chronic cocaine abusers. *American Journal of Drug Alcohol Abuse, 12*(1 & 2), 17–29.

Weissman, M. M., Gershon, E. S., Kidd, K. K., Prusoff, B. A., Leckman, J. F., Dibble, E., Hamovit, J., Thompson, W. D., Pauls, D. L., & Guroff, J. J. (1984). Psychiatric disorder in relatives of probands with affective disorders: The Yale-NIMH collaborative family study. *Archives of General Psychiatry, 41,* 13–21.

Weissman, M. M., Merikangas, K. R., Joh, K., Wickramaratne, P., Prusoff, B. A., & Kidd, K. K. (1986). Family-genetic studies of psychiatric disorders: Developing technologies. *Archives of General Psychiatry, 43,* 1104–1116.

Winokur, G. (1974). The division of depressive illness into depressive spectrum disease and pure depressive disease. *International Pharmacopsychiatry, 9,* 5–13.

Winokur, G., Cadoret, R., Dorzab, J., & Baker, M. (1971). Depressive disease: A genetic study. *Archives of General Psychiatry, 24,* 135–144.

Winokur, G., & Clayton, P. J. (1968). Family history studies, IV: Comparison of male and female alcoholics. *Journal of Studies on Alcohol, 29,* 885–891.

Winokur, G., Morrison, J., Clancy, J., & Crowe, R. (1973). The Iowa 500: Familial and clinical findings favor two kinds of depressive illness. *Comprehensive Psychiatry, 14,* 99–107.

PART THREE

TREATMENT

CHAPTER TWELVE

Cocaine Epidemiology

Mary H. Closser, DO

ROBLEMS WITH ALCOHOL USE have been known to humankind for thousands of years (Vaillant, 1983). Similar problems with cocaine are much more recent as its use has escalated in the United States and other countries over the past 100 years (Gawin & Ellinwood, 1988). The most recent epidemiological phenomena are the spread of cocaine hydrochloride use during the 1970s which has been overshadowed by the epidemic of freebase cocaine use (including crack) that occurred during the 1980s (Rouse, 1991). This chapter describes the most recent epidemiology and clinical characteristics of cocaine users and abusers.

The recentness of the epidemic nature of cocaine use in the United States is reflected in the fact that most methodological studies of cocaine use and consequences has occurred only in the past 10 years. A cocaine dependence syndrome was recognized officially by DSM-III-R as late as 1987 (American Psychiatric Association, 1987). Previously, it had been believed that cocaine had a relatively low addictive potential, no physiological state of tolerance to its effects, and no withdrawal symptoms on cessation. Gawin and Kleber (1988) described evolving ideas of cocaine dependence and emphasized that cocaine does, in fact, produce the tolerance and withdrawal perceived to be essential to dependence. Kosten and Kosten (1990) have addressed the validity of the dependence syndrome across drug classes including cocaine and alcohol; their analyses support the syndrome's validity, while they note the need for future research to refine it and provide a theoretical link between biological and behavioral aspects of the syndrome. The view that cocaine was a benign, recreational drug without important addictive potential has probably contributed to the spread of its use (Clayton, 1985); research advances, improved epidemiological studies, the advent of "crack" and the publicity surrounding its use have disputed this view.

EPIDEMIOLOGY: DEMOGRAPHICS AND CHARACTERIZATION OF USE

Information about the use and abuse of cocaine comes from several sources. The prevalence and incidence of substance use and abuse (or addiction) are monitored differently and, in fact, pose very different problems in measurement. Cocaine use is monitored by national surveillance mechanisms such as the National High School Senior Drug Abuse Survey and the National Household Survey on Drug Abuse. Problems attributable to cocaine use are also monitored by surveillance studies; however, there are no nationally recurring studies of cocaine dependence diagnoses or related psychiatric illnesses. For this information, we rely on the results of the Epidemiologic Catchment Area (ECA) study performed between 1980–1984 and hope for timely new similar studies.

Monitoring the Future: The High School Senior Survey

The 17th annual High School Senior Survey, sponsored by the National Institute on Drug Abuse (NIDA, 1991a) and conducted by the University of Michigan Institute for Social Research, surveyed 15,483 seniors from the graduating class of 1991. The survey also includes data on drug use from a follow-up of 12,000 graduates from 1976–1990. Prevalence of high school seniors ever using cocaine has decreased from peak levels in 1985 of 17.3% to 7.8% in 1991. Those who used during the year preceding the survey declined from 13% to 3.5%, and users during the preceding month declined from 6.7% to 1.4% (Figure 12.1). Crack use has been monitored only during 1989, 1990 and 1991; decreases in use during the past month from 1.4% to 0.7% and decreases in annual use from 3.1% to 1.5% were noted. Overall, the percentage of seniors who used any illicit drug in the year preceding the survey was 29.2%, down from 33.3% in 1990, and from a peak of 52% in 1980 (Figure 12.2).

The High School Survey also contains questions about perceived risk of drug use and drug availability. Those who endorse a risk of harm

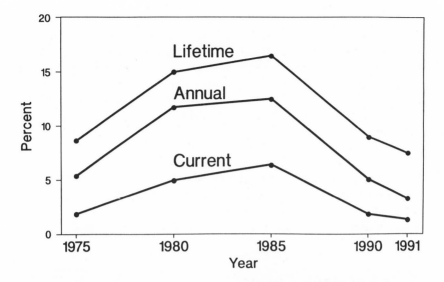

FIGURE 12.1. Cocaine use in the United States 1975–1991. From *Monitoring the Future, 1991* by the National Institute on Drug Abuse, 1991, Washington, DC: U. S. Government Printing Office.

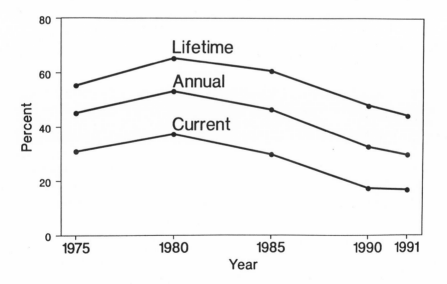

FIGURE 12.2. Illicit drug use in the United States 1975–1991. From *Monitoring the Future, 1991* by the National Institute on Drug Abuse, 1991, Washington, DC: U. S. Government Printing Office.

in using cocaine once or twice has increased dramatically from a low of 16% in 1986 to 53.6% in 1991. Perceived availability of cocaine, however, has shown the first annual decline, from a peak of 58.7% in 1989 stating it was fairly or very easy to get to 51.0% endorsing this idea in 1991 (Table 12.1). These trends may reflect the results on demand reduction of increased education and of indirectly experiencing risk to peers while cocaine availability (supply) remains high (O'Malley, Johnston, & Bachman, 1991).

A major criticism of the High School Survey is that it does not assess drug use in dropouts, who are likely to have even greater drug use. The surveyors did, however, look at the absenteeism rates of respondents to separate those who attend school regularly from those who do not. Although the rates of annual cocaine use are higher in those who are regularly absent, the rates decline significantly as they do in regular attenders (1990 data) (Figure 12.3).

National Household Survey

The findings of the High School Senior Survey parallel the most recent findings announced by the National Household Survey on Drug Abuse-1991 (NIDA, 1991b) which showed significant declines in the current use of illicit drugs. The National Household Survey is a probability-based sample of 32,594 people representative of the U.S. household population aged 12 and over. It gives other measures of

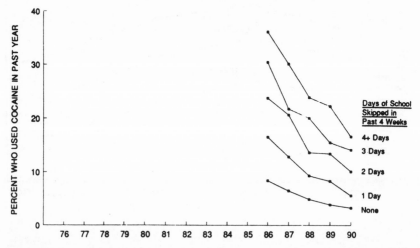

FIGURE 12.3. Trends in annual cocaine use by level of truancy among high school seniors, 1986–1990. From *Monitoring the Future, 1991* by the National Institute on Drug Abuse, 1991, Washington, DC: U. S. Government Printing Office.

TABLE 12.1. Trends in Perceived Availability of Drugs, All Seniors

Percentage saying drugs would be "Fairly easy" or "Very easy" for them to get[b]

Drug[a]	Class of 1975	Class of 1976	Class of 1977	Class of 1978	Class of 1979	Class of 1980	Class of 1981	Class of 1982	Class of 1983	Class of 1984	Class of 1985	Class of 1986	Class of 1987	Class of 1988	Class of 1989	Class of 1990	Class of 1991	'90–'91 change
Marijuana	87.8	87.4	87.9	87.8	90.1	89.0	89.2	88.5	86.2	84.6	85.5	85.2	84.8	85.0	84.3	84.4	85.3	-1.1
Amyl and butyl nitrites	NA	NA	NA	NA	NA	NA	NA	NA	NA	NA	NA	NA	23.9	25.9	26.8	24.4	22.7	-1.7
LSD	46.2	37.4	34.5	32.2	34.2	35.3	35.0	34.2	30.9	30.6	30.5	28.5	31.4	33.3	38.3	40.7	39.5	-1.2
PCP	NA	NA	NA	NA	NA	NA	NA	NA	NA	NA	NA	NA	22.8	24.9	28.9	27.7	27.6	-0.1
Some other psychedelic	47.8	35.7	33.8	33.8	34.6	35.0	32.7	30.6	26.6	26.6	26.1	24.9	25.0	26.2	28.2	28.3	28.0	-0.3
Cocaine	37.0	34.0	33.0	37.8	45.5	47.9	47.5	47.4	43.1	45.0	48.9	51.5	64.2	55.0	58.7	54.5	51.0	-3.58
"Crack"	NA	NA	NA	NA	NA	NA	NA	NA	NA	NA	NA	NA	41.1	42.1	47.0	42.4	39.9	-2.5
Cocaine powder	NA	NA	NA	NA	NA	NA	NA	NA	NA	NA	NA	NA	52.9	50.3	53.7	49.0	46.0	-3.0
Heroin	24.2	18.4	17.9	16.4	18.9	21.2	19.2	20.8	19.3	19.9	21.0	22.0	23.7	28.0	31.4	31.9	30.6	-1.3
Some other narcotic (including methadone)	34.5	26.9	27.8	26.1	28.7	29.4	29.6	30.4	30.0	32.1	33.1	32.2	33.0	35.8	38.3	38.1	34.6	-3.5[a]
Amphetamines	67.8	61.8	58.1	58.5	59.9	61.3	69.5	70.8	68.5	68.2	66.4	64.3	64.5	63.9	64.3	59.7	57.3	-2.4
Barbiturates	60.0	64.4	52.4	60.6	49.8	49.1	54.9	55.2	52.5	51.9	51.3	48.3	48.2	47.8	48.4	45.9	42.4	-3.5[a]
Tranquilizers	71.8	65.5	94.9	64.3	61.4	59.1	60.8	58.9	55.3	54.5	54.7	61.2	48.6	49.1	45.3	44.7	40.8	-3.99
Approximate n	(2627)	(2865)	(3065)	(3598)	(3172)	(3240)	(3578)	(3602)	(3385)	(3289)	(3274)	(3077)	(3271)	(3231)	(2806)	(2549)	(2476)	

Note. From Monitoring the Future, 1991 by the National Institute on Drug Abuse, 1991, Washington, DC: U.S. Government Printing Office.
Level of significance between the two most recent classes: s = .05, ss = .01, sss = .001. NA indicates data not available.
[a] Question asked was "How difficult do you think it would be to get each of the following types of drugs, if you wanted some?"
[b] Answer alternatives were: (1) Probably impossible, (2) Very difficult, (3) Fairly difficult, (4) Fairly easy, and (5) Very easy.

229

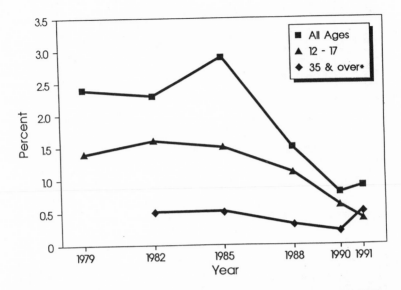

FIGURE 12.4. Trends in past-month cocaine use. From *National Household Survey on Drug Abuse, Population Estimates, 1991* (DHHS Publication No. ADM 91-1732) by the National Institute on Drug Abuse, 1991, Washington, DC: U. S. Government Printing Office.

adolescent drug use but it does not include populations in military installations, nursing homes, dormitories, hospitals, jails, prisons, or among the homeless. The NIDA has conducted this survey every 2–3 years since 1972, and it is now conducted yearly.

Occasional cocaine users (use within the past year in the population over age 12) dropped from 4.1% in 1985 to 3.1% in 1991. The number of current cocaine users (use within the past month) dropped from 2.9% in 1985 to 0.9% in 1991 (Figure 12.4; Table 12.2; Table 12.3). However, among cocaine users, intense use escalated from 647,000 weekly users in 1985 to 855,000 in 1991 despite a temporary decrease in 1990. Cocaine use was most prevalent among those who were unemployed, contrasting with the picture in 1985 wherein the highest prevalence rates were among college-educated, white males on the East and West Coasts. The age group most at risk continued to be those aged 18–25. Crack was used by 17% of cocaine users in 1989 (the first time the use of this form of cocaine specifically was monitored). Current crack use in 1991 was reported by 0.2% of the total sample, or 494,000. Among those aged 18–34, however, current crack use was reported by 0.4%, accounting for 39% of total crack use. These trends correspond to clinical observations that an increasing proportion of those presenting

TABLE 12.2. Trends in Past Year and Past Month Use of Cocaine, 1972–1991

Year	Percent of the household population							
	Total population		Ages 12–17		Ages 18–25		Age 26 and older	
	Past year	Past month	Past year	Past month	Past year	Past month	Past year	Past month
1972	NA	NA	1.5	0.6	NA	NA	NA	NA
1974	NA	NA	2.7	1.0	8.1	3.1	LP	LP
1976	NA	NA	2.3	1.0	7.0	2.0	0.6	LP
1977	NA	1.0	2.6	0.8	10.2	3.7	0.9	LP
1979	NA	2.5	4.2	1.4	19.6	9.3	2.0	0.9
1982	NA	2.3	4.1	1.6	18.8	6.8	3.8	1.2
1985	NA	2.9	4.0	1.5	16.3	7.6	4.2	2.0
1988	4.1	1.5	2.9	1.1	12.1	4.5	2.7	0.9
1990	3.1	0.8	2.2	0.6	7.5	2.2	2.4	0.6
1991	3.1	0.9	1.5	0.4	7.7	2.0	2.5	0.8

Note. NA = Not available; LP = Low precision (no estimate reported). From *National Household Survey on Drug Abuse, Population Estimates, 1991* (DHHS Publication No. ADM 91-1732) by the National Institute on Drug Abuse, 1991, Washington, DC: US Government Printing Office.

for cocaine abuse treatment are young adult, unemployed residents of urban areas; the "typical" cocaine abuser is no longer the upper-middle-class, white, male intranasal user.

Although overall use appears to be declining among those sampled by these surveys, problems from long-term use may just be surfacing, as those who initially began using 4–5 years ago begin to suffer medical and psycho-social difficulties. According to NIDA's DAWN (Drug Abuse Warning Network) data, there was a 5-fold increase in the number of emergency room visits by people using cocaine and a 28-fold increase in the number of visits by smokers of cocaine in 1988 compared with 1984. Freebase or crack cocaine delivers a greater quantity of drug to the body and brain than does

TABLE 12.3. Estimates of Cocaine Use

Use	Total	Ages 12–17	Ages 18–25	Ages 26 & older
Ever used cocaine	23,715,000	491,000	5,099,000	18,125,000
Used in past year	6,383,000	311,000	2,194,000	3,878,000
Current cocaine use	1,892,000	83,000	582,000	1,226,000

Note. From *National Household Survey on Drug Abuse, Population Estimates, 1991* (DHHS Publication No. ADM 91-1732) by the National Institute on Drug Abuse, 1991, Washington, DC: US Government Printing Office.

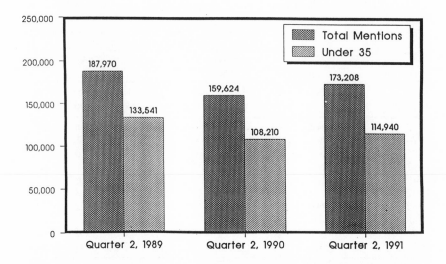

FIGURE 12.5. Drug-related emergency room mentions. From *Drug Abuse Warning Network* by National Institute on Drug Abuse, 1991, Washington, DC: U. S. Government Printing Office.

intranasal use, formerly the most popular, and thus can cause greater medical and psychiatric problems. Declines in survey estimates of overall drug use do not necessarily reflect the continuing epidemic faced by substance abuse treatment providers, who will likely note increasing numbers of cocaine abusers presenting for treatment over the next several years (Siegel, 1985). DAWN has noted a 31% increase in emergency room cocaine (and heroin) mentions from the fourth quarter of 1990 to the second quarter of 1991 (Figure 12.5). It is speculated that this new trend may reflect an increase in reports of medical problems associated with cocaine use.

Overall, National Household Survey data reveal decreasing cocaine use from 1985 to 1991, while indicating that heavy users of either drug represent a greater proportion of all users and appear to be developing greater problems. Although weekly use does not necessarily constitute dependence, 855,000 cocaine users in 1991 used weekly compared with 647,000 users in 1985, an *increase* in numbers of heavy users, not a decline. Given the estimate that 10–25% of current cocaine users have problems (Gawin & Ellinwood, 1988; Adams & Gfroerer, 1991), 290,000–725,000 adults may be at risk. This contrasts with a possible 18.6 million adults with alcohol problems. A critical issue for the treatment and legal control implications of these numbers, however, is that because cocaine is illicit it will be a much more visible problem to treatment and legal systems.

ECA Study Data: Diagnosable Disorders and Risk Factors

Surveys of use suggest the extent of the cocaine epidemic, but they do not measure the psychiatric syndromes and behavioral changes that constitute substance dependence. Surveys of substance dependence and use disorders by the National Institute of Mental Health (NIMH) Epidemiologic Catchment Area program utilized a structured interview, the DIS (Diagnostic Interview Schedule), to study the prevalence and incidence of mental disorders at five sites within the United States. The data were gathered between 1980 and 1984 and consist of survey samples and self-report interviews which were repeated at 1-year follow-up. From the data, nationwide and regional prevalence and incidence rates of alcohol and drug abuse and dependence can be derived. Results of the 1-month prevalence of mental disorders (Regier et al., 1988) revealed an overall combined substance use disorder rate of 3.8% (6.3% in men vs. 1.6% in women). Total substance abuse rates were highest among men aged 18–24 years (9.3%) with 6.0% having alcohol abuse/dependence and 4.8% having drug abuse/dependence. Lifetime prevalence rates for all ages were higher than 1-month prevalence, with alcohol abuse/dependence at 13.7% and drug abuse/dependence 5.9%. Prevalence rates are not available specifically for cocaine abuse/dependence from this study. Given the increasing severity of cocaine use problems among heavy users, it is likely that cocaine now accounts for a greater proportion of overall drug abuse/dependence prevalence rates than was the case during the ECA study. In spite of the expected underreporting of illicit drug use compared with alcohol use, the rate of diagnosable disorders was strikingly higher relative to alcohol than the other surveys of use or problems would suggest. Thus combined alcohol/cocaine abusers might be expected to have much higher rates of dependence than do alcohol abusers alone.

Researchers (Ritter & Anthony, 1991) have since analyzed ECA survey data in regards to factors associated with risk of becoming a cocaine user by comparing individuals who initiated or progressed in significant cocaine use during the follow-up interval with those who had not. An unanticipated finding was that subjects who were initially unemployed but became employed by follow-up were more likely to initiate or progress in cocaine use (possibly facilitated by increased discretionary income). Ritter and Anthony found a significant association between persistent depression and initiation/progression of cocaine use among previous nonusers, a possible manifestation of self-medication. Age and married state at baseline were found to be inversely associated with initiation/progression in cocaine use. Personal income at baseline was positively associated with initiation/progression in cocaine use, although cocaine use is certainly not limited to those with high incomes. Finally, risk of initiating or progressing in cocaine use was higher among those with recent use of marijuana, especially among those with recent use of marijuana and other illicit drugs.

Psychiatric Comorbidity

Other psychiatric disorders are very commonly experienced by substance abusers. Data from the ECA survey revealed that every psychiatric disorder investigated by the study was more likely to occur among alcoholics than nonalcoholics (Helzer & Pryzbeck, 1987). There were especially strong associations between alcoholism and antisocial personality disorder, other substance abuse and mania. Others have studied rates of psychiatric illness in treatment-seeking populations, admittedly a population more likely to be in distress. One such survey of mental disorders in substance abusers seeking treatment (87% alcohol, 12% cocaine abusers) showed that 78% of the sample had a lifetime diagnosable psychiatric disorder and 65% had a current psychiatric disorder diagnosis (Ross, Glaser, & Germanson, 1988). The most common lifetime disorders were antisocial personality disorder, phobias, psychosexual dysfunctions, major depression, and dysthymia. The 18% of patients who abused both alcohol and other drugs (including cocaine) were significantly more psychiatrically impaired than patients with no substance use disorder and patients with either alcohol or other drug abuse but not both. The authors' analyses indicated that the severity of the alcohol and/or drug problem was the best predictor of the co-occurrence of psychiatric disorders. They concluded that psychiatric evaluation of all patients entering substance abuse treatment facilities is imperative.

Of most interest to clinicians treating cocaine abusers have been studies of psychopathology in relatively "pure" cocaine-abusing samples. Studies in cocaine abusers have shown varying rates of affective illness. Weiss and colleagues in 1986 found that 50% of an inpatient sample had an affective disorder (Weiss, Mirin, & Michael, 1986). However, they found a much lower rate of 27% with affective disorder in a larger sample studied several years later (Weiss, Mirin, Griffin, & Michael, 1987). They note that affective illness may have become a less important risk factor for the development of cocaine abuse as cocaine use has become more prevalent. They also note that the cocaine "crash" and subsequent anhedonia can lead to overdiagnosis of affective illness if diagnosis is attempted early in treatment. The cocaine abusers they studied had slightly more affective disorder than did other drug abusers, but had significantly higher rates of cyclothymic disorder (11.4% vs. 2.7%).

Rounsaville et al. (1991) found that 73.5% of a sample of cocaine abusers seeking inpatient or outpatient treatment had another lifetime psychiatric disorder and 55.7% had a current psychiatric disorder. Major depression, hypomania, cyclothymia, anxiety disorders, antisocial personality, and history of childhood attention deficit disorder accounted for most of the diagnoses. Affective disorders and alcoholism usually followed the onset of drug abuse, whereas anxiety disorders, antisocial personality, and attention deficit disorder usually preceded drug abuse (Rounsaville, 1991).

Bunt, Galanter, Lifshutz, & Castaneda (1990) studied a group of cocaine-dependent patients admitted to inpatient psychiatric wards. They found that 88% of the sample predominantly used freebase or crack. Antisocial or borderline personality disorders were found in 40% of the sample and schizophrenia in 33%. Personality-disordered patients used greater quantities of cocaine and began abusing at younger ages than did patients with schizophrenia. The authors note that cocaine abuse has become a major clinical problem among psychiatric patients, often precipitating depression, suicidal ideation, paranoia, anxiety, and auditory hallucinations.

Maternal Cocaine Use: Prevalence and Fetal Effects

The children of mothers using cocaine during pregnancy have become the focus of increasing concern. The number of children so affected is likely proportional to the number of users of cocaine, although much work is needed to further describe short-term and long-term consequences of cocaine use. The National Household Survey reports that 4.8 million or 8% of women aged 15-44 have used an illicit drug in the past month. Of these, 0.5 million or 0.9% used cocaine and 3.9 million or 6.5% used marijuana.

In a prospective study of predominantly poor, minority adolescent mothers (Amaro, Zuckerman, & Cabral, 1989), lifetime use of cocaine was seen to be 23%, use in the past year was 17% and use during pregnancy was 13.8%. In contrast, respective rates of use for alcohol were 84.2% lifetime use, 65.2% use in last year and 52.2% during pregnancy. Compared with nonusers, pregnant adolescent drug users were more likely to be African-American and to report more negative life events and violence during pregnancy. They were also three times more likely to have a male partner who used marijuana or cocaine. Antecedents and correlates of drug use and adolescent pregnancy are described as very similar. The authors note that the most significant risk factor for drug problems besides the adolescent's own drug use may be her partner's drug use.

The effects of maternal cocaine use on the developing fetus have been recognized and studied in recent years. Although there is as yet no clinically defined syndrome with specific diagnostic parameters such as the Fetal Alcohol Syndrome (FAS) (Chasnoff, 1986), significant impairments have been identified in infants born to cocaine-using mothers. Chasnoff et al. (Chasnoff, Griffith, MacGregor, Dirkes, & Burns, 1989) prospectively studied 75 cocaine-using women and divided them into two groups: those who used only during the first trimester of pregnancy and those who used cocaine throughout pregnancy. Perinatal outcomes were compared with those of a matched, nonusing group. Both groups of cocaine-exposed infants showed significant impairment of orientation, motor, and state-regulation behaviors. Women who used cocaine throughout pregnancy had an increased rate of preterm delivery and low birth weight infants as well as an increased rate of intrauterine growth retardation. Term infants born to these mothers had lower mean birth weights, lengths, and head circumferences—consequences, it is believed, of cocaine's constricting effect on uterine and fetal blood vessels.

Data do not yet exist regarding the incidence of cocaine-related problems among infants and children born to cocaine-using mothers, but extrapolating from proportionate rates of alcohol/cocaine use during pregnancy, approximately 4 times as many poor, adolescent mothers use alcohol as cocaine. Given that 2.2 per 1,000 live births may involve FAS in the United States, roughly 0.5 per 1,000 births might involve cocaine-related problems, assuming that the same proportion of problems ensue from use. Much more data is required to clarify this question.

Gender Differences in Use and Abuse of Cocaine and Alcohol

Women who use alcohol have always been the subject of strong societal disapproval, and this disapproval has escalated when targeted at cocaine-using women, particularly pregnant women. The increasing interest in fetal effects of drug and alcohol abuse have led to more research on gender differences in use or abuse of cocaine. The popular notion, however, that cocaine abuse is escalating more among women than among men is not borne out by surveys and may be due to sexual stereotypes persisting in American society (Erickson & Murray, 1989). The rate of current cocaine use for men (1.1%) was double that for women (0.5%) in the 1990 National Household Survey.

The number of young alcoholic women has increased over the past decade and they may have more associated medical and psychosocial problems. Overall, however, women drink less and have lower rates of alcohol problems than men. There are significant sex differences in peak blood alcohol levels, metabolism, onset of alcohol-related diseases such as cirrhosis, as well as in important clinical characteristics (Blume, 1986). Women alcoholics are more likely to report depressive symptoms and to receive depressive disorder diagnoses than men and more often than men report drinking in response to stressors. Women cocaine abusers also are more likely to cite specific psychosocial stressors as reasons for drug use and appear to experience higher rates of depressive disorders (Griffin, Weiss, Mirin, & Lange, 1989). Griffin et al. (1989) also reported that depressive symptoms improved with abstinence much more slowly in women than men, and during early abstinence more severe distress is reported by women than men. Thus depressive symptoms and diagnoses appear to be greater in both alcohol- and cocaine-abusing women seeking treatment and have important clinical implications.

Overlap of Syndromes

There is a very high comorbidity rate between cocaine, alcohol, and other drug dependencies. As described in the ECA data (Helzer & Pryzbeck, 1987), among persons with alcohol abuse or dependence the likelihood of another diagnosis of substance use disorder is 7 times greater than in the overall sample (18% vs. 3.5%). Cocaine abuse/dependence is 35 times more likely to occur in alcoholics than in general population samples. The converse also reveals higher co-occurrence rates for alcohol and drug abuse with 61% of "hard drug" users and 36% of marijuana only users also being alcoholic. The strikingly high rate (84%) of co-occurrence of alcoholism and cocaine dependence was described. Clinical surveys have seen even higher rates of co-occurrence. In a descriptive study of 1,627 patients admitted for substance abuse rehabilitation, Miller, Gold, & Millman (1989) found that 94% of those with cocaine dependence also had alcohol dependence by DSM-III-R criteria. Thus nearly all of the cocaine abusers disabled enough by their addiction to seek inpatient treatment were also alcohol dependent. Outpatient cocaine treatment facilities may observe somewhat lower rates of alcoholism, but these high rates indicate the need for careful assessment and management of likely simultaneous cocaine and alcohol withdrawal syndromes.

SUMMARY

The increasingly high prevalence of cocaine use and abuse in this country, although past its peak, has led to marked changes in the clinical characteristics of patients now presenting for substance abuse treatment in all settings. The numbers of persons using cocaine on a weekly basis has increased in contrast to declines in all other drug use noted. Given a lag time of two to five years between establishment of regular use and treatment seeking, continued high numbers of cocaine abusers can be expected to present at the nation's substance abuse facilities at least over the foreseeable future. Although alcohol remains the most frequently used drug, treatment facilities rarely encounter patients who do not also abuse other drugs, and increasingly, cocaine is the other major drug of choice. Among cocaine abusers, alcohol is almost invariably also abused. Treatment for cocaine abusers can be accomplished in most settings if important demographic and pharmacologic differences between cocaine and other drugs are addressed. In any substance use disorder, co-morbid psychopathology is frequent and appropriate treatment matching based on diagnosis is imperative.

REFERENCES

Adams, E. H., & Gfroerer, J. (1991). Risk of cocaine abuse and dependence. In Susan E. Schober (Ed.), *The epidemiology of cocaine use and abuse* (National Institute on Drug Abuse Research Monograph, DHHS Publication No. ADM 91-1787). Washington, DC: U. S. Government Printing Office.

Amaro, J., Zuckerman, B., & Cabral, H. (1989). Drug use among adolescent mothers: Profile of risk. *Pediatrics, 84*(1), 144–151.

American Psychiatric Association. (1987). *Diagnostic and statistical manual of mental disorders, third edition, revised* (pp. 177–179). Washington, DC: Author.

Blume, S. B. (1986). Women and alcohol: A review. *Journal of the American Medical Association, 256*(11), 1467–1470.

Bunt, G., Galanter, M., Lifshutz, H., & Castaneda, R. (1990). Cocaine/"crack" dependence among psychiatric inpatients. *American Journal of Psychiatry, 147*(11), 1542–1546.

Chasnoff, I. J. (1986). Alcohol use in pregnancy. In I. J. Chasnoff (Eds.), *Drug use in pregnancy: Mother and child* (pp. 75–80). Norwell, MA: MTP Press.

Chasnoff, I. J., Griffith, D. R., MacGregor, S., Dirkes, K., & Burns, K. A. (1989). Temporal patterns of cocaine use in pregnancy. *Journal of the American Medical Association, 261*(12), 1741–1744.

Clayton, R. R. (1985). Cocaine use in the United States: In a blizzard or just being snowed. In N. J. Kozel and E. H. Adams (Eds.), *Cocaine use in America: Epidemiologic and clinical perspectives* (National Institute on Drug Abuse Research Monograph No. 61, pp. 8–34). Washington, DC: U. S. Government Printing Office.

Erickson, P. G., & Murray, G. F. (1989). Sex differences in cocaine use and experiences: A double standard revived? *American Journal of Drug and Alcohol Abuse, 15*(2), 135–152.

Gawin, F. H., & Ellinwood, E. H. (1988). Cocaine and other stimulants: Actions, abuse, and treatment. *New England Journal of Medicine, 318*(18), 1173–1182.

Gawin, F. H., & Kleber, H. D. (1988). Evolving conceptualizations of cocaine dependence. *Yale Journal of Biology and Medicine, 61*, 123–136.

Griffin, M. L., Weiss, R. D., Mirin, S. M., & Lange, U. (1989). A comparison of male and female cocaine abusers. *Archives of General Psychiatry, 46*, 122–126.

Helzer, J. E., & Pryzbeck, T. R. (1987). The co-occurrence of alcoholism with other psychiatric disorders in the general population and its impact on treatment. *Journal of Studies on Alcohol, 49*(1), 219–224.

Kosten, T. A., & Kosten, T. R. (1990). The dependence syndrome concept as applied to alcohol and other substances of abuse. In M. Galanter (Eds.), *Recent developments in alcoholism: Combined alcohol and other drug dependence* (pp. 47–68). New York: Plenum Press.

Miller, N. S., Gold, M. S., & Millman, R. B. (1989). The prevalence of alcohol dependence in cocaine dependence in an inpatient population. *Annals of Clinical Psychiatry, 1*, 93–97.

National Institute on Drug Abuse. (1991a). *Monitoring the Future, 1991*. Washington, DC: U. S. Government Printing Office.

National Institute on Drug Abuse. (1991b). *National Household Survey on Drug Abuse, Population Estimates, 1991* (DHHS Publication No. ADM 91-1732). Washington, DC: U. S. Government Printing Office.

O'Malley, P. M., Johnston, L. D., & Bachman, J. G. (1991). Quantitative and qualitative changes in cocaine use among American high school seniors, college students, and young adults. In Susan E. Schober (Ed.), *The epidemiology of cocaine use and abuse* (DHHS Publication No. ADM 91-1787). Washington, DC: U. S. Government Printing Office.

Regier, D. A., Boyd, J. H., Burke, J. D., Rae, D. S., Myers, J. K., Kramer, M., Robins, L. N., George, L. K., Karno, M., & Locke, B. Z. (1988, November). One-month prevalence of mental disorders in the United States. *Archives of General Psychiatry, 45*, 977–986.

Ritter, C., & Anthony, J. C. (1991). Factors influencing initiation of cocaine use among adults: Findings from the Epidemiologic Catchment Area Program. In Susan E. Schober (Ed.), *The epidemiology of cocaine use and abuse*

(DHHS Publication No. ADM 91-1787). Washington, DC: U. S. Government Printing Office.

Ross, H. E., Glaser, F. B., & Germanson, T. (1988). The prevalence of psychiatric disorders in patients with alcohol and other drug problems. *Archives of General Psychiatry, 45*, 1023–1031.

Rounsaville, B. J. (1991). Psychiatric disorders in treatment-entering cocaine abusers. In Susan E. Schober (Ed.), *The epidemiology of cocaine use and abuse* (DHHS Publication No. ADM 91-1787). Washington, DC: U. S. Government Printing Office.

Rounsaville, B. J., Foley, S., Carroll, K., Budde, D., Prusoff, B. A., & Gawin, F. (1991). Psychiatric diagnosis of treatment seeking cocaine abusers. *Archives of General Psychiatry, 48*(1), 43–51.

Rouse, B. A. (1991). Trends in cocaine use in the general population. In Susan E. Schober (Ed.), *The epidemiology of cocaine use and abuse* (DHHS Publication No. ADM 91-1787). Washington, DC: U. S. Government Printing Office.

Siegel, R. K. (1985). New patterns of cocaine use: Changing doses and routes. In N. J. Kozel & E. H. Adams (Eds.), *Cocaine use in America: Epidemiologic and clinical perspectives* (National Institute on Drug Abuse Research Monograph No. 61, pp. 204–220). Washington, DC: U. S. Government Printing Office.

Vaillant, G. E. (1983). *The natural history of alcoholism.* Cambridge, MA: Harvard University Press.

Weiss, R. D., Mirin, S. M., Griffin, M. L., & Michael, J. L. (1987). Psychopathology in cocaine abusers. *Journal of Nervous Mental Disease, 176*(12), 719–725.

Weiss, R. D., Mirin, S. M., & Michael, J. L. (1986). Psychopathology in chronic cocaine abusers. *American Journal of Drug Alcohol Abuse, 12*, 17–29.

Medical Complications of Cocaine Use

Patrick G. O'Connor, MD, MPH

Grace Chang, MD, MPH

Julia Shi, MD

C OCAINE, ONCE THOUGHT to be a relatively benign drug, has come under increasing scrutiny as a cause of significant morbidity and mortality among its users. In this chapter, we focus on the known medical complications of cocaine use. We first consider the diagnosis and management of patients who present with acute cocaine intoxication and withdrawal. Next, we review the general medical complications associated with cocaine itself. Finally, we review medical complications that are related to specific routes of administration in cocaine users (e.g., intravenous, intranasal, and smoked).

DIAGNOSIS AND MANAGEMENT OF COCAINE INTOXICATION AND WITHDRAWAL

General Management Principles

The first priority in the general management of acute cocaine intoxication is general supportive care and resuscitative measures, if necessary. Assessment of airway obstruction, adequacy of ventilation, vital signs, cardiac rhythm, and level of consciousness warrant immediate attention. The initial determination of the severity of a drug ingestion or poisoning includes the patient's general status and level of consciousness at arrival, alleged drug and dose involved, and complicating clinical situations particular to the patient or to the drug ingested (Gross, 1989).

Patients who are acutely intoxicated may be unable to cooperate with a systematic history, physical, and laboratory examination. Patients may be screened for substance use by direct interview and laboratory analysis of body fluids. There are limitations to each approach, but routine evaluation of substance use is necessary to ensure due consideration of all diagnostic possibilities.

Patient History

Asking the patient about the quantity and frequency of alcohol and other drug consumption is an important means of detecting abuse or dependence (U.S. Preventive Services Task Force, 1989). However, the patient must be able to communicate the necessary information and also be willing to provide accurate information on the amount and type of substance ingested. Whereas some research has demonstrated that patients do provide accurate information on alcohol use (Babor, Stephens, & Marlatt, 1987), information about illicit substances may not be forthcoming when patients have concerns about self-incrimination. In addition, the adulteration of many illicit substances with other psychoactive substance may further obscure the clinical history, insofar as patients are unaware of the exact nature of the additives. Interviewing the patient's companions will have the same potential limitations. Nonetheless, seeking information about the etiology of the acute episode of intoxication allows the clinician to screen for chronic patterns of dysfunctional substance use and refer for substance abuse evaluation and treatment.

Toxicology Screening

Emergency drug screening can provide valuable information to physicians confronted by a confusing clinical presentation with atypical symptoms or signs and little or no history (Kellerman, Fikn, LoGerfo, & Copass, 1987). Urine is the most common specimen for drug testing because it can be collected noninvasively, is available in large volumes, contains higher concentrations of drugs and their metabolites than do other tissues or fluids, is easier to analyze than blood or other tissues, and can be frozen with drugs and their metabolites remaining stable during long-term storage (Council on Scientific Affairs, 1987). Whereas informed voluntary consent ordinarily must be obtained when performing urine tests on any person 18 years of age or older, urine testing should be done without consent when a medical emergency exists (Schwartz, 1988).

The impact of qualitative and quantitative drug screening on the diagnosis and management of emergency service patients has been examined (Kellerman et al., 1987; Sloan et al., 1989; Chang & Astrachan, 1988). While test results do not appear to affect clinical management, they do provide the physician with increased diagnostic certainty and an opportunity to assess the patient's substance use and to offer the appropriate substance abuse referral (Chang & Kosten, in press).

Medical Pharmacology of Cocaine

Cocaine (benzoymethylecgonine) is an alkaloid derived from leaves of the *Eyrthroxylum coca* plant. Cocaine hydrochloride is a water soluble salt which is available for medicinal use.

"Freebase" cocaine is the cocaine alkaloid which is insoluble in water but soluble in alcohol, acetone, oils and ether. It melts at 98° C and vaporizes at high temperatures without decomposing, allowing it to be smoked. Free base cocaine can be absorbed through the mucous membrane and the GI tract (Creglier & Mark, 1986).

The time course of the physiological and subjective effects of a single dose of cocaine is closely correlated with the route of administration and blood levels achieved. An oral dose of 2 mg per kg produces peak effects in about 45 minutes, with a rise in heart rate, blood pressure, decrease in skin temperature, and a 1 mm increase in pupil size (Rowbotham, Jones, Benowitz, & Jacob, 1984). When administered intravenously, intense effects can be achieved with doses one-fifth of that administered orally. When smoked as freebase, cocaine is rapidly absorbed into the pulmonary circulation and is transmitted to the brain in less than 10 seconds (Siegel, 1982).

An intravenous infusion of lethal doses of cocaine in animals produces a predictable physiological sequence, namely, an increase in heart rate, blood pressure, cardiac output, and body temperature, which, combined with a fall in blood pH, causes severe metabolic acidosis. Generalized seizures, cardiopulmonary collapse, and multi-organ failure may ensue. Rapid infusion of lethal doses of cocaine can cause respiratory and cardiac arrest without inducing seizures (Catravas & Waters, 1981).

Cocaine in the blood is rapidly detoxified into water soluble metabolites—benzoylecgonine and ecgonine methyl ester—by plasma and liver cholinesterases and excreted in urine. Cocaine metabolites can be documented in the urine for up to 36 hours depending on the route of administration and the activity of the cholinesterase (Barnett, Hawka, & Resnick, 1981).

The local anesthetic effect of cocaine is due to its ability to block the initiation and conduction of electrical impulses within nerve cells by preventing the rapid increase in cell membrane permeability to sodium ions during depolarization. It blocks the presynaptic reuptake of neurotransmitters norepinephrine and dopamine, producing an excess of transmitter at the postsynaptic receptor sites (Ritchie & Green, 1985). This activates the sympathetic nervous system and produces vasocon- striction, an acute rise in blood pressure, tachycardia, hyperthermia, and a predisposition to ventricular arrhythmia and seizures.

The euphoric effect of cocaine appears to be related to the stimulation of dopaminergic neurotransmission by blocking the reup- take of dopamine. In long-term cocaine use, the nerve terminals may be depleted of dopamine, contributing to the dysphoria that develops during withdrawal and the subsequent compulsive use pattern (Dackis & Gold, 1985). Cocaine use has been described to cause euphoria, dysphoria, and paranoid psychosis in that sequence, depending upon the dose and the chronicity of use (Post, 1975). High-dose cocaine abuse produces disinhibition, impulsiveness, hypervigilance, compulsively repeated actions, and extreme psychomotor agitation as described previously (Rowbotham, 1988).

With the introduction of cocaine freebase and "crack," extremely high blood levels can be achieved rapidly, with subjective and physiological effects similar to those produced by intravenous admini- stration of cocaine. These effects can be maintained for a longer period. Crack has since been established as an important factor in the rise of cocaine use in the 1980s.

Cocaine Intoxication

Cocaine is a sympathomimetic substance that elicits states of heightened alertness, elevated mood, and enhanced psychomotor activity. Cocaine may be taken intranasally ("snorting"), injected intravenously, or smoked as cocaine freebase or "crack."

Central nervous system (CNS) stimulation by high doses of cocaine may result in peculiar stereotyped behavior, bruxism, formication, irritability, restlessness, rhinorrhea, emotional liability, or paranoia. Although some patients may remain fully oriented, they may develop paranoid psychosis similar to that observed in manic–depressive psycho- sis or paranoid schizophrenia. Violent behavior is a possibility. Finally, hyperthermia and grand mal seizures may accompany stimulant toxicity (Weiss & Mirin, 1988).

Stimulation is followed by CNS depression. It may be characterized by paralysis of motor activity, hyperreflexia with eventual areflexia, stupor progressing to coma, loss of vital functions, and even death. Recent data support the causal relationship between increasing dosage of cocaine and a direct toxic effect on the myocardium. Indeed, the occurrence of acute myocardial infarction in any patient younger than 40 years of age without a history of cardiac risk factors suggests the possibility of coronary spasm secondary to cocaine abuse (Ungar, 1989).

Emergency Management

Supportive measures are the first priority in the treatment of cocaine toxicity (Gross, 1989) (Table 13.1). Agitation may respond to benzodiazepines. Management of psychosis can be achieved with chlorpromazine or haloperidol. Haloperidol has been recommended as the pharmacological agent of choice because of its dopaminergic activity (Ungar, 1989). Hyperthermia will require external cooling. Acidification of urine by oral administration of ammonium chloride will hasten urinary excretion of the stimulants. Seizure activity can be controlled by diazepam (Weiss & Mirin, 1988) or phenytoin (Gross, 1989). Severe hypertension and tachycardia have been treated by a variety of agents—propranolol alone or in combination with phentolamine or nitroprusside, or labetalol—but controversy as to their definitive management remains (Gawin & Kleber, 1986).

Withdrawal from CNS stimulants may be accompanied by hypersomnia, depression, fatigue, and apathy, all of which are usually

TABLE 13.1. Emergency Management of Cocaine Use

Immediate Measures	
Examine for:	
Airway obstruction	
Adequacy of ventilation	
Vital signs	
Cardiac rhythm	
Level of consciousness	

Specific Interventions	
Problem	*Treatment*
Agitation	Benzodiazepine
Psychosis	Haloperidol or chlorpromazine
Hyperthermia	External cooling
Seizures	Diazepam or phenytoin
Hypertension and tachycardia	Propanolol ± phentolamine or nitroprusides or labetalol
To hasten excretion	Acidify urine (p. o. ammonium chloride)
Atypical presentation/little history	Urine toxicology screening Direct patient interview
Depression	Psychiatric assessment

transient (Karch, 1989). On the other hand, some clinical reports suggest that stimulant withdrawal can lead to depression of life-threatening intensity that requires hospitalization (Ellison & Jacobs, 1986). The alert clinician will be aware of the possible complications and ensure the appropriate follow-up.

GENERAL MEDICAL COMPLICATIONS OF COCAINE USE

Because of its pharmocological effects on various organ systems, cocaine use can result in specific medical complications regardless of how it is administered (Table 13.2). In clinical practice, the major toxicities of cocaine primarily involve the central nervous system and cardiovascular system. In addition, obstetrical complications have been reported as have other less common toxicities.

Neurological Complications

Cocaine use has been associated with neurological symptoms and diseases including severe headaches, tremor, vertigo, nonspecific dizziness, syncope, blurred vision, ataxia, tinnitus, transient ischemic attacks with transient hemiparesis of unknown origin, choreiform movements, seizures, confusional states, cerebral hemorrhage, cerebral infarction and spinal cord ischemia, and toxic encephalopathy. In one study, the most frequent neurological complications observed at one hospital were seizures, focal neurological deficits, headaches, and transient loss of consciousness (Lowenstein et al., 1987).

Mechanism

The mechanism of cocaine-related neurological events is not clearly understood. Increased dopaminergic transmission is hypothesized to be responsible for the euphoria and addictive behavior caused by cocaine use (Lowenstein et al., 1987; Gold, Dackis, Pattash, Extein, & Washton, 1986). At higher doses, dopamine may cause paranoia, psychosis, and extreme psychomotor hyperactivity (Gold et al., 1986). Chronic cocaine use may lead to dopamine depletion, subsequently expressed as depression, tremors, and/or chorieform movements (Brody, Slovis, & Wrenn, 1990). Cocaine is a known vasoconstrictor, local anesthetic, and CNS stimulant. The enhanced sympathetic activity, cerebral vasocon-

TABLE 13.2. General Medical Complications of Cocaine Use

Neurological	
Symptoms	Headache
	Dizziness
	Syncope
	Focal motor or sensory deficits
	Seizures
Diagnoses	Migraine
	Transient ischemic attacks
	Cerebrovascular accidents
	Seizure disorders
Cardiovascular	
Symptoms	Chest pain
	Shortness of breath
	Dizziness
	Syncope
Diagnoses	Myocardial ischemia
	Myocardial infarction
	Arrhythmias
	Cardiomyopathy
	Myocarditis
	Aortic dissection
Obstetrical	
Symptoms	Abdominal pain
	Vaginal bleeding
	Fetal distress
Diagnoses	Abruptio placentae
	Placenta previa
	Miscarriage
	Developmental abnormalities
Other	
Diagnoses	Renal failure
	Rhabdomyolysis
	Hepatic insufficiency

striction or vasospasm, accompanied by sudden surge of blood pressure following cocaine use, may precipitate ischemic symptoms and even spontaneous bleeding in an otherwise normotensive person (Litchenfeld, Rubin, & Feldman, 1984). Any person with a cerebral structural abnormality such as arterio-venous malformation, aneurysm, or tumor may be at higher risk.

Cocaine itself has been shown to decrease cerebral metabolism in vivo and may thus secondarily cause decrease in cerebral blood flow. In addition, cocaine may potentiate neurotransmission of serotonin by blocking its reuptake, causing an increase in serotonin level at the synapse. Serotonin is one of the most potent vasoconstrictor amines in the cerebral circulation, especially for large and medium sized arteries, and may contribute to the neurological effects of cocaine (Levine et al., 1987). Cocaine in vitro causes enhanced response of platelets to arachnidonic acid, leading to increased thromboxane production and platelet aggregation (Tonga et al., 1985).

Headaches, especially severe migraine, from cocaine use may be related to the combination of disturbed sympathetic, serotonergic, and platelet functions, in that such dysfunctions have been reported in migraine patients (Levine et al., 1987). "Street drug" contaminants such as procainamide, quinidine, amphetamines, phencyclidine, antihistamines, and strychnine have cardiovascular effects that could contribute to decreased cerebral blood flow (Levine et al., 1987).

In acute toxic cocaine encephalopathy, hyperpyrexia, and metabolic acidosis ensue, which along with the effect of the drug on neurotransmitters, may contribute to the development of seizures and coma.

Cerebrovascular Accidents

Cocaine is the recreational drug most frequently associated with cerebrovascular accidents in those stroke victims under 35 years of age, according to a retrospective review of stroke patients aged 17–44 (Kahn & Lowenstein, 1989).

The first reported case of stroke temporally related to cocaine usage was in 1977 (Brust & Richter, 1977). Since then case reports of subarachnoid hemorrhages of saccular aneurysm; intracerebral hemorrhagic strokes secondary to arteriovenous malformation; vasculitis; astrocytoma; and ischemic strokes in all vascular distributions, especially that of the left cerebral artery, middle cerebral artery, and vertebrobasilar artery have been described. Bilateral thalamic infarction, anterior spinal artery ischemia or infarction (Mody, Miller, McIntyre, Cobb, & Goldberg, 1988; Sawaya & Kaminski, 1990), lateral medullary syndrome, multiple cerebral hemorrhage (Green, Kelly, Gabrielsen, Levine, & Vanderzant, 1990), poorly localized basal ganglionic hemorrhage, and bilateral pontine infarction (DeVore & Tucker, 1988) have also been reported. In many cases, angiogram or autopsy have documented anatomical abnormalities. In one study, a predisposing vascular lesion was identified in 78% of cocaine users with subarachnoid hemorrhage and 48% of cocaine users with intracerebral hemorrhage. In a minority of cases, the studies had been normal (Levine et al., 1987).

Klonoff, Andrews, and Obana (1989), have reviewed 47 known cases of cocaine-related stroke and concluded that (1) the apparent incidence of stroke related to cocaine use is increasing; (2) cocaine-associated stroke is primarily a disease of young adults, with patients in their 20's mostly affected, and declines with each additional decade; (3) stroke may occur following any route of cocaine administration, with onset occurring within minutes to as long as a day later; (4) stroke after cocaine use is frequently associated with cerebrovascular abnormalities including intracranial aneurysm and arteriovenous malformations; and (5) in cocaine-associated strokes, the frequency of intracranial hemorrhage exceeds that of cerebral infarction, in contrast to the general population (Klonoff et al., 1989).

Clinical presentations of subarachnoid and intracerebral hemorrhage related to cocaine have been similar; i.e., headache, altered mental status, lateralized deficits, and seizures in varying combinations. Sudden death was also a presenting feature (Green et al., 1990).

Seizures

Seizures following cocaine use were well recognized even before the 1920s. Seizures associated with smoking crack cocaine are not uncommon in adolescents (Schwartz, 1988; Schwartz, 1989). Cocaine-related seizures have been associated with the local anesthetic effects of the drug, similar to that of lidocaine (Sawaya & Kaminski, 1990). Matsuzaki (1978) has shown in rhesus monkies that seizure activity induced by cocaine begins in the temporal lobe and then is generalized. In humans, seizures from cocaine use have been described with generalized tonic–clonic features (Gold et al., 1986; Brody et al., 1990; Schwartz, 1989; Factor, Sanchez Ramos, & Weiner, 1988; Ogunyemi, Locke, Kramer, & Nelson, 1989; Seaman & Gushee, 1990; Merriam, Medaba, & Levine, 1988) and were under 5 minutes in duration (Lowenstein et al., 1987). Complex partial status epilepticus has also been reported (Schwartz, 1989; Merriam et al., 1988). The interval between most recent cocaine use and the seizure was extremely variable, ranging from minutes to 12 hours (Lowenstein et al., 1987). Seizures may occur in first-time users, induced after a single dose of cocaine as well as in chronic addicts (Creglier & Mark, 1986; Merriam et al., 1988).

Of the traditional anticonvulsants, only diazepam and barbiturates have been found to have any preventive effect. Phenytoin is ineffective in animals. Cocaine-induced status epilepticus may be refractory to standard anticonvulsants and may require aggressive treatment to phenobarbital coma (Rowbotham & Lowenstein, 1990).

Cocaine-related seizures associated with anatomical lesions such as cerebrovascular accidents, and brain tumor (Seaman & Gushee, 1990) have been well described. Seizures may also be secondary to cerebral hypoperfusion from cardiac events. Furthermore, hyperpyrexia and metabolic acidosis greatly increase the risk and severity of seizure (Rowbotham, 1988).

Cardiac Complications

Cocaine has been implicated to cause systemic hypertension, tachycardia, supraventricular and ventricular arrhythmias, acute myocardial infarction, and even sudden death. Furthermore, dilated cardiomyopathy, sudden aortic dissection, and myocarditis have been related to the use of cocaine.

Isner et al. (1986), in their review of acute cardiac events temporally related to cocaine abuse, concluded that (1) cardiac consequences of cocaine abuse are not unique to parenteral use of the drug—smoke inhalation, intranasal inhalation, and ingestion of cocaine have also been associated with cardiac complications; (2) underlying heart disease is not a prerequisite for cocaine-related cardiac disorder; (3) seizure activity, a well-documented noncardiac complication of cocaine abuse, is neither a prerequisite for, nor an accompanying feature of, cardiac toxicity of cocaine; and (4) cardiac consequences of cocaine are not limited to massive doses of the drug.

Acute Myocardial Infarction/Myocardial Ischemia

Acute non–Q wave infarction (Wang, Hadidi, Triana, & Bargout, 1987) and Q wave infarction (Rollingher, Balzberg, & MacDonald, 1986) have been associated with cocaine abuse. In many of these patients, myocardial infarction occurs in the absence of significant underlying coronary artery disease (Creglier & Mark, 1985; Schachner, Roberts, & Thompson, 1984; Fernandez, Pichard, & Marchant, 1983; Smith et al., 1987; Zimmerman, Gustagson, & Kemp, 1987; Howard, Hueter, & Davis, 1985). These patients are generally young, without evidence of hyperlipidemia, diabetes mellutis, or hypertension, although cigarette smoking is prevalent. Cocaine definitely represents a potential hazard to anyone with underlying fixed coronary artery disease, whether the abnormality is minor or major (Smith et al., 1987; Wiess, 1986). Smith et al. (1987) reported that the left ascending artery appears to be most affected. Furthermore, myocardial infarction associated with first and only exposure to cocaine has been documented (Wehrie, Widallet, Navetta, & Peter, 1987).

The evidence of cocaine use precipitating coronary artery vasospasm is controversial. It has been postulated that thrombosis in normal or nearly normal arteries seems to have resulted from cocaine abuse leading to acute myocardial infarction, and that such thrombosis could result from prolonged spasm and initial damage (Fischman, Schuster, & Resnekov, 1976; Zimmerman et al., 1987). Nonetheless, in many angiographic studies of patients with normal coronary arteries, ergonovine testing and cold stimulation were negative for vasospasm.

In those patients with fixed coronary artery disease, cocaine causes dose-related increase in heart rate and blood pressure (Wang et al., 1987) secondary to the adrenergic output, and thus predictably increases the double product and myocardial oxygen demand possibly leading to myocardial ischemia and infarction (Creglier & Mark, 1986). In one case report, cocaine was implicated as having a synergistic effect in depressing myocardial function in a heart that had already been compromised by iron deposition associated with hemochromatosis (Goldenberg & Zeldis, 1987). Street cocaine may be mixed with a variety of different diluents including lidocaine, procaine, antihistamines, lactose, and amphetamines which may contribute to the cardiac dysfunction (Creglier et al., 1985). The cardiovascular effect of mixed substance abuse, especially that of cocaine and alcohol, has not been well studied.

The treatment of cocaine-related acute myocardial ischemia/infarction has been according to the standard protocol. One study (Smith et al., 1987) has found thrombolytic therapy to be successful in the selected patients in which it was performed. Nonetheless, Bush (1988) cautioned against the use of thrombolytics in those intravenous drug abusers because of the risk of intracranial bleeding secondary to the increased risk of mycotic aneurysm in this population.

Cardiac Arrhythmias

Cocaine-associated cardiac arrhythmias including sinus tachycardia, supraventricular and ventricular tachycardias, ventricular fibrillation, and asystole have been reported (Creglier & Mark, 1985; Berchinal, Bartall, & Desser, 1978; Boag & Harvard, 1985; Gradman, 1988; Jonsson, O'Meara, & Young, 1983).

In many instances, life-threatening cardiac arrhythmias occur during acute cocaine intoxication, in the context of profound metabolic acidosis resulting from prolonged seizures and/or hyperpyrexia (Gradman, 1988; Jonsson et al., 1983). Arrhythmias related to cardiac ischemia and cardiac infarction are frequently described.

Case reports in which cocaine may have been the primary factor in malignant arrhythmia production are less common (Isner et al., 1986; Creglier & Mark, 1985). The direct arrhythmogenic effect of cocaine may be attributed to the catecholamine outpouring with its use, thus enhancing β-stimulation of the myocardium (Creglier & Mark, 1985).

Cardiomyopathy and Myocarditis

Cocaine has been implicated in several reports as the cause of dilated cardiomyopathy. The patients who suffered coronary artery ischemia or cardiac arrest with stunned myocardium may have "ischemic cardiomyopathy," producing reduced left ventricular ejection fraction and congestive failure (Ascher, Stauffer, & Gaasch, 1988). Other investigators have proposed that cocaine use may have direct or indirect effects producing "toxic cardiomyopathy" with depressed left ventricular function. This depression of myocardial contractility has been attributed to the effect of high levels of circulating catecholamines on the cardiac cells (Chokshi, Moore, Pandian, & Isner, 1989; Duell, 1987), as comparable to patients with diffuse cardiomyopathy secondary to pheochromocytoma (Gradman, 1988).

Acute myocarditis, demonstrated by endomyocardial biopsy, was related to long-term use of freebase cocaine in a young addict (Isner et al., 1986). In this reported case, the myocardial inflammation was successfully treated with prednisone and azathiaprine. The association of myocarditis with cocaine use must be considered inferential at this time (Gradman, 1988), inasmuch as other cases of suspected myocarditis have yielded unsuccessful findings by biopsy.

Acute Aortic Dissection

Several cases of acute aortic dissection attributed to cocaine abuse have been reported. Patients generally presented with crushing, substernal chest pain with radiation. Successful management includes early and accurate diagnosis, and emergency surgical intervention (Gadalata, Hall, & Nelson, 1989; Barth, Bray, & Roberts, 1986). Underlying hypertensive disease, in addition to the elevation of systemic blood pressure following cocaine use, has been postulated to cause aortic dissection (Creglier & Mark, 1985; Edwards & Rubin, 1987).

Obstetric Complications

Peripartum cocaine abuse is common and has increased dramatically over the past several years. The prevalence of cocaine abuse in urban women evaluated by urine toxicology screen during pregnancy was estimated to be 8%–15% (Neerhof, MacGregor, Retsky, & Sullivan, 1989; Frank et al., 1988; Chasnoff, Duns, Schnoll, & Burns, 1985).

Cocaine use has been associated with numerous perinatal factors. Cocaine abusers when compared with nonusers have been found consistently to be less likely to receive prenatal care (MacGregor et al.,

1987; Kaye, Elkind, Goldberg, & Tyton, 1989), have decreased pregnancy weight gain, increased previous history of spontaneous abortions (Frank et al., 1988; Zuckerman et al., 1989; Chasnoff et al., 1985) and elective abortions, more sexually transmitted disease, and prior low birth weight infants (Zuckerman et al., 1989).

The cardiovascular and neurological effects of cocaine pose a definite risk to pregnant mothers and their fetuses. In addition, animal studies have shown that maternal administration of cocaine produced a substantial dose-dependent increase in uterine vascular resistance, maternal hypertension and decreased uteroplacental blood flow (Lindenberg, Alexander, Gendrop, Nencioli, & Williams, 1991). This, in turn, causes decreased fetal oxygenation, fetal hypertension, and fetal tachycardia. Numerous reports of obstetrical complications and perinatal morbidity have been related to the uteroplacental effects of cocaine (Cregler & Mark, 1986).

Chasnoff et al. (1985) have suggested that cocaine use during pregnancy is associated with abruptio placentae after reporting four women who experienced the onset of labor with abruptio placentae immediately after self-injection of cocaine. Subsequent studies (Creglier & Mark, 1986) have reported an increased risk of abruptio placentae. In addition, intrapartum placenta previa is also more prevalent in the cocaine-abusing mothers than in nonusers (Handler, Kistin, Dans, & Ferre, 1991).

There have been frequent reports of preterm labor and/or delivery associated with cocaine use (Neerhof et al., 1989; MacGregor et al., 1987; Little, Snell, Klein, & Gilstrap, 1989). In a prevalence study of illicit drug use as measured by by urine toxicology screening in a group of women with suspected preterm labor, the investigators found that 17% of the women had positive drug screens, and that cocaine was the most commonly abused substance (Ney, Dooley, Keith, Chasnoff, & Socol, 1990).

Adverse perinatal outcomes associated with in utero cocaine exposure include fetal distress in labor with stained amniotic fluid (Chasnoff, Chisum, & Kaplan, 1988), low gestational age, low birth weight, low birth length, and small head circumference (Kaye et al., 1989; Zuckerman et al., 1989; Little et al., 1989; Burkett, Yasin, & Palow, 1990). A neonatal withdrawal syndrome has been described to include tachycardia, tremulousness, poor feeding, and seizures. These symptoms were pronounced in those neonates with positive cocaine testing (Neerhof et al., 1989; Mastrogiannis, Decavalas, Verma, & Tejani, 1990). An increased incidence of congenital malformations especially genitourinary tract (Chasnoff et al., 1987) and cardiac anomalies (Little et al., 1989), has been reported in infants with in utero cocaine exposure when compared with general population. Congenital syphilis was also found to be more prevalent in this group of infants (Burkett et al., 1990). Furthermore, an increased risk of intrauterine and neonatal death (Neerhof et al., 1989) and sudden infant death has been reported in infants born to cocaine-abusing mothers (Creglier & Mark, 1986; Chasnoff, Burns, & Burns, 1987; Ward et al., 1986). Adverse neurological and developmental outcomes including depression of interactive behaviors, depression of state organization, and poor motor regulation have been identified in those infants with perinatal cocaine exposure (Creglier & Mark, 1986; Chasnoff, Griffith, MacGregor, Dirkes, & Burns, 1989).

Chasnoff et al. (1989) reported that infants exposed to cocaine only in the first trimester had birth weight, length, and head circumference similar to drug-free controls, but that those infants exposed to cocaine throughout pregnancy had significantly smaller measurements. Early cessation of cocaine during gestation may prevent some of these adverse consequences.

Cocaine users have been reported to be more likely to use other drugs including opiates, marijuana, tobacco, and alcohol (Little, Snell, Gilstrap, & Johnson, 1990). Whereas mothers who abuse multiple substances were found to have similar adverse perinatal outcomes as cocaine only users, they demonstrated even higher incidence of neonatal withdrawal and congenital anomalies (Neerhof et al., 1989; Little et al., 1990).

As Neerhof et al. (1989) concluded, the prevalence of cocaine abuse and the frequency of adverse perinatal outcomes associated with it emphasize the need to identify substance-abusing mothers during pregnancy. Particular attention should be focused on those women with a history of heavy use of tobacco, alcohol, and marijuana since they are over represented among the cocaine users (Frank et al., 1988). Furthermore, physicians should evaluate those patients with possible preterm labor for illicit drug use (Ney et al., 1990). Identification during pregnancy would enable antenatal surveillance and referral to psychiatric and social services for substance abusing mothers, and long-term neurodevelopmental follow-up for infants exposed to cocaine in utero (Neerhof et al., 19891).

Other Complications

Cocaine use is associated with a variety of other complications. Cocaine-associated acute myoglobinuric renal failure has been reported (Anand, Siami, & Stone, 1989; Krohn, Slowman-Kovacs, & Leapman, 1988; Pogue & Nurse, 1989; Guerin et al., 1989; Bauwens, Boggs, &

Hartwell, 1989; Ahijado, de Vinuesa, & Luno 1990; Steingrub, Sweet, & Teres, 1989). Patients may present with agitation, seizure, hyperthermia, tachycardia, tachypnea, and altered mental status. Metabolic acidosis, bleeding coagulopathy, anuric renal failure with rhabdomyolysis, all with dramatic increases in muscle and liver enzymes, have been documented, leading to multisystem failure (Guerin et al., 1989). Hyperthermia associated with cocaine use may be the primary cause of the toxic metabolic derangement leading to renal failure. Nontraumatic rhabdomyolysis after smoking crack cocaine without hyperthermia has also been reported (Steingrub et al., 1989).

Intestinal ischemia has been described with ingestion and intranasal use of cocaine (Garfia, Valverde, Borondo, Candena, & Lucena, 1990; Nalbandian, Shath, 1985; Mizrahi, Dietrich, & Georgiu, 1988). Early diagnosis and surgical intervention are essential to the therapy. The diagnosis of intestinal ischemia must be considered in cocaine addicts with severe abdominal pain.

Cocaine hepatotoxicity has been well documented to occur in experimental animals (Sluster, Quimby, Bates, & Thompson, 1977). Cocaine-induced hepatotoxicity has also been reported in humans. The mechanism is unclear. It has been postulated that cocaine may cause direct hepatocellular damage (Perino, Warren, & Levine, 1987).

COMPLICATIONS RELATED TO ROUTE OF ADMINISTRATION

Previously we reviewed some medical complications of cocaine use that are specific to cocaine itself, without regard to how it is administered. In this section, we review important route-specific complications (see Table 13.3). Intravenous drug use, for example, results in a number of

TABLE 13.3. Complications of Cocaine Use
Related to Route of Administration

Intravenous	HIV Infection/AIDS
	Hepatitis
	Endocarditis
	Bacteremia/sepsis
	Soft tissue infection (cellulitis, abscess)
Smoked	Pneumothorax
	Pneumomediastinum
	Pulmonary edema
Intranasal	Sinusitis
	Septal perforation

complexities that are more "generic" to the act of injection. Although complications of smoked and intranasal use can also be seen with other drugs, the ones described below are generally associated with cocaine.

Injection Cocaine Use

Intravenous drug use places patients at risk for a variety of specific medical complications with which they may present to primary care providers (Cherubin, 1967; White, 1973; Hahn, Onorato, Jones, & Dougherty, 1989; Stein, 1990; Lindell, Porter, & Langston, 1972). The most prevalent complications are infections that result from the violation of the protective epidermis when a needle is inserted into the skin. Drugs are most commonly injected intravenously ("shooting") when a suitable vein may be found. As an alternative, when accessible veins are lacking, drugs may be injected intradermally ("skin popping"). Intramuscular injection may result in unsatisfactory rates of absorption and is done infrequently. Intraarterial injection is also done infrequently—usually as the result of accidental needle placement (Lindell et al. 1972).

Powdered cocaine is prepared for an injection by dissolving it in a liquid (usually water) and drawing it up into a syringe. It is often mixed with heroin ("speedballing") or other drugs. Addicts will use any of a number of injection sites, depending on vein availability. Arms and legs are often used first. Other sites, such as the neck, come into use once superficial veins become progressively sclerosed. Cocaine addicts will often mix blood with the cocaine in the syringe ("booting") in an effort to modify the "rush" experienced with injection. Sterile needles are often not available, resulting in the frequent use of nonsterile injection equipment ("works"). Needle sharing, either with individuals or in groups ("shooting galleries"), is an injection behavior that carries particular risk for transmission of infections such as AIDS (Marmor, Des Jarlis, & Cohen, 1987).

HIV Infection

The association of HIV infection and AIDS with injection drug use has been well established (Hahn et al., 1989; Marmor et al., 1987; Hardy, Allen, & Morgan, 1985). The contribution of injection drug use to the overall incidence of AIDS in the United States is increasing: 28% of all cases have occurred in drug users, with women and minorities being affected disproportionately (Center for Disease Control, 1991). If exposure to sexual partners who use intravenous drugs is included along with direct needle use, the majority of HIV cases in women are linked to needle use. Obviously, the role of injection drug use in HIV infection is similarly important as an underlying cause of HIV infection in children born to these women (Rogers et al., 1987). In Connecticut, African-Americans and Hispanics account for 54% of all AIDS cases (State of Connecticut Department of Health Services, 1989). Seroprevalence of HIV among black intravenous drug users (IVDUs) was noted to be 45% in one study, compared with 10% in whites (State of Connecticut Department of Health Services, 1989).

The prevalence of HIV infection among IVDUs overall is known to vary widely according to geographical location. In a review by Hahn et al. (1989), seroprevalence rates were found to be highest in the Northeast and Puerto Rico (10–65%), and considerably lower in other parts of the country (0–10%). This study supported prior research suggesting a higher seroprevalence in minorities and noted no relationship of gender or age to HIV infection (Hahn et al., 1989). Data from this study considered primarily IVDUs in drug treatment. Information from those not in treatment is difficult to obtain.

Cocaine use may be independently associated with HIV infection, placing persons at particularly high risk (Chassin et al., 1989; Goldsmith, 1988). For those who use cocaine intravenously, the need to inject more frequently may play a role. Recent work has suggested, however, that cocaine itself, regardless of route, can lead to HIV infection by promoting high-risk sexual behavior (Fullilove, Fullilove, Bowser, & Gross, 1990). Alcohol may have a similar effect through disinhibition (Stall, McKusick, Wiley, Coates, & Ostrow, 1986).

Screening for and diagnosing HIV infection in cocaine users requires great skill and sensitivity. HIV counseling should be offered for all known addicts at an appropriate time. Persons who want to be tested should give informed consent and be given detailed pretest and post-test counseling by a knowledgeable caregiver. This counseling should focus on the meaning of the test and the implication of positive and negative results. Further prevention of HIV spread through safe sexual and drug use behaviors should be emphasized.

Pretest counselling must be done in a careful and thoughtful manner. An assessment should be done of the patient's reasons for being tested, including an extensive evaluation of high-risk behaviors. Information about past testing should be sought. Patients often have misconceptions regarding HIV testing which should be clarified. For example, patients frequently think that a positive result means that they have AIDS. It needs to be clear that HIV testing does not diagnose AIDS—it simply shows past exposure to the virus that causes AIDS and that this diagnosis requires much more clinical data. A negative test may be misinterpreted as a "green light" for ongoing high-risk behaviors that have been "Okay so far." Confidentiality issues must also be explored.

Providers need to be familiar with the state laws regarding confidentiality so that patients are aware who may have access to their test results.

Post-test counseling should be arranged at the time of pretest counseling. Test results should always be given in person so that adequate counseling can be done. For those with a negative test, the discussion should focus on how to increase one's chances of staying negative. It should be noted that an infected person may take up to 6 months to become HIV seropositive.

For those found to be HIV positive, specific steps in evaluation must be taken (Hollander, 1988). Along with a complete history and physical exam, patients should be screened for related diseases, such as syphilis and tuberculosis (see Table 13.4). T-cell subset testing should be performed to assess immune function. T-cell counts are used for staging and to help guide management. After a complete evaluation, treatment options can be discussed. It is crucial that the caregiver be supportive and hopeful. Patients need to know that specific therapies are available to reduce morbidity and mortality, such as antiretroviral drugs and methods for pneumocystitis pneumonia prophylaxis.

Zidovudine (AZT) is currently the primary antiviral therapy used to treat HIV-positive persons. Although it was initially used only in persons with AIDS, Volberding et al (1990) demonstrated that persons with asymptomatic HIV infection who received zidovudine had a slower

TABLE 13.4. The Evaluation and Management of Cocaine Users with HIV Infection

---

Baseline Evaluation
  History and Physical Exam
    Focusing on complications of substance abuse, intravenous drug use, and HIV
    infection
  Laboratory Studies
    Hepatitis serology
    Syphilis serology
    Liver function tests
    T-cell subset studies
  Tuberculosis Screening

Initial Management
  Prevention and management of general complications of substance abuse and HIV
  infection (if indicated)
    Vaccinations (hepatitis B, pneumococcal, influenza)
    Early treatment of syphilis
    Tuberculosis chemoprophylaxis
  HIV specific therapies (if indicated).
    Antiretrovinal therapy (e.g. zidovudine)
    Pneumocystis prophylaxis
    Treatment of specific opportunistic infections

---

rate of disease progression. This benefit was seen only in those asympotomatic persons with T-helper cell counts less than 500. Zidovudine is typically prescribed in a dose of 500 mg per day (in divided doses of 100 mg). Patients on zidovudine need to be monitored closely for side effects, including bone marrow suppression (anemia, leukopenia) and gastrointestinal upset (nausea). Prophylaxis against pneumocystitis pneumonia carinii is recommended for persons with T-helper cell counts less than 200 or in those with a prior episode of pneumonia caused by this organism. Commonly employed therapies include trimethoprim–sulfamethaxosol and aerosolized pentamadine.

Hepatitis

Hepatitis, both acute and chronic, is associated with intravenous drug use (Seeff, 1975). Of the potential etiological agents, hepatitis B virus has been most commonly associated with IVDU. This virus is found in the blood and bodily fluids of persons with active infection and is commonly spread through contaminated needles as well as through sexual activity. During an acute episode of hepatitis, patients will complain of fatigue, anorexia, nausea, vomiting, dark urine, and light stools. Patients with chronic hepatitis may present with more nonspecific symptoms, complications of advanced liver disease, or be asymptomatic.

Studies of hepatitis B serology in addicts have demonstrated that over 50% of have been exposed to hepatitis B virus at some time, and up to 10% may be chronically infected and thus capable of transmitting the disease (Seeff, 1975; Stimmel, Vernace, & Schaffner, 1975). Delta hepatitis infection with hepatitis B occurs in IVDUs and may result in a prolonged and more severe illness (Lettau et al., 1987).

Hepatitis A, which is most often associated with the ingestion of contaminated food or water, has recently been described in IVDUs (Centers for Disease Control, 1988). The source of these infections has been postulated to be contaminated drugs or injection equipment. Hepatitis C (previously referred to as non-A, non-B hepatitis) has also been identified as commonly present in IVDUs (Esteban et al., 1989). As with hepatitis B, chronic disease is possible.

Management of hepatitis in IVDUs who use cocaine or other drugs involves careful assessment and close medical follow-up. All IVDUs should be screened carefully for hepatitis with serologic studies and liver function tests. Those found to be negative for hepatitis B should be offered vaccination. Those who are carriers (hepatitis B surface-antigen positive) need to be cautioned on preventing spread of virus to others. Persons with chronic liver disease (elevated liver enzymes) need to be observed followed longitudinally with avoidance of potential hepatotoxins (alcohol, medications) if possible.

Endocarditis and Bacteremia

Intravenous drug users have long been known to be at high risk for endocarditis (Reisberg, 1979). Bacteria from contaminated needles or from skin enter the blood- stream and may settle on cardiac structures such as valves. Typically, persons with endocarditis cultures present with an acute febrile illness with a variety of nonspecific constitutional symptoms. A new cardiac murmur may be present and blood cultures are persistently positive. Echocardiography will often reveal vegetation on one of the valves.

When culture results are reviewed, *Staphylococcus aureus* is the most common organism found in addicts with endocarditis (Reiner, Gopala-krishna, & Lerner, 1976). Streptococcal and Gram-negative organisms and others may be found as well. Valvular lesions are most often right-sided, with the tricuspid valve the primary site of infection. Therapy for endocarditis is directed towards the organisms isolated on blood culture. Sensitive organisms may be treated with 4 weeks of intravenous antibiotic therapy. One study suggested that in selected patients 2 weeks of combination therapy may be sufficient (Chambers et al., 1988). During therapy, patients need to be monitored closely for complications, including cardiac abcess, valvular failure, and systemic emboli.

Cocaine addicts may be particularly susceptible to endocarditis. In a report by Chambers et al., independent predictors of endocarditis in intravenous drug users with fever were identified (Chambers, Morris, Tucker, & Modin, 1987). A past history of cocaine use was second only to chest radiograph evidence of septic emboli as a predictor of endocarditis in these patients. These authors postulated that features specific to cocaine use, such as patterns of use or methods of drug preparation, may help to explain the predictive value of cocaine use for endocarditis.

Bacteremia without specific evidence of endocarditis is also seen frequently in IVDUs. Up to 60% of bacteremia in such patients may not be associated with documented endocarditis (Stein, 1990). Addicts are well known to be at increased risk for other severe bacterial infections such as pneumonia, osteomyelitis, and CNS infections which may be associated with bacteremia (Haverkos & Lang, 1990).

When a febrile IVDU presents for medical care, the provider faces a challenging task of finding the source. A thorough history and physical exam needs to be done in an effort to identify a focus of infection.

Laboratory studies including a complete blood count, serum chemistry, cultures of body fluids, and chest radiography are often required to supplement the clinical exam. Even when these steps are taken, a source may not be found. In a study done at the Boston City Hospital emergency room, physicians had significant difficulty predicting which patients were bacteremic or had endocarditis (Samet, Shevitz, Fowle, & Singer, 1990). Often when initial evaluation is unrewarding, close follow-up, including hospitalization, may be necessary until a source is found. Other less "acute" sources of fever such as tuberculosis, viral illnesses (including HIV infection), and opportunistic infections in HIV-infected patients need to be considered as well.

Soft-Tissue Infections

Bacterial infections in intravenous drug users may be localized to soft tissues without being associated with bacteremia. These typically occur at injection sites and include cellulitis and abscesses. Bacteria causing skin infections usually include normal skin flora but can include more unusual organisms from contaminated needles. Localized infection can often be treated with oral antibiotics (such as dicloxacillin). Abscesses need to be drained. Patients with local infection that does not respond to antibiotics, or with signs of systemic infection, may need to be switched to intravenous antibiotics. There is evidence that patients who use hygienic injection techniques such as skin cleansing with alcohol may protect themselves from these infections (Herb, Walters, Case, & Pettiti, 1989).

Smoked Cocaine Use

Pulmonary Complications

Chest pain, dyspnea, cough, sputum production, and hemoptysis are common pulmonary symptoms which abusers of freebase crack cocaine present for medical evaluation. Chest radiographs have been helpful in the diagnosis of underlying pulmonary abnormalities. Atelectasis, pneumomediastinum, pneumothorax, and hemopneumothorax have been reported (Eurman et al., 1989).

Smoke and its toxic combustion products from using crack have been shown to reduce mucociliary clearance and to cause bronchiolar damage in both animals and humans. Atelectasis can occur when secretions accumulate in the bronchioles. Immunologically mediated effects of cocaine have also been postulated (Eurman, Potash, Eyler, Paganussi, & Beute, 1989; Kissner, Laurence, Selis, & Flint, 1987).

Spontaneous pneumothorax and pneumomediastinum due to inhalation of cocaine have been described. Inhalation of cocaine involves a deep, prolonged inspiratory effort, often followed by a Valsalva maneuver and violent coughing. The resulting increased intra-alveolar pressures causes rupture of alveoli, with escape of air into the interstitial tissue. The air may dissect centrally along the bronchiovascular sheaths into the mediastinum (Weiner & Putnam, 1987). Decompression of the pneumomediastinum through the mediastinal parietal pleura results in pneumothorax. Less commonly, pneumothorax may result from rupture of visceral pleural blebs (Eurman et al., 1989).

Noncardiogenic pulmonary edema related to cocaine smoking has been reported (Eurman et al., 1989; Cucio, Ok, Cregler & Julet, 1987; Hoffman & Goodman, 1989). Damage to the alveolar capillary membrane by the cocaine smoke may be followed by the transudation of fluid, with resulting diffuse or localized areas of pulmonary edema (Eurman et al., 1989). This abnormality usually resolves within 24–72 hours (Cucio et al., 1987).

Diffuse alveolar hemorrhage (Murray, Albin, Merzner, & Crines, 1988; Walek, Masson, & Siddigui, 1989), pulmonary talc granulomatosis (Ouberd, Bickel, Ingram, & Scott, 1990), bronchiolitis obliterans (Patel, Dutta, & Schonfeld, 1989), severe or life-threatening exacerbation of asthma (Rubin & Neugarten, 1990) have also been associated with cocaine inhalation.

Intranasal Cocaine Use

Chronic intranasal cocaine use can cause nasal symptoms mimicking allergic or vasomotor rhinnitis (Snyder & Snyder, 1985). Hyposmia and anosmia have been reported (Gordon, Moran, Jafek, Eller, & Strahan, 1990). Septal perforations are frequently documented and may occur as early as 3 weeks after "snorting" began (Messinger, 1962). Occasionally, septal necrosis can be severe and accompanied by bleeding, granulation tissue, ulceration, sinusitis, nasal collapse, and even saddle-nose deformity (Kuriloff & Kimmelman, 1989). A combination of irritation from adulterants, ischemia secondary to its intense vasoconstriction effects, and direct trauma may consequently lead to these sinonasal complications. Hot vapors from freebase cocaine have been implicated in causing madarosis (James & Goldenring, 1986).

SUMMARY

Health care providers caring for cocaine users need to be aware of the wide variety of medical complications related to cocaine which may cause patients to seek care. Symptoms and signs relating to intoxication and withdrawal, direct acute and chronic complications of cocaine use, and complications specific to route of administration must be considered in the short- and long-term management of patients. The education of both providers and patients regarding these issues is essential if efforts at prevention and timely management are to be successful.

REFERENCES

Diagnosis and Management of Cocaine Intoxication and Withdrawal

Babor, T. F., Stephens, R. S., & Marlatt, G. A. (1987). Verbal report methods in clinical research on alcoholism: Response bias and its minimization. *Journal of Studies on Alcohol, 48,* 410–424.

Barnett, G., Hawka, R., & Resnick, R. (1981). Cocaine pharmacokinetics in humans. *Journal of Ethnopharmacology, 3,* 353–366.

Catravas, J. D., & Waters, I. N. (1981). Acute cocaine intoxication in the conscious dog: Studies on the mechanism of lethality. *Journal of Pharmacology and Experimental Therapeutics, 217,* 350–356.

Chang, G., & Astrachan, B. M. (1988). The emergency department surveillance of alcohol intoxication after motor vehicle accidents. *Journal of the American Medical Association, 260,* 2533–2536.

Chang, G., & Kosten, T. (in press). Emergency management of acute drug intoxication. In J. H. Lowinson, P. Ruiz, & R. B. Millman (Eds.), *Comprehensive textbook of substance abuse.*

Creglier, L. L., & Mark, H. (1986). Medical complications of cocaine abuse. *New England Journal of Medicine, 315,* 1495–1500.

Council on Scientific Affairs. (1987). Scientific issues in drug testing. *Journal of the American Medical Association, 257,* 3110–3115.

Dackis, C. A., & Gold, M. S. (1985). New concepts in cocaine addiction: The dopamine depletion hypothesis. *Neuroscience and Biobehavioral Reviews, 9,* 469–477.

Ellison, J. M., & Jacobs, D. (1986). Emergency psychopharmacology: A review and update. *Annals of Emergency Medicine, 15,* 962–968.

Gawin, F. H., & Kleber, H. D. (1986). Abstinence symptomatology and psychiatric diagnosis in cocaine abusers. *Archives of General Psychiatry, 43,* 107–113.

Gross, P. L. (1989). Toxiocologic emergencies. In E. W. Wilkins (Ed.), *MGH textbook of emergency medicine* (2nd ed., pp. 395–422). Baltimore, MD: Williams and Wilkins.

Karch, S. B. (1989). Managing cocaine crisis. *Annals of Emergency Medicine, 18,* 228–229.

Kellermann, A. L., Fikn, S. D., LoGerfo, J. P., & Copass, M. K. (1987). Impact of drug screening in suspected overdose. *Annals of Emergency Medicine, 16,* 1206–1216.

Post, R. M. (1975) Cocaine psychosis: A continuum model. *American Journal of Psychiatry, 132,* 225–231.

Ritchie, J. M., & Greene, N. M. (1985). Local anethestics. In A. G. Gilman, L. S. Good, T. W. Rall, & R. Murad (Eds.), *The pharmacological basis of therapeutics* (7th ed., pp. 309–310). New York: Macmillan.

Rowbotham, M. C. (1988). Neurological aspects of cocaine abuse. *Western Journal of Medicine, 149,* 442–448.

Rowbotham, M. C., Jones, R. T., Benowitz, N. L., & Jacob, P. (1984). Trazodone—oral cocaine interactions. *Archives of General Psychiatry, 41,* 895–899.

Schwartz, R. H. (1988). Urine testing in the detection of drugs of abuse. *Archives of Internal Medicine, 148,* 2407–2412.

Siegel, R. K. (1982). Cocaine smoking. *Journal of Psychoative Drugs, 14,* 271–359.

Sloan, E. P., Zalenski, R. J., Smith, R. F. Shaeff, C. M., Chen, E., Keys, N., Crescenzo, M., Barrett, J., & Berman, E. (1989). Toxicology screening in urban trauma patients: Drug prevalence and its relationship to trauma severity and management. *The Journal of Trauma, 29,* 1647–1653.

Ungar, J. R. (1989). Current drugs of abuse. In G. R. Schwartz, N. Buker, B. K. Hanke, M. A. Mangeben, T. Mayer, & G. R. Ungar (Eds.), *Emergency medicine: The essential update* (pp. 210–224). Philadelphia: WB Saunders.

U. S. Preventive Services Task Force. (1989). Screening for alcohol and other drug abuse. *American Family Physician, 40,* 137–146.

Weiss, R. D., & Mirin, S. M. (1988). Intoxication and withdrawal syndromes. In S. E. Hyman (Ed.), *Manual of psychiatric emergencies.* Boston: Little, Brown.

Neurological Complications

Brody, S. L., Slovis, C. M., & Wrenn, K. D. (1990). Cocaine-related medical problems: Consecutive series of 233 patients. *American Journal of Medicine, 88,* 325–331.

Brust, J. C. M., & Richter, R. W. (1977). Stroke associated with cocaine abuse? *New York State Journal of Medicine, 77,* 1473–1475.

Creglier, L. L., & Mark, H. (1986). Medical complications of cocaine abuse. *New England Journal of Medicine, 315,* 1495–1500.

DeVore, R. A., & Tucker, H. M. (1988). Dysphagia and dysarthria as a result of cocaine abuse. *Otolaryngology—Head and Neck Surgery, 98,* 174–175.

Factor, S. A., Sachez Ramos, J. R., & Weiner, W. J. (1988). Cocaine and Tourette's syndrome. *Annuals of Neurology, 23,* 423–424.

Gold, M. S., Dackis, C. A., Pattash, A. L. C., Extein, I., & Washton, A. (1986). Cocaine update: From bench to bedside. *Advances in Alcohol Substance Abuse, 5,* 35–60.

Green, R. M., Kelly, K. M., Gabrielsen, T., Levine, S. R., & Vanderzant, C. (1990). Multiple intracerebral hemorrhages after smoking "crack" cocaine. *Stroke, 83,* 601–602.

Kahn, D. A., & Lowenstein, D. H. (1989). Recreational drug use: A growing risk factor for stroke in young people. *Neurology, 39,* 161.

Klonoff, D. C., Andrews, B. T., & Obana, W. G. (1989). Stroke associated with cocaine use. *Archives of Neurology, 46,* 989–993.

Levine, S. R., Washington, J. M., Moen, M., Kieran, S. N., Junger, S., & Welch, K. M. A. (1987). Crack associated stroke. *Neurology, 37,* 1092–1093.

Levine, S. R., & Welch, K. M. A. (1988). Cocaine and stroke. *Stroke, 19,* 779–783.

Litchenfeld, P. J., Rubin, D. B., Feldman, R. S. (1984). Subarachnoid hemorrhage precipitated by cocaine snorting. *Archives of Neurology, 41,* 223–224.

Lowenstein, D. H., Massa, S. M., Rowbotham, M. C., Collins, S. D., McKinney, H. E., & Simon, R. P. (1987). Acute neurologic and psychiatric complications associated with cocaine abuse. *American Journal of Medicine, 83,* 841–846.

Matsuzaki, M. (1978). Alteration in pattern of EEG activities and convulsant effect of cocaine following chronic administration in the rhesus monkey. *Electroencephalography and Clinical Neurophysiology, 45,* 1–15.

Merriam, A. E., Medaba, A., & Levine, B. (1988). Partial complex status epilepticus associated with cocaine abuse. *Biological Psychology, 23,* 515–518.

Mody, C. K., Miller, B. L., McIntyre, H. B., Cobb, S. K., & Goldberg, M. A. (1988). Neurologic complications of cocaine abuse. *Neurology, 38,* 1189–1193.

Ogunyemi, A. O., Locke, G. E., Kramer, L. D., & Nelsen, L. (1989). Complex partial status epilepticus provoked by "crack" cocaine. *Annals of Neurology, 26,* 785–786.

Rowbotham, M. C. (1988). Neurological aspects of cocaine abuse. *Western Journal of Medicine, 149,* 442–448.

Rowbotham, M. C., Lowenstein, D. H. (1990). Neurologic consequences of cocaine use. *Annual Review of Medicine, 41,* 417–422.

Sawaya, G. R., Kaminski, M. J. (1990). Spinal cord infarction after cocaine use. *Southern Medical Journal, 83,* 601–602.

Schwartz, R. H. (1988). Seizures and syncope in adolescent cocaine abuser. *American Journal of Medicine, 85,* 462.

Schwartz, R. H. (1989). Seizures associated with smoking "crack"—A survey of adolescent "crack" smokers. *Western Journal of Medicine, 150,* 213.

Seaman, M., & Gushee, K. (1990). Investigation of cocaine-related seizures having unsuspected brain tumors. *Annals of Emergency Medicine, 19,* 723–734.

Tonga, G., Tempesta, E., Togue, A. R., Dolci, N., Lebo, B., & Caprino, L. (1985). Platelet responsiveness and biosynthesis of thromboxane and prostacyclin in response to in vitro cocaine treatment. *Haemostasis, 15*, 100–107.

Van Dyke, C., & Byck, R. (1982). Cocaine. *Scientific American, 246*, 128–141.

Cardiac Complications

Ascher, E. K., Stauffer, J. E., & Gaasch, W. H. (1988). Coronary artery spasm, cardiac arrest, transient electrocardiographic Q waves and stunned myocardium in cocaine-associated acute myocardial infarction. *American Journal Cardiology, 61*, 939–941.

Barth, C. W., Bray, M., & Roberts, W. C. (1986). Rupture of ascending aorta during cocaine intoxication. *American Journal of Cardiology, 57*, 496.

Berchinal, A., Bartall, M., & Desser, K. B. (1978). Accelerated ventricular rhythm and cocaine abuse. *Annals of Internal Medicine, 88*, 519.

Boag, F., & Havard, C. W. H. (1985). Cardiac arrhythmia and myocardial ischaemia related to cocaine and alcohol consumption. *Postgraduate Medical Journal, 61*, 997–999.

Bush, H. S. (1988). Cocaine-associated myocardial infarction. A word of caution about thrombolytic therapy. *Chest, 94*, 878.

Chokshi, S. K., Moore, R., Pandian, N. G., & Isner, J. M. (1989). Reversible cardiomyopathy associated with cocaine intoxication. *Annals of Internal Medicine, 111*, 1039–1040.

Creglier, L. L., & Mark, H. (1985). Medical complications of cocaine abuse. *New England Journal of Medicine, 313*, 666–669.

Creglier, L. L., & Mark, H. (1985). Relation of acute myocardial infarction to cocaine abuse. *American Journal of Cardiology, 56*, 794.

Creglier, L. L., & Mark, H. (1986). Cardiovascular dangers of cocaine abuse. *American Journal of Cardiology, 57*, 1185–1186.

Duell, P. B. (1987). Chronic cocaine abuse and dilated cardiomyopathy. *American Journal of Medicine, 83*, 601.

Edwards, J., & Rubin, R. N. (1987). Aortic dissection and cocaine abuse. *Annuals of Internal Medicine, 107*, 779–780.

Fernandez, M. S., Pichard, A. D., Marchant, E. (1983). Acute myocardialinfarction with normal coronary arteries. *Clinical Cardiology, 6*, 553–559.

Fischman, M. W., Schuster, C. R., & Resnekov, L. (1976). Cardiovascular and subjective effects of intravenous cocaine administration in humans. *Archives of General Psychiatry, 33*, 983–989.

Gadalata, D., Hall, M. H., & Nelson, R. L. (1989). Cocaine induced acute aortic dissection. *Chest, 96*, 1203–1206.

Goldenberg, S. P., & Zeldis, S. M. (1987). Fatal acute congestive heart failure in a patient with idiopathic hemochromatosis and cocaine use. *Chest, 92*, 374–375.

Gradman, A. H. (1988). Cardiac effects of cocaine: A review. *Yale Journal of Biology and Medicine, 61*, 137–147.

Haines, J. D., & Sexter, S. (1987). Acute myocardial infarction associated with cocaine abuse. *Southern Medical Journal, 80,* 1326–1327.

Howard, R. E., Hueter, D. C., & Davis, G. J. (1985). Acute myocardial infarction following cocaine abuse in a young woman with normal coronary arteries. *Journal of the American Medical Association, 254,* 95–96.

Isner, J. M., Estes, M., Thompson, P. D., Costanzo-Nordin, M. R., Subramanian, R., Miller, G., Katsas, G., Screeney, K., & Sturner, W. Q. (1986). Acute cardiac events temporally related to cocaine abuse. *New England Journal of Medicine, 315,* 1438–1443.

Jonsson, S., O'Meara, M., & Young, J. (1983). Acute cocaine poisoning: Importance of treating seizure and acidosis. *American Journal of Medicine, 75,* 1061–1064.

Rollingher, I. M., Belzberg, A. S., MacDonald, I. L. (1986). Cocaine-induced myocardial infarction. *Canadian Medical Assocication Journal, 135,* 45–46.

Schachner, J. S., Roberts, B. H., Thompson, P. D. (1984). Coronary artery spasm and myocardial infarction associated with cocaine use. *New England Journal of Medicine, 310,* 1665–1666.

Smith, H. W. B., Liberman, H. A., Brody, S. L., Battey, L. L., Donohue, B. C., & Morris, D. C. (1987). Acute myocardial infarction temporally related to cocaine use. *Annals of Internal Medicine, 107,* 13–18.

Wang, T., Hadidi, F., Triana, F., & Bargout, M. (1987). Morning report at Charity Hospital: Myocardial infarction associated with the use of cocaine. *American Journal of Medical Science, 195,* 569–571.23.

Weiner, D. M., & Putman, C. E. (1987). Pain in the chest in a user of cocaine. *Journal of the American Medical Association, 258,* 2087–2088.

Wehrie, C. S., Widallet, H. J., Navetta, F. I., & Peter, R. H. (1987). Acute myocardial infarction associated with initial cocaine use. *Southern Medical Journal, 89,* 933–934.

Wiess, R. J. (1986). Recurrent myocardial infarction caused by cocaine abuse. *American Heart Journal, 111,* 793.

Zimmerman, F. H. (1987). Cocaine and MI. *Chest, 92,* 767.

Zimmerman, F. H., Gustagson, G. M., & Kemp, H. G. (1987). Recurrent myocardial infarction associated with cocaine abuse in a young man with normal coronary arteries. Evidence for coronary artery spasm culminating on thrombosis. *Journal of the American College of Cardiology, 9,* 964–968.

Obstetric Complications

Burkett, G., Yasin, S., & Palow, K. (1990). Perinatal implications of cocaine exposure. *Journal of Reproductive Medicine, 35,* 35–42.

Chasnoff, I. J., Burns, K. A., & Burns, W. J. (1987). Cocaine use in pregnancy: Perinatal morbidity and mortality. *Neurotoxicology and Teratology, 9,* 291–293.

Chasnoff, I. J., Chisum, G. M., & Kaplan, W. E. (1988). Maternal cocaine use and genitourinary tract malformations. *Teratology, 37,* 201–204.

Chasnoff, I. J., Duns, W. J., Schnoll, S. H., & Burns, K. S. (1985). Cocaine use in pregnancy. *New England Journal of Medicine, 313,* 666–669.

Chasnoff, I. J., Griffith, D. R., MacGregor, S., Dirkes, K., Burns, K. A. (1989) Temporal patterns of cocaine use in pregnancy. Perinatal outcome. *Journal of the American Medical Association, 261,* 1741–1744.

Creglier, L. L., & Mark, H. (1986). Medical complications of cocaine abuse. *New England Journal of Medicine, 315,* 1495–1500.

Frank, D. A., Zuckerman, B. S., Amaro, H., Aboagye, K., Bauchner, H., Cabral, H., Fried, L., Hingson, R., Kayne, H., Levenson, S. M., Parker, S., Reece, H., & Vinci, R. (1988). Cocaine use during pregnancy: prevalence and correlates. *Pediatrics, 82,* 888–895.

Handler, A., Kistin, N., Dans, F., & Ferre, G. (1991). Cocaine use during pregnancy: Perinatal outcomes. *American Journal of Epidemiology, 133,* 818–825.

Kaye, K., Elkind, L., Goldberg, D., & Tyton, A. (1989). Birth outcome for infants of drug abusing mothers. *New York State Journal of Medicine, 89,* 256–261.

Lindenberg, C. S., Alexander, E. M., Gendrop, S. C., Nencioli, M., & Williams, D. G. (1991). A review of the literature on cocaine abuse in pregnancy. *Nursing Research, 40,* 69–75.

Little, B. B., Snell, L. M., Gilstrap, L. D., & Johnston, W. L. (1990). Patterns of multiple substance abuse during pregnancy: Implications for mother and fetus. *Southern Medical Journal, 83,* 507–509, 518.

Little, B. B., Snell, L. M., Klein, V. R., & Gilstrap, L. G. (1989). Cocaine abuse during pregacy: Maternal and fetal complications. *Obstetrics and Gynecology, 73,* 157–160.

MacGregor, S. N., Keith, L. G., Chasnoff, I. J., Rosner, M. A., Chisum, G. M., Shaw, P., & Minogue, J. P. (1987). Cocaine use during pregnancy: Adverse perinatal outcome. *American Journal of Obstetrics and Gynecology, 157,* 686–690.

Mastrogiannis, D. S., Decavalas, G. O., Verma, U., & Tejani, N. (1990). Perinatal outcome after recent cocaine usage. *Obstetrics and Gynecology, 76,* 8–11.

Neerhof, M. G., MaGregor, S. N., Retsky, S. S., & Sullivan, T. P. (1989). Cocaine abuse during pregnancy: Peripartum prevalence and perinatal outcome. *American Journal of Obstetrics and Gynecology, 161,* 633–638.

Ney, J. A., Dooley, S. L., Keith, L. G., & Chasnoff, I. J., & Socol, M. L. (1990). The prevalence of substance abuse in patients with subpected preterm labor. *American Journal of Obstetrics and Gynecology, 162,* 1562–1567.

Ward, S. L., Schuetz, S., Kirshna, V., Bean, X., Wingert, W., Wachsman, L., & Keens, T. G. (1986). Abnormal sleeping ventilatory pattern in infants of substance-abusing mothers. *American Journal of Diseases of Children, 140,* 1015–1020.

Zuckerman, B. S., Frank, D. A., Hingson, R., Amaro, H., Levenson, S.M., Kayne, H., Parker, S., Vinci, R., Aboagye, K., Fried, L. E., Cabral, H., Timperi, R., & Bauchner, H. (1989). Effect of maternal marijuana and cocaine use on fetal growth. *New England Journal of Medicine, 320,* 762–768.

Other Complications

Ahijado, F., de Vinuesa, G., & Luno, J. (1990). Acute renal failure and rhabdomyolysis following cocaine abuse. *Nephron, 54,* 268.

Anand, V., Siami, G., & Stone, W. J. (1989). Cocaine associated rhabomylosis and acute renal failure. *Southern Medical Journal, 82,* 67–69.

Bauwens, J. E., Boggs, J. M., & Hartwell, P. S. (1989). Fatal hyperthermia associated with cocaine use. *Western Journal of Medicine, 150,* 210–212.

Garfia, A., Valverde, J. L., Borondo, J. C., Candenas, I., & Lucena, J. (1990). Vascular lesions in intestinal ischemia induced by cocaine-alcohol abuse: Report of a fatal case due to overdose. *Journal of Forensic Science, 35,* 740–745.

Guerin, J. M., Lustman, C., & Barbotin-Larrieu, F. (1989). Cocaine associated acute myoglobinuric renal failure. *Southern Medical Journal, 82,* 1196–1197.

Krohn, K. D., Slowman-Kovacs, S., & Leapman, S. B. (1988). Cocaine and rhabdomyolysis. *Annals of Internal Medicine, 108,* 639–640.

Mizrahi, S., Laor, D., & Stamler, B. (1988). Intestinal ischemia induced by cocaine abuse. *Archives of Surgery, 123,* 394.

Nalbandian, H., Shath, N., Dietrich, R., & Georgiu, J. (1985). Intestinal ischemia caused by cocaine ingestion: Report of 2 cases. *Surgery, 97,* 375–376.

Perino, L. E., Warren, G. H., & Levine, J. S. (1987). Cocaine induced hepatoxicity in humans. *Gastroenterology, 93,* 176–180.

Pogue, V. A., & Nurse, H. M. (1989). Cocaine associated acute myogloburic renal failure. *American Journal of Medicine, 86,* 183–186.

Sluster, L., Quimby, F., Bates, A., Thompson, M. L (1977). Liver damage from cocaine in mice. *Life Sciences, 20,* 1035–1042.

Steingrub, J. S., Sweet, S., & Teres, D. (1989). Crack-induced rhabdomyolysis. *Critical Care Medicine, 17,* 1073–1074.

Injection Cocaine Use

Centers for Disease Control. (1988). Hepatitis A among drug users. *Morbidity and Mortality Weekly Report, 37,* 297.

Centers for Disease Control. (1991, January). *HIV/AIDS surveillance report* (pp. 1–22). Atlanta, GA: Author.

Chambers, H. F., Miller, R. T., & Newman, M. D. (1988). Right-sided staphylococcis aureus endocarditis in intravenous drug users: Two week combination therapy. *Annals of Internal Medicine, 109,* 619–624.

Chambers, H. F., Morris, L., Tauber, M. G., & Modin, G. (1987). Cocaine use and the risk for endocarditis in intravenous drug users. *Annals of Internal Medicine, 106,* 833–836.

Chassin, R. E., Bacchetti, P., Osmond, D., Brodie, B., Sande, M. A., & Moss, A. R. (1989). Cocaine use and HIV infection in intravenous drug users in San Francisco. *Journal of the American Medical Association, 261,* 561–565.

Cherubin, C. E. (1967). The medical science of narcotic addiction. *Annals of Internal Medicine, 67,* 23–33.

Esteban, J. I., Esteban, R., Viladomiu, L., López-Talavera, J. C., Gonzáles, A., Hernández, J. M., Roget, M., Vargas, V., Genescà, J., Buti. M., & Guardia, J. (1989). Hepatitis C virus antibodies among risk groups in Spain. *Lancet, ii,* 294–295.

Fullilove, R. E., Fullilove, M. T., Bowser, B. F., & Gross, S. A. (1990). Risk of sexually transmitted disease among black adolescent crack users in Oakland and San Francisco, California. *Journal of the American Medical Association, 263,* 851–857.

Goldsmith, M.F. (1988). Sex tied to drugs = STD spread. *Journal of the American Medical Association, 260,* 2009.

Hahn, R. A., Onorato, I. M., Jones, S., & Dougherty, J. (1989). Prevalence of HIV infections among intravenous drug users in the United States. *Journal of the American Medical Association, 261,* 2677–2684.

Hardy, A. M., Allen, J. R., Morgan, W. M. (1985). The incidence of acquired immunodeficiency symdrome in selected populations. *Journal of the American Medical Association, 253,* 215–220.

Haverkos, H. W., & Lang, W. R. (1990). Serious infections other than human immunodeficiency virus among intravenous drug users. *Journal of Infectious Diseases, 161,* 894–899.

Herb, F., Watters, J. K., Case, P., & Pettiti, D. (1989, June). *Endocarditis, subcutaneous abcesses, and other bacterial infections in intravenous drug users and their association with skin-cleansing at injection sites.* Abstract, V International Conference on AIDS.

Hollander, H. (1988). Work-up of the HIV-infected patient. *Infectious Disease Clinics of North America, 2,* 353–358.

Lettau, L. A., McCarthy, J. G., Smith, M. H., Hadler, S. C., Morse, L. J., Ukena, T., Bessette, R., Gurwitz, A., Irvine, W. G., Fields, H. A., Grady, G. F., & Maybard, J. E. (1987). Outbreak of severe hepatitis due to delta and hepatitis B viruses in parenteral drug abusers and their contacts. *New England Jorunal of Medicine, 317,* 1256–1261.

Lindell, T. D., Porter, J. M., & Langston, C. (1972). Intraarterial injections of oral medications—a complication of drug addiction. *New England Journal of Medicine, 287,* 1132–1133.

Marmor, M., DesJarlis, D. C., Cohen, H. (1987). Risk factors for infection with human immunodeficiency virus among intravenous drug users in New York City. *AIDS, 1,* 39–44.

Reiner, N. E., Gopalakrishna, K. V., & Lerner, P. I. (1976). Enterococcal endocarditis in heroin addicts. *Journal of the American Medical Association, 235,* 1861–1863.

Reisberg, B. E. (1979). Infective endocarditis in the narcotic addict. *Progress in Cardiovascular Diseases, 22,* 193–204.

Rogers, M. F., Thomas, P. A., Starcher, E. T., Noa, M. C., Bush, T. J., & Jaffe, H. W. (1987). Acquired immunodeficiency syndrome in children: Report of the CDC National Surveillance, 1982 to 1985. *Pediatrics, 79,* 1008–1011.

Samet, J. H., Shevitz, A., Fowle, J., & Singer, D. E. (1990). Hospitalization decisions in febrile intravenous drug users. *American Journal of Medicine, 89,* 53–57.

Seeff, L. B. (1975). Hepatitis in the drug abusers. *Medical Clinics of North America, 59,* 843–848.

Stall, R., McKusick, L., Wiley, J., Coates, T. J., & Ostrow, D. G. (1986). Alcohol and drug use during sexual activity and compliance with safe sex guidelines: The AIDS Behavioral Research Project. *Health Eduation Quarterly, 13,* 359–361.

Stimmel, B., Vernace, S., & Schaffner, F. (1975). Hepatitis B surface antigen and antibody: A prospective study in asymptomatic drug abusers. *Journal of the American Medical association, 243,* 1135–1139.

Stein, M. D. (1990). Medical complications of intravenous drug use. *Journal of General Internal Medicine, 5,* 249–253.

State of Connnecticut Department of Health Services (1989). *AIDS in Connecticut* (Surveillance Report). Hartford, CT: Author.

Volberding, P. A., Lagakos, S. W., Koch, M. A., Pettinelli, C., Myers, M. W., Booth, D. K., Balfour, H. H., Reichman, R. C., Bartlett, J. A., Hirsch, M. S., Murphy, R. L., Hardy, W. D., Soeiro, R., Fishl, M. H., Bartlett, J. G., Merigan, T. C., Hyslop, N. E., Richman, D. D., Valentine, F. T., Corey, L., & the AIDS Clinical Trials Group of the National Institute of Allergy and Infectious Diseases. (1990). Zidovudine in asymptomatic human immunodeficiency virus infection: A controlled trial in persons with fewer than 500 CD4-positive cells per cubic millimeter. *New England Journal of Medicine, 322,* 941–948.

White, A. G. (1973). Medical disorders in drug addicts. *Journal of the American Medical Association, 223,* 1469–1471.

Smoked Cocaine Use

Cucio, R. A., Ok, H. Y., Creglier, L. L., & Jul, C. C. (1987). Nonfatal pulmonary edema after "free-base" cocaine smoking. *American Review of Respiratory Disease, 136,* 179–181.

Eurman, D. W., Potash, H. I., Eyler, W. R., Paganussi, P. J., & Beute, G. H. (1989). Chest pain and dyspnea related to crack cocaine smoking: value of chest radiography. *Radiology, 172,* 459–462.

Hoffman, C. K., & Goodman, P. C. (1989). Pulmonary edema in cocaine smokers. *Radiology, 172,* 463–465.

Kissner, D. G., Laurence, W. D., Selis, J. E., & Flint, A. (1987). Crack lung: Pulmonary disease caused by cocaine abuse. *American Review of Respiratory Disease, 136,* 1250–1252.

Murray, R. J., Albin, R. J., Mergner, W., & Criner, G. J. (1988). Diffuse alveolar hemorrhage temporally related to cocaine smoking. *Chest, 93,* 427–429.

Ouberd, M., Bickel, J. T., Ingram, E. A., & Scott, G. C. (1990). Pulmonary talc granulomatosis in a cocaine sniffer. *Chest, 98,* 237–239.

Patel, R. C., Dutta, D., & Schonfeld, S. A. (1989). Free-base cocaine use associated with bronchiolitis obliterans organizing pneumonia. *Annals of Internal Medicine, 107,* 186–187.

Rubin, R. B., & Neugarten, J. (1990). Cocaine associated asthma. *American Journal of Medicine, 881,* 438–439.

Walek, J. W., Masson, R. G., & Siddiqui, M. (1989). Pulmonary hemorrhage in a cocaine abuser. *Chest, 96,* 222.

Weiner, D. M., & Putman, C. E. (1987). Pain in the chest in a user of cocaine. *Journal of the American Medical Association, 258,* 2087–2088.

Intranasal Cocaine Use

Gordon, A. S., Moran, D. T., Jafek, B. W., Eller, P. M., & Strahan, R. C. (1990). The effect of chronic cocaine abuse on human olfaction. *Archives of Otolaryngology—Head and Neck Surgery, 116,* 1415–1418.

James, S. M., & Goldenring, J. M. (1986). Madarosis from cocaine use. *New England Journal of Medicine, 314,* 1324.

Kuriloff, D. B., & Kimmelman, C. P. (1989). Osteocartilaginous necrosis of the sinonasal tract following cocaine abuse. *Laryngoscope, 99,* 918–924.

Messinger, E. (1962). Narcotic septal perforations due to drug addiction. *Journal of the American Medical Association, 179,* 964–965.

Snyder, R. D., & Snyder, L. B. (1985). Intranasal cocaine abuse in an allergists office. *Annals of Allergy, 54,* 489–492.

CHAPTER FOURTEEN

Pharmacotherapies

Thomas R. Kosten, MD

THIS CHAPTER REVIEWS various pharmacotherapies for cocaine abuse, starting with four key questions to ask before using this therapeutic strategy: (1) who to treat, (2) when to treat, (3) where to treat, and (4) what treatment agent to use. Each question raises several issues needing consideration before embarking on an essentially new area of therapy which includes no FDA-approved agents for this indication. A careful clinical decision needs to be made based on the risk–benefit ratio for your individual patient. This chapter should help you make a well-informed decision based on the available research data.

WHO TO TREAT

The first issue in the use of pharmacotherapy for cocaine abuse is selecting appropriate patients for treatment. Three types of patients might be considered appropriate candidates for pharmacotherapy: (1) patients with concurrent psychiatric vulnerability, (2) patients with substantial medical risks from continued cocaine use, and (3) patients who have developed neuroadaptation to heavy cocaine use. Heavy cocaine abusers commonly use the high-intensity administration routes of intravenous injection or freebase smoking. These patients not only have markedly high quantities and frequencies of cocaine use, they also get rapid changes in brain levels of cocaine. This combination of large amounts of use and rapid brain changes probably produces functional brain changes in various neurotransmitter systems such as dopamine or serotonin as detailed in Part 2 of this book. Animal studies have shown changes in dopamine receptor sensitivities, and clinical studies have demonstrated abnormalities in prolactin secretion, which is controlled by dopamine (Mendelson et al., 1990). Using position emission tomographic (PET) imaging, Volkow et al. (1990) have also demonstrated persistent abnormalities in dopamine receptor number among heavy cocaine abusers. Finally, neuropsychological testing of chronic cocaine abusers has demonstrated abnormalities (O'Malley, Adams, Heston, & Gawin, 1987). Thus a wide range of preclinical and clinical studies have demonstrated brain abnormalities secondary to heavy chronic cocaine abuse. Reversal of these cocaine-induced neurochemical abnormalities is a core rationale for the use of pharmacotherapeutic interventions.

Whereas cocaine itself may induce neurochemical abnormalities requiring pharmacological intervention, patients with psychiatric vulnerabilities may be adversely affected by cocaine after smaller amounts of use and with lower intensity routes of administration, such as intranasal. Gawin and Kleber (1986) have noted that treatment-seeking cocaine abusers with concurrent psychiatric disorders, such as depression, use significantly less cocaine and are more likely to use it intranasally compared with abusers who do not have psychiatric comorbidity. Treatment- seeking cocaine abusers have substantial rates of psychiatric disorders, with up to 35% being concurrently depressed (Rounsaville et al., 1991; Kleber & Gawin, 1984; Weiss, Mirin, Michael, & Sollogub, 1986). Although it is difficult to demonstrate that these patients are using cocaine to self-medicate dysphoria, it is clear that cocaine worsens their symptoms and can be associated with patients becoming suicidal or psychotic. The inadequacy of cocaine as an antidepressant and the possibility of cocaine inducing further depression has been strongly suggested (Post, Kotin, & Goodwin, 1974; Gawin & Kleber, 1986; Kosten, Rounsaville, & Kleber, 1987). Patients with underlying paranoid psychoses may be sensitive to surprisingly small dosages of cocaine and acutely need pharmacological treatment (Castellani, Petric, & Ellinwood, 1985; McLellan, Woody, & O'Brien, 1979). Pharmacological interventions for these patients need to recognize this underlying psychiatric vulnerability by considering different agents than would be useful for the high-intensity cocaine abuser without underlying psychopathology.

Patients who have significant medical risk from continued cocaine abuse also may be in need of pharmacotherapies. These medical risks include infectious and cardiovascular diseases and, in particular, the development of AIDS. Whereas intravenous cocaine users are at the clearest risk of developing AIDS from their continued cocaine abuse, the phenomenon of "sex for crack" has also led to AIDS transmission through sexual intercourse (Chaisson et al., 1989). Patients who engage in these high-risk behaviors may be good candidates for pharmacological interventions to reduce their cocaine use (Des Jarlais, Friedman, & Hopkins, 1985). Other infectious disease complications, such as endocarditis from intravenous drug use may also be an indication for pharmacotherapy (Cherabin, 1967). When a cocaine abuser has suffered myocardial damage secondary to cocaine use, the use of pharmacotherapies becomes somewhat more complex (Cregler & Mark, 1986; Gay, 1982). If these patients combine cocaine with the treatment medication, their risks of toxic interactions from cocaine may be increased (Ritchie and Greene, 1985). A well-informed clinical judgment of the risks and benefits is critical.

Another area of medical risk involves the pregnant cocaine abuser. Pharmacological management of these women is generally avoided because the potential for significant neonatal problems from cocaine itself may be compounded by continued use of cocaine while taking a treatment medication (Chasnoff, Burns, Schnolls, & Burns, 1986). For the pregnant woman who is dependent on both opiates and cocaine, however, methadone maintenance is recommended (Finnegan, Connaughton, Emich, & Wieland, 1972). Methadone maintenance should be considered for these women, because it is a well-established treatment for opiate dependence, and using it to maintain the pregnant woman in treatment will enable the provider to work with her on the cocaine abuse using psychological approaches. Another important consideration for the pregnant woman who refuses residential treatment is that the methadone program can be used as a conduit to provide prenatal care.

WHEN TO TREAT

The decision about when to initiate or discontinue pharmacotherapy depends on four factors: (1) the precipitants of seeking treatment including psychiatric comorbidity; (2) the phases of recovery; (3) associated psychosocial problems; and 4) relapse potential. Several of these factors—especially (1)—are directly related to the decision about who is an appropriate candidate for pharmacotherapy. Those patients with multiple previous failures at maintaining abstinence without pharmacological treatment are also candidates for pharmacological intervention.

The precipitants for seeking treatment can be classified into four areas: legal, psychosocial, medical, and psychiatric. First is an arrest or other legal pressure. In a 2 1/2-year follow-up of cocaine abusers, we found that legal problems were a frequent precipitant for cocaine abusers seeking treatment (Kosten, Morgan, & Schottenfeld, 1990). Although none of the abusers went to jail for more than a few days, almost all of them substantially reduced or stopped their cocaine abuse for the next 6 months. Thus a relatively minimal criminal justice intervention appeared to have a significant effect (Kosten et al., 1990). Second, family or employer pressures also bring many patients to treatment. With both these criminal justice patients and the patients seeking treatment owing to other social pressures, psychotherapy should be an early approach with pharmacotherapies reserved for those patients who fail to respond to individual, group, or family therapy approaches. Because these patients' support systems can return them to treatment rapidly, if the psychosocial approaches are unsuccessful, there is usually little risk in delaying the pharmacotherapy.

A third precipitant concerns patients who are seeking treatment after acute medical emergencies or drug overdoses; such patients are candidates for more immediate induction into pharmacotherapies. For the intravenous cocaine abuser, abscesses and systemic infections including the development of AIDS can be precipitants for seeking treatment. Freebase or crack cocaine abusers can suffer lung damage from smoking, as well as cardiovascular complications (Weiss, Goldenheim, Mirin, Hale, & Mendelson, 1981). These medical complications need to be carefully considered as indications for pharmacotherapy.

A fourth precipitant and critical consideration in the use of pharmacotherapies is psychiatric comorbidity. Not only are these "dual diagnosis" patients excellent candidates for pharmacotherapy, but the most common comorbid disorder in cocaine abusers, depression, is a significant predictor of increased cocaine use during follow-up if untreated (Kleber & Gawin, 1984; Kosten et al., 1987b; Weiss et al., 1986). The likelihood that cocaine may be used in an effort to self-medicate affective disorders supports the utility of antidepressants in cocaine abuse treatment. Furthermore, pharmacological treatment of depression may be an important preventive strategy to prevent relapse to this self-medication with cocaine. Previous work further suggests that cocaine will intensify depressive symptoms and can be associated with precipitation of suicidality (Post et al., 1974). The other major psychiatric disorder seen in cocaine abusers is antisocial personality disorder. It is important to identify this disorder, because it suggests a poor prognostic indicator. There is no clear role for pharmacotherapy in antisocial patients, but if pharmacotherapy is being considered for them, its initiation may be delayed for several weeks until the patient stabilizes in outpatient therapy.

The second factor in the decision about when to start or stop pharmacotherapy is phase of recovery. Recovery from cocaine abuse can be conceptualized as evolving over a three-phase process. These phases have been heuristically labeled by Gawin and Kleber (1986) as crash, withdrawal, and extinction phases. During the relatively brief crash phase, which may last as long as 2 days, paranoia and suicidality are the most serious concerns. Pharmacological management of these complications may involve the use of neuroleptics, such as haloperidol, and the need for temporary protective care of the patient in an emergency room or a hospital. Among those patients whose crash phase is dominated by sleeping, there may be no indication for medications.

The withdrawal phase, which may persist for several weeks, is more extended than the withdrawal described with other drugs of abuse. Moreover, the symptoms of cocaine withdrawal are primarily depression and anxiety with no clear physiological syndrome. In contrast to the use of medications during opioid withdrawal, there is no clear need for pharmacological intervention to relieve cocaine withdrawal symptoms. The major issue with outpatients in this phase is initiating abstinence and thus reducing the potential for relapse to cocaine abuse. Medications intended to prevent relapse are aimed at the relatively mild withdrawal symptoms of "craving."

This withdrawal phase blends into a phase of extinction or protracted withdrawal, in which conditioned craving may occur in response to a variety of environmental cues. This phase may extend for several months, as relapse to cocaine use becomes closely tied to a limited number of environmental cues that stimulate cocaine craving. This limited craving contrasts with the withdrawal phase when craving is a more pervasive aspect of the abuser's daily life. Medications that are initiated during the withdrawal phase are often discontinued during this extinction phase. Critical considerations during this phase should be given to comorbid psychopathology, because patients with comorbid psychiatric disorders often need more prolonged medication maintenance.

The third factor in treatment decisions is that of psychosocial problems. Because cocaine abuse has many associated legal, social, and employment problems, treatment interventions often need to involve multiple modalities. Legal problems need to be resolved through parole, probation, or court hearings. Family and other social supports need to be reestablished, and mechanisms for future conflict resolution need to be developed. Stable employment is particularly important for those patients whose income had depended on drug sales, and a legal source of future income must be established. Obtaining this source may involve vocational counseling and rehabilitation. Finally, medical stabilization is critical, including the ongoing participation of the patient in medical care, particularly among those patients who are HIV infected.

A fourth factor influencing medication discontinuation is relapse potential. Relapse potential frequently depends on the precipitants that either led to, or were associated with, the patient's seeking treatment. amelioration of the acute medical, legal, or social problems precipitating treatment must occur before establishing a schedule for discontinuing an effective pharmacological treatment. Without this problem resolution, relapse is almost certain. Other critical ingredients in this stabilization are psychotherapy and the longer term involvement of the patient in support systems such as self-help groups (Cocaine Anonymous), family and employers through Employee Assistance Programs (EAP). A final consideration is the control of any concurrent drug abuse, such as alcohol, opioids, or sedatives. Unless other drug abuse is well under control, relapse to cocaine abuse will be quite likely. An important recent consideration has been whether tobacco smoking may be a precipitant for cocaine abuse relapse. Because many cocaine abusers are also tobacco smokers, treatment interventions designed to end the smoking may also be needed.

In order to coordinate this wide range of treatment services with pharmacotherapy, a sophisticated treatment environment is needed. This treatment environment is increasingly a cooperative effort between a physician prescribing medications and a nonphysician psychotherapist or counselor. A nonphysician must cultivate in the patient an attitude that supports medication treatment, because in a nonsupportive or rejecting atmosphere, the patient may use pharmacotherapy as an excuse for continued abuse. Medications can be useful adjuncts, but no psychosocial or psychological problems are going to be resolved by a "magic bullet." Psychotherapeutic approaches can be antagonistic to medication use, and any approach that rejects medications as "drugs to treat drugs" is clearly not a compatible adjunct to pharmacotherapy (Carroll, Fenton, & Gawin, 1987). Finally, stopping any effective medication must be considered a trial in a patient with a chronic relapsing disorder such as cocaine abuse, and a good psychotherapeutic relationship will enable a clinician to restart the medication.

WHERE IS TREATMENT OCCURRING

Prevention of relapse is necessarily an outpatient treatment goal. The primary role of hospitalization is three-fold: to prevent suicide, to control psychosis, and to initiate medications that may prevent relapse during outpatient after care. Initiating medication on an inpatient setting minimizes the risks of cocaine's interacting with a treatment medication during the induction phase. When starting medications with outpatient cocaine abusers, care must be taken to warn the patient of potential interactions between cocaine and the treatment medication. As an example, because tricyclic antidepressants are catecholamine reuptake blockers, high blood pressure could result from combined reuptake blockade of adrenalin by the tricyclic and cocaine (Fischman et al., 1976). Later in treatment this potential interaction is less likely because tricyclics decrease the sensitivity of the postsynaptic adrenergic receptors (Charney, Menkes, & Henninger, 1981). Thus inpatient induction onto various types of anticraving agents for cocaine abuse provides a very safe protocol that will minimize potential medical complications. Outpatient medication induction is widely practiced, however, and has not been associated with any major medical complications.

WHAT TREATMENT AGENT

The pharmacological treatment of cocaine abuse posits a neurochemical substrate underlying both chronic high-intensity periods of abuse (binges) and the "crash" following these high-intensity use periods (Gawin & Kleber, 1986; Gold, Washton, & Dackis, 1985; Spyraki, Fibiger, & Phillips, 1982; Taylor, Ho, & Fagan, 1979; Wise, 1984). A number of parallels have been drawn between the self-administration model of cocaine use in animals and the high-intensity human abuse of cocaine by free-base smokers and intravenous users (Gawin & Kleber, 1984, 1986; Gold et al., 1985). The neurochemical alterations induced by chronic cocaine use in animals, including dopaminergic receptor supersensitivity, may also occur in humans and may respond to agents that reduce receptor sensitivity, such as tricyclic antidepressants (Gawin & Kleber, 1984, 1986; Taylor et al., 1979). Other hypotheses have been that dopamine depletion occurs during chronic cocaine use and that either the amino acid precursor tyrosine or a direct dopamine agonist would ameliorate the cocaine crash (Gold et al., 1985; Tennant, 1985; Tennant & Sagherian, 1987). Based on these neuroadaption models, several studies have sought general agents that may reverse cocaine-induced brain changes and thereby possess anticraving properties, block cocaine euphoria, or decrease cocaine crash and withdrawal symptoms. In our review, clinical studies are divided into open, uncontrolled trials (Tables 14.1, 14.2, 14.3), and blinded, controlled trials (Tables 14.4, 14.5).

Dopaminergic Agents

Dopaminergic agents may be particularly useful in ameliorating early withdrawal symptoms after cocaine binges because these agents appear

TABLE 14.1. Open, Uncontrolled Trials Dopaminergic of Agents

Drug/Reference	*n*	Findings
Amantadine		
(Morgan et al., 1988)	12	Decreased craving
Bromocriptine		
(Teller & Devenyi, 1988)	25	No effect
(Extein, Gross, & Gold, 1989)	10	Decreased early withdrawal symptoms
Carbidopa/L-dopa		
(Rosen et al., 1986)	Unknown	Decreased craving 1st week
Mazindol		
(Berger et al., 1989)	8	Decreased craving
Methylphenidate		
(Gawin et al., 1985)	5	No effect in non-Attention Deficit Disorder
(Khantzian, 1983)	1	Decreased use
Pergolide		
(Malcolm et al., 1991)	21	Decreased craving

TABLE 14.2. Open, Uncontrolled Trials of Antidepressants

Drug/Reference	*n*	Findings
Bupropion		
(Margolin et al., 1991)	6	Decreased craving/use
Desipramine/Lithium		
(Gawin & Kleber, 1984)	16	Decreased use (if dysthymic, Desipramine; if cyclothymic, Lithium)
Desipramine		
(Tennant & Rawson, 1983)	14	Minimal effect
(Kosten et al., 1987)	16	Decreased craving
Imipramine		
(Rosecan, 1983)	14	Decreased craving
Maprotiline		
(Brotman et al., 1988)	9	Decreased use
Phenelzine		
(Golwyn, 1988)	26	Significant abstinence
Trazodone		
(Small & Purcell, 1985)	1	Decreased craving

TABLE 14.3. Open, Uncontrolled Trials of Miscellaneous Agents

Drug/Reference	n	Findings
Antipsychotics		
Chlorpromazine/haloperidol		
(Gawin, 1986)	4	Decreased paranoia
Halperidol		
(Sherer et al., 1989)	5	No physiological change
Flupenthixol		
(Gawin, Allen, et al., 1989)	10	Decreased craving/use
Buprenorphine		
(Kosten et al., 1989)	41	Fewer + urine tests for cocaine
Carbamazepine		
(Halikas et al., 1989)	21	Decreased craving

TABLE 14.4. Blinded, Controlled Trials of Dopaminergic Agents

Drug/Reference	n	Findings
Amantadine (Ama)/Bromocriptine (Br)		
(Giannini et al., 1989)	30	Br > Ama > placebo
(Tennant & Sagherian, 1987)	14	Br = placebo
		Ama > placebo
Bromocriptine		
(Dackis & Gold, 1985)	2	Decreased craving
(Dackis et al., 1987)	13	Decreased evoked craving
(Giannini et al., 1987)	24	Decreased craving
(Kosten et al., 1988)	6	Decreased craving
Bromocriptine/Desipramine (DMI)		
(Giannini et al., 1987)	36	Br > placebo
		Br + DMI > placebo
Desipramine/Amantadine		
(Kosten et al., 1990)	75	Ama > DMI > placebo
(Weddington et al., 1991)	54	DMI = Ama = placebo
Mazindol		
(Diakogiannis et al., 1990)	19	No short-term effect
Buprenorphine		
(Fudala et al., 1990)	162	No effect

TABLE 14.5. Blinded, Controlled Trials of Antidepressants

Drug/Reference	n	Findings
Desipramine (DMI)		
(Giannini et al., 1986)	20	Decreased depressive symptoms
(Tennant & Tarver, 1984)	22	DMI = placebo
Desipramine/Lithium (Li)		
(Gawin, Kleber, et al., 1989)	72	DMI > Li = placebo
Imipramine		
(Rosecan & Klein, 1986)	4	Blocked euphoria
Desipramine/Amantadine (Ama)		
(Kosten et al., 1990)	75	Ama > DMI > placebo
(Weddington et al., 1991)	54	DMI = Ama = placebo

to have their onset of action within a day of starting (Dackis et al., 1987; Gawin & Kleber, 1986; Giannini & Baumgartel, 1987; Khantzian et al., 1984; Kosten, Schumann, & Wright, 1988; Morgan, Kosten, Gawin, & Kleber, 1982; Rosen, Flemenbaum, & Slater, 1986; Tennant & Sagherian, 1987). These agents include amantadine, bromocriptine, L-dopa, methylphenidate, mazindol, and pergolide. Few adequate, placebo-controlled, double-blind studies have been done with any of these agents, but their acute efficacy has been suggested in several single-dose, placebo crossover trials (Dackis, Gold, Sweeney, Byron, & Climko, 1987; Giannini & Baumgartel, 1987; Tennant & Sagherian, 1987). Several trials have examined amantadine at 200 and 300 mg daily and found that it reduces craving and use for several days to a month (Morgan et al., 1987; Handlesman, Chordia, Escovar, Marion, & Lowinson, 1989; Tennant & Sagherian, 1987; Kosten et al., 1990). A controlled trial by Weddington et al. (1991) showed no efficacy for amantadine vs. placebo. Four trials have examined bromocriptine at doses varying from 0.125–0.6 mg three times daily, but have had contradictory results on efficacy owing mostly to dropout from side effects (Dackis et al., 1987; Giannini & Baumgartel, 1987; Kosten et al., 1988; Tennant & Sagherian, 1987). Two open studies of L-dopa and methylphenidate have shown short-term (2-week) reductions in cocaine craving (Khantzian, Gawin, Riordan, & Kleber, 1984; Rosen et al., 1986), although a second trial using methylphenidate found that it increased cocaine use over several weeks of treatment (Gawin, Riordan, & Kleber, 1985). Mazindol has shown promise in an open trial (Berger, Gawin, & Kosten, 1989), but a relatively brief crossover study showed no significant improvement in cocaine craving or use (Diakogiannis, Steinberg, & Kosten, 1990). Pergolide, which has more specific dopamine D2 receptor agonist properties than bromocriptine, has been shown to significantly decrease cocaine craving (Malcolm, Hutto, Phillips, & Ballenger, 1991) without the excessive side effects that often lead to early dropout in bromocriptine studies. This may be due to its lack of D1 receptor antagonism, which characterizes bromocriptine (Goldstein, Lieberman, & Lew, 1980).

Antidepressant Agents

The antidepressant agents have a delayed onset of action in reducing cocaine craving. Desipramine is typical of this class, and its onset of action is usually delayed for approximately 2 weeks. A rationale for use of these drugs has been that they reduce dopaminergic receptor sensitivity and thereby reverse the cocaine-induced supersensitivity. The first study of desipramine examined its acute efficacy (10 days of treatment at a low dose of 75 mg daily) and reported only minimal effectiveness (Tennant & Rawson, 1983). Improved efficacy has been reported since then with higher doses (200–250 mg daily) and longer duration of treatment (4–6 weeks) (Gawin & Kleber, 1984; Kosten, Schumann, Wright, Carney, & Gawin, 1987; Giannini et al., 1986; Tennant & Tarver, 1984; Gawin, Kleber, et al., 1989). The most carefully controlled studies in the cocaine treatment literature have been done with these agents, singly or in combination with dopaminergic agents (Tables 14.4, 14.5) (Tennant & Sagherian, 1987; Giannini, Folts, Feather, & Sullivan, 1989; Giannini & Billett, 1987; Kosten et al., 1990; Weddington et al., 1991;.Giannini et al., 1986; Tennant & Tarver, 1984; Gawin, Kleber, et al., 1989). These studies do not all demonstrate greater efficacy with active medication than placebo, and there is no clear superiority in comparisons between dopaminergic agents and antidepressants. Nonetheless, these trials have shown significant decreases in cocaine use and craving.

Some trials have involved "pure" cocaine abusers, while others have involved methadone-maintained cocaine abusers. In these trials, desipramine has been relatively free of side effects and patients have shown good compliance after an initial dropout rate of 25%–30% during the first 2 weeks of treatment among the nonmethadone patients. This dropout rate may be due to the relatively delayed onset of desipramine's action, and there may be an important role for sequential use of dopaminergic agents in reducing this dropout rate. Few dropouts occur in methadone patients on desipramine, although blood levels may become therapeutic with relatively low desipramine doses owing to impairment of its hepatic metabolism (Kosten et al., 1990). Other antidepressants have been suggested in pilot work including imipramine, maprotiline, phenelzine, and trazodone (Rosecan, 1983; Brotman et al., 1988; Golwyn, 1988; Small & Purcell, 1985), but the results of controlled trials with these agents have not appeared. Future treatment of cocaine abusers may evolve a sequential use of various agents to minimize symptoms and maximize compliance.

Miscellaneous Agents

A number of other agents recently have been used to treat different aspects of cocaine abuse and dependence. Several authors report a decrease in euphoria and/or paranoia with neuroleptics (Gawin & Kleber, 1986; Sherer, Kumor, & Jaffe, 1989; Gawin, Allen, & Humblestone, 1989). Of these, only flupenthixol (not available in the United States at this time) was acceptable to the patients. In this study, flupenthixol decanoate was injected in a population (N = 10) of treatment-resistant patients, resulting in a dramatic decrease in cocaine craving and use, and an increase in treatment retention (Gawin, Allen, et al., 1989). Buprenorphine, a mixed opiate agonist–antagonist, showed initial promise for cocaine-abusing methadone-maintained patients in an open trial (Kosten, Kleber, & Morgan, 1989), but a subsequent double-blind, controlled study was not able to replicate these positive findings (Fudala, Johnson, & Jaffe, 1990). Another study has demonstrated initial promise with the anticonvulsant carbamazepine in the treatment of cocaine-dependent patients (Halikas, Kemp, Kuhn, Carlson, & Crea, 1989). Its use was based upon animal models suggesting a "kindling" mechanism in cocaine abuse, especially in high-dose cocaine bingeing.

CONCLUSION

Pharmacotherapy is not for every cocaine abuser and is clearly best reserved for the severely dependent patient who has not responded to less intensive intervention. A wide range of agents are potentially available, but the research data supporting their use are limited. Even the most closely examined medication, desipramine, has been tested in very few clinical trials, and the results on its utility are not uniform. Much more work is needed in this area, and the delineation of medication-responsive subgroups in cocaine dependence needs to be established. The next few years should provide some of this badly needed data for clinical practice.

REFERENCES

Berger, P. A., Gawin, F. H., Kosten, T. R. (1989). Treatment of cocaine abuse with mazindol. *Lancet, 1*, 283.

Brotman, A. W., Witkie, S. M., Gelenberg, A. J., Falk, W. E., Wojcik, J., & Leahy, L. (1988). An open pilot trial of maprotiline for the treatment of cocaine abuse. *Journal of Clinical Psychopharmacology, 8,* 125–127.

Carroll, K. M., Keller, D. S., Fenton, L. R., & Gawin, R. H. (1987). Psychotherapy for cocaine abusers. In D. Addle (Ed.), *The cocaine crisis.* New York: Plenum.

Chaison, R. E., Bacchetti, P., Osmond, D., Moss, A., Onishi, R. & Carlson, J. (1989). Cocaine use and HIV infection in the intravenous drug users in San Francisco. *Journal of the American Medical Association, 261,* 561–565.

Charney, D. S., Menkes, D. B., & Henninger, G. R. (1981). Receptor sensitivity and the mechanism of action of antidepressant treatment. *Archives of General Psychiatry, 38,* 1160–1180.

Chasnoff, I. J., Burns, E. J., Schnoll, S. H., & Burns, K. A. (1986). Effects of cocaine on pregnancy outcome. In L. S. Harris (Ed.), *Proceedings, problems of drug dependence, 1985* (National Institute on Drug Abuse Research Monograph). Rochville, MD: National Institute on Drug Abuse.

Cherabin, C. E. (1967). The medical sequelae of narcotic addiction. *Annals of Internal Medicine, 67,* 23–30.

Cregler, L. L., & Mark, H. (1986). Medical complications of cocaine abuse. *New England Journal of Medicine, 315,* 1495–1500.

Dackis, C. A., & Gold, M. S. (1985). Bromocriptine as treatment of cocaine abuse. *Lancet, 1,* 1151–1152.

Dackis, C. A., Gold, M. S., Sweeney, D. R., Byron, J. P., & Climko, R. (1987). Single-dose bromocriptine reverses cocaine craving. *Psychiatry Research, 20,* 261–264.

Des Jarlais, D. C., Friedman, S. R., & Hopkins, W. (1985). Risk reduction for the acquired immunodeficiency syndrome among intravenous drug users. *Annals of Internal Medicine, 103,* 755–759.

Diakogiannis, I. A., Steinberg, M., & Kosten, T. R. (1990). *Mazindol treatment of cocaine abuse: double-blind investigation* (National Institute on Drug Abuse Research Monograph No. 105, p. 514). Washington, DC: U. S. Government Printing Office.

Extein, I. L., Gross, D. A., & Gold, M. S. (1989). Bromocriptine treatment of cocaine withdrawal symptoms. *American Journal of Psychiatry, 146,* 403.

Finnegan, L. P., Connaughton, J. F., Emich, J. P., & Wieland, W. F. (1972). Comprehensive care of the pregnant addict and its effect on maternal and infant outcome. *Contemporary Drug Problems, 1,* 795–810.

Fischman, M. W., Schuster, C. R., Resnekov, I., Schick, J. F. E., Krasnegor, N. A., Fennell, W., & Freedman, D. X. (1976). Cardiovascular and subjective effects of intravenous cocaine administration in humans. *Archives in General Psychiatry, 10,* 535–546.

Fudala, P. J., Johnson, R. E., & Jaffe, J. H. (1990). *Outpatient comparison of buprenorphine and methadone* (National Institute on Drug Abuse Research Monograph No. 105, pp. 587-8). Washington, DC: U. S. Government Printing Office.

Gawin, F. H. (1986). Neuroleptic reduction of cocaine-induced paranoia but not euphoria? *Psychopharmacology*, *90*, 142–143.

Gawin, F. H. (1988). Chronic neuropharmacology of cocaine abuse: Progress in pharmacotherapy. *Journal of Clinical Psychiatry*, *49*, S11-17.

Gawin, F. H., Allen, D., & Humblestone B. (1989). Outpatient treatment of crack cocaine smoking with flupenthixol deconoate. *Archives of General Psychiatry*, *46*, 322–325.

Gawin, F. H., & Kleber, H. D. (1984). Cocaine abuse treatment: Open trial with desipramine and lithium carbonate. *Archives of General Psychiatry*, *42*, 903–10.

Gawin, F. H., & Kleber, H. D. (1986). Abstinence symptomatology and psychiatric diagnosis in chronic cocaine abusers. *Archives of General Psychiatry*, *43*, 107–113.

Gawin, F. H., Kleber, H. D., Byck, R., Rounsaville, B. J., Kostin, T. R., Jatlow, P., & Morgan, C. (1989). Desipramine facilitation of initial cocaine abstinence. *Archives of General Psychiatry*, *46*, 117–121.

Gawin, F. H., Riordan, C. A., & Kleber, H. D. (1985). Methylphenidate use in non-ADD cocaine abusers—a negative study. *American Journal of Drug and Alcohol Abuse*, *11*, 193–197.

Gay, G. R. (1982). Clinical management of acute and chronic cocaine poisoning. *Annals of Emergency Medicine*, *11*, 562–572.

Giannini, A. J., & Baumgartel, P. (1987). Bromocriptine in cocaine withdrawal. *Journal of Clinical Pharmacology*, *27*, 267–270.

Giannini, A. J., & Billett, W.(1987). Bromocriptine-desipramine protocol in treatment of cocaine addiction. *Journal of Clinical Pharmacology*, *27*, 549–554.

Giannini, A. J., Folts, D. J., Feather, J. N., & Sullivan, B. S. (1989). Bromocriptine and amantidine in cocaine detoxification. *Psychiatry Research*, *29*, 11–16.

Giannini, A. J., Malone, D. A., Giannini, M. C., & Baumgartel, P. D. (1986). Treatment of depression in chronic cocaine and phencyclidine abuse with desipramine. *Journal of Clinical Pharmacology*, *26*, 211–214.

Ginzberg, H. M., Weiss, S. H., MacDonald, M. G., et al. (1985). HTLV-III exposure among drug users. *Cancer Research*, *45*(Supp), 4605S–4608S.

Gold, M. S., Washton, A. M., & Dackis, C. A. (1985). *Cocaine abuse: Neurochemistry, phenomenology, and treatment* (National Institute on Drug Abuse Research Monograph No. 61). Washington, DC: U. S. Government Printing Office.

Goldsmith, M. F. (1988). Sex tied to drugs = STD spread. *Journal of the American Medical Association*, *260*, 2009.

Goldstein, M., Lieberman, A., & Lew, J. Y. (1990). Interaction of pergolide with central dopaminergic receptors. *Proceedings of the National Academy of Sciences, USA*, *77*, 3725–3728.

Golwyn, D. H. (1988). Cocaine abuse treated with phenelzine. *International Journal of the Addictions*, *23*, 897-905.

Halikas, J., Kemp, K., Kuhn, K., Carlson, G., & Crea, F. (1989). Carbamazepine for cocaine addiction? *Lancet*, *1*, 623–624.

Handlesman, L., Chordia, P. L., Escovar, I. M., Marion, I. J., & Lowinson, J. H. (1989). Amantadine for the treatment of cocaine dependence in methadone maintained patients. *American Journal of Psychiatry, 145*, 533.

Jasinski, D. R., Pevnick, J. S., & Griffith, J. D. (1978). Human pharmacology and abuse of the analgesic buprenorphine. *Archives of General Psychiatry, 35*, 510–516.

Khantzian, E. J. (1983). Cocaine dependence, an extreme case and marked improvement with methylphenidate treatment. *American Journal of Psychiatry, 140*, 784–785.

Khantzian, E. J., Gawin, F. H., Riordan, C., & Kleber, H. D. (1984). Methylphenidate treatment fof cocaine dependence: A preliminary report. *Journal of Substance Abuse Issues, 1*, 107–112.

Kleber, H. D., & Gawin, F. H. (1984). Cocaine abuse: A review of current and experimental treatment. *Journal of Clinical Psychiatry, 45*(12, sec. 2), 18–23.

Kosten, T. R., Gawin, F. H., Morgan, C. H., Nelson, J. C., & Jatlow, P. I. (1990). Evidence for altered desipramine disposition in methadone maintained patients treated for cocaine abuse. *American Journal of Drug and Alcohol Abuse, 16*, 329–336.

Kosten, T. R., Kleber, H. D., Morgan, C. H. (1989). Treatment of cocaine abuse with buprenorphine. *Biological Psychiatry, 26*, 637–639.

Kosten, T. R., Schumann, B., Wright, D., Carney, M. K., & Gawin, F. H. (1987a). A preliminary study of desipramine in the treatment of cocaine abuse in methadone maintenance patients. *Journal of Clinical Psychiatry, 48*, 442–442.

Kosten, T. R., Rounsaville, B. J., & Kleber, H. D. (1987b). A 2.5 year follow-up of cocaine use among opioid addicts. *Archives of General Psychiatry, 12*, 281–284.

Kosten, T. R., Morgan, C. H., & Schottenfeld, R. S. (1990). *Amantidine and desipramine in the treatment of cocaine abusing methadone maintained patients* (National Institute on Drug Abuse Research Monograph No. 105, pp. 510–511). Washington, DC: U. S. Government Printing Office.

Kosten, T. R., Schumann, B., Wright, D. (1988). Bromocriptine treatment of cocaine abuse in methadone maintained patients. *American Journal of Psychiatry, 145*, 381–382.

Lewis, J. W. Buprenorphine. *Drug Alcohol Depend, 14*, 363–372.

Malcolm, R., Hutto, B. R., Phillips, J. D., & Ballenger, J. C. (1991). Pergolide mesylate treatment of cocaine withdrawal. *Journal of Clinical Psychiatry, 52*, 39–40.

Margolin, A., Kosten, T. R., Petrakis, I. L., Avants, S. K., & Kostin, T. A. (1991). Bupropion reduces cocaine abuse in methadone-maintained patients. *Archives of General Psychiatry, 48*, 87.

McLellan, A. T., Woody, G. E., & O'Brien, C. P. (1979) Development of psychiatric illness in drug abusers: Possible role of drug preference. *New England Journal of Medicine, 301*, 1310–1314.

Mello, N. K., & Mendelson, J. H. (1980). Buprenorphine suppresses heroin use by heroin addicts. *Science, 207*, 657–659.

Mendelson, J. H., Teoh, S. K., Lange, U., Mello, N. K., Weiss, R., Skupny, A., & Ellingloc, J. (1988). Anterior pituitary, adrenal and gonadal hormones during cocaine withdrawal. *American Journal of Psychiatry*, *145*, 1094–1098.

Mittleman, R., & Wetli, C. V. (1984). Death caused by recreational cocaine use. *Journal of the American Medical Association*, *252*, 1889–1892.

Morgan, C. H., Kosten, T. R., Gawin, F. H., & Kleber, H. D. (1987). *A pilot trial of amantadine for cocaine abuse* (National Institute on Drug Abuse Research Monograph No. 81, pp. 81–85). Washington, DC: U. S. Government Printing Office.

O'Malley, S. S., Adams, A., Heaton, R. K., & Gawin, F. H. (in press). Neuropsychological impairment in chronic cocaine abusers. *American Journal of Drug and Alcohol Abuse*.

Post, R. M., Kotin, J., & Goodwin, F. K. (1974). The effects of cocaine on depressed patients. *American Journal of Psychiatry*, *131*, 511–517.

Raymond, C. A. (1988). Study of IV drug users and AIDS finds differing infection rate, risk behaviors. *Journal of the American Medical Association*, *260*, 3105.

Ritchie, J. M., & Greene, N. M. (1985). Local anesthetics. In A. G. Gilman, L. S. Goodman, T. W. Rall, & F. Murad (Eds.), *The pharmacological basis of therapeutics* (6th ed., pp. 302–321). New York: Macmillan.

Rogers, T. J., Taub, D. D., Eisenstein, T. K., Geller, E. B., & Adler, M. W. (1990). *Immunomodulatory activity of kappa, mu and delta selective opioid compounds* (National Institute on Drug Abuse Research Monograph No. 105, pp. 82–88). Washington, DC: U. S. Government Printing Office.

Rosecan, J. S. (1983, July). *The treatment of cocaine abuse with imipramine, L-tyrosine, and L-tryptophan*. Paper presented at the 7th World Congress of Psychiatry, Vienna, Austria.

Rosecan, J. S., & Klein D. F. (1986, May). *Imipramine blockade of cocaine euphoria*. Paper presented at the 139th annual meeting of the American Psychiatric Association, Washington, DC.

Rosen, H., Flemenbaum, A., & Slater, V. L. (1986). Clinical trial of carbidopa/L-dopa combination for cocaine abuse. *American Journal of Psychiatry*, *143*, 1493.

Rounsaville, B. J., Anton, S. F., Carroll, K., Budde, D., Prusoff, B. A., & Gawin, F. H. (1991). Psychiatric diagnosis of treatment seeking cocaine abusers. *Archives of General Psychiatry*, *48*, 43–51.

Rowbotham, M. C., Jones, R. T., Benowitz, N. L., & Jacob, P. (1984). Trazodone-oral cocaine interactions. *Archives of General Psychiatry*, *41*, 895–899.

Schmauss, C., & Emrich, H. M. (1985). Dopamine and the action of opiates: A reevaluation of the dopamine hypothesis of schizophrenia. *Biological Psychiatry*, *20*, 1211–1231.

Schmauss, C., Yassouridis, A., & Emrich, H. M. (1987). Antipsychotic effect of buprenorphine in schizophrenia. *American Journal of Psychiatry*, *144*, 1340–1342.

Sherer, M. A., Kumor, K. M., & Jaffe, J. H. (1989). Effects of intravenous cocaine are partially attenuated by haloperidol. *Psychiatry Research, 27*, 117–25.

Small, G. W., & Purcell, J. J. (1985). Trazodone and cocaine abuse. *Archives of General Psychiatry, 42*, 524.

Spyraki, C., Fibiger, H. C., & Philips., A. C. (1982). Cocaine-induced place preference conditioning. Lack of effects of Neuroleptics and 6-hydroxydopamine lesions. *Brain Research, 253*, 195–203.

Taylor, D. L., Ho, B. T., & Fagan, J. D. (1979). Increased dopamine receptor binding in rat brain by repeated cocaine injection. *Communications in Psychopharmacology, 3*, 137–142.

Teller, D. W., & Devenyi, P. (1988). Bromocriptine in cocaine withdrawal—does it work? *International Journal of Addictions, 23*, 1197–1205.

Tennant, F. S., Jr. (1985). Effect of cocaine dependence on plasma phenylalanine and tyrosine levels and on urinary MHPG excretion. *American Journal of Psychiatry, 142*, 1200–1201.

Tennant, F. S., & Rawson, R. (1983). *Cocaine and amphetamine dependence treated with desipramine* (National Institute on Drug Abuse Research Monograph No. 43, pp. 351–355). Washington, DC: U.S. Government Printing Office.

Tennant, F. S., & Sagherian, A. A. (1987). Double-blind comparison of amantidine and bromocriptine for ambulatory withdrawal from cocaine dependence. *Archives of Internal Medicine, 147*, 109–112.

Tennant, F. S., & Tarver, A. L. (1984). *Double-blind comparison of desipramine and placebo in withdrawal from cocaine dependence* (National Institute on Drug Research Abuse Monograph No. 55, pp. 159–163). Washington, DC: U. S. Government Printing Office.

Volkow, N. D., Fowler, J. S., Wolf, A. P., Schlyer, D., Shine, C. Y., Alpert, R., Dewey, S. L., Logan, J., Bendriem, B., Christman, D., Hitzeman, R., & Henn, F. (1990). Effects of chronic cocaine abuse on postsynaptic dopamine receptors. *American Journal of Psychiatry, 147*, 719–724.

Weddington, W. W., Brown, B. S., Haertzen, C. A., Hess, J. M., Mahaffey, J. R., Kolar, A. F., & Jaffe, J. H. (1991). Comparison of amantidine and desipramine combined with psychotherapy for treatment of cocaine dependence. *American Journal of Drug and Alcohol Abuse, 17*, 137–152.

Weiss, R. D., Goldenheim, P.D., Mirin, S. M., Hales, C. A., & Mendelson, J. H. (1981). Pulmonary dysfunction in cocaine smokers. *American Journal of Psychiatry, 138*, 1110–1112.

Weiss, R. D., Mirin, S. M., Michael, J. L., & Sollogub, A. C. (1986). Psychopathology in chronic cocaine abusers. *American Journal of Drug and Alcohol Abuse, 12*, 17–29.

Wise, R. (1984). *Neural mechanisms of the reinforcing action of cocaine* (National Institute on Drug Abuse Research Monograph No. 50, pp. 15–53). Washington, DC: U. S. Government Printing Office.

CHAPTER FIFTEEN

Psychotherapy for Cocaine Abuse: Approaches, Evidence, and Conceptual Models

Kathleen M. Carroll, PhD

THERE HAS BEEN a great deal of interest in recent years in the development and evaluation of pharmacological approaches to the treatment of cocaine abuse. Nevertheless, nonpharmacological treatments, such as psychotherapy and counseling, remain the most widely used approaches to treating cocaine abuse and are available in most drug treatment centers (Onken & Blaine, 1990).

Although psychotherapeutic treatments for cocaine abuse have not yet been widely evaluated in randomized clinical trials, the large number of articles describing various psychotherapeutic treatments suggests their intuitive appeal. Psychotherapies for cocaine abuse described thus far can be broadly categorized as either primarily interpersonal or psychodynamically oriented (e.g., Rounsaville, Gawin & Kleber, 1985; Schiffer, 1988), or primarily behavioral or cognitive–behavioral in orientation (e.g., Anker & Crowley, 1982; Carroll, Rounsaville, & Keller, 1991; O'Brien et al., 1988). Several articles have described psychotherapeutic approaches delivered as a component of a multimodal treatment program (e.g., Rawson, Obert, McCann, Smith, & Ling, 1990; Washton, 1986); almost all clinicians have emphasized the value of self-help groups such as Cocaine Anonymous. Those few reports that have included outcome data consistently point to difficulties met in treating cocaine abusers with a primarily psychotherapeutic approach, including disappointingly high rates of dropout (Anker & Crowley, 1982; Kang et al., 1991; Means et al., 1989), mixed compliance with treatment, and high rates of relapse (Hall, Havassy, & Wasserman, 1991;

Rawson, Obert, McCann & Mann, 1986). This chapter has three parts: (1) a brief overview of Relapse Prevention, the psychotherapy used in the cocaine clinic of the Yale Substance Abuse Treatment Unit; (2) a detailed review of the only randomized clinical trial to date contrasting different psychotherapies for cocaine abuse and with adequate historical controls to evaluate the relative efficacy of psychotherapy and pharmacotherapy; and (3) an explication of possible models for conceptualizing and evaluating the contributions of psychotherapy for cocaine abuse, alone and in combination with pharmacotherapy.

RELAPSE PREVENTION FOR COCAINE ABUSE

Since 1985, the form of psychotherapy most often used in the treatment of ambulatory cocaine abusers at the Yale Substance Abuse Treatment Unit is an adaptation of Marlatt's Relapse Prevention (RP) (Marlatt & Gordon, 1985) for use with cocaine abusers and summarized in a treatment manual (Carroll, 1987). Relapse Prevention therapy is a collection of interdependent techniques based on cognitive–behavioral principles which are intended to enhance self-control in individuals in whom impaired control over cocaine abuse may be a relatively unitary phenomenon or part of a more complex picture of psychiatric disorder or psychosocial disruption.

Our adaptation of RP focuses on specific treatment issues characteristic of the early phases of treatment of cocaine abusers, when abuse of cocaine is likely to be ongoing. Although in many cases RP is conceived as preparation for longer term treatment, the initial focus of this approach is on the inception and maintenance of abstinence from cocaine.

Principles of RP are presented to cocaine abusers in a stratified sequence, with the selection and timing of interventions linked to the patient's current position in the change process: For abusers who remain ambivalent about cessation of cocaine use, initial efforts utilize RP interventions to strengthen the patient's resolve to achieve abstinence. Once the patient's recognition of the need to discontinue cocaine use is solidified, interventions that support the inception of abstinence (altering stimulus control, development of skills for negotiating high-risk situations) are invoked. After a period of relatively stable abstinence is achieved, emphasis is shifted to interventions which promote the long-term prevention of relapse, such as life-style modification.

Described very briefly below are the interventions we most frequently employ with cocaine abusers. These interventions have been developed and described by Marlatt and colleagues (1985); highlighted below are special factors to consider when applying these techniques to cocaine abusers. In addition to proficiency with RP principles, successful application of RP requires that the therapist be familiar with the nature of cocaine abuse so that the therapist may anticipate problems the patient is likely to encounter and thereby help the patient identify effective strategies for avoiding or confronting such problems. For example, therapists should be familiar with the phases of the cocaine abstinence syndrome (Gawin & Kleber, 1986; Chapter 9, this volume) in order to help patients anticipate and develop stage-specific coping strategies, such as development of techniques for conceptualizing and coping with prolonged anhedonia, or preparation for possible resurgence of intense craving for cocaine after extended periods of abstinence, when abusers may assume they are immune to further craving.

Addressing Ambivalence

Rare is the cocaine abuser who seeks treatment without some degree of ambivalence regarding cessation of cocaine use. Moreover, given the substantial external pressures that may precipitate application for treatment, many abusers are highly ambivalent about treatment itself. Ambivalence must be addressed if the patient is to experience himself as an active participant in treatment.

Ambivalence is best addressed early to foster a therapeutic alliance that allows for open exploration of conflicts concerning cessation of cocaine use. To launch a discussion of the patient's struggle around abstinence, help the patient own the decision to stop use through exploring what the patient stands to gain by stopping use, and underscore that cocaine use cannot be divorced from its consequences, we frequently make use of a simplified version of the decision matrix described by Marlatt and Gordon (1985). In this exercise, the therapist divides an index card in half and records the patient's description of all possible benefits of continued cocaine use, however subjective, on one side of the card. Many abusers have initial difficulty in acknowledging positive consequences of continued cocaine use, but most are able to list several justifications like "There's nothing like the coke high," "I feel less anxious with people," "I get most of my money from selling cocaine," "Sex and coke go together," and so on. The therapist encourages the patient to examine the identified positive attributes of continued cocaine use, and with some exploration these are revealed as ultimately negative.

The therapist then asks the patient to list all possible reasons to stop cocaine use and writes these on the other half of the card. These are typically numerous and reflect negative consequences such as "I don't want to lose my job," or "I want to have fewer fights with my wife." Patients are instructed to keep the card in their wallets, preferably near their money: A glimpse of the card when confronted by intense craving for cocaine or a high-risk situation can remind patients of the negative consequences of cocaine use at a time when they are otherwise likely to recall only cocaine euphoria. The power of this concrete reminder was illustrated by a cocaine abuser who removed the card from his wallet before he went out on an evening when he intended to use cocaine, because he felt the card had "stopped me from using" on several previous occasions.

Reducing Cocaine Availability

Abusers are urged to take all possible measures to make cocaine as unavailable—both psychologically and physically—as possible during the initial stages of treatment. When control is fragile, the distinction between cocaine being available in 1 hour versus 1 minute can be critical. Reduced availability of cocaine and associated cues requires that the therapist and patient assess the current availability of cocaine and then formulate the steps to be taken to limit that availability. Again, familiarity with cocaine practices is essential so that the therapist can anticipate stimuli that must be addressed. In our experience these include money and cocaine paraphernalia (pipes, syringes, materials used in the preparation of freebase cocaine, and so on); the therapist should also assess whether other individuals in the patient's home or workplace use cocaine, whether the patient is involved with selling cocaine, and the nature of the patient's cocaine sources.

Many abusers, after an initial brief period of abstinence, will expose themselves to a situation in which cocaine is available, as a test of their ability to withstand temptation. For example, a woman who had altered her route home from work to avoid passing her dealer's house deliberately drove by one evening "just to see if I could do it." Such tests are, with few exceptions, hazardous for the majority of our patients and frequently result in exposure to overwhelming cues and craving. We encourage patients to minimize deliberate exposure to cocaine-related cues and situations as long as possible; in any case, a variety of unforeseeable, "accidental" exposures invariably present themselves as a matter of course.

High-Risk Situations and Coping Strategies

As part of the assessment process for RP, the therapist and patient together compile a list of the conditions or situations that increase the risk of lapses to drug use (high-risk situations). Typical high-risk situations, common to the majority of cocaine abusers, include the availability of money, use of other psychoactive substances, contact with cocaine-using associates, or unstructured time. Other high-risk situations for cocaine abusers are highly idiosyncratic and can often be identified only through careful exploration with the therapist. For example, one man maintained he could not identify any factors that had led to a brief episode of cocaine use. Upon retracing the events of the week, however, it was revealed that the man had had a bitter argument with his wife several days before, concerning his feelings that her efforts to monitor his actions made him her "prisoner." After several days during which he was fully occupied by work and family obligations and watched closely by his wife, he used cocaine at the first opportunity away from her watchful eye. This highlights that strong affects may represent a particularly potent class of high-risk situations, in that cocaine may be used in attempt to alter such negative effects as depression, shame, anger, or disappointment. Similarly, cocaine's initial euphorogenic properties may be sought to enhance positive feelings, and cocaine abusers often report using cocaine when feeling entitled to a reward.

Conditioned Cues and Craving

A special subgroup of high-risk situations requires much emphasis in the treatment of cocaine abusers is that of conditioned cues associated with craving for cocaine. Episodes of intense subjective craving for cocaine are often reported weeks and even months beyond the inception of abstinence. This experience can be both mystifying and disturbing to the abuser and can often culminate in cocaine use if not understood and managed effectively. Give both the frequency and the variety of circumstances in which cocaine is self-administered, for each cocaine user there is a multitude of stimuli previously paired with cocaine use which may act as conditioned cues for cocaine craving. Commonly experienced cues include exposure to cocaine itself or any white crystalline substance resembling cocaine (such as salt, sugar, snow, and even plaster dust), individuals and settings previously associated with cocaine use, and cocaine paraphernalia. For example, former intravenous users participating in research medication trials have reported intense subjective craving when their blood is drawn for determination of blood levels each week.

A first step in addressing the problem of conditioned craving is to provide an explanation of classical conditioning and its putative relationship to cocaine craving. To this end, the therapist might describe Pavlov's classical conditioning paradigm, equating the food with cocaine, the animal's salivation with the experience of cocaine craving, and the bell as the conditioned cue for cocaine. Using this concrete example, the patient can usually identify a number of personal "bells" associated with cocaine craving. The example of Pavlov's experiments is often enough to demystify the experience of craving and help the patient identify and tolerate conditioned craving when it occurs. However, the development of effective coping strategies for conditioned craving is also required. The therapist may then explain the process of extinction of conditioned responses, again using Pavlov's experiments as a concrete example. Here it is conveyed that the experience of craving when not followed by cocaine use will result in reduction of the intensity and frequency of the experience of conditioned craving over time. It is also important to convey the time-limited nature of cocaine craving; that is, conditioned craving usually peaks and dissipates in less than an hour, if not followed by cocaine use. In most cases, an effective strategy for coping with conditioned craving for cocaine is distraction; it is therefore useful to prepare a list of reliable distracting activities with the patient in anticipation of substantial craving in the future. Preparation of such a list may reduce the likelihood of use of other substances, particularly alcohol and marijuana, in ill-fated attempts to deal with craving.

An important area that is relevant to the patient's motivation to use cocaine in general, and in particular when confronted with high risk situations and craving, is the patient's set of expectations about the effects of cocaine. An instrument designed to assess such beliefs and allow them to be addressed in relapse prevention treatment is the Cocaine Expectancy Questionnaire (CEQ) (Jaffe, Kilbey, & Rosenbaum, 1989). See Chapter 7, this volume, for a thorough discussion of the topic.

Apparently Irrelevant Decisions

The strategies described above are used in encouraging the abuser to limit exposure to events or stimuli that may threaten abstinence. As treatment progresses, however, even with the best efforts the abuser will invariably encounter high-risk situations and cocaine itself. Certain exposures are beyond the abusers' control, for example, living in an area where cocaine abounds but where the abuser lacks the wherewithal to relocate his place of residence. There is another class of exposures, however, which patients often experience as beyond their control but which actually involves a process of behaviors determined by the patient himself. Apparently Irrelevant Decisions (Marlatt & Gordon, 1985) refer to those decisions, rationalizations, and minimizations of risk that move the patient closer to, or even ensconced within, high-risk situations but which seem unrelated to the motivation to use cocaine.

For example, an abuser who had been abstinent for several months, driving home from work, turned left rather than right at an intersection in order to enjoy the "scenic route." On this route, he drove past a bar he frequented in the past. Because the day was hot, he stopped for a glass of cola. Once in the bar, however, he decided that insofar as his problems was with cocaine, it would be fine to have a beer. After two beers, however, he ran into a friend who "happened" to have a gram of cocaine, and a relapse ensued. Thus, prior to the relapse, the patient engaged in a series of decisions which, taken together, made him more vulnerable to using cocaine. A critical task of RP is to teach the patient how to recognize and interrupt such a decision chain before the onset of actual use. This often involves familiarizing the patient with his or her distortions of thinking (rationalizations, denial, and so on) such that these may be detected and used by the patient as signals for greater vigilance.

Although it is possible to interrupt a chain of Apparently Irrelevant Decisions at any point prior to the onset of use, it is more difficult toward the end of the chain, when the patient may already be in a high-risk situation where cocaine is available and conditioned cues abound. Therefore we find it desirable to teach the patient how to detect the decisions that commonly occur at the beginning of the chain, when risk, craving, and availability of cocaine are relatively low. This may involve the patients' learning to detect subtle but painful affect states. For instance, the patient in the vignette above was vaguely bored on the day he turned left instead of right, although he was relatively unaware of the connection between his boredom and use of cocaine. After exploring this issue, it became clear that the patient often used cocaine to counter feelings of boredom. He was thereafter able to use this new awareness as a "red flag" signaling the onset of the desire to use.

Life-Style Modification

Life-style modification refers to the need for substance abusers to develop rewarding behavioral alternatives to cocaine use if enduring abstinence is to be achieved. By the time treatment is sought, many cocaine users spend much of their time in acquiring, using, and recovering from cocaine use, to the exclusion of other endeavors and rewards. The abuser may be estranged from friends and family and have few social contacts who do not use drugs. If the abuser is still working, in many cases the job has become only a means of acquiring money to buy cocaine, and the fulfilling or challenging aspects of work have faded. Cocaine-related involvement with the legal system, such as convictions on drug-related charges, may drastically limit an abuser's potential for employment.

To complicate matters further, the process of coping with the aftermath of extended cocaine abuse is both difficult and demanding. Unless the abuser has developed rewarding alternate activities, the frustration of coping with the sequelae of many years of cocaine abuse may be difficult to endure without resorting to cocaine use. One patient who came in for treatment with a cocaine-related debt of $25,000 was working virtually around the clock at three different jobs to pay off this debt. Not surprisingly, after only 1 week with this schedule, the patient felt exhausted and deprived. He felt entitled to a reward, which, because he had developed few gratifying alternatives, was a return to cocaine use.

Patients are thus encouraged to identify and develop fulfilling alternatives to cocaine use. In those cases where premorbid psychosocial functioning was good, patients may devise or rediscover constructive, enjoyable activities with relative ease. A woman with some previous training in painting found a return to this form of creative expression extremely helpful and was able in one instance to paint her experience of craving. However, in most patients the process of life-style modification is much more difficult: Anhedonic cocaine abusers may have difficulty seeing any activity or experience other than cocaine use as enjoyable; all other experiences are perceived as inferior to cocaine use. In such cases, the therapist should stress that anhedonia will dissipate only with continued abstinence and that the patient may find alternative activities more enjoyable than he oe she anticipates they will be. Here the RP therapist may attempt to activate the patient through assignment of a particular activity as homework.

Attendance at 12-step groups may be invaluable in successful life-style modification. Self-help groups provide a number of crucial functions, including an often unique opportunity to initiate contact with other abstinent individuals, facilitating the development of supportive relationships with others who can serve as positive models and provide the basis for hope. Because meetings take place every day, and often several times a day, abusers can easily find a meeting to shore up faltering resolve when craving and other problems become overwhelming.

EMPIRICAL EVIDENCE FOR PSYCHOTHERAPY

Only one randomized clinical trial evaluating purely psychotherapeutic approaches for cocaine abuse has been completed to date. This study (Carroll, Rounsaville, & Gawin, 1991) sought to assess the feasibility of purely psychotherapeutic treatments for cocaine abuse and to contrast two widely different forms of psychotherapy. Forty-two ambulatory

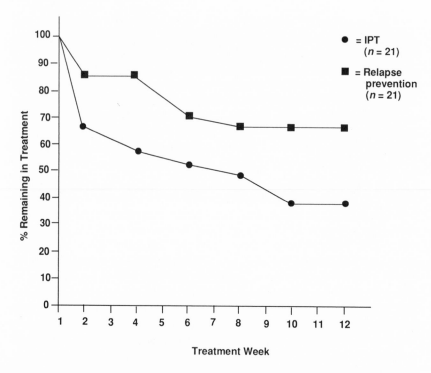

FIGURE 15.1. Treatment retention by group.

cocaine abusers were randomly assigned to either RP (Carroll, 1987), or Interpersonal Psychotherapy (IPT) (Rounsaville, Gawin, & Kleber, 1985), a brief psychodynamic approach adapted for cocaine abusers. This study included important design features such as random assignment to treatments, specification of treatments in manuals, monitoring of treatment delivery to ensure adherence to manual guidelines, use of therapists experienced in the type of treatments they administered, and multidimensional ratings of outcome.

As shown in Figure 15.1, dropout was substantial in both conditions. Half of all subjects who dropped out of treatment (10/20) did so immediately after the first session, with 7 subjects dropping out of IPT with respect to 3 in RP. The trend for improved retention in RP over IPT was consistent throughout the trial. At the end of the 12-week course of treatment, rates of retention were 67% for RP and 38% for IPT, with total dropouts in IPT nearly doubling those who dropped out of RP.

Although both groups showed significant improvement in functioning in virtually all areas assessed, significant differences by treatment type were not seen. However, significant differences did emerge when subjects were stratified by pretreatment severity of cocaine abuse: Among the severe users, those treated with RP were significantly more likely to become abstinent than were high-severity subjects treated with IPT (54% versus 9%, $p < .05$). Subjects with lower levels of severity tended to improve despite type of treatment received. A similar pattern was seen when subjects were stratified by pretreatment severity of psychological symptoms: for subjects high in psychopathology, those in the RP group were much more likely to become abstinent than those treated with IPT (58% versus 14%). In parallel to Woody, McLellean, Luborsky, and O'Brien's (1985) findings for psychotherapy outcome with methadone-maintained opiate addicts, we found cocaine abusers with concurrent depressive disorders tended to improve regardless of treatment received. Cocaine abusers with antisocial personality disorder were significantly more likely than those without this disorder to drop out of treatment and tended not to improve in treatment.

This study suggests that (1) at least some cocaine abusers can be treated successfully with a purely psychotherapeutic approach, and (2) overall response to treatment as well as response to specific forms of psychotherapy may be mediated by patient characteristics. Limitations of the purely psychotherapeutic approaches evaluated here were also revealed: Attrition was substantial in both treatment conditions and was most marked early in treatment (80% of all subjects who dropped out of treatment did so by Week 6). Moreover, although subjects in both conditions demonstrated significant improvement over baseline levels on most measures of outcome, more than half the subjects (23/42) failed to become stably abstinent during treatment.

COMPARISON OF PSYCHOTHERAPY AND PHARMACOTHERAPY: HISTORICAL CONTROLS

Are the limitations of psychotherapy suggested by this study unique to a primarily psychotherapeutic approach? Given that pharmacotherapies are generally perceived as faster acting and more potent than psychotherapy (Karasu, 1982), one might expect improved treatment retention or initiation of abstinence in cocaine abusers receiving pharmacological intervention. In particular, abusers' expectations for medication effects might foster greater retention during the initial weeks of treatment, when rates of attrition are highest.

Because data from direct comparisons of psychotherapy to pharmacotherapy are not yet available, outcomes from our study of psychotherapeutic treatments may be compared with results from a controlled

TABLE 15.1 Comparison of Pharmacotherapy and Psychotherapy Studies

	Pharmacotherapy + psychotherapy[a]			Psychotherapy alone	
Patient category	Desipramine + IPT (n = 24)	Lithium + IPT (n = 24)	Placebo + IPT (n = 24)	RP (n = 21)	IPT (n = 21)
Percent remaining 6 weeks	75.0	45.8	41.7	71.4	52.4
Percent abstinent at 6 weeks	58.3	25.0	16.7	33.3	28.6
Percent abstinent at 12 weeks	—	—	—	57.1	33.3

Note. From "A Comparative Trial of Psychotherapies for Ambulatory Cocaine Abusers: Relapse Prevention and Interpersonal Psychotherapy" by K. M. Carroll, B. J. Rounsaville, and F. H. Gawin, 1991, *American Journal of Drug and Alcohol Abuse, 17*, p. 241. Copyright 1991 by Marcel Dekker, Inc. Reprinted by permission.
IPT = Interpersonal psychotherapy; RP = Relapse prevention.
[a]Data from Gawin et al. (1989).

clinical trial of pharmacotherapies for cocaine abuse also performed at Yale. In this study (Gawin et al., 1989), 72 ambulatory cocaine abusers were randomly assigned to desipramine, lithium, or placebo, each delivered in combination with IPT. Subjects treated in the pharmacotherapy trial can be regarded as historical controls for the psychotherapy study because the following conditions were met (Pocock, 1976): (1) Subjects in both studies were recruited and treated in the same clinic. (2) IPT in both studies was delivered by identical therapists. (3) The two samples are almost identical on pretreatment measures of demographic and psychiatric variables, as well as baseline intensity of cocaine use. (4) Identical subject eligibility criteria were used in both studies, except that subjects in the psychotherapy study did not require medical clearance for pharmacotherapy. (5) Subjects in both studies were evaluated using identical assessment instruments and procedures. Although the likelihood of self-selection may limit the strength of conclusions based on a comparison of the two studies, this comparison is nonetheless useful in demonstrating current conceptions of psychotherapy and pharmacotherapy as treatment for cocaine abuse.

Data contrasting rates of treatment retention and initiation of abstinence from both studies are presented in Table 15.1. The pharmacotherapy study by Gawin et al. (1989) evaluated outcome through 6 weeks of treatment, whereas the psychotherapy study evaluated outcome through 12 weeks. As psychotherapy is generally assumed to require more time to exert its effects (Elkin, Pilkonis, Docherty & Sotsky, 1988b), retention and abstinence data are presented for both time periods.

Several speculations emerge from this comparison regarding the roles and action of psychotherapy and pharmacotherapy in the treatment of cocaine abuse for (1) treatment retention and (2) initiation of abstinence. Considering treatment retention first, the 6-week retention rate for IPT alone in the psychotherapy study (53%) was slightly higher than that of the placebo + IPT combination in the pharmacotherapy study (42%). One interpretation of this finding is the addition of expectations for medication effects in the placebo + IPT combination did little to improve treatment retention over IPT alone. Instead, expectations for medication effects may have resulted in slightly greater attrition when expected benefits of the medication were not forthcoming. Also of note is that the rate of retention through 6 weeks for RP alone in the psychotherapy study (71%) is comparable to that for the desipramine + IPT combination (75%). This suggests that nonpharmacological interventions may have considerable power for keeping cocaine users in treatment, even in the absence of pharmacotherapy. Although retention for the desipramine + IPT combination was markedly higher than that of placebo + IPT, the role of active pharmacotherapy itself in fostering treatment retention is not clear, becuase a pharmacotherapy alone condition was not included in the pharmacotherapy study.

Turning next to a comparison of abstinence rates in the two studies, the expectation that the pharmacotherapy–psychotherapy combinations would exert effects more rapidly than psychotherapy alone was supported. At 6 weeks, the abstinence rate for subjects receiving the desipramine + IPT combination was 58%; abstinence rates for the two psychotherapy-alone conditions were lower and comparable with each other (33% for RP and 28% for IPT). For RP, an additional 6 weeks were required to match the abstinence rate for the pharmacotherapy–psychotherapy combination (the abstinence rate for RP increased to 58% at 12 weeks). This suggests that RP, a skills-training approach, may requires additional opportunities for coping skills to be practiced and implemented.

The lower rate of abstinence at 6 weeks for the placebo + IPT combination (17%) in the pharmacotherapy study, in contrast to that of IPT alone (28%) in the psychotherapy study, is also of interest. Several factors may account for this discrepancy. First, self-selection may have resulted in more psychotherapy- responsive subjects in the psychotherapy study, which may have resulted in better outcome for IPT. Second, for the placebo + IPT group in the pharmacotherapy study, a negative placebo effect (Klerman, 1963) may have undercut the efficacy of IPT, in that patients' expectations for medication effects may have resulted in their making less effort through other means to reduce their cocaine use.

A third possibility exists, which is of particular interest for this chapter: Although IPT in both studies was delivered by the same therapists, differences in conceptions of the role of psychotherapy in the two studies, and hence the context in which the psychotherapy was delivered, may have differentially affected the efficacy of IPT. In the pharmacotherapy study, medications were the change agents of primary interest, and great emphasis was placed on protecting the integrity of the pharmacological components of the treatment. Psychotherapy was conceived as the "ground" against which the impact of the pharmacological agents could be assessed and was not evaluated as a primary change agent; hence delivery of the psychotherapy was not systematically monitored or evaluated. This may have also conveyed to subjects expectations that psychotherapy was a less important or effective component of treatment. Conversely, in the psychotherapy study, the psychotherapies were conceived as powerful change agents and efforts were made to assure that subjects received an adequate "dose" of psychotherapy and therapies were administered optimally. Hence the improved outcome for the IPT-alone condition in the psychotherapy study over the placebo + IPT combination in the pharmacotherapy study may reflect delivery of a more potent form of IPT.

To summarize, data from the above comparison suggest that (1) nonpharmacologic treatments may have an important role in fostering treatment retention, (2) pharmacotherapy may be a more rapidly acting form of treatment than psychotherapy for cocaine abusers, and (3) the often-cited limitations of psychotherapy as treatment for cocaine abuse (high attrition, moderate rates of treatment success) are only partly addressed by combining psychotherapy with desipramine as a pharmacotherapeutic approach.

MODELS FOR THE EVALUATION OF PSYCHOTHERAPY AND PHARMACOTHERAPY

The comparison of this pair of studies also provides two illustrative models for psychotherapy as treatment for cocaine abuse: (1) as a necessary but largely nonspecific support to pharmacotherapy; and (2) as an effective, and in some cases sufficient, treatment in and of itself. The first model suggest that psychotherapy has limited usefulness beyond fostering compliance with pharmacotherapy and implies uniformity of effects from psychotherapy. Data from this comparison suggest that this model of psychotherapy may, in part, have resulted in underestimation of the potential effectiveness of psychotherapy. The second model assumes a broader role for psychotherapy and suggests improved outcome may result from preservation of treatment integrity. Furthermore, it assumes that different forms of treatment may offer unique and specific contributions to outcome.

Which model of psychotherapy is likely to result in more fruitful treatment research with cocaine abuse? Before considering research questions that would follow from adopting different models of psychotherapy as treatment for cocaine abuse, it may be instructive to review models of psychotherapy research from other psychiatric disorders as potential guides.

Opiate Dependence

Successful treatments for opiate dependence have generally involved some combination of psychotherapy and pharmacotherapy, most convincingly demonstrated by the disappointing results typically achieved when either modality is used alone. Purely pharmacological approaches have generally yielded poor retention and limited outcomes, but marked improvements have been noted when a psychotherapeutic component is added to pharmacological interventions such as medication-assisted detoxification (Rawson, Mann, Tennant, & Claybough, 1983), narcotic antagonist programs (Resnick, Washton, & Stone-Washton, 1981) and methadone maintenance (Woody et al., 1983). Conversely, although it is almost impossible to engage opiate addicts in treatment with a purely psychotherapeutic approach (Rounsaville & Kleber, 1985), delivery of psychotherapy within methadone maintenance programs has enabled investigators to rigorously contrast different psychotherapeutic approaches and identify those addicts who benefit most from professional psychotherapy over standard drug counseling during methadone maintenance (e.g., Woody et al., 1983; Rounsaville, Glazer, Wilber, Weissman, & Kleber, 1983). As such, all trials demonstrating efficacy of psychotherapy for opiate addicts have generally involved psychotherapy–pharmacotherapy combinations, and pharmacotherapy may be a necessary condition for successful psychotherapeutic intervention with opiate addicts.

Can this model be applied to the treatment of cocaine abuse? Development of a pharmacological equivalent of methadone for the treatment of cocaine abuse is probably not imminent. Available pharmacological agents for the treatment of cocaine abuse do not approach the effectiveness of methadone for keeping addicts in treatment and reducing illicit substance use. Furthermore, results from our studies and others suggest pharmacologic intervention is not essential for all cocaine abusers. Hence the current model for psychotherapy research among opiate addicts, in which psychotherapy is evaluated as an adjunct to the modal form of treatment (methadone maintenance), has limited usefulness as a model for psychotherapy research with cocaine abusers.

Depression

A more useful model for evaluating psychotherapy, alone and in combination with pharmacotherapy, may come from research on the treatment of depression. In this area, there is a large body of empirical evidence on the efficacy of different psychotherapies, pharmacotherapies, and combinations thereof (Conte, Plutchik, Wild, & Kerasin, 1986; Elkin et al., 1989); well-designed studies have addressed differentiated questions regarding specificity of the different forms of treatment and subtypes of depressives for which different treatments may be most effective (DiMascio et al., 1979: Imber et al., 1990); and conceptual and methodological issues involved in comparing and combining psychotherapy and pharmacotherapies have been addressed in detail (Elkin et al., 1988a, 1988b; Hollon & Beck, 1978).

Current models for research on the treatment of depression may serve as useful guides for psychotherapy research with cocaine abusers, given several parallels in the two disorders and their treatment. In the treatment of depression, as in the treatment of cocaine abuse, response to available pharmacological and psychotherapeutic treatments is incomplete (Karasu, 1990b; Morris & Beck, 1976), relapse after remission of symptoms is frequent (Angst, 1973), patient groups are heterogeneous and may include subtypes with differential response to treatment (Karasu, 1982), and each form of treatment (psychotherapy/pharmacotherapy) may address distinct symptom areas (Klerman, 1975). This body of research has led to current models of treatment that allow for different etiologies of depression, variability in clinical manifestations of depression, heterogeneity in patient groups, and variation in response to available treatments. This model also holds that each form of treatment is powerful and potentially unique. As Karasu (1990b) has noted:

> . . . no single therapy is uniformly successful for all the concomitants of the depressive disorder. For instance, biological variables may override psychological ones, or the reverse. In addition to determining whether treatment should consist of drugs combined with psychotherapy or of psychotherapy alone, examination of the (different) psychotherapies lends itself to a more discriminatory use of each. . . . Psychotherapy may be used

not only by default, that is, to increase compliance with medication or as an alternative for patients who cannot or will not respond to pharmacotherapy, but in itself as an independent intervention. (p. 276)

One could easily substitute "cocaine abuse" for "depression" in the preceding statement as a potential guide for evaluating psychotherapy and pharmacotherapy for cocaine abuse: Because it is unlikely that any single treatment or form of treatment will be adequate for all cocaine abusers, research should address differentiated questions regarding the roles and specific contributions of a variety of treatment approaches: What are the indications for psychotherapy and/or pharmacotherapy for cocaine abuse? Are different psychotherapies differentially effective with different types of cocaine abusers? In combination with different pharmacological agents?

Although treatment research in depression may offer useful models for evaluating psychotherapy and pharmacotherapy, there are noetheless important differences in the two disorders and the available therapies, and these differences that limit the extent to which models from treatment research from depression can be applied to cocaine abuse. Chief among them is that available pharmacological agents cannot be considered "standard" treatments for cocaine abuse as are antidepressants in the treatment of depression. The promising results of the use of tricyclic antidepressants in the therapy of cocaine abuse (Gawin et al., 1989) have not yet been widely replicated. In particular, the efficacy of tricyclic antidepressants as treatment for cocaine abuse may vary by the treatment modality in which they are administered (see Chapter 14, this volume). Nevertheless, as new therapies for cocaine abuse are evaluated, we can continue to draw from research on psychotherapy and pharmacotherapy in the treatment of depression to conceptualize various roles for psychotherapy as treatment for cocaine abuse.

ROLES FOR PSYCHOTHERAPY AS TREATMENT OF COCAINE ABUSE

As Sole Treatment

Initial reports suggest psychotherapy alone may be adequate treatment for some subgroups of cocaine abusers (Carroll, Rounsaville, & Gawin, 1991; Rawson et al., 1986). This leads to two general types of research questions regarding psychotherapy as sole treatment for cocaine abusers: First, which subgroups of cocaine abusers will respond to purely psychotherapeutic treatments? This line of research could include success profiling, in which characteristics of subjects responding well versus poorly to specific psychotherapies are identified retrospectively. For example, psychotherapy "responders" might include cocaine abusers with lower levels of severity, those who can sustain periods of several weeks of abstinence between episodes of cocaine use, or those who are prone to relapse in circumscribed situations.

This line of research would also lead to direct comparisons between psychotherapy and other forms of treatment, particularly pharmacotherapy. In the treatment of depression, many investigations directly contrasting psychotherapy and pharmacotherapy have appeared. These have focused largely on (1) contrasting the efficacy of psychotherapy with respect to pharmacotherapy as a reference condition (e.g., Elkin, Parloff, Hadley & Autry, 1985) and (2) attempting to discern the mode of action and specificity of each form of treatment (e.g., Imber et al., 1990).

In the treatment of cocaine abuse, direct contrasts of psychotherapy with pharmacotherapy might address similar questions. For example, with respect to time course, the effects of drugs may be apparent earlier in treatment than those of psychotherapy, whose effects may require more time to become manifest but endure longer than those of pharmacotherapy. Such a finding would have important implications for treatment: If the effects of pharmacotherapy were found to be transient, then pharmacotherapy would be an appropriate intervention if used to foster initial abstinence, stabilize the patient, and increase availability for psychotherapy, but inappropriate if pharmacotherapy alone were expected to bring about lasting improvement.

Direct contrasts of psychotherapy and pharmacotherapy also would allow detection of specific effects associated with each form of treatment. For example, pharmacotherapy may differentially reduce craving related to alterations in post- synaptic receptor sensitivity (Gawin et al., 1989), whereas some forms of psychotherapy might better address craving that resulted from classical conditioning of particular cocaine cues. Similarly, whereas pharmacotherapy may help abusers achieve initial periods of abstinence, psychotherapies may better address cocaine abusers' motivation to alter their substance use, improve abusers coping skills, and resolve issues related to drug availability. This type of research also could provide guidance regarding indications for psychotherapy or pharmacotherapy for different types of cocaine abusers.

A second general question that could be addressed in research evaluating psychotherapy as sole treatment for cocaine abuse has to do with the efficacy of different types of psychotherapy. In the treatment of depression, there have been many studies contrasting different forms of psychotherapy; in general, this body of work has supported the effectiveness of active psychotherapies over controls but has not demonstrated the superiority of one form of psychotherapy over another (Luborsky, Singer, & Luborsky, 1975; Smith & Glass, 1977). In the treatment of cocaine use, our evaluation of IPT and RP revealed no main effects for treatment but suggested more severe cocaine users as well as those with higher levels of psychiatric severity had better response to RP than IPT. Widely used models of treatment, in particular those derived from the 12-Step model, have not been contrasted with other forms of treatment in order to discern which subgroups of cocaine abuser may respond to different forms of psychotherap eutic intervention.

As Support to Pharmacotherapy

In this model, psychotherapy is seen as providing a minimal supportive structure against which the efficacy of drugs can be evaluated. A psychotherapeutic component is included largely to "warm up the drug," fostering patients' retention in treatment and compliance with pharmacotherapy (Docherty, Marder, Van Kammen, & Siris, 1977; Elkin et al., 1988b). Indeed, few researchers would consider feasible a design in which pharmacotherapy was administered without any supportive or relationship elements (Elkin et al., 1988b; Karasu, 1982, 1990b).

As noted above, this has been the dominant model of psychotherapy in those investigations that have evaluated pharmacotherapies for cocaine abuse. Investigators frequently describe their designs as evaluating drugs as adjuncts to "treatment as usual," which usually consists of psychotherapy or counseling. However, as was suggested in our comparison of psychotherapy and pharmacotherapy studies, in pharmacological trials non-pharmacological components are likely to be de-emphasized relative to the medications being evaluated. Psychotherapy is likely to be implemented as a support to pharmacotherapy rather than as a robust treatment in its own right. Thus, whereas the research question may be posed as What is the incremental effectiveness of adding pharmacotherapy to treatment as usual? in clinical trials of pharmacological agents this often translates in practice to What is the relative effectiveness of active medication or placebo in the context of minimal supportive clinical management?

Limiting conception of psychotherapy to that of a minimal supportive condition in pharmacological trials is likely to have a number of effects, in that the effectiveness of a minimal supportive condition is rarely equal to that of an active psychotherapy (Luborsky et al., 1975; Smith & Glass, 1977). In this context psychotherapy is seen as essentially inert; thus the content, goals, and methods are typically not specified or monitored, with the result that all psychotherapies are conceived as uniform. Active or curative elements that would be included in a psychotherapy condition in which treatment integrity was preserved may be lacking, thereby undercutting the efficacy of the therapy. The unique contributions of psychotherapy are likely to go underemphasized and unassessed. Conclusions regarding the efficacy of psychotherapy based on pharmacological trials (wherein psychotherapy plays a secondary, supportive role) are likely to underestimate the potential efficacy of nonpharmacological treatments.

As a Complementary Treatment

In this model, the efficacy of psychotherapy or pharmacotherapy alone is typically contrasted with the combination of the two. Here each form of treatment is conceived of as having specific and unique therapeutic properties that may interact in a number of ways. Uhlenhuth, Lipman, and Covi (1969) have described four models for such effects: additive (in which the effect of combined treatment equals the sum of their individual effects), potentiation (in which the effect of the combined treatment is greater than the sum of the two individual treatment effects), inhibition (where the combined treatment is less than the sum of their individual effects), and reciprocation (where the effect of the combined treatments equals the individual effect of the more potent intervention). In the treatment of depression, most research on psychotherapy–pharmacotherapy combinations has supported an additive or reciprocal model and has tended not to find evidence supporting inhibition (Rounsaville, Klerman, & Weissman, 1981) or potentiation (Conte et al., 1986) of effects.

There are several advantages of evaluating psychotherapy as a complementary treatment to pharmacotherapy for cocaine abuse. First, because psychotherapy is no longer relegated to a "supportive" role, psychotherapy can be administered at full strength, and so allow maximal effects to emerge and be detected. Psychotherapy and pharmacotherapy are assumed to work through different mechanisms (e.g., desipramine to reverse cocaine-induced neuroadaptation, and psychotherapies such as RP to improve abuser's ability to cope with or avoid high-risk situations and relapse) and to affect different symptoms.

Thus a major potential advantage of psychotherapy–pharmacotherapy combinations in which the integrity of each treatment is protected is that integrative treatments may improve outcome for more symptoms than would either treatment alone. Assuming psychotherapy and pharmacotherapy differentially affect different symptoms, by increasing the number of symptoms potentially improved through combination treatments, one may dramatically improve the "hit rate" among cocaine abusers, who typically present with heterogeneity of symptoms and problems. Such a model also allows for detection of treatment specificity and so would guide future efforts toward patient– treatment matching.

Another advantage of evaluating combination treatments is that potential drawbacks associated with either treatment may be offset by the other. For example, the provision of support through psychotherapy may reduce the potential negative impact of side effects arising from most pharmacotherapies. Similarly, instillation of hope through administration of a drug may support the patient's continuing participation during the early stages of treatment, when a developing therapeutic alliance may be fragile, or until coping skills are mastered and integrated.

If one considers the heterogeneity of cocaine abusers presenting for treatment, the variations in severity of cocaine abuse, and the multidimensionality of cocaine abusers' problems, and the potential value of evaluating both psychotherapy and pharmacotherapy as effective and unique treatment components is further underscored. Extein and Bowers (1979) differentiate between state disorders (e.g., psychoses, severe anxiety, and major depression), described as time-limited, autonomous, and unresponsive to psychotherapeutic intervention; and trait disorders, defined as "dysfunctional qualities which individuals tend to develop and carry throughout life and which become manifest as predictable patterns for interaction and response to stress. Such patterns tend not to be responsive to medication but respond better to psychosocial treatment" (pp. 690–691). State and trait disorders are conceived as independent, but one or both may be present in any individual.

Cocaine abuse (and other forms of substance abuse) can be conceived as having attributes of both state and trait disorders, in varying degrees among different abusers: Pharmacotherapy or other forms of medical intervention are generally essential when state disorders are present (e.g., withdrawal symptoms associated with physical dependence, some forms of drug craving, cocaine-induced psychoses) that would not be expected to respond to psychotherapy. Similarly, psychotherapy may be indicated for those trait aspects of cocaine abuse upon which pharmacotherapy would be expected to have little impact (e.g., fostering motivation to reduce substance use, restricting availability of cocaine, avoidance of situations associated with use, development of non-cocaine-using social supports).

With a state–trait model of substance use disorders, the unique action of each form of a particular approach can be investigated with the goal of developing a model of treatment that is comprehensive and nonexclusionary: At lower severity levels, in the absence of state disorders, psychotherapy alone may be adequate. At higher levels of severity, the presence of state disorders may indicate the need for a combination of psychotherapy and pharmacotherapy, although in some cases the state disorder may be so dominant that it may be futile to initiate psychotherapy until the state disorder resolves and the patient thereby becomes able to participate in psychotherapy.

REFERENCES

Angst, J. (1973). The course of monopolar depression and bipolar psychoses. *Psychiatrica, Neurologica, et Neurochirurgia, 76*, 439–500.

Anker, A. L., & Crowley, T. J. (1982). Use of contingency contracts in specialty clinics for cocaine abuse. In L. S. Harris (Ed.), *Problems of drug dependence, 1981* (National Institute on Drug Abuse Research Monograph No. 41, pp. 452–459). Rockville, MD: National Institute on Drug Abuse.

Carroll, K. M. (1987). *Manual for Relapse Prevention adapted for cocaine abuse.* Unpublished manuscript.

Carroll, K. M., Rounsaville, B. J., & Gawin, F. H. (1991). A comparative trial of psychotherapies for ambulatory cocaine abusers: Relapse prevention and interpersonal psychotherapy. *American Journal of Drug and Alcohol Abuse, 17*, 229–247.

Carroll, K. M., Rounsaville, B. J., & Keller, D. S. (1991). Relapse prevention strategies for the treatment of cocaine abuse. *American Journal of Drug and Alcohol Abuse, 17*, 249–265.

Conte, H. R., Plutchik, R., Wild, K. V., & Karasu, T. B. (1986). Combined psychotherapy and pharmacotherapy for depression. A systematic analysis of the evidence. *Archives of General Psychiatry, 43*, 471–479.

DiMascio, A., Weissman, M. M., Prusoff, B. A. New, C., Zwilling, M., & Klerman, G. L. (1979). Differential symptom reduction by drugs and psychotherapy in acute depression. *Archives of General Psychiatry, 36*, 1450–1456.

Docherty, J. P., Marder, S. R., Van Kammen, D. P., & Siris, S. G. (1977). Psychotherapy and Pharmacotherapy: Conceptual Issues. *American Journal of Psychiatry, 134*, 529–533.

Elkin, I., Parloff, M. B., Hadley, S. W., & Autry, J. H. (1985). NIMH treatment of depression collaborative research program: Background and research plan. *Archives of General Psychiatry, 42*, 305–316.

Elkin, I., Pilkonis, P. A., Docherty, J. P., & Sotsky, S. M. (1988a). Conceptual and methodological issues in comparative studies of psychotherapy and pharmacotherapy: 1. Active ingredients and mechanisms of change. *American Journal of Psychiatry, 145*, 909–917.

Elkin, I., Pilkonis, P. A., Docherty, J. P., & Sotsky, S. M. (1988b). Conceptual and methodological issues in comparative studies of psychotherapy and pharmacotherapy, II: Nature and timing of treatment effects. *American Journal of Psychiatry, 145*, 1070–1076.

Elkin, I., Shea, M. T., Watkins, J. T., Imber, S. D., Sotsky, S. M., Collins, J. F.,

Glass, D. R., Pilkonis, P. A., Leber, W. R., Docherty, J. P., Fiester, S. J., & Parloff, M. B. (1989). National Institute of Mental Health treatment of depression collaborative research program: General effectiveness of treatments. *Archives of General Psychiatry, 46,* 971–982.

Extein, I., & Bowers, M. B. (1979). State and trait in psychiatric practice. *American Journal of Psychiatry, 136,* 690–693.

Gawin, F. H, & Kleber, H. D. (1986). Abstinence symptomatology and psychiatric diagnosis in cocaine abusers. *Archives of General Psychiatry, 43,* 107–113.

Gawin, F. H., Kleber, H. D., Byck, R., Rounsaville, B. J., Kosten, T. R., Jatlow, P. I., & Morgan, C. B. (1989). Desipramine facilitation of initial cocaine abstinence. *Archives of General Psychiatry, 46,* 117–121.

Hall, S. M., Havassy, B. E., & Wasserman, D. A. (1991). Effects of commitment to abstinence, positive moods, stress, and coping on relapse to cocaine use. *Journal of Consulting and Clinical Psychology, 59,* 526–532.

Hollon, S. D., & Beck, A. T. (1978). Psychotherapy and drug therapy: Comparison and combinations. In S. L. Garfield & A. E. Bergin (Eds.), *Handbook of psychotherapy and behavior change* (2nd ed.). New York: Wiley.

Imber, S. D., Pilkonis, P. A., Sotsky, S. M., Elkin, I., Watkins, J. T., Collins J. F., Shea, M. T., Leber, W. R., & Glass, D. R. (1990). Mode-specific effects among three treatments for depression. *Journal of Consulting and Clinical Psychology, 58,* 352–359.

Jaffe, A. J., Kilbey, M. M., & Rosenbaum, G. R. (1989). Cocaine related expectancies: Their domain and implications for treatment. *Pharmacology, Biochemistry, and Behavior, 32*(4), 1094.

Kang, S., Kleinman, P. H., Woody, G. E., Millman, R. B., Todd, T. C., Kemp, J., & Lipton, D. S. (1991). Outcomes for cocaine abusers after one-a-week psychosocial therapy. *American Journal of Psychiatry, 148,* 630–635.

Karasu, T. B. (1982). Psychotherapy and pharmacotherapy: Toward an integrative model. *American Journal of Psychiatry, 32,* 1102–1113.

Karasu, T. B. (1990a). Toward a clinical model of psychotherapy for depression: 1. Systematic comparision of three psychotherapies. *American Journal of Psychiatry, 147,* 133–147.

Karasu, T. B. (1990b). Toward a clinical model of psychotherapy for depression: 2. An integrative and selective treatment approach. *American Journal of Psychiatry, 147,* 269–278.

Klerman, G. L. (1963). Assessing the influence of the hospital milieu upon the effectiveness of psychiatric drug therapy: Problems of conceptualization and of research methodology. *Journal of Nervous and Mental Disease, 137,* 143–154.

Klerman, G. L. (1975). Combining drugs and psychotherapy in the treatment of depression. In M. Greenblatt (Ed.), *Drugs in Combination with other therapies.* New York: Grune & Stratton.

Luborsky, L., Singer, B., & Luborsky, L. (1975). Comparative studies of psychotherapies: Is it true that "Everyone has won and all must have prizes?" *Archives of General Psychiatry, 32,* 995–1007.

Marlatt, G. A., and Gordon, J. R., (Eds.). (1985). *Relapse prevention: Maintenance strategies in the treatment of addictive behaviors.* New York: Guilford.

Means, L. B., Small, M., Capone, D. M., Capone, T. J., Condren, R., Peterson, M., & Hayward, B. (1989). Client demographics and outcome in outpatient cocaine treatment. *International Journal of the Addictions, 24,* 765–783.

Morris, J. B., & Beck, A. T. (1976). The efficacy of antidepressant drugs. In D. F. Klein & R. Gittelman-Klein (Eds.), *Progress in Psychiatric Drug Treatment,* (Vol. 2). New York: Brunner/Mazel.

O'Brien, C. P., Childress, A. R., Arndt, I. O., McLellan, A. T., Woody, G. E., & Maany, I. (1988). Pharmacological and behavioral treatments of cocaine dependence: Controlled studies. *Journal of Clinical Psychiatry, 49,* suppl, 17–22.

Onken, L. S., & Blaine, J. D. (1990). Psychotherapy and counseling research in drug abuse treatment: Questions, problems, and solutions. In L. S. Onken and J. D. Blaine (Eds.), *Psychotherapy and counseling in the treatment of drug abuse* (National Institute on Drug Abuse Research Monograph No. 104, pp. 1–8). Rockville, MD: National Institute on Drug Abuse.

Pocock, S. J. (1976). The combination of randomized and historical controls in clinical trials. *Journal of Chronic Disease, 29,* 175–188.

Rawson, R. A., Mann, A. G., Tennant, F. S., & Clabough, D. (1983). Efficacy of psychotherapeutic counseling during 12-day ambulatory heroin detoxification. In L. S. Harris (Ed.), *Problems of Drug dependence, 1982* (National Institute on Drug Abuse Research Monograph No. 43, pp. 310–314). Rockville, MD: National Institute on Drug Abuse.

Rawson, R. A., Obert, J. L., McCann, M. J., & Mann, A. J. (1986). Cocaine treatment outcome: Cocaine use following inpatient, outpatient, and no treatment. In L. S. Harris (Ed.), *Problems of drug dependence, 1985* (National Institute on Drug Abuse Research Monograph No. 67, pp. 271–277). Rockville, MD: National Institute on Drug Abuse.

Rawson, R. A., Obert, J. L., McCann, M. J., Smith, D. P., & Ling W. (1990). Neurobehavioral treatment for cocaine dependency. *Journal of Psychoactive Drugs, 22,* 159–171.

Resnick, R. B., Washton, A. M., & Stone-Washton, N. (1981). Psychotherapy and naltrexone in opioid dependence. In L. S. Harris (Ed.), *Problems of Drug Dependence, 1980* (National Institute on Drug Abuse research Monograph No. 34, pp. 109–115). Rockville, MD: National Institute on Drug Abuse.

Rounsaville, B. J., Gawin, F. H., & Kleber, H. D. (1985). Interpersonal psychotherapy adapted for ambulatory cocaine abusers. *American Journal of Drug and Alcohol Abuse, 11,* 171–191.

Rounsaville, B. J., Glazer, W., Wilber, C. H., Weissman, M. M., & Kleber, H. D. (1983). Short-term interpersonal psychotherapy in methadone maintained opiate addicts. *Archives of General Psychiatry, 40,* 629–636.

Rounsaville, B. J., & Kleber, H. D. (1985). Psychotherapy/counseling for opiate addicts: Strategies for use in different treatment settings. *International Journal of the Addictions, 20,* 869–896.

Rounsaville, B. J., Klerman, G. L., & Weissman, M. M. (1981). Do psychotherapy and pharmacotherapy for depression conflict? Empirical evidence from a clinical trial. *Archives of General Psychiatry, 38,* 24–29.

Schiffer, F. (1988). Psychotherapy of nine successfully treated cocaine abusers: Techniques and dynamics. *Journal of Substance Abuse Treatment, 5,* 131–137.

Smith, M. L., & Glass, G. V. (1977). Meta-analysis of psychotherapy outcome studies. *American Psychologist, 32,* 752–760.

Uhlenhuth, E. H., Lipman, R. S., & Covi, L. (1969). Combined pharmacotherapy and psychotherapy: Controlled studies. *Journal of Nervous and Mental Disease, 148,* 52–64.

Washton, A. M. (1986). Treatment of cocaine abuse. In L. S. Harris (Ed.), *Problems of drug dependence, 1985* (National Institute on Drug Abuse Research Monograph No. 67, pp. 263–270). Rockville, MD: National Institute on Drug Abuse.

Woody, G. E., Luborsky, L., McLellan, A. T., O'Brien, C. P., Beck, A. T., Blaine, J., Herman, I., & Hole, A. (1983). Psychotherapy for opiate addicts: Does it help? *Archives of General Psychiatry, 40,* 639–645.

Woody, G. E., McLellan, A. T., Luborsky, L., & O'Brien, C. P. (1985). Sociopathy and psychotherapy outcome. *Archives of General Psychiatry, 42,* 1081–1086.

Inpatient Treatment
of Cocaine Addiction

H. Rowland Pearsall, MD
Marc I. Rosen, MD

T HE INPATIENT TREATMENT of cocaine addiction is an intensive intervention that reserved for patients with severe addictions. The logic of this tertiary-care use of inpatient treatment is based in part on tradition growing out of the alcohol and substance abuse treatment literature, and in part on necessity. Because cocaine patients were initially viewed as having a "less severe" addiction that did not require detoxification, the use of the inpatient setting was thought to be most appropriate for those patients with exceptional problems. As we have come to appreciate the power of cocaine's addictive nature, of cocaine urges, and of cocaine withdrawal symptoms, the role of the inpatient treatment unit has been reexamined. Because inpatient treatment beds are a scarce resource in most practice settings, selecting those patients most in need of the intensive services potentially available and structuring the inpatient setting to best meet the needs of those patients is of the utmost importance. The goal of this chapter is to review some of the criteria for selecting patients for admission to an inpatient unit, to discuss the structure and management of such a unit, and to discuss specific therapeutic approaches that may be useful in treating the cocaine-addicted patient. In doing this, we will review some of the relevant clinical information about cocaine addiction and withdrawal as it impacts on problems seen in the inpatient setting and on the treatment process.

OVERVIEW OF COCAINE ADDICTION

No one profile typifies all cocaine users. There are, however, a number of problems that users who may be candidates for inpatient treatment have in common. Most cocaine addicts start out with social, intranasal use. As they gain experience with the drug, some of these users go on to lose control of their use even with the intranasal route of administration. Typically, however, they begin to experiment with smoking cocaine either as freebase or as crack in order to enhance the high. Others turn to intravenous use of cocaine, either alone or as an adjunct to opiates or other drugs. The intravenous and smoked routes of use achieve substantially higher blood levels of the drug much more rapidly, giving a more potent high and a strengthened addiction. Patients presenting with these advanced levels of addiction are the ones most likely to need inpatient services.

By the time most patients present for treatment, their addiction has caused a significant loss of function in the social, psychological, occupational, and medical spheres. What started off as a social drug to use at parties and with friends has become an all-powerful obsession leading to social isolation, loss of relationships with non-drug-using friends, and strained or broken relationships with spouses or significant others. Job performance and attendance become erratic and unpredictable. Cocaine users are often moody, irritable, and paranoid. Because the drug is a powerful stimulant, sleep is frequently decreased during periods of intense use ("runs"). When on a run, job attendance, family obligations, nutrition, and sex are all secondary to continuing the cocaine high. Physical health can suffer from neglect of underlying medical problems, from poor nutrition, and from the consequences of the cocaine use itself. In assessing a patient, clinicians must consider psychiatric, medical, and social problems caused by cocaine abuse.

In the advanced phase of addiction, the psychological state of cocaine abusers is different from that in the early phases. During the early phases, users describe feeling euphoric, all powerful, full of energy, able to do anything. As the addiction progresses, they become paranoid, irritable, and isolative. Following the cocaine high, there is a rapid change in mood with feelings of dysphoria and depression. If more drug is available, users will try to avoid this crash or down period by using more cocaine. The powerful high and the desire to avoid the aversive dysphoria both contribute to the addictive potential of cocaine. These symptoms will become evident in the course of the admission interview and subsequent inpatient treatment.

Many users incorporate other drugs into their cocaine use pattern in order to "smooth out" the euphorigenic and stimulating effects of cocaine. Abuse and/or addiction to other drugs such as alcohol, marijuana, benzodiazepines, and opiates becomes a part of the drug abuse profile of many cocaine addicts and must be considered in preparing a treatment plan and deciding whether considering inpatient admission is indicated.

REVIEW OF OUTCOME STUDIES

Few controlled comparisons have been made of inpatient and outpatient treatment of cocaine abuse, but there are other sources of information on the efficacy of different treatment alternatives. One source is the literature on treatment of alcohol dependence. In a review of this literature, Miller and Hester (1984) conclude that there is no advantage of inpatient over outpatient treatment for chronic alcoholics. Further arguing against the efficacy of hospitalization is the suggestion that shorter inpatient stays are more effective than longer ones. The authors conclude, however, that there may be a place for "matching" a particular type of treatment to a particular type of addict. Studies of cognitive attributes of patients have been used in an effort to match addicts to treatment modalities compatible with these attributes. The authors cite research findings that patients with more severe neuropsychiatric impairment have poorer outcomes and need more intensive treatment; that patients with an internal locus of control respond better to less directive treatment; and that patients with high levels of conformity and authoritarianism do well in Alcoholics Anonymous. Patients have also been matched for severity of their alcohol abuse, with more severe problems generally thought to need more intensive treatment. Alcoholics with more severe problems and those with a positive paternal family history of alcoholism have been unable to succeed in controlled drinking programs. There is also a suggestion in the literature, according to Miller and Hester, that patients who are allowed to choose between several treatment alternatives do better than those assigned to a treatment modality.

Studies attempting to predict which addicts, if any, benefit more from inpatient than outpatient treatment raise several methodological issues. One is the difficulty of randomization. In nonrandomized comparisons of inpatient and outpatient treatment, wealthier and employed patients (better-prognosis patients) who have insurance are more likely to receive inpatient treatment, whereas patients in public systems are more likely to receive outpatient treatment. Most patients would not consent to be randomly assigned to inpatient or outpatient treatment; a sample of addicts who accept randomization is already a self-selected sample. Another set of difficulties comes from defining the type of inpatient treatment provided and comparing that with a similar type of outpatient treatment. Ultimately, the question is not whether inpatient treatment is better than outpatient treatment, but for whom inpatient treatment is better or necessary.

Among studies that have focused more specifically on cocaine addicts, Pettinate et al., (1991) performed an uncontrolled retrospective study at the Carrier Foundation looking at 149 inpatients and 81 outpatients being treated for cocaine abuse. Inpatients began with a 28-day hospitalization, focusing on principles of Narcotics Anonymous, followed by a 12-week low-intensity group therapy. Outpatients were seen approximately 11 hours per week for 6 weeks before being referred to the 12-week follow-up group. The outpatients were 4 times more likely to leave treatment before 1 year (35% vs. 9%). An "opt out" clause allowed outpatients who were failing treatment to be hospitalized; these patients were not counted in the analysis, but likely would have been outpatient dropouts. Because indicating the increased relapse rates for outpatients, the study suggested that patients who had high psychiatric severity and little social support were mismatched with outpatient treatment and had poorer outcomes than outpatients with less severe psychiatric problems and more social support.

Work by other researchers suggests that outpatient treatment for cocaine abuse can be extremely effective with the right population of addicts. In a sample of employed middle-class cocaine addicts, Washton, Gold, and Pottash (1985) reported that 59 of 63 patients completed 3 months of outpatient treatment with a remarkable patient report of 81% remaining abstinent at 7–19 months follow-up. By contrast, a nonrandomized study by O'Brien, Atterman, Walter, Childress, & McLellan (1990) of cocaine-addicted veterans of lower socioeconomic status compared treatment in a 27-hour-per-week outpatient day hospital for 4 weeks with a 4 week inpatient hospitalization which provided comparable services. At the end of the 4 weeks, twice as many cocaine addicts completed the inpatient stay (86%) as completed the day hospital program (43%). However, at 4-month follow-up, there were no significant group differences in reported abstinence during the past month (79% for the day hospital patients and 73% of the inpatients).

All of this work points out the difficulty in systematically studying inpatient versus outpatient treatment approaches. Issues of patient assessment and matching appropriate patients to appropriate treatment seem crucial to achieving the best possible treatment outcomes.

THE DECISION TO ADMIT

Assessing patients for admission involves a complex decision-making process. Some of the factors that complicate the decision whether to admit include the condition of the patient, the setting of the evaluation, the environment in which the patient is functioning, and the extent of the addiction. An evaluating clinician needs to take into account all of these factors so as to make a recommendation for a treatment approach that is likely both to succeed and to be best for the patient.

One important variable is the condition or sobriety of the patient at the time of evaluation. Many patients present for evaluation while still actively using cocaine or other drugs. Assessing such a patient while he or she is high adds to the complexity of the workup and makes it more difficult to engage the patient in meaningful decisions about his or her life and treatment options. Acutely intoxicated patients should ideally be contained until the effects of the drug subside and they are sober. Other patients may present already sober, often after a recently concluded cocaine binge, with concerns about their ability to maintain abstinence. With the sober patient, one can make a more reasoned assessment of the pattern of abuse, social strengths and supports, previous treatment efforts and their outcome, and the patient's motivation to stop using cocaine. Once a patient is sober, he or she is more easily engaged in the treatment process. The guidelines outlined later offer some specific suggestions as to which types of these patients should be considered for inpatient treatment.

Where the patient is evaluated is a second variable that may complicate making the decision to admit. The acutely intoxicated patient may begin to come down during the evaluation and want to leave, or become irritable, impulsive, and paranoid. In an office setting, it may be impossible to stop the patient from leaving to get more drug. The clinician must appreciate the limitations of a particular setting and change settings if the situation so warrants. The outpatient office offers little structure to contain a patient who is high and starts to become paranoid, or who begins to come down from the high and later wants to leave to get high again. This type of patient may be better treated in an emergency room (ER), which offers a high degree of structure. However, the ER setting can often be intimidating, institutional, impersonal, and, overall, not conducive to engaging a paranoid drug abuser in the treatment process. Further complicating an ER evaluation is that the ER clinician is often a stranger to the patient and unfamiliar with the case. The currently sober patient may be put off by this and would be more easily engaged in an office atmosphere.

The environment in which the patient is functioning also impacts on the alternatives for treatment. Patients with intact families who have not given up and are willing to assist in getting the patient to outpatient treatment initially will facilitate the outpatient therapy. The presence of a stable job to provide structure, as well as the possibility of involving an employee assistance program to help the patient in recovery, are also factors that may allow an attempt at outpatient therapy. If there are 12-step program sponsors involved who can provide structure and support, an inpatient stay may be avoided. If the patient has no family or other supports, and the primary social network is among substance-abusing peers, then an inpatient stay may be needed.

The extent of addiction to cocaine and/or other drugs is another important factor. An intranasal abuser of cocaine for several months has a much better chance of successfully using outpatient services than does someone who has been freebasing daily for the past 2 years. For some patients who have been abusing opiates or alcohol along with cocaine, a medical detoxification from one of more of these drugs may need to be done in an inpatient setting.

In summary, the more severe, refractory addictions require inpatient treatment. Poor prognostic signs for outpatient treatment include lack of social supports, lack of 12-step program involvement, and multiple addictions. Inpatient treatment is comparatively expensive, and patients who have not had previous treatment should be encouraged to attempt outpatient treatment if they are able. Offering patients the option to try outpatient treatment with a plan for hospitalization if they relapse may allow some marginal patients to avoid an inpatient stay.

SPECIFIC ADMISSION GUIDELINES

Specific guidelines for admission to inpatient treatment are listed in Table 16.1.

Self-destructive and/or suicidal behavior, aggressive/violent behavior, and psychiatric symptoms such as paranoia, psychosis, or severe depression describe a broad group of emotional or psychiatric reasons to consider inpatient admission. Often, when patients are acutely high from cocaine, they can present with symptoms of paranoia or psychosis. Engaging the patient in outpatient plan under such circumstances may be impossible, and inpatient admission, at least to treat the acute psychiatric symptoms, may be necessary. If these resolve in a few days, then an appropriate disposition can be made to an outpatient setting if the clinical picture suggests that this will be workable.

TABLE 16.1. Admission Guidelines for Inpatient Cocaine Treatment

Psychiatric
    Self-destructive or suicidal behavior
    Aggressive/violent behavior
    Severe psychiatric symptoms (e.g., paranoia, psychosis, depression, mania)
Medical
    Presence of complicating medical problems
    Presence of other addictions requiring detoxification
Historical
    Recurrent failure of outpatient treatment
Environmental
    Pending legal action or court mandated treatment
    Presence of acute life stressors, (e.g., death of a loved one)
    Severe psychosocial consequences (e.g., loss of job or family)

The presence of complicating medical problems is another reason to consider immediate admission to either a medical or chemical-dependency setting. Acute medical problems such as cardiac arrhythmias, infections, or severe malnutrition obviously need immediate attention. More chronic medical problems can be treated electively on an outpatient basis if the patient can be engaged enough in treatment to reliably follow up with needed treatments. If significant doubt exists, then the decision to admit must take into account the potential consequences of a particular medical problem being left unattended owing to the patient's continued addiction.

If there is evidence of addiction to other substances, then inpatient admission needs to be considered. Alcohol is commonly abused by those addicted to cocaine, and the possibility of alcohol withdrawal, delirium tremens, and alcohol-related seizures should be assessed. Likewise, addiction to sedative hypnotics and benzodiazepines should be screened for, because withdrawal from these substances can be life-threatening. Addiction to opium derivatives such as heroin or to the various synthetic opioids also requires evaluation. Opiate detoxification may be needed, and continued use of these drugs will almost certainly lead to relapse in outpatient therapy.

Failure of previous outpatient efforts indicates a patient who should be considered for a more intensive type of treatment. Factors to consider include the degree of success of the previous efforts, period of sobriety achieved, reasons for failure of previous efforts (e.g., therapist left after a year vs. patient never attended), and the patient's current attitude toward resuming an outpatient-type approach. A patient who has done well with extended periods of sobriety and who is motivated to resume outpatient treatment is a good candidate to succeed. Conversely, a patient with five ER visits who has never followed through on outpatient appointments may warrant a more intensive inpatient phase of treatment in an effort to engage him or her in longer term outpatient therapy afterward.

The presence of severe psychosocial stressors, legal consequences, and acute life stresses may be thought of as the environmental factors in assessing for inpatient admission. Often the loss of family or a job is the motivating factor for seeking help. The reality of severe financial problems as a consequence of drug use may complicate the family situation or represent a separate problem area. Sometimes patients have pending legal problems as a consequence of their cocaine use, and the realizaton of this consequence, or an actual court mandate or lawyer recommendation, is the motivation to seek treatment. When these circumstances exist, they need to be considered in the decision to admit. If patients have experienced recent severe stress such as the death of a parent, spouse, or child, some intensive therapy may be needed in a structured, safe environment before the patient is ready for outpatient work. The incidence of relapse in the face of such unresolved external stressors is very high. Only those patients with strong outside supports such as family, 12-step sponsors, or good existing outpatient therapy linkages have much chance of remaining abstinent in these circumstances.

Any of these factors may be pivotal in deciding to recommend inpatient treatment. Particularly when multiple factors are present, the scale may tip toward inpatient treatment as most likely to be helpful. For the clinician, each case becomes a weighing of the best available facts to determine the most clinically appropriate action.

ENGAGING THE PATIENT IN TREATMENT

Once the clinician has decided in favor of inpatient treatment the next job is to engage the patient. This may be easier to do when the patient presents seeking help, but even then, the patient may be resistant to a recommendation for inpatient treatment. Patients are afraid and may question why outpatient treatment would not do as well. The clinician must be prepared to explain the rationale behind suggesting inpatient treatment. Engaging family support for the recommendation can be very useful because the family is often desperate for help to deal with the situation and has already accepted the necessity of an intensive intervention to stabilize the situation. They may also have gone through several attempts at outpatient treatment and be willing to confront the patient with his or her previous promises and failures in an effort to get the addict to accept more intensive treatment.

Some patients come to evaluation via the police or the ER and express little or no interest in pursuing treatment, even though they may meet several of the guidelines outlined above for inpatient admission. Getting through to these patients represents a major challenge. Some might argue that the apparent lack of motivation is such an overwhelming negative factor and poor prognostic sign that it is not worth the effort to try to retain such patients in treatment. Unfortunately, these very patients are the ones who will almost certainly be back in the ER, clinic, or office in a week or two if nothing is done to change the pattern. They are also a group at very high risk for all of the negative medical and social consequences of drug use, for themselves and their families.

As mentioned earlier, patients who are high or intoxicated at the time of the evaluation will have impaired judgement. Allowing a period to "sober up" may permit them to reflect more realistically on their options and on the need for structured treatment. Similarly, after a day or two, a reluctant patient who is in denial may be able to begin to see the extent of his or her addiction and its consequences. The difficulty is in convincing the patient to stay in treatment, even if only for a few days, to have the chance of becoming engaged in the inpatient milieu.

Most states do not allow for the easy commitment of patients strictly for treatment of substance abuse, and the clinician must find ways to persuade patients to entertain the idea of treatment on a voluntary basis. Doing this requires time and patience. Paranoid, suspicious, and manipulative, patients must come to trust that the clinician is giving them the best possible advice on how to change their life. The clinician should be knowledgeable about the basics of substance abuse and about the nature of the treatment program being recommended. Substance abusers are highly proficient in sensing a clinician's uncertainties, and if doubt exists about the effectiveness of a program, either because the clinician does not really feel it is helpful or because he or she just does not know much about the program, it is much harder to engage the patient. It is sometimes helpful to have the patient talk with a substance abuse counselor or recovering person such as a 12-step sponsor, but clinicians without this background can still engage patients successfully. Generally, patients will respond to the facts. Confrontation about the reality of the situation and the consequences to be faced can be a powerful ally in engaging the patient. The same factors that led the clinician to recommend intensive inpatient treatment can also lead a patient to the same conclusion when the information is presented in a straightforward and logical manner.

ASSESSMENT

A cornerstone of the assessment for inpatient cocaine treatment is a comprehensive drug history, which serves both therapeutic and diagnostic purposes by detailing the drug-related problems in a patient's life prior to entry into the hospital. It helps the clinician penetrate the patient's denial and establishes the need for treatment. The Addiction Severity Index (ASI) (McLellan et al., 1980) is one tool that can serve as a useful initial data base for evaluation of the patient. The ASI is a clinician-rated structured interview that asks patients detailed questions about their functioning in each of the following areas: physical health, employment and support systems, drug and alcohol use, legal status, family and social relationships, and psychological problems. The ASI includes questions in language that may prompt addicts to remember details they might otherwise overlook. For instance, the questions about medical issues ask specifically how many days in the past 30 days the patient was bothered by medical problems, and asks specifically about overdoses and overnight stays in emergency rooms for detoxification. The ASI's drug use section should be supplemented by a more detailed cocaine use history. This is best accomplished thorough an experienced clinician's interview using a structured interview tool such as the Quantitative Cocaine Inventory. It can be useful to ask patients to write a diary of the history of their cocaine use, which can be expanded to include concomitant use of other drug.

Another potentially important area to assess is the set of expectations associated with the patients' cocaine use. Cocaine users' thoughts and beliefs about how cocaine affects them have important implications for treatment. Direct attempts to change patient expectations can make treatment more effective. An instrument designed to assess the patient's beliefs about the effects of cocaine is the Cocaine Expectancy Questionnaire (CEQ) (Jaffe, Kilbey, & Rosenbaum, 1989; Jaffe & Kilbey, 1992), a self report measure. The reader is referred to Chapter 7 for a thorough discussion of the assessment and use of cognitive factors to treat cocaine abuse.

Cocaine has undoubtedly become a central feature of the addict's life-style by the time he or she seeks admission to the hospital. It is critical in the assessment to determine the people, places, and things associated with cocaine use, because the addict will need to have these cues removed from the environment wherever possible, prior to discharge from the hospital. Detailed questions should focus on from whom and where the addict obtains his or her cocaine. The places where cocaine is stored, at home or at work, should be identified and any hidden cocaine should be confiscated. The people with whom the addict uses and secures cocaine need to be identified. If the patient does not wish to identify these people, this generally indicates a denial of the need for help, a wish to continue associating with these people, and/or a distrust of the treaters. These issues need to confronted. There should be a detailed discussion of the patient's financial status. For many addicts, having cash is a stimulus to use cocaine, and access to large amounts of cash may need to be curtailed. Patients often feel under pressure to repay old debts, and may plan to use cocaine or other drug dealing as a means to raise cash. Although the addict's intent is not to relapse, the result in inevitable, and the issue of engaging in such potentially dangerous behavior needs to be confronted early in treatment. Finally, it is important to ascertain how much the addict has told significant others about the addiction. As treatment progresses, the addict will need to enlist significant others as supporters of abstinence. In our experience, reluctance to disclose the addiction to significant others is a poor prognostic sign.

There are protean medical manifestations of cocaine use. Below are listed several of the signs to look for on admission physical exam and medical history:

1. *Vital signs.* Heart rate, blood pressure, and respiratory rate may all be increased if the patient used cocaine immediately prior to admission. Hyperpyrexia (increased temperature) is seen with large use of toxic amounts of cocaine. Elevations in these vital signs may also indicate impending withdrawal from other drugs.

2. *Weight.* Cocaine addiction may lead to weight loss because of cocaine's actions as an appetite suppressant, and the addict's self-neglect. The addict's weight will generally increase in the hospital, and this can be pointed out as a measure of progress.

3. *Skin.* Skin should be examined for needle tracks, and "skin popping" blisters. Occasionally these are hidden by tattoos.

   Because cocaine binge use requires frequent reinjections (owing to cocaine's short half-life), most intravenous users have tracks.

4. *Head, eyes, ears, nose, and throat.* Ocular fundi should be examined for emboli. Intranasal users frequently have local damage to the nasal mucosa and septum, leading to chronic rhinitis. Dental problems are common owing to neglect of self-care and cocaine's local anesthetic effects.

5. *Lungs.* Lung damage may be manifested as an increased respiratory rate or abnormal breath sounds. Possible etiologies

include pulmonary hypertension owing to contaminants of intravenous drug use and direct damage from inhalation of freebase cocaine.

6. *Cardiac*. Murmurs may reflect valve damage from endocarditis. A history of cocaine-induced chest pain may reflect cocaine toxicity, panic attacks, or early atherosclerotic disease.

7. *Abdomen*. Hepatosplenomegaly or hepatic tenderness may be present.

8. *Gynecological*. Sexually transmitted diseases are common in this population. Exposure to gonococcis, trichomonae, and *Treponema pallidum* (syphilis) should all be considered.

9. *Extremities*. Emboli from injected contaminants may be present. Septic emboli are often manifestations of endocarditis. Abscesses and phlebitis often occur at injection sites.

10. *Neurological*. Mental status changes are discussed later. Stereotypies may be present, such as bruxism, or picking tics owing to tactile hallucinations. There may be mild parkinsonian features such as myoclonic tremors and bradykinesias. Focal neurological signs suggest a prior cerebrovascular accident.

Admission laboratory work should include serum electrolytes, blood urea nitrogen, creatinine, complete blood count with differential, liver function tests, screening for syphilis, a pregnancy test in women, and hepatitis B antigen profile (some would recommend hepatitis D antigen as well). HIV testing should be offered, as these patients are at increased risk of exposure to HIV, and the diagnosis of HIV positivity requires medical follow-up. Discussion of this testing may need to be deferred until later in the hospitalization; the patient should not be intoxicated during pre-test counseling. It is recommended that a screening skin test for tuberculosis be placed on patients at risk. An electrocardiagram should also be obtained. One study found that 8 of 21 consecutive male patients admitted to a 28-day inpatient cocaine treatment program had an episode of ST segment elevation during the first several weeks of their withdrawal (Nademanee et al., 1989). A chest roentgenogram is only indicated if there are pulmonary symptoms. Pulmonary function tests may be indicated for heavy freebase users.

As discussed in previous chapters, cocaine withdrawal symptoms are usually mild and self-limited. No medication has demonstrated efficacy in furthering abstinence in inpatients. The most distressing symptom of the crash phase of cocaine withdrawal, as defined by Gawin and Kleber (1986), is insomnia. Crashing patients may crave sleep more than they crave cocaine, and it is appropriate to treat insomnia on the inpatient ward with short-acting benzodiazepines. Initial treatment should be aimed at providing crashing or withdrawing patients a quiet, nonstimulating environment. Later as patients experience more craving, treatment needs to focus on keeping them busy in groups and therapy.

PSYCHOTROPIC MEDICATIONS

Patients may present to the inpatient unit in a state of acute intoxication, delirium, or psychosis. The symptoms of cocaine intoxication include feelings of activation, euphoria, disinhibition, and increased self-esteem. More severe toxicity is indicated by confusion, paranoia, and psychosis. The delirious patient may have symptoms of muscle twitching, seizures, and even cardiac and focal neurological symptoms; these need to be managed in a general hospital setting. The treatment of the less critical symptoms during the first few days consists of careful observation, and helping to protect the patient from dangerous or self-destructive behavior. A short-acting benzodiazapine such as lorazepam can be very useful in the initial phase of treatment to help with sleep disturbance and episodic agitation. Given in sufficient doses, lorazepam can be as effective as neuroleptics for behavioral control, but with fewer side-effects.

Patients who are dependent on other substances may require medical detoxification and frequent monitoring of vital signs and withdrawal symptoms. Concomitant dependence on high-dose benzodiazepines or alcohol can be managed with a long-half-life benzodiazepine such as diazepam. Patients addicted to high-dose benzodiazepines can be begun on diazepam at approximately 40% of their reported daily benzodiazepine consumption and the dosage tapered by 10% per day (Harrison, Bust, Naranjo, Kaplan, & Sellers, 1984). In patients who are abusing opiates, the need for detoxification can be determined by injection of 0.8 mg of intramuscular naloxone (Wang, Wiesen, Lamid, & Rod, 1974); only opiate-dependent patients will have opiate withdrawal symptoms precipitated within 30 minutes of the challenge. Detoxification can be accomplished using clonidine and naltrexone (Vining, Kosten, & Kleber, 1988). In patients who need to be detoxified from both opiates and benzodiazepines, the patient should be stabilized on diazepam, and then sequentially withdrawn from first the opiates and then the diazepam. Alternatively, a patient can be stabilized on methadone, and then be withdrawn from benzodiazepines first, followed by the methadone later.

For the first several days after hospitalization, a psychiatric diagnosis may be difficult to make. Acute cocaine intoxication and abstinence can mimic an organic syndrome with cognitive impairment, mania, depression, or attention deficit disorder. When feasible, making a formal psychiatric diagnosis should be deferred for a week, or until after abstinence symptoms have cleared. Symptomatic treatment can be offered for the acute psychiatric problems, and, as noted above, lorazepam is an effective and safe medication for many patients.

After the patient has been thus stabilized any underlying psychiatric disorders that complicated the treatment picture can be addressed. The diagnosis of depression requires symptoms of depression lasting for 1–2 weeks after last cocaine use. During this time, the patient should be observed for suicidal ideation on the unit. In some cases, it may be possible to obtain a history of depression that antedated cocaine use. In most of these patients, we believe that desipramine is the drug of choice. In addition to providing effective antidepressant treatment, desipramine has been shown in a double-blind placebo-controlled trial to facilitate the achievement of abstinence and lower cocaine craving (Gawin et al., 1989). The clinician should be alert to side effects unique to this population, including the jitteriness from desipramine-triggered cocaine craving (Weiss, 1988). Another side effect sometimes seen early in treatment with desipramine is a worsening of anxiety and panic symptoms. This is especially true in patients in whom cocaine has triggered panic attacks, or in whom cocaine has exacerbated an underlying panic disorder. In panic disorder patients, the desipramine dose needs to be titrated up more slowly. Another drug that has antidepressant and potentially anticraving efficacy is buproprion (Margolin et al., 1991). Treatment of depression with monoamine oxidase (MAO) inhibitors is extremely risky in cocaine addicts because of the potential hypertensive interaction with cocaine. In patients who do not respond to desipramine, consideration can be given to trying other tricyclic antidepressants such as nortriptyline, or to a trial of fluoxetine.

Other affective disorders such as mania or cyclothymia may be treated with lithium or carbamazepine. Use of carbamazepine may confer the additional benefit of some reduction in cocaine craving. Symptoms of inattention, impulsivity, and hyperactivity that persist after 1 week of hospitalization should be corroborated with a developmental history to rule out a diagnosis of attention deficit disorder. Antisocial personality disorder is a common comorbid diagnosis in cocaine addicts, and generally portends a poor response to pharmacological interventions.

Several unique features of prescribing medications to cocaine addicts warrant mentioning. These patients are extremely sensitive to side effects and have often been amateur pharmacists. They should be told in advance about side effects and that these are common, normal reactions to these medications which will improve with time. Patients should be explicitly warned against adjusting doses, especially with medications like the tricyclic antidepressants. Because of prior drug use, these patients tend to assume that more of any given medication will work better and faster.

ELEMENTS OF TREATMENT

Framing the Treatment Experience: Orientation and Treatment Contract

It is useful to think about the treatment experience as a cohesive process having an introductory or orientation phase to engage and evaluate the patient, a treatment phase, and a discharge phase. Within this process are multiple roles and perspectives for both staff and patients. What the staff should expect from the patient changes over the course of an inpatient stay, as should the expectations of the patients themselves.

For the staff, the initial task must be to evaluate and engage the patient. From the time of admission, the inpatient experience must work toward involving the patient in treatment. Staff must be aware that the patient may be in denial about his or her illness and not reject the patient because he or she evidently lacks motivation for treatment. If the patient is acutely intoxicated or the drug use status is uncertain, staff must take care to monitor mental status and to help the new patient understand the routine of the inpatient unit. An initial psychiatric evaluation should be followed by a more detailed evaluation once the patient is sober.

Patients need to be oriented to their expected behavior and treatment participation on the inpatient unit. An orientation group specifically set aside to introduce patients to the unit, can be an efficient and orderly method of transmitting necessary information to the patient. This, in combination with an individual orientation to the unit rules and expectations, is usually sufficient.

Once the patient is oriented to the treatment milieu, development of a treatment contract should be considered. This is a written document that outlines the rules and expectations of the treatment program along with the patient's identified goals in treatment. The patient has an opportunity to read and discuss the contract and can then be asked to sign it as an acknowledgement that the basic expectations of treatment are understood. This also acknowledges patients' initial goals of being on the inpatient unit. Once the treatment team has developed a more comprehensive plan of treatment, particular items relevant to a specific patient can be added.

Staff should expect the patient to become more involved in treatment after the first few days in the hospital. Initially, denial is common, and staff should expect to see an emerging and changing history from the patient as denial subsides. The amount of drug use, the consequences, and the reactions of others in the patient's life are all likely to undergo modification during the first phase of treatment. Helping patients come to terms with their addiction—that it is real, and that it has caused real consequences—is the staff goal.

As part of the orientation and treatment, it is helpful to involve any available family as early as possible. Just as with patients, so do family members need to understand the rules and expectations of the inpatient unit. On occasion family members may feel distrusted because of visiting restrictions or other unit rules, and the need for such restrictions must be explained to both the patient and family during the initial orientation. Often, families have their own dysfunctional nature, and failure to fully involve the family in how the unit works and what will be happening to their relative over the course of treatment can leave the family vulnerable to manipulation by the patient that may subvert the treatment process. An equally undesirable outcome is for families to undermine a patient's sobriety by trying to reinvolve the patient in a family crisis. Staff should maintain an open line of communication with any involved family members and make sure that they have a specific staff member to contact with questions.

Specific Elements of the Treatment Program and Milieu

The content of treatment programs varies and there is no single correct mix in structuring a program. Programs need to be flexible enough to meet the needs and diversity of their particular patient population. There are, however, some major components that are a part of almost all treatment programs for cocaine and other substance abuse.

Most treatment is organized around a milieu and group treatment program. Part of the group program should be educational and deal with the concepts of cocaine addiction, specific effects of cocaine and other drugs, and relapse prevention. The 12-step approach, as embodied in the philosophy of Alcoholics Anonymous and applied to cocaine addiction through the work of Cocaine Anonymous, is one of the most widespread of recovery methods. These so-called fellowship programs provide both an organizing structure and a nationwide self-help network that can supplement other structured outpatient care. The use of step groups, daily meditation, and life story groups can all enhance the inpatient program. The presence of speakers at 12-step meetings can offer role models for patients and provide living proof that it is possible to conduct one's life without using drugs.

The milieu itself deserves some explanation, in that there are some special considerations in managing a unit where substance abuse and cocaine addiction are treated. The nature of addiction to cocaine and other drugs includes patient urges to use the drugs and the fact that relapse is common. Part of the goal of the inpatient unit should be to provide a safe, drug-free environment in which the patient can begin the recovery process. To do this it is necessary to closely monitor all visitors to the unit, including the patient's family. During the detoxification phase of treatment, patients may be asked to have no visitors. At this point in treatment, the addict is at high risk to make bad decisions and may ask visitors to bring drugs into the hospital setting. Later, patients should be asked to prepare a list of people with whom they would like to visit and who would be supportive in the recovery process. Anyone outside immediate family should be considered carefully by the treatment team before allowing them to visit. Unfortunately, many people with severe addictions have few friends who are not also drug users, and it is dangerous for both the patient and others on the unit if these active users also come to visit. In some cases other family members may be significant abusers of either drugs or alcohol. Whether they should visit needs to be considered carefully and perhaps allowed only in the context of their participation in family treatment of some type or with staff-supervised visits.

With the outside boundaries of the unit monitored, it is still necessary to provide an internal check of the security of the unit. This is usually done by obtaining periodic urine drug screening tests. The frequency with which these tests should be performed varies between programs, from once or twice a week with an additional urine sample obtained any time the patient is off the unit on any unsupervised activity, to daily on a routine basis. It is advisable to obtain a urine sample at times when a patient's behavior seems odd or out of character with what the staff has come to expect. This level of monitoring is necessary to insure the safety of all patients on the unit and the integrity of the treatment program.

When ordering a urine drug screen it is useful to understand exactly what type of laboratory methods will be used and what the results will mean. Thin-layer chromatography (TLC) is a commonly used technique to screen urine for the presence of illicit substances. It is inexpensive to perform and gives a rapid, qualitative answer as to the presence or absence of the screened-for substances. It is not, however, particularly sensitive or specific (in most laboratories), and after 12–24 hours cocaine and its metabolites are usually no longer detectable.

Enzyme multiplied immunoassay test (EMIT) technology is more sensitive and somewhat more expensive. Cocaine can be detected for 2–3 days. Gas chromatography in combination with mass spectroscopy provides highly sensitive results which can both detect small amounts of drugs and provide a quantitative measure of exactly how much was present. This added precision comes at added cost and may not be needed in some situations. For example, a urine drug screen obtained within an hour or two following a patient's return from a visit home can be screened using TLC or EMIT technology and would probably provide an adequate answer to the question of whether the patient maintained sobriety while outside the hospital setting. On the other hand, a rumor of drug use on the unit over the weekend cannot be effectively investigated on Monday afternoon using TLC, and a more sensitive drug screen will be needed if accurate data are to be obtained.

Managing the Psychosocial Aspects of Treatment

Most patients with serious addiction problems have created havoc in their lives outside the hospital prior to admission. In order to provide the best possible chance of recovery, these outside problems must be addressed either by the patient or the treatment team. Financial difficulties are common and should be discussed in a straightforward manner with the patient, and if necessary, the family. If the patient is unemployed, part of the treatment plan may call for examination of employment alternatives, vocational training, contacting the old employer to see if a job can be retrieved, working with employee assistance personnel, and making the patient aware of benefits such as unemployment insurance. As mentioned earlier, patients may have legal problems resulting from their cocaine use. Theft, drug dealing, motor vehicle accidents, and assaultive behavior toward family all represent common consequences of severe cocaine addiction. The treatment program cannot solve these problems for the patient. However, an awareness of the problems and an effort to help the patient solve them is needed. Advice or information about how to contact an attorney or legal aid service can help bring some order to a situation that may otherwise be overwhelming and lead to relapse rather than resolution.

Family therapy is an extremely valuable part of the treatment armamentarium for this population. The family is usually frustrated with the patient's inability to stop using drugs, but often there are numerous codependent behaviors that unwittingly contribute to an individual being able to continue abusing drugs. Therapy sessions with the family and patient plus participation in a larger, multifamily group program have both proven helpful in providing education and treatment for all members of the family. Studies suggest that intervening in the family system may be one of the most influential treatment approaches for this population, and whenever possible the inpatient unit should use this in the patient's treatment program.

CRITERIA FOR DISCHARGE

Some guidelines that can be applied in assessing a patient's readiness for discharge are shown in Table 16.2. As with admission criteria, no one factor governs the decision that a patient is now ready for transition to outpatient therapy, and usually a combination of factors suggests when the patient is ready.

DISCHARGE PLANNING

Once the patient completes an inpatient stay, there must be a transition to follow-up outpatient care. Planning for this should be integrated into the inpatient program from the time of admission. Failure to engage the patient in outpatient aftercare leads to relapse in virtually all patients. Some of the treatment interventions mentioned previously should become part of the transition process from inpatient to outpatient treatment. Attendance at 12-step meetings that have begun on the inpatient unit should continue in the community. It is helpful to have patients begin attending some community 12-step meetings even in advance of formal discharge from the hospital. Family work can continue on an outpatient basis, and connection to either individual or family counselors should be made prior to discharge whenever possible.

It is helpful for inpatient clinicians to become familiar with the outpatient treatment resources in the community, including substance

TABLE 16.2. Criteria for Discharge

Substance abuse recovery
　Drug urges are under control
　Patient is able to make a commitment to recovery
　Patient is able to acknowledge addiction (steps 1 & 2 of 12-step program)
Psychiatric
　Psychiatric symptoms (mood, anxiety, paranoia) are stable
Environmental
　Outside problems have a plan of action
　Family, treatment team, and patient all feel patient is ready to leave
　Outpatient follow-up is in place

abuse programs and psychiatric resources for dual-diagnosis patients. The interface between psychiatric problems such as depression and chemical dependency on cocaine is frequently problematic. One needs to appreciate that not all substance abuse programs will accept or feel comfortable with managing the outpatient follow-up of patients with psychiatric problems, especially if they are on psychotropic medication. These factors need to be considered when making an outpatient referral.

During the inpatient stay, some patients will be identified who are clearly in need of a continued highly structured, long-term treatment approach. Residential programs that provide this type of structure are generally in short supply but can be lifesaving for some patients. Other structured options include halfway house settings, structured apartment programs, and day hospital programs. For patients lacking the time-structuring benefits of employment, the day hospital can be a useful transitional tool. When day hospitals are considered, it is best to find programs with expertise in chemical dependency.

CONCLUSIONS

Inpatient treatment is a limited resource that should be used wisely to benefit those patients most in need. A well-structured program should provide for a comprehensive evaluation of the patient's needs including psychiatric, medical, social, legal, family, and substance abuse recovery. The program needs to work toward rapidly engaging the patient in treatment and toward a smooth transition back to the community. The use of pharmacotherapy to enhance the recovery process should be evaluated on an individual basis as part of the treatment plan for every patient.

REFERENCES

Gawin, F. H, & Kleber, H. D. (1986). Abstinence symptomatology and psychiatric diagnosis in cocaine abusers: Clinical observations. *Archives of General Psychiatry, 43*, 107–113.

Gawin, F. M., Kleber, H. D., Byck, R., Rounsaville, B. J., Kosten, T. R., Jatlow, P. I., & Morgan, C. (1989). Desipramine facilitation of initial cocaine abstinence. *Archives of General Psychiatry, 46*, 117–121.

Harrison, M., Busto, U., Naranjo, A., Kaplan, H. L., & Sellers, E. M.(1984). Diazepam tapering in detoxification for high-dose benzodiazepine abuse. *Clinical Pharmacology and Therapeutics, 36*(4), 527–533.

Jaffe, A. J., & Kilbey, M. M. (1992). *The Cocaine Expentancy Questionnaire (CEQ): Its construction and predictive utility.* Manuscript submitted for publication.

Jaffe, A. J., Kilbey, M. M., & Rosenbaum, G. R. (1989). Cocaine related expectancies: Their domain and implications for treatment. *Pharmacology, Biochemistry, and Behavior, 32*(4), 1094.

Margolin, A., Kostin, T. R., Petrakis, I., Avants, S. K., & Kosten, T. A. (1991). Buproprion reduces cocaine abuse in methadone maintained patients. *Archives of General Psychiatry, 48*, 87.

McLellan, A., Luborsky, L., Moody, G., & O'Brien, C. (1980). An improved diagnostic evaluation instrument for substance abuse patients: The addiction severity scale index. *Journal of Nervous and Mental Disease, 168*, 26–33.

Miller, W. R., & Hester, R. K. (1984). The effectiveness of alcoholism treatment: What research reveals. *Treating Addictive Behaviors Processes of Change.* New York: Plenum Press.

Nademanee, K., Gorelick, D., Josephson, M., Ryan, M., Wildins, J., Robertson, H., Mody, F. V., & Intrachot, V. (1989). Myocardial ischemia during cocaine withdrawal. *Annals of Internal Medicine, 111*, 876–880.

O'Brien, C. P., Alterman, A. L., Walter, D., Childress, A. R., & McLellan, A. T. (1990). *Evaluation of cocaine dependence treatment.* (National Institute on Drug Abuse Research Monograph No. 95). Washington, DC: U. S. Government Printing Office.

Pettinati, H. M., Myers, K., Evans, V. D., Jensen, J. M., Tracy, J. I., Kaplan, F. N., & Ruetsch, C. R. (1991, June). *The differences in attrition and early outcome of inpatient versus outpatient treatment for cocaine dependence.* Abstract presented at the meeting of the Committee for the Problems of Drug Dependence, Palm Beach, FL.

Vining, E., Kosten, T. R., & Kleber, H. D. (1988). Clinical utility of rapid clonidine-naltrexone detoxification for opioid abusers. *British Journal of Addictions, 83*, 567–575.

Wang, R. I. H., Wiesen, R. L., Lamid, S., & Roh, B. L. Rating the presence of opiate dependence. *Clinical Pharmacology and Therapeutics, 16*, 653–658.

Washton, A. M., Gold, M. S., & Pottash, A. C. (1985). Treatment outcome in cocaine abusers. In L. Harris (Ed.), *Problems of drug dependence 1985* (National Institute on Drug Abuse Research Monograph No. 67). Washington, DC: U. S. Government Printing Office.

Weiss, R. D. (1988). Relapse to cocaine abuse after initiating desipramine treatment. *Journal of the American Medical Association, 260*(17), 2545–2546.

CHAPTER SEVENTEEN

Comorbid Psychopathology and Cocaine Addiction

Douglas M. Ziedonis, MD

COCAINE ADDICTS often present for treatment with complaints of psychiatric symptoms. The clinician must try to make an accurate assessment in order to develop a comprehensive treatment plan that addresses both the substance abuse problems and psychiatric symptoms. The relationship of psychopathology and substance abuse is complex. Psychiatric patients may use drugs to self-medicate symptoms and are at risk to become drug dependent. Substance abuse in psychiatric patients can change the symptomatology, prognosis, and treatment of psychiatric illness. In addition, any drug use by psychiatric patients may lead to increased psychiatric and medical symptoms. Primary substance abusers can develop psychiatric symptoms from their drug use and/or life situation, with a deleterious effect on the course of their substance abuse disorder. In recent years, patients with a mental illness and a substance abuse disorder have been labeled "dual diagnosis" patients. These dually diagnosed patients are being identified more frequently in both the mental health and chemical dependence treatment systems, and many clinicians in these settings require new knowledge and skills in improving treatment of, and attitude toward, these patients. Understandably, clinicians in both fields have requested additional training in "dual diagnosis" issues (Brown, Ridgely, Pepper, Levine, & Ryglewicz, 1989).

In general, dually diagnosed patients tend to seek professional treatment more frequently, have a poorer prognosis, require additional treatment approaches including medications, and require modifications to traditional approaches such as the 12-step recovery, relapse prevention, social skills training, medical and psychiatric strategies, and counseling approaches. Traditional chemical dependence treatment and mental health treatment approaches have been inadequate for this population, and patients have been shuffled between the two systems because they fail to fit into the artificially created treatment slots labeled "psychiatric" or "substance abuse."

The "dual diagnosis" label has been helpful in increasing the awareness of this clinical problem and in forcing clinicians, administrators, and researchers to focus on this population. Unfortunately, this term simplifies the complexities of this population, and clinicians at both mental health and chemical dependence programs use the "dual diagnosis" term as if it represented a unique entity. In actuality, "dual diagnosis" is a broad term that represents a complex and heterogeneous group of patients with many subtypes requiring specific treatment approaches. Dual-diagnosis patients can have a wide range of psychiatric and substance abuse disorders, including the abuse of alcohol, cocaine, opiates, benzodiazepines, nicotine, and marijuana. Dually diagnosed patients often have more than just one substance abuse disorder and one mental illness. They are often polydrug addicts, may have a serious medical condition such as AIDS, and may have more than one psychiatric disorder.

This chapter focuses on the cocaine abuser with psychiatric comorbidity, emphasizing diagnostic and specific treatment approaches. "Subtyping" the cocaine addicts by psychiatric disorders has been suggested because of the high prevalence of psychiatric conditions. These subtypes appear to be clinically relevant because of the differences in clinical presentations, family history information, prognosis, and response to specific treatment approaches (Weiss & Mirin, 1986). This chapter focuses on six psychiatric diagnostic subtypes:

1. Affective disorders—depression and bipolar disorder
2. Anxiety disorders—including phobia, generalized anxiety, and panic disorder
3. Attention deficit disorder
4. Personality disorders—including the antisocial, narcissistic, and borderline patient
5. Schizophrenia—the chronically mentally ill patient
6. Cognitive disorders—traumatic brain injury, AIDS dementia, and withdrawal from drugs

Subtyping dually diagnosed patients demonstrates the heterogeneity of this population and the need for specific treatment approaches. For example, the chronically mentally ill patient with a diagnosis of schizophrenia and cocaine abuse requires a very different strategy than the cocaine addict with concurrent depression, antisocial personality, and alcohol abuse. Usually the psychiatric diagnosis dictates the balance in emphasis between the addiction and psychological models. Of course, even within subtypes there are subgroups of patients based on specific psychiatric disorders, gender, race, treatment responsiveness, and level of motivation for treatment. Also, the specific needs of individual patients must be evaluated and addressed in matching specific treatment approaches to specific patients.

Clinicians' attitudes are often challenged in the treatment of the dually diagnosed patient. Often, clinicians believe in the disease concept only for their area of expertise. The use of medications (pharmacotherapy) in treatment may require an attitudinal adjustment for the chemical dependence specialist. Many dually diagnosed patients require the use of medications for either their mental illness or their substance abuse disorder or both.

DIAGNOSTIC ISSUES

An initial evaluation of any patient in either a mental health or chemical dependence setting should include a mental status examination and a review of the patient's use of alcohol and other drugs. A mental status examination should include a patient's general appearance, including behavior and attitude toward the clinician; the state of alertness; ability to attend and concentrate; orientation to time and place; mood and affect, including sleep patterns, appetite, suicidal or homicidal ideation; thought or perceptual disturbances, including hallucinations and delusions; and cognitive abilities, including memory, fund of knowledge, and ability to read and write. In reviewing drug usage, consider issues of loss of control, insight into problems, concurrent medical problems, and psychosocial complications.

Each patient should be asked about his or her previous substance abuse and psychiatric treatment. This information should include the previous diagnoses, severity of illness, the type of treatment (e.g., methadone, antidepressants or other medications, electroconvulsive therapy, behavioral therapy, supportive therapy), intensity of treatment (outpatient, inpatient, partial hospitalization), and length of treatment (dates). Also, patients should be asked questions about their family history for substance abuse and psychiatric disorders.

An initial evaluation should include asking about medical conditions and use of prescribed medications. Psychiatric symptoms can develop not only from the intoxication/withdrawal of alcohol and other abused substances, but also from the use of prescription drugs like benzodiazepines, barbiturates, steroids, antihypertensives, nonster-oidals, antihistamines, and antibiotics. There are many medical conditions that can mimic psychiatric conditions, including endocrine disorders (thyroid), systemic and/or central nervous system infections (neurosyphilis, HIV/AIDS), collagen vascular disorders (lupus), neurological disorders (multiple sclerosis, temporal lobe seizures), and cardiac disorders. Also a patient's trauma history should be explored for possible traumatic brain injury (Skinner, Holt, Schuller, Roy, & Israel, 1984). These medically induced organic mental disorders tend to include symptoms of delirium like agitation, confusion, disorientation, and diminished sensorium, but also include anxiety, depression or mania, mood lability, bizarre thoughts, and a variety of hallucinations. Given the poor self-care of many addicts and the likelihood of consequent medical problems, patients should have a physical exam that includes routine laboratory blood tests, and monitoring of vital signs.

Urine toxicology and Breathalyzer tests are important parts of the diagnostic process. In evaluating a positive or negative test result, the clinician should be aware of the time required for a drug to be metabolized. This knowledge improves the usefulness and interpretability of the test results. Most patients will admit to cocaine use if a urine test is obtained; however, chronically mentally ill patients frequently still deny an use of cocaine even after being tested and/or receiving a positive test result.

Efforts should be made to obtain information from the patient's family or friends. Like traditional substance abusers, dually diagnosed patients will attempt to protect their drug supply, deny using drugs, and minimize the consequences of their usage. These collateral contacts can be invaluable sources of information on the patient and the family history, and often these individuals can help in the treatment process. A strong family history of either a substance use disorder or a psychiatric disorder may be clinically important. Of note, cocaine abusers with a strong family history for affective disorders are at higher risk for an underlying affective disorder (Weiss, Mirin, Griffin, & Michael, 1988).

Clinicians are urged to make a psychiatric diagnosis on the basis of DSM-III-R diagnostic criteria (American Psychiatric Association, 1987). Using diagnostic criteria helps the clinician to focus on the differences between symptoms versus syndromes, such as drinking and alcoholism, sadness and major depression, and nervousness and panic disorder. For example, a patient with a major depression diagnosis would have substantial depressive symptoms which lasted for most of the day, interfered with functioning, and occurred nearly every day for at least a 2-week period (Schuckit & Monteiro, 1988; American Psychiatric Association, 1987).

Some clinicians and researchers have used structured instruments to help in the diagnostic assessment. Several studies comparing the different instruments suggest that the special nature of the dual-diagnosis population favors a clinician-administered structured interview, such as the SCID (Structured Clinical Interview for DSM-III-R). The combination of a clinical assessment and a structured interview can lead to a more reliable and valid diagnosis than can either approach alone (Ford, Hillard, Giesler, Lassen, & Thomas, 1989).

An initial approach to tease apart the psychiatric and drug induced symptoms is to obtain an extensive history on the development of both substance abuse and mental illness. Consider drawing out a timeline (Schuckit & Monteiro, 1988), noting when the patient first met criteria for a psychiatric disorder and when for a substance abuse disorder. In establishing a timeline, the clinician emphasizes diagnoses not symptoms, and makes an effort to disentangle the time course of the disorders. The primary disorder develops first, and the secondary disorder occurs in the context of the primary disorder. Determination of the primary disorder requires that a careful history be taken from both the patient and collateral persons. Also, a primary or coexisting disorder can be made if a new disorder developed during any periods of abstinence of 3 or more months (Schuckit & Monteiro, 1988). Some practical problems in organizing the timeline include patients' varying ability to recall information, the fact that many patients have few protracted drug-free periods, and that the typical onset of mental illness occurs in which many patients already have developed a substance abuse disorder. Patients with a primary psychiatric disorder can be started on pharmacotherapy, earlier if necessary.

Without a clear history of a primary psychiatric disorder, the diagnosis of a primary or coexisting psychiatric disorder in the context of recent drug use is difficult. The clinician should try to do the evaluation after a period of prolonged abstinence from cocaine and other drugs, ideally 6 weeks. During the evaluation, the clinician should document recent drug use and track the time a patient maintains abstinence.

Recent drug use can cause a variety of psychiatric symptoms, and these symptoms can vary depending on whether they are associated with chronic cocaine use, intoxication, acute withdrawal, and protracted withdrawal states. The psychiatric symptoms can include paranoia/psychosis, mood lability, euphoria, sleep disturbance, appetite disturbance, grandiosity, depression, agitation, irritability, anhedonia, suicidal ideation, and anxiety (Post, Kotin, & Goodwin, 1974; Gawin & Kleber, 1986). Many cocaine addicts complain of severe psychiatric symptoms on initial evaluation, but most of these symptoms are temporary and are secondary to the pharmacological properties of cocaine. An initial preliminary diagnosis made after the first 2 weeks of cocaine abstinence should exclude most of the psychiatric symptoms caused by acute intoxication and acute withdrawal.

Although waiting 6 weeks may result in a more accurate diagnosis, the clinician must treat severe psychiatric symptoms immediately. For example, a patient who recently stopped bingeing on cocaine may develop acute suicidal ideation and severe depressive symptoms, which are the result of the biological effects of cocaine withdrawal. This patient's suicidal ideation must be addressed and inpatient monitoring considered. The cause of the symptoms does not affect the acute treatment plan, but will influence the long-term prognosis and treatment. Ultimately, this patient's symptoms may resolve quickly and be secondary to cocaine's effects. The accuracy of a diagnosis should improve by one's continued observation of a patient's condition over time (Schuckit & Monteiro, 1988).

A careful psychiatric and substance abuse evaluation is essential in designing a specific treatment plan. However, the treatment plan should not be based on a polarization of "primary versus secondary" diagnostic clusters; a diagnosis should predict treatment but not necessarily eliminate a type of treatment modality. For example, an addict with primary depression may receive traditional antidepressant pharmacotherapy, and an addict with secondary depression should not be excluded from consideration for pharmacotherapy. Continued research is needed in both the assessment of dual-diagnosis patients in general and the treatment of the various specific dual-diagnosis subtypes.

EPIDEMIOLOGY: RATES OF COMORBID PSYCHIATRIC DISORDERS

Several epidemiological studies have investigated the rates of cocaine abuse and psychiatric disorders in a variety of settings and cohorts. Some studies occurred in treatment-seeking cohorts, whereas others evaluated non-treatment-seeking community populations. Studies of treatment-seeking populations were done in different clinical settings including inpatient versus outpatient sites and primary psychiatric clinics versus primary substance abuse clinics. Also, studies in similar clinical settings vary by different populations (e.g., those in inner-city, suburban, or Veterans Administration clinics). Also, assessment strategies in the studies varied according to which standardized diagnostic instruments were used, whether or not a friend or family member was interviewed for collateral information, diagnostic criteria or categories (e.g., DSM-III-R and Research Diagnostic Criteria [RDC]) were used, the timing of the assessment relative to the last use of cocaine, and whether the primary versus secondary disorder distinction was considered or ignored. These methodological and site differences explain some of the variability in the reported rates of comorbidity. Overall, these epidemiological studies demonstrate clearly that cocaine abusers have high rates of psychiatric comorbidity and that high rates of cocaine abuse are found in psychiatric patients (Rounsaville et al., 1991; Regier et al., 1990).

In addition, the reader must distinguish between "lifetime" rates and "current" rates of the disorders. Obviously, lifetime rates will be higher and include current rates. Most studies of psychiatric illness in cocaine abusers have not been longitudinal studies; the latter might be able to assess the temporal sequencing of the disorders. Schottenfeld, Carroll, and Rounsaville have written an excellent in-depth review of these epidemiological studies (Schottenfeld, Carroll, & Rounsaville, in press).

The National Institute of Mental Health's ECA study (Regier et al., 1990) evaluated the prevalence of rates of mental disorders, alcohol use disorders, and other drug use disorders by interviewing 20,291 people with e Diagnostic Interviewing Schedule using DSM-III criteria. The estimated lifetime prevalence rates were 13.5% for alcohol use disorders and 6.1% for other drug use disorders, with only 0.2% having a cocaine use disorder. The current prevalence rates are 2.8% for alcohol use disorders and 1.3% for all other drug use disorders.

Of the people with a cocaine use disorder, 76.1% had another comorbid psychiatric disorder, which is 11.3 times greater than the general population (based on 11.3 odds ratio [OR]). Also, relative to other substance use disorders, the rate of psychiatric comorbidity is 36.6% for those with an alcohol use disorder (OR of 2.3) and 53.1% for those with any other drug disorder (OR of 4.5).

In the ECA study, cocaine use disorders were associated with schizophrenia (16.7%, OR of 8.1), affective disorders (34.7%, OR of 8.6), anxiety disoders (33%, OR of 11), and DSM-III antisocial personality disorder (42.7%, OR of 12.3). The community sample ECA study data can be used for comparison with the treatment-seeking samples like the New Haven Cocaine Diagnostic Study (Rounsaville et al., 1991).

The New Haven Cocaine Diagnostic Study (Rounsaville et al., 1991) reported current and lifetime psychiatric disorders in substance abuse treatment-seeking cocaine addicts. Patients were evaluated in both an inpatient ($n = 149$) and outpatient setting ($n = 149$), and there were no significant differences between these groups. The typical patient was a 28-year-old, white (64%), lower social class (76% Hollingshead class 4 or 5), intranasal-cocaine-abusing (47%) male (69%). Twenty-seven percent of these patients had a current affective disorder (61.5% lifetime), and 15.7% a current anxiety disorder (22.1% lifetime). The current diagnosis of alcoholism was diagnosed in 28.9% of the patients, with a lifetime prevalence of 61.1%. Compared with the general population, these patients had a higher rate of *current* major depression (4.7%), alcoholism (28.9%), minor bipolar disorders (e.g., hypomania, 2%; cyclothymic personality, 20%), anxiety disorders (phobia, 12%; generalized anxiety, 3.7%), antisocial personality disorder (33% by DSM-III criteria; 7.7% by RDC criteria), and history of childhood attention deficit disorder (34.9%). Alcoholism and mood disorders (depression and minor bipolar) appeared to follow the onset of cocaine abuse, whereas the other psychiatric disorders preceded the cocaine abuse (Rounsaville et al., 1991). Of note, because many cocaine addicts also abuse alcohol, they are vulnerable to alcohol mood-altering affects.

Compared with non-treatment-seeking cocaine abusers, treatment seekers use cocaine in a higher intensity manner, have longer periods of depression, and have more adverse consequences associated with cocaine use, including drug overdoses and losses of jobs and relationships. The high rates of psychopathology in treatment-seeking cocaine abusers can be explained in part by "Berkson's bias," which suggests that patients with more problems are more likely to go for treatment (Berkson, 1946; Rounsaville et al., 1991).

The lifetime prevalence of schizophrenic disorders was only 1.3% in the New Haven Cocaine Study (Rounsaville et al., 1991). This low rate in substance abuse treatment-seeking populations contrasts with data from psychiatric treatment-seeking populations. In general, psychiatric patients abuse drugs at a higher rate than that for the general population, with some variability in the prevalence of specific drug diagnosis based on specific psychiatric diagnoses. For example, schizophrenic patients tend to abuse amphetamines and cocaine more than do other psychiatric patients or normal controls, with reported prevalence of cocaine-abusing schizophrenics ranging from 15–25% (Schneier & Siris, 1987; Dixon, Haas, Weiden Sweeney, & Frances, 1991; Galanter & Castaneda, 1988).

TREATMENT SYSTEM ISSUES

Treating the dual-diagnosis patient often requires that the clinician interact with professionals from a variety of services (alcohol and drug abuse, mental health, and criminal justice, to name a few). Until recently, interaction and coordination among these services has been limited; unfortunately, the current treatment system still has many barriers to integration of care. As more dually diagnosed patients are being recognized, treatment services are changing their programs and staffing patterns. Traditional 12-Step chemical dependence programs are learning to integrate other approaches like relapse prevention, psychiatric assessment and treatment approaches, and the medical model, including the use of pharmacotherapies. Traditional mental health programs are integrating 12-Step approaches, codependence treatment, and Relapse Prevention.

Dual-diagnosis treatment services are being organized in a multitude of ways. For some dual-diagnosis subtypes (depression, anxiety, personality disorders), modified traditional chemical dependence treatment approaches are providing complete dual-diagnosis treatment packages with minor modifications in staff and program. Chronically mentally ill patients tend to slip through traditional services, or they are able to receive both mental-health and chemical dependence treatment by attending multiple treatment sites either concurrently or sequentially. New dual diagnosis treatment programs for the chronically mentally ill are developing with integrated chemical-dependence and mental health services in one program (Minkoff & Drake, 1991).

Dual-Diagnosis Treatment Approaches for the Cocaine Addict

The remainder of this chapter focuses on the six psychiatric diagnosis "subtypes" of cocaine addicts discussed earlier:

1. Affective disorders—depression and bipolar (manic–depressive) disorder
2. Anxiety disorders—including phobia, generalized anxiety, and panic disorder
3. Attention deficit disorder.
4. Personality disorders—including the antisocial, narcissistic, and borderline patient
5. Schizophrenia—the chronically mentally ill patient
6. Cognitive Disorders—traumatic brain injury, AIDS dementia, and withdrawal from drugs

In general, the treatment of the dually diagnosed patient must address both the mental illness and the substance abuse disorder by integrating treatment approaches from each field, including both pharmacotherapy and psychotherapy. Of note, pharmacotherapy is used to a greater extent in this subpopulation than in the general addict population. In chemical dependence treatment programs, the staff must receive extra education on the use of medications, including the practical aspects of medication monitoring and the psychology of prescribing medications. The practical issues include monitoring side effects, medication blood levels, compliance, target symptoms that are to change with treatment; and explaining risks and benefits to the patient. Patients should also be warned about using nonaddictive medication in an addictive manner. When prescribing medications, the staff must be aware of how they and the patient perceive the use of medication. The message should be clear that the medication is only one part of the treatment process. Also, providing the staff and patients with Alcoholics Anonymous literature such as *The A.A. Member: Medications and Other Drugs* (Alcoholics Anonymous, 1984) can help focus a discussion on the differences between addictive and nonaddictive medications and on the official position of A.A., which suggests leaving medical decisions to treatment providers. Also, some dually diagnosed patients will need to be maintained on medications for years, like a diabetic receiving insulin (e.g., bipolar and schizophrenic patients) (Ziedonis & Kosten, 1991b).

AFFECTIVE DISORDERS

Depression

Although lifetime and current affective disorders are very common in cocaine addicts, most patients presenting for treatment have depressive symptoms and do not meet diagnostic criteria for depression. Depressive symptoms in these cocaine addicts may result from a variety of causes including the biological effects of cocaine withdrawal. Of note, however, is that the intensity of these initial depressive symptoms appears to be independent of other cocaine withdrawal symptoms such as the intensity of cocaine craving in newly abstinent chronic cocaine users (Ho, Cambor, Bodner, & Kreek, 1991). For many cocaine addicts, there is an initial improvement in depressive symptoms during the first month of treatment, with some patients maintaining this improved mood state. Unfortunately, many patients experience a reemergence of the depressive symptoms including difficulty concentrating, anxiety, fatigue, boredom, anhedonia, loss of sex drive, irritability, and insomnia. These symptoms occur after 6 weeks of abstinence and can last for months during a stage of recovery often referred to as "the wall" (Rawson, Obert, McCann, Smith, & Ling, 1990). During this time a patient is particularly vulnerable to resume cocaine use and discontinue treatment. Depressive symptoms can also be a reflection of the psychosocial consequences of cocaine addiction or a coexisting depressive disorder. Often, patients entering treatment have recently experienced a large number of life crises and significant life events, and depressions related to psychosocial consequences tend to be classified as reactive depressions.As mentioned earlier, many cocaine addicts abuse alcohol, and alcohol can potentiate the depressive symptoms of cocaine withdrawal.

The "self-medication theory" has been used to explain the use of cocaine in some people who have depressive symptoms. This theory suggests that people self-select a particular type of drug (cocaine, opiates, or alcohol) based on particular psychological characteristics or psychiatric diagnoses. For some people, the energizing properties of cocaine are thought to help overcome boredom, emptiness, and fatigue related to depression, personality disorder, or alcoholism. Also, some people develop severe depressive symptoms during cocaine withdrawal and are caught in a cycle of trying to medicate these withdrawal feelings. For other people, the use of cocaine leads to increased assertiveness, self-esteem, and frustration tolerance, which has been thought to relate to an addict's disturbances in "self-regulation," including an inability to recognize, tolerate, and regulate affect. Some people have chosen cocaine because it helps them augment a hyperactive life-style and fulfill an exaggerated need for self-sufficiency (Khantzian, 1985).

In treating the depressed cocaine addict, the clinician must assess for suicidality. Regardless of the etiology of the depressive symptoms, suicidal thoughts must be taken seriously because the incidence of suicide among substance abusers is about 20 times higher than among the general population. The risk for suicidality tends to increase with a history of prior suicide attempts, when a patient has a suicide plan, when the plan involves a lethal method that is accessible, with impaired judgment (including intoxication), with a family history of suicide, and when a patient lacks a support system (Blumenthal, Marzuk, & Mann, 1988). It is noteworthy that, depressed patients also can have a negative paradoxical reaction to cocaine use, including tearfulness and extreme mood lability (Post et al., 1974), and be at further risk for suicidality.

In general, a diagnosis of depression is a predictor of poor treatment response in opiate addicts (Rounsaville, Kosten, Weissman, & Kleber, 1986) and cocaine-dependent methadone maintained patients (Ziedonis & Kosten, 1991a). These outcomes can be improved when traditional psychiatric and substance abuse treatment approaches are integrated, including psychotherapy and pharmacotherapy.

Psychotherapy of depressed cocaine addicts should be specific to the stage of recovery and include individual, group, and family modalities. The initial focus should be on achieving and maintaining abstinence from drugs. The treatment plan should include opportunities for the patient to ventilate depressive feelings. Specific psychiatric approaches for treating depression include interpersonal psychotherapy (Weissman, Klerman, Rounsaville, Chevron, & Neu, 1982) and cognitive therapy (Beck, Rush, Shaw & Emery, 1979). Both of these specific approaches can be adapted easily to the structure of substance abuse relapse prevention strategies (Marlatt & Gordon, 1985; Carroll, Rounsaville, & Keller, 1991). Assertiveness training and mood management can also be helpful techniques (Hall, Munoz, & Reus, 1991).

In addition to psychotherapy, patients should be evaluated for the use of pharmacotherapy. Patients with primary depression often require pharmacotherapy, and a variety of antidepressants are available with different side effect profiles. Like substance abuse disorders, primary depression is a relapsing condition, and medications are often used as a form of maintenance treatment for 6 months to as long as several years. Cocaine addicts who are diagnosed with a secondary depression disorder should also be considered for pharmacotherapy. Dopamine agonists and tricyclic antidepressants have been helpful in stabilizing depressive symptoms and decreasing cocaine craving and use in cocaine addicts with secondary depression (Ziedonis & Kosten, 1991a, 1991b).

Bipolar Disorder

Cocaine addicts have a high rate for bipolar disorder as well as depression. A patient with bipolar disorder can present for treatment either in a depressed, hypomanic/manic, or mixed state. Interestingly, many of these dually diagnosed patients have their most persistent use of cocaine when hypomanic/manic and not when depressed (Weiss et al., 1988). Cocaine abuse during mania may be the result of the impaired judgment characteristic of mania. In addition to enhancing mania, cocaine usage can precipitate mania (Weiss et al., 1988). Generally speaking, some bipolar patients enjoy their hypomanic/manic phase and minimize the risk of a bipolar relapse owing to poor compliance with their nonaddictive mood-stabilizing medication (lithium or carbamazepam). Treatment of cocaine addicts with bipolar disorder should include an educational component on both disorders, including the importance of maintaining medication compliance and the role of psychosocial stressors. Both disorders can be confusing to families, and they should also receive education on both disorders. Family members can be enlisted to help the patient see warning signs of an impending bipolar relapse. Lithium has been shown to be effective in the treatment of the cocaine addict with bipolar disorder

(Nunes, McGrath, Wager, & Quitkin, 1990). The use of other medications for this subtype has not been studied extensively.

ANXIETY

A diagnosis of generalized anxiety disorder (GAD) is made with more severe, chronic anxiety symptoms, including autonomic responses (palpitations, diarrhea, sweating, urinary frequency), insomnia, fatigue, sighing, and trembling. GAD can include depressive symptoms. A family history of an anxiety disorder can provide information on genetic loading for diagnostic purposes and understanding family dynamics. Making a diagnosis of GAD in a cocaine addict is complicated because symptoms of protracted abstinence include anxiety, and the addict can become anxious in dealing with early recovery issues like financial problems, drug craving, and interpersonal problems. Specific GAD treatment approaches should initially focus on nonpharmacological approaches including supportive therapy, relaxation techniques, meditation, and self-hypnosis. Initial pharmacotherapy approaches should focus on non-addictive medications such as β-blockers or the use of buspirone. Buspirone has shown little abuse potential or withdrawal syndrome and has been shown to be effective in improving treatment outcome in anxious alcoholics (Kranzler & Meyer, 1989). More research is needed in this area of pharmacotherapy, and future projects should consider integrating psychotherapy approaches.

Panic disorder is manifested by the sudden and dramatic onset of anxiety symptoms which last for a short time, minutes to hours. The panic attack occurs without a clear precipitant and in patients with or without chronic anxiety. Symptoms are often perceived by patients as medical and have a strong autonomic nervous system component, including increased pulse, blood pressure, chest pain, shortness of breath, choking, sweating, abdominal pain; and often include a feeling of impending doom. Treatment should include supportive therapy and educational approaches; however, this disorder can be very disabling and the use of pharmacotherapy should be considered. Again, the use of nonaddictive medications should be the first pharmacotherapy approach, including tricyclic antidepressants, β-blockers, and carbamazepine.

Patients who demonstrate anxiety with specific fears have a phobic disorder. Phobic fears are persistent and intense and out of proportion to the stimulus, may make little sense to the sufferer, and will lead to an avoidance of the feared object or situation. Included are social phobias, simple phobias, and agoraphobia. The most common of these is agoraphobia, which includes multiple phobias with chronic anxiety and specific fears of open or closed places, crowded places, or being alone. Many patients with agoraphobia also have panic attacks, and this combination can be psychiatrically disabling. In this situation, the clinician may consider the use of a benzodiazepine, such as clonazepam, for a short time until the tricyclic antidepressant takes full effect. (Zweben & Smith, 1989). In general, phobias can be treated with behavioral therapy approaches, including exposing the patient to the feared object in a controlled manner using specific techniques like systematic desensitization, flooding, and implosion. Some phobias may benefit from a trial of tricyclic antidepressants (Quitkin, Rifkin, Kaplan, Klein, & Oaks, 1972).

ATTENTION DEFICIT DISORDER, RESIDUAL

Attention deficit disorder (ADD) is a childhood disorder which can continue into adulthood and has features of a personality disorder. The adults have symptoms of increased distractibility, impulsiveness, restlessness, and quick temper (Gittelman, Mannuzza, & Shenker, 1985). The diagnosis in adults is difficult, and the evaluation should include a longitudinal history from childhood with input from the patient and a resource person (perhaps a parent). Several researchers noted an interesting association of this disorder with cocaine addicts (Khantzian, Gawin, Kleber, & Riordan, 1984). Some of these dually diagnosed addicts reported that they only used cocaine in low doses on a daily basis. Initially, researchers speculated that these addicts may be self-medicating their ADD with cocaine, and several patients were treated with stimulant medication. In spite of this initial enthusiasm, however, the risks of giving an addictive medication to an addict proved to outweigh the benefits. In general, the use of a tricyclic antidepressants or a dopamine agonist is a more appropriate pharmacotherapy choice for cocaine addicts with ADD, residual (Cocores, Patel, Gold, & Pottash, 1987).

PERSONALITY DISORDERS

The most common personality disorders associated with cocaine abuse are antisocial, borderline, and narcissistic personality disorders. Making an Axis II diagnosis is difficult because many of the symptoms manifested by an addict in early treatment can resemble a personality disorder, including using defenses of denial, excuse making, blaming, lying, minimizing, vagueness, anger, victim role playing, and grandiosity. Also, many addicts carry out antisocial activities related to obtaining cocaine. Antisocial personality (ASP) disorder is the most common personality disorder in substance abusers; however, the choice of diagnostic criteria used can influence the determination of ASP. The DSM-III method focuses on behavioral criteria and does not require antisocial behaviors to exist independently of substance abuse. The RDC criteria exclude antisocial behaviors that result during substance abuse. Given this difference in diagnostic criteria, one should not be surprised at the variability in rates of current ASP diagnosis in cocaine abusers (33% with DSM-III and 7.7% with RDC) (Rounsaville et al., 1991). These two diagnostic methods may differentiate two types of ASP patients with different prognostic and treatment implications. The stricter RDC criteria diagnosis may indicate a subtype who are "true/idiopathic psychopaths" who have an early onset of ASP with both antisocial behavior and antisocial character structure, including the inability to experience guilt or remorse or to form meaningful relationships. This ASP type has a poor prognosis. The patients diagnosed as ASP only by DSM-III criteria may be a subtype of "symptomatic psychopaths" who demonstrate antisocial behavior in the context of drug abuse, but who show signs of remorse, anxiety, guilt, and ability to form meaningful relationships. This ASP type can have a coexistent diagnosis of an anxiety or depression disorder, and predicts a better prognosis and ability to relate to the therapist (Gerstley, Alterman. McLellan, & Woody, 1990).

Addicts with ASP engage in high-risk behaviors and are at an increased risk for exposure to the HIV virus secondary to needle sharing (especially with the "speedball" combination of cocaine and heroin) and for high-risk sexual behaviors (Brooner, Bigelow, Greenfield, Strain, & Schmidt, 1991). Also, there appears to be a strong association between any patient with a high level of psychological distress and high-risk needle-sharing behaviors (Metzger et al., 1991). The treatment and prevention implications of these findings are an increased role for HIV testing among all dually diagnosed patients and an increased need for effective education on HIV transmission, high-risk behaviors, and AIDS. Also, approaches to help patients modify high-risk behaviors should be included in the treatment program.

In general, severe personality disorders have been difficult to treat. An understanding of the underlying dynamics can be important; however, the patient's defenses are not to be interpreted or abruptly changed, but rather brought to the addict's attention, with the goal of developing substitutes for these defenses. Clinicians should use their resources in an effort to provide a structure in which the patient's self-destructive behaviors can be minimized (Vaillant, 1975).

SCHIZOPHRENIA: THE CHRONICALLY MENTALLY ILL PATIENT

The rate of schizophrenia in cocaine abusers is higher than the general population, and the reported range is 1–17%. However, cocaine abuse is prevalent among schizophrenics, with published studies suggesting rates of at leat 15–20% and more recent data in clinical settings indicating rates of about 50% (Brady et al., 1990; Rounsaville et al., 1991; Schneier & Siris, 1987; Regier et al., 1990).

Schizophrenic patients who abuse cocaine tend to require more psychiatric hospitalizations, have a poorer prognosis and compliance with treatment, and be at greater risk for suicide. However compared with non-drug abusing schizophrenics, these dually diagnosed patients have less severe symptoms of schizophrenia (Dixon, Haas, Weiden, Sweeney, & Francis, 1991).

Cocaine affects the same area of the brain in which schizophrenics have abnormalities. This area includes neurons that contain the neurotransmitter dopamine. This biological relationship may partly explain the exacerbation of schizophrenia symptoms with cocaine use. Cocaine can also potentiate the side effects of antipsychotic medication, including an apparent increase in tardive dyskinesia (Brady et al., 1990).

There have been few studies on treatment approaches for the schizophrenic cocaine abuser (Galanter & Castaneda, 1988; Hellerstein & Meehan, 1987; Kofoed, Kanier, Walsh, & Atkinson, 1986). However, novel psychotherapy and pharmacotherapy approaches are currently being designed.

One such progam is the Dual Diagnosis Relapse Prevention (DDRP) program at Yale which provides treatment for drug-abusing schizophrenics and integrates pharmacotherapy and psychotherapy approaches (Ziedonis, Jaffe, Davis, Petrakis, & Hogan, 1991). The psychotherapy component merges traditional chemical dependence relapse prevention approaches (Marlatt & Gordon, 1985; Carroll et al., 1991) with traditional mental health social skills training approaches, including medication management and psychiatric symptom management (Liberman, De Risi, & Mueser, 1989). An important element of the DDRP program is that of recruiting staff who are "dually trained" and providing continued inservice training.

This unique outpatient treatment approach is part of a complete treatment package that includes standard mental health outpatient treatment, vocational rehabilitation, and modified chemical dependence treatment. The DDRP program has three phases, which are specific both to the patient's commitment to treatment and to his or her stage in the recovery process. Phase I is the "engagement" phase. The patient is assessed, and attempts are made to enhance the patient's motivation for dual-diagnosis treatment. Patients remain in this phase for at least the first month, and longer if they cannot sustain abstinence from drugs. Some of these dually diagnosed patients need to be convinced to accept their psychiatric illness, whereas others need to accept their drug addiction. Enticements to improve compliance with treatment include small items like occasional lunches and opportunities for socialization, and larger items like providing assistance in obtaining basic necessities like food, shelter, and clothing; help in accessing entitlement programs; and vocational rehabilitation.

Phase II, Commitment to Treatment, is designed for patients in the early recovery phase. Patients can stay at this level unless they have two cocaine "slips," whereupon they must return to the Phase I group. In this phase, the clinician works with the patient to accept long-term abstinence-oriented treatment. This can be a slower process in the dually diagnosed population, especially if non-DDRP clinicians are not committed to this goal.

Phase III, Transition to Recovery and Well-Being, includes patients who have acquired 3 months of sobriety and psychiatric stability, and who are maintaining an active involvement in treatment and commitment to an abstinence life-style with appropriate psychiatric care.

The specifics of this treatment approach are described in manuals for the staff and the patients. The manual is divided into four sections. Section I, General Concepts and Vocabulary, serves as an introduction to the disease model and the parallels of mental illness and addiction. Patients' interpersonal and vocational skills are assessed, and they are provided a framework to improve general communication and problem-solving skills. Of note, these dually diagnosed patients tend to have better interpersonal and vocational skills than do other schizophrenics, which actually may have resulted in their increased involvement in the drug abuse culture. The vocabulary of the different treatment approaches are discussed including 12-step, relapse prevention, and psychiatric approaches.

In Section II, Identifying Early Warning Signs and High Risk Situations, patients uncover their own internal and external cues/triggers for drug craving and use, with a strong emphasis on relating these issues to internal mood states and their own psychiatric condition. Patients are helped to recognize how negative external situations relate to increased psychiatric symptoms and drug use. Family systems issues are addressed, including the issue of "expressed emotion." Cocaine abuse relapse prevention issues focus on the "seemingly irrelevant decisions," characteristics/phenomenology of past relapses/"slips," and discussion of drug dreams and relapse fantasies.

Section III, Developing Coping Skills, deals with specific skill development including problem-solving applications (e. g., drug refusal exercises, managing a "slip," getting help from others, plans to handle cravings and urges), time structuring (especially weekends), and coping skills (stress management, relaxation skills, efficacy-enhancing imagery, anger and other mood management). Also, patients are supported in developing skills in managing their medications and psychiatric symptoms.

Section IV, Maintaining Healthy Coping Responses, focuses on continued self-monitoring of psychiatric and substance abuse issues, craving control, abstinence violation techniques, social skills training, relationship issues, and independent living and general life-style changes.

This treatment approach focuses on "recovery" as a lifelong process for improving health and well-being. Both the cocaine abuse and the schizophrenia must be addressed without a focus on which problem is primary. The patient's goals include compliance with abstinence and appropriate medication, however the initial goal is maintaining program attendance.

Modified 12-step groups (Double Trudgers; Mentally Ill Chemical Abusers [MICA]) are part of the treatment package in most cases and most patients attend the 12-Step Meeting at this institution. Patients are prepared for outside meetings through participation in these groups and through education on the 12-step literature about medications (Alcoholics Anonymous, 1984). The modified 12-step group encourages the recruitment of a traditional sponsor and a maintenance of the primary counselor for support.

In addition to the psychotherapy approach, which sets the stage for treatment, pharmacotherapy is integrated into treatment. Patients are stabilized on their psychiatric medication for schizophrenia and are considered for substance abuse treatment pharmacotherapies. Specific cocaine abuse treatment pharmacotherapies have been researched in nonpsychotic patients but not in psychotic patients. In the context of the innovative DDRP program, an outpatient pilot study evaluated the effectiveness of using the antidepressant desipramine in a 12-week open trial for 12 cocaine abusing schizophrenics. Overall, these patients reported less cocaine craving, less cocaine use, decreased cocaine urine tests for cocaine, improved psychiatric stability, no new medical problems; and maintained excellent program retention. Eighty-three percent of the patients (10 of 12) treated with desipramine stayed in treatment for at least 12 weeks. The dosage of desipramine (100–150 mg) was lower than usual because of the altered metabolism when used in combination with neuroleptics. Additional research is needed in this use of pharmacotherapy, and these pilot results should be considered with guarded optimism (Ziedonis, Richardson, Lee, Petrakis, & Kosten, in press). The antidepressant imipramine has been used effectively in schizophrenics with postpsychosis depression (Siris, 1990). In addition to the use of pharmacotherapy for cocaine abuse, this program has had a good experience with the use of naltrexone or disulfuram (Antabuse) in schizophrenic patients who have polydrug problems. The dosage of disulfuram tends to be lower than 500 mg (usually 250 mg), but can be safe and effective (Kingsbury & Salzman, 1990).

COGNITIVE DISORDERS

The subtype of the cocaine addict with a cognitive disorder is often overlooked. Because many treatment programs are based on cognitive learning, patients with cognitive deficits are not likely to benefit from these approaches. To make it possible for these addicts to learn, a change in the educational process is often required. Addicts are at risk for trauma, including traumatic brain injury. Other medical causes of cognitive deficits include AIDS dementia and drug intoxication/ withdrawal. A careful mental status examination should include screening for cognitive functioning: consider the Mini-Mental Status Examination. Sophisticated neuropsychological testing can be considered, including the Halstead-Reitan and the Luria-Nebraska test batteries. Testing can be helpful in making a diagnosis, planning treatment, assessing prognosis, and monitoring improvements in functioning. Patients with cognitive deficits often require specialized treatment depending on the severity of the deficits, the possibility for improvement, the location of the brain dysfunction, the patient's motivation for recovery, family supports, and the preexisting intellectual skills and personality characteristics.

CONCLUSION

This chapter focused on the issues of cocaine addiction and psychiatric comorbidity. This problem is complex and may require new paradigms in approaching diagnosis and treatment. Comorbidity appears to be an interactive process rather than a simple cause-and-effect relationship, as suggested by the primary and secondary diagnostic distinction. Even specific psychiatric subtypes are heterogeneous and may require unique treatment approaches. There is a need for research on differential diagnosis and specific treatment approaches for the different psychiatric subtypes in cocaine addiction. Also, clinicians in both the chemical dependence and mental health fields need continuing education on comorbidity issues. With new skills and knowledge in this area, clinicians' attitudes toward these patients can change. In working with these patients at this time, clinicians should consider integrating traditional chemical dependence and mental health approaches. For new clinical advances to occur, clinicians, researchers, and administrators must approach the problem together.

REFERENCES

Alcoholics Anonymous. (1984). *The A. A. member: Medications and other drugs.* New York: Alcoholics Anonymous World Services.

American Psychiatric Association. (1987). *Diagnostic and statistical manual of mental disorders* (3rd ed., rev.). Washington, DC: Author.

Anthony, J. C., & Trinkoff, A. M. (1988). United States epidemiologic data on drug use and abuse: How are they relevant to testing abuse liability of drugs? In M. W. Fischman & N. K. Mello (Eds.), *Testing for abuse liability of drugs in humans* (National Institute on Drug Abuse Research Monograph No. 92, pp. 241–266). Washington, DC: U. S. Government Printing Office.

Aronson, T. A., & Craig, T. J. (1986). Cocaine precipitation of panic disorder. *American Journal of Psychiatry, 143*, 643–645.

Beck, A. T., Rush, A. J., Shaw, B. F., & Emery, G. (1979). *Cognitive therapy of depression.* New York: Guilford Press.

Berkson, J. (1946). Limitations of the application of the 4-fold table analyses to hospital data. *Biometrics, 2*, 47–53.

Blumenthal, S. J. (1988). A guide to risk factors, assessment, and treatment of suicidal patients. *Medical Clinics of North America, 72*, 937–971.

Brady, K., Anton, R., Ballenger, J. C., Lydiard, R. B., Adinoff, B., & Selander, J. (1990). Cocaine abuse among schizophrenic patients. *American Journal of Psychiatry, 147*, 1164–1167.

Brooner, R. K., Bigelow, G. E., Greenfield, L., Strain, E. C., & Schmidt, C. W. (1990). Intravenous drug abusers with antisocial personality disorder: High rate of HIV-1 infection. In L. Harris (Ed.), *Problems of drug dependence, 1990: Proceedings of the 52nd annual scientific meeting of the Committee on Problems of Drug Dependence* (National Institute on Drug Abuse Research Monograph No. 105, DHHS Publication No. ADM 91–1753, pp. 488–489). Washington, DC: U. S. Government Printing Office.

Brown, U. B., Ridgely, M. S., Pepper, B, Levine, I. S., & Ryglewicz, H. (1989). The dual crisis: Mental illness and substance abuse. *American Psychologist, 44*(3), 565–569.

Carroll, K. M., Rounsaville, B. J., & Keller, D. S. (1991). Relapse prevention strategies for the treatment of cocaine abuse. *American Journal of Drug and Alcohol Abuse, 7*(3), 249–265.

Chitwood, D. D., & Morningstar, P. C. (1985). Factors which differentiate cocaine users in treatment from nontreatment users. *International Journal of the Addictions, 20*, 449–459.

Cocores, J. A., Patel, M. D., Gold, M. S., & Pottash, A. C. (1987). Cocaine abuse, attention deficit disorder, and bipolar disorder. *Journal of Nervous and Mental Disease, 175*(7), 431–432.

Dilsauer, S. (1987). The pathophysiologies of substance abuse and affective disorders: An integrative model. *Journal of Clinical Psychopharmacology, 7*, 1–10.

Dixon, L., Haas, G., Weiden, P. J., Sweeney, J., & Frances, A. J. (1991). Drug abuse in schizophrenic patients: Clinical correlates and reasons for use. *American Journal of Psychiatry, 148*, 224–230.

Evans, K., & Sullivan, J. M. (1990). *Dual diagnosis: Counseling the mentally ill substance abuser.* New York: Guilford Press.

Ford, J., Hillard, J. R., Giesler, L. J., Lassen, K. L., & Thomas, H. (1989). Substance abuse/mental illness: Diagnostic issues. *American Journal of Drug and Alcohol Abuse, 15*, 297–307.

Galanter, M., & Castaneda, R. (1988). Substance abuse among general psychiatric patients: Place of presentation, diagnosis, and treatment. *American Journal of Drug and Alcohol Abuse, 14*, 211–235.

Gawin, F. H., & Kleber, H. D. (1986). Abstinence symptomatology and psychiatric diagnosis in cocaine abusers. *Archives of General psychiatry, 43*, 107–113.

Gawin, F. H., Kleber, H. D., Byck R., et al. (1989). Desipramine facilitation of initial cocaine abstinence. *Archives of General Psychiatry, 46*, 117–121.

Gerstley, L. J., Alterman, A. I., McLellan, A. T., & Woody, G. E. (1990). Antisocial personality disorder in patients with substance abuse disorders: A problematic diagnosis? *American Journal of Psychiatry, 147*, 173–178.

Gianni, A. J., Malone, D. A., Gianni, M. C., et al. (1986). Treatment of depression in chronic cocaine and phencyclidine abuse with desipramine. *Journal of Clinical Pharmacology, 26*, 211–214.

Gittelman, R., Mannuzza, S., & Shenker, R. (1985). Hyperactive boys almost grown up. *Archives of General Psychiatry, 42*, 937–947.

Grant, I., & Reed, R. Neuropsychology of alcohol and drug abuse. In A. Alterman (Ed.), *Substance abuse and psychopathology.* New York: Plenum Press.

Hall, S. M., Munoz, R., & Reus, V. (1991, December). *Depression and smoking treatment: A clinical trial of an affect regulation treatment.* Paper presented at the 53rd annual scientific meeting of the Committee on Problems of Drug Dependence, Palm Beach, FL.

Hellerstein, D. J., & Meehan, B. (1987). Outpatient group therapy for schizophrenic substance abusers. *American Journal of Psychiatry, 144*, 1337–1339.

Ho, A., Cambor, R., Bodner, G., & Kreek, M. J. (1991, December). *Intensity of craving is independent of depression in newly abstinent chronic cocaineusers.* Abstract presented at the 53rd annual scientific meeting of the Committee on Problems of Drug Dependence, Palm Beach, FL.

Kaufman, E. (1989). The psychotherapy of dually diagnosed patients. *Journal of Substance Abuse Treatment, 6*, 9–18.

Khantzian, E. J. (1985). The self-medication hypothesis of addictive disorders: Focus on heroin and cocaine dependence. *American Journal of Psychiatry, 142*, 259–1264.

Khantzian, E. J., Gawin, F., Kleber, H. D., & Riordan, C. E. (1984). Methylphenidate (Ritalin) treatment of cocaine dependence—A preliminary report. *Journal of Substance Abuse Treatment, 1*, 1198–1199.

Kingsbury, S. J., & Salzman, C. (1990). Disulfiram in the treatment of alcoholic patients with schizophrenia. *Hospital and Community Psychiatry, 41*(2), 133–134.

Kofoed, L., Kania, J., Walsh, T., & Atkinson, R. M. (1986). Outpatient treatment of patients with substance abuse and coexisting psychiatric disorders. *American Journal of Psychiatry, 143*, 867–872.

Kosten, T. R. (1990). Pharmacotherapeutic interventions for cocaine abuse: Matching patients to treatments. *American Journal of Drug and Alcohol Abuse, 16*, 329–336.

Kosten, T. R., & Kleber, H. D. (1988). Differential diagnosis of psychiatric comorbidity in substance abusers. *Journal of Substance Abuse Treatment, 5*, 201–206.

Kranzler, H. R., & Meyer, R. E. (1989). An open trial of buspirone in alcoholics. *Journal of Clinical Psychopharmacology, 9*(5), 379–380.

Lader, M. (1987). Assessing the potential for buspirone dependence or abuse and effects of its withdrawal. *American Journal of Medicine, 82*, (Suppl. 5A), 20–26.

Leff, J. A., & Vaughn, C. (1985). *Expressed emotion in families.* New York: Guilford Press.

Liberman, R. P., DeRisi, W. J., & Mueser, K. T. *Social skills training for psychiatric patients.* Elmsford, NY: Pergamon Press.

Marlatt, G. A., & Gordon., J. K. (Eds.) (1985). *Relapse prevention: Maintenance strategies in the treatment of addictive behaviors.* New York: Guilford Press.

Marzuk, P. M., & Mann, J. (1988). Suicide and substance abuse. *Psychiatric Annals, 18*, 639–645.

McLellan, A. T., Luborsky, L., Woody, G. E., et al. (1983). Predicting response to alcohol and drug abuse treatment: Role of psychiatric severity. *Archives of General Psychiatry, 40*, 620–625.

Metzger, H. Y., Woody, G. E., Druley, P., DePhillips, D., Navaline, H., McLellan, A. T., & O'Brien, C. P. (1991). Psychiatric symptoms, high risk behaviors and HIV positivity among methadone patients. (National Institute on Drug Abuse Research Monograph No. 105, DHHS Publication No. ADM 91–1753, pp. 490–491). Washington, DC: U. S. Printing Office.

Meyer, R. E. (1986). *Psychopathology and addictive disorders*. New York: Guilford Press.

Minkoff, K., & Drake, R. E. (Eds.) (1991). Dual diagnosis of major mental illness and substance disorder. *New Directions For Mental Health Services, 50*.

Nunes, E. V., McGrath, P. J., Wager, S., & Quitkin, F. M. (1990). Lithium treatment for cocaine abusers with bipolar spectrum disorders. *American Journal of Psychiatry, 147*, 655–657.

Nunes, E. V., Quitkin, F. M., Brady, R., Stewart, J., & Post, T. (1991). Imipramine treatment of depressed drug abusers. *1991 New Research Program and Abstracts* (Abstract No. NR281, p. 115). Washington, DC: American Psychiatric Association.

Perry, J. C. (1985). Depression in borderline personality disorder: Lifetime prevalence at interview and longitudinal course of symptoms. *American Journal of Psychiatry, 142*(1), 15–21.

Post, R. M., Kotin, J., Goodwin, F. R. (1974). The effects of cocaine on depressed patients. *American Journal of Psychiatry, 131*, 511–517.

Quitkin, F. M., Rifkin, A., Kaplan, J., Klein, D. F., & Oaks, G. (1972). Phobic anxiety syndrome complicated with drug dependence and addiction. *Archives of General Psychiatry, 27*, 159–162.

Rawson, R. A., Obert, J. L., McCann, M. J., Smith, D. P., & Ling, W. Neurobehavioral treatment for cocaine dependency. *Journal of Psychoactive Drugs, 22*, 159–171.

Regier, D. A., Farmer, M. E., Rae, D. S., Locke, B. Z., Keith, S. J., Judd, L. L., & Goodwin, F. K. (1990). Comorbidity of mental disorders with alcohol and other drug abuse: Results from the epidemiologic catchment area (ECA) study. *Journal of the American medical Association, 264*, 2511–2518.

Rounsaville, B. J., Anton, S. F., Carroll, K., Budde, D., Prusoff, B. A., & Gawin, F. H. (1991). Psychiatric diagnosis of treatment-seeking cocaine abusers. *Archives of General Psychiatry, 48*, 43–51.

Rounsaville, B. J., Kosten, T. R., Weissman, M. M., & Kleber, H. D. (1986). Prognostic significance of psychiatric disorders in treated opiate addicts. *Archives of General Psychiatry, 43*, 739–745.

Schneier, F. R., & Siris, S. G. (1987). Review of psychoactive substance use and abuse in schizophrenia. *Journal of Nervous and Mental Disease, 175*(11), 641–652.

Schottenfeld, R., Carroll, K. M., & Rounsaville, B. J. (in press). Comorbid psychiatric disorders and cocaine abuse. In F. Tims (Ed.), *Advances in cocaine treatment* (National Institute on Drug Abuse Research Monograph). Washington, DC: U. S. Government Printing office.

Schuckit, M. A., & Monteiro, M. G. (1988). Alcoholism, anxiety, and depression. *British Journal Of Addictions, 83*, 1373–1380.

Siris, S. G. (1990). Pharmacological treatment of substance abusing schizophrenic patients. *Schizophrenia Bulletin, 16*, 111–122.

Skinner, H. A., Holt, S., Schuller, R., Roy, J., & Israel, Y. (1984). Identification of alcohol abuse using laboratory tests and a history of trauma. *Annals of Internal Medicine, 101*, 847–851.

Vaillant, G. E. (1975). Sociopathy as a human process. *Archives of General Psychiatry, 32*, 178–183.

Weiss, R. D., & Mirin, S. M. (1986). Subtypes of cocaine Abusers. *Psychiatric Clinics of North America, 9*, 91–101.

Weiss, R. D., Mirin, S. M., Griffin, M. L., & Michael, J. (1988). Psychopathology in cocaine abusers: Changing trends. *The Journal of Nervous and Mental Disease, 176*, 719–725.

Weissman, M. M., Klerman, G., Rounsaville, B. J., Chevron, E. S., & Neu, C. (1982). Short-term interpersonal psychotherapy (IPT) for depression: Description and efficacy. In J. C. Anchin & D. J. Keisler (Eds.), *Handbook of interpersonal psychotherapy.* New York: Pergamon Press.

Woody, G. E., McLellan, A. T., Luborsky, L., et al. (1984). Severity of psychiatric symptoms as a predictor of benefits from psychotherapy: The Veterans Administration-Penn Study. *American Journal of Psychiatry, 141*, 1172–1177.

Ziedonis, D. M., Jaffe, A., Davis, E., Petrakis, I., & Hogan, I. (1991) Relapse prevention group therapy is effective in the treatment of the mentally ill substance abuser. In *1991 New Research Program and Abstracts* (Abstract No. NR283, p. 116). Washington, DC: American Psychiatric Association.

Ziedonis, D. M., & Kosten, T. R. (1991a). Depression as a prognostic factor for pharmacological treatment of cocaine dependency. *Psychopharmacology Bulletin, 27*(3) 337–343.

Ziedonis, D. M., & Kosten, T. R. (1991b). Pharmacotherapy improves treatment outcome in depressed cocaine addicts. *Journal of Psychoactive Drugs, 23*(4), 417–425.

Ziedonis, D. M., Richardson, T. C., Lee, E., Petrakis, I., & Kosten, T. R. (in press). Adjunctive desipramine in the treatment of cocaine abusing schizophrenics. *Psychopharmacology Bulletin.*

Zweben, J. E. (1987). Recovery oriented psychotherapy: Facilitating the use of 12 step programs. *Journal of Psychoactive Drugs, 19*, 243–251.

Zweben, J. E., & Smith, D. E. (1989). Considerations in using psychotropic medication with dual diagnosis patients in recovery. *Journal of Psychoactive Drugs, 21*, 221–228.

CHAPTER EIGHTEEN

Cocaine Abuse within Methadone Maintenance Programs

Susan M. Stine, MD, PhD

TREATMENT OF ADDICTIVE BEHAVIOR has suffered from cyclical fluctuations in public opinion between the extremes of the biological models, which postulate etiologies such as receptor abnormalities for these disorders, and the criminal model, which considers addiction to be "willful misconduct." Addressing this general problem in his Albert Lasker Award Lecture, Vincent Dole (1988) said, "[T]he Supreme Court affirmed the denial of veterans' benefits to alcoholics on the grounds that their condition is due to 'willful misconduct,' an opinion that . . . made explicit the widespread prejudice against addicts, one that if carried to logical limits would deny treatment to a skier with a broken leg or a sun-bather with skin cancer."

Methadone maintenance has been a particularly polarized issue among substance abuse treatment professionals as well as within society in general. Even among methadone maintenance programs themselves, there are conflicting philosophies. In this context, other substance abuse such as that of cocaine presents special challenges for the treatment professional.

Cocaine use in methadone programs is a widespread problem and continues to increase. In a study conducted by the U.S. General Accounting Office (1990), in 8 of 24 treatment programs, 20–40 percent of patients used cocaine. Not only does serious cocaine abuse occur in methadone programs, but there is also evidence that cocaine use may increase for some patients during methadone maintenance (Kosten, Rounsaville, & Kleber, 1987). A variety of theoretical explanations can be postulated for the worsening of cocaine use during treatment with methadone, and it is not clear to what extent this problem may be iatrogenic. Furthermore, whether or not methadone treatment in some way exacerbates cocaine abuse, the structure of the methadone program presents particular challenges and, as I will describe, special opportunities for cocaine abuse treatment. To maximize these opportunities, it is important to minimize ideological distortions and develop empirical approaches to this problem. This chapter first summarizes the context of the problem and its treatment, that is, the structure of the methadone programs. The relationship of this specialized treatment of opiate dependence to the etiology or exacerbation of cocaine abuse is then considered theoretically from behavioral and pharmacological perspectives. Finally, clinical interventions, both behavioral and pharmacological, are considered.

THE CONTEXT: THE METHADONE PROGRAM STRUCTURE

Methadone programs can vary widely with respect to their program design, view of outcome goals, and even their use of methadone itself. The above-mentioned GAO report (1990), based on a study of 24 methadone maintenance programs in eight states, confirms that there is no typical methadone maintenance treatment program. The use of methadone as a method of drug treatment for heroin addiction started in the early 1960s and expanded in the 1970s. In 1988, approximately 100,000 heroin addicts received methadone maintenance in more than 650 programs nationwide. Programs can be found in rural and suburban areas as well as in inner cities, and differ with respect to private, public, and not-for-profit status. Heroin addicts span the socio-economic range from poor to rich, uneducated to professional. Problems associated with heroin addicts include homelessness, mental illness, tuberculosis, pneumonia, HIV infection, and numerous other debilitating diseases.

Methadone maintenance programs are more effective when linked with comprehensive treatment services, according to a major study sponsored by the National Institute on Drug Abuse (Ball, Lane, Myers, & Friedman, 1988). This in-depth 3-year study of six methadone maintenance treatment programs noted that effective programs reduced intravenous (IV) drug use and needle sharing among most heroin addicts, thus reducing the risk of contracting or spreading the HIV virus through needle use. However, the study found marked differences in the effectiveness of various programs in reducing IV drug use. Many programs offer a variety of rehabilitation services and therapy and often do this within a context of a highly structured behavioral design.

By combining the use of methadone with counseling and other services treatment programs attempt to help heroin addicts stop using street drugs and lead more stable and productive lives. An ongoing philosophical debate has surrounded the use of methadone maintenance since its development as a treatment method. Some treatment practitioners believe drug-free treatment is the only valid method. They discount the efficacy of methadone maintenance on the grounds that it merely substitutes one narcotic drug for another. In contrast, other treatment practitioners view methadone as a medication for treating heroin addiction, and some compare it to taking insulin for diabetes. Some programs consider methadone as a treatment for heroin dependence alone, and do not attempt to address concurrent abuse of other drugs. Most programs, however, also focus on other drug abuse in addition to opiates, although they vary with respect to the particular drugs addressed and with respect to the severity of the interventions. Programs also differ with respect to the goal of ultimately achieving a drug-free state.

ETIOLOGY OF COCAINE ABUSE IN METHADONE PROGRAMS

A variety of possible factors have been cited as contributing to the problem of cocaine abuse in methadone programs. For example, polydrug abuse has, in recent years, been much more normative than in the past, and cocaine has been fashionable and more readily available. In addition, cocaine euphoria is not dampened by methadone, as is the opiate high. Finally, the availability of methadone allows addicts the opportunity to buy cocaine with money once targeted for heroin.

Methadone maintenance treatment itself may be associated with increased cocaine abuse among certain patients because it may prolong the pleasurable effects and diminish the dysphoric aftereffects of cocaine (Kosten et al., 1987). Conversely, greater cocaine dependence is associated with less severe opiate withdrawal in opiate-dependent subjects (Kosten, Jacobsen, & Kosten, 1989), and with less severe naloxone-precipitated opiate withdrawal (Kosten, 1990). This effect was also demonstrated in rats (Kosten, 1990). If cocaine attenuates the severity of opiate withdrawal, this may place methadone-maintained patients at risk, because many report mild withdrawal sensations near the end of their 24-hour dosing schedule. Understanding the interaction of cocaine and methadone and optimizing methadone dosage is clearly of crucial importance in the effective treatment of methadone-maintained patients.

In the routine management of patients in methadone programs, two broad categories of intervention are used concurrently: (1) behavioral, and (2) pharmacological (methadone dose). Further, any dosage manipulation has in itself a behavioral meaning and therefore acts in both behavioral and pharmacological categories.

Behavioral Considerations in Etiology of Cocaine Abuse in Methadone Programs

Substance abuse behavior is maintained by both positive reinforcement (euphoria) and negative reinforcement (relief of dysphoria, i.e., withdrawal symptoms or unpleasant drug effects) (Wise, 1988). Therefore, any manipulation of opiate dose that changes this behavior may be expected to influence one or both of these factors.

There is evidence for the reciprocal action of opiates and cocaine on negative reinforcement. Both cocaine attenuation of opiate withdrawal (Kosten, 1989, 1990) and opiate attenuation of the unpleasant effects of cocaine (Kosten, Rounsaville, & Kleber, 1987, 1988) have been reported. The interaction of opiates and cocaine in the achievement of drug-induced euphoria (positive reinforcement) is even more clear, especially in "speedball" (heroin + cocaine) abusers, and has been frequently observed in the literature. Thus it is clear that opiates and cocaine each have the potential to act as reinforcement for the abuse of the other.

Additionally, many routine interventions used in methadone programs consist of behavioral manipulations that do not directly relate to the response to the drug itself. For example, such interventions as take-home privileges provide behavioral incentives that reinforce drug-free behavior in a different "currency" other than drug-related pleasure or dysphoria (e.g., personal free time, self-esteem). The ways in which such incentives for opiate abstinence affect other drug abuse behavior are not clear. For example, increased free time and decreased program contact given as a reward for opiate abstinence could increase risk for cocaine abuse in the opiate-dependent but "street"-opiate-abstinent patient.

Role of Neurobiology and Pharmacology in the Etiology of Cocaine Abuse in Methadone Programs

Although the subject cannot be reviewed in detail here, there is abundant evidence for interaction of cocaine and opiates in the neurobiology of reward. Opioid receptor density in brain reward areas such as the ventral tegmental area (VTA) and nucleus accumbens (NAC) is altered as a result of chronic cocaine exposure in the rat (Hammer, 1989). The importance of the ascending dopaminergic pathway from the VTA to the NAC for brain reward with cocaine and opiates, as well as other reinforcing drugs, is supported by a large body of evidence (Koob & Bloom, 1988). In addition to the VTA–NAC pathway, there is also evidence from electrophysiological experiments in the rat for opiate effects on other, as yet unidentified, NAC afferent systems (Hakan & Hendrikson, 1989).

With respect to pharmacology, there have been several studies in animals examining the effect of opiates on cocaine self-administration. Intravenous cocaine self-injection behavior was shown to be suppressed by morphine pretreatment (Stretch, 1977). The opiate antagonist naloxone reversed this effect. Buprenorphine, a mixed agonist–antagonist, has also been shown to decrease cocaine self-administration in monkeys (Mello, Mendelson, Bree, & Lucas, 1989).

These results are complex, in that some of the reports cited above reports indicate that opiate agonists place addicts at higher risk for cocaine abuse, whereas other studies suggest that these drugs can attenuate cocaine use. One possible explanation for these mixed observations could be that the effect of opioid agonists on cocaine use is dose dependent. For example, a low methadone dose that does not result in cross tolerance to opiate euphoria may also permit greater cocaine euphoria than a higher methadone dose. Indeed, opiate receptor blockade in animals can block some effects of cocaine (Houdi, Bardo, & Van Loon, 1989). Thus it is possible that in methadone maintained patients, tolerance to a higher dose of methadone diminishes whatever a component of cocaine reward is opioid mediated.

Cocaine effects on opiate withdrawal may be another factor in cocaine abuse in methadone programs. Clinically, the effect of cocaine on opiate withdrawal symptoms has been noted since the 1870s (Clarke, 1989). Among the historical proponents of cocaine use to treat opiate addicts was Freud in 1882 (Clarke, 1989; Freud, 1975). Recently, there have been renewed empirical observations of the attenuation of opiate withdrawal by cocaine in adults entering maintenance treatment for opiate addiction (Kosten, 1990), and in infants (Finnegan, Mellott, Ryan, & Wapner, 1991).

Thus, biologically and pharmacologically, an argument can be made for both opiate-agonist-induced increased risk and opiate-agonist attenuated risk for cocaine abuse. At this time, these opposing sets of data cannot be resolved. One testablehypothesis is that this is a dose-related effect of opiates. This possibility is considered below.

TREATMENT INTERVENTIONS FOR COCAINE ABUSE IN METHADONE MAINTENANCE PROGRAMS

Behavioral Approaches

With respect to the behavioral component of methadone maintenance treatment, a range of behavioral interventions have been implemented to manage the growing problem of cocaine use. Many of these interventions have not been adequately evaluated for effectiveness. A recent review found only three studies that specifically evaluated the effectiveness of behavioral intervention for cocaine use among methadone patients (Condelli, Fairbank, Dennis, & Rachal, 1991). Those interventions were: confrontation about urine tests positive for cocaine (Chambers, Taylor, & Moffett, 1972), withdrawing patients from methadone if they continue to use cocaine (Black, Dolan, Penk, Rabinowitz, & DeFord, 1987); and rewarding patients with take-home doses of methadone for not using cocaine (Magura, Casriel, Goldsmith, Strug, & Lipton, 1988) (Table 18.1). The studies were in diverse clinical settings but appeared to reduce cocaine use from 16–37%. Although one of these studies demonstrated reduced methadone dose, no study has examined the effects of increasing methadone dose. Further, no study was designed to specifically exclude pharmacological effects and treat purely behavioral effects.

Pharmacological Approaches: The Role of Methadone Dose

Methadone programs have different philosophies and practices regarding the appropriate dosage level. Ball et al. (1988) believe that an adequate dose of methadone is necessary to stop heroin use. These investigators found that 60 mg is the lowest effective methadone dose and that low-dose maintenance (20–40 mg) is "inappropriate." The optimal daily dose of methadone for maintenance has been reported to be the quantity that will hold the blood level in the 150–600 mg/mL range (Dole, 1988). This concentration is generally achieved by a 60–80 mg oral methadone dose although in some cases higher doses may be needed (Dole, 1988). Although the exact therapeutic blood level for methadone is not clearly established, if the activity of hepatic microsomal enzymes has been increased by interaction with other medications being taken concurrently (Kreek, Garfield, Gutjahr, & Giusti, 1976, Tong, Pond, Kreek, Jaffery, & Benowitz, 1981), or for unknown reasons the elimination of methadone has been accelerated (Tennant, 1987), even

100 mg per day may fail to hold the blood methadone level in a therapeutic range for the full 24 hours. Such a fluctuation could subject a patient to significant abstinence symptoms each day and lead to poor therapeutic results. Tusel, Banys, and Sees (1990) have reported that the rate of decline of methadone levels, rather than the peak or trough levels, is correlated with treatment outcome. In that study, slow metabolizers showed higher rates of treatment retention than did fast metabolizers. This is consistent with the hypothesis that abstinence symptoms may be a significant impediment to successful treatment. When cocaine abuse is considered, the question of methadone dose takes on a new dimension. It is not known how methadone itself affects the risk of cocaine abuse on a biological–pharmacological level.

The difficulty of separating behavioral and pharmacological interventions in the everyday operation of a methadone program is now widely recognized. Nevertheless, understanding of the biological mechanisms of cocaine abuse risk and of biological treatment strategies is essential. Methadone programs generally respond to concurrent cocaine abuse by lowering methadone dose or "detoxing" the patient from the program as a disciplinary action. However, I am aware of no efforts to do the opposite—that is, to increase the methadone dose in response to cocaine abuse. Lowering doses in response to cocaine abuse in a methadone program may result in decreased efficacy of the treatment of opiate dependence, because higher methadone doses have been shown to be more effective in a variety of studies (Hargraves, 1983; Stitzer, McCall, Bigelow, & Liebson, 1984; Stine, 1991a, 1991b; Higgins, Stitzer, Bigelow, & Liebson, 1986). Recently two studies examined the effect of increased methadone dose in combination with increased take-home doses on cocaine and polydrug abuse in methadone programs. One study showed no effect of dose (Kirby, Stitzer, & Brockish, in press), whereas the other showed that the combination of high dose and take-home privileges was most effective (Rhoades, Ronith, Kirby, Cowan, & Grabowski, 1990). Both studies, however, combined a nonpharmacological variable (take-home dose) with a pharmacological variable and were not able to distinguish the effect of methadone dose alone. "High" doses used were also relatively low in the above studies (50 mg and 80 mg respectively). In all cases, increased dose was a response to abstinence (negative urine toxicology) rather than a response to cocaine abuse. Thus the possibility that high-dose methadone may be therapeutic for cocaine abuse, as it is for opiate abuse, has not been adequately investigated.

Some early data from the West Haven Veterans Administration Medical Center support such a role for high-dose methadone. We have compared two protocols in two sites in the Yale Department of Psychiatry. In one protocol, methadone dose was raised in response to each cocaine-positive urine test. Of patients treated under this protocol (n = 22), 33% were successfully treated (stopped cocaine use). In another protocol, methadone dose was raised in response to each cocaine-positive urine test to a maximum of 120 mg daily. Six patients have entered this protocol to date, and all six responded to this treatment by stopping cocaine abuse (Table 18.2). Thus the increasing methadone dose contingency treatment was more effective (100% vs. 33%, p = .005, Fisher's exact test).

A case history illustrates our experience with this treatment:

Mr. A, a 37-year-old employed single black male who is HIV positive, entered our program in June. This was his second methadone main-tainance program (MMP). His substance use began at age 13 with alcohol, and at age 16 he used marijuana and intravenous heroin. At age 30 he began to use cocaine. He has been arrested three times (larceny, violation of probation, trespassing). He has been in treatment four times, twice in the late 1970s. In 1987 he entered his first MMP, but was discharged after 8 months for continued drug use and failure to pay his treatment bill. In the 6 months prior to entering our program, he reported using heroin (4–5 bags daily) and alcohol (1/2 pint daily). Although he reported using only heroin and alcohol prior to entering our program, his very first urine test was strongly positive for cocaine. By August he was clearly on a cocaine run. We began increasing his methadone dose in mid-August. By October 17th he was being maintained at 120 mg of methadone per day. On that same date he used cocaine for the last time. Since that date his urine tests have been negative. After 1 1/2 months abstinence, Mr. A's methadone main-tainance dose was decreased.

These results suggest that a methadone dose contingency treatment program that increases methadone dose in response to cocaine abuse may be a successful treatment for cocaine abuse in methadone maintenance programs. This study is limited by its smallness, and by its design (two reporting sites, open treatment protocol). Furthermore, both pharmacological and behavioral mechanisms are involved in this treatment and cannot be separated in the current study. A dose contingency protocol with randomized double-blind assignment to increasing dose, decreasing dose, or behavioral contingency alone (counseling without dose change) is clearly indicated as a next step. A future study should also include measurements of cocaine craving and high, and of opiate withdrawal symptoms. Methadone blood levels should also be monitored to rule out pharmacokinetic explanations for nonresponse.

Other Pharmacological Approaches

There are currently no widely accepted pharmacotherapies for cocaine abuse, but there is a growing literature on this subject, as well as an expanding list of candidates for potential cocaine pharmacotherapy. This subject is described in detail in Chapter 14 of this book and therefore will not be presented extensively here. A brief list of potential agents includes desipramine (Arndt, Dorozynski, Woody, McLellan, & O'Brien, 1988; Kosten et al., 1990), other antidepressants such as bupropion (Margolin, Kosten, Avants, & Petrakis, 1991), and fluoxetine (Batki et al., 1990; Grabowski, Kirby, Elk, Cowan, & Rhoades, 1991), dopaminergic agonists such as mazindol (Berger, Gawin, & Kosten, 1989), bromocriptine (Dackis, Gold, Davies, & Sweeney, 1985; Dackis, Gold, Sweeney et al., 1987), and amantadine (Kosten, 1989) and antagonists (flupenthixol) as well as assorted other agents, such as carbamazepine (Sharpe, 1991), clozapine (Witkin, Minkel, Terry, Pontecorvo, & Katz, 1991), ondansetron (Sullivan, Jasinski, Preston, Testa, & Bell, 1991).

Perhaps the best-studied pharmacotherapy for cocaine is desipramine (DMI). DMI has been shown in a placebo-controlled double-blind study to be an effective therapy for some cocaine abusers (Gawin et al., 1989). There is some preliminary evidence that DMI is also effective for cocaine abuse in a methadone maintenance program (Kosten et al., 1987). A blinded, placebo-controlled study, however, revealed no significant effect of DMI on cocaine abuse in this population (Arndt, Dorozynski, Woody, McLellan, & O'Brien, 1990). A further study has reported an increase in desipramine serum levels associated with methadone treatment (Maany et al., 1989). This may account in part for repeated complaints of side effects at relatively low doses of DMI in methadone patients. Methadone-maintained patients treated with DMI have also been reported to have lower 2-hydroxy-metabolite/desipramine ratios than do other cocaine abusers and depressed patients (Kosten et al., 1990). Although it remains conjectural whether methadone inhibits hydroxylation of desipramine, it is clear that pharmacokinetic factors complicate attempts to extend studies of cocaine pharmacotherapies to a methadone-maintained population.

In considering pharmacotherapies for cocaine, attention should also be given to a phasic model of cocaine recovery, that is, to crash, withdrawal, and extinction, and to patient typology (Kosten, 1989). For example, depressed patients who are cocaine abusers patients may respond better to DMI treatment. This effort to match patient to treatments is still in early stages. When extending these findings to methadone patients, the challenge will be to further define the influence of phase of opiate recovery on such treatment matching.

Buprenorphine represents a unique and promising potential therapeutic agent in that it has been studied primarily as an alternative to methadone maintenance—that is, as a treatment for opiate addiction—and serendipitously has been found useful for treatment of cocaine abuse as well in this population. This use is investigational, in that the only FDA-approved use for buprenorphine is for analgesia at a substantially lower dose than that used for opioid abuse treatment (0.2 mg vs. 2–16 mg daily). Buprenorphine is an opiate analgesic which exhibits both agonist and antagonist effects and has been used in clinical trials for treatment of opiate dependence for many years (Jasinski, Peynick, & Griffith, 1978). Buprenorphine was shown to block the effects of morphine in opiate addicts, but chronic treatment with buprenorphine is accompanied by a low level of physical dependence. Only a mild, opiate-like withdrawal has been observed after stopping 8 weeks of buprenorphine treatment.

Studies of buprenorphine in opiate abusers have found that subjects stopped the self-administration of heroin. In doses of 2, 4, and 8 mg, sublingually, buprenorphine has been shown to be effective in maintaining abstinence and keeping patients in treatment (Kosten, Kleber, & Morgan, 1989a, 1989b).

These same authors also report that buprenorphine maintenance has been associated with less cocaine abuse in opiate-dependent subjects when compared with methadone maintenance (Kosten, et al., 1989a, 1989b). The mechanism of buprenorphine action is not clear, although it is proposed that the opiate agonist component or the agonist–antagonist combination (as opposed to the antagonist action) is critical for the effect on cocaine self-administration (Mello et al., 1989). This is because naltrexone and naloxone, pure antagonists, do not decrease cocaine self-administration in primates (Killian, Bonese, & Schuster, 1978; Goldberg, Woods, & Schuster, 1971) or in rodents (Ettenberg, Pettit, Bloom, & Koob, 1982; Condelli et al., 1986).

CONCLUSION

The basic foundation for effective management of cocaine abuse in a methadone maintenance program must be adherence to known standards of care to assure that the program is effective for opiate abuse. For example, the program should be structured, provide adequate rehabilitation, and adequate methadone dose. Although further study is needed to determine the interaction of methadone dose and cocaine abuse, prelimi-nary evidence indicates that higher methadone doses are more effective. Behavioral incentives (e.g., take-home privileges) for cocaine abstinence are also effective and are easily implemented in the context of the behavioral structure of a methadone program. Other pharmacological interventions are not discussed in detail in this chapter, but may be useful for certain subtypes of patient. For example, the depressed patient may respond to DMI. The interaction of methadone and these other agents (e.g., changes in blood level) should be considered. As treatment matching becomes more extensively studied, the choice of proper agents for subgroups should become clearer. New pharmacological treatment for opiate dependence (e.g., buprenorphine) may also have a beneficial effect on cocaine abuse.

Although risk may increase in methadone programs owing to methadone–cocaine interaction, and responsibility for the treater be-comes greater (especially in the context of public health risks such as AIDS), methadone programs also have special resources. Not only methadone itself, but also structured behavioral programs for psychoso-cial rehabilitation, as well as close collaboration with probation/parole officers and other outside support structures, offer a unique opportunity to increase retention and effectiveness of cocaine abuse treatment.

REFERENCES

Arndt, I., Dorozynsky, L., Woody, A., McLellan, A., & O'Brien, C. (1990). *Desipramine treatment of cocaine abuse in methadone maintained outpatients* (National Institute on Drug Abuse Research Monograph No. 95, pp. 322–333). Washington, DC: U. S. Government Printing Office.

Ball, J., Lange, W., Myers C., & Friedman, S. (1988). Reducing the risk of AIDS through methadone maintenance treatment. *Journal of Health and Social Behavior, 29*(3), 214–226.

Batki, S. L., Manfredi, L. B., Sorensen, J. L., Jacob, P., Dumontet, R., & Jones, R. T. (1990). Fluoxetine for cocaine abuse in methadone patients: Preliminary findings. *Proceedings of the 52nd Annual Meeting of the Committee for Problems in Drug Dependence Meeting* (National Institute on Drug Abuse Research Monograph No. 105, pp. 516–517). Washington, DC: U. S. Government Printing Office.

Berger, P., Gawin, F., & Kosten, T. R. (1989). Treatment of cocaine abuse with mazindol. *Lancet, 1*(8632), 283.

Black, J. L., Dolan, M. P., Penk, W. E., Robinowitz, R., & DeFord, H. A. (1987). The effect of increased cocaine use on drug treatment. *Addictive Behaviors, 12,* 289–292.

Chambers, C. D, Taylor, W. J. R., & Moffett, A. D. (1972). The incidence of cocaine abuse among methadone maintenance patients. *The International Journal of the Addictions, 7*(3), 427–441.

Clarke, M. J. (1989). Cocaine and morphine withdrawal. *Lancet, 2*(8659), 381–382.

Condelli, W., Fairbank J., Dennis M., & Rachal, J. (1991). Cocaine use by clients in methadone programs: Significance, scope, and behavioral interventions. *Journal of Substance Abuse Treatment, 8,* 203–212.

Dackis, C. A., Gold, M. S., Davies, R. K., & Sweeney, D. R. (1985). Bromocriptine: Treatment for cocaine abuse and the dopamine depletion hypothesis. *International Journal of Psychiatry in Medicine, 15*(2), 125–135.

Dackis, C. A., Gold, M. S., Sweeney, D. R., Byron, J. P., & Climko, R. (1987). Single-dose bromocriptine reverses cocaine craving. *Psychiatry Research, 20,* 261–264.

Dole, V. P. (1988). Implications of methadone maintenance for theories of narcotic action. *Journal of the American Medical Association, 260,* 3025–3029.

Ettenberg, A., Pettit, H. O., Bloom, F. E., & Koob, G. F. (1982). Heroin and cocaine intravenous self-administration in rats: Mediation by separate neural systems. *Psychopharmacology* [Berlin], *78,* 204-209

Finnegan, L. P., Mellott, J. M., Ryan, L. M., & Wapner, R. J. (1991). In J. M. Lakoski, M. P. Galloway, & F. J. White (Eds.), *Cocaine: Pharmacology, physiology, and clinical strategies.* Boca Raton: CRC Press.

Freud, S. (1975). *Cocaine Papers* (R. Byck, ed.). New York: Stonehill.

Gawin, F. H., Kleber, H. D., Byck, R., Rounsaville, B. J., Kosten, T. R., Jatlow, P. I., & Morgan, C. (1989). Desipramine facilitation of initial cocaine abstinence. *Archives of General Psychiatry, 46*(2), 117–121.

Goldberg, S. R., Woods, J. H., & Schuster, C. R. (1971). Nalorphine-induced changes in morphine self-administration in rhesus monkeys. *Journal of Pharmacology and Experimental Therapeutics, 176*(2), 464–471.

Grabowski, J., Kirby, K., Elk, R., Cowan, C., & Rhoades, H. (1991). Fluoxetine and behavioral factors in treatment of cocaine dependence. *Proceedings of the 53rd Annual Scientific Meeting of the Committee for Problems in Drug Dependence* (National Institute on Drug Abuse Research Monograph No. 119, p. 352). Washington, DC: U. S. Government Printing Office.

Hakan, R. L., & Hendrikson, S. J. (1989). Opiate influences in Nucleus accumbens neuronal electrophysiology: Dopamine and non-dopamine mechanisms. *Journal of Neuroscience, 9*(10) 3538–3546.

Hammer, R. P., Jr. (1989). Cocaine alters opiate receptor binding in critical brain reward regions. *Synapse, 3,* 55–60.

Hargraves, W. A. (1983). Methadone dosage and duration for maintenance treatment. In J. R. Cooper, E. Altman, B. S. Brown, & D. Czechowicz (Eds.), *Research on the treatment of narcotic addiction: State of the art* (DHHS Publication No. ADM83-1281). Rockville, MD: National Institute on Drug Abuse.

Higgins, S. T., Stitzer, M. L., Bigelow, G. E., & Liebson, I. A. (1986).

Contingent methadone delivery: Effects on illicit opiate use. *Drug and Alcohol Dependence, 17*(4), 311–322.

Houdi, A. A., Bardo, M. T., & Van Loon, G. R. (1989). Opioid mediation of cocaine-induced hyperactivity and reinforcement. *Brain Research, 497,* 195–198.

Jasinski, D. R., Peynick, J. S., & Griffith, J. D. (1978). Human pharmacology and abuse potential of the analgesic buprenorphine. *Archives of General Psychiatry, 35*(4), 501–516.

Killian, A. K., Bonese, K., & Schuster, C. R. (1978). The effects of naloxone on behavior maintained by cocaine and heroin injection in the rhesus monkey. *Drug and Alcohol Dependence, 3*(4), 243–251.

Kirby, K. C., Stitzer, M. L., & Brockish. M. (in press). Contingency management aftercare for polydrug abuse in methadone maintenance patients. *Proceedings of the 53rd Annual Scientific Meeting of the Committee for Problems in Drug Dependence* (National Institute on Drug Abuse Research Monograph No. 119, p. 474). Washington, DC: U. S. Government Printing Office.

Koob, G. F., & Bloom, F. E. (1988). Cellular and molecular mechanisms of drug dependence. *Science, 242,* 715–723.

Kosten, T. R. (1989). Pharmacotherapeutic interventions for cocaine abuse— Matching patients to treatments. *Journal of Nervous and Mental Disease, 177*(7), 379–389.

Kosten, T. A. (1990). Cocaine attenuates the severity of naloxone-precipitated opioid withdrawal. *Life Sciences, 47*(18), 1617–1623.

Kosten, T. R, Gawin, F. H., Morgan, C., Nelson, J. C., & Jatlow, P. (1990). Desipramine and its 2-hydroxy metabolite in patients taking or not taking methadone. *American Journal of Psychiatry, 147,* 1379–1380.

Kosten, T. A, Jacobsen, L. S., & Kosten, T. R. (1989). Severity of precipitated opiate withdrawal predicts drug dependence by DSM-III-R criteria. *American Journal of Drug and Alcohol Abuse, 15*(3), 237–250.

Kosten, T. R., Kleber, H. D., & Morgan, C. (1989a). Treatment of cocaine abuse with buprenorphine. *Biological Psychiatry, 26*(6), 637–639.

Kosten, T. R., Kleber, H. D., & Morgan, C. (1989b). Role of opioid antagonists in treating intravenous cocaine abuse. *Life Sciences, 44*(13), 887–892.

Kosten, T. R., Rounsaville, B. J., & Kleber, H. D. (1987). A 2.5 year follow-up of cocaine use among treated opioid addicts: Have our treatments helped? *Archives of General Psychiatry, 44*(3), 281–284.

Kosten, T. R., Rounsaville, B. J., & Kleber, H. D. (1988). Antecedents and consequences of cocaine abuse among opioid addicts: A 2.5 year follow-up. *The Journal of Nervous and Mental Disease, 176*(3), 176–181.

Kreek, M. J., Garfield, J. W., Gutjahr, C. L., & Giusti, L. M. (1976). Rifampin-induced methadone withdrawal. *New England Journal of Medicine, 294*(20), 1104–1106.

Maany, I., Dhopesh, V., Arndt, I., Burke, W., Woody, G., & O'Brien, C,P. (1989). Increase in desipramine serum levels associated with methadone treatment. *American Journal of Psychiatry, 146*(12), 1611–1613.

Magura, S., Casriel, C., Goldsmith, D. S., Strug, D. L., & Lipton, D. S. (1988). Contingency contracting with polydrug-abusing methadone patients. *Addictive Behaviors, 13*(1), 113–118.

Margolin, A., Kosten, T. R., Avants, S. K., & Petrakis, I. (1991). Pre- and post-treatment cue reactivity in cocaine addicts treated with bupropion. *Proceedings of the 53rd Annual Scientific Meeting of the Committee for Problems in Drug Dependence* (National Institute on Drug Abuse Research Monograph No. 119, p. 463). Washington, DC: U. S. Government Printing Office.

Mello, N. K., Mendelson, J. H., Bree, M. P., & Lukas, S. E. (1989). Buprenorphine suppresses cocaine self-administration by Rhesus monkeys. *Science, 245*(4920), 859–862.

Newman, R. G., & DesJarlais, D. C. (1991). Criteria for judging methadone maintenance programs. *Journal of the American Medical Association, 265*(17), 2190–2191.

Rhoades, H., Ronith, E., Kirby, K., Cowan, K., & Grabowski, J. (1990). Joint action of methadone dose and take home dose frequency in treatment compliance. *Proceedings of the 52rd Annual Scientific Meeting of the Committee for Problems in Drug Dependence* (National Institute on Drug Abuse Research Monograph No. 160, p. 453). Washington, DC: U. S. Government Printing Office.

Sharpe, L. G., Jaffe, J. H., Nouvet, F. J., & Katz, J. (1990). Nonspecific effects of carbamazepine on cocaine self-administration in rats. *Proceedings of the 52nd Annual Scientific Meeting for the Committee for Problems in Drug Dependence* (National Institute on Drug Abuse Research Monograph No. 160, p. 405). Washington, DC: U. S. Government Printing Office.

Stine, S. M., Burns, B., & Kosten, T. (1991a). Methadone dose and cocaine abuse [Letter to editor]. *American Journal of Psychiatry, 148*(9), 1268.

Stine, S. M., Freeman, M. S., Burns, B., & Kosten, T. (1991b). Effect of methadone dose contingency treatment on cocaine abuse in a methadone program. *Proceedings of the 53rd Annual Scientific Meeting of the Committee for Problems in Drug Dependence* (National Institute on Drug Abuse Research Monograph No. 119, p. 477). Washington, DC: U. S. Government Printing Office.

Stitzer, M. L., McCaul, M. E., Bigelow, G. E., & Liebson, I. A. (1984). Chronic opiate use during methadone detoxification: Effects of a dose increase treatment. *Drug and Alcohol Dependence, 14*(1), 37–44.

Strain, E. C., Stitzer, M. L., Bigelow, G. E., & Liebson, I. A. (1991). Methadone dosing level: Effect on treatment outcome. *Proceedings of the 53rd Annual Scientific Meeting of the Committee for Problems in Drug Dependence* (National Institute on Drug Abuse Research Monograph No. 119, p. 357). Washington, DC: U. S. Government Printing Office.

Stretch, R. (1977). Discrete trial control of morphine self- injection behavior in squirrel monkeys: Effects of naloxone, morphine, and chlorpromazine. *Canadian Journal of Physiology and Pharmacology, 55*(4), 778–790.

Sullivan, J. T., Jasinski, D. R., Preston, K. L., Testa, M., & Bell, J. (1991).

Cocaine blocking effects of ondansetron (OND). *Proceedings of the 53rd Annual Scientific Meeting of the Committee for Problems in Drug Dependence* (National Institute on Drug Abuse Research Monograph No. 119, p. 466). Washington, DC: U. S. Government Printing Office.

Tennant, F. S., Jr. (1987). Inadequate plasma concentrations in some high-dose methadone maintenance patients. *American Journal of Psychiatry, 144*(10), 1349–1350.

Tong, T. G., Pond, S. M., Kreek, M. J., Jeffery, N. F., & Benowitz, N. L. (1981). Phenytoin-induced methadone withdrawal. *Annals of Internal Medicine, 94*(3), 349–351.

Tusel, D., Banys, P., & Sees, K. (1990). The effect of rate of methadone metabolism on treatment outcome. *Proceedings of the 52rd Annual Scientific Meeting of the Committee for Problems in Drug Dependence* (National Institute on Drug Abuse Research Monograph No. 160, p. 454). Washington, DC: U. S. Government Printing Office.

U. S. General Accounting Office. (1990, March). *Methadone maintenance—Some treatment programs are not effective: Greater federal oversight needed* (Report to the Chairman of the Select Committee on Narcotics Abuse and Control, House of Representatives; GAO Publication No. HRD-90-104). Washington, DC: U. S. Government Printing Office.

Wise, R. A. (1988). The neurobiology of craving: Implication for the understanding and treatment of addiction. *Journal of Abnormal Psychology, 97*(2), 118–132.

Witkin, J. M., Minkel, M., Terry, P., Pontecorvo, M., & Katz, J. (1991). Blockade of the locomotor stimulant effects of cocaine by potential antipsychotic agents active at sigma binding sites. In *Proceedings of the 53rd Annual Scientific Meeting of the Committee for Problems in Drug Dependence* (National Institute on Drug Abuse Research Monograph No. 119, p. 341). Washington, DC: U. S. Government Printing Office.

CHAPTER NINETEEN

Pregnancy and Women's Issues

Judy Grossman, DrPH
Richard Schottenfeld, MD

ERINATAL ADDICTION has reemerged as a public health crisis because of the number of women of childbearing age abusing cocaine. The effects on maternal health, family functioning, and child development have alerted service providers and policymakers to the growing need for prevention, early intervention, and effective treatment of pregnant substance abusers. The economic burden of drug-exposed infants is enormous, with increased dollars being spent on neonatal intensive care, early intervention programs, and foster care. The indirect societal costs are just beginning to be realized.

Treatment services for pregnant substance abusers are in short supply. More importantly, few programs have been designed for the special needs of this population. The majority of drug-addicted women have associated social, psychological, medical, and economic problems that must be considered as part of a comprehensive service delivery system. Programs should be family centered to include the developmental needs of mothers and children, and to support women in their parenting role. The challenges are multifaceted: Pregnant substance abusers need adequate prenatal care, drug treatment, and services to promote healthy mother–child interaction.

EPIDEMIOLOGY

There has been a marked increase in the number of women addicted to cocaine (U.S. Department of Health and Human Services, 1988). Based on national statistics, 15% of women of childbearing age are substance abusers (U.S. General Accounting Office, 1990). Although national cocaine prevalence rates for young adults have shown a downward trend from 7.6% in 1985 to 2.2% in 1990 (National Institute on Drug Abuse, 1990), this decline is not reflected in the number of pregnant substance abusers from disadvantaged urban areas in need of treatment.

Because of methodological limitations, the reliability of prevalence rates for drug-exposed infants is a matter of concern. In a nationwide survey of 36 hospitals conducted by the National Center for Perinatal Addiction and Education, it was estimated that 11% of the deliveries were exposed to illicit substances. Investigators then calculated that as many as 375,000 infants may be affected by their mothers' drug use each year (Chasnoff, 1989). The projections for cocaine exposure range from 100,000 infants affected each year (U.S. General Accounting Office, 1990) to reports that there will be about 4 million cocaine exposed infants and children in 10 years who will need special services (Wheeler Clinic, 1991).

Across studies, the rate of cocaine use among pregnant women averages approximately 10%–11%, although there is great variability between hospitals, with rates approaching 50% in some centers (Chasnoff, 1989; Jones & Lopez, 1990). Methods of identification are an important consideration. Hospitals that used rigorous testing procedures had rates 3–5 times that of hospitals with less systematic methods (Chasnoff, 1989). In a study conducted at Boston City Hospital, 18% of the prenatal sample were cocaine users, based on self report or urine assays. Of the 114 cocaine users, 24% would have been misclassified if toxicological screenings had not been performed (Zuckerman et al., 1989). Variability can also be explained by the type of provider. As reported for Pinellas County, Florida, there were no differences in illicit drug use by race or socioeconomic status (Chasnoff, Harvey, Landress & Barrett, 1990). There were, however, differences in the choice of drug and rates of reporting.

A pilot study conducted over a 1 month period at Yale New Haven Hospital demonstrated that 9% of women in labor and delivery and 47% of those from the prenatal clinic reported cocaine use during pregnancy (Viscarello, Mayes, DeGennaro & Granger, 1990). Subsequent to that survey, data collected at the prenatal clinic over a 3-month period indicated that 32% of the women reported lifetime use of cocaine, and 15% reported continued use of cocaine during pregnancy. This is clearly an undercount because urine assays were not part of the identification process. From our experience, there is great variability month to month, and prevalence estimates should be used with caution.

EFFECTS OF COCAINE ON MOTHER AND CHILD

Biological Risk

Cocaine exposure has both direct and indirect effects on the fetus. A powerful central nervous system stimulant, cocaine affects the mother's cardiovascular system. During pregnancy, cocaine causes uterine vaso-constriction, which results in lack of oxygen and nutrients to the fetus, thereby causing poor fetal growth (Woods, Plessinger, & Clark, 1987). Reported consequences of cocaine exposure in pregnancy include spontaneous abortion, premature onset of labor, and abruptio placentae (Acker, Sachs, Tracey & Wise, 1983; Bingol, Fuchs, Diaz, Stone, & Gromish, 1987; Cherukuri, Minkoff, Feldman, Parekh, & Glass, 1988).

The teratogenic effect most consistently related to cocaine exposure has been intrauterine growth retardation (Bingol et al., 1987; Cherukuri et al., 1987; Little, Snell, Klein, & Gilstrap, 1989; MacGregor et al., 1987; Oro & Dixon, 1987; Zuckerman et al., 1989). Low birth weight increases the risk of infant mortality and morbidity, making the child vulnerable to illness and neurobehavioral conditions. According to the National Hospital Discharge Survey, drug-exposed infants are twice as likely to be of low birth weight (U.S. General Accounting Office, 1990).

The evidence for other perinatal outcomes such as congenital malformations, cerebral infarction, and neonatal seizures is less consis-tent (Bingol et al., 1987; Chasnoff, Bussey, Savich & Stack, 1986; Chasnoff, Griffith, MacGregor, Dirkes, & Burns, 1989). For example, animal studies by Mahalik, Gautieri, & Mann (1980) did find that cocaine exposure increased fetal anomalies compared with controls, whereas reports by other investigators (Church, Dintcheff, & Gessner, 1988; Fantel & MacPhail, 1982) did not support such results. There are positive findings for congenital anomalies for cocaine-exposed infants (Bingol et al., 1987; Chasnoff, Chisum & Kaplan, 1988; Chavez, Mulinare & Cordero, 1989; Little et al., 1989), but it must be noted that clinical studies associating cocaine exposure with congenital malforma-tions have not consistently controlled for exposure to other substances that may cause some of the same abnormalities.

Early reports on the temporal pattern of drug use suggested that continued drug use during pregnancy is associated with low birth weight, prematurity, and intrauterine growth retardation, but that women who become abstinent after the first trimester have better neonatal outcomes (Chasnoff et al., 1989). There was no significant difference, however, between first-trimester use and or continued use of cocaine on neurobehavioral effects in the neonate. These reports were based on a small number of women, many of whom may have used multiple combinations of drugs; thus the results are not generalizable to the entire population of cocaine-abusing women.

Findings of depressed interactive behavior and poor state control have been reported by several groups (Chasnoff, Burns, Schnoll, & Burns, 1985; Griffith, 1988). Although longitudinal studies are limited, there is some evidence of persistent central nervous system dysfunction and problems in attention regulation and state control. Anecdotal and media reports, classroom observations, and increasing referrals to special education are suggestive of long-term learning and developmental deficits. It is important to realize, however, that many of these long-term behavioral problems may result from impaired parent–child interaction in multiproblem families where substance abuse continues throughout childhood. This is an area that requires much more rigorous investigation.

Environmental, Familial, and Psychosocial Risk Factors

The combination of constitutional vulnerability and environmental and psychosocial risk factors does increase the incidence of dysfunction. First, a multivariate risk model should include the social context—factors such as stress, poverty, and lack of social support. Second, the model should include psychological and familial variables that affect maternal competence and coping skills.

Pregnant substance abusers from inner cities experience multiple stressors such as poor health, inadequate housing, single-parent households, large families, and inadequate resources. Poor health practices and unhealthy life-styles increase the rates of anemia, infection, sexually transmitted disease, trauma, and abuse. The data at Yale New Haven Hospital indicate that pregnant substance abusers enter prenatal care later, have higher rates of unregistered deliveries, more emergency room visits, and more missed appointments than do their non-drug-abusing counterparts. (Report of the Committee on Infant Mortality, 1991). Overall, the percentage of women receiving adequate prenatal care has decreased and this is only exacerbated for pregnant addicts who have increased medical and psychosocial risk (Expert Panel on the Content of Prenatal Care, 1989).

Poverty, a chronic enduring stressor, is also a significant risk factor for low birth rate and associated rates of early childhood morbidity (Klerman, 1991). The increasing number of female-headed households is associated with the feminization of poverty and the declining economic status of women and children (Sidel, 1986).

The cumulative effect of stressful life events such as separations, legal actions, or hospitalization may intensify chronic, enduring stressors. Daily hassles are another risk as these women attempt to negotiate the fragmented human-service delivery system with its lengthy waiting periods and unfriendly or uncaring attitudes.

Social support may be inadequate or indeed a source of stress for the woman. Partners are often substance abusers, and women are frequently introduced to drugs, and supplied drugs, by men. Partners may be unavailable to provide financial, emotional, or parenting support. Drug-free social networks are less likely in substance-affected environments with high rates of drug-related crime and street dealing. It becomes even more difficult to cope with high-risk situations and cocaine cravings when drug use is rampant in the neighborhood (Finnegan, 1990). Young children often experience chaotic and dangerous home environments where personal safety and basic needs are urgent priorities.

Women may turn to drugs to relieve the pain caused by problematic relationships or isolation from others. Drug addiction may be a way of coping with the demands of parenting and household responsibilities, and the sense of helplessness that surrounds these women's daily routines. Child-care options are limited, and women have little time to themselves.

Psychosocial problems are another risk factor that influences parenting practices. Pregnant substance abusers sometimes lack the psychological and social resources needed to promote recovery and healthy maternal behaviors. Such resources can decrease the effects of life stress on family functioning and child development. Studies demonstrate that disadvantaged women with young children have very high rates of depression, and this is associated with child adjustment problems (Belle, 1982). Depression is particularly likely among cocaine-abusing women, as documented by several studies of comorbidity and cocaine abuse (Gawin & Kleber, 1988; Kleinman et al., 1990).

Additionally, lack of mastery and internal control are related to maternal well-being and feelings of perceived helplessness in caregiving. Disadvantaged women may perceive themselves as worthless and incapable of effecting change in their lives. The resultant passivity and depression may influence readiness for treatment. Low self-esteem is characteristic of the population. In addition, issues of guilt and shame become evident as women admit to cocaine use during pregnancy. This may include reactions to unwanted or unplanned pregnancies.

Substance abuse is often an intergenerational problem. A high percentage of drug-abusing women have grown up in substance-abusing families where they are exposed to family disruption, violence, and abuse

(Finklestein, 1990). Partners and family members often enable the woman's drug use rather than support abstinence and recovery. Dysfunctional relationships and poor role models create deficits that affect later caretaking behaviors.

In summary, environmental and psychosocial risk factors may act independently or interact with predisposing cocaine exposure to produce poor perinatal outcomes. It is the cumulative effect of risk factors that leads to obstetrical complications and childhood morbidity.

Recommendations for Research

The scientific challenge is to gather epidemiological and clinical data for resource allocation and the development of treatment services. To measure the direct effects of cocaine exposure in utero it is necessary to control for confounding variables such as the amount and frequency of other substances used, as well as for maternal health and nutrition. Statistical models should also include sociodemographic and environmental risk factors, which may be independently associated with developmental psychopathology (Rutter, 1987; Sameroff, Seifer, Barocas, Sax, & Greenspan, 1987).

TREATMENT

There is a severe shortage of treatment services for pregnant substance abusers. A survey by the National Association of State Alcohol and Drug Abuse Directors (Wheeler Clinic, 1991) estimated that 280,000 pregnant women needed treatment, but that less than 11% of women received care. Similarly, a multihospital survey by the U.S. Select Committee on Children, Youth and Families (1989) reported that two thirds of hospitals had no place to refer women for drug treatment. Many programs do not accept pregnant women because of inadequate medical resources and concerns about liability. An increasing number of residential slots are being funded, but this does not begin to meet the demand. A reasonable goal is to provide a range of services—residential, in-patient, out-patient, day treatment, and self-help—to match patient's needs with available resources.

Family Systems Model

Most treatment programs have been based on male-oriented, individual treatment. This stems from a medical model, in which the individual is the target of intervention. A family systems approach is more appropriate when designing programs for women. Because drug abuse affects not only the woman but also the entire family, treatment models must provide family-centered services.

Treatment programs for substance-abusing pregnant women and mothers must address the woman's addiction and her role as caretaker. Programs should be designed to address the developmental needs of mother and child, and the mother–child relationship. This mutuality between mother and child becomes central to the recovery process.

Maternal drug use affects parental competence and child development and adaptation. Just as the child is shaped by the caretaking environment (Sameroff & Seifer, 1983), parenting behavior is shaped by child characteristics and the mother's personal and social resources for coping. The mother's developmental history and early childhood experience influence her ability to nurture her infant and provide competent parenting.

The dynamic relationship between mother and child is also influenced by the larger social systems in which they live. Drug treatment cannot be separated from the social, psychological, and environmental forces that exert an influence on the mother's addiction and her parenting practices. This includes the interactions between family, social network, community, and sociocultural factors (Bronfenbrenner, 1977). This dynamic interplay between multiple systems affects mother, child, and family health.

Ecological models of parenting include the psychological resources of the mother, characteristics of the child, and contextual sources of stress and support (Abidin, 1983; Belsky, 1984). The combination of a vulnerable infant, maternal psychopathology, and lack of healthy social supports can lead to dysfunctional parenting (Burns & Burns, 1988). The greatest deficits occur when perinatal distress interacts with environmental deprivation and sociodemographic factors (Werner & Smith, 1982).

Treatment programs for substance-abusing pregnant women should be based on theories of women's psychological development, which stress the central importance of connectedness to others. Treatment models based on self-in-relation theories emphasize the woman's relationship skills and the need to include significant others in the treatment process (Miller, 1976).

Women who abuse cocaine typically enter treatment after they have had children, or during pregnancy when they are motivated and/or identified and referred for treatment. This situation demands a family-centered approach to care. Unfortunately, this is a period of conflicting interests and rights (American Bar Association, 1990). The criminalization of pregnant addicts reflects the prevailing moralistic attitudes of anger and blame rather than a therapeutic stance. Counteracting this trend is the new attitude towards separate and specialized women's programs. Legislation to support additional funding for women's programs is a response to the growing prevalence of perinatal addiction and the need to develop new models of practice.

A family systems model includes comprehensive and coordinated services to women and children. Such an approach necessitates multidisciplinary action and interagency collaboration to meet the multiple needs of families. Maternal drug addiction is a family matter. For this reason, human service providers should combine individual, family, and ecologically planned interventions that strengthen and support the entire family system.

THE MOTHERS PROJECT

The Mothers Project is a model program for cocaine-dependent pregnant women and their children in New Haven, Connecticut. Funded by the National Institute on Drug Abuse, it is a collaborative effort of the APT (Addiction, Prevention, and Treatment) Foundation; the Substance Abuse Treatment Unit; the Yale University Department of Psychiatry; the Child Study Center; and the Departments of Obstetrics and Gynecology, Pediatrics, Epidemiology, and Public Health. The goal of The Mothers Project is to evaluate the effectiveness of comprehensive, family-centered treatment services for substance-abusing pregnant women.

The program provides early outreach and identification of pregnant substance abusers, and comprehensive medical and social services to women and their children. The components of The Mothers Project include specialized prenatal care; individual, group, and family counseling; on-site day care; and family support.

Pregnancy is a critical time to intervene in the drug behavior of women. It is a period of vulnerability and change, yet it also affords time for intensive interventions that can improve maternal and child health. For this reason, routine prenatal care at Yale New Haven Hospital includes screening for eligibility for The Mothers Project. Pregnant women who self-report current cocaine use and/or test positive on a urine assay are invited to enroll in the program. Women may also obtain services through self-referral or referral from community agencies. Treatment begins during pregnancy and continues 6 months postpartum.

Prenatal Care

Women who enter The Mothers Project are referred to the Perinatal Chemical Dependency Center at Yale New Haven Hospital for specialized prenatal care. This includes medical and psychosocial risk assessment, advocacy, and active outreach. The integration of medical services with drug treatment and family-centered care improves access and enhances the quality and continuity of care. The obstetrical staff are sensitive to the social and cultural backgrounds of the patients and responsive to their complex needs. Care is provided in a nonjudgmental atmosphere in which adequate time and attention is given to each patient. A research nurse coordinator provides liaison activities between the obstetrical services and the day treatment program. This ensures adequate communication and coordination of services.

Individual and Group Treatment

The conceptual model for the day treatment program is based on coping skills in relation to the multiple roles of women: drug user, parent, partner, worker/homemaker, and player. The goals of treatment include the development of personal resources and social skills to cope with high-risk situations for drug use and the demands of everyday living. Coping strategies foster empowerment, which helps women reduce stress, depression, cocaine cravings, and the sense of hopelessness that often accompanies drug dependence.

The parenting curriculum includes didactic material and informal question-and-answer periods with a developmental pediatrician. Topics include prenatal development and danger signs in pregnancy, nutrition, infant care, emergency first aid and safety, and child behavior. Developmental specialists also provide individual and group sessions on topics such as infant handling techniques, children's play, language development, and mother-child interaction. The parenting curriculum is designed to increase maternal coping skills through in vivo training, modeling, and feedback.

Women's issues are a central focus of group treatment. Many of the women share a history of failed relationships, abusiveness, and abandonment. Based on theories of women's psychological development, the discussions focus on relational issues and connection to others. Specific topics include intimacy, sex roles, sexuality, dependency, female guilt and shame, and assertiveness.

Empowerment is an important theme in treatment programs for low-income women. Women are helped to develop assertiveness, self-esteem, and control over their lives. As the women gain confidence and self-respect, they are able to take greater responsibility for their recovery.

Relapse prevention therapy is designed to foster the acquisition of skills to cope with high-risk situations, cocaine cravings, peer pressure, mood management, leisure time, and irrational thinking that often lead to relapse. The strategies include behavior change and cognitive restructuring.

Because problematic relationships, including physical abuse by a partner or the partner's drug use, often contribute to relapse, special groups and referral sources are being developed for the partners of women in the program. The relationship between the client and her mother are also a concern because pregnant substance abusers are confronted with the emotional issues of mothering and nurturance. Grandmothers may be a significant child care resource for temporary placement of children. Finally, sisterhood and mutually supportive relationships with other women are encouraged. It is important for substance-abusing pregnant women to begin to build drug-free relationships and engage in healthy leisure activities.

Role satisfaction and personal goal setting are topics of group and individual treatment. There is a progression from daily and weekend planning to cope with high-risk situations, to long-range plans for education and job training. Personal goal setting and achievement are significant for the women in that they contribute to their sense of empowerment and ability to create change in their lives. Educational and vocational assessment and referrals are services offered during the transitional phase of the program, the final 3 months when aftercare plans and the utilization of healthy support systems are stressed.

Throughout the day, the women have opportunities to engage in verbal and activity-based therapy. This combination is essential for behaviorally oriented treatment. Group activities include daily living skills to improve personal hygiene, home management, budgeting, and use of community resources. Some of these activities are reinforced through home-based family support services.

Family Support Services

Family support workers provide family-centered, home-based interventions to the substance-abusing pregnant woman and her family. These services are a critical component of the program. Family support workers provide outreach to bring women into the program and assist them in complying with treatment, and they help the women develop drug-free supports outside the treatment program, using existing family and community resources. Through their relationship, the family support worker helps the woman identify and solve problems that affect her ability to parent competently. Time may be spent on securing housing assistance and transportation, and in preparation for the new baby.

Family support workers are women from the same ethnic background and same or similar communities as those families being served by the program. Although they are not professionally trained, the workers bring with them experience in successful parenting, the ability to negotiate social service systems, connections with the community, credibility, and a strong sense of affiliation with the client. Each worker is teamed with a rehabilitation counselor for effective case management. Through formal training and close supervision, the family support workers are able to form and sustain a supportive and trusting relationship with the client. They provide practical and psychological support and help the family to obtain necessary services.

Family-centered, home-based services have emerged as a method of child protection and family preservation. Since 1985, the Family Support Service Program of the Yale Child Study Center has provided services for children at risk of abandonment. In addition to services for victims of child abuse and neglect and for HIV-infected children, services are now being provided to cocaine-exposed children. The program has been successful in keeping families together and improving outcomes for children.

Day Care

An on-site therapeutic day care center, an integral part of The Mothers Project, operates during the hours of the day treatment program. Women bring their infants and preschool children to the center where they participate in developmentally appropriate activities while the mothers attend individual and group sessions. The day care staff provides diagnostic and therapeutic services to these high-risk children and their families. Most of the children have been exposed to perinatal and environmental risk, so that developmental delay and early signs of psychopathology are common. Daycare staff assess each child and then implement home-based and center-based early intervention services. Some of the most frequently presenting problems include expressive language delay, disorganized and aggressive behavior, difficulty with transitions, extreme passivity, and an absence of expressed emotion.

The children's services complement the program for mothers. There are identified time slots for mother–child activities, and fluidity between the two components is encouraged. The center functions as a laboratory for learning, with opportunities to observe role models and practice parenting techniques. As part of the effort to improve maternal coping skills and increase the mother's knowledge of child development, it is vital to identify maternal attitudes that may interfere with attachment and interactive behaviors between mother and infant. During case conferences, the project staff discuss mother, child, and family functioning, and collaborate on individualized treatment plans.

There is empirical evidence that social support is an important influence on early childhood development and maternal behavior (Shonkoff, 1984). For this reason, the program emphasizes formal and informal support systems for high-risk families. The combination of center-based and home-based services reinforces parenting skills and a stable caretaking environment. Family support workers are able to observe maternal—child interaction in the home and reinforce the woman's self-concept as that of a competent parent.

Day care is an integral part of The Mothers Project. Although the targeted patient is the woman and her cocaine-exposed infant, all children from high-risk environments can benefit from early intervention services. Developmental day care is cost effective, and it provides both short- and long-term benefits to the family.

SUMMARY

The Mothers Project is designed to provide comprehensive, family-centered services to cocaine-dependent pregnant women and children. The goal is to strengthen and support the entire family system. Some of the barriers to treatment found elsewhere, such as lack of child care, difficult access, and unfriendly attitudes on the part of service providers have been eliminated. Active case-finding and outreach are additional strategies to bring pregnant women into treatment. Foremost, a caring community has been established that welcomes women in a safe and supportive environment.

Substance-abusing pregnant women have complex needs, and lack of compliance remains a significant barrier to success. Furthermore, the combination of isolation, denial, and attitudes of blame keep women from fully utilizing available services. Treatment models must address the social, emotional, and economic conditions that contribute to the woman's illness and recovery. Systemic and programmatic changes are necessary. The Mothers Project includes many of the important components of family-centered care: specialized prenatal services, drug treatment, day care, and family support.

REFERENCES

Abidin, R. R. (1983). *Parenting Stress Index Manual (PSI)*. Charlottesville, VA: Pediatric Psychology Press.

Acker, D., Sachs, B., Tracey, K. J., & Wise, W. (1983). Abruptio placentae associated with cocaine use. *American Journal of Obstetrics and Gynecology, 146*, 220–221.

American Bar Association. (1990). *Drug exposed infants and their families: Coordinating responses of the legal, medical and child protection system.* Washington, DC: Center on Children and the Law.

Belle, I. (Ed.). (1982) *Lives in stress.* Beverly Hills, CA: Sage Publications.

Belsky, J. (1984). The determinants of parenting. *Child Development, 55*, 83–95.

Bingol, N., Fuchs, M., Diaz, V., Stone, R. K., & Gromisch, D. S. (1987). Teratogenicity of cocaine in humans. *Journal of Pediatrics, 110*, 93–96.

Bronfenbrenner, U. (1977, July). Toward an experimental ecology of human development. *American Psychologist, 513*–530.

Burns, M. J., & Burns, K. A. (1988). Parenting dysfunction in chemically dependent women. In I. J. Chasnoff (Ed.), *Drugs, alcohol, pregnancy and parenting.* Norwell, MA: Kluwer Academic.

Chasnoff, I. J. (1989). Drug use and women: Establishing a standard of care. In D. E. Hutchings (Ed.), *Prenatal use of licit and illicit drugs.* New York: New York Academy of Sciences.

Chasnoff, I. J., Burns, W. J., Schnoll, S. H., & Burns, K. A. (1985). Cocaine use in pregnancy. *New England Journal of Medicine, 313,* 666–669. Chasnoff, I. J., Bussey, M. E., Savich, R., & Stack, C. M. (1986). Perinatal cerebral infarction and maternal cocaine use. *Journal of Pediatrics, 108*, 456–459.

Chasnoff, I. J., Chisum, G. M., & Kaplan, D. (1988). Maternal cocaine use and genitourinary tract malformations. *Teratology, 37*, 201–204.

Chasnoff, I. J., Griffith, D. R., MacGregor, S., Dirkes, K., & Burns, K. A. (1989). Temporal matters of cocaine use in pregnancy. Perinatal outcome. *Journal of the American medical Association, 261*, 1741–1744. Chasnoff, I. J., Landress, H. J., & Barrett, M. E. (1990). The prevalence of illicit drug or alcohol abuse during pregnancy and discrepancies in mandatory reporting in Pinellas County, Florida. *New England Journal of Medicine, 322*, 102–106.

Chavez, G. F., Mulinare, J., & Cordero, J. F. (1989). Maternal cocaine use during early pregnancy as a risk factor for congenital urogenital anomalies. *Journal of the American Medical Association, 262*, 795–798.

Cherukuri, R., Minkoff, H., Feldman, J., Parekh, A., & Glass, L. (1988). A cohort study of alkaloidal cocaine ("crack") in pregnancy. *Obstetrics and Gynecology, 72*, 147–151.

Church, M. W., Dintcheff, B. A., & Gessner, P. K. (1988). Dose-dependent consequences of cocaine on pregnancy outcome in the Long-Evans rat. *Neurotoxicology and Teratology, 10*, 51–58.

Expert Panel on the Content of Prenatal Care.(1989). *Caring for our future: The content of prenatal care.* Washington, DC: Public Health Service, U. S. Department of Health and Human Services.

Fantel, A. G., & MacPhail, B. J. (1982). The teratogenicity of cocaine. *Teratology, 26,* 17–19.

Finklestein, N. (1990, September). *Treatment issues: Women and substance abuse.* Paper prepared for the National Coalition on Alcohol and Drug Dependent Women and Their Children, presented at Healthy Women, Healthy Pregnancies, Healthy Infants: Emerging Solutions in the Face of Alcohol and Other Drugs Problems, Miami, FL.

Finnegan, W. (1990, September 10). Out there: 1. *The New Yorker,* pp. 51–86.

Finnegan, W. (1990, September 17). Out there: 2. *The New Yorker,* pp. 60–88.

Gawin, F. H., & Kleber, H. D. (1988). Evolving conceptualizations of drug dependence. *Yale Journal of Biology and Medicine, 61,* 123–136.

Griffith, D. R. (1988). The effects of perinatal cocaine exposure on infant neurobehavior and early maternal infant interactions. In I. J. Chasnoff (Ed.), *Drugs, alcohol, pregnancy and parenting.* Norwell, MA: Kluwer Academic.

Jones, C. L., & Lopez, R. (1990). Drug use and pregnancy. In R. R. Merkatz & J. E. Thompson. (Eds.), *New perspectives on prenatal care* (pp. 273–319). New York: Elsevier.

Kleinman, P. H., Miller, A. B., Millman, R. B., Woody, G. E., Todd, T., Kemp, T., & Lipton, D. (1990). Psychopathology among cocaine abusers entering treatment. *Journal of Nervous and Mental Disease, 178,* 442–447.

Klerman, L. V. (1991). *Alive and well? A research and policy review of health programs for poor young children.* New York: National Center for Children in Poverty.

Little, B. B., Snell, L. M., Klein, V. R., & Gilstrap, L. C., III. (1989). Cocaine abuse during pregnancy: Maternal and fetal implications. *Obstetrics and Gynecology, 73,* 157–160.

MacGregor, S. N., Keith, L. G., Chasnoff, I. J., Rosner, M. A., Chisum, G. M., Shan, P., & Minogues, J. P. (1987). Cocaine use during pregnancy: Adverse perinatal outcome. *American Journal of Obstetrics and Gynecology, 157,* 686–690.

Mahalik, M. P., Gautieri, R. F., & Mann, D. E. (1980). Teratogenic potential of cocaine hydrochloride in CF-1 mice. *Journal of Pharmaceutical Science, 69,* 703–706.

Miller, J. B. (1976). *Toward a new psychology of women.* Boston: Beacon Press.

National Institute on Drug Abuse. (1990). *National Household Survey on Drug Abuse.* Rockville, MD: Author.

Oro, A. S., & Dixon, S. D. (1987). Perinatal cocaine and methamphetamine exposure: Maternal and neonatal correlates. *Journal of Pediatrics, 111,* 571–578.

Report of the Committee on Infant Mortality. (1991). New Haven, CT: Yale University School of Medicine.

Rutter, M. (1987). Psychosocial resilience and protective mechanisms. *American Journal of Orthopsychiatry, 57,* 316–331. Sameroff, A. J., & Seifer, R.

(1983). Familiar risk and child competence. *Child Development*, *54*, 1254–1268.

Sameroff, A. J., Seifer, R., Barocas, R., Zax, M., & Greenspan, S. (1987). Intelligent quotient scores of four year-old children. Social–environmental risk factors. *Pediatrics*, *79*, 343–350.

Shonkoff, J. P. (1984). Social support and the development of vulnerable children. *American Journal of Public Health*, *74*, 310–312.

Sidel, R. (1986). *Women and children last*. New York: Penguin Books.

U. S. Department of Health and Human Service. (1988). *National household survey on drug abuse: Population estimates 1985* (DHHS Publication No. 871539). Washington DC: U. S. Government Printing Office.

U. S. General Accounting Office. (1990). *Drug exposed infants: A generation at risk*. Washington, DC: U. S. Government Printing Office.

U. S. Select Committee Hearing on Children, Youth and Families. (1989). *Addicted infants and their mothers*. Washington, DC: U. S. Government Printing Office.

Viscarello, R., Mayes, L. C., DeGennaro, N., & Granger, R. (1990). *The prevalence of cocaine use among women in labor*. Unpublished manuscript, Yale School of Medicine, Department of Obstetrics, New Haven, CT.

Werner, E. E., & Smith, R. S. (1982). *Vulnerable but not invincible: A longitudinal study of resilient children & youth*. New York: McGraw–Hill.

Wheeler Clinic. (1991). *Drug-exposed babies raise many issues*. Plainview, CT: Connecticut Alcohol and Drug Abuse Commission.

Woods, J. R., Plessinger, M. A., & Clark, K. E. (1987). Effect of cocaine on uterine blood flow and fetal oxygenation. *Journal of the American Medical Association*, *257*, 957–961.

Zuckerman, B., Frank, D. A., Hingson, R., Amaro, H., Levenson, S. M., Kayne, H., Parker, S., Vinci, R., Aboagye, K., Fried, L. E., Cabral, H., Timperi, R., & Bauchner, H. (1989) Effects of maternal marijuana and cocaine use on fetal growth. *New England Journal of Medicine*, *320*, 762–768.

CHAPTER TWENTY

Matching Patients to Treatment

Thomas R. Kosten, MD

IN THE PRECEDING CHAPTERS we have reviewed the history, epidemiology, psychology, neurobiology, and treatment of cocaine dependence. A wide spectrum of the American population has been exposed to cocaine, and many people have become cocaine-dependent, from the affluent stockbroker down to the grade school student, from the hard-core criminal to the pregnant mother. Whereas the neurobiology of cocaine's actions in these divergent populations appears to be similar, the treatment approaches have varied depending upon the psychosocial needs of these different patient populations. Matching of patients to appropriate treatments requires a consideration of treatment setting (inpatient, outpatient, or residential), treatment modality (focusing on psychotherapy or pharmacotherapy), and ancillary interventions (such as legal and vocational services for the antisocial addict or prenatal services and parenting skills for the pregnant addict). Ideally, this matching is based on clinical need, but availability of resources has also become a significant consideration for matching services to substance abusers' needs. With the more expensive and less commonly available resources such as inpatient hospitalization, significant limitations have evolved in the criteria for severity of patient pathology necessary for hospital admission, as well as those for duration of stay. On the other hand, outpatient modalities, particularly those involving group therapies with drug abuse counselors and minimal ancillary services, can be quite inexpensive and are more widely available. In many cases, the necessary cost–benefit analyses to make intelligent choices in the allocation of scarce resources do not exist, and decisions are based on economically biased clinical judgments.

In the matching of patients to appropriate treatments, several principles are evolving within the cocaine abuse field. These principles include (1) criteria for the use of inpatient hospitalization, (2) the role of pharmacotherapy in attaining abstinence and preventing relapse, and (3) the importance of intensive outpatient interventions for treatment retention. First, because the withdrawal syndrome from cocaine dependence is generally not viewed as needing medical intervention, inpatient treatment for this purpose alone is not necessary. However, the suicidality and psychosis that can accompany the "crash" from cocaine may require inpatient care, and the management of comorbid psychiatric disorders in cocaine abusers will benefit from an inpatient setting. This inpatient stay may be particularly helpful for induction onto psychotropic medications, facilitation of initial abstinence, and reducing relapse to cocaine abuse by establishing adequate aftercare. Second, a general role for pharmacotherapy in cocaine dependence is evolving, although this remains a research issue. The clearest indications for pharmacotherapy are in "dual-diagnosis" patients—those with concurrent psychotic, affective, or anxiety disorders and cocaine dependence. Third, because these pharmacotherapies are not effective in isolation, intensive outpatient interventions including day hospitals, and the use of cognitive behavioral therapies such as relapse prevention therapy are valuable.

The matching of patients to appropriate levels of care, whether inpatient, day hospital, outpatient, or brief professional interventions coupled with self-help groups, requires a comprehensive psychosocial evaluation of the patient. As previously stated, the patient with major psychiatric comorbidity, such as psychosis or suicidal depression, will usually not be manageable outside the inpatient setting. Those patients with less severe comorbidity, including antisocial personality disorder, may benefit substantially from a day hospital program with regular urine monitoring and daily attendance at group treatment sessions. These programs can be coupled with self-help groups such as Cocaine Anonymous, which will help the patient build a strong and lasting support network. In some cases, these day hospital programs may also be important as a step down after relatively brief inpatient hospitalization, particularly among psychotic cocaine abusers. Day programs are ideal settings for building the social skills for competitive employment and for longer term recovery from substance dependence.

The outpatient setting is the most common treatment site for substance abusers and may range from thrice-weekly group therapy to once-weekly brief counseling and urine monitoring. Outpatient care is usually essential as an aftercare plan for those patients completing hospitalization or a day treatment program, and it can be the primary intervention for the cocaine abuser without comorbid psychopathology. With this relatively lower level intervention, however, a more intensive intervention should be available as a backup for those patients who do not sustain abstinence. Important specialized variations in these outpatient programs are the work release program in conjunction with the criminal justice system, and employment-related treatment programs, wherein urine monitoring may be more frequent than is usual with weekly drug counseling.

The least restrictive level of intervention is a professional evaluation followed by primary referral to self-help groups. This minimal treatment is generally not appropriate with a cocaine-dependent patient. Although long- term investment in self-help groups is an important tool in sustained recovery, new patients usually are unable to maintain their involvement in self-help groups without continued professional encouragement. The role of relatively brief educational programs and other limited professional involvement in the prevention of cocaine abuse is recognized and important, but not in treatment of dependence. The peer counseling and self-help approach may have a particular role in the adolescent substance abuser who is still experimenting with drugs and not dependent on cocaine. All cases of cocaine abusers who come to professional attention deserve a careful assessment of three areas: (1) their substance abuse, (2) any comorbid psychopathology, and (3) their support system for remaining drug free. Only with this information can appropriate triage be made to a level of care that will meet the patient's needs.

Once a setting for care has been determined, the type of intervention needs to be carefully considered. Psychotherapy is the mainstay of treatment for cocaine dependence. Several specific interventions for cocaine abuse, particularly cognitive behavioral interventions, have been developed. The addition of pharmacotherapies to psychotherapy can substantially improve treatment outcome owing to synergistic interactions. The role of these pharmacotherapies has been primarily demonstrated in the facilitation of initial abstinence from cocaine, although longer term relapse prevention might also be facilitated. A range of medications may be used, as reviewed in Chapter 14, and an optimal match between particular medications and patients in various diagnostic subgroups may be possible. Comorbid affective disorders seem particularly good prognostic indicators for the use of antidepressant therapy in cocaine abusers. Early results are also suggesting a substantial role for antidepressants in the psychotic cocaine abuser who is concurrently maintained on an antipsychotic agent. Small subgroups of patients have also been identified, such as patients with adult attention deficit disorder who may benefit from selected pharmacotherapies such as methylphenidate. Work appears to be rapidly evolving on patient–treatment matching with pharmacotherapies as well as on the interactive effects of psychotherapy with pharmacotherapy, particularly relapse prevention therapy with desipramine. A critical consideration is that pharmacotherapies alone have limited utility and that they function best in a context of intensive psychotherapies such as twice-weekly outpatient treatment or even day hospital treatment. The need for pharmacotherapies during inpatient treatment appears to be limited, because cocaine withdrawal includes no medically serious symptoms. Instead, inpatient treatment can be a setting for induction on medications for subsequent outpatient treatment.

As cocaine abuse and dependence has reached progressively younger adolescents, the role of ancillary services has become increasingly important. For the middle-class, cocaine-abusing businessman or professional, there is a limited need for ancillary services to build social skills or provide vocational rehabilitation. However, among adolescents whose schooling is frequently disrupted by addiction to crack cocaine and who have not been part of the work force or health care system, many fundamental ancillary services are needed. Young adult crack abusers referred by the criminal justice system frequently need not only legal counseling, but also vocational services and substantial social rehabilitation. Some of these services can be provided in an outpatient context when done within work-release and day hospital programs. For other, more seriously antisocial, cocaine-dependent patients, treatment for 12–18 months in long-term residential facilities is needed. In these residential settings, many of the ancillary services are provided.

Pregnant cocaine-abusing women comprise another group needing extensive ancillary services. Most of these women are young unwed mothers who often become the sole parent in their families. When these mothers fail in their parental responsibilities, extended families including grandparents are given the burden of raising the crack-addicted baby. A key role of treatment is to get the mother reinvolved with her child. Thus drug abuse programs must provide adequate postnatal as well as prenatal care of the mother and infant. Expensive but essential are programs to provide not only drug abuse counseling but also prenatal obstetrical care and follow-up in parenting skills.

The complexities of treating cocaine dependence, even in those patients with abundant resources, are illustrated by Mr. A, who required a complex mix of inpatient and outpatient treatments, with individual psychotherapy and pharmacotherapy as well as ancillary family counseling.

Mr. A, aged 30, sought treatment after he had used freebase cocaine for 2 years. He worked as a manager in the family business and was not managing the company well. He would spend hours in his locked office, refusing to answer telephone calls or knocks on his door, because he was smoking freebase cocaine.

He liked the high from cocaine and felt that it improved his performance at work, at least initially. At the beginning, he used cocaine episodically in weekly binges of 12–24 hours, but he was using it daily toward the end of his cocaine career. After 2 years, he was more than $100,000 in debt for cocaine purchases and sought treatment because of intense pressure from cocaine dealers who wanted to be paid.

Treatment began with a 6-week hospitalization in a general psychiatric setting because of the intense dysphoria that followed cessation of use. Mr. A was initially suicidal, but this resolved within 2 days. His mood gradually improved, along with his appetite and his ability to sleep. Tricyclic antidepressant medication (desipramine) was prescribed after the first week to help with his continued depression and cocaine craving. After the first week of inpatient treatment, couples meetings began with his wife, who was 6 months pregnant. Following discharge, weekly meetings were held for 6 months in an outpatient setting.

Clearly there were significant problems both on the job and at home. Mr. A had not been available in either setting because of his cocaine use. His mother and his wife each blamed the other for Mr. A's cocaine abuse. Therapy focused on the couple and on encouraging the wife to assert some control in the relationship and to stop externalizing responsibility to her in-laws. Instead of blaming her husband's mother for his drug use, Mrs. A needed to take a more active stance against the cocaine abuse and acknowledge her own capacity to influence her husband.

Because of Mrs. A's inability to accept much responsibility and her belief that his family was responsible for her husband's problems, the financial affairs of Mr. and Mrs. A were placed in the hands of an attorney whom both Mr. A and his mother trusted, rather than directly under the control of the wife. This action was essential to prevent financial disaster and to minimize the potential for cocaine abuse relapse by limiting available funds.

Couples treatment then addressed issues related to the pregnancy, contingency plans should Mr. A abuse cocaine again, and an improved alliance between the wife and her mother-in-law. In all these areas, the couple needed to become more balanced in their responsibilities, Mrs. A needed to adopt a tougher stance in setting limits for her husband. Most of these issues were addressed through routine structural family therapy techniques, including the assignment of tasks to be performed at home and reviewed in the therapy sessions.

Cocaine abuse was monitored through laboratory studies of urine specimens obtained 3 times per week; study results were made available to the couple's therapist. It had been agreed that, if cocaine were detected in the urine, Mr. A was to be hospitalized for at least 4 weeks. This contingency plan proved necessary and was utilized 1 month after the baby was born. Cocaine use had been suspected in the 2 weeks prior to the delivery, when Mr. A failed to give two urine specimens, but the therapist compromised by having Mr. A return to the agreed schedule of urine monitoring. In retrospect, this was the first test of the limit-setting ability of the therapy. A compromise was necessary at that time because Mrs. A did not want Mr. A in a psychiatric hospital when she delivered. Limit setting can be effective only if the drug-free spouse supports it.

This case clearly shows the need for coordination of complex, interlocking treatments that challenge any therapist. With the poor patient, doing more with less is difficult and more efficient approaches are needed. Relapse prevention therapy groups may have a major role, as may self-help groups. With the more impaired "dual-diagnosis" patient, who may have polydrug abuse as well as a comorbid psychiatric disorder, a major problem in treatment delivery may be to arrive at an accurate diagnosis and then develop appropriate treatments. The following case illustrates these difficulties.

Mr. T a 35-year-old black male, was brought to the ER in a coma after the police found him lying on the street at 11 p.m. Physical examination disclosed fresh needle marks on his legs and old track marks on his arms. His pupils were pinpoint, his respiration was depressed, and his overall condition was suggestive of opioid overdose. A dose of 0.4 mg naloxone was given subcutaneously, and he became alert within a few minutes. Repeat naloxone dosages were given 30 minutes and 60 minutes later. Urine and blood specimens were sent to the toxicology laboratory for cocaine and opioid testing. Over the next few hours, the patient went from incoherent ramblings to elaboration of a paranoid delusion that he was sent by the "Holy Ghost" to cure AIDS. Owing to severe agitation, restraints were needed. Results of toxicology testing indicated recent cocaine use, and a tentative diagnosis of cocaine delusional disorder was made. The patient also appeared to have opioid withdrawal symptoms, including goose flesh, sweating, dilated pupils, and vomiting.

He was medicated with chlorpromazine 300 mg, but continued to be quite psychotic and minimally sedated. He reported having been treated for "anxiety" over several years at the local community mental health center, but he was actually being treated for paranoid schizophrenia with haloperidol, which he had not been taking over the last few weeks. His clinician at the mental health center knew that Mr. T used drugs of some sort and had repeatedly tried to get him to stop, since she felt that it markedly interfered with his rehabilitation program. In addition, he had recently tested positive for HIV antibodies. With this additional information, a spinal tap was done to rule out opportunistic infection. Because the cerebrospinal fluid analysis proved normal, transfer was arranged to a psychiatric hospital with a tentative diagnosis of relapsed paranoid schizophrenia. Mr. T's symptoms gradually resolved over a 3-week hospitalization with reinstitution of the haloperidol.

The patient's cocaine use and his HIV status were important components of his presentation. Cocaine probably precipitated psychosis in this "speedballing" schizophrenic, but this was not a typical brief cocaine psychosis. Instead of the 12–24 hours usually needed for resolution of a cocaine psychosis, this patient's psychosis did not substantially improve over the 2 days that he was held in the emergency room. He clearly had an underlying psychotic disorder. The patient's HIV status was relevant as a precipitant of an intentional overdose. When asked about his understanding of the HIV test results, the patient responded, "I know this is a death sentence, and I wanted to get it over fast." This suicidality was an important indicator for hospitalization and stresses the importance of careful follow-up after HIV testing.

In summary, treatment matching based on setting of treatment, type of therapy, and availability of ancillary services holds significant promise for the future. Because of our limited understanding of the neurobiology of cocaine dependence, treatment matching can not yet take advantage of biological criteria, particularly when attempting to match up pharmacotherapies with appropriate candidates. The clinical criteria outlined here should become more sophisticated as we come to understand the psychological factors contributing to cocaine abuse (e.g., conditioned responses and cognitive factors) and as we link these conditioning factors to a neurobiological substrate. With substance dependence the potential for rational treatment matching and for developing targeted treatments is greater than that with psychiatric disorders, because we have a clear understanding of the etiological agent and can produce both animal and human models of the disorder. This gives us an excellent ability to investigate cocaine dependence and to develop rational therapies. Significant advances should be possible over the next few years, as we come to understand this disorder and develop new treatments. This combination of better understanding and new treatment tools will inevitably lead to the identification of more homogeneous patient subgroups for treatment interventions and to the implementation of more efficacious treatments.

Index